Fuzzy Logic Theory and Applications

Part I and Part II

Fuzzy Logic Theory and Applications

Part I and Part II

Lotfi A Zadeh
University of California, Berkeley, USA

Rafik A Aliev
Azerbaijan State Oil and Industry University, Azerbaijan

 **World Scientific**

NEW JERSEY · LONDON · SINGAPORE · BEIJING · SHANGHAI · HONG KONG · TAIPEI · CHENNAI · TOKYO

Published by

World Scientific Publishing Co. Pte. Ltd.

5 Toh Tuck Link, Singapore 596224

USA office: 27 Warren Street, Suite 401-402, Hackensack, NJ 07601

UK office: 57 Shelton Street, Covent Garden, London WC2H 9HE

Library of Congress Cataloging-in-Publication Data

Names: Zadeh, Lotfi A. (Lotfi Asker), author. | Aliev, R. A. (Rafik Aziz ogly), author.
Title: Fuzzy logic theory and applications : Part I and Part II / by Lotfi A. Zadeh (UC Berkeley),
    Rafik A. Aliev (Azerbaijan State Oil and Industry University, Azerbaijan).
Description: New Jersey : World Scientific, 2018.
Identifiers: LCCN 2018009989 | ISBN 9789813238176 (hc : alk. paper)
Subjects: LCSH: Fuzzy logic. | Fuzzy sets. | Fuzzy mathematics. |
    Logic, Symbolic and mathematical.
Classification: LCC QA9.64 .Z33 2018 | DDC 511.3/13--dc23
LC record available at https://lccn.loc.gov/2018009989

British Library Cataloguing-in-Publication Data

A catalogue record for this book is available from the British Library.

For any available supplementary material, please visit
http://www.worldscientific.com/worldscibooks/10.1142/10936#t=suppl

Desk Editor: Anthony Alexander

Typeset by Stallion Press
Email: enquiries@stallionpress.com

Printed in Singapore

To the memory of my wife Aida Alieva

Rafik A. Aliev

Preface

Nowadays, voluminous textbooks and monographs in fuzzy logic are devoted only to separate or some combination of separate facets of fuzzy logic. There is a lack of a single book that presents a comprehensive and self-contained theory of fuzzy logic and its applications.

This unique compendium includes all the principal facets of fuzzy logic such as logical, fuzzy-set-theoretic, epistemic and relational. Theoretical problems are prominently illustrated and illuminated by numerous carefully worked-out and thought-through examples.

Part I, "Fuzzy Logic Theory" written by Lotfi A. Zadeh and Rafik A. Aliev, brings the fundamentals of fuzzy sets and fuzzy logic, and is organized into eight chapters. Chapter 1 is devoted to fuzzy sets which are class of objects with a continuum of grades of membership. The nations of inclusion, union, intersection, complement, relation, convexity, etc., and various properties of fuzzy sets are described. Operations on fuzzy sets and fuzzy numbers are illustrated by many examples. In this chapter, extensions of fuzzy sets, such as Type-2 fuzzy sets, Intuitionistic fuzzy sets, Rough sets and Neutrosophic sets are also considered.

Chapter 2 covers the basics of fuzzy logic to describe an imprecise logical system in which the truth-values are fuzzy subsets of the unit interval with linguistic labels. In this chapter, main emphasis is put on fuzzy logic-based approximate reasoning. This chapter also includes extended fuzzy logic which adds to fuzzy logic an essential capability — the capability to deal with unprecisiated imperfect information.

Chapter 3 is devoted to the restriction concept which opens the door to construction of mathematical solutions of computational problems which are stated in a natural language. Different types of restrictions and computations with them are given.

Chapter 4 presents fuzzy probabilities which are assumed to be fuzzy rather than real numbers. It is shown how such probabilities may be estimated from fuzzy data and a basic relation between joint, conditional and marginal fuzzy probabilities is established.

Chapter 5 covers the fuzzy function concept. Different definitions of fuzzy functions, integrability and differentiability of fuzzy functions are considered.

Chapter 6 presents several basic concepts relating to the characterization of fuzzy systems. Main emphasis is given to the definition of a fuzzy system and its state. Basic principles of fuzzy rule-based system are also described in this chapter.

Chapter 7 is devoted to Z-number theory-extensions of fuzzy arithmetic. Basically, the concept of a Z-number relates to the issue of reliability of information. Thus, real-world information is often represented in a framework of Z-number-based evaluations. The main critical problems that naturally arise in processing Z-information are computation and reasoning with Z-information. These problems are considered in detail in this chapter.

Chapter 8 presents the generalized theory of uncertainty, which is based on the fuzzy logic concept. Concomitantly, existing theories of uncertainty are based on the probability theory. The generalized theory of uncertainty (GTU) departs from the existing theories in essential ways. First, the thesis that information is statistical in nature is replaced by a much more general thesis that information is a generalized constraint, with statistical uncertainty being a special, albeit important case. The chapter concludes with examples of computations with uncertain information described in natural language.

Part II, written by experts in applied fields of their specialization who developed and used advanced techniques of fuzzy logic, includes 11 chapters edited by Lotfi A. Zadeh and Rafik A. Aliev.

Chapter 9 is devoted to restriction-based semonties which is a generalization of truth-conditional and possible-word semantics. In the following, precisiation of propositions through the use of restriction-based semantics is discussed in greater detail. The point of departure in restriction-based semantics is an unconventional definition of the concept of a proposition. Considered in this chapter concept of precisiation of meaning opens the door to computation with natural language.

Chapter 10 focuses on the conceptual and algorithmic developments of information granules.

The concepts of granular mappings which form the cornerstone of granular calculations by expanding upon numerical mappings and augmenting originally available numeric results are considered. The quality of the information granules is evaluated and optimized *vis-à-vis* the coverage of the experimental data and their specificity.

Chapter 11 reintroduces the concept of complex fuzzy sets and complex fuzzy logic and surveys the current state of complex fuzzy logic, complex fuzzy sets theory, and related applications. Recent applications of the theory in complex fuzzy-based algorithms and complex fuzzy inference systems are given.

Chapter 12 covers the application of fuzzy logic to control problems. It emphasizes that the idea of linguistic control algorithms is a brilliant generalization of the human experience to use linguistic rules with vague predicates in order to formulate control actions. The formalizations of this concept by fuzzy set theory brought it to the field of control by using the apparatus of approximate reasoning. The main paradigm of fuzzy control which is that the control algorithm is a knowledge-based algorithm described by the methods of fuzzy logic is considered.

Chapter 13 shows that the vagueness of preferences and imperfect decision-relevant information require using suitable decision model which would be fundamentally different to the existing precise utility models. Precise utility models cannot reflect the vagueness of preferences, vagueness of objective conditions and outcomes, imprecise beliefs, etc. It is proposed as a decision theory, which is capable of dealing with vague preferences and imperfect information. The theory discussed here is based on a fuzzy-valued non-expected utility model representing linguistic preference relations and imprecise beliefs. Application results of the suggested decision theory are discussed.

Chapter 14 analyzes the issue of interpretability of fuzzy systems comprehensively in terms of semantics. The developed interpretability criteria apply to all aspects of fuzzy system designing: interpretability of fuzzy sets and rules, parameterized triangular norms, weights of importance and discretization points. In this chapter, a hybrid algorithm for selection of the structure and parameters of a fuzzy system, constructed on the basis of the genetic and the imperialist algorithms, is also introduced.

Chapter 15 discusses fuzzy reinforcement learning. Fuzzy learning algorithm to solve fuzzy dynamic programming problem is considered.

Chapter 16 proposes a class of adaptive networks that are functionally equivalent to fuzzy inference systems. The proposed architecture is referred to as adaptive neuro-fuzzy inference system (ANFIS), which stands for adaptive network-based fuzzy inference system or semantically equivalently, adaptive neuro-fuzzy inference system. The effectiveness of ANFIS with the hybrid learning rule is tested through simulation examples.

Chapter 17 presents fundamentals of fuzzy expert systems. Different types of fuzzy expert systems are discussed. Main emphasis is done on the shell of fuzzy expert system ESPLAN, suggested by authors. The problems connected with fuzzy knowledge representation in knowledge base of this system and the inference organization are discussed.

Chapter 18 considers the application of logistic regression analysis to fuzzy cognitive maps. Author suggests the model construction of complex systems with fuzzy cognitive maps which gives quite a simple method for simulating the diversified phenomena of the real world. Application of both logistic and multinomial logistic regression models to practical problems is considered.

Chapter 19 is devoted to the application of fuzzy logic in medicine. The chapter mainly introduces a results of fuzzy signal processing and a health checkup data analysis method on fuzzy interval $[0, 1]$.

This volume will be a useful reference guide for academics, practitioners, graduates and undergraduates in fuzzy logic and its applications.

Lotfi A. Zadeh
Rafik A. Aliev

About the Authors

 **Lotfi A. Zadeh** is a Professor at the Graduate School, Computer Science Division, Department of EECS, University of California, Berkeley. He is the Director of Berkeley Initiative in Soft Computing.

Lotfi A. Zadeh is an alumnus of the University of Tehran, MIT, and Columbia University. He joined the Department of Electrical Engineering at UC Berkeley in 1959.

Lotfi A. Zadeh is a Fellow of the IEEE, AAAS, ACM, AAAI, and IFSA. He is a member of the National Academies of Sciences of different countries. He is the recipient of a series of medals and prizes such as the IEEE Education Medal, the IEEE Medal of Honor, the Honda Prize, the SOFT Scientific Contribution Memorial Award of the Japan Society for Fuzzy Theory, the IEEE Millennium Medal, the Norbert Wiener Award of the IEEE Systems, Man and Cybernetics Society, the Franklin Institute Medal, the High State Award "Friendship Order", from the President of the Republic of Azerbaijan. He has published over 200 single-authored papers related to the conception and design of information/intelligent systems and is serving on the editorial boards of over 70 journals.

He is the creator of the theories of Z-transform, fuzzy logic, soft computing, computing with words, Z-numbers, and other theories.

Rafik A. Aliev received his post-graduate and Ph.D. degrees from the Institute of Control Problems, Moscow, USSR, in 1967 and 1975, respectively. His major fields of study are decision theory with imperfect information, arithmetic of Z-numbers, fuzzy logic, soft computing and control theory. He is a Professor and the Head of the Department of the joint MBA Program between the Georgia State University (Atlanta, GA, USA) and the Azerbaijan State University of Oil and Industry (Baku, Azerbaijan), and a Visiting Professor with the University of Siegen, (Siegen, Germany) and with Near East University, (Nicosia, North Cyprus). He is also an invited speaker at Georgia State University, (Atlanta, GA).

Dr. Aliev is a regular Chairman of the International Conferences on Fuzzy Logic and Soft Computing. He is an Editor of the *Journal of Advanced Computational Intelligence and Intelligent Informatics* (Japan), and an Associate Editor of the *Information Sciences* journal and other journals. He is the author of several monographs published by World Scientific, Springer, Technik Verlag, and other publishers. He was awarded the USSR State Prize in field of Science (1983), Lifetime Achievement Award, USA (2014), and International Fuzzy Systems Association Fuzzy Fellow Award (2015).

About the Contributors

Lotfi A. Zadeh

Professor at the Graduate School, Computer Science Division,
Department of EECS, University of California, Berkeley
E-mail: zadeh@berkeley.edu

Rafik A. Aliev

Professor, Joint MBA Program, Georgia State University, USA,
Azerbaijan State Oil and Industry University, Azerbaijan
Postal address: 20 Azadlig Ave., AZ1010 Baku, Azerbaijan
E-mail: raliev@asoa.edu.az

Witold Pedrycz

Professor, Department of Electrical & Computer Engineering,
University of Alberta, Canada
Postal address: Canada, Edmonton AB T6R 2V4 Canada
E-mail: wpedrycz@ualberta.ca

Dan E. Tamir

Professor, Department of Computer Science,
Texas State University San Marcos, Texas, USA
Postal address: USA, Texas, San Marcos Office, Comal 311F;
Round Rock Office, Avery 464X
E-mail: dt19@txstate.edu

Naphtali D. Rishe

Eminent Chair Professor of Computer Science, The Inaugural
Outstanding University Professor,
Florida International University,
Postal address: USA, Miami, High Performance Database Research
Center, School of Computing and Information Sciences,
University Park, FIU ECS-243, FL 33199
E-mail: rishe@fiu.edu

Abraham Kandel

Professor, Chairman, Computer Science and Engineering
Department, University of South Florida
Postal address: USA, Tampa, Florida 33620
E-mail: abraham.kandel.fiu@gmail.com

Hao Ying

Professor, Department of Electrical and Computer Engineering,
Wayne State University, USA
Postal address: USA, Michigan, Wayne State University,
42 W Warren Ave, Detroit, MI 48202, 5050 Anthony
Wayne Drive Engineering Building, Room 3144
E-mail: hao.ying@wayne.edu

Dimitar Filev

Executive Technical Leader, Autonomous Vehicles & Controls R&A,
Research & Innovation Center, Ford Motor Company, Rm. 1343,
Postal address: USA, 2101 Village Rd., Dearborn, MI 48121
E-mail: dfilev@ford.com

Leszek Rutkowski

Professor, Institute of Computational Intelligence,
Czestochowa University of Technology,
Postal address: Poland, Czestochowa,
Czestochowa University of Technology,

Institute of Computational Intelligence,
Armii Krajowej 36, 42-200
E-mail: leszek.rutkowski@iisi.pcz.pl

Hamid R. Berenji

Senior Research Scientist with Intelligent Inference Systems
Corporation at the Computational Sciences Division of NASA Ames
Research Center in Moffett Field, California
Postal address: Intelligent Inference Systems Corp.
Artificial Intelligence Research Branch, MS: 269-2,
NASA Ames Research Center Mountain View, CA 94035
E-mail: berenji@ptolomey.arc.nasa.gov

J.-S. Roger Jang

Professor, Department of Computer Science and Information
Engineering, National Taiwan University, Taiwan
Postal address: Taiwan, Taipei, No. 1, Section 4,
Roosevelt Rd, Da'an District, 10617
E-mail: jang@mirlab.org

Vesa A. Niskanen

Ph.D., Adjunct Professor (Computational Intelligence, ICT,
general methodology, e-learning), University of Helsinki
Postal address: Finland, Helsinki, University of Helsinki,
Department of Economics & Management, P.O. Box 27, 00014
E-mail: vesa.a.niskanen@helsinki.fi

Yutaka Hata

Ph.D. (Doctor of Engineering), Himeji Institute of Technology
Postal address: Japan, Kobe, Kobe Information Science Campus,
Computational Science Center Building,
7-1-28 Minatojima-minamimachi, Chuo-ku, Hyogo 650-0047
E-mail: hata@comp.eng.himeji-tech.ac.jp

Contents

Preface   vii

About the Authors   xiii

About the Contributors   xv

Part I   Fuzzy Logic Theory   1
     Lotfi A. Zadeh and Rafik A. Aliev

Chapter 1   Fuzzy Sets   3

     1.1   Introduction   3
     1.2   Definitions   4
     1.3   Some Properties of $\cup$, $\cap$, and Complementation .   7
     1.4   Algebraic Operations on Fuzzy Sets   8
     1.5   Convexity   11
     1.6   Examples on Operations on Fuzzy Sets   19
     1.7   Fuzzy Arithmetic   44
     1.8   Extensions of Fuzzy Sets   57
         1.8.1   Type-2 fuzzy sets and numbers   57
         1.8.2   Intuitionistic fuzzy sets   60
         1.8.3   Rough sets   62
         1.8.4   Neutrosophic set   63

Chapter 2   Fuzzy Logic   65

2.1   Introduction   65
2.2   Fuzzy Logic   68
2.3   Approximate Reasoning   80
2.4   Analysis of Different Fuzzy Logics   85
2.5   Extended Fuzzy Logic   113
      2.5.1   Introduction   114
      2.5.2 f-geometry and f-transformation   118

Chapter 3   Restriction Concept   125

3.1   Introduction to Restriction Concept   125
      3.1.1   Computation with restrictions   129
3.2   Truth and Meaning   132
      3.2.1   Truth qualification: Internal and external
            truth values   140

Chapter 4   Fuzzy Probabilities   147

4.1   Introduction   147
4.2   The Concept of Fuzzy Probability   148

Chapter 5   Fuzzy Functions   163

5.1   Definition of Fuzzy Functions   163
5.2   Integrability and Differentiability of Fuzzy
      Functions   165

Chapter 6   Fuzzy Systems   169

6.1   Introduction   169
6.2   System, Aggregate and State   171
6.3   State Equations for Fuzzy Systems   172
6.4   Fuzzy Rule-based System   183

Chapter 7   Z-number Theory   **189**

   7.1   Introduction   189
   7.2   Computation with Z-numbers   193
       7.2.1   Computation with continuous
              Z-numbers   193
       7.2.2   Computation with discrete
              Z-numbers   202
   7.3   Standard Division of Discrete Z-numbers   211

Chapter 8   Generalized Theory of Uncertainty   **213**

   8.1   Introduction   214
   8.2   The Concept of NL-Computation   217
   8.3   The Concept of Precisiation   219
   8.4   The Concept of Cointensive Precisiation   222
   8.5   A Key Idea — The Meaning Postulate   226
   8.6   The Concept of a Generalized
       Constraint   227
   8.7   Principal Modalities of Generalized
       Constraints   228
   8.8   The Concept of Bimodal Constraint/
       Distribution   233
   8.9   The Concept of a Group Constraint   236
   8.10   Primary Constraints, Composite Constraints and
        Standard Constraints   237
   8.11   The Generalized Constraint Language and
        Standard Constraint Language   238
   8.12   The Concept of Granular Value   239
   8.13   The Concept of Protoform   241
   8.14   The Concept of Generalized-Constraint-Based
        Computation   244
   8.15   Protoformal Deduction Rules   247

8.16   Examples of Computation/Deduction   253
    8.16.1 The Robert example   254
    8.16.2 The tall Swedes problem   255
    8.16.3 Tall Swedes and tall Italians   258
    8.16.4 Simplified trip planning   258

Part II   Applications and Advanced Topics of Fuzzy Logic   261

Lotfi A. Zadeh and Rafik A. Aliev (Eds.)

Chapter 9   Restriction-based Semantics   263

Lotfi A. Zadeh

9.1   Precisiation of Meaning   263
    9.1.1   Canonical form of p: $cf(p)$ 267
9.2   The Concept of Explanatory Database (ED) . . .   267

Chapter 10   Granular Computing: Principles and Algorithms   277

Witold Pedrycz

10.1   Introduction   277
10.2   Information Granularity: Selected Examples . . .   278
    10.2.1 Image processing   279
    10.2.2 Processing and interpretation of time
        series   279
    10.2.3 Granulation of time   280
    10.2.4 Data summarization   280
10.3   Formal Platforms of Information Granularity . .   284
10.4   Characterization of Information Granules:
    Coverage and Specificity   287
10.5   The Design of Information Granules   291
    10.5.1 The principle of justifiable granularity . .   292
    10.5.2 Augmentations of the principle of
        justifiable granularity   298

        10.5.2.1 Weighted data 298

        10.5.2.2 Inhibitory data 299

10.6   Information Granularity as a Design Asset in

      System Modeling 301

      10.6.1 Granular mappings 301

      10.6.2 Granular aggregation: An enhancement of

            aggregation operations through allocation

            of information granularity 304

      10.6.3 Development of granular models of higher

            type 305

10.7   Concluding Comments 307

Chapter 11 Complex Fuzzy Sets and Complex
**   Fuzzy Logic. An Overview of**
**   Theory and Applications   309**

           Dan E. Tamir, Naphtali D. Rishe and
           Abraham Kandel

11.1   Introduction 309

11.2   Complex Fuzzy Logic and Set Theory 312

      11.2.1 Complex fuzzy sets 312

      11.2.2 Complex fuzzy logic 313

11.3   Generalized Complex Fuzzy Logic 314

      11.3.1 Propositional and first-order predicate

            complex fuzzy logic 314

      11.3.2 Complex fuzzy propositions and inference

            examples 316

      11.3.3 Complex fuzzy inference example 317

11.4   Generalized Complex Fuzzy Class Theory 318

      11.4.1 Complex fuzzy classes and connectives

            examples 320

11.5   Pure Complex Fuzzy Classes 320

11.6   Recent Developments in the Theory and

      Applications of CFL and CFS 321

11.6.1 Advances in the theoretical foundations of CFL/CFS 321

11.6.2 Applications of CFL/CFS 322

11.7 Conclusion 325

Chapter 12 Introduction to Fuzzy Logic Control 327

Hao Ying and Dimitar Filev

12.1 Introduction 327

12.2 The Mamdani Fuzzy Controller 329

12.2.1 Fuzzification module 330

12.2.2 Fuzzy rules 332

12.2.3 Fuzzy inference mechanism and defuzzification 336

12.3 Design of Fuzzy Controllers 339

12.3.1 Selection of membership functions 339

12.3.2 Rule-base 340

12.3.3 Implementation 342

12.4 Multiple-Output, Single-Input (MISO) Mamdani Fuzzy Controllers 342

12.5 Takagi–Sugeno (TS) Fuzzy Controllers 344

12.6 Fuzzy Control Versus Conventional Control . . . 346

12.6.1 Advantages of fuzzy control 347

12.6.2 Disadvantages of fuzzy control 348

12.7 Applicability of Fuzzy Control 350

Chapter 13 Fuzzy Decision-Making 353

Rafik A. Aliev

13.1 Introduction 353

13.2 Definitions 362

13.3 Decision Model 366

13.4 Examples 374

13.4.1 Zadeh's two boxes problem 374

13.4.2 Investment problem 380

Chapter 14 Selected Interpretability Aspects of Fuzzy Systems for Classification   **401**

Leszek Rutkowski

14.1 Introduction 401

    14.1.1 Attempts at systematizing solutions for interpretability of fuzzy systems 404

    14.1.2 Solutions proposed in this chapter 405

14.2 Description of a Fuzzy System for Classification 406

    14.2.1 Rule base 406

    14.2.2 Defuzzification process 407

    14.2.3 Aggregation and inference operators . . . 408

14.3 A Hybrid Genetic-Imperialist Algorithm for Automatic Selection of Structure and Parameters of a Fuzzy System 410

    14.3.1 Encoding of potential solutions 411

    14.3.2 Evaluation of potential solutions 413

    14.3.3 Processing of potential solutions 414

14.4 Interpretability Criteria of a Fuzzy System for Classification 420

    14.4.1 Complexity evaluation criterion 420

    14.4.2 Fuzzy sets readability evaluation criterion 421

        14.4.2.1 Criterion for assessing similarity of fuzzy sets width 424

    14.4.3 Fuzzy rules readability evaluation criteria 425

        14.4.3.1 Criterion for assessing fuzzy rules activity 426

    14.4.4 Criterion for assessing the readability of weights values in the fuzzy rule base 427

    14.4.5 Criterion for assessing the readability of aggregation and inference operators 429

14.4.6 Criterion for assessing the defuzzification
mechanism   431
14.5 Simulations   432

Chapter 15 Fuzzy Reinforcement Learning   445

Hamid R. Berenji

15.1 The GARIC Architecture   445
15.2 The ACFRL Algorithm   447
15.3 Fuzzy *Q*-Learning to Solve Fuzzy Dynamic
Programming   451

**Chapter 16 Adaptive Neuro-Fuzzy Inference
Systems (ANFISs)   453**

J.-S. Roger Jang

16.1 Introduction   453
16.2 ANFIS Architecture   454
16.3 Hybrid Learning Algorithm   458
16.4 Learning Methods That Cross-Fertilize ANFIS
and RBFN   461
16.5 ANFIS as a Universal Approximator   462
16.5.1 Stone–Weierstrass theorem   462
16.5.2 Algebraic closure — Multiplicative   464
16.6 Simulation Examples   465
16.6.1 Practical considerations   465
16.6.2 Example 1: Modeling a two-input sinc
function   467
16.6.3 Example 2: Modeling a three-input
nonlinear function   469
16.6.4 Example 3: Online identification in control
systems   471
16.6.5 Example 4: Predicting chaotic time
series   476
16.6.6 Example 5: Dimensionality reduction for
ANFIS   486
16.7 Extensions and Advanced Topics   491

Chapter 17 Fuzzy Expert Systems 495

Rafik A. Aliev

17.1 Introduction 495
17.2 Fuzzy Expert Systems Using Bayes-Shortliffe
Approach 496
    17.2.1 Structure of the system 496
    17.2.2 Knowledge representation 497
    17.2.3 Inference 500
17.3 Examples 502
    17.3.1 The expert system for scheduling of
           oil-refinery production 502
    17.3.2 Fuzzy hypotheses generating and
           accounting systems 503
    17.3.3 Forecasting of conflicts 504

Chapter 18 Application of Logistic Regression Analysis to Fuzzy Cognitive Maps 507

Vesa A. Niskanen

18.1 Introduction 507
18.2 Fuzzy Cognitive Maps 508
18.3 Logistic and Multinomial Logistic Regression
Analysis 510
18.4 Application Examples 512
    18.4.1 The city-health model 513
    18.4.2 The liquid tank model 522
18.5 Conclusions 528

Chapter 19 Fuzzy Logic in Medicine 531

Yutaka Hata

19.1 Introduction 531
19.2 Fuzzy Signal Processing-Trans-Skull Brain
Imaging 532
    19.2.1 Characteristics with respect to echo
           shape, λ_f 534

19.2.2 Characteristics with respect to magnitude
of echo amplitude, λ_α   535

19.2.3 Characteristic value with respect to
location, λ_{th}   535

19.3   Health Checkup Data Analysis   541

Bibliography   547

Index   577

Part I
Fuzzy Logic Theory

Chapter 1

Fuzzy Sets

A fuzzy set is a class of objects with a continuum of grades of membership. Such set is characterized by a membership (characteristic) function which assigns to each object a grade of membership ranging between zero and one. The notions of inclusion, union, intersection, complement, relation, convexity, etc., are extended to such sets, and various properties of these notions in the context of fuzzy sets are described. In particular, a separation theorem for convex fuzzy sets is proved without requiring that the fuzzy sets be disjoint [501].

1.1. Introduction

More often than not, the classes of objects encountered in the real physical world do not have precisely defined criteria of membership. For example, the class of animals clearly includes dogs, horses, birds, etc. as its members, and clearly excludes such objects as rocks, fluids, plants, etc. However, such objects as starfish, bacteria, etc. have an ambiguous status with respect to the class of animals. The same kind of ambiguity arises in the case of a number such as 10 in relation to the "class" of all real numbers which are much greater than 1.

Clearly, the "class of all real numbers which are much greater than 1," or "the class of beautiful women," or "the class of tall men," do not constitute classes or sets in the usual mathematical sense of these terms. Yet, the fact remains that such imprecisely defined "classes" play an important role in human thinking, particularly in the domains of pattern recognition, communication of information, and abstraction.

3

The purpose of this chapter is to explore in a preliminary way some of the basic properties and implications of a concept which may be used in dealing with "classes" of the type cited above. The concept in question is that of a *fuzzy set*, that is, a "class" with a continuum of grades of membership. As will be seen in the sequel, the notion of a fuzzy set provides a convenient point of departure for the construction of a conceptual framework which parallels in many respects the framework used in the case of ordinary sets, but is more general than the latter and, potentially, may prove to have a much wider scope of applicability, particularly in the fields of pattern classification and information processing. Essentially, such a framework provides a natural way of dealing with problems in which the source of imprecision is the absence of sharply defined criteria of class membership rather than the presence of random variables.

We begin the discussion of fuzzy sets with several basic definitions.

1.2. Definitions

Let X be a space of points (objects), with a generic element of X denoted by x. Thus, $X = \{x\}$.

A fuzzy set (class) A in X is characterized by a *membership (characteristic) function* $\mu_A(X)$ which associates with each point in X a real number in the interval $[0, 1]$, with the value of $\mu_A(X)$ at x representing the "grade of membership" of x in A. Thus, the nearer the value of $\mu_A(X)$ *to* unity, the higher the grade of membership of x in A. When A is a set in the ordinary sense of the term, its membership function can take on only two values 0 and 1, with $\mu_A(X) = 1$ or 0 according as x does or does not belong to A. Thus, in this case, $\mu_A(X)$ reduces to the familiar characteristic function of a set A. (When there is a need to differentiate between such sets and fuzzy sets, the sets with two-valued characteristic functions will be referred to as *ordinary sets* or simply *sets*.)

Example: Let X be the real line R^1 and let A be a fuzzy set of numbers which are much greater than 1. Then, one can give a precise, albeit subjective, characterization of A by specifying $\mu_A(X)$ as a function on R^1. Representative values of such a function might be: $\mu_A(0) = 0$; $\mu_A(1) = 0$; $\mu_A(10) = 0.2$; $\mu_A(100) = 0.95$; $\mu_A(500) = 1$.

It should be noted that, although the membership function of a fuzzy set has some resemblance to a probability function when X is a countable set (or a probability density function when X is a continuum), there are essential differences between these concepts which will become clearer in the sequel once the rules of combination of membership functions and their basic properties have been established. In fact, the notion of a fuzzy set is completely non-statistical in nature.

We begin with several definitions involving fuzzy sets which are obvious extensions of the corresponding definitions for ordinary sets.

A fuzzy set is *empty* if and only if its membership function is identically zero on X.

Two fuzzy sets A and B are *equal*, written as $A = B$, if and only if $\mu_A(X) = \mu_B(X)$ for all x in X. (In the sequel, instead of writing $\mu_A(X) = \mu_B(X)$ for all x in X, we shall write more simply $\mu_A = \mu_B$.)

The *complement* of a fuzzy set A is denoted by A' and is defined by

$$\mu_{A'} = 1 - \mu_A \tag{1.1}$$

As in the case of ordinary sets, the notion of containment plays a central role in the ease of fuzzy sets. This notion and the related notions of union and intersection are defined as follows.

Containment. A is contained in B (or, equivalently, A is a subset of B, or A is smaller than or equal to B) if and only $\mu_A \leqq \mu_B$. In symbols

$$A \subset B \Leftrightarrow \mu_A \leqq \mu_B \tag{1.2}$$

Union. The *union* of two fuzzy sets A and B with respective membership functions $\mu_A(X)$ and $\mu_B(B)$ is a fuzzy set C, written as $C = A \cup B$, whose membership function is related to those of A and B by

$$\mu_C(X) = \text{Max}[\mu_A(X), \mu_B(X)], \quad x \in X \tag{1.3}$$

or, in abbreviated form,

$$\mu_c = \mu_A \vee \mu_B \qquad (1.4)$$

Note that $\cup$ has the associative property, that is, $A \cup (B \cup C) = (A \cup B) \cup C$.

A more intuitively appealing way of defining the union is the following: The union of A and B is the smallest fuzzy set containing both A and B. More precisely, if D is any fuzzy set which contains both A and B, then it also contains the union of A and B.

To show that this definition is equivalent to (1.3), we note, first, that C as defined by (1.3) contains both A and B, since

$$\text{Max}[\mu_A, \mu_B] \geqq \mu_A$$

and

$$\text{Max}[\mu_A, \mu_B] \geqq \mu_B$$

Furthermore, if D is any fuzzy set containing both A and B, then

$$\mu_D \geqq \mu_A$$

$$\mu_D \geqq \mu_B$$

and hence

$$\mu_D \geqq \text{Max}[\mu_A, \mu_B] = \mu_C$$

which implies that $C \subset D$. $\square$

The notion of an intersection of fuzzy sets can be defined in an analogous manner. Specifically:

Intersection. The *intersection* of two fuzzy sets A and B with respective membership functions $\mu_A(X)$ and $\mu_B(X)$ is a fuzzy set C, written as $C = A \cap B$, whose membership function is related to those of A and B by

$$\mu_C(X) = \text{Min}[\mu_A(X), \mu_B(X)], \quad x \in X \qquad (1.5)$$

or, in abbreviated form,

$$\mu_c = \mu_A \wedge \mu_B \qquad (1.6)$$

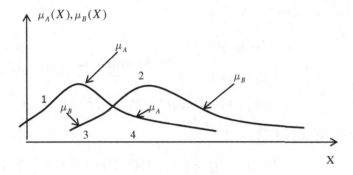

Fig. 1.1. Illustration of the union and intersection of fuzzy sets in R^1.

As in the case of the union, it is easy to show that the intersection of A and B is the *largest* fuzzy set which is contained in both A and B. As in the case of ordinary sets, A and B are *disjoint* if $A \cap B$ is empty. Note that $\cap$, like $\cup$, has the associative property.

The intersection and union of two fuzzy sets in R^1 are illustrated in Fig. 1.1. The membership function of the union comprises curve segments 1 and 2; that of the intersection comprise segments 3 and 4 (heavy lines).

Note that the notion of "belonging", which plays a fundamental role in the case of ordinary sets, does not have the same role in the case of fuzzy sets. Thus, it is not meaningful to speak of a point x "belonging" to a fuzzy set A except in the trivial sense of $\mu_A(X)$ being positive.

Less trivially, one can introduce two levels α and $\beta(0 < \alpha < 1, 0 < \beta < 1, \alpha > \beta)$ and agree to say that (1.1) "x belongs to A" if $\mu_A(X) \geqq \alpha$; (1.2) "x does not belong to A" if $\mu_A(X) \leqq \beta$, and (1.3) "x has an indeterminate status relative to A" if $\beta < \mu_A(X) < \alpha$. This leads to a three-valued logic [241] with three truth values: $T(\mu_A(x) \geqq \alpha)$, $F(\mu_A(x) \leqq \beta)$, and $U(\beta < \mu_A(X) < \alpha)$.

1.3. Some Properties of $\cup$, $\cap$, and Complementation

With the operations of union, intersection, and complementation defined as in (1.3), (1.5), and (1.1), it is easy to extend many of the basic identities which hold for ordinary sets to fuzzy sets. As examples, we have

$$(A \cup B)' = A' \cap B' \Bigg\} \text{ De Morgan's laws} \quad (1.7)$$
$$(A \cap B)' = A' \cup B' \qquad\qquad\qquad\qquad (1.8)$$

$$C \cap (A \cup B) = (C \cap A) \cup (C \cap B) \qquad (1.9)$$

Distributive laws

$$C \cup (A \cap B) = (C \cup A) \cap (C \cup B) \qquad (1.10)$$

These and similar equalities can be readily established by showing that the corresponding relations for the membership functions of A, B, and C are identities. For example, in the case of (1.7), we have

$$1 - \text{Max}[\mu_A, \mu_B] = \text{Min}[1 - \mu_A, 1 - \mu_B] \qquad (1.11)$$

which can be easily verified to be an identity by testing it for the two possible cases: $\mu_A(x) > \mu_B(x)$ and $\mu_A(x) < \mu_B(x)$.

Similarly, in the case of (1.10), the corresponding relation in terms of μ_A, μ_B and μ_C is

$$\text{Max}[\mu_C, \text{Min}[\mu_A, \mu_B]] = \text{Min}[\text{Max}[\mu_C, \mu_A], \text{Max}[\mu_C, \mu_B]] \qquad (1.12)$$

which can be verified to be an identity by considering the six cases:

$$\mu_A(x) > \mu_B(x) > \mu_C(x), \mu_A(x) > \mu_C(x) > \mu_B(x)$$
$$\mu_B(x) > \mu_A(x) > \mu_C(x), \mu_B(x) > \mu_C(x) > \mu_A(x) \qquad (1.13)$$
$$\mu_C(x) > \mu_A(x) > \mu_B(x), \mu_C(x) > \mu_B(x) > \mu_A(x)$$

Essentially, fuzzy sets in X constitute a distributive lattice with a 0 and 1 [74].

1.4.   Algebraic Operations on Fuzzy Sets

In addition to the operations of union and intersection, one can define a number of other ways of forming combinations of fuzzy sets and relating them to one another. Among the more important of these are the following.

Algebraic product. The algebraic product of A and B is denoted by $A\,B$ and is defined in terms of the membership functions of A and B by the relation

$$\mu_{AB} = \mu_A\mu_B \tag{1.14}$$

Clearly,

$$A\,B \subset A \cap B \tag{1.15}$$

Algebraic sum. The *algebraic sum* of A and B is denoted by $A + B$ and is defined by

$$\mu_{A+B} = \mu_A + \mu_B \tag{1.16}$$

provided the sum $\mu_A + \mu_B$ is less than or equal to unity. Thus, unlike the algebraic product, the algebraic sum is meaningful only when the condition $\mu_A(x) + \mu_B(x) \leqq 1$ is satisfied for all x.

Absolute difference. The *absolute difference* of A and B is denoted by $|A - B|$ and is defined by

$$\mu_{|A-B|} = |\mu_A - \mu_B|$$

Note that in the case of ordinary sets $|A - B|$ reduces to the relative complement of $A \cap B$ in $A \cup B$.

Convex combination. A convex combination of two vectors μ and g is usually meant to be a linear combination of μ and g of the form $\lambda\mu + (1 - \lambda)g$, in which $0 \leq \lambda \leq 1$. This mode of combining μ and g can be generalized to fuzzy sets in the following manner.

Let A, B, and Λ be arbitrary fuzzy sets. The *convex combination of A, B, and Λ* is denoted by $(A, B; \Lambda)$ and is defined by the relation

$$(A, B; \Lambda) = \Lambda A + \Lambda' B \tag{1.17}$$

where Λ' is the complement of Λ. Written out in terms of membership functions, (1.17) reads

$$\mu_{(A,B;\Lambda)}(x) = \mu_A(x)\mu_\Lambda(x) + [1 - \mu_\Lambda(x)]\mu_B(x), \quad x \in X \tag{1.18}$$

A basic property of the convex combination of A, B, and Λ is expressed by

$$A \cap B \subset (A, B; \Lambda) \subset A \cup B \text{ for all } \Lambda \qquad (1.19)$$

This property is an immediate consequence of the inequalities

$$\text{Min}[\mu_A(x), \mu_B(x)] \leqq \lambda \mu_A(x) + (1 - \lambda)\mu_B(x)$$

$$\leqq \text{Max}[\mu_A(x), \mu_B(x)], \quad x \in X \qquad (1.20)$$

which hold for all λ in [0, 1]. It is of interest to observe that, given any fuzzy set C satisfying $A \cap B \subset C \subset A \cup B$, one can always find a fuzzy set Λ such that $C = (A, B; \Lambda)$. The membership function of this set is given by

$$\mu_\Lambda(x) = \frac{\mu_C(x) - \mu_B(x)}{\mu_A(x) - \mu_B(x)}, \quad x \in X \qquad (1.21)$$

Fuzzy relation. The concept of a relation (which is a generalization of that of a function) has a natural extension to fuzzy sets and plays an important role in the theory of such sets and their applications — just as it does in the case of ordinary sets. In the sequel, we shall merely define the notion of a fuzzy relation and touch upon a few related concepts.

Ordinarily, a relation is defined as a set of ordered pairs [194], e.g., the set of all ordered pairs of real numbers x and y such that $x \geq y$. In the context of fuzzy sets, a fuzzy relation in X is a fuzzy set in the product space $X \times X$. For example, the relation denoted by $x \gg y$, $x, y \in R^1$, may be regarded as a fuzzy set A in R^2, with the membership function of A, $\mu_A(x, y)$, having the following (subjective) representative values: $\mu_A(10, 5) = 0, \mu_A(100, 10) = 0, 7, \mu_A(100, 1) = 1$, etc.

More generally, one can define an *n-ary fuzzy relation* in X as a fuzzy set A in the product space $X \times X \times \cdots \times X$. For such relations, the membership function is of the form $\mu_A(x_1, \ldots, x_n)$ where $x_i \in X$, $i = 1, \ldots, n$.

In the case of binary fuzzy relations, the *composition* of two fuzzy relations A and B is denoted by $B \circ A$ and is defined as a fuzzy relation in X whose membership function is related to those of A

and B by

$$\mu_{B \circ A}(x, y) = \operatorname{Sup}_v \operatorname{Min}[\mu_A(x, v), \mu_B(v, y)]$$

Note that the operation of composition has the associative property

$$A \circ (B \circ C) = (A \circ B) \circ C$$

Fuzzy sets induced by mappings. Let T be a mapping from X to a space Y. Let B be a fuzzy set in Y with membership function $\mu_B(y)$. The inverse mapping T^{-1} induces a fuzzy set A in X whose membership function is defined by for all x in X which are mapped by T into y.

$$\mu_A(x) = \mu_B(y), \quad y \in Y \qquad (1.22)$$

Consider now a converse problem in which A is a given fuzzy set in X, and T, as before, is a mapping from X to Y. The question is: What is the membership function for the fuzzy set B in Y which is induced by this mapping?

If T is not one-one, then an ambiguity arises when two or more distinct points in X, say x_1 and x_2, with different grades of membership in A, are mapped into the same point y in Y. In this case, the question is: What grade of membership in B should be assigned to y?

To resolve this ambiguity, we agree to assign the larger of the two grades of membership to y. More generally, the membership function for B will be defined by where $T^{-1}(y)$ is the set of points in X which are mapped into y by T.

$$\mu_B(y) = \operatorname*{Max}_{x \in T^{-1}(y)} \mu_A(x), \quad y \in Y \qquad (1.23)$$

1.5. Convexity

As will be seen in the sequel, the notion of convexity can readily be extended to fuzzy sets in such a way as to preserve many of the properties which it has in the context of ordinary sets. This notion appears to be particularly useful in applications involving pattern classification, optimization and related problems.

In what follows, we assume for concreteness that X is a real Euclidean space E^n.

Convexity. A fuzzy set A is *convex* if and only if the sets Γ_α defined by

$$\Gamma_\alpha = \{x | \mu_A(x) \geq \alpha\} \tag{1.24}$$

are convex for all α in the interval $(0, 1]$.

An alternative and more direct definition of convexity is the following: A is *convex* if and only if

$$\mu_A[\lambda x_1 + (1 - \lambda)x_2] \geq \text{Min}[\mu_A(x_1), \mu_A(x_2)] \tag{1.25}$$

for all x_1 and x_2 in X and all λ in $[0, 1]$. Note that this definition does not imply that $\mu_A(x)$ must be a convex function of x. This is illustrated in Fig. 1.2 for $n = 1$.

To show the equivalence between the above definitions, note that if A is convex in the sense of the first definition and $\alpha = \mu_A(x_1) \leq \mu_A(x_2)$, then $x_2 \in \Gamma_\alpha$, and $\lambda x_1 + (1 - \lambda)x_2 \in \Gamma_\alpha$ by the convexity of Γ_α. Hence,

$$\mu_A[\lambda x_1 + (1 - \lambda)x_2] \geq \alpha = \mu_A(x_1) = \text{Min}[\mu_A(x_1), \mu_A(x_2)]$$

Conversely, if A is convex in the sense of the second definition and $\alpha = \mu_A(x_1)$, then Γ_α may be regarded as the set of all points x_2 for which $\mu_A(x_2) \geq \mu_A(x_1)$. In virtue of (1.25), every point of the form $\lambda x_1 + (1 - \lambda)x_2$, $0 \leq \lambda \leq 1$, is also in Γ_α and hence Γ_α is a convex set.

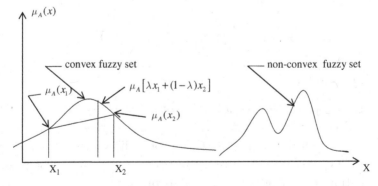

Fig. 1.2. Convex and non-convex fuzzy sets in E^1.

A basic property of convex fuzzy sets is expressed by the following theorem.

Theorem 1.1. *If A and B are convex, so is their intersection.*

Proof. Let $C = A \cap B$. Then

$$\mu_C[\lambda x_1 + (1 - \lambda)x_2]$$
$$= \text{Min}[\mu_A[\lambda x_1 + (1 - \lambda)x_2], \mu_B[\lambda x_1 + (1 - \lambda)x_2]] \quad (1.26)$$

Now, since A and B are convex,

$$\mu_A[\lambda x_1 + (1 - \lambda)x_2] \geq \text{Min}[\mu_A(x_1), \mu_A(x_2)]$$
$$\mu_B[\lambda x_1 + (1 - \lambda)x_2] \geq \text{Min}[\mu_B(x_1), \mu_B(x_2)] \quad (1.27)$$

and hence

$$\mu_C[\lambda x_1 + (1 - \lambda)x_2]$$
$$\geq \text{Min}[\text{Min}[\mu_A(x_1), \mu_A(x_2)], \text{Min}[\mu_B(x_1), \mu_B(x_2)]] \quad (1.28)$$

or equivalently

$$\mu_C[\lambda x_1 + (1 - \lambda)x_2] \geq \text{Min} \begin{bmatrix} \text{Min}[\mu_A(x_1), \mu_B(x_1)], \\ \text{Min}[\mu_A(x_2), \mu_B(x_2)] \end{bmatrix} \quad (1.29)$$

and thus

$$\mu_C[\lambda x_1 + (1 - \lambda)x_2] \geq \text{Min}[\mu_C(x_1), \mu_C(x_2)] \quad (1.30)$$

$\square$

Boundedness. A fuzzy set A is *bounded* if and only if the sets $\Gamma_\alpha = \{x | \mu_A(x) \geq \alpha\}$ are bounded for all $\alpha > 0$, that is, for every $\alpha > 0$, there exists a finite $R(\alpha)$ such that $\|x\| \leq R(\alpha)$ for all x in Γ_α.

If A is a bounded set, then for each $\epsilon > 0$, there exists a hyperplane H such that $\mu_A(x) \leq \epsilon$ for all x on the side of H which does not contain the origin. Consider the set $\Gamma_\epsilon = \{x | \mu_A(x) \geq \epsilon\}$. By hypothesis, this set is contained in a sphere S of radius $R(\epsilon)$. Let H be any hyper plane supporting S. Then, all points on the side of H which does not contain the origin lie outside or on S, and hence for all such points, $\mu_A(x) \leq \epsilon$.

Lemma 1.1. *Let A be a bounded fuzzy set and let $M = \text{Sup}_x \mu_A(x)$. (M will be referred to as the maximal grade in A.) Then there is at least one point x_0 at which M is essentially attained in the sense that, for each $\epsilon > 0$, every spherical neighborhood of x_0 contains points in the set $Q(\epsilon) = \{x | \mu_A(x) \geq M - \epsilon\}$.*

Proof. Consider a nested sequence of bounded sets $\Gamma_1, \Gamma_2, \ldots,$ where $\Gamma_n = \{x | \mu_A(x) \geq M - M/(n+1)\}$, $n = 1, 2 \ldots$. Note that Γ_n is non-empty for all finite n as a consequence of the definition of M as $M = \text{Sup}_x \mu_A(x)$ (we assume that $M > 0$).

Let x_n be an arbitrarily chosen point in $\Gamma_n, 1, 2, \ldots$. Then, $x_1, x_2, \ldots,$ is a sequence of points in a closed bounded set Γ_1. By the Bolzano–Weierstrass theorem, this sequence must have at least one limit point, say x_0, in Γ_1. Consequently, every spherical neighborhood of x_0 will contain infinitely many points from the sequence $x_1, x_2, \ldots,$ and, more particularly, from the subsequence $x_{N+1}, x_{N+2}, \ldots,$ where $N \geq M/\epsilon$. Since the points of this subsequence fall within the set $Q(\epsilon) = \{x | \mu_A(x) \geq M - \epsilon\}$, the lemma is proved.   □

Strict and strong convexity. A fuzzy set A is *strictly convex* if the sets Γ_α, $0 < \alpha \leq 1$ are strictly convex (that is, if the midpoint of any two distinct points in Γ_α lies in the interior of Γ_α). Note that this definition reduces to that of strict convexity for ordinary sets when A is such a set.

A fuzzy set A is *strongly convex* if, for any two distinct points x_1 and x_2, and any λ in the open interval $(0, 1)$

$$\mu_A[\lambda x_1 + (1 - \lambda)x_2] > \text{Min}[\mu_A(x_1), \mu_A(x_2)]$$

Note that strong convexity does not imply strict convexity or vice versa. Note also that if A and B are bounded, so is their union and intersection. Similarly, if A and B are strictly (strongly) convex, their intersection is strictly (strongly) convex.

Let A be a convex fuzzy set and let $M = \text{Sup}_x \mu_A(x)$. If A is bounded, then, as shown above, either M is attained for some x, say x_0, or there is at least one point, x_0 at which M is essentially attained in the sense that, for each $\epsilon > 0$, every spherical neighborhood of x_0 contains points in the set $Q(\epsilon) = \{x | M - \mu_A(x) \leqq \epsilon\}$. In particular, if A is strongly convex and x_0 is attained, then x_0 is unique. For, if $M = \mu_A(x_0)$ and $M = \mu_A(x_1)$, with $x_1 \neq x_0$, then $\mu_A(x) > M$ for $x = 0.5x_0 + 0.5x_1$, which contradicts $M = \text{Max}_x \mu_A(x)$.

More generally, let $C(A)$ be the set of all points in X at which M is essentially attained. This set will be referred to as the *core* of A. In the case of convex fuzzy sets, we can assert the following property of $C(A)$.

Theorem 1.2. *If A is a convex fuzzy set, then its core is a convex set.*

Proof. It will suffice to show that if M is essentially attained at x_0 and x_1, $x_1 \neq x_0$, then it is also essentially attained at all x of the form $x = \lambda x_0 + (1 - \lambda)x_1, 0 \leqq \lambda \leqq 1$.

To the end, let P be a cylinder of radius ϵ with the line passing through x_0 and x_1 as its axis. Let x_0' be a point in a sphere of radius ϵ centering on x_0 and x_1' be a point in a sphere of radius ϵ centering on x_1 such that $\mu_A(x_0') \geqq M - \epsilon$ and $\mu_A(x_1') \geqq M - \epsilon$. Then, by convexity of A, for any point u on the segment $x_0' x_1'$, we have $\mu_A(u) \geqq M - \epsilon$. Furthermore, by the convexity of P, all points on $x_0' x_1'$ will lie in P.

Now, let x be any point in the segment $x_0 x_1$. The distance of this point from the segment $x_0' x_1'$ must be less than or equal to ϵ, since $x_0' x_1'$ lies in P. Consequently, a sphere of radius ϵ centering on x will contain at least one point of the segment $x_0' x_1'$ and hence will contain at least one point, say ω, at which $\mu_A(\omega) \geqq M - \epsilon$. This establishes that M is essentially attained at x and thus proves the Theorem 1.2. $\square$

Corollary. *If $X = E^1$ and A is strongly convex, then the point at which M is essentially attained is unique.*

Shadow of a fuzzy set. Let A be a fuzzy set in E^n with membership function $\mu_A(x) = \mu_A(x_1, \ldots, x_n)$. For notational simplicity, the notion of the *shadow* (projection) of A on a hyperplane H will be defined below for the special case where H is a coordinate hyperplane, e.g., $H = \{x | x_1 = 0\}$.

Specifically, the *shadow* of A on $H = \{x|x_1 = 0\}$ is defined to be a fuzzy set $S_H(A)$ in E^{n-1} with $\mu_{S_H(A)}(x)$ given by

$$\mu_{S_H(A)}(x) = \mu_{S_H(A)}(x_2, \ldots, x_n) = \mathrm{Sup}_{x_1}\mu_A(x_1, \ldots, x_n)$$

Note that this definition is consistent with (1.23).

When A is a convex fuzzy set, the following property of $S_H(A)$ is an immediate consequence of the above definition: If A is a convex fuzzy set, then its shadow on any hyperplane is also a convex fuzzy set.

An interesting property of the shadows of two convex fuzzy sets is expressed by the following implication:

$$S_H(A) = S_H(B) \quad \text{for all } H \Rightarrow A = B$$

To prove this assertion, it is sufficient to show that if there exists a point, say x_0, such that $\mu_A(x_0) \neq \mu_B(x_0)$, then there exists a hyperplane H such that $\mu_{S_H(A)}(x_0^*) \neq \mu_{S_H(B)}(x_0^*)$, where x_0^* is the projection x_0 of on H.

Suppose that $\mu_A(x_0) = \alpha > \mu_B(x_0) = \beta$. Since B is a convex fuzzy set, the set $\Gamma_B = \{x|\mu_B(x) > \beta\}$ is convex, and hence there exists a hyperplane F supporting Γ_B and passing through x_0. Let H be a hyperplane orthogonal to F, and let x_0^* be the projection of x_0 on H. Then, since $\mu_B(x) \leqq \beta$ for all x on F, we have $\mu_{S_H(B)}(x_0^*) \leqq \beta$. On the other hand, $\mu_{S_H(A)}(x_0^*) \geqq \alpha$. Consequently, $\mu_{S_H(B)}(x_0^*) \neq \mu_{S_H(A)}(x_0^*)$, and similarly for the case where $\alpha < \beta$.

A somewhat more general form of the above assertion is the following: Let A, but not necessarily B, be a convex fuzzy set, and let $S_H(A) = S_H(B)$ for all H. Then $A = \mathrm{conv}\, B$, where conv B is the convex hull of B, that is, the smallest convex set containing B. More generally, $S_H(A) = S_H(B)$ for all H implies conv $A = \mathrm{conv}\, B$.

Separation of convex fuzzy sets. The classical separation theorem for ordinary convex sets states, in essence, that if A and B are disjoint convex sets, then there exists a separating hyperplane H such that A is on one side of H and B is on the other side.

It is natural to enquire if this theorem can be extended to convex fuzzy sets, without requiring that A and B be disjoint, since the condition of disjointness is much too restrictive in the case of fuzzy sets. It turns out, as will be seen in the sequel, that the answer to this question is in the affirmative.

As a preliminary, we shall have to make a few definitions. Specifically, let A and B be two bounded fuzzy sets and let H be a hypersurface in E^n defined by an equation $h(x) = 0$, with all points for which $h(x) \geq 0$ being on one side of H and all points for which $h(x) \leq 0$ being on the other side.

Let K_H be a number dependent on H such that $\mu_A(x) \leq K_H$ on one side of H and $\mu_B(x) \leq K_H$ on the other side. Let M_H be Inf K_H. The number $D_H = 1 - M_H$ will be called the degree of separation of *A and B by H.*

In general, one is concerned not with a given hypersurface H, but with a family of hypersurfaces $\{H_\lambda\}$, with λ ranging over, say, E^m. The problem, then, is to find a member of this family which realizes the highest possible degree of separation.

A special case of this problem is one where the H_λ are hyperplanes in E^n, with λ, ranging over E^n. In this case, we define the degree of separability of A and B by the relation

$$D = 1 - \bar{M} \qquad (1.31)$$

where

$$\bar{M} = \text{Inf}_B M_H \qquad (1.32)$$

with the subscript λ, omitted for simplicity.

Among the various assertions that can be made concerning D, the following statement is, in effect, an extension of the separation theorem to convex fuzzy sets.

Theorem 1.3. *Let A and B be bounded convex fuzzy sets in E^n, with maximal grades M_A and M_B, respectively* $[M_A = \text{Sup}_x \mu_A(x), M_B = \text{Sup}_x \mu_B(x)]$. *Let M be the maximal grade for the intersection $A \cap B$ $(M = \text{Sup}_x \text{Min}[\mu_A(x), \mu_B(x)])$. Then $D = 1 - M$.*

In plain words, the theorem states that the highest degree of separation of two convex fuzzy sets A and B that can be achieved

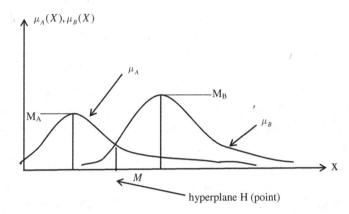

Fig. 1.3. Illustration of the separation theorem for fuzzy sets in E^1.

with a hyperplane in E^n is one minus the maxima l grade in the intersection $A \cap B$. This is illustrated in Fig. 1.3 for $n = 1$.

Proof. It is convenient to consider separately the following two cases: (1) $M = \text{Min}(M_A, M_B)$ and (2) $M < \text{Min}(M_A, M_B)$. Note that the latter case rules out $A \subset B$ or $B \subset A$.

Case 1. For concreteness, assume that $M_A < M_B$, so that $M = M_A$ Then, by the property of bounded sets already stated, there exists a hyperplane H such that $\mu_B(x) \leq M$ for all x on one side of H. On the other side of H, $\mu_A(x) \leq M$ because $\mu_A(x) \leq M_A = M$ for all x.

It remains to be shown that there does not exist an $M' < M$, and a hyperplane H' such that $\mu_A(x) \leq M'$ on one side of H' and $\mu_B(x) \leq M'$ on the other side.

This follows at once from the following observation. Suppose that such H' and M' exist, and assume for concreteness that the core of A (that is, the set of points at which $M_A = M$ is essentially attained) is on the plus side of H'. This rules out the possibility that $\mu_A(x) \leq M'$ for all x on the plus side of H' and hence necessitates that $\mu_A(x) \leq M'$ for all x on the minus side of H', and $\mu_B(x) \leq M'$ for all x on the plus side of H'. Consequently, over all x on the plus side of H'

$$\text{Sup}_x \text{Min}[\mu_A(x), \mu_B(x)] \leq M'$$

and likewise for all x on the minus side of H'. This implies that, over all x in X, $\text{Sup}_x\text{Min}[\mu_A(x), \mu_B(x)] \leqq M'$, which contradicts the assumption that $\text{Sup}_x\text{Min}[\mu_A(x), \mu_B(x)] = M > M'$.

Case 2. Consider the convex sets $\Gamma_A = \{x|\mu_A(x) > M\}$ and $\Gamma_B = \{x|\mu_B(x) > M\}$. These sets are non-empty and disjoint, for if they were not there would be a point, say u, such that $\mu_A(u) > M$ and $\mu_B(u) > M$, and hence $\mu_{A\cap B}(u) > M$, which contradicts the assumption that $M = \text{Sup}_x\mu_{A\cap B}(x)$.

Since Γ_A and Γ_B are disjoint, by the separation theorem for ordinary convex sets, there exists a hyperplane H such that Γ_A is on one side of H (say, the plus side) and Γ_B is on the other side (the minus side). Furthermore, by the definitions of Γ_A and Γ_B, for all points on the minus side of H, $\mu_A(x) \leqq M$, and for all points on the plus side of H, $\mu_B(x) \leqq M$.

Thus, we have shown that there exists a hyperplane H which realizes $1 - M$ as the degree of separation of A and B. The conclusion that a higher degree of separation of A and B cannot be realized follows from the argument given in Case 1. This concludes the proof of the theorem. $\qquad\square$

The separation theorem for convex fuzzy sets appears to be of particular relevance to the problem of pattern discrimination. Its application to this class of problems as well as to problems of optimization will be explored in subsequent notes on fuzzy sets and their properties.

1.6. Examples on Operations on Fuzzy Sets [17]

Equality of fuzzy sets

Two fuzzy sets A and B are said to be equal if and only if

$$\forall x \in X \quad \mu_A(x) = \mu_B(x) \quad A = B$$

The support and the crossover point of a fuzzy set. The singleton

The support of a fuzzy set A is the ordinary subset of X that has non-zero membership in A:

$$\text{supp } A = A^{+0} = \{x \in X, \mu_A(x) > 0\}$$

The elements of x such as $\mu_A(x) = 1/2$ are the crossover points of A.

A fuzzy set that has only one point in X with $\mu_A = 1$ as its support is called a singleton.

The height of a fuzzy set. Normal and subnormal sets

The height of A is

$$\text{hgt}(A) = \sup_{x \in X} \mu_A(x)$$

that is, the least upper bound of $\mu_A(x)$.

A is said to be normalized iff $\exists\, x \in X$, $\mu_A(x) = 1$. This definition implies $\text{hgt}(A) = 1$. Otherwise, A is called subnormal fuzzy set.

The empty set $\emptyset$ is defined as

$$x \in X,\ \mu_\emptyset(x) = 0,\ \text{of course}\ \forall x \in X,\ \mu_X(x) = 1$$

Example:

$$A = 0.3/20 + 0.5/22 + 1.0/25 + 0.8/27 + 0.4/30$$

Here, the universe X is

$$X = \{15, 20, 22, 25, 27, 30, 33, 35\}$$

$$\text{supp } A = \{20, 22, 25, 27, 30\}$$

A is normalized, i.e., $25 \in X, \mu_A(25) = 1$,

$$\text{hgt}(A) = \sup_{x \in X} \mu_A(x) = \sup_{x \in 15,\ldots,35} \{0, 0.3, 9.5, 1.0, 0.8, 0.4\} = 1$$

α-level fuzzy sets

One of the important ways of representation of fuzzy sets is α-cut method. Such type of representation allows us to use properties of crisp sets and operations on crisp sets in fuzzy set theory.

The (crisp) set of elements that belongs to the fuzzy set A at least to the degree α is called the α-level set:

$$A^\alpha = \{x \in X,\ \mu_A(x) \geq \alpha\}$$

$A^\alpha = \{x \in X,\ \mu_A(x) > \alpha\}$ is called "strong α-level set" or "strong α-cut".

Let us consider a simple example.

$$A = 0.2/x_1 + 0.5/x_2 + 0.8/x_3 + 1.0/x_4$$

The level set of A is $\{0.2, 0.5, 0.8, 1.0\}$. Then the α-level sets are

$$A^{0.2} = \{x_1, x_2, x_3, x_4\}$$

$$A^{0.5} = \{x_2, x_3, x_4\}$$

$$A^{0.8} = \{x_3, x_4\}$$

$$A^{1.0} = \{x_4\}$$

Now, we introduce fuzzy set A_α, defined as

$$A_\alpha(x) = \alpha A^\alpha(x) \tag{1.33}$$

Then the original fuzzy set A may be defined as $A = \bigcup_{\alpha \in [0,1]} A_\alpha$. $\cup$ denotes the standard fuzzy union.

In our example,

$$A_{0.2} = 0.2/x_1 + 0.2/x_2 + 0.2/x_3 + 0.2/x_4$$

$$A_{0.5} = 0/x_1 + 0.5/x_2 + 0.5/x_3 + 0.5/x_4$$

$$A_{0.8} = 0/x_1 + 0/x_2 + 0.8/x_3 + 0.8/x_4$$

$$A_{1.0} = 0/x_1 + 0/x_2 + 0/x_3 + 1.0/x_4$$

The union of these four fuzzy sets gives

$$A = A_{0.2} \cup A_{0.5} \cup A_{0.8} \cup A_{1.0}$$

The representation of A by union of fuzzy sets A_α is usually referred to as a decomposition of A. Below we give decomposition theorem of fuzzy sets.

Theorem 1.4. *For every $A \in F(X)$,*

$$A = \bigcup_{\alpha \in [0,1]} A_\alpha \tag{1.34}$$

where A_α is defined by (1.33), $F(X)$ denotes the fuzzy power set of X. Proof of this theorem is given in [246].

The cardinality of a fuzzy set

When X is a finite set, the scalar cardinality $|A|$ of a fuzzy set A on X is defined as

$$|A| = \sum_{x \in A} \mu_A(x)$$

Sometimes $|A|$ is called the power of A.

$\|A\| = |A|/|X|$ is the relative cardinality.

When X is infinite, $|A|$ is defined as

$$|A| = \int_X \mu_A(x) dx$$

Example: $A = 0/1 + 0.3/2 + 0.6/3 + 0.9/4 + 1.0/5 + 0.7/6 + 0.4/7 + 0.2/8 + 0.1/9 + 0/10$. For the fuzzy set A, the cardinality is

$$|A| = 0.3 + 0.6 + 0.9 + 1.0 + 0.7 + 0.4 + 0.2 + 0.1 = 4.2$$

Its relative cardinality is

$$\|A\| = \frac{4.2}{10} = 0.42$$

Fuzzy set inclusion

Given fuzzy sets $A, B \in F(X)$, A is said to be included in $B(A \subseteq B)$ or A is a subset of B if $\forall x \in X$, $\mu_A(x) \leq \mu_B(x)$.

When the inequality is strict, the inclusion is said to be strict and is denoted as $A < B$.

Representations and constructing of fuzzy sets

It was mentioned above that each fuzzy set is uniquely defined by a membership function.

In the literature, one can find different ways in which membership functions are represented.

List representation

If universal set $X = \{x_1, x_2, \ldots, x_n\}$ is a finite set, membership function of a fuzzy set A on X $\mu_A(x)$ can be represented as table.

Such table lists all elements in the universe X and the corresponding membership grades as shown below

$$A = \mu_A(x_1)/x_1 + \cdots + \mu_A(x_n)/x_n = \sum_{i=1}^{n} \mu_A(x_i)/x_i$$

Here, symbol/(slash) does not denote division, it is used for correspondence between an element in the universe X (after slash) and its membership grade in the fuzzy set A (before slash). The symbol $+$ connects the elements (does not denote summation).

If X is a finite set, then

$$A = \int_X \mu_A(x)/x$$

Here, symbol $\int_X$ is used for denoting a union of elements of set X.

Example: An operator in an enterprise wants to classify the quality of fruits production. The values at the variable "Quality" and elements of the universe $X = \{0, 1, 2, \ldots, 10\}$ are given in Table 1.1.

Fuzzy set $A \cong$ highest from Table 1.1 may be represented as

$$A \cong \text{highest} = 0.1/0 + 0.1/1 + 0.2/2 + 0.3/3 + 0.4/4 + 0.5/5$$
$$+ 0.6/6 + 0.7/7 + 0.8/8 + 0.9/9 + 1.0/10$$

Table 1.1. The values of the variable "quality".

Quality	$x \in X$
Very low	0
Almost low	1
Low	2
Better than low	3
Almost average	4
Average	5
Better than average	6
Almost high	7
High	8
Better than high	9
Highest	10

Graphical representation

Graphical description of a fuzzy set A on the universe X is suitable in case when X is one or two-dimensional Euclidean space. Simple typical shapes of membership functions are usually used in fuzzy set theory and practice (see Table 1.2).

Example: Assume, for instance, a group of women aged near 30. In this case, we may define intuitively fuzzy sets $A_1 = $ *very young*, $A_2 = $ *young*, $A_3 = $ *yet young*, $A_4 = $ *young for somebody* as shown in Fig. 1.4.

Fuzzy n-cube representation

All fuzzy sets on universe X with n elements can be represented by points in the n-dimensional unit cube-n-cube.

Assume that universe X contains n elements $X = \{x_1, x_2, \ldots, x_n\}$. Each element x_i, $i = \overline{1, n}$ can be viewed as a coordinate in the n-dimensional Euclidean space. A subset of this space for which values of each coordinate are restricted in [0,1] is called n-cube. Vertices of the cube, i.e., bit list $(0, 1, \ldots, 0)$ represent crisp sets. The points inside the cube define fuzzy subsets.

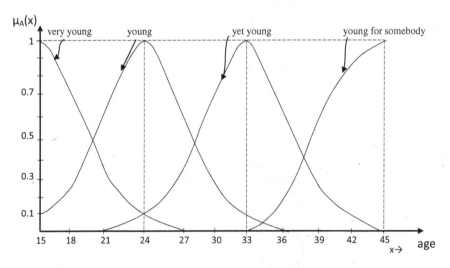

Fig. 1.4. Graphical representation of membership function.

Analytical representation

In case if universe X is infinite, it is not effective to use the above considered methods for representation of membership functions of a fuzzy sets. In this case, it is suitable to represent fuzzy sets in an analytical form, which describes the shape of membership functions.

There are some typical formulas describing frequently used membership functions in fuzzy set theory and practice.

For example, bell-shaped membership functions often are used for representation of fuzzy sets. These functions are described by the formula:

$$\mu_A(x) = c \cdot \exp\left(-\frac{(x-a)^2}{b}\right)$$

which is defined by three parameters, a, b and c (Fig. 1.5).

The triangular membership functions are frequently used in fuzzy arithmetics for describing fuzzy numbers. These membership functions can be represented by the formula:

$$\mu_A(x) = \begin{cases} \dfrac{x - a_1}{a_2 - a_1}r & \text{if } a_1 \leq x \leq a_2 \\ \dfrac{a_3 - x}{a_3 - a_2}r & \text{if } a_2 \leq x \leq a_3 \\ 0 & \text{otherwise} \end{cases}$$

which is fully defined by the four parameters a_1, a_2, a_3 and r (Fig. 1.6).

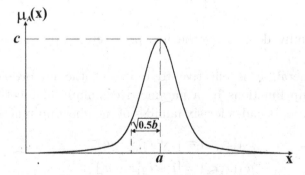

Fig. 1.5. Bell-shaped membership function.

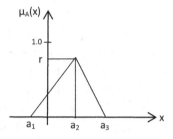

Fig. 1.6. A triangular membership functions.

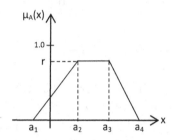

Fig. 1.7. A trapezoidal membership function.

Trapezoidal membership functions are also quite useful. These functions may be described by the formula:

$$\mu_A(x) = \begin{cases} \dfrac{x - a_1}{a_2 - a_1}r & \text{if } a_1 \leq x \leq a_2 \\ r & \text{if } a_2 \leq x \leq a_3 \\ \dfrac{a_4 - x}{a_4 - a_3}r & \text{if } a_3 \leq x \leq a_4 \\ 0 & \text{otherwise} \end{cases}$$

which is fully defined by the five parameters, a_1, a_2, a_3, a_4 and r (Fig. 1.7).

In general, it is effective to represent the important typical membership functions by a parametrized family of functions. The following are formulas for six families of membership functions

$$\mu_A(x, c_1) = [1 + c_1(x - a)^2]^{-1} \tag{1.35}$$

$$\mu_A(x, c_2) = [1 + c_2|x - a|]^{-1} \tag{1.36}$$

$$\mu_A(x, c_3, d) = [1 + c_3|x - a|^d]^{-1} \tag{1.37}$$

$$\mu_A(x, c_4, d) = \exp[-c_4|x - a|^d] \tag{1.38}$$

$$\mu_A(x, c_5) = \max\{0, [1 - c_5|x - a|]\} \tag{1.39}$$

$$\mu_A(x, c_6) = c_6 \exp\left[-\frac{(x - a)^2}{b}\right] \tag{1.40}$$

Here, $c_i > 0$, $i = \overline{1, 6}$, $d > 1$ are parameters, a denotes the elements of corresponding fuzzy sets with the membership grade equal to unity. Table 1.2 summarizes the graphical and analytical representations of frequently used membership functions (MF).

The problem of constructing membership functions is the problem of knowledge engineering.

There are many methods for estimation of membership functions. They can be classified as follows:

1. Membership functions based on heuristics.
2. Membership functions based on reliability concepts with respect to the particular problem.
3. Membership functions based on more theoretical demand.
4. Membership functions as a model for human concepts.
5. Neural networks based construction of membership functions.

The heuristic methods for estimation of the membership use partial information about it, such as the values that membership function takes at a finite number of samples in the universe of discourse.

For example, in order to build the membership function of the fuzzy set A = "young" or "old," the following formula is used:

$$\mu_{young}(x) = \begin{cases} 0 & \text{if } x \le 25 \\ 1/(1 + ((x - 25)/5)^{-2}) & \text{if } x > 25 \end{cases}$$

$$\mu_{old}(x) = \begin{cases} 0 & \text{if } x < 50 \\ 1/(1 + ((x - 50)/5)^{-2}) & \text{if } x \ge 50 \end{cases}$$

When membership function is estimated with respect to the particular problem, i.e., for fuzzy mathematical programming problem, some of its parameters are chosen relative to the particular problem.

Table 1.2. Typical membership functions (MFs).

Type of MFs	Graphical representation	Analytical representation
Triangular MF		$\mu_A(x) = \begin{cases} \dfrac{x-a_1}{a_2-a_1}\, r & \text{if } a_1 \leq x \leq a_2 \\[2mm] \dfrac{a_3-x}{a_3-a_2}\, r & \text{if } a_2 \leq x \leq a_3 \\[2mm] 0 & \text{otherwise} \end{cases}$
Trapezoidal MF		$\mu_A(x) = \begin{cases} \dfrac{x-a_1}{a_2-a_1}\, r & \text{if } a_1 \leq x \leq a_2 \\[2mm] r & \text{if } a_2 \leq x \leq a_3 \\[2mm] \dfrac{a_4-x}{a_4-a_3}\, r & \text{if } a_3 \leq x \leq a_4 \\[2mm] 0 & \text{otherwise} \end{cases}$

$$\mu_A(x) = \begin{cases} 0 & \text{if } x \le a_1 \\ 2\left(\dfrac{x-a_1}{a_3-a_1}\right)^2 & \text{if } a_1 < x < a_2 \\ 1 - 2\left(\dfrac{x-a_1}{a_3-a_1}\right)^2 & \text{if } a_2 \le x < a_3 \\ 1 & \text{if } a_3 \le x \end{cases}$$

$$\mu_A(x) = c \cdot \exp\left(-\frac{(x-a)^2}{b}\right)$$

S-shaped MF

Bell-shaped MF

Most useful membership function in this area is linear or piecewise linear function with relativity parameters, where the parameter a is chosen with respect to given problem.

The estimation methods of membership functions based on more theoretical demand use axioms, probability density functions and so on.

Let's consider operations on fuzzy sets. There exist three standard fuzzy operations: fuzzy intersection, union and complement which are generalization of the corresponding classical set operations.

For example,

$$\mu(x) = 1 - x/a \quad x \in [0, a]$$

Let A and B be two fuzzy sets in X with the membership functions μ_A and μ_B, respectively. Then the operations of intersection, union and complement are defined as given below.

Fuzzy standard intersection and union

The intersection ($\cap$) and union ($\cup$) of fuzzy sets A and B can be calculated by the following formulas:

$$\forall x \in X \quad \mu_{A \cap B}(x) = \min(\mu_A(x), \mu_B(x))$$

$$\forall x \in X \quad \mu_{A \cup B}(x) = \max(\mu_A(x), \mu_B(x))$$

where $\mu_{A \cap B}(x)$ and $\mu_{A \cup B}(x)$ are the membership functions of $A \cap B$ and $A \cup B$, respectively.

Example:

$$A = 0.15/2 + 0.41/3 + 0.66/4 + 0.85/5 + 0.97/6 + 1.0/7 + 0.9/8$$
$$+ 0.6/9 + 0.42/10 + 0.3/11 + 0.18/12 + 0.1/13 + 0.03/14$$
$$B = 0.05/5 + 0.1/6 + 0.16/7 + 0.25/8 + 0.35/9 + 0.47/10$$
$$+ 0.62/11 + 0.8/12 + 0.94/13 + 1.0/14 + 0.97/15$$
$$+ 0.83/16 + 0.5/17 + 0.2/18 + 0.07/19$$
$$A \cap B = 0.05/5 + 0.1/6 + 0.16/7 + 0.25/8 + 0.35/9 + 0.42/10$$
$$+ 0.3/11 + 0.18/12 + 0.1/13 + 0.03/14$$

(see Fig. 1.8).

$$A = 0.07/2 + 0.2/3 + 0.4/4 + 0.63/5 + 0.87/6 + 1.0/7 + 0.89/8$$
$$+ 0.5/9 + 0.2/10 + 0.07/11$$
$$B = 0.05/6 + 0.11/7 + 0.21/8 + 0.32/9 + 0.46/10 + 0.69/11$$
$$+ 0.87/12 + 1.0/13 + 0.9/14 + 0.5/15 + 0.25/16 + 0.09/18$$
$$A \cup B = 0.07/2 + 0.2/3 + 0.4/4 + 0.63/5 + 0.87/6 + 1.0/7 + 0.89/8$$
$$+ 0.5/9 + 0.46/10 + 0.69/11 + 0.87/12 + 1.0/13 + 0.9/14$$
$$+ 0.5/15 + 0.25/16 + 0.09/18$$

(see Fig. 1.9).

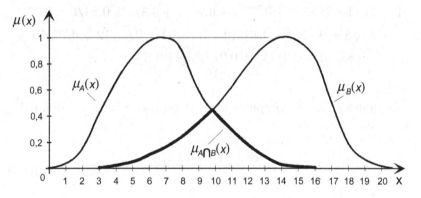

Fig. 1.8. Intersection of fuzzy sets.

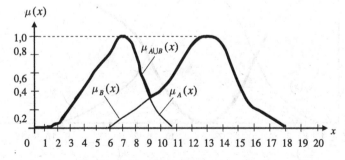

Fig. 1.9. Union of fuzzy sets.

Standard fuzzy complement

The complement A^c of A is defined by the membership function:

$$\forall x \in X \quad \mu_{A^c}(x) = 1 - \mu_A(x)$$

As already mentioned, $\mu_A(x)$ is interpreted as the degree to which x belongs to A. Then by the definition $\mu_{A^c}(x)$ can be interpreted as the degree to which x does not belong to A.

Example:

$$A = 0/1 + 0.05/2 + 0.14/3 + 0.27/4 + 0.5/5 + 0.76/6 + 0.93/7$$
$$+ 1.0/8 + 0.96/9 + 0.84/10 + 0.62/11 + 0.37/12 + 0.25/13$$
$$+ 0.16/14 + 0.09/15 + 0.03/16 + 0/17$$
$$\overline{A} = 1.0/1 + 0.95/2 + 0.86/3 + 0.73/4 + 0.5/5 + 0.24/6 + 0.07/7$$
$$+ 0/8 + 0.04/9 + 0.16/10 + 0.38/11 + 0.63/12 + 0.75/13$$
$$+ 0.84/14 + 0.91/15 + 0.97/16 + 1.0/17$$

(see Fig. 1.10).

In general, fuzzy complement of A type c A^c may be defined by a function

$$c : [0, 1] \rightarrow [0, 1]$$

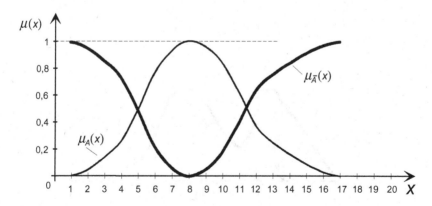

Fig. 1.10. Complement of fuzzy sets.

which assigns a value $A^c(x)$ to each membership grade $\mu_A(x)$. As it is shown in [246], function c must satisfy the following axiomatic requirements:

$$c(0) = 1 \quad \text{and} \quad c(1) = 1$$

for all $a, b \in [0, 1]$, if $a \leq b$, then $c(a) \geq c(b)$; c is a continuous function:

$$c(c(a)) = a \quad \text{for each} \quad a \in [0, 1]$$

For example, the threshold-type complements

$$c(a) = \begin{cases} 1 & \text{if } a \leq t \\ 0 & \text{if } a > t \end{cases}$$

are general fuzzy complements. Here, $t \in [0, 1]$ is the threshold of c.

The standard fuzzy operations do not satisfy the law of excluded middle $A \cup A^c = X$ and the law of contradiction $A \cap A^c = 0$ of classical set theory. But commutativity, associativity, idempotency, distributivity, and De Morgan laws are held for standard fuzzy operations.

For fuzzy union, intersection and complement operations, there exist a broad class of functions. Functions that qualify as fuzzy intersections and fuzzy unions are defined as t-norms and t-conorms.

t-norms

t-norm is a binary operation in $[0, 1]$, i.e., a binary function t from $[0, 1]$ into $[0, 1]$ that satisfies the following axioms:

$$t(\mu_A(x), 1) = \mu_A(x) \tag{1.41}$$

if $\mu_A(x) \leq \mu_C(x)$ and $\mu_B(x) \leq \mu_D(x)$, then

$$t(\mu_A(x), \mu_B(x)) \leq t(\mu_C(x), \mu_D(x)) \tag{1.42}$$

$$t(\mu_A(x), \mu_B(x)) = t(\mu_B(x), \mu_A(x)) \tag{1.43}$$

$$t(\mu_A(x), t(\mu_B(x), \mu_C(x))) = t(t(\mu_A(x), \mu_B(x), \mu_C(x))) \tag{1.44}$$

Here, (1.41) is boundary condition, (1.42)–(1.44) are conditions of monotonicity, commutativity and associativity, respectively.

The function t takes as its arguments the pair consisting of the element membership grades in set A and set B, and yields membership grades of the element in the $A \cap B$

$$(A \cap B)(x) = t[A(x), B(x)] \quad \forall x \in X$$

The following are frequently used t-norm-based fuzzy intersection operations:

Standard intersection

$$t_0(\mu_A(x), \mu_B(x)) = \min\{\mu_A(x), \mu_B(x)\} \tag{1.45}$$

Algebraic product

$$t_1(\mu_A(x), \mu_B(x)) = \mu_A(x) \cdot \mu_B(x) \tag{1.46}$$

Example

Fuzzy sets A and B are given.

$$A = 0.1/1 + 0.24/2 + 0.4/3 + 0.63/4 + 0.82/5 + 0.94/6 + 1.0/7$$
$$+ 0.98/8 + 0.91/9 + 0.76/10 + 0.57/11 + 0.35/12 + 0.2/13$$
$$+ 0.1/14 + 0.04/15$$
$$B = 0.02/4 + 0.09/5 + 0.2/6 + 0.32/7 + 0.46/8 + 0.61/9 + 0.76/10$$
$$+ 0.88/11 + 0.96/12 + 1.0/13 + 0.96/14 + 0.85/15 + 0.62/16$$
$$+ 0.37/17 + 0.2/18 + 0.09/19$$

Then intersection of fuzzy sets A and B are in accordance to (1.46) defined as

$$\mu_{A \cap B} = \mu_{A \cdot B} = 0/3 + 0.01/4 + 0.07/5 + 0.19/6 + 0.32/7 + 0.45/8$$
$$+ 0.55/9 + 0.58/10 + 0.5/11 + 0.34/12 + 0.2/13 + 0.96/14$$
$$+ 0.03/15 + 0/16$$

(see Fig. 1.11).

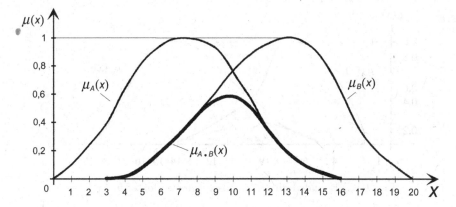

Fig. 1.11. Algebraic product intersection of fuzzy sets.

Bounded difference

$$t_2(\mu_A(x), \mu_B(x)) = \mu_{A \cap B}(x) = \max(0, \mu_A(x) + \mu_B(x) - 1)$$

$$(1.47)$$

Example

Fuzzy sets A and B are given:

$$A = 0.03/1.0 + 0.15/2 + 0.5/3 + 0.77/4 + 0.93/5 + 1.0/6 + 0.96/7$$
$$+ 0.85/8 + 0.71/9 + 0.55/10 + 0.4/11 + 0.27/12 + 0.18/13$$
$$+ 0.11/14 + 0.05/15 + 0.01/16$$

$$B = 0.04/5 + 0.1/6 + 0.17/7 + 0.28/8 + 0.4/9 + 0.55/10 + 0.71/11$$
$$+ 0.89/12 + 0.98/13 + 1.0/14 + 0.93/15 + 0.65/16 + 0.2/17$$
$$+ 0.06/18 + 0.01/19$$

The intersection of A and B in accordance to (1.47) is

$$A \cap B = 0/1 + 0/2 + 0/3 + 0/4 + 0/5 + 0.1/6 + 0.13/7 + 0.13/8$$
$$+ 0.11/9 + 0.1/10 + 0.11/11 + 0.16/12 + 0.16/13 + 0.11/14$$
$$+ 0/15 + 0/16 + 0/17 + 0/18 + 0/19$$

(see Fig. 1.12).

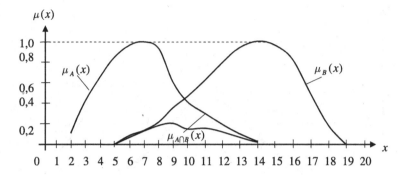

Fig. 1.12. Bounded difference-based intersection of fuzzy sets.

Drastic intersection

$$t_3(\mu_A(x), \mu_B(x)) = \begin{cases} \min\{\mu_A(x), \mu_B(x)\} & \text{if } \mu_A(x) = 1 \\ & \text{or } \mu_B(x) = 1 \\ 0 & \text{otherwise} \end{cases} \quad (1.48)$$

For four fuzzy intersections, the following is true:

$$t_3(\mu_A(x), \mu_B(x)) \leq t_2(\mu_A(x), \mu_B(x)) \leq t_1(\mu_A(x), \quad (1.49)$$
$$\mu_B(x)) \leq t_0(\mu_A(x), \mu_B(x))$$

t-conorms

t-conorm is a binary operation in $[0, 1]$, i.e., a binary function S: $[0, 1] \times [0, 1] \rightarrow [0, 1]$ that satisfies the following axioms (boundary condition)

$$S(\mu_A(x), 0) = \mu_A(x) \quad (1.50)$$

if $\mu_A(x) \leq \mu_C(x)$ and $\mu_B(x) \leq \mu_D(x)$ then (monotonicity)

$$S(\mu_A(x), \mu_B(x)) \leq S(\mu_C(x), \mu_D(x)) \quad (1.51)$$

(commutativity)

$$S(\mu_A(x), \mu_B(x)) = S(\mu_B(x), \mu_A(x)) \quad (1.52)$$

(associativity)

$$S(\mu_A(x), S(\mu_B(x), \mu_C(x))) = S(S(\mu_A(x), \mu_B(x), \mu_C(x))) \quad (1.53)$$

The function S yields membership grade of the element in the set $A \cup B$ on the argument which is the pair consisting of the same elements membership grades in set A and B

$$(A \cup B)(X) = S[A(x), B(x)] \quad (1.54)$$

The following are frequently used t-conorm-based fuzzy union operations.

Standard union

$$S_0(\mu_A(x), \mu_B(x)) = \max\{\mu_A(x), \mu_B(x)\} \quad (1.55)$$

Algebraic sum

$$S_1(\mu_A(x), \mu_B(x)) = \mu_A(x) + \mu_B(x) - \mu_A(x) \cdot \mu_B(x) \quad (1.56)$$

Example: Fuzzy sets A and B are given

$$A = 0.03/1 + 0.1/2 + 0.28/3 + 0.52/4 + 0.75/5 + 0.94/6 + 1.0/7$$
$$+ 0.96/8 + 0.87/9 + 0.71/10 + 0.55/11 + 0.4/12 + 0.28/13$$
$$+ 0.19/14 + 0.16/15 + 0.06/16 + 0.02/17$$
$$B = 0/1 + 0/2 + 0/3 + 0.02/4 + 0.06/5 + 0.12/6 + 0.17/7 + 0.25/8$$
$$+ 0.35/9 + 0.5/10 + 0.68/11 + 0.82/12 + 0.95/13 + 1.0/14$$
$$+ 0.95/15 + 0.62/16 + 0.35/17 + 0.17/18 + 0.06/19$$

Then in accordance to (1.56), union of fuzzy A and B is

$$A \hat{+} B = 0.03/1 + 0.1/2 + 0.28/3 + 0.52/4 + 0.75/5 + 0.94/6$$
$$+ 1.0/7 + 0.96/8 + 0.91/9 + 0.86/10 + 0.86/11 + 0.88/12$$
$$+ 0.96/13 + 1.0/14 + 0.95/15 + 0.62/16 + 0.35/17$$
$$+ 0.17/18 + 0.06/19$$

(see Fig. 1.13).

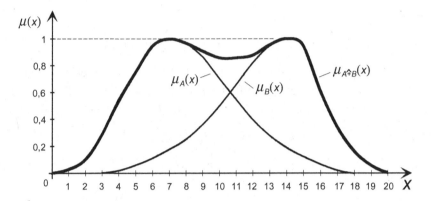

Fig. 1.13. Algebraic sum-based union of fuzzy sets.

Bounded sum

$$S_2(\mu_A(x), \mu_B(x)) = \min\{1, \mu_A(x) + \mu_B(x)\} \qquad (1.57)$$

Example: Fuzzy sets A and B are given.

$$A = 0.06/1 + 0.17/2 + 0.31/3 + 0.5/4 + 0.67/5 + 0.82/6 + 0.93/7$$
$$+ 1.0/8 + 0.98/9 + 0.89/10 + 0.46/11 + 0.6/12 + 0.45/13$$
$$+ 0.33/14 + 0.23/15 + 0.14/16 + 0.08/17 + 0.03/18$$
$$B = 0.03/4 + 0.08/5 + 0.15/6 + 0.26/7 + 0.4/8 + 0.55/9 + 0.7/10$$
$$+ 0.85/11 + 0.95/12 + 1.0/13 + 0.96/14 + 0.85/15 + 0.6/16$$
$$+ 0.33/17 + 0.18/18 + 0.09/19$$

Then in accordance to (1.57), the union of A and B is

$$\mu_{A \cup B} = 0.06/1 + 0.17/2 + 0.31/3 + 0.53/4 + 0.75/5 + 0.97/6$$
$$+ 1.0/7 + 1.0/8 + 1.0/10 + 1.0/11 + 1.0/12 + 1.0/13$$
$$+ 1.0/14 + 1.0/15 + 0.64/16 + 0.41/17 + 0.21/18$$
$$+ 0.09/19$$

(see Fig. 1.14).

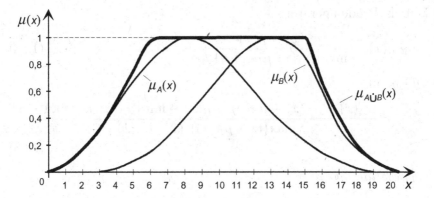

Fig. 1.14. Bounded sum-based union of fuzzy sets.

Drastic union

$$S_3(\mu_A(x), \mu_B(x)) = \begin{cases} \max\{\mu_A(x), \mu_B(x)\} & \text{if } \mu_A(x) = 0 \\ & \text{or } \mu_B(x) = 0 \quad (1.58) \\ 1 & \text{otherwise} \end{cases}$$

For four fuzzy union operations, the following is true:

$$S_0(\mu_A(x), \mu_B(x)) \leq S_1(\mu_A(x), \mu_B(x)) \leq S_2(\mu_A(x)$$
$$\mu_B(x)) \leq S_3(\mu_A(x), \mu_B(x)) \quad (1.59)$$

Parametrized families of t-norms and t-conorms

Different authors suggested parametrized families of t-norms and t-conorms in order to adapt them to context in which they are used. The following are examples of some parametrized t-norms and t-conorms.

Yager operation

$$\mu_{A \cap B}(x) = 1 - \min\{1, ((1 - \mu_A(x))^\gamma + (1 - \mu_B(x))^\gamma)^{\frac{1}{\gamma}}\}, \quad \gamma \geq 1 \tag{1.60}$$

$$\mu_{A \cup B}(x) = \min\{1, ((\mu_A(x))^\gamma + (\mu_B(x))^\gamma)^{\frac{1}{\gamma}}\}, \quad \gamma \geq 1 \tag{1.61}$$

Dubois–Prade operator

$$\mu_{A \cap B}(x) = \frac{\mu_A(x) \cdot \mu_B(x)}{\max\{\mu_A(x), \mu_B(x), \gamma\}} \tag{1.62}$$

$\mu_{A \cup B}(x)$

$$= \frac{\mu_A(x) + \mu_B(x) - \mu_A(x) \cdot \mu_B(x) - \min\{\mu_A(x), \mu_B(x), 1 - \gamma\}}{\max\{(1 - \mu_A(x)), (1 - \mu_B(x)), \gamma\}} \tag{1.63}$$

Aggregation operation

Aggregation operation on n fuzzy sets is defined by a function

$$l : [0, 1]^n \rightarrow [0, 1]$$

Let's give fuzzy sets $A_1, A_2, \ldots, A_n$ defined on X. Function l produces an aggregate fuzzy set A by corresponding operating on membership functions of these sets for each $x \in X$

$$A(x) = l(A_1(x), \ldots, A_n(x))$$

Function l must satisfy boundary conditions, be monotonic increasing and continuous function. The following are examples of aggregation operations.

Generalized means

$$l_g(\mu_{A_1}, \mu_{A_2}, \ldots, \mu_{A_n}) = \left(\frac{\mu_{A_1}^\gamma + \mu_{A_2}^\gamma + \cdots + \mu_{A_n}^\gamma}{n} \right)^{\frac{1}{\gamma}} \tag{1.64}$$

where $\gamma \in R(\gamma \neq 0)$ is the parameter that indicates the type of different means.

When $\gamma = 1$ (arithmetic mean),

$$l_1(\mu_{A_1}, \mu_{A_2}, \ldots, \mu_{A_n}) = \frac{1}{n}(\mu_{A_1} + \mu_{A2} + \cdots + \mu_{A_n}) \tag{1.65}$$

Ordered weighted averaging operations

$$l_N(\mu_{A_1}, \mu_{A_2}, \ldots, \mu_{A_n}) = w_1 \mu_{B_1} + w_2 \mu_{B_2} + \cdots + w_n \mu_{B_n} \tag{1.66}$$

where $\sum_{i=1}^n w_i = 1$, μ_{B_i} is the largest element in $\mu_{A_1}, \mu_{A_2}, \ldots, \mu_{A_n}$.

Cartesian product of fuzzy sets

The Cartesian product of fuzzy sets $A_1, A_2, \ldots, A_n$ on universes $X_1, X_2, \ldots, X_n$, respectively, is a fuzzy set in the product space $X_1 \times X_2 \times \cdots \times X_n$ with the membership function

$$\mu_{A_1 \times A_2 \times \cdots \times A_n}(x) = \min_i \{\mu_{A_i}(x_i) | x = (x_1, x_2, \ldots, x_n), x_i \in X_i\}$$

(1.67)

Power of fuzzy sets

mth power of a fuzzy set A^m is defined as

$$\mu_{A^m}(x) = [\mu_A(x)]^m, \quad \forall x \in X, \quad \forall m \in R^+ \tag{1.68}$$

where R^+ is positively defined set of real numbers.

Concentration and dilation of fuzzy sets

Let A be fuzzy set on the universe:

$$A = \{x, \mu_A(x)/x \in X)$$

Then the operator $\text{Con}_m A = \{(x, [\mu_A(x)]^m)/x \in X\}$ is called concentration of A and the operator $\text{Dil}_n A = \{(x, \sqrt{\mu_A(x)})/x \in X\}$ is called dilation of A.

Example: Concentration of fuzzy set.

$$A = 0.03/1 + 0.1/2 + 0.21/3 + 0.37/4 + 0.57/5 + 0.8/6 + 0.96/7$$
$$+ 1.0/8 + 0.94/9 + 0.7/10 + 0.42/11 + 0.27/12 + 0.17/13$$
$$+ 0.09/14 + 0.03/15$$
$$A^2 = 0.0009/1 + 0.01/2 + 0.044/3 + 0.137/4 + 0.325/5 + 0.64/6$$
$$+ 0.92/7 + 1.0/8 + 0.884/9 + 0.49/10 + 0.174/11 + 0.07/12$$
$$+ 0.03/13 + 0.01/14 + 0.0009/15$$

(see Fig. 1.15).

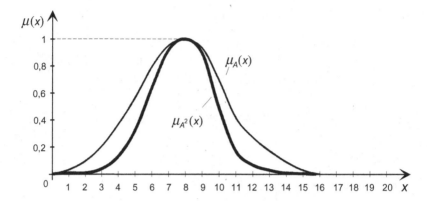

Fig. 1.15. Concentration of fuzzy sets.

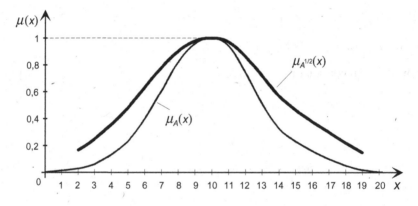

Fig. 1.16. Dilation of fuzzy sets.

Dilation of fuzzy set.

$$A = 0.03/2 + 0.06/3 + 0.13/4 + 0.23/5 + 0.4/6 + 0.61/7 + 0.82/8$$
$$+ 0.96/9 + 1.0/10 + 0.94/11 + 0.74/12 + 0.51/13 + 0.33/14$$
$$+ 0.23/15 + 0.16/16 + 0.1/17 + 0.05/18 + 0.02/19$$

$$A^{1/2} = 0.17/2 + 0.25/3 + 0.36/4 + 0.48/5 + 0.63/6 + 0.78/7$$
$$+ 0.9/8 + 0.98/9 + 1.0/10 + 0.97/11 + 0.86/12 + 0.72/13$$
$$+ 0.57/14 + 0.48/15 + 0.4/16 + 0.3/17 + 0.22/18 + 0.15/19$$

(see Fig. 1.16).

The examples of conversions of fuzzy sets using the concentration and dilation operations are shown below:

$$A = \int \mu_A(x)/x$$

$$\text{Very } A = \int [\mu_A(x)]^2/x$$

$$\text{Very very } A = \int [\mu_A(x)]^4/x$$

$$\text{More or less } A = \int \sqrt{\mu_A(x)}/x$$

$$\text{A little } A = \int \sqrt[4]{\mu_A(x)}/x$$

$$\text{Not } A = \int 1 - \mu_A(x)/x$$

$$\text{Not very much } A = \int 1 - [\mu_A(x)]^2/x$$

Difference of fuzzy sets

Difference of fuzzy sets is defined by the formula:

$$\forall x \in X, \quad \mu_{A|-|B}(x) = \max(0, \mu_A(x) - \mu_B(x)) \qquad (1.69)$$

$A|-|B$ is the fuzzy set of elements that belong to A more than to B.

Example: Let's give sets A and B

$$A = 0.08/1 + 0.23/2 + 0.45/3 + 0.7/4 + 0.86/5 + 0.96/6 + 1.0/7$$
$$+ 0.98/8 + 0.92/9 + 0.82/10 + 0.67/11 + 0.47/12 + 0.3/13$$
$$+ 0.13/14$$
$$B = 0.03/6 + 0.08/7 + 0.18/8 + 0.34/9 + 0.55/10 + 0.7/11$$
$$+ 0.84/12 + 0.94/13 + 0.99/14 + 1.0/15 + 0.96/16 + 0.82/17$$
$$+ 0.6/18 + 0.2/19$$

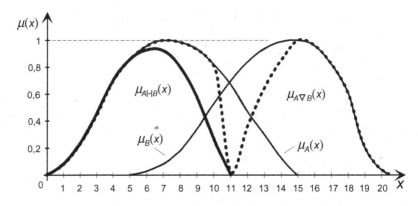

Fig. 1.17. Difference of fuzzy sets.

Then difference fuzzy sets A and B in accordance to (2.44) is defined as

$$A| - |B = 0.08/1 + 0.23/2 + 0.45/3 + 0.7/4 + 0.86/5 + 0.93/6$$
$$+ 0.92/7 + 0.8/8 + 0.58/9 + 0.27/10 + 0/11$$

(see Fig. 1.17).

Symmetrical difference of fuzzy sets A and B is the fuzzy set $A\nabla B$ of elements that belong more to A than to B:

$$\forall x \in X \quad \mu_{A\nabla B}(x) = |\mu_A(x) - \mu_B(x)|$$

Symmetrical difference is determined as

$$A\nabla B = 0.08/1 + 0.23/2 + 0.45/3 + 0.7/4 + 0.86/5 + 0.96/6 + 1.0/7$$
$$+ 0.98/8 + 0.92/9 + 0.82/10 + 0.03/11 + 0.36/12 + 0.65/13$$
$$+ 0.86/14 + 1.0/15 + 0.96/16 + 0.82/17 + 0.6/18 + 0.2/19$$

(see Fig. 1.17).

1.7. Fuzzy Arithmetic

Fuzzy arithmetic is an important constituent of numerical analysis and main tool for dealing with uncertainly in a computationally effective way. The main concept and kernel of fuzzy arithmetic is fuzzy number [236].

Fuzzy number

A fuzzy number is a fuzzy set A on R which possesses the following properties: (a) A is a normal fuzzy set; (b) A is a convex fuzzy set; (c) α-cuts of A, A^α are a closed interval for every $\alpha \in (0,1]$; (d) the support of A, A^{+0} is bounded.

In Fig. 1.18, some basic types of fuzzy numbers are shown. For example, "around 2", "large," etc.

Arithmetic operation on fuzzy numbers

There are different methods for developing fuzzy arithmetic. In this section, we present three methods.

Method based on the extension principle

By this method, basic arithmetic operations on real numbers are extended to operations on fuzzy numbers. Let A and B be two fuzzy numbers and * denote any of the four arithmetic operations $\{+, -, \cdot, :\}$.

A fuzzy set A^*B on R can be defined by the equation

$$\forall z \in R \quad \mu_{(A*B)}(z) = \sup_{z=x*y} \min[\mu_A(x), \mu_B(y)] \qquad (1.70)$$

It is shown [246] that $A*B$ is fuzzy number and the following theorem has been formulated and proved.

Theorem 1.5. *Let* $* \in \{+, -, \cdot, :\}$, *and let* A, B *denote continuous fuzzy numbers. Then, the fuzzy set* A^*B *defined by* (1.70) *is a continuous fuzzy number.*

Then for four basic arithmetic operations on fuzzy numbers, we can write

$$\mu_{(A+B)}(z) = \sup_{z=x+y} \min[\mu_A(x), \mu_B(y)] \qquad (1.71)$$

$$\mu_{(A-B)}(z) = \sup_{z=x-y} \min[\mu_A(x), \mu_B(y)] \qquad (1.72)$$

$$\mu_{(A \cdot B)}(z) = \sup_{z=x \cdot y} \min[\mu_A(x), \mu_B(y)] \qquad (1.73)$$

$$\mu_{(A:B)}(z) = \sup_{z=x:y} \min[\mu_A(x), \mu_B(y)] \qquad (1.74)$$

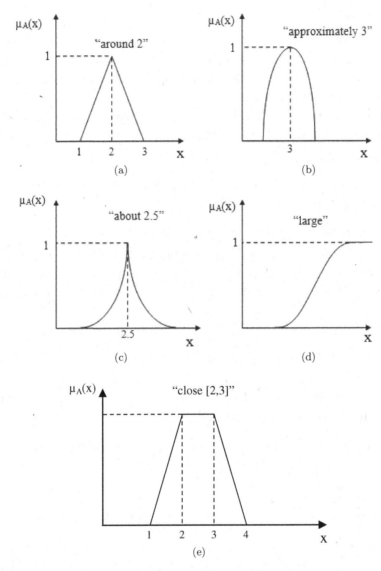

Fig. 1.18. Types of fuzzy numbers.

Example. Fuzzy addition

$$A = (\tilde{3}) = 0.3/1 + 0.6/2 + 1/3 + 0.6/4 + 0.3/5$$

$$B = (\widetilde{11}) = 0.5/10 + 1/11 + 0.5/12$$

$$A + B = (0.3 \wedge 0.5)/(1 + 10) + (0.6 \wedge 0.5)/(2 + 10)$$
$$+ (1 \wedge 0.5)/(3 + 10) + (0.6 \wedge 0.5)/(4 + 10)$$
$$+ (0.3 \wedge 0.5)/(5 + 10) + (0.3 \wedge 1)/(1 + 11)$$
$$+ (0.6 \wedge 1)/(2 + 11) + (1 \wedge 1)/(3 + 11) + (0.6 \wedge 1)/(4 + 11)$$
$$+ (0.3 \wedge 1)/(5 + 11) + (0.3 \wedge 0.5)/(1 + 12)$$
$$+ (0.6 \wedge 0.5)/(2 + 12) + (1 \wedge 0.5)/(3 + 12)$$
$$+ (0.6 \wedge 0.5)/(4 + 12) + (0.3 \wedge 0.5)/(5+12)$$
$$A + B = 0.3/11 + 0.5/12 + 0.5/13 + 0.5/14 + 0.3/15$$
$$+ 0.3/12 + 0.6/13 + 1/14 + 0.6/15 + 0.3/16 + 0.3/13$$
$$+ 0.5/14 + 0.5/15 + 0.5/16 + 0.3/17$$

Applying the maximum operator,

$$A + B = 0.3/11 + (0.5 \vee 0.3)/12 + (0.5 \vee 0.6 \vee 0.3)/13$$
$$+ (0.5 \vee 1 \vee 0.5)/14 + (0.3 \vee 0.6 \vee 0.5)/15$$
$$+ (0.3 \vee 0.5)/16 + 0.3/17$$
$$A + B = 0.3/11 + 0.5/12 + 0.6/13 + 1/14 + 0.6/15$$
$$+ 0.5/16 + 0.3/17$$

Example. Fuzzy product

$$A = \tilde{2} = \left\{ \frac{0.6}{1} + \frac{1}{2} + \frac{0.8}{3} \right\}$$

$$B = \tilde{6} = \left\{ \frac{0.8}{5} + \frac{1}{6} + \frac{0.7}{7} \right\}$$

$$A \times B = \left\{ \frac{0.6}{1} + \frac{1}{2} + \frac{0.8}{3} \right\} \times \left\{ \frac{0.8}{5} + \frac{1}{6} + \frac{0.7}{7} \right\}$$

$$= \left\{ \frac{\min(0.6, 0.8)}{5} + \frac{\min(0.6, 1)}{6} + \cdots + \frac{\min(0.8, 1)}{18} \right.$$

$$+ \frac{\min(0.8, 0.7)}{21} \bigg\}$$

$$= \left\{ \frac{0.6}{5} + \frac{0.6}{6} + \frac{0.6}{7} + \frac{0.8}{10} + \frac{1}{12} + \frac{0.7}{14} + \frac{0.8}{15} + \frac{0.8}{18} + \frac{0.7}{21} \right\}$$

Method based on interval arithmetic and α-cuts

This method is based on representation of arbitrary fuzzy numbers by their α-cuts and use interval arithmetic to the α-cuts. Let $A, B \in R$ be fuzzy numbers and * denote any of four operations. For each $\alpha \in (0, 1]$, the α-cut of $A * B$ is expressed as

$$(A * B)^{\alpha} = A^{\alpha} * B^{\alpha} \tag{1.75}$$

Example: The following fuzzy numbers A and B are given (Fig. 1.19):

$$\mu_A(x) = \begin{cases} 0 & \text{for } x < -1 \text{ and } x > 4 \\ (x+1)/2 & \text{for } -1 \leq x \leq 1 \\ (4-x)/3 & \text{for } 1 \leq x \leq 4 \end{cases} \tag{1.76}$$

$$\mu_B(x) = \begin{cases} 0 & \text{for } x < 2 \text{ and } x > 6 \\ (x-2)/2 & \text{for } 2 \leq x \leq 4 \\ (6-x)/2 & \text{for } 4 \leq x \leq 6 \end{cases} \tag{1.77}$$

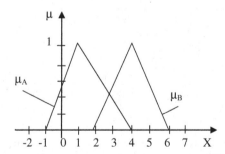

Fig. 1.19. Fuzzy numbers A and B.

Then their α-cut are $A^\alpha = [a_1^\alpha, a_2^\alpha]$; $B^\alpha = [b_1^\alpha, b_2^\alpha]$ and

$$A(a_1^\alpha) = (a_1^\alpha + 1)/2 = \alpha$$
$$A(a_2^\alpha) = (4 - a_2^\alpha)/3 = \alpha$$

From these, we obtain

$$a_1^\alpha = 2\alpha - 1$$
$$a_2^\alpha = 4 - 3\alpha$$

Hence,

$$A^\alpha = [2\alpha - 1, 4 - 3\alpha]$$

Similarly, for fuzzy number B,

$$B(b_1^\alpha) = (b_1^\alpha - 2)/2 = \alpha$$
$$B(b_2^\alpha) = (6 - b_2^\alpha)/2 = \alpha$$

From these, we obtain

$$b_1^\alpha = 2\alpha + 2$$
$$b_2^\alpha = 6 - 2\alpha$$

that is

$$B^\alpha = [2\alpha + 2, 6 - 2\alpha]$$

Then

$$(A + B)^\alpha = [2\alpha - 1, 4 - 3\alpha] + [2\alpha + 2, 6 - 2\alpha] = [4\alpha + 1, 10 - 5\alpha]$$

which is the α-cut representation of the sum of the given fuzzy numbers A and B.

Since $\alpha \in (0, 1]$, the range of the left endpoint of the interval is $(1, 5]$ and the range of its right endpoint is $[15, 16]$. This means that

$$4\alpha + 1 = x \text{ when } x \in (1, 5]$$

and

$$10 - 5\alpha = x \text{ when } x \in [5, 10)$$

Solving these equations for α, we obtain

$$\alpha = (x - 1)/4 = (A + B)(x) \text{ when } x \in (1, 5]$$
$$\alpha = (10 - x)/5 = (A + B)(x) \text{ when } x \in [5, 10)$$

That is, the membership function $A + B$, corresponding to the α-cut representation, is expressed by the formula (see Fig. 1.20):

$$\mu_{A+B}(x) = \begin{cases} 0 & \text{for } x < 1 \text{ and } x > 10 \\ (x - 1)/4 & \text{for } 1 \leq x \leq 5 \\ (10 - x)/5 & \text{for } 5 \leq x \leq 10 \end{cases}$$

Subtraction

Subtraction of given fuzzy numbers A and B can be defined as

$$(A - B)^{\alpha} = A^{\alpha} - B^{\alpha} = [a_1^{\alpha} - b_2^{\alpha}, a_2^{\alpha} - b_1^{\alpha}], \quad \forall \alpha \in [0, 1] \qquad (1.78)$$

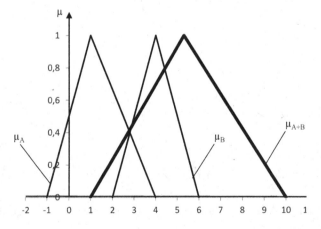

Fig. 1.20. Addition of two triangular fuzzy numbers A and B.

We can determine (1.78) by addition of the image B^- to A

$$\forall \alpha \in [0,1], B^{\alpha^-} = [-b_2^\alpha, -b_1^\alpha] \tag{1.79}$$

Then we have

$$\mu_{A-B}(x) = \begin{cases} 0 & \text{for } x < -7 \text{ and } x > 2 \\ (x+7)/4 & \text{for } -7 \leq x \leq -3 \\ (2-x)/5 & \text{for } -3 \leq x \leq 2 \end{cases}$$

Example: To calculate the product of fuzzy numbers A and B given in (1.76)–(1.77) $A \cdot B$, we have first to calculate the α-cut representation of $A \cdot B$:

$$(A \cdot B)^\alpha = [2\alpha - 1, 4 - 3\alpha] \cdot [2\alpha + 2, 6 - 2\alpha]$$

Applying the rule of interval multiplication, we find that the expression for the α-cuts differ in the intervals $\alpha \in (0, 0.5]$:

$$(A \cdot B)^\alpha = \begin{cases} [-4\alpha^2 + 14\alpha - 6, 6\alpha^2 - 26\alpha + 24] & \text{for } \alpha \in (0, 0.5] \\ [4\alpha^2 + 2\alpha - 2, 6\alpha^2 - 26\alpha + 24] & \text{for } \alpha \in (0.5, 1] \end{cases}$$

The resulting membership function $A \cdot B$, whose graph is shown in Fig. 1.21 is defined by the formula

$$\mu_{A \cdot B}(x) = \begin{cases} 0 & \text{for } x < -6 \text{ and } x > 24 \\ \dfrac{7 - \sqrt{25 - 4x}}{4} & \text{for } -6 \leq x < 0 \\ \dfrac{-1 + \sqrt{9 + 4x}}{4} & \text{for } 0 \leq x < 4 \\ \dfrac{13 - \sqrt{25 + 6x}}{6} & \text{for } 4 \leq x \leq 24 \end{cases}$$

Multiplication of fuzzy number A in R by ordinary numbers $k \in R^+$ is performed as follows:

$$\forall A \subset R \quad kA^\alpha = [ka_1^\alpha, ka_2^\alpha]$$

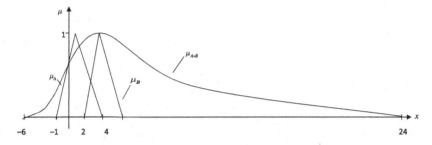

Fig. 1.21. Multiplication of two fuzzy numbers.

Division

Division of two fuzzy numbers A and B is defined by

$$A^\alpha : B^\alpha = [a_1^\alpha, a_2^\alpha] : [b_1^\alpha, b_2^\alpha] \quad \forall \alpha \in [0,1]$$

Example: Using basically the same procedure described for the previous three operations, we obtain α-cut representation

$$\left(\frac{A}{B}\right)^\alpha = \begin{cases} \left[\dfrac{2\alpha - 1}{2\alpha + 2}, \dfrac{4 - 3\alpha}{2\alpha + 2}\right] & \text{for } \alpha \in (0, 0.5] \\[3ex] \left[\dfrac{2\alpha - 1}{6 - 2\alpha}, \dfrac{3 - 2\alpha}{2\alpha + 2}\right] & \text{for } \alpha \in (0.5, 1] \end{cases}$$

and the membership function

$$\mu_{\frac{A}{B}}(x) = \begin{cases} 0 & \text{for } x < -1 \text{ and } x > 2 \\[2ex] \dfrac{2x + 1}{2 - 2x} & \text{for } -1 \le x \le 0 \\[2ex] \dfrac{6x + 1}{2x + 2} & \text{for } 0 \le x \le \dfrac{1}{4} \\[2ex] \dfrac{4 - 2x}{4x + 3} & \text{for } \dfrac{1}{4} \le x \le \dfrac{5}{6} \\[2ex] \dfrac{4 - 2x}{2x + 3} & \text{for } \dfrac{5}{6} \le x \le 2 \end{cases}$$

Fuzzy minimum and maximum of fuzzy numbers

The set R of real numbers has linear order. For $\forall x, y \in R$, the pair $(R, \le)$ as mentioned above is a lattice. Fuzzy numbers do not have the structure of linear order, they can be ordered partially. In ordering of fuzzy numbers it is necessary to extend the lattice operation max and min to fuzzy minimum min and fuzzy maximum max. Consider two fuzzy numbers $A, B \subset R$. Fuzzy minimum and fuzzy maximum we can define as

$$\min(A, B)(z) = \sup_{z=\min(x,y)} \min[A(x), B(y)] \qquad (1.80)$$

$$\max(A, B)(z) = \sup_{z=\max(x,y)} \min[A(x), B(y)] \qquad (1.81)$$

By using α-cuts, we define

$$\forall \alpha \in [0, 1] \quad \min(A^\alpha, B^\alpha) = [\min(a_1^\alpha, b_1^\alpha), \min(a_2^\alpha, b_2^\alpha)] \qquad (1.82)$$

$$\max(A^\alpha, B^\alpha) = [\max(a_1^\alpha, b_1^\alpha), \max(a_2^\alpha, b_2^\alpha)] \qquad (1.83)$$

Example: Let us consider the example illustrated in Fig. 1.22, where $\forall x \subset R$:

$$\mu_A(x) = \begin{cases} 0, & x \le -3 \\ x/3 + 1, & -3 \le x \le 0 \\ -x/5 + 1, & 0 \le x \le 5 \\ 0, & x \ge 5 \end{cases}$$

$$\mu_B(x) = \begin{cases} 0, & x \le -5 \\ x/7 + 5/7, & -5 \le x \le 2 \\ -x/2 + 2, & 2 \le x \le 4 \\ 0, & x \ge 4 \end{cases}$$

If $\forall x \in [0, 1]$ then we have:

$$A^\alpha = [3\alpha - 3, -5\alpha + 5]$$
$$B^\alpha = [7\alpha - 5, -2\alpha + 4]$$

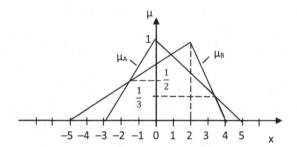

Fig. 1.22. Fuzzy numbers A and B.

Therefore, for a minimum,

$$\min(A^\alpha, B^\alpha) = [\min(3\alpha - 3, 7\alpha - 5), \min(-5\alpha + 5, -2\alpha + 4)]$$

$$= \begin{cases} [7\alpha - 5, -2\alpha + 4] & 0 \leq \alpha \leq \dfrac{1}{3} \\[2mm] [7\alpha - 5, -5\alpha + 5] & \dfrac{1}{3} \leq \alpha \leq \dfrac{1}{2} \\[2mm] [3\alpha - 3, -5\alpha + 5] & \dfrac{1}{2} \leq \alpha \leq 1 \end{cases}$$

From this, we obtain the following result:

$$\mu_{\min(A,B)}(x) = \begin{cases} 0 & \text{for } x \leq -5 \text{ and } x \geq 4 \\[2mm] x/7 + 5/7 & \text{for } -5 \leq x \leq -1\dfrac{1}{2} \\[2mm] x/3 + 1 & \text{for } -1\dfrac{1}{2} \leq x \leq 0 \\[2mm] -x/5 + 1 & \text{for } 0 \leq x \leq 3\dfrac{1}{3} \\[2mm] -x/2 + 2 & \text{for } 3\dfrac{1}{3} \leq x \leq 4 \end{cases}$$

Figure 1.23 shows a sketch of $\min(A, B)$.

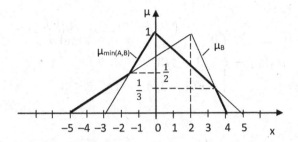

Fig. 1.23. Minimum of fuzzy numbers A and B.

To find the maximum value, we draw

$$\max(A^\alpha, B^\alpha) = [\max(3\alpha - 3, 7\alpha - 5), \max(-5\alpha + 5, -2\alpha + 4)]$$

$$= \begin{cases} [3\alpha - 3, -5\alpha + 5] & 0 \leq \alpha \leq \dfrac{1}{3} \\[2mm] [3\alpha - 3, -2\alpha + 4] & \dfrac{1}{3} \leq \alpha \leq \dfrac{1}{2} \\[2mm] [7\alpha - 5, -2\alpha + 4] & \dfrac{1}{2} \leq \alpha \leq 1 \end{cases}$$

From this, we obtain the following result:

$$\mu_{\max(A,B)}(x) = \begin{cases} x/3 + 1 & \text{for } -3 \leq x \leq -1.5 \\[2mm] x/7 + 5/7 & \text{for } -1.5 \leq x \leq 2 \\[2mm] -x/2 + 1 & \text{for } 2 \leq x \leq 3\dfrac{1}{3} \\[2mm] -x/5 + 1 & \text{for } 3\dfrac{1}{3} \leq x \leq 5 \\[2mm] 0 & \text{for } x \leq -3 \text{ and } x \geq 5 \end{cases}$$

A sketch of this is shown in Fig. 1.24.

Absolute value of fuzzy number

Absolute value of fuzzy number is defined as

$$\text{abs}(A) = \begin{cases} \max(A, -A) & \text{for } R^+ \\ 0 & \text{for } R^- \end{cases}$$

Example. Let

$$
\mu_A(x) = \begin{cases}
0 & x < -4 \text{ and } x > 3 \\
x/3 + 4/3 & -4 \le x \le -1 \\
-x/4 + 3/4 & -1 \le x \le 3
\end{cases}
$$

then

$$
\mu_{\text{abs}(A)}(x) = \begin{cases}
0 & x < 0 \text{ and } x > 4 \\
x/4 + 3/4 & 0 \le x \le 1 \\
-x/3 + 4/3 & 1 \le x \le 4
\end{cases}
$$

(see Fig. 1.25).

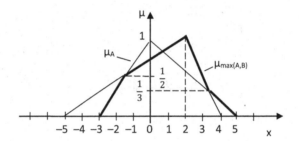

Fig. 1.24. Maximum of fuzzy numbers A and B.

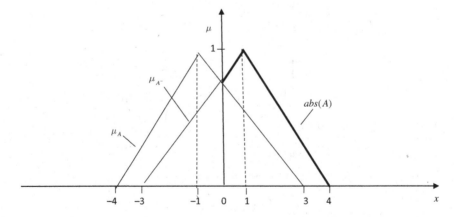

Fig. 1.25. Absolute value of fuzzy number A.

1.8. Extensions of Fuzzy Sets

1.8.1. *Type-2 fuzzy sets and numbers*

Fuzzy Type-2 sets possess more expressive power to create models adequately describing uncertainty. The three-dimensional membership functions of Type-2 fuzzy sets provide additional degrees of freedom that make it possible to directly and more effectively model uncertainties.

Type-2 fuzzy set ([21, 95, 234, 235, 299, 300, 302, 303, 305, 394, 554]). Type-2 fuzzy set (T2 FS) in the universe of discourse X can be represented as follows:

$$\tilde{A} = \{((x, u), \mu_{\tilde{A}}(x, u)) | \forall x \in X, \forall u \in J_x \subseteq [0, 1]\} \qquad (1.84)$$

where $0 \leq \mu_{\tilde{A}}(x, u) \leq 1$. The Type-2 fuzzy set $\tilde{A}$ also can be represented as follows:

$$\tilde{A} = \int_{x \in X} \int_{u \in J_x} \mu_{\tilde{A}}(x, u) / (x, u) = \int_{x \in X} \left[\int_{u \in J_x} \mu_{\tilde{A}}(x, u) / u \right] / x$$
$$(1.85)$$

where x is the primary variable, $J_x \subseteq [0, 1]$ is the primary membership of x, u is the secondary variable. $f(x) = \int_{u \in J_x} \mu_{\tilde{A}}(x, u) / u$ is the secondary membership function at x. $\iint$ denotes the union over all admissible x and u.

If X is a discrete set with elements $x_1, \ldots, x_n$ then Type-2 fuzzy set $\tilde{A}$ can be as follows:

$$\tilde{A} = \sum_{x \in X} \left[\sum_{u \in J_x} f_x(u) / u \right] / x = \sum_{i=1}^{n} \sum_{u \in J_x} [f_x(u) / u] / x_i \qquad (1.86)$$

Interval Type-2 Fuzzy set. As special case of a general T2 FS, Interval Type-2 fuzzy sets uses a subinterval of $[0, 1]$ as its membership value. Interval Type-2 fuzzy sets (IT2 FSs) in comparison with general T2 FSs are more effective from computational point of view. This fact made IT2 FSs a widely used framework for design of fuzzy systems.

When all $\mu_{\tilde{A}}(x, u) = 1$ in (5.2) then $\tilde{A}$ is an interval Type-2 fuzzy set (IT2 FS).

Consequently IT2 FS can be expressed as

$$\tilde{A} = \int_{x \in X} \int_{u \in J_X} 1/(x, u), \quad J_x \subseteq [0, 1] \tag{1.87}$$

First we consider some properties of Type-2 fuzzy sets. To indicate second order uncertainty one can use the concept of the footprint of uncertainty.

The footprint of uncertainty (FOU) of a Type-2 fuzzy set $\tilde{A}$ is a region with boundaries covering all the primary membership points of elements x, and is defined as follows [21, 95, 96, 295, 298–301, 303, 305–307]:

$$\text{FOU}(\tilde{A}) = \bigcup_{x \in X} J_x \tag{1.88}$$

Embedded fuzzy sets. The embedded Type-2 fuzzy set of Type-2 fuzzy set $\tilde{A}$ is defined as follows [300]:

$$\tilde{A}_0 = \int_{x \in X} [f_x(\theta)/\theta]/x \tag{1.89}$$

where θ is the element, which can be chosen from each interval J_x. For discrete case, $\tilde{A}_0$ is defined as follows:

$$\tilde{A}_0 = \sum_{i=1}^{R} [f_{x_i}(\theta_i)/\theta_i]/x_i$$

Let's consider theoretic operations on Type-2 fuzzy sets. Two Type-2 fuzzy sets $\tilde{A}$ and $\tilde{B}$ in a universe X with membership functions $\mu_{\tilde{A}}(x)$ and $\mu_{\tilde{B}}(x)$ are given:

$$\mu_{\tilde{A}}(x) = \int_u f_x(u)/u$$

and

$$\mu_{\tilde{B}}(x) = \int_w g_x(w)/w$$

where $u, w \subseteq J_x$ indicate the primary memberships of x and $f_x(u), g_x(w) \in [0, 1]$ indicate the secondary memberships (grades) of x. Using Zadeh's Extension Principle, the membership grades for union, intersection and complement of Type-2 fuzzy sets $\tilde{A}$ and $\tilde{B}$ can be defined as follows [235]:

Union:

$$\tilde{A} \cup \tilde{B} \Leftrightarrow \mu_{\tilde{A} \cup \tilde{B}}(x) = \mu_{\tilde{A}}(x) \sqcup \mu_{\tilde{B}}(x)$$
$$= \int_u \int_w (f_x(u) * g_x(w))/(u \vee w) \qquad (1.90)$$

Intersection:

$$\tilde{A} \cap \tilde{B} \Leftrightarrow \mu_{\tilde{A} \cap \tilde{B}}(x) = \mu_{\tilde{A}}(x) \sqcap \mu_{\tilde{B}}(x) = \int_u \int_w (f_x(u) * g_x(w))/(u * w) \qquad (1.91)$$

Complement:

$$\tilde{A} \Leftrightarrow \mu_{\tilde{A}}(x) = \neg \mu_{\tilde{A}}(x) = \int_u f_x(u)/(1-u) \qquad (1.92)$$

Here, $\sqcap$ and $\sqcup$ are intersection/meet and union/join operations on two membership function Type-2 fuzzy sets, $*$ indicates the chosen t-norm.

***t*-norm.** A t-norm can be extended to be a conjunction in Type-2 logic and an intersection in Type-2 fuzzy set theory, such as a Minimum t-norm and a Product t-norm [355].

***t*-conorm.** A t-conorm of operation can be used to stand for a disjunction in Type-2 fuzzy logic and a union in Type-2 fuzzy set theory, such as maximum t-conorm.

Type reduction. To defuzzify Type-2 fuzzy sets, one can use type reduction procedure. By this procedure, we can transform a Type-2 fuzzy set into a Type-1 fuzzy set. The centroid of a Type-2 set, whose domain is discretized into points, can be defined as follows [234]:

$$C_{\tilde{A}} = \int_{\theta_1} \cdots \int_{\theta_N} [\mu_{D_1}(\theta_1) * \cdots * \mu_{D_N}(\theta_N)] / \frac{\sum_{i=1}^N x_i \theta_i}{\sum_{i=1}^N \theta_i}$$

where $D_i = \mu_{\tilde{A}}(x_i)$, $\theta_i \in D_i$.

Type-2 fuzzy number. Let $\tilde{A}$ be a Type-2 fuzzy set defined in the universe of discourse R. If $\tilde{A}$ is normal, $\tilde{A}$ is a convex set, and the support of $\tilde{A}$ is closed and bounded, then $\tilde{A}$ is a Type-2 fuzzy number.

1.8.2.   *Intuitionistic fuzzy sets* [40–42]

Universe U and its subset A are given. The set

$$A^* = \{\langle x, \mu_A(x), v_A(x)\rangle | x \in U\}$$

where

$$0 \le \mu_A(x) + v_A(x) \le 1$$

is called intuitionistic fuzzy set (IFS). Functions $\mu_A : U \to [0,1]$ and $v_A : U \to [0,1]$ represent degree of membership and non-membership function $\pi_A : U \to [0,1]$ through

$$\pi(x) = 1 - \mu(x) - v(x)$$

represents degree of indeterminacy. For standard fuzzy set A. $\pi_A(X) = 0$ for each $x \in U$.

Geometrical and probabilistic relations between standard and IFSs are discussed below. In classical fuzzy set theory $\neg\mu = 1 - \mu$. The geometrical interpretation is shown in Fig. 1.26.

As it is shown in Fig. 1.27, situation for IFS is different:

The geometrical sums of both degrees are smaller than 1. In probabilistic interpretation for ordinary fuzzy sets,

$$p(\mu \vee \neg\mu) = p(\mu) + p(\neg\mu) = 1$$

In the IFS case,

$$p(\mu \vee \neg\mu) \le 1$$

Fig. 1.26. Geometrical interpretation of ordinary fuzzy set.

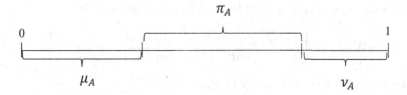

Fig. 1.27. Geometrical interpretation of intuitionistic fuzzy set (IFS).

Some operations over IFSs are shown below. For every two IFSs A and B, we have [40]

$$A \subset B \text{ iff } (\forall x \in U)(\mu_A(x) \leq \mu_B(x) \,\&\, v_A(x) \geq v_B(x))$$

$$A = B \text{ iff } (\forall x \in U)(\mu_A(x) = \mu_B(x) \,\&\, v_A(x) = v_B(x))$$

$$\bar{A} = \{\langle x, v_A(x), \mu_A(x)\rangle | x \in U\}$$

$$A \cap B = \{\langle x, \min(\mu_A(x), \mu_B(x)), \max(v_A(x), v_B(x))\rangle | x \in U\}$$

$$A \cup B = \{\langle x, \max(\mu_A(x), \mu_B(x)), \min(v_A(x), v_B(x))\rangle | x \in U\}$$

$$A + B = \{\langle x, \mu_A(x) + \mu_B(x) - \mu_A(x).\mu_B(x), v_A(x).v_B(x)\rangle | x \in U\}$$

$$A.B = \{\langle x, \mu_A(x).\mu_B(x), v_A(x) + v_B(x) - v_A(x).v_B(x)\rangle | x \in U\}$$

There are different types of negations operations [42]. For example,

$$\neg A = \{\langle x, 1 - sg(\mu_A(x)), sg(\mu_A(x))\rangle | x \in U\}$$

where

$$sg(x) = \begin{cases} 1 & \text{if } x > 0 \\ 0 & \text{if } x \leq 0 \end{cases}$$

Different implications can be defined over IFSs. Below two implication operators over IFSs are given [213].

$$X_1 = \{\langle x, \max(v_A(x), \min(\mu_A(x), \mu_B(x))),$$

$$\min(\mu_A(x), v_B(x)))\rangle | x \in U\}$$

$$X_2 = \{\langle x, 1 - sg(\mu_A(x) - \mu_B(x)), v_B(x).sg(\mu_A(x) - \mu_B(x))\rangle | x \in U\}$$

The weight operator over IFSs is defined as follows [41]:

$$W(A) = \left\{ \left\langle x, \frac{\sum_{y \in U} \mu_A(y) \cdot}{card(U)}, \frac{\sum_{y \in U} \nu_A(y)}{card(U)} \right\rangle \bigg| x \in U \right\}$$

where $card(U)$ is cardinality of the set U.

1.8.3. *Rough sets*

The traditional rough sets were introduced in Ref. [344]. It is a useful tool in processing incomplete and insufficient information.

It is useful for data mining and data analysis of discrete attribute value space. Because of their property of indiscernibility relation, it is difficult to directly apply rough sets on continuous value space. Combination of fuzzy sets and rough sets gives a useful tool for describing and modeling uncertain and impressive information.

The fuzzy rough sets were proposed in Refs. [131, 132, 367]. Traditional rough sets are based on the equivalence relation, in fuzzy rough sets, a fuzzy equivalence is used [367, 446].

A fuzzy binary relation R on universe U is called a fuzzy equivalence relation if R satisfies the reflexivity $(R(x, x) = 1)$, symmetry $(R(x, y) = R(y, x))$ and the sup-min transitivity $R(x, y) \geq \sup \min_{z \in U} \{R(x, z), R(z, y)\}$). U and R defined on the fuzzy approximation space (FAS) $F_{AS} = (U, R)$. The corresponding equivalence class $[x]_R$ with $x \in U$ is defined as a fuzzy set $[x]_R(y) = R(x, y)$ on U. Using fuzzy approximation space, the definition of fuzzy rough approximations (FRA) is given in Ref. [446].

Given a border implicator I, t-norm t and the power set $F(U)$ of universe U, the fuzzy lower and upper approximations of a fuzzy set $X \in F(U)$ are defined as two fuzzy sets with respect to I, T and the fuzzy approximation space $F_{AS} = (U, R)$ as

$$\underline{F_{AS}}_I(X)(x) = \inf_{y \in U} I(R(x, y), X(y)) \tag{1.93}$$

$$\overline{F_{AS}}^T(X)(x) = \sup_{y \in U} T(R(x, y), X(y))$$

$\underline{F_{AS}}_I(X)$ and $\overline{F_{AS}}^T(X)$ are called I-lower and T-upper fuzzy rough approximations of X in F_{AS}.

Given a FAS $F_{AS} = (U, R)$ a border implicator I, t-norm T, a pair of fuzzy sets (A_L, A_U) $(A_L, A_U) \in F(U) \times F(U)$ is called a (I, T)-fuzzy rough set in F_{AS} iff $(A_L, A_U) = (F_{ASI}(X), \overline{F_{AS}}^T(X))$ for some fuzzy sets $X \in F(U)$ [446].

In the case of [131, 132], the fuzzy rough sets can be denoted as a fuzzy sets pair $(R_*(X), R^*(X))$ for fuzzy equivalence relation R and fuzzy set $X \in F(U)$. Here, the $R_*(X)$ and $R^*(X)$ are defined as

$$R_*(X)(x) = \inf_{y \in U} \max\{1 - R(x, y), X(y)\} \qquad (1.94)$$

$$R_*(X)(x) = \sup_{y \in U} \min\{R(x, y), X(y)\}$$

1.8.4. *Neutrosophic set* [418]

To present the neutrosophic set, we need to introduce the neutrosophic (components) T, I, F which denotes the membership, indeterminacy, and non-membership values, respectively. Also it is needed to introduce the $]^-0, 1^+[$ which is the non-standard unit interval.

Let T, I, F be real standard or non-standard subsets of $]^-0, 1^+[$, with

$$\sup T = t\_\text{sup}, \ \inf T = t\_\text{inf}$$

$$\sup I = i\_\text{sup}, \ \inf I = i\_\text{inf}$$

$$\sup F = f\_\text{sup}, \ \inf F = f\_\text{inf}$$

and

$$n\_\text{sup} = t\_\text{sup} + i\_\text{sup} + f\_\text{sup}$$

$$n\_\text{inf} = t\_\text{inf} + i\_\text{inf} + f\_\text{inf}$$

Let U be a universe of discourse, and $M \in U$. X from U $x(T, I, F)$ with respect to the set M belongs to U as $t\%$ true, $i\%$ indetermine, and $f\%$ false, where t varies in T, i varies in I, f varies in F.

For example, $x(0.5,0.2,0.3)$ belongs to M with a probability of 50% x is in A with a probability of 30% x is not in A, and the rest is undecidable.

For example, a cloud is a neutrosophic set. Its borders are ambiguous, and each element belongs with a neutrosophic probability to the set.

Let's consider neutrosophic set operations. Assume that the sets A and B over the universe U are given, $x = x(T_1, I_1, F_1) \in A$ and $x = x(T_2, I_2, F_2) \in B$.

Complement of A:

If $x(T_1, I_1, F_1) \in A$, then $x(\{1^+\}\theta T_1, \{1^+\}\theta I_1, \{1^+\}\theta F_1) \in C(A)$.

Intersection:

If $x(T_1, I_1, F_1) \in A$, $x(T_2, I_2, F_2) \in B$, then $x(T_1 \otimes T_2, I_1 \otimes I_2, F_1 \otimes F_2) \in A \cap B$.

Union:

If $x(T_1, I_1, F_1) \in A$, $x(T_2, I_2, F_2) \in B$, then $x(T_1 \oplus T_2 \theta T_1 \otimes T_2, I_1 \oplus I_2 \theta I_1 \otimes I_2, F_1 \oplus F_2 \theta F_1 \otimes F_2) \in A \cup B$.

Difference:

If $x(T_1, I_1, F_1) \in A$, $x(T_2, I_2, F_2) \in B$, then $x(T_1 \theta T_1 \otimes T_2, I_1 \theta I_1 \otimes I_2, F_1 \theta F_1 \otimes F_2) \in A \backslash B$ because $A \backslash B = A \cap C(B)$.

Cartesian product:

If $x(T_1, I_1, F_1) \in A$, $y(T', I', F') \in B$, then $(x(T_1, I_1, F_1), y(T', I', F')) \in A \times B$.

M is a subset of N:

If $x(T_1, I_1, F_1) \in M \Rightarrow x(T_2, I_2, F_2) \in N$, where $\inf T_1 \leq \inf T_2$, $\sup T_1 \leq \sup T_2$, and $\inf F_1 \geq \inf F_2$, $\sup F_1 \geq \sup F_2$.

Chapter 2

Fuzzy Logic

The term fuzzy logic (FL) is used in this chapter to describe an imprecise logical system, in which the truth-values are fuzzy subsets of the unit interval with linguistic labels such as *true, false, not true, very true, quite true, not very rue and not very false*, etc. The truth-value set, T, of FL is assumed to be generated by a context-free grammar, with a semantic rule providing a means of computing the meaning of each linguistic truth-value in T as a fuzzy subset of [0,1].

Since T is not closed under the operations of negation, conjunction, disjunction and implication, the result of an operation on truth-values in T requires, in general, a linguistic approximation by a truth-value in T. As consequence, the truth tables and the rules of inference in fuzzy logic are (i) inexact and (ii) dependent on the meaning associated with the primary truth-value *true* as well as the modifiers *very, quite, more or less*, etc. [513].

2.1. Introduction

It is a truism that much of human reasoning is approximate rather than precise in nature. As a case in point, we reason in approximate terms when we decide on how to cross a traffic intersection, which route to take to a desired destination, how much to bet in poker and what approach to use in proving a theorem. Indeed, it could be argued, rather convincingly, that only a small fraction of our thinking could be categorized as precise in either logical or quantitative terms.

Perhaps the simplest way of characterizing fuzzy logic is to say that it is a logic of approximate reasoning. As such, it is a logic whose distinguishing features are (i) fuzzy truth-values expressed in linguistic terms, e.g., true, very true, more or less true, rather true, not true, false, not very true and not very false, etc.; (ii) imprecise truth tables; and (iii) rules of inference whose validity is approximate rather than exact. In these respects, fuzzy logic differs significantly from standard logical systems ranging from the classical Aristotelian logic [284] to inductive logics [204] and many-valued logics with set-valued truth-values [370].

An elementary example of approximate reasoning in fuzzy logic is the following variation on a familiar Aristotelian syllogism.

$$A1 : \text{Most men are vain}$$
$$A2 : \text{Socrates is a man}$$

$$A3 : \text{It is likely that Socrates is vain} \qquad (2.1)$$

or

$$A'3 : \text{It is very likely that Socrates is vain}$$

In this example, both A_3 and A'_3 are admissible approximate consequents of A_1 and A_2, with the degree of approximation depending on the definitions of the *terms most, likely and very* as fuzzy subsets of their respective universes of discourse. For example, assume that most and likely are defined as fuzzy subsets of the unit interval by membership functions of the form shown in Fig. 2.1, and let *very* be defined as a modifier which squares the compatibility function of its operand. Then A'_3 is a better approximation than A_3 to the exact consequent of A_1 and A_2 provided very *likely*, as a fuzzy subset of $[0, 1]$, is a better approximation than *likely* to the *fuzzy* subset *most*. This is assumed to be the case in Fig. 2.1.

Additional examples of approximate reasoning in fuzzy logic are the following. (u_1 and u_2 are numbers.)

$$A_1 : u_1 \text{ is small}$$
$$A_2 : u_1 \text{ and } u_2 \text{ are approximately equal}$$

$$A_3 : u_2 \text{ is more or less small} \qquad (2.2)$$

$$A_1 : (u_1 \text{ is small}) \text{ is very true}$$
$$A_2 : (u_1 \text{ and } u_2 \text{ are } approximately \text{ equal}) \text{ is very true}$$

$$A_3 : (u_2 \text{ is } more \text{ or } less \text{ small}) \text{ is true} \qquad (2.3)$$

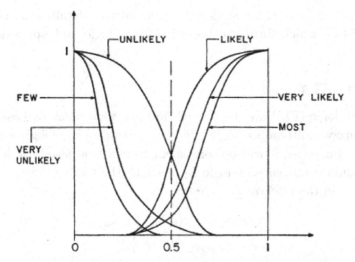

Fig. 2.1. Membership functions (not to scale) of most, likely, very likely, unlikely, few and very unlikely. Note that unlikely and likely are symmetric with respect to #=0.5; very likely is the square of likely; and very unlikely is the square of unlikely.

The italicized words in these examples represent labels of fuzzy sets. Thus, a fuzzy proposition of the form "u_1 is small", represents the assignment of a fuzzy set (or, equivalently, a unary fuzzy relation) labeled small as a value of u_1. Similarly, the fuzzy proposition "u_1 and u_2 are *approximately equal*, represents the assignment of a binary fuzzy relation approximately equal to the ordered pair (u_1, u_2). And, the nested fuzzy proposition "$(u_1$ *is small) is very true*" represents the assignment of a fuzzy truth-value *very true* to the fuzzy proposition $(u_1$ *is small*).

As will be seen in Section 2.3, the above examples may be viewed as special instances of a model of reasoning in which the process of inference involves the solution of a system of relational assignment equations. Thus, in terms of this model, *approximate reasoning* may be viewed as the determination of an *approximate* solution of a system of relational assignment equations in which the assigned relations are generally, but not necessarily, fuzzy rather than nonfuzzy subsets of a universe of discourse.

In what follows, we shall outline in greater detail some of the main ideas which form the basis for fuzzy logic and approximate reasoning.

2.2.   Fuzzy Logic

A fuzzy logic (FL) may be viewed, in part, as a fuzzy extension of a nonfuzzy multi-valued logic which constitutes a base logic for FL. For our purposes, it will be convenient to use as a base logic for FL the standard Lukasiewicz logic L_1 in which the truth-values are real numbers in the interval $[0, 1]$ and

$$v(\neg p) \triangleq 1 - v(p) \tag{2.4}$$

$$v(p \vee q) \triangleq \max(v(p), v(q)) \tag{2.5}$$

$$v(p \wedge q) \triangleq \min(v(p), v(q)) \tag{2.6}$$

$$v(p \Rightarrow q) = \min(1, 1 - v(p) + v(q)) \tag{2.7}$$

where $v(p)$ denotes the truth-value of a proposition p, $\neg$ the negation, $\wedge$ is the conjunction, $\vee$ is the disjunction and $=>$ is the implication. In what follows, however, it will be more convenient to denote the negation, conjunction and disjunction by *not, and, or*, respectively, reserving the symbols $\neg, \wedge$ and $\vee$ to denote operations on truth-values, with $\wedge \triangleq \min$ and $\vee \triangleq \max$.

The truth-value set of FL
The truth-value set of FL is assumed to be a countable set T of the form

$$T = \begin{cases} \text{true, false, not true, very true, not very true,} \\ \text{more or less true, rather true, not very true} \\ \text{and not very false}, \dots \end{cases} \tag{2.8}$$

Each element of this set represents a fuzzy subset of the truth-value set of L_1 i.e., $[0, 1]$. Thus, the *meaning* of a linguistic truth-value, τ, in y is assumed to be a fuzzy subset of $[0, 1]$.

More specifically, let $\mu_\tau : [0, 1] \to [0, 1]$ denote the compatibility (or membership) function of τ. Then the meaning of τ, as a fuzzy subset of [0,1], is expressed by

$$\tau = \int_0^1 \mu_\tau(v)/v \qquad (2.9)$$

where the integral sign denotes the union of fuzzy singletons $\mu_\tau(v)/v$, with $\mu_\tau(v)/v$, signifying that the compatibility of the numerical truth-value v with the linguistic truth-value τ is $\mu_\tau(v)$ or, equivalently, that the grade of membership of v in the fuzzy set labeled τ is $\mu_\tau(v)$.

If the support of τ is a finite subset $\{v_1, \ldots, v_n\}$ of $[0, 1]$, τ may be expressed as

$$\tau = \mu_1/v_1 + \cdots + \mu_n/v_n \qquad (2.10)$$

or more simply as

$$\tau = \mu_1 v_1 + \cdots + \mu_n v_n \qquad (2.11)$$

when no confusion between μ_i and v_i in a term of the form $\mu_i v_i$ can arise.

Note that $+$ in (2.10) plays the role of the union rather than the arithmetic sum.

As a simple illustration, suppose that the meaning of true is defined by

$$\begin{aligned}
\mu(v) &= 0 & \text{for} \quad & 0 \le v \le \alpha \\
\mu(v) &= 2\left(\frac{v-\alpha}{1-\alpha}\right)^2 & \text{for} \quad & \alpha \le v \le \frac{\alpha+1}{2} \\
\mu(v) &= 1 - 2\left(\frac{v-1}{1-\alpha}\right)^2 & \text{for} \quad & \frac{\alpha+1}{2} \le v \le 1
\end{aligned} \qquad (2.12)$$

where α is a point in $[0, 1]$.

Then, we may write

$$\text{true} \triangleq \int_\alpha^{\frac{1}{2}(\alpha+1)} 2\left(\frac{v-\alpha}{1-\alpha}\right)^2 \Big/ v + \int_{\frac{1}{2}(\alpha+1)}^1 \left(1 - 2\left(\frac{v-1}{1-\alpha}\right)^2\right) \Big/ v^2$$

$$(2.13)$$

If $v_1 = 0$, $v_2 = 0.1, \ldots, v_{11} = 1$, then *true* might be defined by, say,

$$true = 0.3/0.6 + 0.5/0.7 + 0.7/0.8 + 0.9/0.9 + 1/1 \qquad (2.14)$$

In terms of the meaning of true, the truth-value false may be defined as

$$false \int_0^1 \mu_{true}(1 - v)/v \qquad (2.15)$$

while not true is given by

$$not\ true = \int_0^1 (1 - \mu_{true}(v))/v \qquad (2.16)$$

Thus, as a fuzzy set, *not true* is the complement of *true* whereas *false* is the truth-value of the proposition *not p*, if *true* is the truth-value of *p*. In the case of (2.11), this implies that

$$false \triangleq \neg true = 1/0 + 0.9/0.1$$
$$+ 0.7/0.2 + 0.5/0.3 + 0.3/0.4 \qquad (2.17)$$

and

$$Not\ true \triangleq true' = 1/(0 + 0.1 + 0.2 + 0.3 + 0.5)$$
$$+ 0.7/0.6 + 0.5/0.7 + 0.3/0.8 + 0.1/0.9 \quad (2.18)$$

where $\neg$ stands for negation and $'$ denotes the complement.

More generally, the truth-value set of FL is characterized by two rules: (i) a *syntactic rule*, which we shall assume to have the form of a context free grammar G such that

$$\mathcal{T} = L(G) \qquad (2.19)$$

that is, $\mathcal{T}$ is the language generated by G; and (ii) a *semantic rule*, which is an algorithmic procedure for computing the meaning of the elements of $\mathcal{T}$. Generally, we shall assume that F contains one or more *primary terms* (e.g., *true*) whose meaning is specified *a priori* and which form the basis for the computation of the meaning of the other terms in $\mathcal{T}$. The truth values in $\mathcal{T}$ are referred to as *linguistic* truth-values in order to differentiate them from the numerical truth-values of L_1.

As a simple illustration, suppose that T is of the form

$$T = \{true,\ false,\ not\ true,\ very\ true,\ very\ very\ true,\ not\ very\ true$$
$$not\ true\ and\ not\ false,\ true\ and(not\ false\ or\ not\ true),\ldots\}$$

$$(2.20)$$

It can readily be verified that T can be generated by a context-free grammar G whose production system is given by

$$
\begin{array}{ll}
T \to A & C \to D \\
T \to T\ or\ A & C \to E \\
A \to B & D \to very\ D \\
A \to A\ and\ B & E \to very\ E \qquad (2.21) \\
B \to C & D \to true \\
B \to not\ C & E \to false \\
C \to (T) &
\end{array}
$$

In this grammar, T, A, B, C, D and E are nonterminals; *and true, false, very, not, and, or, (,)* are terminals. Thus, a typical derivation yields

$$T => A => A\ and\ B => B\ and\ B => not\ C\ and\ B => not$$
$$E\ and\ B => not\ very\ E\ and\ B => not\ very\ false\ and\ B =>$$
$$not\ very\ false\ and\ not\ C => not\ very\ false\ and\ not\ D => not$$
$$very\ false\ and\ not\ very\ D => not\ very\ false\ and\ not\ very\ true$$

$$(2.22)$$

If the syntactic rule for generating the elements of T is expressed as a context-free grammar, then the corresponding semantic rule may be conveniently expressed by a system of productions and relations in which each production in G is associated with a relation between the fuzzy sub-sets representing the meaning of the terminals and nonterminals [533]. For example, the production $A \to A$ and B induces the relation

$$A_L = A_R \cap B_R \qquad (2.23)$$

where A_L, A_R, and B_R represent the meaning of A and B as fuzzy subsets of $[0,1]$ (the subscripts L and R serve to differentiate between the symbols on the left- and right-hand sides of a production), and $\cap$ denotes the intersection. Thus, in effect, (2.23) defines the meaning of the connective *and*.

With this understanding, the dual system corresponding to (2.21) may be written as

$$
\begin{aligned}
T &\to A & T_L &= A_R \\
T &\to T \text{ or } A & T_L &= T_R \cup A_R \\
A &\to B & A_L &= B_R \\
A &\to A \text{ and } B & A_L &= A_R \cap B_R \\
B &\to C & B_L &= C_R \\
B &\to \text{not } C & B_L &= C_R' \\
C &\to (T) & C_L &= T_R \\
C &\to D & C_L &= D_R \\
C &\to E & C_L &= E_R \\
D &\to \text{very } D & D_L &= (D_R)^2 \\
E &\to \text{very } E & E_L &= (E_R)^2 \\
D &\to \text{true} & D_L &= \text{true} \\
E &\to \text{false} & E_L &= \text{false}
\end{aligned}
\tag{2.24}
$$

This dual system is employed in the following manner to compute the meaning of a composite truth-value in $\mathcal{T}$.

(1) The truth-value in question, e.g., *not very true and not very false*, is parsed by the use of an appropriate parsing algorithm for G [8], yielding a syntax tree such as shown in Fig. 2.2. The leaves of this syntax tree are (a) primary terms whose meaning is specified a priori; (b) names of modifiers, connectives and negation; and (c) markers such as parentheses which serve as aids to parsing.

(2) Starting from the bottom, the primary terms are assigned their meaning and, using the equations of (2.24), the meaning of nonterminals connected to the leaves is computed. Then, the subtrees which have these nonterminals as their roots are deleted,

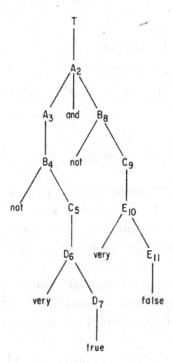

Fig. 2.2. Syntax tree for the linguistic truth-value not very true and not very false.

leaving the nonterminals in question as the leaves of the pruned tree. This process is repeated until the meaning of the term associated with the root of the syntax tree is derived.

In applying this procedure to the syntax tree shown in Fig. 2.2, we first assign to true and false the meaning expressed by (2.9) and (2.15). Then, we obtain in succession

$$D_7 = true$$
$$E_{11} = false$$
$$D_6 = D_7^2 = true$$
$$E_{10} = E_{11}^2 = false^2$$
$$C_5 = D_6 = true^2$$
$$C_9 = E_{10} = false^2$$

$$B_4 = C_5' = (true^2)'$$
$$B_8 = C_9' = (false^2)'$$
$$A_3 = B_4 = (true^2)'$$
$$A_2 = A_3 \cap B_8 = (true^2)' \cap (false^2)' \qquad (2.25)$$

and finally,

$$not\ very\ true\ and\ not\ very\ false = (true^2)' \cap (false^2)' \qquad (2.26)$$

where $\mu_{true^2} = (\mu_{true})^2$ and likewise for μ_{false^2}.

It should be noted that the truth-values in (2.8) involve just one modifier, *very*, whose meaning is characterized by (2.24). As defined by (2.24), *very* has the effect of squaring the compatibility function of its operand.

This simple approximation should not be viewed, of course, as an accurate representation of the complex and rather varied ways in which *very* modifies the meaning of its operands in a natural language discourse.

In addition to *very*, the more important of the modifiers which may be of use in generating the linguistic truth-values in $\mathcal{T}$ are: *more or less, rather, quite, essentially, completely, somewhat, and slightly*. As in the case of *very*, the meaning of such modifiers may be defined — as a first approximation — in terms of a set of standardized operations on the fuzzy sets representing their operands. Better approximations, however, would require the use of algorithmic techniques in which a definition is expressed as a fuzzy recognition algorithm which has the form of a branching questionnaire [515].

What is the rationale for using the linguistic truth-values of FL in preference to the numerical truth-values of L_1? At first glance, it may appear that we are moving in a wrong direction, since it is certainly easier to manipulate the real numbers in [0,1] than the fuzzy subsets of $[0, 1]$. The answer is two-fold. First, the truth-value set of Li is a continuum whereas that of FL is a countable set. More importantly, in most applications to approximate reasoning, a small finite subset of the truth-values of FL would, in general, be sufficient because each truth-value of FL represents a fuzzy subset rather than a single element of $[0, 1]$. Thus, we gain by trading the large number of simple truth-values of L_1 for the small number of less simple truth-values of FL.

The second and related point is that approximate reasoning deals, for the most part, with propositions which are fuzzy rather than precise, e.g., "Vera is *highly intelligent*", "Douglas is *very inventive*", "Berkeley is *close* to San Francisco", "It is *very likely* that Jean-Paul will *succeed*" etc. Clearly, the fuzzy truth-values of FL are more commensurate with the fuzziness of such propositions than the numerical truth-values of L_1.

Operations on linguistic truth-values

So far, we have focused our attention on the structure of the truth-value set of FL. We turn next to some of the basic questions relating to the manipulation of linguistic truth-values which are labels of fuzzy subsets of $[0, 1]$.

To extend the definitions of negation, conjunction, disjunction and implications in L_1 to those of FL, it is convenient to employ an extension principle for fuzzy sets which may be stated as follows [514].

Let f be a mapping from V to W and let A be a fuzzy subset of V expressed as

$$A = \int_v \mu_A(v)/v \qquad (2.27)$$

or, in the finite case, as

$$A = \mu_1 v_1 + \cdots + \mu_n v_n \qquad (2.28)$$

where μ_A is the compatibility function of A, with $\mu_A(v)$ and μ_i denoting, respectively, the compatibilities of v and $v_i, i = 1, \ldots, n$, with A.

Then, the image of A under f is a fuzzy subset, $f(A)$, of W defined by

$$f(A) = \int_w \mu_A(v)/f(v) \qquad (2.29)$$

or, in the case of (2.28),

$$f(A) = \mu_1 f(v_1) + \cdots + \mu_n f(v_n) \tag{2.30}$$

where $w = f(v)$ is the image of v under f. In effect, (2.29) and (2.30) extend the domain of definition of f from points in V to fuzzy subsets of V.

More generally, let $*$ denote a mapping (or a relation) from the Cartesian product $U \times V$ to W. Thus, expressed in infix form, we have

$$w = u * v, \quad u \in U, \quad v \in V, \quad w \in W \tag{2.31}$$

where w is the image of u and v under $*$.

Let A and B be fuzzy subsets of U and V, respectively, expressed as

$$A = \int_U \mu_A(u)/u \tag{2.32}$$

$$B = \int_V \mu_B(u)/v \tag{2.33}$$

or

$$A = \mu_1 u_1 + \cdots + \mu_m u_m \tag{2.34}$$

$$B = u_1 v_1 + \cdots + u_n v_n \tag{2.35}$$

Then, the image of $A \times B$ under $*$ is a fuzzy subset, $A * B$, of W defined by

$$A * B = \int_W (\mu_A(u) \wedge \mu_B(v))/(u * v) \tag{2.36}$$

or, in the case of (2.34) and (2.35),

$$A * B = \sum_{i,j} (\mu_i \wedge v_j)/u_i * v_j, \quad i = 1, \ldots, m, \quad j = 1, \ldots, n \tag{2.37}$$

provided u and v are non-interactive [514] in the sense that the assignment of a value to u does not affect the values that may be assigned to v, and vice-versa. A convenient feature of (2.37) is that the expression for $A * B$ may be obtained quite readily through term by term multiplication of (2.34) and (2.35), and employing the identities

$$(\mu_i u_i) * (\nu_i \nu_j) = (\mu_i \wedge \nu_j)/u_i * \nu_j \qquad (2.38)$$

and

$$a_k w_k + \beta_k w_k = (\alpha_k \vee \beta_k) w_k \qquad (2.39)$$

for combination and simplification.

To apply the extension principle to the definition of negation, conjunction, disjunction and implication in FL, it is expedient to use (2.11), since it is easy to extend the resulting definitions to the case where the truth values are of the form (2.9).

Specifically, let p and q be fuzzy propositions whose truth-values are fuzzy sets of the form

$$\nu(p) = \mu_1 \nu_1 + \cdots + \mu_m \nu_m \qquad (2.40)$$
$$\nu(q) = u_1 \nu_1 + \cdots + u_n \nu_n \qquad (2.41)$$

For example, p might be "Eugenia is *very kind*", with the truth-value of p being *very true*, while q might be "Fania was *very healthy*", with the truth-value of q being *more or less* true.

Applying (2.30) to (2.40), the expression for the truth-value of the proposition *not p* is found to be

$$v(not\ p) = \mu_1/(1 - v_1) + \cdots + \mu_m/(1 - v_m) \qquad (2.42)$$

For example, if *true* is defined by (2.14) and $v(p) = very\ true$, then

$$very\ true = 0.9,/0.6 + 0.25/0.7 + 0.9,/0.8 + 0.81/0.9, +1/1 \qquad (2.43)$$

and $v(not\ p) = 0.09/0.4 + 0.25/0.3 + 0.49/0.2 + 0.81/0.1 + 1/0$

$$(2.44)$$

which in view of (2.14) may be expressed as

$$v(not\ p) = very\ false \qquad (2.45)$$

In this example, the truth-value of *not p* is an element of. In general, however, this will not be the case, so that a fuzzy truth-value, ϕ, obtained as a result of application of (2.30) or (2.37) would normally have to be approximated by a linguistic truth-value, ϕ^*, which is in $\mathcal{T}$. The relation between ϕ^* and ϕ will be expressed as

$$\phi^* = LA[\phi] \qquad (2.46)$$

where LA is an abbreviation for *linguistic approximation*. Note that a linguistic approximation to a given ϕ will not, in general, be unique.

At present, there is no simple or general technique for finding a "good" linguistic approximation to a given fuzzy subset of V. In most cases, such an approximation has to be found by ad hoc procedures, without a precisely defined criterion of the "goodness" of approximation. In view of this, the standards of precision in computations involving linguistic truth-values are, in general, rather low. This, however, is entirely consistent with the imprecise nature of fuzzy logic and its role in approximate reasoning.

Turning to the definitions of conjunction, disjunction and implication in FL, we obtain on application of (2.37) to (2.5), (2.6) and (2.7)

$$\nu t(p \text{ and } q) = LA[\nu(p) \wedge \nu(q)] = LA[(\mu_1 u_1 + \cdots + \mu_m u_m)$$

$$\wedge\, (u_1 \nu_1 + \cdots + u_n \nu_n)] = A\left[\sum_{i,j}(\mu_i \wedge v_j)/u_i \wedge v_j\right]$$

$$(2.47)$$

$$\nu(p \text{ or } q) = LA[\nu(p) \vee \nu(q)] = LA[(\mu_1 u_1 + \cdots + \mu_m u_m)$$

$$\vee\, (u_1 \nu_1 + \cdots + u_n \nu_n)] = LA\left[\sum_{i,j}(\mu_i \wedge v_i)/u_i \vee v_j\right]$$

$$(2.48)$$

and similarly

$$\nu(p => q) = LA\left[\sum_{i,j}(\mu_i \wedge v_j)/(1 \wedge (1 - (u_1 - \nu_j)))\right] \qquad (2.49)$$

As an illustration, suppose that

$$\nu(p) = \text{true} = 0.6/0.8 + 0.9/0.9 + 1/1 \qquad (2.50)$$

and

$$\nu(q) = \text{not true} = 1/(0 + 0.1 + \cdots + 0.7) + 0.4/0.8 + 0.1/0.9 \quad (2.51)$$

Then

$$\nu(\text{not } p) = 0.6/0.2 + 0.9/0.1 + 1/0 \qquad (2.52)$$

and

$$\nu(p \text{ and } q) = LA[\nu(p) \wedge \nu(q)]$$
$$= LA[1/(0 + \cdots + 0.7) + 0.4/0.8 + 0.1/0.9]$$
$$= \text{not true} \qquad (2.53)$$

Applying the same technique to the computation of the truth-value of the proposition *very p* (e.g., if $p \triangleq$ Evan is *very smart*, then *very p* $\triangleq$ Evan *is very very smart*), we have

$$v(\text{very } p) = LA[v^2(p)] = LA[(\mu_1 u_1 + \cdots - +\mu_m u_m)^2]$$
$$= LA[\mu_1 u_1^2 + \cdots + \mu_m u_m^2] \qquad (2.54)$$

and for the particular case where

$$v(p) = \text{true} = 0.6/0.8 + 0.9/0.9 + 1/1 \qquad (2.55)$$

(2.54) yields

$$v(\text{very } p) = LA[0.6/0.64 + 0.9/0.81 + 1/1] \qquad (2.56)$$

$$v(\text{very } p) \cong \text{more or less true} \qquad (2.57)$$

if the modifier *more or less* is defined by

$$\mu_{\text{more or less } A} = (\mu_A)^{1/2} \qquad (2.58)$$

where A is a fuzzy subset of U, and μ_A and $\mu_{\text{more or less } A}$ are the compatibility functions of A and *more or less A*, respectively. It should be noted that the approximation of the bracketed expression in (2.56) by (2.57) is low in precision.

2.3.   Approximate Reasoning

It is rather illuminating as well as convenient to view the process of reasoning as the solution of a system of relational assignment equations. Specifically, consider a fuzzy proposition, p, of the form

$$p \triangleq u \text{ is } A \tag{2.59}$$

or, more concretely

$$p \triangleq \text{Mark is tall} \tag{2.60}$$

in which A is a fuzzy subset of a universe of discourse U and u is an element of a possibly different universe V. Conventionally, p would be interpreted as "u is a member of A", (e.g., "Mark is a member of the class of *tall* men"). However, if A is a fuzzy rather than a nonfuzzy subset of U, then it is not meaningful to assert that u is a member of A — if "is a member of" is interpreted in its usual mathematical sense.

We can get around this difficulty by interpreting "u is A" as the assignment of a unary fuzzy relation A as the value of a variable which corresponds to an implied attribute of u. For example, "Mark is tall", would be interpreted as the assignment equation.

$$\text{Height(Mark)} = \text{tall} \tag{2.61}$$

in which Height(Mark) is the name of a variable and tall is its assigned linguistic value. Similarly, the proposition

$$p \triangleq \text{Mark is tall and Jacob is not heavy} \tag{2.62}$$

Is equivalent to two assignment equations

$$\text{Height(Mark)} = \text{tall} \tag{2.63}$$

and

$$\text{Weight(Jacob)} = \text{not heavy} \tag{2.64}$$

In which both tall and not heavy are fuzzy subsets of the real line which may be characterized by their respective compatibility functions μ_{tall} and $\mu_{not\ heavy}$. As a further example, consider the proposition

$$p \triangleq \text{Mark is } much\ taller\ than \text{ Mac} \qquad (2.65)$$

In this case, the relational assignment equation may be expressed as

$$(\text{Height(Mark)}, \text{Height(Mac)}) = much\ taller\ than \qquad (2.66)$$

In which the linguistic value on the right-hand-side represents a binary fuzzy relation in $R \times R(R \triangleq$ real line) which is assigned to the variable on the left-hand-side of (2.66).

More generally, let $U_1,...,U_n$ be a collection of universes of discourse, and let $(u_1, \ldots, u_n)$ be an n-tuple in the Cartesian product $U_1 \times \cdots \times U_n$. By a *restriction on* $(u_1, \ldots, u_n)$ denoted by $R(u_1, \ldots, u_n)$, is meant a fuzzy relation in $U_1 \times \cdots \times U_n$ which defines the compatibility with $R(u_1, \ldots, u_n)$ of values that are assigned to $(u_1, \ldots, u_n)$. As a simple example, if u is a real number and $R(u)$ is the fuzzy set

$$R(u) = 1/0 + 1/1 + 0.8/2 + 0.5/3 + 0.2/4 \qquad (2.67)$$

then 2 may be assigned as a value to u with compatibility 0.8.

Now if p is a proposition of the form

$$p(u_1, \ldots, u_n) \text{ is } A \qquad (2.68)$$

where A is an n-ary fuzzy relation in $U_1 \times \cdots \times U_n$, then (2.68) may be interpreted as the assignment equation

$$R(u_1, \ldots, u_n) = A \qquad (2.69)$$

which for simplicity may be written as

$$(u_1, \ldots, u_n) = A \qquad (2.70)$$

In this sense, a collection of propositions of the form

$$p_i \triangleq (u_{i_1}, \ldots, u_{i_k}) \text{ is } A_i \qquad (2.71)$$

where $(i_1, \ldots, i_k)$ is a subsequence of the index sequence $(1, \ldots, n)$, translates into a collection of assignment equations of the form

$$R(u_1, \ldots, u_n) = A_i, \quad i = 1, 2, \ldots, n \qquad (2.72)$$

or more simply

$$(u_{i_1}, \ldots, u_{i_k}) = A_i \qquad (2.73)$$

For example, the propositions

$$p \triangleq u_1 \text{ is small} \qquad (2.74)$$

and

$$q \triangleq u_1 \text{ and } u_2 \text{ are } approximately\ equal \qquad (2.75)$$

translate into the relational assignment equations

$$u_1 = \text{small} \qquad (2.76)$$

and

$$(u_1, u_2) = approximately\ equal \qquad (2.77)$$

As was stated in the Introduction, the process of inference may be viewed as the solution of a system of relational assignment equations. In the case of (2.76) and (2.77), for example, solving these equations for u_2 yields

$$u_2 = LA[small \circ approximately\ equal] \qquad (2.78)$$

where $\circ$ denotes the composition of fuzzy relations and LA stands for linguistic approximation. Thus, if

$$small = 1/1 + 0.6/2 + 0.2/3 \qquad (2.79)$$

and

$$approximately\ equal = 1/((1,1) + (2,2) + (3,3) + (4,4))$$
$$+ 0.5/((1,2) + (2,1) + (2,3) + (3,2)$$
$$+ (3,4) + (4,3))(3.22) \qquad (2.80)$$

then by expressing (2.78) as the max–min product of the relation matrices for *small* and *approximately equal*, we obtain

$$u_2 = LA[1/1 + 0.6/2 + 0.5/3 + 0.2/4]$$
$$\cong more\ or\ less\ small \qquad (2.81)$$

as a rough linguistic approximation to the bracketed fuzzy set. This explains the way in which the consequent u_2 is *more or less small,* was inferred in the second example in the Introduction.

Stated in somewhat more general terms, the compositional rule of *inference* expressed by (2.76), (2.77) and (2.78) may be summarized as follows, where A and B are fuzzy relations expressed in linguistic terms and $\mathrm{LA}[A \circ B]$ is a linguistic approximation to their composition. The rationale for the compositional rule of inference can readily be understood by viewing the composition of A and B as the projection on U_2 of the intersection of B with the cylindrical extension of A.

$$A_1 : u_1 \text{ is } A$$
$$A2 : u_1 \text{ and } u_2 \text{ are } B \qquad (2.82)$$
$$A3 : u_2 \text{ is } \mathrm{LA}[A \circ B]$$

and

$$A_1 : u_l \text{ and } u_2 \text{ are } A$$
$$A_2 : u_2 \text{ and } u_3 \text{ are } B \qquad (2.83)$$
$$\overline{\phantom{A_3 : u_1 \text{ and } u_3 \text{ are } LA[A \circ B]}}$$
$$A_3 : u_1 \text{ and } u_3 \text{ are } LA\,[A \circ B]$$

More specifically, if $R(u_{i_1}, \dots, u_{i_k})$ is a fuzzy relation in $U_1 \times \cdots \times U_{i_k}$, then its cylindrical extension, $\bar{R}(u_{i_1}, \dots, u_{i_k})$ is a fuzzy relation in $U_1 \times \cdots \times U_n$ defined by

$$\bar{R}(u_1, \dots, u_{ik}) = R(u_{i_1}, \dots, u_{i_k}) \times U_{j_1} \times \cdots \times U_{j_l} \qquad (2.84)$$

where $(j_1, \dots, j_l)$ is the index sequence complementary to $(i_l, \dots i_k)$ (e.g., if $n = 6$ and $(i_1, i_2, i_3, i_4) = (2, 4, 5, 6)$, then $(j_1, j_2) = (1, 3)$).

Now suppose that we have translated a given set of propositions into a system of relational assignment equations each of which is of the form

$$(u_{r1}, \dots, u_{rs}) = R_r \qquad (2.85)$$

where R_r is a fuzzy relation in $U_{r1} \times \cdots \times U_{rs}$. To solve this system for, say, $(u_{j1}, \dots, u_{j_i})$, we form the intersection of the cylindrical extensions of the R_r and project the resulting relation on $U_{j1} \times \cdots \times U_{j_i}$. Thus, in symbols,

$$(u_{j1}, \ldots, u_{j_i}) = \text{Proj}_{U_{j_1} \times \cdots \times U_{J_i}} \underset{r}{\cap} \bar{R}_r \qquad (2.86)$$

which subsumes (2.82) and (2.83) as special cases. In this sense, as stated in the Introduction, the process of inference may be viewed as the solution of a system of relational assignment equations.

In the foregoing discussion, we have limited our attention to propositions of the form "u is A". How, then, could we treat nested propositions of the form

$$p_1(u \text{ is } A_1) \text{ is } \tau \qquad (2.87)$$

e.g., (Lisa is *young*) is *very true*, where A_1 is a fuzzy subset of U and τ is a linguistic truth-value? It can readily be shown [515] that a proposition of the form (2.87) implies

$$p_2 \triangleq u \text{ is } A_2 \qquad (2.88)$$

where A_2 is given by the composition

$$A_2 = \mu_{A1}^{-1} \circ \tau$$

in which μ_{A1} is the membership function of A_1 and μ_{A1}^{-1} is its inverse (Fig. 2.3).

It is this relation between p_2 and p_1 that in conjunction with the compositional rule of inference provides the basis for the approximate inference

$$(u_1 \text{ is } A) \text{ } is \text{ } \tau_1$$
$$(u_1 \text{ and } u_2 \text{ are } B) \text{ is } \tau_2 \qquad (2.89)$$
$$(u_1 \text{ and } u_2 \text{ are } C) \text{ is } \tau_3$$

where A, B, C, are fuzzy relations; τ_1, τ_2 and τ_3 are linguistic truth values; and C and τ_3 satisfy the approximate equality

$$\mu_C^{-1} \circ \tau_3 \cong (\mu_A^{-1} \circ \tau_1) \circ (\mu_B^{-1} \circ \tau_2) \qquad (2.90)$$

between the fuzzy set $\mu_C^{-1} \circ \tau_3$, on the one hand, and the composition of $\mu_A^{-1} \circ \tau_1$ and $\mu_B^{-1} \circ \tau_2$, on the other.

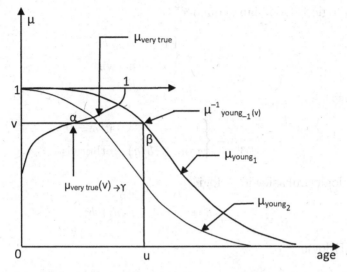

Fig. 2.3. The membership function associated with the nested proposition $p \triangleq$ (Lisa is young) is very true, where $\mu_{young2} = \mu_{young1}^{-1} \circ$ *very true*.

2.4.   Analysis of Different Fuzzy Logics [17, 20]

Here we denote the truth values of premises A and B through $T(A) = a$ and $T(B) = b$.

The implication operation in analyzed logics [12, 370] has the following form:

(1) min-logic

$$a \underset{\min}{\rightarrow} b = \begin{cases} a & \text{if } a \leq b \\ b & \text{otherwise} \end{cases}$$

(2) $S^{\#}$-logic

$$a \underset{S\#}{\rightarrow} b = \begin{cases} 1 & \text{if } a \neq 1 \text{ or } b = 1 \\ 0 & \text{otherwise} \end{cases}$$

(3) S-logic ("Standard sequence")

$$a \underset{S}{\rightarrow} b = \begin{cases} 1 & \text{if } a \leq b \\ 0 & \text{otherwise} \end{cases}$$

(4) G-logic ("Gödelian sequence")

$$a \underset{G}{\rightarrow} b = \begin{cases} 1 & \text{if } a \leq b \\ b & \text{otherwise} \end{cases}$$

(5) G43-logic

$$a \underset{G43}{\rightarrow} b = \begin{cases} 1 & \text{if } a = 0 \\ \min{(1, b/a)} & \text{otherwise} \end{cases}$$

(6) L-logic(Lukasiewicz's logic)

$$a \underset{L}{\rightarrow} b = \min(1, 1 - a + b)$$

(7) KD-logic

$$a \underset{KD}{\rightarrow} b = ((1 - a) \vee b) = \max(1 - a, b)$$

(8) ALI1-logic

$$a \underset{ALI1}{\rightarrow} b = \begin{cases} 1 - a & \text{if } a < b \\ 1 & \text{if } a = b \\ b & \text{if } a > b \end{cases}$$

(9) ALI2-logic

$$a \underset{ALI2}{\rightarrow} b = \begin{cases} 1 & \text{if } a \leq b \\ (1 - a) \wedge b & \text{if } a > b \end{cases}$$

(10) ALI3-logic

$$a \underset{ALI3}{\rightarrow} b = \begin{cases} 1 & \text{if } a \leq b \\ b/[a + (1 - b)] & \text{otherwise} \end{cases}$$

The comparative analysis of the first seven logics has been given in Ref. [51]. The analysis of these seven logics has shown that only *S*- and *G*-logics satisfy the classical principle of Modus Ponens and allow development of improved rule of fuzzy conditional inference.

At the same time the value of truthness of the implication operation in G-logic is equal either to 0 or 1; and only the value of truthness of logical conclusion is used in the definition of the implication operation in S-logic. Thus the degree of "fuzziness" of implication is decreased, which is a considerable disadvantage and restricts the use of these logics in approximate reasoning.

Considering the first seven logics to be well known, we give below the main logical connectives and properties of fuzzy logics ALI1-ALI3 and their comparative semantic analysis [13]. Logical connectives in logic ALI1 are given in Table 2.1.

Thus, the considered theory of fuzzy sets differs from the existing theories in new operation of union $(\overset{1}{\cup})$ and intersection $(\underset{1}{\cap})$. The value of negation is calculated as $T(\neg A) = 1 - T(A)$.

Table 2.1. Logical connectives in logic ALI1.

Name of connective	Designation of connective	Value of connective
Tautology	$\overset{.}{A}$	1
Contradiction	$\overset{\circ}{A}$	0
Disjunction	$A \overset{1}{\vee} B$	$a, a + b > 1$
		$1, a + b = 1$
		$b, a + b < 1$
Negation	$\neg A$	$(1 - a)$
Conjunction	$A \underset{1}{\wedge} B$	$a, a + b < 1$
		$0, a + b = 1$
		$b, a + b > 1$
Equivalence	$A \underset{1}{\leftrightarrow} B$	$1 - ka, a < b$
		$1, a = b$
		$1 - kb, a > b$
Sheffer's connective	$A \overset{1}{|} B$	$1 - a, a + b < 1$
		$1, a + b = 1$
		$1 - b, a + b > 1$
Pearce's connective	$A \overset{1}{\downarrow} B$	$1 - a, a + b > 1$
		$0, a + b = 1$
		$1 - b, a + b < 1$

In its turn, the connectives $\overset{1}{|}$ and $\overset{1}{\downarrow}$ are expressed as negation of $\overset{}{\underset{1}{\wedge}}$ and $\overset{1}{\vee}$, respectively, and contradiction and tautology as

$$T(\overset{\circ}{A}) = T(A \underset{1}{\wedge} \neg A); \quad T(\dot{A}) = T(A \overset{1}{\vee} \neg A)$$

For this fuzzy logic the following properties are true:

(1) Non-commutativity: $a \overset{1}{\vee} b \neq b \overset{1}{\vee} a$; $a \underset{1}{\wedge} b \neq b \underset{1}{\wedge} a$. This property is directly derived from the equations:

$$a \overset{1}{\vee} b = \begin{cases} a, & a+b > 1; \\ 1, & a+b = 1; \\ b, & a+b < 1; \end{cases} \quad b \overset{1}{\vee} a = \begin{cases} b, & a+b > 1 \\ 1, & a+b = 1 \\ a, & a+b < 1 \end{cases}$$

Note that this fuzzy logic can become commutative, if the following type of inversion is used:

$$\neg a = \begin{cases} 1, & a = 0 \\ 0, & a \neq 0 \end{cases}$$

(2) Absence of associativity of disjunction and conjunction

$$a \underset{1}{\wedge} (b \underset{1}{\wedge} c) \neq (a \underset{1}{\wedge} b) \underset{1}{\wedge} c; \quad a \overset{1}{\vee} (b \overset{1}{\vee} c) \neq (a \overset{1}{\vee} b) \overset{1}{\vee} c$$

(3) Partial idempotence

$$a \underset{1}{\wedge} a = \begin{cases} a, & a \neq 0,5; \\ 0, & a = 0,5; \end{cases} \quad a \overset{1}{\vee} a = \begin{cases} 1, & a = 0,5 \\ a, & a \neq 0,5 \end{cases}$$

(4) Absence of distributivity

$$(a \overset{1}{\vee} b) \underset{1}{\wedge} c \neq (a \underset{1}{\wedge} c) \overset{1}{\vee} (b \underset{1}{\wedge} c)$$

$$(a \underset{1}{\wedge} b) \overset{1}{\vee} c \neq (a \overset{1}{\vee} c) \underset{1}{\wedge} (b \overset{1}{\vee} c)$$

(5) Satisfaction of De Morgan's law generalized for the case of $M = [0, 1]$

$$\overline{a \underset{1}{\wedge} b} = \overline{a} \overset{1}{\vee} \overline{b}; \quad \overline{a \overset{1}{\vee} b} = \overline{a} \underset{1}{\wedge} \overline{b}$$

Note that the following three properties take place:

$$(1)\ a \underset{1}{\wedge} 0 = \begin{cases} a, & a \neq 1, \\ 0, & a = 1; \end{cases} \quad (2)\ a \overset{1}{\vee} 1 = \begin{cases} 1, & a \leq 0, \\ a, & a > 0; \end{cases} \quad (3)\ \overline{(a)} = a$$

ALI2 logic is a commutative fuzzy logic, in which the degree of truthness of the implication operation is determined considering the degrees of truthness of the premise and conclusion. This logic allows implementation of the fuzzy conditional inference rule, which satisfies criteria of both M. Mizumoto and Modus Ponens. The logical connectives used in ALI2 logic are shown in Table 2.2.

It is evident that the considered fuzzy sets theory differs from the existing ones with new operations of union $(\overset{2}{\cup})$ and $(\underset{2}{\cap})$ intersection.

The values of negation, connectives $\overset{2}{|}$ and $\overset{2}{\downarrow}$, contradiction and tautology are defined as in ALI1 logic.

Note that the following properties are true for this fuzzy logic.

(1) Commutativity $a \underset{2}{\wedge} b = b \underset{2}{\wedge} a; \quad a \overset{2}{\vee} b = b \overset{2}{\vee} a$

(2) Associativity $a \underset{2}{\wedge} (b \underset{2}{\wedge} c) = (a \underset{2}{\wedge} b) \underset{2}{\wedge} c; \quad a \overset{2}{\vee} (b \overset{2}{\vee} c) = (a \overset{2}{\vee} b) \overset{2}{\vee} c$

(3) Partial idempotence

$$a \underset{2}{\wedge} a = \begin{cases} 0, & a \leq 0,5; \\ a, & a > 0,5; \end{cases} \quad a \overset{2}{\vee} a = \begin{cases} 1, & a \geq 0,5 \\ a, & a < 0,5 \end{cases}$$

(4) Distributivity

$$(a \overset{2}{\vee} b) \underset{2}{\wedge} c = (a \underset{2}{\wedge} c) \overset{2}{\vee} (b \underset{2}{\wedge} c); \quad a \overset{2}{\vee} (b \underset{2}{\wedge} c) = (a \overset{2}{\vee} b) \underset{2}{\wedge} (a \overset{2}{\vee} c)$$

Table 2.2. Logical connectives in logic ALI2.

Name of connective	Designation of connective	Value of connective
Tautology	A	1
Contradiction	$\overset{o}{A}$	0
Negation	$\neg A$	$1 - a$
Disjunction	$A \overset{2}{\vee} B$	$\begin{array}{ll} 1, & a+b \geq 1 \\ \min(a,b), & a+b < 1 \end{array}$
Conjunction	$A \underset{2}{\wedge} B$	$\begin{array}{ll} 0, & a+b \leq 1 \\ \max(a,b), & a+b > 1 \end{array}$
Implication	$A \underset{2}{\to} B$	$\begin{array}{ll} 1, & a \leq b \\ \min[(1-a),b], & a > b \end{array}$
Equivalence	$A \underset{2}{\leftrightarrow} B$	$\begin{array}{ll} \min[a,1-b)], & a < b \\ 1, & a = b, \\ \min[(1-a),b], & a > b \end{array}$
Sheffer's connective	$A \overset{2}{\mid} B$	$\begin{array}{ll} 1, & a+b \leq 1 \\ \min[(1-a), & (1-b)], \\ & a+b > 1 \end{array}$
Pearce's connective	$A \overset{2}{\downarrow} B$	$\begin{array}{ll} 0, & a+b \geq 1 \\ \max[(1-a), & (1-b)], \\ & a+b < 1 \end{array}$

(5) Satisfaction of De Morgan's laws generalized for the case $M = [0, 1]$

$$\begin{cases} \overline{a \underset{2}{\wedge} b} = \overline{a} \overset{2}{\vee} \overline{b}; \\ \overline{a \overset{2}{\vee} b} = \overline{a} \underset{2}{\wedge} \overline{b}; \end{cases} \qquad \begin{cases} a \overset{2}{\vee} (a \underset{2}{\wedge} b) = a \\ a \underset{2}{\wedge} (a \overset{2}{\vee} b) = a \end{cases}$$

Note that the following three properties also take place

$$a \underset{2}{\wedge} 0 = 0; \quad a \overset{2}{\vee} 1 = 1; \quad (a) = a$$

Main logical connectives of ALI3 logic are represented in Table 2.3.

Table 2.3. Logical connectives in logic ALI3.

Name of connective	Designation of connective	Value of connective
Tautology	$\overset{.}{A}$	1
Contradiction	$\overset{o}{A}$	0
Negation	$\neg A$	$1 - a$
Disjunction	$A \overset{3}{\vee} B$	$\begin{cases} 1, & a + b \geq 1 \\ b/[2 - (a+b)], & a + b < 1 \end{cases}$
Conjunction	$A \underset{3}{\wedge} B$	$\begin{cases} 0, & a + b \leq 1 \\ 1 - [(1-a)/(a+b)], & a + b > 1 \end{cases}$
Implication	$A \underset{3}{\to} B$	$\begin{cases} 1, & a \leq b \\ b/[a + (1-b)], & a > b \end{cases}$
Equivalency	$A \underset{3}{\leftrightarrow} B$	$\begin{cases} a/[b + (1-a)], & a < b \\ 1, & a = b \\ b/[a + (1-b)], & a > b \end{cases}$
Sheffer's connective	$A \overset{3}{\mid} B$	$\begin{cases} 1, & a + b \leq 1 \\ (1-b)/(a+b), & a + b > 1 \end{cases}$
Pearce's connective	$A \overset{3}{\downarrow} B$	$\begin{cases} 0, & a + b \geq 1 \\ 1 - b/[2 - (a+b)], & a + b < 1 \end{cases}$

ALI3 fuzzy logic is identical to ALI1 fuzzy logic for its properties. Hence we will illustrate only the most important property of them, the property of non-commutativity.

$$a \overset{3}{\vee} b = \begin{cases} 1, & a + b \geq 1 \\ \dfrac{b}{2 - (a+b)}, & a + b < 1 \end{cases}$$

$$b \overset{3}{\vee} a = \begin{cases} 1, & a + b \geq 1 \\ \dfrac{a}{2 - (a+b)}, & a + b < 1 \end{cases}$$

Hence, it is obvious

$$a \overset{3}{\vee} b \neq b \overset{3}{\vee} a, \quad a + b < 1$$

$$a \underset{3}{\wedge} b = b \underset{3}{\wedge} a, \quad a + b \geq 1$$

Implication operations are conveniently represented in form of the implicative transition tables for eleven-valued logic. Such table for the ALI1-logic has the following form (Table 2.4).

Such table for ALI2 logic looks as follows (Table 2.5).

Table 2.4. Implicative transition table for logic ALI1.

					$\overrightarrow{\text{ALI1}}$						
					b						
a	0	0.1	0.2	0.3	0.4	0.5	0.6	0.7	0.8	0.9	1
0	1	1	1	1	1	1	1	1	1	1	1
0.1	0	1	0.9	0.9	0.9	0.9	0.9	0.9	0.9	0.9	0.9
0.2	0	0.1	1	0.8	0.8	0.8	0.8	0.8	0.8	0.8	0.8
0.3	0	0.1	0.2	1	0.7	0.7	0.7	0.7	0.7	0.7	0.7
0.4	0	0.1	0.2	0.3	1	0.6	0.6	0.6	0.6	0.6	0.6
0.5	0	0.1	0.2	0.3	0.4	1	0.5	0.5	0.5	0.5	0.5
0.6	0	0.1	0.2	0.3	0.4	0.5	1	0.4	0.4	0.4	0.4
0.7	0	0.1	0.2	0.3	0.4	0.5	0.6	1	0.3	0.3	0.3
0.8	0	0.1	0.2	0.3	0.4	0.5	0.6	0.7	1	0.2	0.2
0.9	0	0.1	0.2	0.3	0.4	0.5	0.6	0.7	0.8	1	0.1
1	0	0.1	0.2	0.3	0.4	0.5	0.6	0.7	0.8	0.9	1

Table 2.5. Implicative transition table for logic ALI2.

					$\overrightarrow{\text{ALI2}}$						
					b						
a	0	0.1	0.2	0.3	0.4	0.5	0.6	0.7	0.8	0.9	1
0	1	1	1	1	1	1	1	1	1	1	1
0.1	0	1	1	1	1	1	1	1	1	1	1
0.2	0	0.1	1	1	1	1	1	1	1	1	1
0.3	0	0.1	0.2	1	1	1	1	1	1	1	1
0.4	0	0.1	0.2	0.3	1	1	1	1	1	1	1
0.5	0	0.1	0.2	0.3	0.4	1	1	1	1	1	1
0.6	0	0.1	0.2	0.3	0.4	0.4	1	1	1	1	1
0.7	0	0.1	0.2	0.3	0.3	0.3	0.3	1	1	1	1
0.8	0	0.1	0.2	0.2	0.2	0.2	0.2	0.2	1	1	1
0.9	0	0.1	0.1	0.1	0.1	0.1	0.1	0.1	0.1	1	1
1	0	0	0	0	0	0	0	0	0	0	1

Table 2.6. Implicative transition table for logic ALI3.

| | | | | | $\overrightarrow{\text{ALI3}}$ | | | | | | |
| | | | | | b | | | | | | |
a	0	0.1	0.2	0.3	0.4	0.5	0.6	0.7	0.8	0.9	1
0	1	1	1	1	1	1	1	1	1	1	1
0.1	0	1	1	1	1	1	1	1	1	1	1
0.2	0	1/11	1	1	1	1	1	1	1	1	1
0.3	0	1/12	2/11	1	1	1	1	1	1	1	1
0.4	0	1/13	1/6	3/11	1	1	1	1	1	1	1
0.5	0	1/14	2/13	1/4	4/11	1	1	1	1	1	1
0.6	0	1/15	1/7	3/13	1/3	5/11	1	1	1	1	1
0.7	0	1/16	2/15	3/14	4/13	5/12	6/11	1	1	1	1
0.8	0	1/17	1/8	1/5	2/7	5/13	1/2	7/11	1	1	1
0.9	0	1/18	2/17	3/16	4/15	5/14	6/13	7/12	8/11	1	1
1	0	1/19	1/9	3/17	1/4	1/3	3/7	7/13	2/3	9/11	1

Implicative transition table for ALI3 fuzzy logic is given in Table 2.6.

Let us consider the analytical expression for defining double implication operations for proposed fuzzy logic ALI1–ALI3 [17]:

$$a \underset{\text{ALI1}}{\leftrightarrow} b = \begin{cases} 1 - ka & \text{if } a < b \\ 1 & \text{if } a = b \\ 1 - kb & \text{if } a > b \end{cases}$$

$$a \underset{\text{ALI2}}{\leftrightarrow} b = \begin{cases} 1 & \text{if } a = b \\ 0 & \text{if } (ka = 1) \vee (kb = 1) \\ \min[(\neg a \wedge b), (\neg b \wedge a)] & \text{otherwise} \end{cases}$$

$$a \underset{\text{ALI3}}{\leftrightarrow} b = \begin{cases} 1 & \text{if } a = b \\ 0 & \text{if } (a = 0) \vee (b = 0) \\ \min\left[\dfrac{a}{b + \neg a}, \dfrac{b}{a + \neg b}\right] & \text{otherwise} \end{cases}$$

where $ka = \max(a, 1 - a)$.

It is obvious that for the fuzzy logic ALI1 the degree to which a set is the subset of its complement is equal to the degree to which this set is empty. It should also be mentioned that the semantic analysis given in [12, 14, 17, 28] as well as the analysis given above show a significant analogy between features of fuzzy logics ALI1 and KD. However, as it will be shown below, the fuzzy logic ALI1, unlike the KD logic, has a number of advantages. For example, ALI1 logic satisfies the condition $\mu_A x \wedge (\mu_A x \rightarrow \mu_B x) \leq \mu_B x$ necessary for development of fuzzy conditional inference rules. ALI2 and ALI3 logics satisfy this inequality as well. This allows them to be used for the formalization of improved rules of fuzzy conditional inference and for the modeling of various systems, which is considered in Chapter 6.

Lately in fuzzy sets research the great attention is paid to the development of fuzzy conditional inference rules (CIR) [14, 20, 49, 51, 162, 246, 289, 312, 370, 480]. This is connected with the feature of the natural language to contain a certain number of fuzzy concepts (F-concepts), therefore we have to make logical inference in which the preconditions and conclusions contain such F-concepts. The practice shows that there is a huge variety of ways in which the formalization of rules for such kind of inferences can be made. The development of the conditional logic rules embraces mainly three types of fuzzy propositions:

$$P_1 = \text{IF } x \text{ is } A \text{ THEN } y \text{ is } B$$

$$P_2 = \text{IF } x \text{ is } A \text{ THEN } y \text{ is } B$$

$$\text{Otherwise } C$$

$$P_3 = \text{IF } x_1 \text{ is } A_1 \text{ AND } x_2 \text{ is } A_2 \text{ AND} \ldots x_n \text{ is } A_n \text{ then } y \text{ is } B.$$

The conceptual principle in the formalization of fuzzy rules is the Modus Ponens inference (separation) rule that states:

$$\text{IF } (\alpha \rightarrow \beta) \text{ is true and } \alpha \text{ is true THEN } \beta \text{ is true.}$$

The methodological base for this formalization is the compositional rule is given above. Using this rule, it was formulated some

inference rules in which both the logical preconditions and consequences are conditional propositions including F-concepts. Later
E. Mamdani [289] suggested inference rule, which like Zadeh's rule
was developed for the logical proposition of type $P1$. In other words
the following type F-conditional inference is considered:

Proposition 1: IF x is A THEN y is B

Proposition 2: x is A'

---

conclusion: y is B'

where A and A' are F-concepts represented as F-sets in the universe
U; B is F-conceptions or F-set in the universe V. It follows that B'
is the consequence represented as a F-set in V.

To obtain a logical conclusion based on the CIR, Propositions 1
and 2 must be transformed accordingly to the form of binary
F-relation $R(A_1(x), A_2(y))$ and unary F-relation $R(A_1(x))$. Here
$A_1(x)$ and $A_2(y)$ are defined by the attributes x and y which take
values from the universes U and V, respectively. Then

$$R(A_1(x)) = A' \tag{2.91}$$

According to Zadeh–Mamdani's inference rule $R(A_1(x), A_2(y))$
is defined as follows.

The maximin conditional inference rule

$$R_m(A_1(x), A_2(y)) = (A \times B) \cup (\neg A \times V) \tag{2.92}$$

The arithmetic conditional inference rule

$$R_a(A_1(x), A_2(y)) = (\neg A \times V) \oplus (U \times B) \tag{2.93}$$

The mini-functional conditional inference rule

$$R_c(A_1(x), A_2(y)) = A \times B \tag{2.94}$$

where $\times, \cup$ and $\neg$ is the Cartesian product, union, and complement
operations, respectively; $\oplus$ is the limited summation.

Thus, in accordance with Refs. [289, 501, 506] the logical consequence $R(A_2(y))$, can be derived as follows:

$$R(A_2(y)) = A'^{\circ}[(A \times B)] \cup [\neg A \times U)]$$
$$R(A_2(y)) = A'^{\circ}[(\neg A \times V)] \oplus [U \times B)]$$

or

$$R(A_2(y)) = A' \circ (A \times B)$$

where $\circ$ is the F-set maximin composition operator.

On the base of these rules the conditional inference rules for type P_2 were suggested in Ref. [49]:

$$R_4(A_1(x), A_2(y)) = [(\neg A \times V) \oplus (U \times B)] \cap [(A \times V) \oplus (U \times C)]$$
$$(2.95)$$
$$R_5(A_1(x), A_2(y)) = [(\neg A \times V) \cup (U \times B)] \cap [(A \times V) \cup (U \times C)]$$
$$(2.96)$$
$$R_6(A_1(x), A_2(y)) = [(A \times B) \cup (\neg A \times C)] \qquad (2.97)$$

Note that in Ref. [49] also the fuzzy conditional inference rules for type P_3 were suggested:

$$R_7(A_1(x), A_2(y)) = \left[\bigcap_{i=\overline{1,n}}(\neg A_i \times V)\right] \oplus [(U \times B)] \quad (2.98)$$

$$R_8(A_1(x), A_2(y)) = \left[\bigcap_{i=\overline{1,n}}(\neg A_i \times V)\right] \cup [(U \times B)] \quad (2.99)$$

$$R_9(A_1(x), A_2(y)) = \left[\bigcap_{i=\overline{1,n}} A_i\right] \times B \qquad (2.100)$$

In order to analyze the effectiveness of rules we use some criteria for F-conditional logical inference suggested in Ref. [162]. The idea of these criteria is to compare the degree of compatibility of some fuzzy conditional inference rules with the human intuition when making approximate reasoning. These criteria are the following:

| Criterion I | Precondition 1: IF x is A THEN y is B |
| | Precondition 2: x is A |

	Conclusion: y is B
Criterion II-1	Precondition 1: IF x is A THEN y is B
	Precondition 2: x is very A

	Conclusion: y is very B
Criterion II-2	Precondition 1: IF x is A THEN y is B
	Precondition 2: x is very A

	Conclusion: y is B
Criterion III	Precondition 1: IF x is A THEN y is B
	Precondition 2: x is more or less A

	Conclusion: y is more or less B
Criterion IV-1	Precondition 1: IF x is A THEN y is B
	Precondition 2: x is not A

	Conclusion: y is unknown
Criterion IV-2	Precondition 1: IF x is A THEN y is B
	Precondition 2: x is not A

Conclusion : y is not B

In Ref. [162], it was shown that in Zadeh–Mamdani's rules the relations R_m, R_0 and R_c do not always satisfy the above criteria. For instance, for R_m the following results can be derived. If $A' = A$ and

$$
\begin{aligned}
B'_m &= A \circ [(A \times B) \cup (\neg A \times V)] \\
&= \int_U \mu_A(u)|u \circ \int_{U \times V} (\mu_A(u) \wedge \mu_B(v)) \vee (1 - \mu_A(u))/(u, v) \\
&= \int_V \bigvee_{u \in U} [\mu_A(u) \wedge ((\mu_A(u) \wedge \mu_B(v)) \vee (1 - \mu_A(u)))]/v
\end{aligned}
$$

we derive

$$S_m(\mu_A(u)) = \mu_A(u) \wedge ((\mu_A(u) \wedge \mu_B(v)) \vee (1 - \mu_A(u)))$$

Since for $u \in U$ the membership function $\mu_A(u)$ takes all values from the interval $[0,1]$, then

$$\bigvee_{u \in U} S_m(\mu_A(u)) = \begin{cases} \mu_B(v) & \mu_B(v) > 0,5 \\ 0,5 & \mu_B(v) \leq 0,5 \end{cases}$$

and $B'_m = \int_V \bigvee_{u \in U} S_m(\mu_A(u))/v$, then it is clear that $B'_m \neq B$, that shows that criterion I is not satisfied.

For $A' = A^2$ (very A) we have

$$S'_m(\mu_A(u)) = \mu_A(u) \wedge [(\mu_A(u) \wedge \mu_B(v)) \vee (1 - \mu_A(u))]$$

and

$$\bigvee_{u \in U} S'_m(\mu_A(u)) = \begin{cases} \mu_B(v) & \mu_B(v) > (3 - \sqrt{5})/2 \\ (3 - \sqrt{5})/2 & \mu_B(v) \leq (3 - \sqrt{5})/2 \end{cases}$$

Thus,

$$B'_m = \int_V \bigvee_{u \in U} S'_m(\mu_A(u))/v + \text{very } B$$

i.e., $B'_m \neq B$, therefore criteria II-1 and II-2 are not satisfied.

For $A' = $ (more or less A) criterion III is not satisfied, while criterion IV-1 is.

For the arithmetical operator R_a with

$$B'_a = A^{\alpha\circ}[(\neg A \times V) \oplus (U \times B)]$$

the following results have been obtained:

(a) for $A' = A$

$$\bigvee_{u \in U} S_0(\mu_A(u), 1) = [1 + \mu_B(v)]/2$$

or

$$B'_a = \int_V \bigvee_{u \in U} S_0(\mu_A(u), 1)/v = \int_V \frac{1 + \mu_A(v)}{2} \bigg/ v$$

i.e., $B'_a \neq B$ and criterion I is not satisfied;

(b) for $A' = A^2$ (very A) it was shown that

$$B'_a = \int_V \frac{3 + 2\mu_B(v) - \sqrt{5 + 4\mu_B(v)}}{2} \bigg/ v$$

but very $B = \int_V \mu_B^2(v)/v$, thus, $B'_a \neq B^2$ (very B), i.e., criterion II-1 is not satisfied and for $B_a \neq B$ $B = \int_V \mu_B(v)/v$, i.e., criterion II-2 is not satisfied;

(c) for $A' = A^{0.5}$ (more or less A) the following takes place:

$$B'_a = \int_V \frac{-1 + \sqrt{5 + 4\mu_B(v)}}{2} \bigg/ v$$

$$\neq \int_V \mu_B^{0,5}(v)/v = \text{(more or less B)}$$

Thus, criterion III is not satisfied while criterion IV-1 is.

For the case of mini-operational rule R_c it has been found that criteria I and II-2 are satisfied while criteria II-1 and III are not.

IF $A' = \text{not } A$ THEN

$$B'_c = (\neg A) \circ (A \times B) = \begin{cases} \int_V 0,5/v, & \mu_B(v) \geq 0,5 \\ \int_V \mu_B(v)/v, & \mu_B(v) \leq 0,5 \end{cases}$$

this proves that the criteria IV-1 and IV-2 are not satisfied. In other words, logical conclusions for the first three rules do not always satisfactorily match our intuition. It is easy to notice that the rules $R_4 - R_9$ are simple modifications of Zadeh–Mamdani's inference rules regarding the propositions P_2 and P_3. Therefore, they do not satisfy criteria I–IV either.

In Ref. [162], an important generalization was made that allows some improvement to the mentioned F-conditional logical inference rules. It was shown there that for the conditional proposition arithmetical rule defined by Zadeh

$$P_1 = \text{IF } x \text{ is } A \text{ THEN } y \text{ is } B$$

the following takes place

$$R_a(A_1(x), A_2(y)) = (\neg A \times V) \oplus (U \times B)$$

$$= \int_{U \times V} 1 \wedge (1 - \mu_A(u) + \mu_B(v))/(u, v)$$

The membership function for this F-relation is

$$1 \wedge (1 - \mu_A(u) + \mu_B(v))$$

that obviously meets the implication operation or the Ply-operator for the multi-valued logic L (by Lukasiewicz), i.e.,

$$T(P \underset{L}{\rightarrow} Q) = 1 - (1 - T(P) + T(Q)) \qquad (2.101)$$

where $T(P \underset{L}{\rightarrow} Q), T(P)$ and $T(Q))$ are the truth values for the logical propositions $P \underset{L}{\rightarrow} Q, P$ and Q, respectively.

In other words, these expressions can be considered as adaptations of implication in the L-logical system to a conditional proposition.

Having considered this fact, the following expression was derived:

$$R_a(A_1(x), A_2(y)) = (\neg A \times V) \oplus (U \times B)$$

$$= \int_{U \times V} 1 \wedge (1 - \mu_A(u) + \mu_B(v))/(u, v)$$

$$= \int_{U \in V} (\mu_A(u) \underset{L}{\rightarrow} \mu_B(v))/(u, v)$$

$$= (A \times V) \underset{L}{\rightarrow} (U \times B) \qquad (2.102)$$

In Ref. [162], an opinion was expressed that the implication operation or the Ply-operator in expression (2.102) may belong to any multi-valued logical system. The following are guidelines for deciding which logical system to select for developing F-conditional logical inference rules [162].

Let F-sets A from U and B from V are given in the form:

$$A = \int_V \mu_A(u)/u, \quad B = \int_V \mu_B(v)/v$$

Then, as mentioned above, the conditional logical proposition $P1$ can be transformed to the F-relation $R(A_1(x), A_2(y))$ by adaptation of the Ply-operator in multi-valued logical system, i.e.,

$$R(A_1(x), A_2(y)) = A \times V \to U \times B$$
$$= \int_{U \times V} (\mu_A(u) \to \mu_B(v))/(u, v) \quad (2.103)$$

where the values $\mu_A(u) \to \mu_B(v)$ are depending on the selected logical system.

Assuming $R(A_1(x)) = A$ we can conclude a logical consequence $R(A_2(y))$, then using the CIR for $R(A_1(x))$ and $R(A_1(x), A_2(y))$, then

$$R(A_2(y)) = A \circ R(A_1(x), A_2(y))$$
$$= \int_U \mu_A(u)/u \circ \int_{U \times V} \mu_A(u) \to \mu_B(v))/(u, v)$$
$$= \int_V \bigvee_{u \in V} [\mu_A(u) \wedge (\mu_A(u) \to \mu_B(v))] \quad (2.104)$$

For the criterion I to be satisfied, one of the following equalities must hold true

$$R(A_2(y)) = B$$

$$\text{or} \bigvee_{u \in V} [\mu_A(u) \wedge (\mu_A(u) \to \mu_B(v))] = \mu_B(v) \quad (2.105)$$

$$\text{or } \mu_A(u) \wedge (\mu_A(u) \to \mu_B(v)) \leq \mu_B(v)$$

the latter takes place for any $u \in U$ and $v \in V$ or in terms of truth values:

$$T(P \wedge (P \to Q)) \leq T(Q) \qquad (2.106)$$

The following two conditions are necessary for formalization of F-conditional logical inference rules:

1. The conditional logical inference rules (CIR) must meet the criteria I–IV;
2. The CIR satisfy the inequality (2.106).

As was shown above, the logical inference for conditional propositions of type P_1 is of the following form:

$$\begin{array}{l} \text{Proposition 1 : IF } x \text{ is } A \text{ THEN } y \text{ is } B \\ \underline{\text{Proposition 2 : } x \text{ is } A'} \\ \\ \text{Conclusion : } y \text{ is } B' \end{array} \qquad (2.107)$$

where A, B, and A' are F-concepts represented as F-sets in U, V, and V, respectively, which should satisfy the criteria I, II-1, III, and IV-1.

For this inference if the Proposition 2 is transformed to an unary F-relation in the form $R(A_1(x)) = A'$ and the Proposition 1 is transformed to an F-relation $R(A_1(x), A_2(y))$ defined below, then the conclusion $R(A_2(y))$ is derived by using the corresponding F-conditional logical inference rule, i.e.,

$$R(A_2(y)) = R(A_1(x))^{\circ} R(A_1(x), A_2(y)) \qquad (2.108)$$

where $R(A_2(y))$ is equivalent to B' in (2.18).

Fuzzy Conditional Inference Rule 1

Theorem 2.1. *If the F-sets A from U and B from V are given in the traditional form:*

$$A = \int_U \mu_A(u)/u; \quad B = \int_V \mu_B(v)/v \qquad (2.109)$$

and the relation for the multi-valued logical system ALI1

$$R_1(A_1(x), A_2(y)) = A \times V \underset{ALI1}{\rightarrow} U \times B$$

$$= \int_{U \times V} \mu_A(u)/(u,v) \underset{ALI1}{\rightarrow} \underset{ALI1}{\rightarrow} \int_{U \times V} \mu_B(v)/(u,v)$$

$$= \int_{U \times V} (\mu_A(u) \underset{ALI1}{\rightarrow} \mu_B(v))/(u,v) \qquad (2.110)$$

where

$$\mu_A(u) \underset{ALI1}{\rightarrow} \mu_B(v) = \begin{cases} 1 - \mu_A(u), & \mu_A(u) < \mu_B(v) \\ 1, & \mu_A(u) = \mu_B(v) \\ \mu_B(v), & \mu_A(u) > \mu_B(v) \end{cases}$$

then the criteria I–IV are satisfied.

Proof is given in Ref. [17].

Fuzzy Conditional Inference Rule 2

Theorem 2.2. *If the F-sets A from U, and B from V are the same as in (2.109) and the binary relation $R_2(A_1(x), A_2(y))$ for logical multi-valued system ALI2 is defined as follows:*

$$R_2(A_1(x), A_2(y)) = A \times V \underset{ALI2}{\rightarrow} U \times B$$

$$= \int_{U \times V} \mu_A(u) \underset{ALI2}{\rightarrow} \mu_B(v)/(u,v) \qquad (2.111)$$

where

$$\mu_A(u) \underset{ALI2}{\rightarrow} \mu_B(v) = \begin{cases} 1, \mu_A(u) \le \mu_B(v) \\ (1 - \mu_A(u)) \wedge \mu_B(v) \\ \mu_A(u) > \mu_B(v) \end{cases}$$

then the criteria I-IV *are satisfied.*

Proof is given in Ref. [17].

Fuzzy Conditional Inference Rule 3

Theorem 2.3. *If F-sets A from U and B from V are the same as in (2.109) and the binary relation $R_3(A_1(x), A_2(y))$ for logical system ALI3 takes the form:*

$$R_3(A_1(x), A_2(y)) = A \times V \underset{ALI3}{\rightarrow} U \times B$$

$$= \int_{U \times V} \mu_A(u) \underset{ALI3}{\rightarrow} \mu_B(v)/(u,v) \quad (2.112)$$

where

$$\mu_A(u) \underset{ALI3}{\rightarrow} \mu_B(v) = \begin{cases} 1, & \mu_A(u) \le \mu_B(v) \\ \dfrac{\mu_B(v)}{\mu_A(u) + (1 - \mu_B(v))}, & \mu_A(u) > \mu_B(v) \end{cases}$$

then the criteria I–IV *are satisfied.*

Proof is given in Ref. [17].

The following example for the logical multi-valued system ALI1 can be shown as an illustration of the suggested inference rules.

Example:

Let $U = V = 0 + 1 + 2 + 3 + 4 + 5 + 6 + 7 + 8 + 9 + 10$,

$A = small = 1/0 + 0.8/1 + 0.6/2 + 0.4/3 + 0.2/4$,

$B = average = 0.2/2 + 0.4/3 + 0.8/4 + 1/5 + 0.8/6 + 0.4/7 + 0.2/8$.

Then the F-conditional proposition

IF x *is small* THEN y *is average*

boils down to a binary relation of the following type:

$$R(A_1(x), A_2(y)) = [small] \times V \underset{\text{ALI1}}{\rightarrow} U \times [average] =$$

=

	0	1	2	3	4	5	6	7	8	9	10
0	0	0	0.2	0.4	0.8	1	0.8	0.4	0.2	0	0
1	0	0	0.2	0.4	1	0.2	1	0.4	0.2	0	0
2	0	0	0.2	0.4	0.4	0.4	0.4	0.4	0.2	0	0
3	0	0	0.2	1	0.6	0.6	0.6	1	0.2	0	0
4	0	0	1	0.8	0.8	0.8	0.8	0.8	1	0	0
5	1	1	1	1	1	1	1	1	1	1	1
6	1	1	1	1	1	1	1	1	1	1	1
7	1	1	1	1	1	1	1	1	1	1	1
8	1	1	1	1	1	1	1	1	1	1	1
9	1	1	1	1	1	1	1	1	1	1	1
10	1	1	1	1	1	1	1	1	1	1	1

Let $R(A_1(x)) = small$, then $R(A_2(y))$

$= [small] \circ R_1(A_1(x)),\ (A_2(y))$

$= 0.2/2 + 0.4/3 + 0.8/4 + 1/5 + 0.8/6 + 0.4/7 + 0.2/8$

$= average.$

When $R_1(A_1(x)) = very\ small$, we get

$R(A_2(y)) = [very\ small] \circ R_1(A_1(x)),(A_2(y))$

$= [small]^2 \circ R_1(A_1(x),\ A_2(y))$

$= 0.04/2 + 0.16/3 + 0.64/4 + 1/5 + 0.64/6 + 0,16/7 + 0,04/8$

$= [average]^2 = very\ average$

If $R(A_2(y)) = not\ small$, then we get

$R(A_2(y)) = [not\ small] \circ R_1(A_1(x),\ A_2(y))$

$= 0 + 1 + 2 + 3 + 4 + 5 + 6 + 7 + 8 + 9 + 10 = unknown = V.$

In ordinary language this inference can be illustrated as follows:

IF x is *small* THEN y is *average*

$x = small$

$y = average$

IF x is *small* THEN y is *average*

$x = very\ small$

$y = very\ average$

IF x is *small* THEN y is *average*

$x = not\ small$

$y = unknown$

Some features of R_1, R_2, and R_3. Let's describe some interesting features of the F-relation R_1 defined in (2.110), R_2 defined in (2.111), and R_3 defined in (2.112).

Relationship 2.1

Assume that the F-conditional relation P_1 is given in the form:

$$P_{11} = \text{IF } x \text{ is } A \text{ THEN } y \text{ is } B$$
$$P_{12} = \text{IF } y \text{ is } B \text{ THEN } z \text{ is } C \qquad (2.113)$$
$$P_{13} = \text{IF } x \text{ is } A \text{ THEN } z \text{ is } C$$

where A, B, and C are F-concepts given as F-sets in the form

$$A = \int_U \mu_A(u)/u, \quad B = \int_V \mu_B(v)/v, \quad C = \int_W \mu_C(w)/w$$

Assume that $R_2(A_1(x), A_2(y))$; $R_2(A_2(y), A_3(z))$ and $R_2(A_1(x), A_3(z))$ are F-relations that translate the relations P_{11}, P_{12} and P_{13} using the rule (2.111) (note that the aforesaid is true for R_3 defined in (2.110) and (2.112) as well). Then when the conditions:

$$\left. \begin{array}{ll} \exists u \in U/\mu_A(u) = 0 & \exists u' \in U/\mu_A(u') = 1 \\ \exists v \in V/\mu_B(v) = 0 & \exists v' \in V/\mu_B(v') = 1 \\ \exists w \in W/\mu_C(w) = 0 & \exists w' \in W/\mu_C(w') = 1 \end{array} \right\} \qquad (2.114)$$

are satisfied the equality

$$R_2(A_1(x), A_3(x)) = R_1(A_1(x), A_2(y)) \circ R_2(A_2(y), A_3(z)) \qquad (2.115)$$

as well as the F-conditional propositions

$$P_{11} = \text{IF } x \text{ is } A \text{ THEN } y \text{ is } B$$
$$P_{12} = \text{IF } y \text{ is } B \text{ THEN } z \text{ is } C$$
$$P_{13} = \text{IF } x \text{ is } A \text{ THEN } z \text{ is } C$$

take place.

Proof is given in Ref. [17].

Now we consider the formalization of the fuzzy conditional inference rules for the conditional proposition of type P_2.

As it was shown above, one of the well known forms of the conditional inference is the following:

IF x is A THEN y is B ELSE y is C

For such form of the conditional proposition the following logical inference rule can take place

$$R(A_1(x), A_2(y)) = [(A \times V) \to (U \times B)] \cap (\neg A \times V) \to (U \times C)]$$

Assume that $R(A_1(x)) = A$, then

$$R(A_2(y)) = A \circ R(A_1(x), A_2(y))$$

$$= \int_U \mu_A(u)/u \circ \int_{U \times V} (\mu_A(u) \to \mu_B(v))$$

$$\wedge \, ((1 - \mu_A(u)) \to \mu_C(v))/(u, v)$$

$$= \int_V \bigvee_{u \in U} \{\mu_A(u) \wedge [(\mu_A(u) \to \mu_B(v))$$

$$\wedge \, ((1 - \mu_A(u)) \to \mu_C(v))]/v\} \qquad (2.116)$$

For the criterion I to be satisfied it is necessary that either $R(A_2(y)) = B$ or the equality

$$\bigvee_{u \in U} \{\mu_A(u) \wedge [(\mu_A(u) \to \mu_B(v)) \wedge ((1 - \mu_A(u)) \to \mu_C(v))] = \mu_B(v)\}$$

$$(2.117)$$

takes place. In other words, for $\forall v \in V$ the following must hold true:

$$\mu_A(u) \wedge [(\mu_A(u) \to \mu_B(v)) \wedge ((1 - \mu_A(u)) \to \mu_C(v))] \le \mu_B(v)$$

$$(2.118)$$

It is obvious that

IF $A \subset U$ THEN $B \subset V$ and $C \subset V$.

The logical precondition C, which is generally either unknown or equal to $\neg B$, i.e., meets the criterion IV is especially interesting.

Let's consider the case when $C = \neg B = $ not B. i.e., the following form of F-conditional logical inference takes place:

Proposition 1: IF x is A THEN y is B ELSE y is NOT B
Proposition 2: x is A'

Conclusion: y is B'

Let's show the formalization of some inference rules for the proposition of type P_2 considered in above form of F-conditional logical inference.

Fuzzy Conditional Inference Rule 4

Theorem 2.4. *If F-sets A from U and B from V are defined and the binary relation $R_1(A_1(x)), A_2(y))$ for S-logical multi-valued system takes the form*

$$R_{S1}(A_1(x), A_2(y)) = (A \times V \underset{S}{\rightarrow} U \times B)$$

$$\cap(\neg A \times V \underset{S}{\rightarrow} U \times \neg B) = \int_{U \times V} \left[\mu_A(u) \underset{S}{\rightarrow} \mu_B(v) \right]$$

$$\wedge \ [(1 - \mu_A(u)) \underset{S}{\rightarrow} (1 - \mu_B(v))]/(u, v)$$

$$(2.119)$$

where

$$[\mu_A(u) \underset{S}{\rightarrow} \mu_B(v)] \wedge [(1 - \mu_A(u)) \underset{S}{\rightarrow} (1 - \mu_B(v))]$$

$$= \begin{cases} 1 & \text{if } \mu_A(u) = \mu_B(v) \\ 0 & \text{if } \mu_A(u) \neq \mu_B(v) \end{cases}$$

then the criteria I–IV are satisfied.

Proof is given in Ref. [17].

Fuzzy Conditional Inference Rule 5

Theorem 2.5. *If F-sets A from U and B from V are defined as in (2.109), and the binary relation $R_{11}(A_1(x), A_2(y))$ in logical* *multi-valued system ALI1 takes the form*

$$R_{11}(A_1(x), A_2(y)) = (A \times V \underset{ALI1}{\to} U \times B)$$

$$\cap(\neg A \times V \underset{ALI1}{\to} U \times \neg B) = \int_{U \times V} (\mu_A(u) \underset{ALI1}{\to} \mu_B(v))$$

$$\wedge \ [(1 - \mu_A(u)) \underset{ALI1}{\to} (1 - \mu_B(v))]/(u, v)$$

$$(2.120)$$

where

$$(\mu_A(u) \underset{ALI1}{\to} \mu_B(v)) \wedge [(1 - \mu_A(u)) \underset{ALI1}{\to} (1 - \mu_B(v))]$$

$$= \begin{cases} 1 - \mu_B(v) & \text{if } \mu_A(u) < \mu_B(v) \\ 1 & \text{if } \mu_A(u) = \mu_B(v) \\ \mu_B(v) & \text{if } \mu_A(u) > \mu_B(v) \end{cases}$$

then criteria I–IV are satisfied.

Proof is given in Ref. [17].

Fuzzy Conditional Inference Rule 6

Theorem 2.6. *If F-sets A from U and B from V are defined like in (2.109), and the binary relation $R_{22}(A_1(x), A_2(y))$ in logical multi-valued system ALI2 takes the form*

$$R_{22}(A_1(x), A_2(y)) = (A \times V \underset{ALI2}{\to} U \times B) \wedge (\neg A \times V_2 \underset{ALI2}{\to} U \times \neg B)$$

$$= \int_{U \times V} (\mu_A(U) \underset{ALI2}{\to} \underset{ALI2}{\to} \mu_B(v))$$

$$\wedge \ [(1 - \mu_A(u)) \underset{ALI2}{\to} (1 - \mu_B(v))]$$

$$\underset{ALI2}{\to} (1 - \mu_B(v))/(u, v) \qquad (2.121)$$

where

$$R_{22}(A_1(x), A_2(y)) = (\mu_A(u) \underset{ALI2}{\to} \mu_B(v))$$

$$\wedge \ [(1 - \mu_A(u)) \underset{ALI2}{\to} (1 - \mu_B(v))]$$

$$= \begin{cases} \mu_A(u) \wedge (1 - \mu_B(v)) & \text{if } \mu_A(u) < \mu_B(v) \\ 1 & \text{if } \mu_A(u) = \mu_B(v) \\ (1 - \mu_A(u)) \wedge \mu_B(v) & \text{if } \mu_A(u) > \mu_B(v) \end{cases}$$

$$(2.122)$$

then criteria I–IV are satisfied.

Proof is given in Ref. [17].

Fuzzy Conditional Inference Rule 7

Theorem 2.7. *If F-sets A from U and B from V are defined as in (2.141) and the binary relation $R_{33}(A_1(x), A_2(y))$ in logical multivalued system ALI3 takes the form*

$$R_{33}(A_1(x), A_2(y)) = (A \times V \underset{ALI3}{\rightarrow} U \times B) \cap (\neg A \times V \underset{ALI3}{\rightarrow} U \times \neg B)$$

$$= \int_{U \times V} (\mu_A(u) \underset{ALI3}{\rightarrow} \mu_B(v))$$

$$\wedge \; [(1 - \mu_A(u)) \underset{ALI3}{\rightarrow} (1 - \mu_B(v))]/(u, v) \qquad (2.123)$$

where

$$R_{33}(A_1(x), A_2(y)) = (\mu_A(u) \underset{ALI3}{\rightarrow} \mu_B(v))$$

$$\wedge \; [(1 - \mu_A(u)) \underset{ALI3}{\rightarrow} (1 - \mu_B(v))]$$

$$= \begin{cases} \dfrac{1 - \mu_B(v)}{(1 - \mu_A(u)) + \mu_B(v)} & \text{if } \mu_A(u) < \mu_B(v) \\ 1 & \text{if } \mu_A(u) = \mu_B(v) \\ \dfrac{\mu_B(v)}{\mu_A(u) + (1 - \mu_B(v))} & \text{if } \mu_A(u) > \mu_B(v) \end{cases}$$

$$(2.124)$$

then criteria I–IV are satisfied.

Proof is given in Ref. [17].

It should be noted that in formalizing the *F*-conditional logical inference rules for conditional proposition of P_2 type a combination of the logical systems can be used as well; in this case the binary relations can take the form:

$$R_{\text{SALI1}}, R_{\text{SALI2}}, R_{\text{SALI3}}, R_{\text{ALI1S}}, R_{\text{ALI2S}}, R_{\text{ALI3S}}, R_{\text{ALI1ALI2}}, R_{\text{ALI1ALI3}}$$

Now we need to find out what is the connection or relationship between B and C.

Lemma 2.1. *If the logical proposition:*

$$IF \ x \ is \ A \ THEN \ y \ is \ B \ ELSE \ y \ is \ C$$

takes place, then for logical consequence B and C from V we get the following relationship: $C \subseteq B$.

Proof is given in Ref. [17].

Corollary 2.1. *The expression $B \subseteq C$, i.e., $B \rightarrow C$ then is transformed to the relation*

$$R(A_1(x), A_2(y)) = (A \rightarrow B) \cap (\neg A \rightarrow C) = (A \rightarrow C) \cap (\neg A \rightarrow C)$$

In other words the conditional proposition
    IF x is A THEN y is C ELSE y is C,
i.e., logical conclusion B is omitted, and the inference rule becomes nonsense.

Formalization of the fuzzy conditional inference rules for the conditional proposition of type P_3.

Let's consider the following widely used form of conditional proposition

$$IF \ x_1 \ is \ A_1, x_2 \ is \ A_2, \ldots, x_n \ is \ A_n \ THEN \ y \ is \ B,$$

i.e., in this case the binary relation $R(A_1(x), A_2(y))$ is represented as

$$[\cap_i A_i] \times V \rightarrow U \times B.$$

Assume then that $R(A_1(x)) = \underset{i}{\cap} A_i' = A^{*'}$, then

$$R(A_2(y)) = A^{*'} \circ R(A_1(x), A_2(y))$$

$$= \int_U \mu_{A^{*'}}(u)/u \circ \int_{U \times V} \mu_{A^*}(u) \to \mu_B(v)/(u,v)$$

$$= \int_V \underset{u \in U}{\vee} [\mu_{A^{*'}}(u) \wedge (\mu_{A^*}(u) \to \mu_B(v))]/v$$

In order to satisfy the criterion I, the following equality must hold

$$\underset{u \in U}{\vee} [\mu_{A^{*'}}(u) \wedge (\mu_{A^*}(u) \to \mu_B(v))] = \mu_B(v), \qquad (2.125)$$

for arbitrary $v \in V$. This equality, in turn leads to the following inequality

$$\mu_{A^{*'}}(u) \wedge (\mu_{A^*}(u) \to \mu_B(v)) \le \mu_B(v)) \qquad (2.126)$$

or in full form

$$[\overset{n}{\underset{i}{\wedge}} \mu_{A_i'}(u)] \wedge ([\overset{n}{\underset{i}{\wedge}} \mu_{A_i}(u)] \to \mu_B(v)) \le \mu_B(v) \qquad (2.127)$$

For such form of conditional proposition the following type of F-conditional logical inference takes place:

Precondition 1: IF x_1 is A_1, x_2 is $A_2, \dots$, x_n is A_n THEN y is B
Precondition 2: x_1 is A_1', x_2 is $A_2', \dots$, x_n is A_n'

Conclusion: y is B'

Now we consider the F-conditional logical inference rules for conditional propositions of type P_3.

Theorem 2.8. *If $A_i \subseteq U$ are logical preconditions and the following logical proposition takes place:*
    IF x_1 is A_1, and x_2 is $A_2, \dots$, and x_n is A_n THEN y is B, also $\underset{i}{\cap} A_i = \emptyset$ (empty), $\forall i = \overline{1, n}$, then the logical conclusion B' is unknown.

Proof is given in Ref. [17].

Corollary 2.2. *In order for the conclusion B' to logical proposition of type P_3 to take place*

IF x_1 is A_1, x_2 is $A_2, \ldots, x_n$ is A_n THEN y is B

the following is necessary: the subset A_i, $A_i \subseteq U$, must be connected, i.e., $\bigcap_i A_i \neq 0$.

The application practice of the *F*-conditional proposition of type P_3 has shown that the most effective is the following combined inference rule

$$R(A_2(y)) = R(A_1(x)) \circ R(A_1(x), A_2(y))$$
$$= R(A_1(x)) \circ \{[(\bigcap_i A_i) \times V \to U \times B]$$
$$\bigcap [\neg(\bigcap_i A_i) \times V \to U \times \neg B]\} \qquad (2.128)$$

2.5. Extended Fuzzy Logic [543]

Fuzzy logic adds to bivalent logic an important capability — a capability to reason precisely with imperfect information. Imperfect information is information which in one or more respects is imprecise, uncertain, incomplete, unreliable, vague or partially true. In fuzzy logic, results of reasoning are expected to be provably valid, or p-valid for short. Extended fuzzy logic adds an equally important capability — a capability to reason imprecisely with imperfect information. This capability comes into play when precise reasoning is infeasible, excessively costly or unneeded. In extended fuzzy logic, p-validity of results is desirable but not required. What is admissible is a mode of reasoning which is fuzzily valid, or f-valid for short. Actually, much of everyday human reasoning is f-valid reasoning.

f-valid reasoning falls within the province of what may be called unprecisiated fuzzy logic, FLu. FLu is the logic which underlies what is referred to as f-geometry. In f-geometry, geometric figures are drawn by hand with a spray pen — a miniaturized spray can. In Euclidean geometry, a crisp concept, C, corresponds to a fuzzy concept, f-C, in f-geometry. f-C is referred to as an f-transform of C, with C serving as the prototype of f-C. f-C may be interpreted as the result of execution of the instructions: Draw C by hand with a spray pen. Thus, in f-geometry we have f-points, f-lines, f-triangles, f-circles, etc. In addition, we have f-transforms of higher-level concepts: f-parallel, f-similar, f-axiom, f-definition, f-theorem, etc. In f-geometry, p-valid reasoning does not apply. Basically, f-geometry may be viewed as an f-transform of Euclidean geometry.

What is important to note is that f-valid reasoning based on a realistic model may be more useful than p-valid reasoning based on an unrealistic model.

2.5.1.   *Introduction*

The extended fuzzy logic, FLe, is a venture into unchartered territory — a territory in which reasoning and formalisms are quasi-mathematical rather than mathematical. The following is a very brief exposition of some of the basic ideas which underlie FLe. It should be stressed that what follows is just the first step toward construction of extended fuzzy logic and an exploration of its implications and applications.

Science deals not with reality but with models of reality. In large measure, scientific progress is driven by a quest for better models of reality. In constructing better models of reality, a problem that has to be faced is that as the complexity of a system, S, increases, it becomes increasingly difficult to construct a model, $M(S)$, which is both cointensive, that is, close-fitting, and precise. This applies, in particular, to systems in which human judgment, perceptions and emotions play a prominent role. Economic systems, legal systems and political systems are cases in point.

As the complexity of a system increases further, a point is reached at which construction of a model which is both cointensive and precise is not merely difficult — it is impossible. It is at this point that extended fuzzy logic comes into play.

Actually, extended fuzzy logic is not the only formalism that comes into play at this point. The issue of what to do when an exact solution cannot be found or is excessively costly is associated with a vast literature. Prominent in this literature are various approximation theories [50], theories centered on bounded rationality [415], qualitative reasoning [470], commonsense reasoning [276, 320] and theories of argumentation [444]. Extended fuzzy logic differs from these and related theories both in spirit and in substance. The difference will become apparent in Section 2.5.2, in which the so-called f-geometry is used as an illustration.

To develop an understanding of extended fuzzy logic, FLe, it is expedient to start with the following definition of fuzzy logic, FL. Fuzzy logic is a precise conceptual system of reasoning, deduction and computation in which the objects of discourse and analysis are, or are allowed to be, associated with imperfect information. Imperfect information is information which in one or more respects is imprecise, uncertain, incomplete, unreliable, vague or partially true. In fuzzy logic, the results of reasoning, deduction and computation are expected to be provably valid (p-valid) within the conceptual structure of fuzzy logic.

There are many misconceptions about fuzzy logic. The principal misconception is that fuzzy logic is fuzzy. The stated definition underscores that fuzzy logic is precise. In fuzzy logic precision is achieved through association of fuzzy sets with membership functions and, more generally, association of granules with generalized constraints [546]. What this implies is that fuzzy logic is what may be called precisiated logic.

At this point, a key idea comes into play. The idea is that of constructing a fuzzy logic, FLu, which, in contrast to FL, is unprecisiated. What this means is that in FLu membership functions and generalized constraints are not specified, and are a matter of perception rather than measurement. To stress the contrast between FL and FLu, FL may be written as FLp, with p standing for precisiated.

A question which arises is: What is the point of constructing FLu — a logic in which provable validity is off the table? But what is not off the table is what may be called fuzzy validity, or f-validity for short. As will be shown in Section 2.2, a model of FLu is f-geometry — a geometry in which figures are drawn by hand with a spray pen, without the use of a ruler or compass. Actually, everyday human reasoning is preponderantly f-valid reasoning. Humans have a remarkable capability to perform a wide variety of physical and mental tasks without any measurements and any computations. In this context, f-valid reasoning is perception-based. In FLu, there are no formal definitions, theorems or p-valid proofs.

The concept of unprecisiated fuzzy logic provides a basis for the concept of extended fuzzy logic, FLe. More specifically, FLe is the result of adding FLu to FL(FLp),

$$FLe = FL + FLu,$$

with FLu playing the role of an extension of, or addendum to, FL.

Expressing FLe as the sum of FL and FLu has important implications. First, to construct a definition of FLe it is sufficient to delete the word "precise" from the definition of FL. With this deletion, the definition of FLe reads:

Extended fuzzy logic, FLe, is a conceptual system of reasoning, deduction and computation in which the objects of discourse and analysis are, or are allowed to be, associated with imperfect information. Imperfect information is information which in one or more respects is imprecise, uncertain, incomplete, unreliable, vague or partially true. In extended fuzzy logic, the result of reasoning, deduction or computation is not expected to be provably valid.

Second, and more importantly, f-valid reasoning is not admissible in FL, but is admissible in FLe when p-valid reasoning is infeasible, carries an excessively high cost or is unneeded. In many realistic settings, this is the norm rather than exception. The following very simple example is a case in point.

I hail a taxi and ask the driver to take me to address A. There are two versions: (a) I ask the driver to take me to A the shortest way; and (b) I ask the driver to take me to A the fastest way. Based on his/her experience, the driver chooses route (a) for (a) and route (b) for (b).

In version (a) if there is a map of the area it is possible to construct the shortest way to A. This would be a p-valid solution. Thus, for version (a) there exists a p-valid solution but the driver's choice of route (a) may be viewed as an f-valid solution which in some sense is good enough.

In version (b), it is not possible to construct a cointensive model of the system and hence it is not possible to construct a p-valid solution. The problem is rooted in uncertainties related to traffic conditions, timing of lights, etc. In fact, if the driver had asked me to define what I mean by "the fastest way," I could not come up with an answer to his/her question. Thus, in version (b) there exists an f-valid solution, but a p-valid solution does not exist.

Basically, extended fuzzy logic, FLe, results from lowering of standards of cointension and precision in fuzzy logic, FL. In effect, extended fuzzy logic adds to fuzzy logic a capability to deal imprecisely with imperfect information when precision is infeasible, carries a high cost or is unneeded. This capability is a necessity when repeated attempts at constructing a theory which is both realistic and precise fail to achieve success. Cases in point are the theories of rationality, causality and decision-making under second order uncertainty, that is, uncertainty about uncertainty.

A useful analogy is the following. In bivalent logic, the writing/ drawing instrument is a ballpoint pen. In fuzzy logic, the writing/ drawing instrument is a spray pen — a miniature spray can — with an adjustable, precisely specified spray pattern and a white marker for the centroid of the spray pattern, with the marker serving the purpose of precisiation when it is needed. Such a pen will be referred to as precisiated. In unprecisiated fuzzy logic, the spray pen has an adjustable spray pattern and a white marker which are not precisiated. In extended fuzzy logic, there are two spray pens — a precisiated spray pen and an unprecisiated spray pen.

In summary, there are three principal rationales for the use of extended fuzzy logic. First, when a p-valid solution is infeasible. Second, when a p-valid solution carries an excessively high cost; and third, when there is no need for a p-valid solution, that is, when an f-valid solution is good enough. In much of everyday human reasoning, it is the third rationale that is preponderant.

There is an important point to be made. f-validity is a fuzzy concept and hence is a matter of degree. When a chain of reasoning leads to a conclusion, a natural question is: What is the possibly fuzzy degree of validity, call it the validity index, of the conclusion? In most applications involving f-valid reasoning a high validity index is a desideratum. How can it be achieved? Achievement of a high validity index is one of the principal objectives of extended fuzzy logic. It should be noted that in many realistic settings, the question of whether or not a conclusion has a high validity index may be a matter of argumentation.

To take a step toward construction of modes of reasoning which lead to conclusions which are associated with high validity indices, it is expedient to go back to the origin of logical reasoning — Euclidian geometry. This is what is done in the following.

2.5.2. *f-geometry and f-transformation*

In the world of Euclidean geometry, Weg, the drawing instruments are: ruler, compass and ballpoint pen. The underlying logic is the familiar bivalent, Aristotelian logic. In the world of f-geometry, Wfg, the only drawing instrument is an unprecisiated spray pen, and drawing is done by hand. Figures in Wfg are fuzzy in appearance. In f-geometry, the underlying logic is unprecisiated fuzzy logic, FLu. f-Geometry differs both in spirit and in substance from Poston's fuzzy geometry [362], coarse geometry [376], fuzzy geometry of Rosenfeld [380], fuzzy geometry of Buckley and Eslami [85], fuzzy geometry of Mayburov [294], and fuzzy geometry of Tzafestas [449]. The underlying logic in these fuzzy geometries is FL(FLp).

The counterpart of a crisp concept, C, in Weg, is a fuzzy concept, f-C or, when more convenient, $^*C$, in Wfg (Fig. 2.4). f-C is referred to as an f-transform of C, with C playing the role of the prototype of f-C. It is helpful to visualize a fuzzy transform of C as the result of execution of the instruction: Draw C by hand with a spray pen. Note that there is no formal definition f-transformation.

For example, the f-transform of a point is an f-point, the f-transform of a line is an f-line, the f-transform of a triangle is an f-triangle, the f-transform of a circle is an f-circle and the f-transform of parallel is f-parallel (Fig. 2.5).

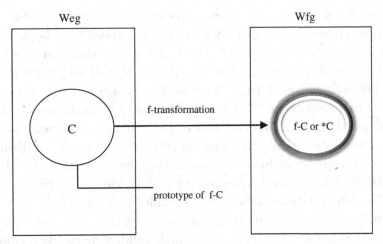

Fig. 2.4. *f*-transformation and *f*-geometry. Note that fuzzy figures, as shown, are not hand drawn. They should be visualized as hand drawn figures.

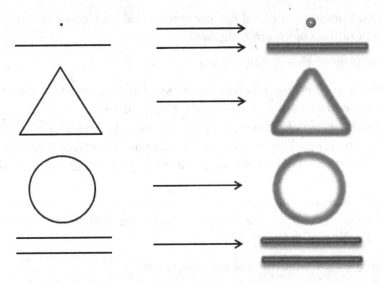

Fig. 2.5. Examples of *f*-transformation.

Note that *f*-transformation is one-to-many. *f*-transformation may be applied to relations. Thus, in Wfg we have the concepts of *f*-parallel, *f*-similar, *f*-congruent, etc. Furthermore, *f*-transformation may be applied to higher-level concepts, e.g., axiom, definition, principle, proof, theorem, truth, etc. In addition, f-transformation may be applied to concepts drawn from fields other than f-geometry. Examples: f-convex, f-linear, f-stable, etc. Of particular importance in f-geometry is the concept of f-theorem [514].

The cointension of f-C is a qualitative measure of the proximity of f-C to its prototype, C. A fuzzy transform, f-C, is cointensive if its cointension is high. Unless stated to the contrary, f-transforms are assumed to be cointensive. The concept of f-transform is distinct from the concept of fuzzy transform (Perfilieva transform) of Perfilieva [361]. In summary, f-geometry may be viewed as the result of application of f-transformation to Euclidean geometry.

A key idea in f-geometry is the following: if C is p-valid then its f-transform, f-C, is f-valid with a high validity index. As a simple example, consider the definition, D, of parallelism in Euclidean geometry.

D: Two lines are parallel if for any transversal that cuts the lines the corresponding angles are congruent.

f-transform of this definition reads:

f-D: Two f-lines are f-parallel if for any f-transversal that cuts the lines the corresponding f-angles are f-congruent.

Similarly, in Euclidean geometry, two triangles are similar if the corresponding angles are congruent. Correspondingly, in f-geometry two f-triangles are f-similar if the corresponding angles are f-congruent.

An f-theorem in f-geometry is an f-transform of a theorem in Euclidean geometry. As a simple example, an elementary theorem, T, in Euclidean geometry is:

T: the medians of a triangle are concurrent.

A corresponding theorem, f-T, in f-geometry is:

f-T: the f-medians of an f-triangle are f-concurrent.

An important f-principle in f-geometry, referred to as the validation principle, is the following. Let p be a p-valid conclusion drawn from a chain of premises $p_1, \ldots, p_n$. Then, using the star notation, $^*p$ is an f-valid conclusion drawn from $^*p_1, \ldots, ^*p_n$, and $^*p$ has a high validity index. It is this principle that is employed to derive f-valid conclusions from a collection of f-premises. As a very simple illustration, consider two triangles A and B. In Euclidean geometry, if A and B are similar then the corresponding sides are in proportion. The validation principle leads to the following assertion in f-geometry. If A and B are f-similar f-triangles then the corresponding sides are in f-proportion.

In f-geometry, an f-proof may be (a) empirical or (b) logical. An empirical f-proof involves experimentation. Consistent with the validation principle, a logical f-proof is an f-transform of a proof in Euclidean geometry. As an illustration, consider the f-theorem:

f-T: the f-medians of an f-triangle are f-concurrent.

With reference to Fig. 2.6, the logical f-proof of this theorem follows at once from the property of f-similar triangles. The f-theorem and its f-proof are f-transforms of their counterparts in Euclidean geometry. But what is important to note is that the f-theorem and its f-proof could be arrived at without any reference to their counterparts in Euclidean geometry. This suggests an intriguing possibility of constructing, in various fields, independently arrived at systems of f-concepts, f-definitions, f-theorems, f-proofs and,

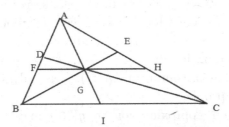

D,E are f-midpoints
DE is f-parallel to BC
FH is f-parallel to BC
AGI is an f-line passing through
f-point G
f-triangles EGH and EBC are f-similar

f-triangles DFG and DBC are f-similar
f-proportionality of corresponding sides of
f-triangles implies that G is f-midpoint of
FH
G is f-midpoint of FH implies that I is
f-midpoint of BC implies that the
f-medians are f-concurrent

Fig. 2.6. f-proof of the f-theorem: f-midpoints of an f-triangle are f-concurrent.

more generally, f-reasoning and f-computation. In the conceptual world of such systems, p-validity has no place.

As was alluded to earlier, the concept of f-transformation is not limited to Euclidean geometry — it has broad applicability. f-transformation may be applied to concepts, definitions and theorems drawn from various fields. As an elementary example, consider the definition of a convex set, A, in a linear vector space, U.

D: A is a convex set in U if for any points x and y in A every point in the segment xy is in A. The f-transform of this definition is the definition of an f-convex set, f-A. Specifically,

f-D:f-A is an f-convex set in U if for any f-points x and y in f-A every f-point in the f-segment xy is in f-A.

An elementary property of convex sets is:

T: if A and B are convex sets, so is their f-intersection $A \cap B$.

An f-transform of T reads:

f-T: if A and B are f-convex sets, so is their f-intersection f-$A \cap f$-B.

More generally,

T: if A and B are convex fuzzy sets, so is their intersection.

Applying f-transformation to T, we obtain the theorem:

f-T: if A and B are f-convex fuzzy sets, so is their f-intersection.

A basic problem which arises in computation of f-transforms is the following. Let g be a function, a functional or an operator. Using the star notation, let an f-transform, $^*C$, be an argument of g. The problem is that of computing $g(^*C)$. Generally, computing $g(^*C)$ is not a trivial problem.

An f-valid approximation to $g(^*C)$ may be derived through application of an f-principle which is referred to as precisiation/imprecisiation principle or P/I principle, for short [40]. More specifically, the principle may be expressed as

$$g(^*C) \; ^* \; = \; ^*g(C)$$

where $^* =$ should be read as approximately equal. In words, $g(^*C)$ is approximately equal to the f-transform of $g(C)$. As an illustration,

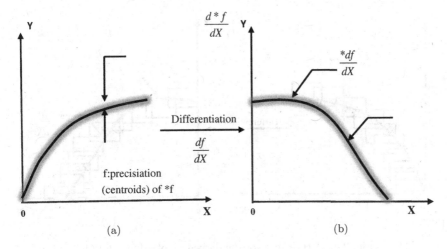

Fig. 2.7. f-transform of the derivative of an f-transform.

if g is the operation of differentiation and $^*C$ is an f-function, $^*f$, shown in Fig. 2.7(a), then the f-derivative of this function is an f-function shown in Fig. 2.7(b).

If C is a real number and $^*C$ is approximately C, then the P/I principle asserts that $g(^*C)$ is approximately equal to approximately $g(C)$. More generally, if C is a function from reals to reals, $^*C$ is the fuzzy graph of C [541] and g is the operation of differentiation, then the derivative of the fuzzy graph of C is approximately equal to the fuzzy graph of the derivative of C. An example is shown in Fig. 2.8.

In one guise or another, the P/I principle is widely used in science and engineering. What should be a matter of concern, however, is that it is common practice to present the results of an analysis in which the principle is employed without a qualification to the effect that the results are f-valid rather than p-valid, and that there is no guarantee that the validity index of results is high.

In large measure, extended fuzzy logic is perception-based rather than measurement-based. Perceptions are intrinsically imprecise, reflecting the bounded ability of human sensory organs, and ultimately the brain, to resolve detail and store information. The intrinsic imprecision of perceptions underlies the intrinsic imprecision of a major component of extended fuzzy logic — the unprecisiated

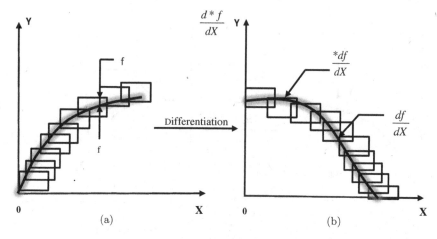

Fig. 2.8. f-transform of the derivative of a fuzzy graph.

fuzzy logic. As was alluded to earlier, reasoning in unprecisiated fuzzy logic — f-valid reasoning — is quasi-mathematical rather than mathematical. This is what sets unprecisiated fuzzy logic apart from other logical systems, including precisiated fuzzy logic, FL.

The importance of extended fuzzy logic derives from the fact that it adds to fuzzy logic an essential capability — the capability to deal with unprecisiated imperfect information. In many realistic settings, decision-relevant information falls into this category. In addition, what should be underscored is that in dealing with many real-world problems an f-valid solution based on a realistic model may be more useful than a p-valid solution based on an unrealistic model.

Chapter 3

Restriction Concept

A precise definition of truth is formulated in this chapter. The theory outlined in the chapter is a departure from traditional theories of truth and meaning. In the suggested theory, truth values are allowed to be described in the natural language. For example, more or less true, almost true, usually true, etc. Such truth values are referred in this theory as linguistic truth values. Linguistic truth values are not allowed in traditional logical systems, but are routinely used by humans in everyday reasoning and everyday discourse. The centerpiece of this theory is a deceptively simple concept — the concept of a restriction. The suggested theory opens the door to the construction of mathematical solutions of computational problems, which are stated in the natural language.

3.1. Introduction to Restriction Concept [30]

A restriction $R(X)$ on variable X may be viewed as information about X. More concretely, $R(X)$ may be expressed in a canonical form, $CF(R(X))$,

$$CF(R(X)) : X \text{ isr } R$$

A restriction is precisiated if X, R and r are mathematically well defined. Precisiation of restrictions plays a pivotal role in RCT. Precisiation of restrictions is a prerequisite to computation with restrictions. Here is an example of a simple problem which involves computation with restrictions.

Usually Robert leaves his office at about 5 pm.
Usually it takes Robert about an hour to get home from work.
At what time does Robert get home?

Humans have a remarkable capability to deal with problems of this kind using approximate, everyday reasoning. One of the important contributions of RCT is that RCT opens the door to construction of mathematical solutions of computational problems which are stated in a natural language. There are many types of restrictions. A restriction is singular if R is a singleton.

Example: $X = 5$. A restriction is non-singular if R is not a singleton. Non-singularity implies uncertainty. A restriction is direct if the restricted variable is X. A restriction is indirect if the restricted variable is of the form f(X).

Example: $R(p) : \int_a^b \mu(u)p(u)du$ is likely, is an indirect restriction on p.

In the sequel, the term restriction is sometimes applied to R.

The principal types of restrictions are: possibilistic restrictions, probabilistic restrictions and Z-restrictions.

- *Possibilistic restriction* $(r = blank)$

$$R(X) : X \text{ is } A$$

where A, is a fuzzy set in a space, U, with the membership function, μ_A. A plays the role of the possibility distribution of X,

$$\text{Poss}(X = u) = \mu_A(u)$$

Example:

$$\underset{\uparrow}{X} \quad \text{is} \quad \underset{\uparrow}{\text{small}}$$

restricted variable   restricting relation (fuzzy set)

The fuzzy set small plays the role of the possibility distribution of X (Fig. 3.1).

Example:

Leslie is taller than Ixel $\rightarrow$

$(\underset{\uparrow}{\text{Height(Leslie)}}, \text{Height(Ixel)})$ is $\underset{\uparrow}{\text{taller}}$

restricted variable   restricting relation (fuzzy relation)

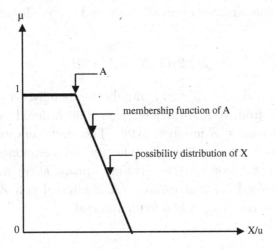

Fig. 3.1. Possibilistic restriction ox X.

The fuzzy relation taller is the possibility distribution of ((Height (Leslie), Height (Ixel)).

- *Probabilistic restriction* $(r = p)$

$$R(X) : X \text{ isp } p$$

where p is the probability density function of X,

$$\text{Prob}(u \leq X \leq u + du) = p(u)du$$

Example:

$$X \text{ isp } \frac{1}{\sqrt{2\pi}} \exp(-(X - m)^2/2\sigma^2)$$

         ↑   ↑

restricted variable   restricting relation (probability density function)

- *Z-restriction* $(r = z)$

A Z-restriction is expressed as

$$R(X) : X \text{ is } Z$$

where Z is a combination of possibilistic and probabilistic restrictions defined as

$$Z : \text{Prob}(X \text{ is } A) \text{ is } B$$

in which A and B are fuzzy numbers. Usually, A and B are labels drawn from a natural language. The ordered pair, (A, B), is referred to as a Z-number [548]. The first component, A, is a possibilistic restriction on X. The second component, B, is a possibilistic restriction on the certainty (probability) that X is A, X is a real-valued random variable. A Z-interval is a Z-number in which the first component is a fuzzy interval.

Examples:

Probably Robert is tall $\rightarrow$ Height(Robert) is (tall; probable)
Usually temperature is low $\rightarrow$ Temperature is (low; usually)
Usually X is A

is a Z-restriction when A is a fuzzy number.

A Z-valuation is an ordered triple of the form (X, A, B), and (A, B) is a Z-number. Equivalently, a Z-valuation (X, A, B), is a Z-restriction on X,

$$(X, A, B) \rightarrow X \text{ is } (A, B)$$

Examples:

(Age(Robert), young, very likely)

(Traffic, heavy, usually)

A natural language may be viewed as a system of restrictions. In the realm of natural languages, restrictions are predominantly possibilistic. For this reason, in this paragraph we focus our attention on possibilistic restrictions. For simplicity, possibilistic restrictions are assumed to be trapezoidal.

Example: Figure 3.2 shows a possibilistic trapezoidal restriction which is associated with the fuzzy set middle-age.

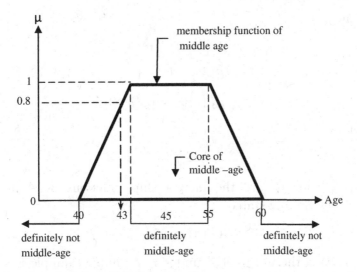

Fig. 3.2. Trapezoidal possibilistic restriction on age.

Note: Parameters are context-dependent.

3.1.1. *Computation with restrictions*

Computation with restrictions plays an essential role in RCT. In large measure, computation with restrictions involves the use of the extension principle [501, 514]. A brief exposition of the extension principle is presented in the following. The extension principle is not a single principle. The extension principle is a collection of computational rules in which the objects of computation are various types of restrictions. More concretely, assume that Y is a function of $X, Y = f(X)$, where X may be an n-ary variable. Assume that what we have is imperfect information about X, implying that what we know is a restriction on $X, R(X)$. The restriction on $X, R(X)$, induces a restriction on $Y, R(Y)$. The extension principle is a computational rule which relates to computation of $R(Y)$ given $R(X)$. In what follows, we consider only two basic versions of the extension principle. The simplest version [501] is one in which the restriction is possibilistic and direct. This version of the extension principle reduces computation of $R(Y)$ to the solution of a variational problem,

$$Y = f(X)$$

$$R(X) : X \text{ is } A$$

$$R(Y) : \mu_Y(v) = \sup_u(\mu_A(u))$$

subject to

$$v = f(u)$$

where μ_A and μ_Y are the membership functions of A and Y, respectively. Simply stated,

$$\text{If } X \text{ is } A \text{ then } Y \text{ is } f(A)$$

where $f(A)$ is the image of A under f. A simple example is shown in Fig. 3.3.

An inverse version of this version of the extension principle is the following:

$$Y = f(X)$$

$$R(Y) : Y \text{ is } B$$

$$R(X) : \mu_A(u) = (\mu_B(f(u)))$$

Simply stated, A is the pre-image of B under f (Fig. 3.4).

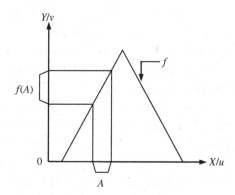

Fig. 3.3. Possibilistic version of the basic extension principle. $f(A)$ is the image of A under f. What is shown is a trapezoidal approximation to $f(A)$.

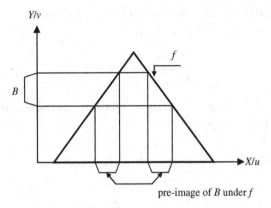

pre-image of *B* under *f*

Fig. 3.4. Inverse version of the basic possibilistic extension principle. The induced restriction on X is the pre-image of B, the restriction on Y.

A slightly more general version [514] is one in which $R(X)$ is possibilistic and indirect.

$$Y = f(X)$$

$$R(X) : g(X) \text{ is } A$$

$$R(Y) : \mu_Y(v) = \sup_u(\mu_A(g(u)))$$

subject to

$$v = f(g(u))$$

Example:

Given, p: Most Swedes are tall.

Question, q: What is the average height of Swedes?

The first step involves precisiation of p and q. For this purpose, it is expedient to employ the concept of a height density function, h.

$h(u)du = fraction$ of Swedes whose height lies in the interval

$$[u, u \mid du]$$

If h_{min} and h_{max} are, respectively, the minimum and maximum heights in the population, we have

$$\int_{h_{min}}^{h_{max}} h(u)du = 1$$

In terms of the height density function, precisiations of q and p, q^* and p^*, may be expressed as

$$q^* :? h_{ave} = \int_{h_{min}}^{h_{max}} uh(u)du$$

$$p^* : \int_{h_{min}}^{h_{max}} \mu_{tall}(u)h(u)du \text{ is most}$$

where μ_{tall} is the membership function of tall. Applying the basic, indirect, possibilistic version of the extension principle, computation of h_{ave} is reduced to the solution of the variational problem

$$\mu_{h_{ave}}(v) = \sup_h \mu_{most}\left(\int_{h_{min}}^{h_{max}} \mu_{tall}(u)h(u)du\right)$$

subject to

$$v = \int_{h_{min}}^{h_{max}} uh(u)du$$

and

$$\int_{h_{min}}^{h_{max}} h(u)du = 1$$

In RCT, for purposes of reasoning and computation what are needed — in addition to possibilistic versions of the extension principle — are versions in which restrictions are probabilistic restrictions and Z-restrictions. These versions of the extension principle are described in Ref. [550].

3.2. Truth and Meaning

There is a close relationship between the concept of truth and the concept of meaning. To assess the truth value of a proposition, p, it is necessary to understand the meaning of p. However, understanding the meaning of p is not sufficient. What is needed, in addition, is precisiation of the meaning of p. Precisiation of the meaning of p involves representation of p in a form that is mathematically well defined and lends itself to computation. In RCT, formalization of the concept of truth is a byproduct of formalization of the concept of meaning. In the following, unless stated to the contrary, p is assumed to be a proposition drawn from a natural language. Typically, propositions drawn from a natural language are fuzzy propositions, that is, propositions which contain fuzzy predicates and/or fuzzy quantifiers and/or fuzzy probabilities.

The point of departure in RCT consists of two key ideas: the meaning postulate, MP, and the truth postulate, TP. MP relates to precisiation of the meaning of p. More concretely, a proposition is a carrier of information. Information is a restriction. Reflecting these observations, MP postulates that the precisiated meaning of p — or simply precisiated p — may be represented as a restriction. In symbols, p may be expressed as

$$p \to X \text{ isr } R$$

where X, R and r are implicit in p. The expression X isr R is referred to as the canonical form of p, $\mathrm{CF}(p)$. In general, X is an n-ary variable and R is a function of X. Basically, X is a variable such that p is a carrier of information about X. X is referred to as a focal variable of p. In large measure, the choice of X is subjective.

Examples:

p : Robert is young Age (Robert) is young

$\qquad\qquad\quad \uparrow \qquad\qquad\qquad\quad \uparrow$

$\qquad\qquad\quad X \qquad\qquad\qquad\quad R$

p : Most Swedes are tall $\to$

Proportion(tall Swedes/Swedes) is most

$\qquad\quad \uparrow \qquad\qquad\qquad\quad \uparrow$

$\qquad\quad X \qquad\qquad\qquad\quad R$

p : Robert is much taller than most of his friends $\to$ Height (Robert) is much taller than most of his friends

p : Usually it takes Robert about an hour to get home from work $\rightarrow$ Travel time from office to home is (approximately 1 h, usually).

The truth postulate, TP, relates the truth value of p to its meaning. More concretely, consider the canonical form

$$\mathrm{CF}(p) : X \text{ isr } R$$

TP postulates that the truth value of p is the degree to which X satisfies R.

In RCT, truth values form a hierarchy: First-order (ground level), second order, etc. First order truth values are numerical. For simplicity, numerical truth values are assumed to be points in the interval (Fig. 3.5).

A generic numerical truth value is denoted as nt. Second-order truth values are linguistic.

Examples: Quite true, possibly true. A generic linguistic truth value is denoted as lt. In RCT, linguistic truth values are viewed as restrictions on numerical truth values. In symbols, $lt = R(nt)$. A generic truth value is denoted as t. t can be nt or lt.

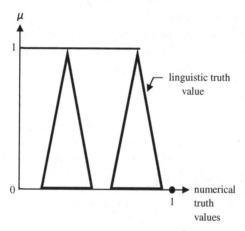

Fig. 3.5. Hierarchy of truth values. A numerical truth value is first-order (ground level) truth value. A linguistic truth value is a second-order truth value. A linguistic truth value is a restriction on numerical truth values. Typically, a linguistic truth value is a fuzzy set or, equivalently, a possibility distribution.

Typically, X and R are described in a natural language. To compute the degree to which X satisfies R it is necessary to precisiate X and R. In RCT, what is used for this purpose is the concept of an explanatory database, ED [525, 549]. Informally, ED is a collection of relations which represent the information which is needed to precisiate X and R or, alternatively, to compute the truth value of p. Example. Consider the proposition, p: Most Swedes are tall. In this case, the information consists of three relations, TALL[Height;μ], MOST[Proportion;μ] and POPULATION[Name;Height]. In TALL, μ is the grade of membership of Height in tall. In MOST, μ is the grade of membership of Proportion — a point in the unit interval — in most. In POPULATION, Height is the height of Name, where Name is a variable which ranges over the names of Swedes in a sample population. Equivalently, and more simply, ED may be taken to consist of the membership function of tall, μ_{tall}, the membership function of most, μ_{most}, and the height density function, h. h is defined as the fraction, $h(u)du$, of Swedes whose height is in the interval $[u, u + du]$.

X and R are precisiated by expressing them as functions of ED. Precisiated X, R and p are denoted as X^*, R^* and p^*, respectively. Thus,

$$X^* = f(ED), \quad R^* = g(ED)$$

The precisiated canonical form, $\text{CF}^*(p)$, is expressed as X^* is$r^* R^*$. At this point, the numerical truth value of p, nt_p, may be computed as the degree to which X^* satisfies R^*. In symbols,

$$nt_p = tr(ED)$$

in which tr is referred to as the truth function (Fig. 3.6).

What this equation means is that an instantiation of ED induces a value of nt_p. Varying instantiations of ED induces what is referred to as the truth distribution of p, denoted as $\text{Tr}(p|ED)$. The truth distribution of p may be interpreted as the possibility distribution of ED given p, expressed as $\text{Poss}(ED|p)$. Thus, we arrive at an important equality

$$\text{Tr}(p|ED) = \text{Poss}(ED|p).$$

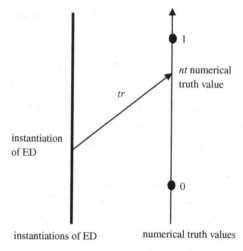

Fig. 3.6. A numerical truth value, nt, is induced by an instantiation of ED. tr is the truth function.

In RCT, the precisiated meaning of p is expressed in three equivalent forms. First, as the precisiated canonical form, $CF^*(p)$. Second, as the truth distribution of p, $Tr(p|ED)$. Third, as the possibility distribution, $Poss(ED|p)$. These representations of the precisiated meaning of p play an essential role in RCT. The precisiated meaning of p may be viewed as the computational meaning of p. Of the three equivalent definitions stated above, the definition that is best suited for computational purposes is that which involves the possibility distribution of ED. Adopting this definition, what can be stated is the following.

Definition 3.1. The precisiated (computational) meaning of p is the possibility distribution of ED, $Poss(ED|p)$, which is induced by p.

Example: Consider the proposition, p: Robert is tall. In this case, ED consists of Height(Robert) and the relation TALL[Height; μ] or, equivalently, the membership function μ_{tall}. We have,

$$X = \text{Height(Robert)}, \quad R = \text{tall}$$

The canonical form reads

$$\text{Height(Robert) is tall}$$

The precisiated X and R are expressed as

$$X^* = \text{Height(Robert)}, \quad R^* = \text{tall}$$

where tall is a fuzzy set with the membership function, μ_{tall}.

The precisiated canonical form reads

$$\text{Height(Robert) is tall}$$

Note that in this case the unprecisiated and precisiated canonical forms are identical. The truth distribution is defined by

$$nt_{\text{p}} = \mu_{\text{tall}}(h)$$

where h is a generic value of Height(Robert).

The basic equality reads

$$\text{Tr}(p|h) = \text{Poss}(h|p)$$

More specifically, if $h = 175$ cm and $\mu_{\text{tall(175cm)}} = 0.9$, then 0.9 is the truth value of p given $h = 175$ cm, and the possibility that $h = 175$ cm given p (Fig. 3.7).

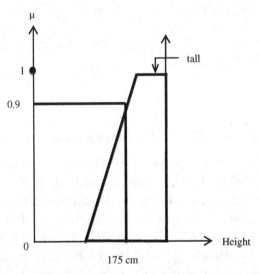

Fig. 3.7. $0.9 =$ Truth value of the proposition Robert is tall given that Robert's height is 175 cm. $0.9 =$ possibility that Robert's height is 175 cm, given the proposition Robert is tall.

Example: Robert is *handsome*. In this case, assume that we have a sample population of men, $Name_1, \ldots, Name_n$ with μ_i being the grade of membership of $Name_i$ in the fuzzy set *handsome*. The meaning of p is the possibility distribution associated with the fuzzy set *handsome* — the possibility distribution which is induced by p. The possibility that $Name_i$ is *handsome* is equal to the grade of membership of $Name_i$ in *handsome*.

Example: Consider the proposition, p: Most Swedes are tall. In this case, $X = $ Proportion(tall Swedes/Swedes) and $R = $ most. The canonical form of p is Proportion(tall Swedes/Swedes) is most. The precisiated X and R may be expressed as

$$X^* = \int_{h_{\min}}^{h_{\max}} h(u)\mu_{\text{tall}}(u)du$$

$$R^* = \text{most}$$

where most is a fuzzy set with a specified membership function, μ_{most}.
The precisiated canonical form reads

$$\text{CF}^*(p) : \int_{h_{\min}}^{h_{\max}} h(u)\mu_{\text{tall}}(u)du \text{ is most}$$

The truth distribution, $\text{Tr}(p|\text{ED})$, is defined by computing the degree, nt_p, to which X^* satisfies R^*,

$$nt_p = \mu_{\text{most}}\left(\int_{h_{\min}}^{h_{\max}} h(u)\mu_{\text{tall}}du\right).$$

Note that an instantiation of ED induces a numerical truth value, nt_p.

Example: Consider the proposition, p: Robert is much taller than most of his friends. In this case, assume that $X = $ *Proportion* of friends of Robert in relation to whom Robert is much taller, and $R = $ most. The explanatory database, ED, consists of the relations FRIENDS[Name;μ], HEIGHT[Name;Height], MUCH. TALLER[$Height_1$;$Height_2$;μ], and Height(Robert). Equivalently, ED may be expressed as $\mu_F(Name_i)$, h_i, and $\mu_{MT}(h, h_i)$, $i = 1, \ldots, n$. In this ED, $h = $ Height(Robert), $h_i = $ Height $(Name_i)$, $\mu_F(Name_i) = $ grade of membership of $Name_i$ in the fuzzy set of friends of Robert, and $\mu_{MT}(h, h_i) = $ grade of membership of (h, h_i) and the fuzzy set much taller. Precisiated X and R are expressed as,

$$X^* = \left(\frac{1}{n} \sum_i \mu_{MT}(h, h_i) \wedge \mu_F(\text{Name}_i) \right), \quad R^* = \text{most}$$

The precisiated meaning of p is expressed as,

$$\text{Poss}(ED|p) = \mu_{\text{most}} \left(\frac{1}{n} \sum_i \mu_{MT}(h, h_i) \wedge \mu_F(i) \right)$$

where $\wedge$ denotes conjunction.

The concept of an instantiated ED in RCT is related to the concept of a possible world in traditional theories. Similarly, the concept of a possibility distribution of the explanatory database is related to the concept of intension.

Precisiation of meaning is the core of RCT and one of its principal contributions. A summary may be helpful.

The point of departure is a proposition, p, drawn from a natural language. The objective is precisiation of p.

1. Choose a focal variable, X, by interpreting p as an answer to the question: What is the value of X? Identify the restricting relation, R. R is function of X. At this point, X and R are described in a natural language.
2. Construct the canonical form, $\text{CF}(p) = X$ is$r$ R.
3. Construct an explanatory database, ED. To construct ED, ask the question: What information is needed to express X and R as functions of ED? Alternatively, ask the question: What information is needed to compute the truth value of p?
4. Precisiate X and R by expressing X and R as functions of ED. Precisiated X and R are denoted as X^* and R^*, respectively.
5. Construct the precisiated canonical form, $\text{CF}^*(p) : X^*$ isr^*R^*.
6. Equate precisiated p to $\text{CF}^*(p)$.
7. $\text{CF}^*(p)$ defines the possibility distribution of ED given p, $\text{Poss}(ED|p)$.
8. $\text{CF}^*(p)$ defines the truth distribution of the truth value or p given ED, $\text{Tr}(p|ED)$.

9. $\text{Poss}(ED|p) = \text{Tr}(p|ED)$.

10. Define the precisiated (computational) meaning of p as the possibility distribution of ED given p, $\text{Poss}(ED|p)$. More informatively, the precisiated (computational) meaning of p is the possibility distribution, $\text{Poss}(ED|p)$, together with the procedure which computes $\text{Poss}(ED|p)$.

3.2.1.   *Truth qualification: Internal and external truth values*

A truth-qualified proposition is a proposition of the form $t\,p$, where t is the truth value of p. t may be a numerical truth value, nt, or a linguistic truth value, lt. Example. It is quite true that Robert is tall. In this case, $t =$ quite true and $p =$ Robert is tall. A significant fraction of propositions drawn from a natural language are truth-qualified. An early discussion of truth-qualification is contained in Ref. [517]. Application of truth-qualification to a resolution of Liar's paradox is contained in Ref. [520].

In a departure from tradition, in RCT a proposition, p, is associated with two truth values — internal truth value and external truth value. When necessary, internal and external truth values are expressed as Int(truth value) and Ext(truth value), or $\text{Int}(p)$ and $\text{Ext}(p)$.

Informally, the internal numerical truth value is defined as the degree of agreement of p with an instantiation of ED. Informally, an external numerical truth value of p is defined as the degree of agreement of p with factual information, F. More concretely, an internal numerical truth value is defined as follows:

Definition 3.2.

$$\text{Int}(nt_p) = tr(\text{ED}).$$

In this equation, ED is an instantiation of the explanatory database, $\text{Int}(nt_p)$ is the internal numerical truth value of p, and tr is the truth function which was defined earlier.

More generally, assume that we have a possibilistic restriction on instantiations of ED, $\text{Poss}(\text{ED})$. This restriction induces a possibilistic restriction on nt_p which can be computed through the use of the extension principle. The restriction on nt_p may be expressed as $tr(\text{Poss}(ED))$. The fuzzy set, $tr(\text{Poss}(ED))$, may be approximated by the membership function of a linguistic truth value. This leads to the following definition of an internal linguistic truth value of p.

Definition 3.3.

$$\text{Int}(lt_p) \approx tr(\text{Poss}(ED))$$

In this equation, $\approx$ should be interpreted as a linguistic approximation. In words, the internal linguistic truth value, $\text{Int}(lt_p)$, is the image — modulo linguistic approximation — of the possibility distribution of ED under the truth function, tr. It is important to note that the definition of linguistic truth value which was stated in the previous subsection is, in fact, the definition of internal linguistic truth value of p (Fig. 3.8).

Poss(ED), $tr(\text{Poss}(ED))$ and lt_p are fuzzy sets. For simplicity, denote these fuzzy sets as A, B and C, respectively. Using the extension principle, computation of lt_p reduces to the solution of

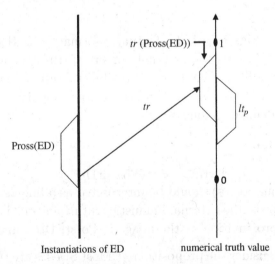

Fig. 3.8. A linguistic truth value, lt_p, is induced by a possibilistic restriction on instantions of ED, Poss(ED). lt_p is a linguistic approximation to the image of Poss(ED) under tr.

the variational problem,

$$\mu_B(\mathrm{v}) = \sup_u \mu_A(u)$$

subject to

$$v = tr(u)$$

$$\mu_C \approx \mu_B$$

The external truth value of p, Ext(p), relates to the degree of agreement of p with factual information, F. In RCT, factual information may be assumed to induce a possibilistic restriction on ED, Poss(ED$|F$). In particular, if F instantiates ED, then the external truth value is numerical. This is the basis for the following definition.

Definition 3.4. The external numerical truth value of p is defined as

$$\mathrm{Ext}(nt_p) = tr(\mathrm{ED}|F)$$

where ED is an instantiation of the explanatory database induced by F.

Example: In Fig. 1.7, if the factual information is that Robert's height is 175 cm, then the external numerical truth value of p is 0.9.

More generally, if F induces a possibilistic restriction on instantiations of ED, Poss(ED$|F$), then the external linguistic truth value of p may be defined as follows:

Definition 3.5.

$$\mathrm{Ext}(lt_p) \approx tr(\mathrm{Poss}(\mathrm{ED}|F))$$

In this equation, $\approx$ should be interpreted as a linguistic approximation. In words, the external linguistic truth value of p is — modulo linguistic approximation — the image of Poss(ED$|F$) under tr.

Example: Consider the proposition, p: Most Swedes are tall. Assume that the factual information is that the average height of Swedes is around 170 cm. Around 170 cm is a fuzzy set defined by its membership function, $\mu_{\text{ar.170cm}}$. In terms of the height density function, h, the average height of Swedes may be expressed as

$$h_{\text{ave}} = \int_{h_{\min}}^{h_{\max}} uh(u)du$$

The explanatory database consists of μ_{tall}, μ_{most} and h. Assuming that μ_{tall} and μ_{most} are fixed, the possibilistic restriction on ED is induced by the indirect possibilistic restriction

$$\int_{h_{\min}}^{h_{\max}} uh(u)du \text{ is around 170 cm}$$

which is equivalent to the possibility distribution of h expressed as

$$\text{Poss}(h|h_{\text{ave}}) = \mu_{\text{ar.170cm}}\left(\int_{h_{\min}}^{h_{\max}} uh(u)du\right)$$

An important observation is in order. An internal truth value modifies the meaning of p. An external truth value does not modify the meaning of p; it places in evidence the factual information, with the understanding that factual information is a possibilistic restriction on the explanatory database.

How does an internal truth value, t, modify the meaning of p? Assume that the internal truth value is numerical. The meaning of p is the possibility distribution, $\text{Poss}(\text{ED}|p)$. The meaning of nt_p is the pre-image of nt under the truth function, tr. In other words, the meaning of p, expressed as the possibility distribution, $\text{Poss}(\text{ED}|p)$, is modified to the possibility distribution $\text{Poss}(\text{ED}|nt_p)$. If the internal truth value is linguistic, lt_p, the modified meaning is the pre-image of lt_p, $\text{Poss}(\text{ED}|lt_p)$, under tr (Fig. 3.9). More concretely, using the inverse version of the basic extension principle, we can write

$$\mu_{\text{Poss}(\text{ED}|lt_p)}(u) = \mu_{\text{tr}(\text{Poss}(\text{ED}|lt_p))}(tr(u))$$

where u is an instantiation of ED, $\mu_{\text{Poss}(\text{ED}|lt_p)}$ and $\mu_{\text{tr}(\text{Poss}(\text{ED}|lt_p))}$ are the membership functions of $\text{Poss}(\text{ED}|lt_p)$ and $tr(\text{Poss}(\text{ED}|lt_p))$, respectively.

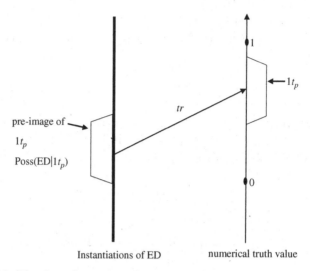

Fig. 3.9. Modification of meaning of p. Modified meaning of p is the pre-image of $1t_p$ under tr.

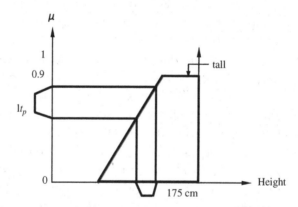

Fig. 3.10. An internal linguistic truth value modifies the meaning of p.

Example: In Fig. 3.7, the pre-image of 0.9 is 175 cm. The meaning of p is the possibility distribution of tall. The truth value 0.9 modifies the possibility distribution of tall to Height(Robert) = 175 cm. More generally, when the truth value is linguistic, lt_p, the modified meaning of p is the pre-image of lt_p under tr (Fig. 3.10).

There is a special case which lends itself to a simple analysis. Assume that lt is of the form h true, where h is a hedge exemplified by quite, very, almost, etc. Assume that p is of the form X is A, where A is a fuzzy set. In this case, what can be postulated is that truth-qualification modifies the meaning of p as follows:

$$h \text{ true}(X \text{ is } A) = X \text{ is} h\ A$$

hA may be computed through the use of techniques described in early papers on hedges [257, 509].

Example: (usually true) snow is white = snow is usually white.

Example: (see Fig. 3.11)
    It is very true that Robert is tall = Robert is very tall.
    A word of caution is in order. Assume that there is no hedge. In this case, the equality becomes

$$\text{true}(X \text{ is } A) = X \text{ is } A$$

If truth is bivalent, and true is one of its values, this equality is an agreement with the school of thought which maintains that propositions p and p is true have the same meaning. In RCT, p and p is true do not have the same meaning. There is a subtle difference. More concretely, the meaning of p relates to the agreement of p with a possibilistic restriction on ED. The meaning of p is

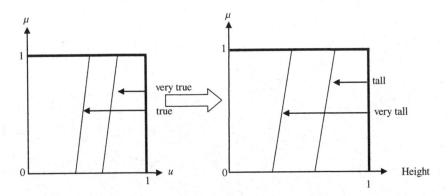

Fig. 3.11. Meaning — modification induced by truth-qualification.

true relates to a possibilistic restriction which is induced by factual information.

When lt_p is an external truth value, the meaning of p is not modified by lt_p. In RCT, a simplifying assumption which is made regarding the factual information, F, is that F may be described as a possibility distribution of instantiations of ED, Poss(ED$|F$). The external truth value, lt_p, identifies the factual information as the pre-image of lt_p under tr,

$$\text{Ext}(lt_p) = tr(\text{Poss}(\text{ED}|F))$$

$$F = \text{Poss}(\text{ED}|\text{Ext}(lt_p))$$

Truth-qualification in RCT is paralleled by probability-qualification in probability theory and by possibility-qualification in possibility theory. Truth-qualification, probability-qualification and possibility-qualification are intrinsically important issues in logic, information analysis and related fields.

Chapter 4

Fuzzy Probabilities

The conventional approaches to decision analysis are based on the assumption that the probabilities which enter into the assessment of the consequences of a decision are known numbers. In most realistic settings, this assumption is of questionable validity since the data from which the probabilities must be estimated are usually incomplete, imprecise or not totally reliable.

In the approach outlined in this chapter, the probabilities are assumed to be fuzzy rather than real numbers. It is shown how such probabilities may be estimated from fuzzy data and a basic relation between joint, conditional and marginal fuzzy probabilities is established. Manipulation of fuzzy probabilities requires, in general, the use of fuzzy arithmetic, and many of the properties of fuzzy probabilities are simple generalizations of the corresponding properties of real-valued probabilities.

4.1. Introduction

Computer-assisted decision analysis is likely to play an increasingly important role in applications such as command and control in which vast amounts of information in the database exceed the capacity of the unassisted human mind to assess the consequences of various alternatives and choose that action which is optimal with respect to a set of specified criteria.

An issue which complicates the determination of an optimal action is that in most realistic settings the information which is available to the decision-maker is imprecise, incomplete or not totally reliable. In the conventional approaches to decision analysis,

147

uncertain information is treated probabilistically, with probabilities assumed to be known in numerical form. In an alternative approach which is described in this paper, a more realistic assumption is made, namely, that probabilities are known imprecisely as fuzzy rather than crisp numbers. Such probabilities — which will be referred to as fuzzy probabilities — are exemplified by the perceptions of likelihood which are commonly labeled as *very likely, unlikely, not very likely,* etc. [514].

The concept of fuzzy probability is distinct from that of second-order probability (i.e., a probability-value which is characterized by its probability distribution) and contains that of interval-valued probability as a special case. As will be seen in the sequel, in our formulation of the concept of fuzzy probability, the uncertainty in probability is characterized by a possibility [516] rather than probability distribution. In our view, the use of possibility rather than probability in this context leads to a more effective way of dealing with uncertain probabilities and provides a basis for a natural generalization of classical probability theory.

4.2.   The Concept of Fuzzy Probability

Theories of subjective probability provide ways of eliciting probability judgments but do not have much to say about the processes by which such judgments are formed. To relate this issue to the concept of fuzzy probability, it is instructive to consider an elementary example of a situation in which an imprecise perception of probability is formed and in which the underlying uncertainty is possibilistic rather than probabilistic in nature. Specifically, consider the following question, in which the italicized words have a fuzzy meaning: An *urn* contains approximately n balls of various sizes, of which several are large? What is the probability that a ball drawn at random is *large?*

If the information-bearing terms in the question, namely, approximately n several and large were real numbers, the answer to the question would be a numerical probability. But, since these terms are fuzzy rather than real numbers, it should be expected that the desired probability like the data on which it is based is a fuzzy number i.e., a fuzzy probability.

This conclusion may be stated more succinctly as a principle, namely: Fuzzy information induces fuzzy probabilities. What is important to note is that this principle is at variance with the traditional Bayesian point of view which implies that probabilities are real numbers regardless of the nature of the underlying data.

To support our principle, we have to be able to demonstrate how fuzzy probabilities may be computed from fuzzy data. To this end, it is necessary. first. to provide a mechanism for counting the number of elements in a fuzzy set, i.e., for determining its cardinality or. more generally. its measure. We need this mechanism to precisiate the meaning of fuzzy descriptions such as several large balls and to be able to answer fuzzy questions like, "How many combat-ready ships are there in the vicinity of the Persian Gulf?"

In what follows, we shall limit our discussion of the cardinality of fuzzy sets to what is needed to enable us to define fuzzy probabilities in more concrete terms than we have done so far. A more detailed discussion of related issues may be found in Refs. [514, 517, 519].

Consider a fuzzy set A which is represented as

$$A = \mu_1/u_1 + \cdots + \mu_n/u_n \tag{4.1}$$

where μ_i, $i = 1, \ldots, n$ is an element of a universe of discourse U, μ_i is the grade of membership of u_i in A, and $+$ denotes the union rather than the arithmetic sum.

Strictly speaking, it is not meaningful to ask for a count of the elements of U which are in A, since some of the elements of U may be in A "to a degree." Nevertheless, it is useful to have one or more extensions of the conventional concept of cardinality which make it meaningful to speak of the "count" of elements of a fuzzy set. One such extension, which was suggested by Deluca and Termini [120], is the power of A. which is defined as the arithmetic sum of the grades of membership in A of all elements of C'. For our purposes, it is preferable to refer to this count as the sigma-count of A and write

$$\sum \text{Count}(A) \overset{\Delta}{=} \sum_i \mu_i \tag{4.2}$$

with the understanding that, when appropriate, the right-hand member of (4.2) may be rounded to the nearest integer.

Example: Assume that U is comprised of the elements a, b, c, d, e and f. Then

$$\sum \text{Count}(0.8/a + 0.3/b + 0.8/c + 1/d + 0.2/e) = 3$$

An alternative extension which was suggested in Ref. [507] defines the count of A *as a fuzzy number.* More specifically, let A_α be the α-level-set of A i.e., the nonfuzzy set defined by [507]

$$A_\alpha \overset{\Delta}{=} \{u_i | \mu_A(u_i) \geq \alpha\} \quad o > \alpha \geq 1, \quad u_i \in U, \quad i = 1, \ldots, n \quad (4.3)$$

where $\mu_i \overset{\Delta}{=} \mu_A(u_i)$, $i = 1, \ldots, n$ is the grade of membership of u_i in A. Then, as shown in [507]. A_α may be expressed in terms of the A, by the relation

$$A = \sum_\alpha \alpha A_\alpha \qquad (4.4)$$

where $\sum$ stands for the union and αA_α is a fuzzy set whose membership function is defined by

$$\mu_{\alpha A_\alpha}(u) = \alpha \quad \text{for} \quad u \in A_\alpha = 0 \quad \text{elsewhere} \qquad (4.5)$$

For example, if $U = \{a, b, c, d, e, f\}$ and

$$A = 0.8/a + 0.3/b + 0.8/c + 1/d + 0.2/e \qquad (4.6)$$

then $A_1 = \{d\}; A_{0.8} = \{a, c, d\}; A_{0.3} = \{a, b, c, d\}; A_{0.2} = \{a, b, c, d, e\}$; and (4.4) becomes

$$A = 1/d + 0.8/(a + c + d) + 0.3/(a + b + c + d)$$
$$+ 0.2/(a + b + c + d + e) \qquad (4.7)$$

Now, let $\text{Count}(A_\alpha)$ denote the count of elements of the nonfuzzy set A_α. Then, the FGCount of A, where F stands for fuzzy and G stands for greater than, is defined as the fuzzy number

$$\text{FGCount}(A) \stackrel{\Delta}{=} \sum_\alpha \alpha/\text{Count}(A_\alpha) \tag{4.8}$$

with the understanding that any gap in the $\text{Count}(A_\alpha)$ may be filled by a lower count with the same α. For example, for A defined by (4.6) we have

$$\text{FGCount}(A) = 1/1 + 0.8/3 + 0.6/4 + 0.22/5$$
$$= 1/0 + 1/1 + 0.8/2 + 0.8/3 + 0.6/4 + 0.2/5 \tag{4.9}$$

Let $A \downarrow$ denote A sorted in descending order and let $NA \downarrow$ denote the fuzzy number resulting from replacing the mth element in $A \downarrow$ by μ_m/m and adding the element $1/0$. For example, if

$$A = 0.6/a + 0.9/b + 1/c + 0.6/d + 0.2/e \tag{4.10}$$

then

$$A \downarrow = 1/c + 0.9/b + 1/c + 0.6/a + 0.6/d + 0.2/e \tag{4.11}$$
$$NA \downarrow = 1/0 + 1/1 + 0.9/2 + 0.6/3 + 0.6/4 + 0.2/5 \tag{4.12}$$

In terms of this notation, then, the definition of $\text{FGCount}(A)$ stated (A) earlier (4.8) may be expressed more succinctly as

$$\text{FGCount}(A) = NA \downarrow \tag{4.13}$$

To illustrate the use of the concepts defined above, we shall show how to arrive at an answer to a question raised earlier, namely, "How many combat-ready ships are there in the vicinity of the Persian Gull?"

Assume that in the database we have a relation LIST [Name; μCR; $\mu\,\text{Pr}\,ox$] which lists the name of each ship; its degree of combat-readiness, μCR; and its degree of proximity to the Persian Gulf, $\mu\,\text{Pr}\,ox$.

Furthermore, we assume that only those ships are to be considered whose degree of proximity to the Persian Gulf exceeds a specified threshold, say 0.6.

From the relation LIST we can derive another relation LIST [Name; $\mu CR \wedge \mu \Pr ox$] in which $\mu CR \wedge \mu \Pr ox$ denotes the combined degree of combat-readiness and proximity to the Persian Gulf. For example, if the degrees of combat-readiness and proximity of a ship S1 are 0.8 and 0.7, respectively, then the combined degree will be assumed to be the smaller of the two degrees, i.e., 0.7. More generally, in place of $\wedge$ (min) any desired mode of aggregation may be employed to express the combined degree as a function of its constituents.

To be specific, assume that the relation LIST[Name; $\mu CR/ \mu \Pr ox$] reads

LIST Name	$\mu CR \wedge \mu \Pr ox$
S1	0.9
s2	1
s3	0.6
s4	0.7
s5	0.8
S6	0.7
s7	0.9
S8	1
S9	0.8

The $\sum$-count of LIST is found to be given by

$$\sum \text{Count(LIST)} = 8$$

On the other hand, using the definition of FGCount, we obtain the fuzzy number

$$\text{FGCount(LIST)} = 1/0 + 1/1 + 1/2 + 0.9/4 + 0.8/5$$
$$+ 0.8/6 + 0.7/7 + 0.7/8 + 0.6/9$$

A constituent such as 0.8/6 in this number signifies that there are six ships whose combined degree of combat-readiness and proximity to the Persian Gulf is greater than or equal to 0.8.

In addition to providing a basis for answering questions of the form "How many objects are there which satisfy a set of specified fuzzy criteria?". the concept of cardinality serves also as a means of precisiation of descriptions of the form QAU, where Q is a fuzzy quantifier, e.g., several, many, few, etc.: A is a fuzzy adjective, e.g., tall, combat-ready, blue, young, etc.; and 0 is the description of an object, e.g., ball, ship, car, man, etc. As will be seen in the sequel, the ability to precisiate the meaning of such expressions plays an essential role in the computation of fuzzy probabilities.

As a concrete illustration, consider the description

$$d \overset{\Delta}{=} \text{several large balls} \tag{4.14}$$

Using test-score semantics [523], the meaning of d may be defined as a test procedure which yields the degree of compatibility of d with a database which consists of a collection $D = \{b, \ldots, b, \ldots, \}$ of in balls of various sizes. More specifically, let $\mu_{\text{LARGE}}(b_i)$ be the degree to which a ball, b_i, $i = 1, \ldots, m$, is large. Furthermore, let, μ_{SEVERAL} denote the membership function of the fuzzy quantifier several. Then, on employing the $\sum$ count of large balls. we have

$$\sum \text{Count(LARGE BALL)} = \sum_{i=1}^{m} \mu_{\text{LARGE}}(b_i) \tag{4.15}$$

and hence the degree to which this count satisfies the constraint induced by the quantifier several is given by

$$\tau = \mu_{\text{SEVERAL}} \left(\sum_{i}^{m} \mu_{\text{LARGE}}(b_i) \right) \tag{4.16}$$

As shown in Ref. [521], the degree of compatibility, τ may be interpreted as the possibility of the database, D, given the description $d \overset{\Delta}{=}$ several large balls.

Alternatively, the compatibility of d with D may be computed by using the FGCount.

Thus, let τ_1

$$\tau_1 \overset{\Delta}{=} \mu_{\text{LARGE}}(b_i) \wedge \cdots \wedge \mu_{\text{LARGE}}(b_m)$$

represent the degree to which the constraint on the size of the balls is satisfied. Now, the degree to which the constraint on the number of balls is satisfied is given by

$$\tau_2 = \mu_{\text{SEVERAL}}(m) \tag{4.17}$$

and hence the degree to which both constraints are satisfied may be expressed as

$$\tau = \tau_1 \wedge \tau_2$$

$$= \mu_{\text{SEVERAL}}(m) \wedge \mu_{\text{LARGE}}(b_1) \wedge \cdots \wedge \mu_{\text{LARGE}}(b_m) \tag{4.18}$$

where $\wedge$ denotes the min operator in infix form. This expression for the compatibility of d and D corresponds to what is referred to in Ref. [523] as a compartmentalized interpretation of the description $d \overset{\Delta}{=}$ several large balls.

The foregoing analysis provides us with 2 means of precisiating the meaning of descriptions of the general form QAO, of which $d \overset{\Delta}{=}$ several large balls is a typical instance. With this means, then, we can address the issue of computing fuzzy probabilities when the underlying data contain fuzzy descriptions.

As a concrete illustration, we shall consider a slightly simplified version of a question that was posed earlier. Specifically:

An urn contains m balls of various sizes, of which several are large. What is the probability that a ball drawn at random is large?

The simplification-which is not essential-is that the number of balls in the urn is assumed to be m rather than *approximately* m. Furthermore, in the representation of the meaning of "*several large balls*" we shall employ the $\sum$ Count rather than the FGCount.

Assume that the urn, U, consist of the balls $b_1, \ldots, b_m$ with $\mu_{\text{LARGE}}(b_i)$, $i = 1, \ldots, m$ representing the grade of membership of b_i in the fuzzy set LARGE. Now from (4.16) it follows that the possibility of U given the datum "The urn contains several large balls" is

$$\tau = \mu_{\text{SEVERAL}} \left(\sum_{i=1}^{m} \mu_{\text{LARGE}}(b_i) \right)$$

On the other hand, if a ball is chosen at random, the probability of the fuzzy event "The chosen ball is large" is given by (see [503])

$$q \overset{\Delta}{=} \text{Prob}\{\text{ball is large}\} = \frac{1}{m} \sum_{i=1}^{m} \mu_{\text{LARGE}}(b_i) \qquad (4.19)$$

Consequently the possibility that Prob{ball is large} may take a value, say, v, is

$$\text{Poss}\{q = v\} = \mu_{\text{SEVERAL}}(mv) \qquad (4.20)$$

or equivalently,

$$\prod_q = \frac{\text{SEVERAL}}{m} \qquad (4.21)$$

where $\prod_q$ denotes the possibility distribution of q [517] and SEVERAL is interpreted as a fuzzy number. For example, if $m = 10$ and

$$\text{SEVERAL} = 0.4/3 + 0.8/4 + 1/5 + 1/6 + 0.6/7 + 0.3/8 \qquad (4.22)$$

then

$$\prod_q = 0.4/0.3 + 0.8/0.4 + 1/0.5 + 1/0.6 + 0.6/0.7 + 0.3/0.8 \qquad (4.23)$$

is the possibility distribution of the fuzzy number which represents the fuzzy probability that a ball drawn at random is large.

As was pointed out earlier, the fuzziness in the probability of drawing a large ball is induced by the fuzziness in our knowledge of the number of large balls in the urn. In this connection, it should be noted that. if instead of being given the $\sum$ Count of large balls we were given the FGCount of large balls. the expression for fuzzy probability would become

$$F\,\text{Prob}\{\text{ball is large}\} = \frac{\text{FGCount(LARGE)}}{m} \qquad (4.24)$$

where $F\,\text{Prob}$ identifies the probability in question as a fuzzy probability which is the ratio of the fuzzy number FGCount(LARGE) and the nonfuzzy number tn. Stated in this form. the fuzzy probability

F Prob{ball is large}: becomes closely related to the probability distribution function of the random variable which is associated with the membership function of LARGE.

There is a significant difference between the results expressed by (4.21) and (4.24) that is in need of clarification.

In the case of (4.21). it is tacitly assumed that the probability of drawing a large ball is a real number whose possibility distribution is expressed by (4.21). In the case of (4.24), on the other hand, the probability is assumed to be a fuzzy rather than a real number.

To differentiate between these interpretations, the probabilities expressed by (4.21) and f (4.24) will be referred to disjunctive fuzzy probability and conjunctive fuzzy probability, respectively. We shall rely on the context to indicate whether a fuzzy probability should be interpreted in a disjunctive or conjunctive sense.

To view the computation of fuzzy probability from a broader perspective, let $U = \{u_1, \ldots, u_m\}$ be a finite universe of discourse and let X be a variable which takes the values $u_1, \ldots, u_m$ with a uniform probability $(1/m)$. Now if A is a nonfuzzy subset of U, the probability of the proposition or. equivalently, of the event

$$p \overset{\Delta}{=} X \in A \tag{4.25}$$

is given by

$$\text{Prob}\{X \in A\} = \frac{\text{Count}(A)}{m} \tag{4.26}$$

More generally, if A is a fuzzy subset of U then the probability of the fuzzy proposition or. equivalently, of the fuzzy event

$$p \overset{\Delta}{=} X \text{ is } A \tag{4.27}$$

may be expressed in two distinct ways: (a) as a nonfuzzy probability

$$\text{Prob}\{X \text{ is } A\} \overset{\Delta}{=} \frac{\sum \text{Count}(A)}{m} \tag{4.28}$$

and (b) as a fuzzy probability

$$F \text{Prob}\{X \text{ is } A\} \overset{\Delta}{=} \frac{\text{FGCount}(A)}{m} \tag{4.29}$$

with the understanding that (4.29) is implied by

$$\text{Prob}\{X \text{ is } A\} \triangleq \frac{\text{Count}(A_\alpha)}{m} \tag{4.30}$$

where A_α is the α-level-set of A.

Furthermore, if A and B are fuzzy subsets of U, then the joint fuzzy probability of the fuzzy events $p \triangleq X$ and $q \triangleq X$ is B is given by

$$F \text{Prob}\{X \text{ is } A, X \text{ is } B\} = \frac{\text{FGCount}(A \cap B)}{m} \tag{4.31}$$

Correspondingly, the conditional fuzzy probability of p given q may be defined as the fuzzy number

$$F \text{Prob}\{X \text{ is } A, \ X \text{ is } B\} = \sum_\alpha \alpha \left/ \frac{\text{Count}(A_\alpha \cap B_\alpha)}{\text{Count}(B_\alpha)} \right. \tag{4.32}$$

where $\sum$ stands for the union rather than the arithmetic sum and $\text{Count}(B_\alpha) \neq 0$. From (4.31) and (4.32) we can deduce the basic identity for fuzzy probabilities:

$$F \text{Prob}\{X \text{ is } A, \ X \text{ is } B\} = F \text{Prob}\{X \text{ is } A\} \otimes F \text{Prob}\{X \text{ is } B\} \tag{4.33}$$

where $\otimes$ is the product of fuzzy numbers [128, 311]. This identity may be viewed as a natural generalization of the familiar relation:

$$\text{Prob}\{X \in A, \ X \in B\} = \text{Prob}\{X \in B\}\text{Prob}\{X \in A | X \in B\} \tag{4.34}$$

which holds when A and B are non-fuzzy probabilities of fuzzy events defined via the $\sum$ Count as in (4.28).

In the foregoing discussion, we have assumed that the probability distribution on U is uniform. More generally, if $\text{Prob}(u_i) \triangleq p_i$,

$i = 1, \ldots, m$ and $p_1 + \cdots + p_m = 1$ then (4.29) become

$$F\mathrm{Prob}\{X \text{ is } A\} = \sum_\alpha \alpha/\mathrm{Prob}(A_\alpha) \qquad (4.35)$$

where

$$\mathrm{Prob}(A_\alpha) \overset{\Delta}{=} \mathrm{Prob}\{x \in A_\alpha\} \qquad (4.36)$$

Similarly, if X and Y take values in $U = \{u_1, \ldots, u_m\}$ and $V = \{v_1, \ldots, v_n\}$ respectively, and

$$\mathrm{Prob}(u_1, v_1) \overset{\Delta}{=} p_{ij}, \quad i = 1, \ldots, m, \quad j = 1, \ldots, n$$

then

$$F\,\mathrm{Prob}\{X \text{ is } A,\ Y \text{ is } B\} = \sum_\alpha \alpha \Big/ \mathrm{Prob}(X \in A_\alpha, Y \in B_\alpha) \quad (4.37)$$

$$F\,\mathrm{Prob}\{X \text{ is } A,\ Y \text{ is } B\} = \sum_\alpha \alpha \Big/ \mathrm{Prob}(X \in A_\alpha | Y \in B_\alpha) \quad (4.38)$$

and

$$F\,\mathrm{Prob}\{X \text{ is } A,\ X \text{ is } B\}$$
$$= F\,\mathrm{Prob}\{Y \text{ is } B\} \otimes F\mathrm{Prob}\{X \text{ is } A | Y \text{ is } B\} \quad (4.39)$$

which reduces to (4.33) when $X = Y$. By analogy with numerical probabilities, the fuzzy events X is A and Y is B will be said to *independent* if

$$F\,\mathrm{Prob}\{X \text{ is } A | Y \text{ is } B\} = F\,\mathrm{Prob}\{X \text{ is } A\} \qquad (4.40)$$

which implies that

$$F\,\mathrm{Prob}\{X \text{ is } A | Y \text{ is } B\} = F\,\mathrm{Prob}\{X \text{ is } A\} \otimes F\,\mathrm{Prob}\{Y \text{ is } B\}$$
$$(4.41)$$

In addition to the cases discussed above, there is another important way in which fuzzy information induces fuzzy probabilities. More specifically. consider the case where an individual, I, is faced with the decision of whether or not to insure his or her car. To find that choice which maximizes the expected utility, it is necessary to know, among other parameters, the probability that I's car may be stolen. How could this probability be determined?

Just a little reflection makes it clear that the desired probability cannot be deduced from the statistics of car thefts, since I's car — and the way in which it is driven, parked and garaged — is unique. Furthermore, there is no way in which I can obtain the desired probability by experimentation. What we see in this case is a paradigm of a well known paradox in probability theory which raises serious questions with regard to the meaning-fullness of the concept of probability in application to unique events.

One way of getting around the difficulty with uniqueness is to relate probability to similarity, with similarity viewed as a fuzzy relation [507]. Thus, suppose that we wish to estimate the probability that an object, u. which is an element of a finite universe of discourse U, belongs to A, a subset of U. To this end, let S be a fuzzy similarity relation which associates with each element $u \in U$ its degree of similarity to a, $u_s(u, a)$. Then $\mu_s(u, a)$ may be regarded as the membership function of a fuzzy set, $S(u)$. of objects which are similar to a.

In terms of the similarity relation S, the probability Prob$\{a \in A\}$ may be defined via the $\sum$ Count or the FGCount of the intersection of $S(a)$ and A. Thus,

$$\text{Prob}(a \in A) \triangleq \frac{\sum \text{Count}(S(a) \cap A)}{\text{Count}(U)} \qquad (4.42)$$

where $S(a) \cap A$ denotes the intersection of the fuzzy set $S(a)$ with A [503].

If the similarity relation were known precisely (4.42) would yield a numerical value of a belonging to A. But, in general, this would not be the case, with the result that the expression for the probability Prob$\{a \in A\}$ would be a fuzzy number. In this sense, then estimates of probability based on similarity will, in general, be fuzzy rather than real numbers.

To make the point more concretely, assume that the imprecision in S is modeled by treating S as a fuzzy relation of type 2 [516], which implies that the degree of similarity of a and u, $\mu_s(a,u)$, is taken to be a fuzzy number. More specifically, assume that $\mu_s(a,u)$ is a fuzzy number ϕ whose membership function μ_ϕ is a π-function [517], that is,

$$
\begin{aligned}
\vec{a}(u,\delta,\gamma) &= 0 && \text{for } u \leq \gamma - \delta \\
&= 2\left(\frac{u-\gamma+\delta}{\delta}\right)^2 && \text{for } \gamma - \delta \leq \frac{\delta}{2} \\
&= 1 - 2\left(\frac{u-\gamma}{\delta}\right)^2 && \text{for } \gamma - \frac{\delta}{2} \leq u \leq 7 \\
&= 1 - 2\left(\frac{\gamma-u}{\delta}\right)^2 && \text{for } \gamma \leq u \leq \gamma + \frac{\delta}{2} \\
&= 2\left(\frac{\gamma+\delta-u}{\delta}\right)^2 && \text{for } \gamma + \frac{\delta}{2} \leq u \leq \gamma + \delta \\
&= 0 && \text{for } u \geq \gamma + \delta \qquad (4.43)
\end{aligned}
$$

where γ is the peak of ϕ and δ is its bandwidth. Then, as shown in [128], the sum of fuzzy numbers of this form is a number of the same form whose peak and bandwidth are respectively, the arithmetic sums of the peaks and bandwidths of their summands. In this way, the numerator of (4.42) evaluates to a fuzzy number which upon division by the count of U yields the fuzzy probability of a belonging to A.

Since the principle of maximization of expected utility plays a central role in decision analysis, it is important to be able to evaluate fuzzy expectations of the general form

$$
E = (g_1 \otimes p_1) \oplus (g_2 \otimes p_2) \oplus \cdots \oplus (g_n \otimes p_n), \qquad (4.44)
$$

where $\otimes$ and $\oplus$ represent fuzzy multiplication and addition, respectively; $p_1, \ldots, p_n$ are fuzzy probabilities; and $g_1, \ldots, g_n$ are fuzzy gains (or utilities). Expressions of the form (4.44) can readily be computed by the use of fuzzy arithmetic. This and related issues are discussed in greater detail in Refs. [3, 19, 21, 28, 46, 128, 135, 136, 223, 311, 331, 441, 443, 467, 478].

In most realistic applications of decision analysis the underlying probabilities are fuzzy rather than real numbers. In general, fuzzy probabilities are induced by fuzzy data and may be determined by (a) employing the concept of cardinality of fuzzy sets, and (b) using fuzzy arithmetic to compute the ratios, products and sums of counts of elements in such sets.

Chapter 5

Fuzzy Functions

Classical crisp functions are important in mathematical modeling. Fuzzy modeling is based on fuzzy functions. Fuzzy functions may be obtained as an extension of a crisp function to map fuzzy sets to fuzzy sets. Fuzzy functions may be described by using methods such as the extension principle and the alpha cuts-based method. Different properties such as differentiability and integrability of a fuzzy function are considered in this chapter.

5.1. Definition of Fuzzy Functions

First we use Zadeh's extension principle to define fuzzy functions. It is known that the distance between two fuzzy numbers is expressed as [364]:

$$D(A, B) = \sup_{\alpha \in [0,1]} \{\max\{|A^-(\alpha) - B^-(\alpha)|, |A^+(\alpha) - B^+(\alpha)|\}\}$$

Assume that two fuzzy subsets A and B on U and V respectively are given. Using extension principle, one can find function f to induce a fuzzy-valued function F

$$F(A, B)(z) = \begin{cases} \sup_{f(x,y)=z}\{\min\{A(x), B(y)\}\}, & f^{-1}(z) \neq \phi \\ 0, & f^{-1}(z) = \phi \end{cases}$$

where $f^{-1}(z) = \{(x, y) \in U \times V : f(x, y) = z \in W\}$. Function F is called a fuzzy function induced by the extension principle. The theorem given in Ref. [2] restricts f to construct function F.

In Ref. [327], it is proved that if f is a continuous function, then F is a well-defined function with α-cut

$$(F(A, B))_\alpha = f(A_\alpha, B_\alpha)$$

In Ref. [158], it is proved that if f is a function, then the following conditions are equivalent: f is continuous, and F is continuous with respect to the metric D.

There are different definitions of fuzzy functions. In Ref. [326], a fuzzy function from X to Y is defined as a mapping $p : X \times Y \to [0, 1]$. In Ref. [129], it is shown that a mapping $p : X \times Y \to [0, 1]$ is a fuzzy function if for all $x \in X$ there exists $y \in Y$ such that $p(x, y) > 0$.

A fuzzy-number-valued function $F:[a, b] \to E^1$ is said to be continuous at $x_0 \in [a, b]$ if for each $\varepsilon > 0$ there is a $\delta > 0$ such that $D(f(x), f(x_0)) < \varepsilon$ whenever $x \in [a, b]$ with $|x - x_0| < \delta$. If f is continuous at each $x \in [a, b]$, then we say f is continuous on $[a, b]$. Here E^1 is the space of fuzzy numbers.

A fuzzy-number-valued function $F:[a, b] \to E^1$ is called Riemann integrable on $[a, b]$ if there exists $I \in E^1$ with the property: $\forall \varepsilon > 0$, $\exists \delta > 0$ such that for any division of $[a, b]\, d : a = x_0 < x_1 < \cdots < x_n = b$ norm $\nu(d) < \delta$, and for any points $\xi_i \in [x_i, x_{i+1}] i = \overline{0, n - 1}$ we have

$$D \left(\sum_{i=0}^{n-1} F(\xi_i)(x_{i+1} - x_i), I \right) < \varepsilon$$

Then

$$I = \int_a^b F(x)\,dx$$

Theorem 5.1 ([180, 492]). *If fuzzy-number-valued function $F : [a, b] \to E^1$ is continuous (with respect to the metric D) and for each $x \in [a, b]$, F has the parametric representation*

$$[F(x)]_\alpha = [F_\alpha^-(x), F_\alpha^+(x)]$$

then $\int_a^b F(x)dx$ exists, belongs to E^1 and is parametrized by

$$\left[\int_a^b F(x)dx\right]_\alpha = \left[\int_a^b F_\alpha^-(x)dx, \int_a^b F_\alpha^+(x)dx\right]$$

Assume that $F(x)$ is a fuzzy-number-valued function defined on interval $[a, \infty)$. The integral

$$\int_a^\infty f(x)dx = \lim_{t\to\infty} \int_a^t f(x)dx$$

converges and is equal to the value of limit [491].

Let's $(\Omega, \sum, \mu)$ denotes a σ-finite measure space. If $F : \Omega \to E$ is a fuzzy-number-valued function and B is a subset of R, then $F^{-1}(B)$ is the fuzzy subset of Ω. F is called measurable if for every B of R the fuzzy set $F^{-1}(B)$ is measurable.

5.2. Integrability and Differentiability of Fuzzy Functions

A measurable function $F : F(\omega) = \{(F_\alpha^-(\omega), F_\alpha^+(\omega)|0 \le \alpha \le 1\}$ is called integrable if for each $\alpha \in [0, 1]$, F_α^- and F_α^+ are integrable. Then integral of F over $A \in \sum$ is defined by

$$\int_A Fd\mu = \left\{\left(\int_A F_\alpha^- d\mu, \int_A F_\alpha^+ d\mu\right) \Big| 0 \le \alpha \le 1\right\}$$

Below an important result on the properties of integral of fuzzy function is given.

Proposition 5.1 ([59]). *The fuzzy integral has the following properties.*

(i) If $f, g : [a, b] \to E^1$ are integrable and $\lambda, \gamma \in R$ we have

$$\int_a^b (\lambda f(x) + \gamma g(x))dx = \lambda \int_a^b f(x)dx + \gamma \int_a^b g(x)dx$$

(ii) If $f : [a, b] \to E^1$ is integrable and $c \in [a, b]$, then

$$\int_a^c f(x)dx + \int_c^b f(x)dx = \int_a^b f(x)dx$$

(iii) If $c \in E^1$ and $f : [a, b] \to E^1$ has constant sign on $[a, b]$, then

$$\int_a^b c \cdot f(x)dx = c \int_a^b f(x)dx$$

Let's consider derivatives of fuzzy functions. Let F be a fuzzy function and $x_0 \in R$. The fuzzy function F is differentiable at x_0, if there exists the mapping

$$h_{x_0} : a \mapsto \frac{dF^{(-1)}(x_0)}{dx}(a)$$

as an element of $H^{(-1)}(R)$. Here $H(R)$ is the set of all fuzzy numbers.

If f is differentiable at x_0, then the function $f'(x_0) = [h_{x_0}]^{(-1)}$ is the derivative of f at the point x_0 [225]. Derivative of a fuzzy function at a point is a fuzzy number. Therefore, it is possible to define the derivative of f, which will be a fuzzy function.

One of the basic notions related to differentiability of a fuzzy function is Hukuhara differentiability:

Definition 5.1 ([59]). A function $f : [a, b] \to E^1$ is called Hukuhara differentiable if for $h > 0$ sufficiently small the H-differences $f(x + h) \ominus f(x)$ and $f(x) \ominus f(x - h)$ exist and if there exist an element $f'(x) \in E^1$ such that

$$\lim_{h \searrow 0} \frac{f(x + h) \ominus f(x)}{h} = \lim_{h \searrow 0} \frac{f(x) \ominus f(x - h)}{h} = f'(x)$$

The fuzzy number $f'(x)$ is called the Hukuhara derivative of f at x.

An analogous definition of differentiability of a fuzzy function is formulated in terms of α-cuts:

Definition 5.2 ([59]). The Seikkala derivative of a fuzzy-number-valued function $f : [a, b] \to E^1$ is defined by

$$f'(x)_\alpha = [(f_\alpha^-(x))', (f_\alpha^+(x))'],$$

$0 \le \alpha \le 1$, provided that it defines a fuzzy number $f'(x) \in E^1$.

In Refs. [59, 60], authors introduce new generalized differentiability concepts for fuzzy valued functions as a generalization of Hukuhara differentiability. It is shown that if $F :]a, b[\to E^1$ and

$x_0 \in]a, b[$ is strongly generalized differentiable at x_0 if there exists an element $f'_G(x_0) \in E^1$, such that for all $h > 0$ sufficiently small

(i) $\exists f(x_0 + h)\theta_H f(x_0), f(x_0)\theta_H f(x_0 - h)$ and

$$\lim_{h \searrow 0} \frac{f(x_0 + h)\theta_H f(x_0)}{h} = \lim_{h \searrow 0} \frac{f(x_0)\theta_H f(x_0 - h)}{h} = f'_G(x_0)$$

or (ii) $\exists f(x_0)\theta_H f(x_0 + h), f(x_0 - h)\theta_H f(x_0)$ and

$$\lim_{h \searrow 0} \frac{f(x_0)\theta_H f(x_0 + h)}{(-h)} = \lim_{h \searrow 0} \frac{f(x_0 - h)\theta_H f(x_0)}{(-h)} = f'_G(x_0)$$

or (iii) $\exists f(x_0 + h)\theta_H f(x_0), f(x_0 - h)\theta_H f(x_0)$ and

$$\lim_{h \searrow 0} \frac{f(x_0 + h)\theta_H f(x_0)}{h} = \lim_{h \searrow 0} \frac{f(x_0 - h)\theta_H f(x_0)}{(-h)} = f'_G(x_0)$$

or (iv) $\exists f(x_0)\theta_H f(x_0 + h), f(x_0)\theta_H f(x_0 - h)$ and

$$\lim_{h \searrow 0} \frac{f(x_0)\theta_H f(x_0 + h)}{(-h)} = \lim_{h \searrow 0} \frac{f(x_0)\theta_H f(x_0 - h)}{(h)} = f'_G(x_0)$$

Taking into account difficulties related to existence of Hukuhara difference, Bede and his colleagues introduced a more general concept of fuzzy derivative which is based on the concept of generalized Hukuhara difference (for more details, see Ref. [59] and the references here in):

Definition 5.3 ([59]). Let $x_0 \in (a, b)$. Then the fuzzy gH-derivative of a function $f : [a, b] \to E^1$ at x_0 is defined as

$$f'_{\text{gH}}(x_0) = \lim_{h \to 0} \frac{1}{h}[f(x_0 + h) \ominus_{\text{gH}} f(x_0)]$$

If $f'_{\text{gH}}(x_0) \in E^1$ exists, then we say that f is generalized Hukuhara differentiable (gH-differentiable for short) at x_0($\ominus_{\text{gH}}$ is the gH-difference).

Chapter 6

Fuzzy Systems

Many of the systems encountered in the real-world; are too complex and/or too ill-defined to be susceptible of exact analysis. The concept of a fuzzy set, that is, a class which of intermediate admits grades of membership in it, opens the possibility of analyzing such systems both qualitatively and quantitatively by allowing the input and/or the output and/or the state of the system to range over fuzzy sets. In this chapter, several basic concepts relating to the characterization of fuzzy systems are considered.

6.1. Introduction

What we still lack, and lack rather acutely, are methods for dealing with systems which are too complex or too ill-defined to admit of precise analysis. Such systems pervade life sciences, social sciences, philosophy, economics, psychology and many other "soft" fields. Furthermore, they are encountered in what are normally regarded as "non-soft" fields when the complexity of a system rules out the possibility of analyzing it by conventional mathematical means, whether with or without the aid of computers. Many examples of such systems are found among large-scale traffic control systems, pattern recognition systems, machine translators, large-scale information processing systems, large-scale power distribution networks, neural networks and games such as chess, checkers, etc.

Perhaps the major reason for the ineffectiveness of classical mathematical techniques in dealing with systems of high order of complexity lies in their failure to come to grips with the issue of fuzziness, that is, with imprecision which stems not from randomness but from a lack of sharp transition from membership in a class to non-membership in it. It is this type of imprecision which arises when one speaks, for example, of the class of real numbers which are much larger 10, than since the real numbers cannot be divided dichotomously into those that are much larger than 10 and those that are not. The same applies to classes such as "tall men", "good strategies for playing chess", "pairs of numbers which are approximately equal to one another", "systems which are approximately linear", etc. Actually, most of the classes encountered in the real world are of this fuzzy, imprecisely defined, kind. What sets such classes apart from classes which are well defined in the conventional mathematical sense is the fuzziness of their boundaries. In effect, in the case of a class with a fuzzy boundary, an object may ha a grade of membership in it which lies somewhere between full membership and non-membership.

Why is fuzziness *so* relevant to complexity? Because no matter what the nature of a system is, when its complexity exceeds a certain threshold it becomes impractical or computationally in feasible to make precise assertions about it. For example, in the case of chess the size of the decision tree so is large that it is impossible, in general, to find a precise algorithmic solution to the following problem: Given the position of pieces on the board, determine an optimal next move. Similarly, in the case of a large-scale traffic control system, the complexity of the system precludes the possibility of precise evaluation of its performance. Thus, any significant assertion about the performance of such a system must necessarily be fuzzy in nature, with the degree fuzziness increasing with the complexity of the system.

How can fuzziness be made a part of system theory? A tentative step in this direction was taken in Refs. [504, 505, 547] in which the notions of a fuzzy system were introduced. In what follows, we shall proceed somewhat further in this direction, focusing our attention on the definition of a fuzzy system and its state. It should be emphasized, however, that the task of constructing a complete theory of fuzzy systems one is of very considerable magnitude, and that what we shall have to say about fuzzy systems in the sequel is conceptual framework for dealing with such systems in both qualitative and quantitative ways.

6.2. System, Aggregate and State

For simplicity, we shall restrict our attention to time-invariant discrete-time systems in which t, time, ranges over integers, and the input and output at time t are real-valued.

In the theory of non-fuzzy discrete-time systems, it is customary to introduce the notion of state at the very outset by defining a system a through its state equations:

$$x_{t+1} = f(x_t, u_t) t = \ldots, -1, 0, 1, \ldots \qquad (6.1)$$

$$y_t = g(x_t, u_t)$$

where u_t denotes the input at time t, y_t is the output at time t and x_t is the state at time t, with the ranges of u_t, y_t and x_t denoted by U, Y and X, respectively. Let A be a fuzzy set in $X \times Y$. In this way, A is characterized by two mappings, $f : X \times U \to X$ and $g : X \times U \to Y$. The space X is called the state space of A, and a point α in X is called a state of A.

Let u denote an input sequence starting at, say, $t = 0$. Thus, $u = u_0, u_1, \ldots, u_\ell$ where $u_t \in U, t = 0, 1, \ldots, \ell, \ell =$ non-negative integer. The set of all sequences whose elements are drawn from U will be denoted by U^*.

Now, to each state α in X and each input sequence $u = u_0$, $u_1, \ldots, u_\ell$ in U^* will correspond an output sequence $y = y_0 y_1 \cdots y_\ell$ in Y^*. The pair of sequences (u, y) is called an input–output pair of length $\ell + 1$. The totality of input–output pairs, (u, y), of varying lengths which correspond to a particular state α in X will be referred to as an aggregate of input–output pairs, or simply an aggregate, $A(\alpha)$, with α playing the role of a label for this aggregate. The union

$$A = \underset{\alpha \in X}{U} A(\alpha)$$

represents the totality of input–output pairs which correspond to all the states of A. It is this totality of input–output pairs that we shall equate with A.

The fact that a state is merely a label for an aggregate suggests that the concept of an aggregate be accorded a central place among the basic concepts of system-theory. This is done implicitly in Refs. [500, 504], and explicitly in Ref. [505]. The point of departure in the theory developed in Ref. [500] is the definition of a system as a collection of input–output pairs. An aggregate, then, may be defined as a subset of input–output pairs which satisfy certain consistency conditions, with a state playing the role of a name for an aggregate.

In what follows, we shall first generalize to fuzzy systems the conventional approach in which a system is described through its state equations. Then we shall indicate a connection between the notion of a fuzzy algorithm and a fuzzy system. Finally, we shall present in a summary from some of the basic definitions relating to the notion of an aggregate and briefly touch upon their generalization to fuzzy systems.

6.3.   State Equations for Fuzzy Systems

Let u_t, y_t and x_t denote, respectively, the input, output and state of a system A at time t. Such a system is said to be deterministic if it is characterized by state equations of the from

$$x_{t+1} = f(x_t, u_t) t = \cdots - 1, 0, 1, 2, \ldots \qquad (6.2)$$

$$y_t = g(x_t, u_t) \qquad (6.3)$$

in which f and g are mappings from $X \times U$ to X and Y, respectively. A is said to be non-deterministic if x_{t+1} and/or y_t are not uniquely determined by x_t and u_t. Let $X^{t+1}(x_t, u_t)$ and $Y^t(x_t, u_t)$ or X^{t+1} and Y^t, for short, denote, respectively, the state of possible values of x_{t+1} and y_t, given x_t and u_t. Then (6.2) and (6.3) can be replaced by equations of the form

$$X^{t+1} = F(x_t, u_t) \qquad (6.4)$$

$$Y^t = G(x_t, u_t) \qquad (6.5)$$

where F and G are mappings from $X \times U$ into the space of subsets of X and Y, respectively. Thus, a non-deterministic system is characterized by equations of the form (6.4) and (6.5), in which X^{t+1} and Y^t are subsets of X and Y, respectively.

The next step in the direction of further generalized is to assume that X^{t+1} and Y^t are fuzzy rather than non-fuzzy sets in X and Y, respectively. In this case, we shall say that A is a fuzzy discrete-time system. Clearly, such a system reduces to a non-deterministic system when X^{t+1} and Y^t are non-fuzzy sets. In turn, a non-deterministic system reduces to a deterministic system when X^{t+1} and Y^t are single points (singletons) in their respective spaces.

Let $\mu_X(x_{t+1}|x_t, u_t)$ and $\mu_Y(y_t|x_t, u_t)$ denote the membership functions of X^{t+1} and Y^t, respectively, given x_t and u_t. Then we can say that A is characterized by the two membership functions $\mu_X(x_{t+1}|x_t, u_t)$ and $\mu_Y(y_t|x_t, u_t)$, which define conditioned fuzzy sets X in and Y, respectively, involving x_t and u_t as parameters.

To illustrate, suppose that $X = R$. Then A is a fuzzy system if its characterization contains statements such as: "If an input $u_t = 5$ is applied to A in state $x_t = (3, 5, 1)$ at time t, then the state A of at time $t + 1$ will be in the *vicinity* of the point $(7, 3, 5)$". Here, the set of points in X in which lie in the vicinity of a given point α is a fuzzy set in X. Such a set may be characterized by a membership function such as

$$\mu(x) = \left(\exp -\frac{1}{k} \|x - \alpha\| \right) \qquad (6.6)$$

where x is a point in X, $\|x - \alpha\|$ denotes a norm of the vector $x - \alpha$ and k is a positive constant.

By analogy with non-fuzzy systems, a fuzzy system A will be said to be memoryless if the fuzzy set Y^t is independent of x_t that is, if its membership function is of the form $\mu_Y(y_t|u_t)$. Just as a non-fuzzy memoryless system is characterized by a graph $y_t = g(u_t)$, $u_t \in U$, so a fuzzy memoryless system is characterized by a fuzzy graph which is a family of fuzzy sets $\{Y^t(u_t), u_t \in U\}$.

In the case of a memoryless system, to such point u_t in U corresponds a fuzzy set $Y^t(u_t)$, or Y^t for short, in Y. Thus, we can write

$$Y^t = G(u_t) \; t = \cdots, -1, 0, 1, 2, \ldots \tag{6.7}$$

where G is a function from R^1 to the space of fuzzy sets in Y. Consequently this implies that if U^t is a fuzzy set in U set characterized by a membership function. Then to U^t will correspond the fuzzy set Y^t defined by the membership function

$$\mu_Y(y_t) = \bigvee_{u_t}(\mu_U(u_t) \wedge \mu_Y(y_t|u_t)) \tag{6.8}$$

where $\vee$ and $\wedge$ denote the supremum and minimum, respectively. Thus, (6.8) establishes a relation between U^t and Y^t which can be expressed as

$$Y^t = G_0(U^t) \; t = \cdots, -1, 0, 1, 2, \ldots \tag{6.9}$$

where G_0 is a function from the space of fuzzy sets in U to the space of fuzzy sets in Y.

The important point to be noted is here that Eq. (6.7) which expresses Y^t as a function of u induces Eq. (6.9), which expresses Y^t as a function of U^t. As should be expected, (6.9) reduces to (6.7) when U^t is taken to be the singleton $\{u_t\}$.

Intuitively, (6.7) and (6.9) may be interpreted as follows. If A is a fuzzy memoryless system, then to every non-fuzzy input u_t at time t corresponds a unique fuzzy output which is represented by a conditioned fuzzy set Y^t in Y. The membership function of this fuzzy set is given by $\mu_Y(y_t|u_t)$.

If the input to A is fuzzy, i.e., is a fuzzy set U^t in U, then the corresponding fuzzy output Y^t is given uniquely by (6.9). The membership function for Y^t is expressed by (6.8).

As a very simple example, suppose that U and Y are finite sets: $U = \{1, 2, 3\}$ and $Y = \{1, 2, 3\}$. Furthermore, suppose that if the input u_t is 1, then the output is a fuzzy set described verbally as "y_t is approximately equal to 1." Similarly, if $u_t = 2$, then y_t is approximately equal to 2, and if $u_t = 3$, then y_t is approximately equal to 3. More concretely, we assume that $\mu_Y(y_t|u_t)$ is defined by the table:

$$\mu_Y(1|1) = 1; \quad \mu_Y(2|1) = 0.3; \quad \mu_Y(3|1) = 0.1;$$
$$\mu_Y(1|2) = 0.2; \quad \mu_Y(2|2) = 1; \quad \mu_Y(3|2) = 0.2;$$
$$\mu_Y(1|3) = 0.1; \quad \mu_Y(2|3) = 0.2; \quad \mu_Y(3|3) = 1;$$

Now assume that the input is a fuzzy set described verbally as "u_t is close to 1", and characterized by the membership function

$$\mu_U(1) = 1; \quad \mu_U(2) = 0.2; \quad \mu_U(3) = 0.1$$

Then, by using (6.8) the response to this fuzzy input is found to be fuzzy set defined by the membership function

$$\mu_Y(1) = 1; \quad \mu_Y(2) = 0.3; \quad \mu_Y(3) = 0.2$$

It is convenient to regard (6.9) as a mapping from names of fuzzy sets in U to names of fuzzy sets in Y. In many cases of practical interest such a mapping can be adequately characterized by a finite, and perhaps even fairly small, number of points (ordered pairs (U, Y)) on the graph of G_0. For example, G_0 might be characterized approximately by a table such as shown below (for simplicity we suppress the subscript t in u_t and y_t).

U^t	Y^t
$\widetilde{1}$	$\widetilde{1}$
$\widetilde{1.1}$	$\widetilde{1.3}$
$\widetilde{1.2}$	$\widetilde{1.6}$
$\widetilde{1.3}$	$\widetilde{2}$
$\widetilde{1.4}$	$\widetilde{2.5}$
$\widetilde{1.5}$	$\widetilde{2.9}$
$\widetilde{1.6}$	$\widetilde{2.5}$
$\widetilde{1.7}$	$\widetilde{2.1}$
$\widetilde{1.8}$	$\widetilde{1.8}$
$\widetilde{1.9}$	$\widetilde{1.6}$
$\widetilde{2}$	$\widetilde{1.5}$
$\widetilde{2.1}$	$\widetilde{1.5}$
$\vdots$	$\vdots$
$\widetilde{3}$	$\widetilde{1.5}$

where $\widetilde{x}, \widetilde{x} \in R$ is the name for the fuzzy set of real numbers which are approximately equal to x. Such a set may be characterized quantitatively by a membership function. In many practical situations a very approximate description of this membership function would be sufficient. In this way, Eq. (6.9) can serve the purpose of an approximate characterization of a fuzzy memoryless system.

Turning to non-memoryless fuzzy systems, consider a system A which is characterized by state equations of the form

$$X^{t+1} = F(x_t, u_t) \tag{6.10}$$

$$Y^t = G(x_t, u_t) \tag{6.11}$$

where F is a function from the product space $X \times U$ the space of fuzzy sets in X, G is a function from $X \times U$ to the space of fuzzy sets in Y, X^{t+1} denotes a fuzzy set in X which is conditioned on x_t, u_t and Y_t denotes a fuzzy set in Y which, like X^{t+1}, is conditioned on x_t and u_t. X^t and Y^t represent, respectively, the fuzzy state and output of a at time t and are defined by the membership functions $\mu_X(x_{t+1}|x_t, u_t)$ and $\mu_Y(y_t|x_t, u_t)$.

Equations (6.10) and (6.11) relate the fuzzy state at time $t+1$ and the fuzzy output at time to the non-fuzzy state and non-fuzzy input at time t. As in the case of a memoryless system, we can deduct from these equations — by repeated application of the state equations for A for the case where the state at t time or the input at time t or both are fuzzy.

Specifically, let us assume that the state at time is a fuzzy set characterized by a membership function $\mu_X(x_t)$. Then, we deduce from (6.10) and (6.11)

$$\mu_X(x_{t+1}) = \bigvee_{x_t}(\mu_x(x_t) \wedge \mu_X(x_{t+1}|x_t, u_t)) \qquad (6.12)$$

$$\mu_Y(y_t) = \bigvee_{x_t}(\mu_x(x_t) \wedge \mu_Y(y_t|x_t, u_t)) \qquad (6.13)$$

which in symbolic form may be expressed as

$$X^{t+1} = F_0(X^t, u_t) \qquad (6.14)$$

$$Y^t = G_0(X^t, u_t) \qquad (6.15)$$

Note that $\mu_X(x_{t+1})$ and $\mu_x(x_t)$ represent different membership functions. Strictly speaking, we should write them as $\mu_{X^{t+1}}(x_{t+1})$ and $\mu_{X^t}(x_t)$, respectively.

In what follows, to simplify the appearance of equations such as (6.11) and (6.12), we shall omit the subscripts X and Y in membership functions.

By n-fold iteration of (6.14) and (6.15), we can obtain expressions for X^{t+1+n} and Y^{t+n}, $n = 1, 2, 3, \ldots$, in terms of X^t and $u_t, \ldots, u_{t+n}$. For example, for $n = 1$, we have

$$X^{t+2} = F_0(F_0(X^t, u_t), u_{t+1}) \qquad (6.16)$$

$$Y^{t+1} = G_0(F_0(X^t, u_t), u_{t+1}) \qquad (6.17)$$

or more compactly

$$X^{t+2} = F_1(X^t, u_t, u_{t+1}) \qquad (6.18)$$

$$Y^{t+1} = G_1(X^t, u_t, u_{t+1}) \qquad (6.19)$$

To express (6.18) and (6.19) in terms of membership functions, we note that on replacing t with $t+l$ in (6.12) and (6.13), we obtain

$$\mu(x_{t+2}) = \bigvee_{x_{t+1}} \left(\mu(x_{t+1}) \wedge \mu(x_{t+2}|x_{t+1}, u_{t+1}) \right) \tag{6.20}$$

$$\mu(y_{t+1}) = \bigvee_{x_{t+1}} \left(\mu(x_{t+1}) \wedge \mu(y_{t+1}|x_{t+1}, u_{t+1}) \right) \tag{6.21}$$

Then, on substituting $\mu(x_{t+1})$ from (6.12) into (6.20) and (6.21), we get

$$\mu(x_{t+2}) = \bigvee_{x_{t+1}} \left(\bigvee_{x_t}(\mu(x_t) \wedge \mu(x_{t+1}|x_t, u_t)) \wedge \mu(x_{t+2}|x_{t+1}, u_{t+1}) \right) \tag{6.22}$$

$$\mu(y_{t+1}) = \bigvee_{x_{t+1}} \left(\bigvee_{x_t}(\mu(x_t) \wedge \mu(x_{t+1}|x_t, u_t)) \wedge \mu(y_{t+1}|x_{t+1}, u_{t+1}) \right) \tag{6.23}$$

which by virtue of the distributivity of $\vee$ and $\wedge$ may be expressed as

$$\mu(x_{t+2}) = \bigvee_{x_{t+1}} \bigvee_{x_t}(\mu(x_t) \wedge \mu(x_{t+1}|x_t, u_t) \wedge \mu(x_{t+2}|x_{t+1}, u_{t+1})) \tag{6.24}$$

$$\mu(y_{t+1}) = \bigvee_{x_{t+1}} \bigvee_{x_t}(\mu(x_t) \wedge \mu(x_{t+1}|x_t, u_t) \wedge \mu(y_{t+1}|x_{t+1}, u_{t+1})) \tag{6.25}$$

and likewise for larger values of n. It should be noted that these relations are fuzzy counterparts of the corresponding expressions for stochastic systems, with $\vee$ and $\wedge$ replacing product and sum, respectively, and membership functions replacing probability functions.

In the above analysis, we have assumed that the successive inputs $u_t, \ldots, u_{t+n}$ are non-fuzzy. On this basis, we can obtain expressions for $X^{t+1}, \ldots, X^{t+n+1}$ and $Y^t, \ldots, Y^{t+n}$ in terms of X^t and $u_t, \ldots, u_{t+n}$. It is natural to raise the question of what are the corresponding expressions for $X^{t+1}, \ldots, X^{t+n+1}$ and $Y^t, \ldots, Y^{t+n}$ when the successive inputs are fuzzy.

First, let us focus our attention on the state Eqs. (6.4) and (6.5), in which F and G are functions from $X \times U$ to fuzzy sets in X and Y, respectively. Suppose that both the input at time t and the state at time t are fuzzy. What would be the expressions for the membership functions of X^{t+1} and Y^t in this simple case?

Let $\mu(x_t, u_t)$ denote the membership function of the fuzzy set whose elements are ordered pairs (x_t, u_t). Then, we can express the membership functions of X^{t+1} and Y^t as follows:

$$\mu(x_{t+1}) = \bigvee_{x_t} \bigvee_{u_t} (\mu(x_t, u_t) \wedge \mu(x_{t+1}|x_t, u_t)) \qquad (6.26)$$

$$\mu(y_t) = \bigvee_{x_t} \bigvee_{u_t} (\mu(x_t, u_t) \wedge \mu(y_t|x_t, u_t)) \qquad (6.27)$$

These formulae assume a simpler form when $\mu(x_t, u_t)$ can be expressed as

$$\mu(x_t, u_t) = \mu(x_t) \wedge \mu(u_t) \qquad (6.28)$$

where $\mu(x_t)$ and $\mu(u_t)$ denote, respectively, the membership function of the fuzzy state and the fuzzy input at time t. In this case, we shall say that the fuzzy sets X^t and U^t are noninteracting. Essentially, the notion of nonintersection of fuzzy sets corresponds to the notion of independence of random variables.

The assumption that X^t and U^t are noninteracting fuzzy sets is a reasonable one to make in many cases of practical interest. Under this assumption, (6.26) and (6.27) reduce to

$$\mu(x_{t+1}) = \bigvee_{x_t} \bigvee_{u_t} (\mu(x_t) \wedge \mu(u_t) \wedge \mu(x_{t+1}|x_t, u_t)) \qquad (6.29)$$

$$\mu(y_t) = \bigvee_{x_t} \bigvee_{u_t} (\mu(x_t) \wedge \mu(u_t) \wedge \mu(y_t|x_t, u_t)) \qquad (6.30)$$

In symbolic form, (6.29) and (6.30) can be expressed as

$$X^{t+1} = F_{00}(X^t, U^t) \qquad (6.31)$$

$$Y^t = G_{00}(X^t, U^t) \qquad (6.32)$$

where F_{00} and G_{00} are, respectively, functions from the product space of fuzzy sets in X and fuzzy sets in U to the space of fuzzy sets in

X and fuzzy sets in Y. Thus, (6.31) expresses the fuzzy state at time $t+1$ as a function of the fuzzy state at time t and the fuzzy input at time t. Similarly, (6.32) expresses the fuzzy output at time t as a function of the fuzzy state at time t and the fuzzy input at time t. Note that (6.31) is induced by (6.10), which expresses the fuzzy state at time $t+1$ as a function of the non-fuzzy state at time t and the non-fuzzy input at time t. The same is true of (6.32) and (6.11).

When X, U and Y are finite sets, the above equations can be written more compactly by expressing the membership functions in matrix or vector form. Specifically, suppose that X, for example, is a finite set $X = \{x^1, \ldots, x^m\}$. For each input u_t, let $M(u_t)$ denote a matrix whose (i,j)th element is given by

$$M_{ij}(u_i) = \mu(x^i | x^j, u_i)$$

Also, let $\tilde{x}_{t+1}$ and $\tilde{x}_t$ be column vectors whose ith elements are $\mu(x_{t+1})$ and $\mu(x_t)$, respectively, evaluated at x_{t+1} and x_t equal to $x^i, i = 1, \ldots, m$. Then, (6.12) and (6.13) may be written in matrix from as

$$\tilde{x}_{t+1} = M(u_i)\tilde{x}_t$$

where the right-hand member should be interpreted as the matrix product of $M(u_t)$ and $\tilde{x}_t$, with $+$ replaced by $\vee$ and product by $\wedge$. Similarly, (6.24) and (6.25) become

$$\tilde{x}_{t+2} = M(u_{t+1})M(u_t)\tilde{x}_t$$

$$\tilde{y}_{t+1} = M_Y(u_{t+1})M(u_t)\tilde{x}_t$$

where $M_Y(u_{t+1})$ is defined in the same way as $M(u_t)$, with y_{t+1} replacing x_{t+1} in the definition of the latter, and likewise for $\bar{y}_{t+1}$. More generally, for $n = 1, 2, \ldots$, we can write

$$\tilde{x}_{t+n+1} = M(u_{t+n}) \cdots M(u_t)\tilde{x}_t$$

$$\tilde{y}_{t+n} = M_Y(u_{t+n})M(u_{t+n-1}) \cdots M(u_t)\tilde{x}_t$$

When both x_t and u_t are fuzzy, we can no longer employ the matrix notation to simplify expressions such as (6.12) and (6.13). However, some notational simplification, particularly in the case of expressions like (6.24) and (6.25) may be achieved by the use of the tensor notation or the notation commonly employed in dealing with bilinear forms.

A simple numerical example will serve to illustrate the use of the formulae derived above. Specifically, let us consider a fuzzy system with binary input and output, $U = Y = \{0, l\}$, and finite state space $X = \{\alpha, \beta, \gamma\}$. Suppose that the membership functions $\mu(x_{t+1}|x_t, u_t)$ and $\mu(y_t|x_t, u_t)$ for this system are characterized by the following tables:

$\mu(x_{t+1}|x_t, U_t)$:

	$u_t = 0$			$u_t = 1$		
x_{t+1} x_t	α	β	γ	α	β	γ
α	1	0.8	0.6	0.8	0.5	1
β	0.7	0.2	1	0.2	1	0.6
γ	0.3	0.3	0.4	0.9	0.7	1

$\mu(y_t|x_t, u_t)$:

	$u_t = 0$		$u_t = 1$	
y_t x_t	0	1	0	1
α	0.8	0.3	0.6	0.3
β	1	0.1	0.5	1
γ	0.8	0.7	0.3	0.2

Further, assume X^t and U^t are characterized by the membership functions tabulated below:

$$\mu(\alpha) = 1; \quad \mu(\beta) = 0.8; \quad \mu(\gamma) = 0.4$$

$$\mu(0) = 1; \quad \mu(1) = 0.3$$

Then, using (6.29) and (6.30) and employing matrix multiplication (with the operations $\vee$ and $\wedge$ replacing sum and product), we can readily compute the values of the membership functions of X^{t+1} and Y^t at the points $\alpha, \beta, \gamma, 0$, and 1, respectively. These values are

$$\mu(\alpha) = 1 \quad \mu(\beta) = 0.8 \quad \mu(\gamma) = 0.8$$
$$\mu(0) = 0.8 \quad \mu(1) = 0.4$$

It should be noted that, as in the case of a memoryless fuzzy system, (6.31) and (6.32) can be used to provide an approximate characterization of a non-memoryless fuzzy system. To illustrate, let us employ the convention introduced earlier, namely, using the symbol $\tilde{x}$ to denote the name of a fuzzy set or real numbers which are approximately equal to x. Then, viewed as relations between names of fuzzy sets, (6.31) and (6.32) may take the appearance of tables such as shown below:

X^{t+1}:

U^t \ X^t	$\tilde{1}$	2	$\tilde{3}$	4
$\tilde{0}$	2	$\tilde{1}$	4	$\tilde{3}$
$\tilde{1}$	$\tilde{3}$	4	$\tilde{1}$	$\tilde{3}$

Y^{t+1}:

U^t \ X^t	$\tilde{1}$	2	$\tilde{3}$	4
$\tilde{0}$	$\tilde{0}$	$\tilde{1}$	$\tilde{1}$	$\tilde{0}$
$\tilde{1}$	$\tilde{1}$	$\tilde{0}$	$\tilde{1}$	$\tilde{1}$

More generally, the entries in these tables would be names for fuzzy sets in X, U and Y, and only a finite number of such names would be used as representative samples (paradigms) of the fuzzy sets in the irrespective spaces.

So far, we have restricted our attention to the case where a single fuzzy input U^t is applied to A in state X^t. For this case, we found expressions for X^{t+1} and Y^t in terms of X^t and U^t. The same approach can readily be extended, however, to the case where the input is a sequence of non-interacting fuzzy inputs $U^t U^{t+1} \ldots U^{t+n}$, $n \geq 1$. The assumption of non-interaction implies that

$$\mu(u_t, \ldots, u_{t+n}) = \mu(u_t) \wedge \mu(u_{t+1}) \wedge \cdots \wedge \mu(u_{t+n}) \tag{6.33}$$

To illustrate, let $n = 1$. Then by applying to (6.24) and (6.25), we obtain

$$\mu(x_{t+2}) = \bigvee_{x_{t+1}} \bigvee_{x_t} \bigvee_{u_t} \bigvee_{u_{t+1}} (\mu(x_t) \wedge \mu(x_{t+1}|x_t, u_t)$$

$$\wedge \mu(x_{t+2}|x_{t+1}, u_{t+1}) \wedge \mu(u_t) \wedge \mu(u_{t+1})) \tag{6.34}$$

$$\mu(y_{t+1}) = \bigvee_{x_{t+1}} \bigvee_{x_t} \bigvee_{u_t} \bigvee_{u_{t+1}} (\mu(x_t) \wedge \mu(x_{t+1})|x_t, u_t)$$

$$\wedge \mu(y_{t+1}|x_{t+1}, u_{t+1}) \wedge \mu(u_t) \wedge \mu(u_{t+1})) \tag{6.35}$$

6.4. Fuzzy Rule-based System

Fuzzy rule-based system (FRBS) (Fig. 6.1) is based on highly parallel, modular granular model which consist of fuzzy rules of the form

If ⟨input variable X_1 is A_{1i}⟩ and

⟨output variable X_1 is A_{2i}⟩ and .....

Then ⟨output variable is B_1 $i = 1, 2, \ldots, n$⟩

Here, A_i and B_i are information granules. FRBS is performed in multidimensional input space, fuzzy inputs aggregated by the t-norm.

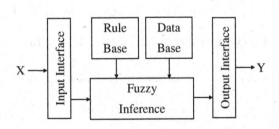

Fig. 6.1. Fuzzy rule-based system.

Multi-input multi-output fuzzy system is described as follows

If X_1 is A_1 and X_2 is A_2 and ..... and X_n is A_n

then Y_1 is B_1 and Y_2 is B_2 and ..... and Y_m is B_m

FRBS also can be based on functional fuzzy rules

$$\text{If X is } A_i \text{ then } y = f(x, a_i)$$

$$f : X \rightarrow Y$$

$$x \in R^n$$

Here, $f(\cdot)$ may be linear or nonlinear functions.

Construction of FRBS includes following steps:

- determination of the fuzzy input and output;
- association of the input and output variables;
- formalization fuzzy relations for each rule;
- aggregation of rules.

Input interface performs function (attribute) of (input) is (value)

If $p : X_1$ is A_1 and X_2 is A_2 and ..... and X_n is A_n

A fuzzy relation P on $X_1 \times X_1 \times \cdots X_n$ is defined as

$$P(x_1, x_2, \ldots, x_n) = A_1(x_1)tA_2(x_2)t \ldots tA_n(x_n)$$
$$= T_{i=1}^{n} A_i(x_i) \text{ here } t(T) = t\text{-norm}$$

For disjunctive canonical form

$$q : X_1 \text{ is } A_1 \text{ or } X_2 \text{ is } A_2 \text{ or} \ldots \ldots \text{ or } X_n \text{ is } A_n$$

Here X_i are fuzzy (linguistic) variables, A_i are fuzzy sets on X_i, $i = 1, 2, \ldots, n$

Q on $X_1 \times X_1 \times \cdots X_n$ is determined as follows.

$$\text{Here } s(S) = t\text{-conorm}$$

$$Q(x_1, x_2, \ldots, x_n) = A_1(x_1)sA_2(x_2)s \ldots sA_n(x_n) = S_{i=1}^{n} A_i(x_i)$$

Rule base in Fig. 6.1 is described as

> If X is A then Y is $B \equiv$ relationship between X and Y

Fuzzy relation R is determined as

$$R(x, y) = f(A(x), B(y)) \forall (x, y) \in X \times Y$$

$$f : [0, 1]^2 \to [0, 1]$$

Here, f can be fuzzy conjunction, fuzzy disjunction and fuzzy implication.

Fuzzy rule base can be presented in different formats:

Fuzzy graph

R_i : If X is A_i then Y is B_i is a fuzzy granule in $X \times Y$, $i = 1, \ldots, n$

Fuzzy implication rule base

R_i : If X is A_i then Y is B_i is a fuzzy implication, $i = 1, \ldots, n$

Functional fuzzy rule base

R_i : If X is A_i then $y = f_i(x)$ is a functional fuzzy rule, $i = 1, \ldots, n$

Fuzzy graph $\equiv R$ is a set of fuzzy granules

$$R = \bigcup_{i=1}^{N} R_i = \bigcup_{i=1}^{N} (A_i \times B_i)$$

General form of fuzzy graph is

$$R(x, y) = \mathop{S}_{i=1}^{N} [A_i(x) t B_i(y)]$$

Fuzzy implication

Fuzzy implication presents each fuzzy rule R_i. Relation R in this case is determined as

$$R = \bigcap_{i=1}^{N} R_i = \bigcap_{i=1}^{N} f_i = \bigcap_{i=1}^{N} (A_i \Rightarrow B_i)$$

In general form

$$R = \mathop{T}_{i=1}^{N} f_i(A_i(x), B_i(y))$$

Data base of FRBS contains universes, scaling functions of input and output variables, granulation of the universes membership functions.

- Granulation
    - granular constructs in the form of fuzzy points,
    - granules along different regions of the universes.
- Construction of membership functions:
    - expert knowledge,
    - learning from data.

Fuzzy inference in FRBS is defined as

$$B(y) = \sup\{A(x)tR(x,y)\} \; x \in X$$

X is A(fuzzy set on X)

(X,Y) is R(fuzzy relation on $X \times Y$)

Y is B(fuzzy set on Y)

Compositional rule of inference in FRBS is performed as

$$X \text{ is } A$$

$$(X,Y) \text{ is } R$$

$$Y \text{ is } B$$

$$B = A \circ R$$

$$X \text{ is } A$$

$$(X,Y) \text{ is } R$$

$$Y \text{ is } A \circ R$$

FRBS is universal approximator with algebraic product t-norm in antecedent, rule semantics via algebraic product, rule aggregation via ordinary sum, Gaussian membership functions, sup-min compositional rule of inference, point wise inputs and centroid defuzzification [353].

FRBS may be constructed by expert-based or data driven development. In first case knowledge provided by domain experts. In data-driven case the following procedure is used. Given a finite set of input/output pairs

$$\{(x_k, y_k), \ k = 1, \ldots, M\}$$

$$x_k = [x_{1k}, x_{2k}, \ldots, x_{nk}] \in R^n$$

$$z_k = [x_k, y_k] \in R^{n+1}, k = 1, \ldots, M$$

Clustering $z_k = [x_k, y_k] \in R^{n+1}, k = 1, \ldots, M$ (e.g., using FCM)

$$v_1, v_2, \ldots, v_N \quad v_i \in R^{n+1}, \quad i = 1, \ldots, n \text{ is obtained.}$$

We have to mention that fuzzy clusters ≡ fuzzy rules.

Main design issues of FRBS are consistency and completeness. Consistency of rules may be defined as follows.

$$R_i : \text{ If } X \text{ is } A_i \text{ then } Y \text{ is } B_i$$

$$R_j : \text{ If } X \text{ is } A_j \text{ then } Y \text{ is } B_j$$

$$\text{cons}(i, j) = \sum_{i=1}^{M} \{|B_i(y_k) - B_j(y_k)| \Rightarrow |A_i(x_k) - A_j(x_k)|\}$$

Completeness of rules is satisfied if all data points are represented through some fuzzy set

$$\max_{i=1,\ldots,M} A_i(x_k) > 0 \quad \text{for all } k = 1, 2, \ldots, M$$

and input space completely covered by fuzzy sets

$$\max_{i=1,\ldots,M} A_i(x_k) > \delta \quad \text{for all } k = 1, 2, \ldots, M$$

Chapter 7

Z-number Theory

The concept of a Z-number has a potential for many applications, especially in the realms of computation with probabilities and events described in NL. Of particular importance are applications in economics, decision analysis, risk assessment, prediction, anticipation, planning, biomedicine and rule-based manipulation of imprecise functions and relations.

Thus, real-world information is often represented in a framework of Z-number-based evaluations. Such information is referred to as Z-information. The main critical problems that naturally arises in processing Z-information are computation and reasoning with Z-information. The existing literature devoted to computation with Z-numbers is quite scarce.

Many numbers, especially, in fields such as economics and decision analysis, are in reality Z-numbers, but they are not treated as such, because it is much simpler to compute with numbers than with Z-numbers. Basically, the concept of a Z-number is a step toward formalization of the remarkable human capability to make rational decisions in an environment of imprecision and uncertainty.

7.1. Introduction

Decisions are based on information. To be useful, information must be reliable. Basically, the concept of a Z-number relates to the issue of reliability of information. A Z-number, Z, has two components, $Z = (A, B)$. The first component, A, is a restriction (constraint) on the values which a real-valued uncertain variable, X, is allowed to take. The second component, B, is a measure of reliability (certainty) of the first component. Typically, A and B are described in a natural language. The concept of a Z-number has a potential for many applications, especially in the realms of economics, decision analysis, risk assessment, prediction, anticipation and rule-based characterization of imprecise functions and relations.

In the real world, uncertainty is a pervasive phenomenon. Much of the information on which decisions are based is uncertain. Humans have a remarkable capability to make rational decisions based on information which is uncertain, imprecise and/or incomplete. Formalization of this capability, at least to some degree, is a challenge that is hard to meet. It is this challenge that motivates the concepts and ideas of Z-number theory.

The ordered triple (X, A, B) is referred to as a Z-valuation. A Z-valuation is equivalent to an assignment statement, X is (A, B). X is an uncertain variable if A is not a singleton. In a related way, uncertain computation is a system of computation in which the objects of computation are not values of variables but restrictions on values of variables. In Z-number theory, unless stated to the contrary, X is assumed to be a random variable. For convenience, A is referred to as a value of X, with the understanding that, strictly speaking, A is not a value of X but a restriction on the values which X can take. The second component, B, is referred to as certainty. Closely related to certainty are the concepts of sureness, confidence, reliability, strength of belief, probability, possibility, etc. When X is a random variable, certainty may be equated to probability. Informally, B may be interpreted as a response to the question: How sure are you that X is A? Typically, A and B are perception-based and are described in a natural language. A collection of Z-valuations is referred to as Z-information. It should be noted that much of everyday reasoning and decision-making is based, in effect, on Z-information. For purposes of computation, when A and B are described in a natural language, the meaning of A and B is precisiated (graduated) through association with membership functions, μ_A and μ_B, respectively (Fig. 7.1).

The membership function of A, μ_A, may be elicited by asking a succession of questions of the form: To what degree does the number, a, fit your perception of A? Example: To what degree does 50 min fit your perception of about 45 min? The same applies to B. The

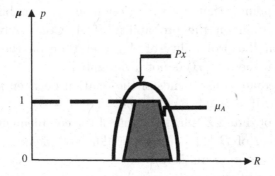

Fig. 7.1. Membership function of A and probability density function of X.

fuzzy set, A, may be interpreted as the possibility distribution of X. The concept of a Z-number may be generalized in various ways. In particular, X may be assumed to take values in R^n, in which case A is a Cartesian product of fuzzy numbers. Simple examples of Z-valuations are:

(anticipated budget deficit, close to 2 million dollars, very likely)
(price of oil in the near future, significantly over 100 dollars/barrel, very likely)

If X is a random variable, then X is A represents a fuzzy event in R. The probability of this event, p, may be expressed as [503]:

$$p = \int_R \mu_A(u)p_X(u)du$$

where p_X is the underlying (hidden) probability density of X. In effect, the Z-valuation (X, A, B) may be viewed as a restriction (generalized constraint) on X defined by:

$$\mathrm{Prob}(X \text{ is)is } B$$

What should be underscored is that in a Z-number, (A, B), the underlying probability distribution, p_X, is not known. What is known is a restriction on p_X which may be expressed as:

$$\int_R \mu_A(u)p_X(u)du \text{ is } B$$

A subtle point is that B is a restriction on the probability measure of A rather than on the probability of A. Conversely, if B is a restriction on the probability of A rather than on the probability measure of A, then (A, B) is not a Z-number.

An immediate consequence of the relation between p_X and B is the following. If $Z = (A, B)$ then $Z' = (A', 1 - B)$, where A' is the complement of A and Z' plays the role of the complement of Z. $1 - B$ is the antonym of B [445]. Example: The complement of $Z = (A;$ likely) is $Z' = ($not $A;$ unlikely).

An important qualitative attribute of a Z-number is informativeness. Generally, but not always, a Z-number is informative if its value has high specificity, that is, is tightly constrained [481], and its certainty is high. Informativeness is a desideratum when a Z-number is a basis for a decision. A basic question is: When is the informativeness of a Z-number sufficient to serve as a basis for an intelligent decision?

The concept of a Z-number is based on the concept of a fuzzy granule [518, 521, 542]. It should be noted that the concept of a Z-number is much more general than the concept of confidence interval in probability theory. There are some links between the concept of a Z-number, the concept of a fuzzy random number and the concept of a fuzzy random variable [87, 236, 326]. An alternative interpretation of the concept of a Z-number may be based on the concept of a fuzzy-set-valued random variable [518].

Assume that U is a finite set, $U = \{u_1, \ldots, u_n\}$. We can associate with X a possibility distribution, μ, and a probability distribution, p, expressed as

$$\mu = \mu_1/u_1 + \cdots + \mu_n/u_n$$

$$p = p_1 \backslash u_1 + \cdots + p_n \backslash u_n$$

in which μ_i/u_i means that μ_i, $i = 1, \ldots, n$, is the possibility that $X = u_i$. Similarly, $p_i \backslash u_i$ means that p_i is the probability that $X = u_i$.

The possibility distribution, μ, may be combined with the probability distribution, p, through what is referred to as confluence.

More concretely,

$$\mu : p = (\mu_1, p_1)/u_1 + \cdots + (\mu_n, p_n)/u_n$$

It is convenient to express a generalization of the basic if-then rule to Z-numbers in terms of Z-valuations. More concretely,

if (X, A_X, B_X) then (Y, A_Y, B_Y).

Example: If (anticipated budget deficit, about two million dollars, very likely) then (reduction in staff, about 10%, very likely)

7.2. Computation with Z-numbers

7.2.1. *Computation with continuous Z-numbers* [26]

Definition 7.1 (A Continuous Z-number [548]). A continuous Z-number is an ordered pair $Z = (A, B)$ where A is a continuous fuzzy number playing a role of a fuzzy constraint on values that a random variable X may take:

$$X \text{ is } A$$

and B is a continuous fuzzy number with a membership function $\mu_B :$ $[0, 1] \rightarrow [0, 1]$, playing a role of a fuzzy constraint on the probability measure of A:

$$P(A) \text{ is } B$$

concept of a continuous Z^+-number is closely related to the concept of a continuous Z-number. Given a continuous Z-number $Z = (A, B)$, Z^+-number Z^+ is a pair consisting of a continuous fuzzy number, A, and a random number R:

$$Z^+ = (A, R)$$

where A plays the same role as it does in a continuous Z-number $Z = (A, B)$ and R is described by pdf p_R, such that $P(A) = \int_{\mathcal{R}} \mu_A(x) p_R(x) dx$, $P(A) \in \text{supp}(B)$.

Definition 7.2 (Probability measure of a continuous fuzzy number [503]). Let X be a continuous random variable with pdf p. Let A be a continuous fuzzy number describing a possibilistic restriction on values of X. A probability measure of A denoted $P(A)$ is defined as

$$P(A) = \int_{\mathcal{R}} \mu_A(x)p(x)dx$$

Let $Z_1 = (A_1, B_1)$ and $Z_2 = (A_2, B_2)$ be continuous Z-numbers describing values of random variables X_1 and X_2. Assume that it is needed to compute $Z_{12} = Z_1 * Z_2, * \in \{+, -, \cdot, /\}$.

At the *first step* we compute $A_{12} = A_1 + A_2$ by using arithmetic of fuzzy numbers.

At the *second step* it is needed to compute discretized μ_{p_j}. Construction of continuous μ_{p_j} requires solving a complex variational problem. Discretization of μ_{p_j} leads to reducing of computational complexity. It allows to achieve a required tradeoff between accuracy and computational efficiency. We recall that "true" pdfs p_1 and p_2 are unknown, and we have to consider all the pdfs p_1 and p_2 satisfying the available restrictions:

$$\sum_{i=1}^{n_j} \mu_{A_j}(x_{ji})p_j(x_{ji}) \text{ is } B_j$$

described by a membership function as

$$\mu_{p_j}(p_j) = \mu_{B_j}\left(\sum_{i=1}^{n_j} \mu_{A_j}(x_{ji})p_j(x_{ji})\right), \quad j = 1,2 \qquad (7.1)$$

Thus, a fuzzy number $B_j, j = 1, 2$ plays the role of a soft constraint on a value of a probability measure of A_j. In other words, an element $h_j \in B_j, i = 1, 2$ is induced by some probability distribution p_j. We will use discretized version of $B_j, j = 1, 2$, i.e., the latter will be described as discrete fuzzy sets [25, 30]. This is more practical as we will deal with finite number of probability distributions underlying $B_j, j = 1, 2$. We will split up supp(B_j) into discrete elements $b_{jl}, l = 1, \ldots, m$ such that the spacing is the constant interval $\Delta b_j = b_{jl+1} - b_{jl}, l = 1, \ldots, m-1$. For example, consider $B_j = (0.6, 0.7, 0.8)$. Let us discretize the support of this fuzzy number into $m = 9$ points as follows: $b_{j1} = 0.6, b_{j2} = 0.625, \ldots, b_{j9} = 0.8$. Therefore, the following discretized fuzzy number will be obtained:

$$B = 0/0.6 + 0.25/0.625 + 0.5/0.65 + 0.75/0.675 + 1/0.7$$
$$+ 0.75/0.725 + 0.5/0.75 + 0.25/0.775 + 0/0.8$$

Any $b_l, l = 1, \ldots, m$ is induced by some probability distribution p_{jl} as $b_{jl} = \sum_{i=1}^{n_j} \mu_{A_j}(x_{ji}) p_{jl}(x_{ji})$.

In this case basic values $b_{jl} \in \text{supp}(B_j)$; $j = 1, 2$; $l = 1, \ldots, m$ of a fuzzy number $B_j, j = 1, 2$ are values of a probability measure of A_j, $b_{jl} = P(A_j)$ Thus, given b_{jl}, we have to find such pdf p_{jl} which satisfies $b_{jl} = (\mu_{A_j}(x_{j1}) p_{jl}(x_{j1}) + \mu_{A_j}(x_{j2}) p_{jl}(x_{j2}) + \cdots + \mu_{A_j}(x_{jn_j}) p_{jl}(x_{jn_j}))$. At the same time we know that p_{jl} has to satisfy:

$$\sum_{i=1}^{n_j} p_{jl}(x_{ji}) = 1, p_{jl}(x_{ji}) \geq 0$$

$$\sum_{i=1}^{n_j} p_{jl}(x_{ji}) x_{ji} = \frac{\sum_{i=1}^{n_j} \mu_{A_j}(x_{ji}) x_{ji}}{\sum_{i=1}^{n_j} \mu_{A_j}(x_{ji})} \quad \text{(compatibility conditions)}$$

Therefore, the following goal programming problem should be solved to find p_j

$$\mu_{A_j}(x_{j,1}) p_{jl}(x_{j,1}) + \mu_{A_j}(x_{j,2}) p_{jl}(x_{j,2}) + \cdots$$
$$+ \mu_{A_j}(x_{j,n_j}) p_{jl}(x_{j,n_j}) \rightarrow b_{jl} \quad (7.2)$$

subject to

$$p_{jl}(x_{j,1}) + p_{jl}(x_{j,2}) + \cdots + p_{jl}(x_{j,n_j}) = 1$$
$$p_{jl}(x_{j,1}), p_{jl}(x_{j,2}), \ldots, p_{jl}(x_{j,n_j}) \geq 0 \quad (7.3)$$

$$\sum_{i=1}^{n_j} p_{jl}(x_{j,i}) x_{j,i} = \frac{\sum_{i=1}^{n_j} \mu_{A_j}(x_{j,i}) x_{j,i}}{\sum_{i=1}^{n_j} \mu_{A_j}(x_{j,i})} \quad \text{(compatibility conditions)}$$

$$(7.4)$$

Let us now use new notations. At first, we fix $j \in \{1, 2\}$, choose points $x_{j,i}$ and denote $c_{j,i} = \mu_{A_j}(x_{j,i})$ for $i = 1, \ldots, n_j$. Second, we choose m and fix an index $l \in \{1, \ldots, m\}$. Third, we compute $\gamma_j =$

$\sum_{i=1}^{n_j} c_{j,i}$, $\beta_j = \frac{1}{\gamma_j} \sum_{i=1}^{n_j} c_{j,i} x_{j,i}$ and solve the linear goal programming problem with n_j variables $v_1, v_2, \ldots, v_{n_j}$:

$$c_{j,1} v_1 + c_{j,2} v_2 + \cdots + c_{j,n_j} v_{n_j} \to b_{j,l} \tag{7.5}$$

subject to

$$\begin{aligned} v_1 + v_2 + \cdots + v_{n_j} &= 1 \\ v_1, v_2, \ldots, v_n &\geq 0 \end{aligned} \tag{7.6}$$

$$x_{j,1} v_1 + x_{j,2} v_2 + \cdots + x_{j,n_j} v_{n_j} = \beta_j \tag{7.7}$$

Having obtained the solution vector $v_i, i = 1, 2, \ldots, n_j$ the values of the probabilities $p_{j,l}(x_{j,l})$, for the fixed indices j and l, are given by the found values v_i. Thus, each pdf $p_{j,l}(x_{j,l})$ is approximated at the same points $x_{j,l}, i = 1, 2, \ldots, n_j$ for all l. Next, as $p_{j,l}$ is obtained given $b_{j,l}$, the membership degree of $p_{j,l}$ in the fuzzy set of distributions is $\mu_{p_j}(p_{j,l}) = \mu_{B_j}(b_{j,l})$, $j = 1, 2$, that is $\mu_{p_j}(p_j) = \mu_{B_j}\left(\sum_{i=1}^{n_j} \mu_{A_j}(x_{j,i}) p_{j,l}(x_{j,i})\right)$. Thus, to construct a fuzzy set of pdfs p_j, it is needed to solve simple goal linear programming problems (7.5)–(7.7). Let us mention that discretized $p_{j,l}$ can be further approximated by continuous pdfs of the type assumed for the considered real-world problem (e.g., normal pdf).

At the *third step* we compute discretized $\mu_{p_{12}}$. The fuzzy sets of pdfs $p_{1l_1}, l_1 = 1, \ldots, m$ and $p_{2l_2}, l_2 = 1, \ldots, m$ induce the fuzzy set of convolutions p_{12s} with the membership function defined as

$$\mu_{p_{12}}(p_{12s}) = \max_{p_{1l_1}, p_{2l_2}} \left[\mu_{p_1}(p_{1l_1}) \wedge \mu_{p_2}(p_{2l_2}) \right] \tag{7.8}$$

subject to

$$p_{12s} = p_{1l_1} \circ p_{2l_2} \tag{7.9}$$

where $\wedge$ is min operation. Depending on operation convolution (7.9) is determined. Let us mention that the number of pdfs p_j is equal to the number of points of discretized B_j, m. Thus, to construct all the convolutions p_{12s}, one will consider m^2 possible combinations of p_1 and p_2. Therefore, the number of convolutions p_{12s} is in general equal to $m^2 : p_{12s}, s = 1, \ldots, m^2$. It is natural that the value of m is chosen on the basis of computational efficiency and accuracy trade-off.

At the *third step* we need to compute approximated $\mu_{B_{12}}$. At first we should compute probability measure of $A_{12} = A_1 * A_2$ given p_{12}, that is, compute probability measure $P(A_{12})$ of the fuzzy event X_{12} *is A_{12}* as

$$P(A_{12}) = \sum_{i=1}^{n} \mu_{A_{12}}(x_{12,i})p_{12s}(x_{12,i})$$

Thus, when p_{12} is known, $P(A_{12})$ is a number $P(A_{12}) = b_{12}$. However, what is only known is a fuzzy restriction on pdfs p_{12s} described by the membership function $\mu_{p_{12}}$. Therefore, $P(A_{12})$ will be a fuzzy set B_{12} with the membership function $\mu_{B_{12}}$ defined as follows:

$$\mu_{B_{12}}(b_{12s}) = \max \mu_{p_{12s}}(p_{12s}) \tag{7.10}$$

subject to

$$b_{12s} = \sum_{i=1}^{n} \mu_{A_{12}}(x_i)p_{12s}(x_i) \tag{7.11}$$

The sense of Eqs. (7.10)–(7.11) is as follows. In general, several convolutions p_{12s} may induce the same numeric value of probability measure $b_{12s} = P(A_{12})$ as a basic value of the fuzzy set B_{12}. Then, the membership degree $\mu_{B_{12}}(b_{12s})$ is equal to the maximum of the membership degrees $\mu_{p_{12s}}(p_{12s})$ of all the convolutions p_{12s} which induce the value of $b_{12s} = P(A_{12}) = \sum_{i=1}^{n} \mu_{A_{12}}(x_i)p_{12s}(x_i)$. As a result, $Z_{12} = Z_1 * Z_2$ is obtained as $Z_{12} = (A_{12}, B_{12})$.

Examples:

Computation of addition of continuous Z-numbers

Consider computation of $Z_{12} = Z_1 + Z_2$ for the following continuous Z-numbers with components as trapezoidal fuzzy numbers (TFNs): $Z_1 = ((1,2,3),(0.7,0.8,0.9))$, $Z_2 = ((7,8,9),(0.4,0.5,0.6))$. For clarity of presentation and better understanding for readers, suppose that the pdfs underlying the considered Z-numbers are normal pdfs. However, any other type of pdfs may be used (as it is mentioned above, there is a wide class of methods for operations over random variables in existence). The procedures of computation of $Z_{12} = Z_1 + Z_2$ are given below.

At the *first step*, we computed $A_{12} = A_1 + A_2$ [17, 236, 246]: $A_{12} = (8, 10, 12)$.

At the *second step* we realize, that "true" pdfs p_1 and p_2 are not exactly known, but only fuzzy restrictions $\mu_{p1}()$ and $\mu_{p2}()$ for p_1 and p_2 are available which are induced by B_1 and B_2 respectively. Therefore, we should extract distributions p_j, $j = 1, 2$ underlying B_j, $j = 1, 2$ and compute the membership degrees $\mu_{p_j}(p_j)$, $j = 1, 2$.

Next, we extract distributions p_{jl}. For simplicity, we omit compatibility condition. Let us consider an extraction of distributions p_{1l}. For example, let us uniformly split B_1 to 11 points and take the fourth basic value of the support of B_1 : $b_{1,4} = 0.76$. Also, taking into account that we deal with multiplication of membership degrees $\mu_{A_1}(x_{ji})$ by values of pdf $p_{1l}(x_{ji})$ to be found, we need to discretize A_1. Let us have the following discretization:

$$A_1 = 0/1 + 0.2/1.2 + 0.4/1.4 + 0.6/1.6 + 0.8/1.8$$
$$+ 1/2 + 0.8/2.2 + 0.6/2.4 + 0.4/2.6 + 0.2/2.8 + 0/3$$

Then by using the corresponding notations, we rewrite as follows:

$$0v_1 + 0.2v_2 + 0.4v_3 + 0.6v_4 + 0.8v_5 + 1v_6$$
$$+ 0.8v_7 + 0.6v_8 + 0.4v_9 + 0.2v_{10} + 0v_{11} \rightarrow 0.76$$

subject to

$$v_1 + v_2 + \cdots + v_{11} = 1$$
$$v_1, v_2, \ldots, v_{11} \geq 0$$

The solution of this problem is the following:

$$v_1 = 0, \quad v_2 = 0, \quad v_3 = 0.007, \quad v_4 = 0.12, \quad v_5 = 0.2, \quad v_6 = 0.25,$$
$$v_7 = 0.2, \quad v_8 = 0.14, \quad v_9 = 0.07, \quad v_{10} = 0.009, \quad v_{11} = 0$$

Therefore, the obtained probability distribution comes in the form

$$p_{1,4} = 0/1 + 0/1.2 + 0.007/1.4 + 0.12/1.6 + 0.2/1.8$$
$$+ 0.25/2 + 0.2/2.2 + 0.14/2.4 + 0.07/2.6 + 0.009/2.8 + 0/3$$

In a continuous framework, this distribution can be approximated by normal pdf $p_{1,4} \approx N(2, 0.31)$ as in this example we consider normal random variables. However, we can consider also different cases.

By using this procedure, given all the basic values $b_{1l}, l = 1, \ldots,$ 11 we have obtained all the probability distributions p_{1l}, $l = 1,$ $2, \ldots, 11$. Analogously, we obtain probability distributions $p_{2l}, l = 1, 2, \ldots, 11$. For this purpose, we use the following discretization:

$$A_2 = 0/7 + 0.2/7.2 + 0.4/7.4 + 0.6/7.6 + 0.8/7.8$$
$$+ 1/8 + 0.8/8.2 + 0.6/8.4 + 0.4/8.6 + 0.2/8.8 + 0/9$$

Also, let us consider $b_{2,4} = 0.46$. Then we will deal with the following problem:

$$0v_1 + 0.2v_2 + 0.4v_3 + 0.6v_4 + 0.8v_5 + 1v_6$$
$$+0.8v_7 + 0.6v_8 + 0.4v_9 + 0.2v_{10} + 0v_{11} \rightarrow 0.46$$

subject to

$$v_1 + v_2 + \cdots + v_{11} = 1$$
$$v_1, v_2, \ldots, v_{11} \geq 0$$

The solution of this problem is the following:

$$v_1 = 0.31, \quad v_2 = 0.53, \quad v_3 = 0.46, \quad v_4 = 0.39, \quad v_5 = 0.56,$$
$$v_6 = 0.35, \quad v_7 = 0.56, \quad v_8 = 0.39, \quad v_9 = 0.46, \quad v_{10} = 0.53,$$
$$v_{11} = 0.45$$

Therefore, the obtained probability distribution comes in the form

$$p_{2,4} = 0.31/0 + 0.53/1 + 0.46/2 + 0.39/3 + 0.56/4 + 0.35/5 + 0.56/6$$
$$+ 0.39/7 + 0.46/8 + 0.53/9 + 0.45/10$$

In a continuous framework, this distribution can be approximated by normal pdf $p_{2,4} \approx N(8, 0.76)$.

Let us now consider determination of the membership degrees $\mu_{p_1}(p_{1,4})$ and $\mu_{p_2}(p_{2,4})$. For example, given distributions p_{14} and p_{24}

considered above, one has

$$\int_{\mathcal{R}} \mu_{A_1}(x_1) \frac{1}{0.31\sqrt{2\pi}} e^{-\frac{(x_1-2)^2}{2(0.31)^2}} dx_1 = 0.76$$

$$\int_{\mathcal{R}} \mu_{A_2}(x_2) \frac{1}{0.91\sqrt{2\pi}} e^{-\frac{(x_2-8)^2}{2(0.76)^2}} dx_2 \approx 0.46$$

Therefore, $\mu_{p_1}(p_{1,4}) = \mu_{B_1}(0.76) = 0.6$ and $\mu_{p_2}(p_{2,4}) = \mu_{B_2}(0.46) = 0.6$. Analogously, we computed the membership degrees of for all the considered p_1 and p_2.

At the *third step*, given $\mu_{p_1}()$ and $\mu_{p_2}()$, we should determine the fuzzy restriction $\mu_{p_{12}}()$ over all the convolutions p_{12} (obtained from all the considered p_1 and p_2). For example, the membership degree of this fuzzy restriction for the convolution

$$
\begin{aligned}
p_{12s} &= p_{1,4} \circ p_{2,4} \\
&= N(2, 0.31) \circ N(8, 0.76) = N(2+8, \sqrt{0.31^2 + 0.76^2}) \\
&= N(10, 0.83) \text{ of } p_{14} \text{ and } p_{24} \text{ obtained above is}
\end{aligned}
$$

$$\mu_{p_{12}}(p_{12s}) = \mu_{p_1}(p_{1,4}) \wedge \mu_{p_2}(p_{2,4}) = 0.6 \wedge 0.6 = 0.6$$

Analogously, we computed the degrees for all the considered p_{12} (let us mention that a fuzzy set of distributions p_1 and a fuzzy set of distributions p_2 induce a fuzzy set of convolutions p_{12}). Let us mention that if there is some complexities in construction of p_{12} (for example, the case of product of random variables), we can construct discrete convolution p_{12} as it is done in Ref. [30].

As one can see, the optimization and computation problems solved above which lead to construction of $\mu_{p_{12}}$ is relatively simple. The use of discretized analogs reduces computation complexity as makes us free on solving specific nonlinear variational problem with some type of pdfs p_1 and p_2 (normal, exponential etc.) in a practical case.

At the *fourth step*, we proceed to construction of discretized B_{12} as a soft constraint on a probability measure $P(A_{12})$. First we need to compute values of probability measure $P(A_{12})$ for the obtained convolutions p_{12}. For example, $P(A_{12})$ computed with respect to

$p_{12} = N(10, 0.83)$ considered above is

$$P(A_{12}) = \int_{\mathcal{R}} \mu_{A_{12}}(x_{12}) \frac{1}{0.83\sqrt{2\pi}} e^{-\frac{(x-10)^2}{2(0.83)^2}} dx_{12} \approx 0.67$$

The computed $P(A_{12})$ is one possible value within the fuzzy restriction B_{12} to be constructed, and we can say that one basic value of B_{12} is found as $b_{12s} = 0.67$. We can write $\mu_{B_{12}}(b_{12} = \int_{\mathcal{R}} \mu_{A_{12}}(x_{12})p_{12}(x_{12})dx_{12}) = \mu_{p_{12}}(p_{12})$. Next, taking into account that $\mu_{p_{12}}(p_{12} = (10, 0.8)) = 0.6$, we obtain $\mu_{B_{12}}(b_{12s} = 0.67) = 0.6$ for $b_{12s} = \int_{\mathcal{R}} \mu_{A_{12}}(x_{12})\frac{1}{0.8\sqrt{2\pi}}e^{-\frac{(x_{12}-10)^2}{2(0.8)^2}} dx_{12}$. By carrying out analogous computations, we constructed B_{12}.

Thus, the result of addition $Z_{12} = (A_{12}, B_{12})$ is obtained. The obtained B_{12} can be approximated as a TFN $B_{12} = (0.62, 0.72, 0.79)$. Thus, the found result of addition is $Z_{12} = (A_{12}, B_{12}) \approx ((8, 10, 12), (0.62, 0.72, 0.79))$.

Computation of multiplication of continuous Z-number

Consider computation of $Z_{12} = Z_1 \cdot Z_2$ for the Z-numbers given in the previous example. First, $A_{12} = A_1 \cdot A_2$ is found. Second $R_1 \cdot R_2$ is found as convolution p_{12} of distributions determined. Let us mention that in contrast to addition and subtraction, the convolution of normal distributions for the case of multiplication is not a normal distribution. However, it can be approximated by a normal distribution $p_{12} \approx N(m_{12}, \sigma_{12})$ as it is shown in Ref. [475]. For the pdfs, considered in the previous example the convolution is

$$p_{12} \approx N(16, 5.5)$$

Second, it is needed to compute membership degrees $\mu_{p_1}(p_1)$ and $\mu_{p_2}(p_2)$ of p_1 and p_2. These distributions and membership degrees were determined in the previous example.

Third, the membership degrees of the convolutions p_{12} are obtained on the basis of $\mu_{p_1}(p_1)$ and $\mu_{p_2}(p_2)$ analogously to the cases of addition and subtraction. Indeed, $\mu_{p_{12}}(p_{12})$ for p_{12} obtained above is $\mu_{p_{12}}(p_{12}) = 0.6$.

Fourth, we compute B_{12}. For this, we compute values of probability measure $P(A_{12})$ with respect to the obtained convolutions p_{12}. For example, $P(A_{12})$ computed for p_{12} considered above is $P(A_{12}) = b_{12} = 0.67$.

Therefore, we can compute approximated $\mu_{B_{12}}$. For example, $\mu_{B_{12}}(b_{12} = 0.67) = 0.8$ Thus, $Z_{12} = (A_{12}, B_{12})$ as the result of multiplication is obtained. The obtained A_{12}, B_{12} can be approximated as TFNs $A_{12} = (7, 16, 27)$, $B_{12} = (0.35, 0.55, 0.75)$. Thus, the result is $Z_{12} \approx ((7, 16, 27), (0.35, 0.55, 0.75))$.

7.2.2.   *Computation with discrete Z-numbers* [15]

Definition 7.3 (A discrete fuzzy number [93, 94, 455, 461]).
A fuzzy subset A of the real line $\mathcal{R}$ with membership function $\mu_A :$ $\mathcal{R} \to [0, 1]$ is a discrete fuzzy number if its support is finite, i.e., there exist $x_1, \ldots, x_n \in \mathcal{R}$ with $x_1 < x_2 < \cdots < x_n$, such that $\text{supp}(A) = \{x_1, \ldots, x_n\}$ and there exist natural numbers s, t with $1 \leq s \leq t \leq n$ satisfying the following conditions:

1. $\mu_A(x_i) = 1$ for any natural number i with $s \leq i \leq t$,
2. $\mu_A(x_i) \leq \mu_A(x_j)$ for each natural numbers i, j with $1 \leq i \leq j \leq s$,
3. $\mu_A(x_i) \geq \mu_A(x_j)$ for each natural numbers i, j with $t \leq i \leq j \leq n$.

Definition 7.4 (Probability measure of a discrete fuzzy number [25, 503]). Let A be a discrete fuzzy number. A probability measure of A denoted $P(A)$ is defined as

$$P(A) = \sum_{i=1}^{n} \mu_A(x_i)p(x_i)$$

$$= \mu_A(x_{j1})p_j(x_{j1}) + \mu_A(x_{j2})p_j(x_{j2}) + \cdots + \mu_A(x_{jn_j})p_j(x_{jn_j})$$

Below we present a definition of addition of discrete fuzzy numbers suggested in Ref. [17–20]. In this definition, non-interactive fuzzy numbers are considered.

Definition 7.5 (Addition of discrete fuzzy numbers [93, 94, 455, 461]). For discrete fuzzy numbers A_1, A_2 their addition $A_{12} =$

$A_1 + A_2$ is the discrete fuzzy number whose α-cut is defined as

$$A_{12}^\alpha = \{x \in \{\text{supp}(A_1) + \text{supp}(A_2)\}| \min\{A_1^\alpha + A_2^\alpha\}$$
$$\leq x \leq \max\{A_1^\alpha + A_2^\alpha\}\},$$

where $\text{supp}(A_1) + \text{supp}(A_2) = \{x_1 + x_2 | x_j \in \text{supp}(A_j), j = 1, 2\}$, $\min\{A_1^\alpha + A_2^\alpha\} = \min\{x_1 + x_2 | x_j \in A_j^\alpha), j = 1, 2\}$, $\max\{A_1^\alpha + A_2^\alpha\} = \max\{x_1 + x_2 | x_j \in A_j^\alpha, j = 1, 2\}$ and the membership function is defined as

$$\mu_{A_1+A_2}(x) = \sup\{\alpha \in [0, 1] | x \in \{A_1^\alpha + A_2^\alpha\}\}$$

The authors of the present paper suggest several definitions be used in the suggested arithmetic of discrete Z-numbers (Definitions 7.6–7.10). In these definitions, as well as in Definition 7.5, non-interactive fuzzy numbers are considered.

Definition 7.6 (Standard subtraction of discrete fuzzy numbers). For discrete fuzzy numbers A_1, A_2 their standard subtraction $A_{12} = A_1 - A_2$ is the discrete fuzzy number whose α-cut is defined as

$$A_j^\alpha = \{x \in \{\text{supp}(A_1) - \text{supp}(A_2)\}| \min\{A_1^\alpha - A_2^\alpha\}$$
$$\leq x \leq \max\{A_1^\alpha - A_2^\alpha\}\}$$

where

$$\text{supp}(A_1) - \text{supp}(A_2) = \{x_1 - x_2 | x_j \in \text{supp}(A_j), j = 1, 2\}$$
$$\min\{A_1^\alpha - A_2^\alpha\} = \min\{x_1 - x_2 | x_j \in A_j^\alpha, j = 1, 2\}$$
$$\max\{A_1^\alpha - A_2^\alpha\} = \max\{x_1 - x_2 | x_j \in A_j^\alpha, j = 1, 2\}$$

and the membership function is defined as

$$\mu_{A_1-A_2}(x) = \sup\{\alpha \in [0, 1] | x \in \{A_1^\alpha - A_2^\alpha\}\}$$

For the standard subtraction one has:

$$A_2 + (A_1 - A_2) \neq A_1.$$

Definition 7.7 (Hukuhara difference of discrete fuzzy numbers). For discrete fuzzy numbers A_1, A_2 their Hukuhara difference denoted $A_1 -_h A_2$ is the discrete fuzzy number A_{12} such that

$$A_1 = A_2 + A_{12}$$

Hukuhara difference exists only if $n \geq m$. Denote $\text{supp}(A_1) = \{x_{11}, \ldots, x_{1n}\}$, $A_1^\alpha = \{x_{1\,1_\alpha}^\alpha, \ldots, x_{1\,n_\alpha}^\alpha\}, 1_\alpha, n_\alpha \in \{1, \ldots, n\}$ and $\text{supp}(A_2) = \{x_{21}, \ldots, x_{2m}\}$, $A_2^\alpha = \{x_{2\,1_\alpha}^\alpha, \ldots, x_{2\,m_\alpha}^\alpha\}, 1_\alpha, m_\alpha \in \{1, \ldots, m\}$. Hukuhara difference A_{12}, where $\text{supp}(A_{12}) = \{x_1, \ldots, x_k\}$, $A_{12}^\alpha = \{x_{l_\alpha}, \ldots, x_{r_\alpha}\}, l_\alpha, r_\alpha \in \{1, \ldots, k\}$ exists if and only if cardinality of A_1^α is not lower than that of A_2^α for any $\alpha \in (0,1]$, and the following is satisfied:

$$A_1^\alpha = \bigcup_{i=1}^{r_\alpha - l_\alpha + 1} A_{1,i}^\alpha$$

where $A_{1,i}^\alpha = \{x_{1\,i1}^\alpha, \ldots, x_{1\,im}^\alpha\}, x_{1\,i(j+1)}^\alpha - x_{1\,ij}^\alpha = x_{2(j+1)}^\alpha - x_{2j}^\alpha, j = 1, \ldots, m; \alpha \in (0,1]$.

Definition 7.8 (Multiplication of discrete fuzzy numbers). For discrete fuzzy numbers A_1, A_2 their multiplication $A_{12} = A_1 \cdot A_2$ is the discrete fuzzy number whose α-cut is defined as

$$A_j^\alpha = \{x \in \{\text{supp}(A_1) \cdot \text{supp}(A_2)\}| \min\{A_1^\alpha \cdot A_2^\alpha\}$$
$$\leq x \leq \max\{A_1^\alpha \cdot A_2^\alpha\}\}$$

where

$$\text{supp}(A_1) \cdot \text{supp}(A_2) = \{x_1 \cdot x_2 | x_j \in \text{supp}(A_j), j = 1, 2\}$$
$$\min\{A_1^\alpha \cdot A_2^\alpha\} = \min\{x_1 \cdot x_2 | x_j \in A_j^\alpha, j = 1, 2\}$$
$$\max\{A_1^\alpha \cdot A_2^\alpha\} = \max\{x_1 \cdot x_2 | x_j \in A_j^\alpha, j = 1, 2\}$$

and the membership function is defined as

$$\mu_{A_1 \cdot A_2}(x) = \sup\{\alpha \in [0,1] | x \in \{A_1^\alpha \cdot A_2^\alpha\}\}$$

Definition 7.9 (Standard division of discrete fuzzy numbers). For discrete fuzzy numbers A_1, A_2 given that $0 \notin \text{supp}(A_2)$ their standard division $A_{12} = A_1/A_2$ is the discrete fuzzy number whose

α-cut is defined as

$$A_{12}^\alpha = \{x \in \{\text{supp}(A_1)/\text{supp}(A_2)\}|\min\{A_1^\alpha/A_2^\alpha\}$$
$$\leq x \leq \max\{A_1^\alpha/A_2^\alpha\}\}$$

where

$$\text{supp}(A_1)/\text{supp}(A_2) = \{x_1/x_2|x_j \in \text{supp}(A_j), j = 1, 2\}$$
$$\min\{A_1^\alpha/A_2^\alpha\} = \min\{x_1/x_2|x_j \in A_j^\alpha, j = 1, 2\}$$
$$\max\{A_1^\alpha/A_2^\alpha\} = \max\{x_1/x_2|x_j \in \text{supp}(A_j), j = 1, 2\}$$

and the membership function is defined as

$$\mu_{A_1/A_2}(x) = \sup\{\alpha \in [0,1]|x \in \{A_1^\alpha/A_2^\alpha\}\}$$

For the standard division one has:

$$A_2 \cdot (A_1/A_2) \neq A_1$$

Definition 7.10 (A discrete Z-number [15, 25, 30]). A discrete Z-number is an ordered pair $Z = (A, B)$ where A is a discrete fuzzy number playing a role of a fuzzy constraint on values that a random variable X may take:

$$X \text{ is } A$$

and B is a discrete fuzzy number with a membership function μ_B : $\{b_1, \ldots, b_n\} \rightarrow [0,1]$, $\{b_1, \ldots, b_n\} \subset [0,1]$, playing a role of a fuzzy constraint on the probability measure of A

$$P(A) \text{ is } B.$$

Let $Z_1 = (A_1, B_1)$ and $Z_2 = (A_2, B_2)$ be discrete Z-numbers describing imperfect information about values of real-valued random variables X_1 and X_2. Consider the problem of computation of addition $Z_{12} = Z_1 + Z_2$.

The addition $A_1 + A_2$ of discrete fuzzy numbers is defined in accordance with Definition 7.5.

Z-numbers are based on the use of a sets of linguistic terms. Such sets can be represented by ordinal linguistic scales. In the considered case, one may consider the ordinal linguistic scales with, for example, eleven linguistic terms $\mathcal{M} = \{VL, L, \ldots, M, \ldots, H, VH\}$, where the letters denote linguistic terms *very low, low, ..., medium, ..., high, very high* and $\mathcal{N} = \{U, NVL, \ldots, L, \ldots, VL, EL\}$, where the letters denote linguistic terms *unlikely, not very likely, ..., likely, ..., very likely, extremely likely.* The terms of the considered scales are ordered in an increasing order: $VL \prec L \prec \cdots \prec M \prec \cdots \prec H \prec VH$ and $U \prec NVL \prec \cdots \prec L \prec \cdots \prec VL \prec EL$. Therefore, one can consecutively number the linguistic terms in the considered scales and arrive at an ordered set $L = \{0, 1, \ldots, n\}$.

Consideration of discrete Z-numbers instead of their continuous counterparts also allows us to significantly improve tradeoff between adequacy and universality from the one side and computational complexity from the other side. Concerning loss of accuracy as a result of proceeding from continuous forms of membership functions and probability distributions to discrete forms, in many problems it may not be significant from qualitative point of view. As it will be shown, operations over discrete Z-numbers involve only linear programming problems but not nonlinear variational problems.

Computation with discrete Z-numbers is conducted by using (7.1)–(7.11). Let us consider standard subtraction $Z_{12} = Z_1 - Z_2$ of discrete Z-numbers $Z_1 = (A_1, B_1)$ and $Z_2 = (A_2, B_2)$.

First, we construct the fuzzy sets

$$\mu_{p_{jl}}(p_{jl}) == \mu_{B_j}\left(\sum_{k=1}^{n_j} \mu_{A_j}(x_{jk})p_{jl}(x_{jk})\right),$$

$j = 1, 2,\ l = 1, \ldots, m$ by solving (7.5)–(7.7).

Second, the fuzzy set of convolutions $p_{12s}, s = 1, \ldots, m^2$, with the membership function constructed by solving (7.8)–(7.9), where convolution is computed.

At the *third step,* we proceed to construction of B_{12}. First we should compute probability measure of $A_{12} = A_1 - A_2$ given p_{12}, i.e., to compute probability of the fuzzy event X is A_{12}. Finally, we compute a fuzzy set B_{12} according to (7.10)–(7.11). As a result, $Z_{12} = Z_1 - Z_2$ is obtained as $Z_{12} = (A_{12}, B_{12})$.

Let us consider multiplication $Z_{12} = Z_1 \cdot Z_2$ of $Z_1 = (A_1, B_1)$ and $Z_2 = (A_2, B_2)$. We construct the fuzzy sets $\mu_{p_{jl}}(p_{jl})$, $l = 1, \ldots, m$, and the fuzzy set of convolutions p_{12s}, $s = 1, \ldots, m^2$, with the membership function defined by solving (7.8)–(7.9).

At the next step probability measure of $A_{12} = A_1 \cdot A_2$ is computed Finally, a fuzzy set B_{12} is constructed according to (7.10)–(7.11). As a result, $Z_{12} = Z_1 \cdot Z_2$ is obtained as $Z_{12} = (A_{12}, B_{12})$.

Let us consider standard division $Z_{12} = Z_1/Z_2$ of $Z_1 = (A_1, B_1)$ and $Z_2 = (A_2, B_2)$, where $0 \notin \mathrm{supp}(A_2)$.

We construct the fuzzy sets $\mu_{p_{jl}}(p_{jl})$, $j = 1, 2$, $l = 1, \ldots, m$ and the fuzzy set of convolutions p_{12s}, $s = 1, \ldots, m^2$, with the membership function defined by solving (7.8)–(7.9).

At the next step probability measure of A_{12} is computed.

Finally, a fuzzy set B_{12} is constructed according to (7.10)–(7.11). As a result, $Z_{12} = Z_1/Z_2$ is obtained as $Z_{12} = (A_{12}, B_{12})$.

Examples: Let us consider computation of an addition $Z_{12} = Z_1 + Z_2$ of two discrete Z-numbers $Z_1 = (A_1, B_1)$ and $Z_2 = (A_2, B_2)$ given:

$$A_1 = 0/1 + 0.3/2 + 0.5/3 + 0.6/4 + 0.7/5 + 0.8/6 + 0.9/7 + 1/8$$
$$+ 0.8/9 + 0.6/10 + 0/11$$

$$B_1 = 0/0 + 0.5/0.1 + 0.8/0.2 + 1/0.3 + 0.8/0.4 + 0.7/0.5 + 0.6/0.6$$
$$+ 0.4/0.7 + 0.2/0.8 + 0.1/0.6 + 0/1;$$

$$A_2 = 0/1 + 0.5/2 + 0.8/3 + 1/4 + 0.8/5 + 0.7/6 + 0.6/7 + 0.4/8$$
$$+ 0.2/9 + 0.1/10 + 0/11$$

$$B_2 = 0/0 + 0.3/0.1 + 0.5/0.2 + 0.6/0.3 + 0.7/0.4 + 0.8/0.5 + 0.9/0.6$$
$$+ 1/0.7 + 0.9/0.8 + 0.8/0.6 + 0/1.$$

At the *first step* of computation of Z_{12} we proceed to the discrete Z^+-numbers. Let us consider $Z_1^+ = (A_1, R_1)$ and $Z_2^+ = (A_2, R_2)$ where R_1 and R_2 are the following discrete probability distributions R_1 and R_2:

$$p_1 = 0.27\backslash 1 + 0\backslash 2 + 0\backslash 3 + 0.0027\backslash 4 + 0.04\backslash 5 + 0.075\backslash 6 + 0.11\backslash 7$$
$$+ 0.15\backslash 8 + 0.075\backslash 9 + 0.0027\backslash 10 + 0.27\backslash 11$$

$$p_2 = 0.09\backslash 1 + 0\backslash 2 + 0.18\backslash 3 + 0.32\backslash 4 + 0.18\backslash 5 + 0.1\backslash 6 + 0.036\backslash 7$$
$$+ 0\backslash 8 + 0\backslash 9 + 0\backslash 10 + 0.09\backslash 11$$

At the *second step* we should determine the discrete Z^+-number

$$Z_{12}^+ = (A_1 + A_2, R_1 + R_2)$$

In accordance with the approach suggested, here we first compute $A_{12} = A_1 + A_2$.

$$A_{12} = \bigcup_{\alpha \in [0,1]} \alpha A_{12}^\alpha$$

where $A_{12}^\alpha = \{x \in \{\mathrm{supp}(A_1) + \mathrm{supp}(A_2)\} | \min\{A_1^\alpha + A_2^\alpha\} \le x \le \max\{A_1^\alpha + A_2^\alpha\}\}$. We will use $\alpha = 0, 0.1, \ldots, 1$.

The resulting A_{12} is found as follows

$$A_{12} = 0/1 + 0/2 + 0.19/3 + 0.36/4 + 0.5/5 + 0.58/6 + 0.65/7$$
$$+ 0.73/8 + 0.8/9 + 0.87/10 + 0.93/11 + 1/12 + 0.9/13$$
$$+ 0.8/14 + 0.73/15 + 0.7/16 + 0.6/17 + 0.45/18 + 0.3/19$$
$$+ 0.17/20 + 0.086/21$$

Next we compute $R_1 + R_2$ as a convolution $p_{12} = p_1 \circ p_2$ of the considered p_1 and p_2.

For example, compute $p_{12}(x)$ for $x = 4$. The latter can be $x = x_{11} + x_{23} = 1 + 3 = 4$, $x = x_{13} + x_{21} = 3 + 1 = 4$ or $x = x_{12} + x_{22} = 2 + 2 = 4$. Then

$$p_{12}(4) = p_1(1)p_2(3) + p_1(3)p_2(1) + p_1(2)p_2(2)$$
$$= 0.27 \cdot 0.18 + 0 \cdot 0.09 + 0 \cdot 0 = 0.0486$$

The p_{12} obtained is given below:

$$p_{12} = 0\backslash 1 + 0.0243\backslash 2 + 0\backslash 3 + 0.0486\backslash 4 + \cdots$$
$$+ 0.007\backslash 19 + 0.0002\backslash 20 + 0.0243\backslash 21.$$

Thus, $Z_{12}^+ = (A_1 + A_2, R_1 + R_2) = (A_1 + A_2, p_{12})$ is obtained.

At the *second step* we realize, that "true" probability distributions p_1 and p_2 are not exactly known, but only fuzzy restrictions $\mu_{p_1}()$ and $\mu_{p_2}()$ for p_1 and p_2 are available which are induced by $\tilde{B}_1$ and $\tilde{B}_2$ respectively. We compute the membership degrees $\mu_{p_j}(p_j)$, $j = 1, 2$, of the fuzzy restrictions given the solutions of the goal linear programming problems.

Let us consider determination of the membership degrees $\mu_{p_1}(p_1)$ and $\mu_{p_2}(p_2)$ for distributions p_1 and p_2 considered above. It is known that

$$\mu_{p_1}(p_1) = \mu_{B_1}\left(\sum_{k=1}^{n_1} \mu_{A_1}(x_{1k})p_1(x_{1k})\right)$$

and as for p_1 considered above we have

$$\sum_{k=1}^{n_1} \mu_{A_1}(x_{1k})p_1(x_{1k})$$

$$= 0 \cdot 0.27 + 0.3 \cdot 0 + 0.5 \cdot 0 + 0.6 \cdot 0.003 + 0.7 \cdot 0.04 + 8 \cdot 0.075$$

$$+ 0.9 \cdot 0.11 + 1 \cdot 0.15 + 0.8 \cdot 0.075 + 0.6 \cdot 0.002 + 0 \cdot 0.27 = 0.4$$

then $\mu_{p_1}(p_1) = \mu_{B_1}(0.4) = 0.8$.

Analogously we find that $\mu_{p_2}(p_2) = 1$ for p_2 considered above.

Finally, we compute the membership degrees of for all the considered p_1 and p_2.

At the *third step*, we should determine the fuzzy restriction $\mu_{p_{12}}()$ over all the convolutions p_{12} obtained from all the considered p_1 and p_2.

It is clear that the fuzzy restriction $\mu_{p_{12}}()$ is induced fuzzy restrictions $\mu_{p_1}()$ and $\mu_{p_2}()$.

For example, the membership degree of this fuzzy restriction for the convolution p_{12} obtained above is

$$\mu_{p_{12}}(p_{12}) = \mu_{p_1}(p_1) \wedge \mu_{p_2}(p_2) = 0.8 \wedge 1 = 0.8.$$

Analogously, we computed the degrees for all the considered p_{12}.

At the *fourth step*, we should proceed to construction of B_{12} as a soft constraint on a probability measure $P(\Lambda_{12})$. First we need to compute values of probability measure $P(A_{12})$ based on Definition 7.4 by using the obtained convolutions p_{12}.

For example, $P(A_{12})$ computed with respect to p_{12} considered above is

$$P(A_{12}) = \sum_{k=1}^{n_1} \mu_{A_{12}}(x_{12k})p_{12}(x_{12k}) = 0 \cdot 0 + 0 \cdot 0.243 + 0.19 \cdot 0$$
$$+ 0.36 \cdot 0.0486 + 0.087 \cdot 0.5 + \cdots + 0.086 \cdot 0.243 = 0.63$$

As the computed $P(A_{12})$ is one possible value of probability measure within the fuzzy restriction B_{12} to be constructed, we can say that one basic value of B_{12} is found as $b_{12} = 0.63$.

Now we recall that

$$\mu_{B_{12}}\left(b_{12} = \sum_{k=1}^{n_1} \mu_{A_{12}}(x_{12k})p_{12}(x_{12k})\right) = = \mu_{p_{12}}(p_{12})$$

Then given $\mu_{p_{12}}(p_{12}) = 0.8$, we obtain $\mu_{B_{12}}(b_{12} = 0.63) = 0.8$ for

$$b_{12} = \sum_{k=1}^{n_1} \mu_{A_{12}}(x_{12k})p_{12}(x_{12k})$$

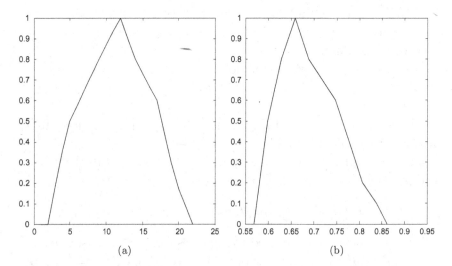

Fig. 7.2. The results of addition of the discrete Z-numbers: (a) A_{12}, (b) B_{12}.

By carrying out analogous computations, we constructed $\tilde{B}_{12}$ as follows:

$$B_{12} = 0/0.56 + 0.5/0.60 + 0.8/0.63 + 1/0.66 + 0.8/0.69 + 0.7/0.72$$
$$+ 0.6/0.75 + 0.4/0.78 + 0.2/0.81 + 0.1/0.84 + 0/0.86 + 0/1$$

Thus, the result of addition $Z_{12} = (A_{12}, B_{12})$ is obtained, where A_{12}, B_{12} are shown in Fig. 7.2.

7.3. Standard Division of Discrete Z-numbers

Let us consider standard division $Z_{12} = Z_1/Z_2$ of $Z_1 = (A_1, B_1)$ and $Z_2 = (A_2, B_2)$, where $0 \notin \text{supp}(A_2)$ considered in previous example.

Let us consider standard division of the considered Z-numbers.

Again, first we compute $A_{12} = A_1/A_2$ and convolution $p_{12} = p_1 \circ p_1$.

The obtained results are shown below:

the fuzzy number $A_{12} = A_1/A_2$:

$$A_{12} = A_1/A_2$$
$$= 0.07/0.36 + 0.1/0.375 + \cdots + 1/1.6 + \cdots + 0.17/100 + 0/121,$$

the convolution:

$$p_{12} = 0.025\backslash 1 + 0\backslash 2 + \cdots + 0\backslash 1.6 + \cdots + 0\backslash 100 + 0.025\backslash 121$$

Next we compute membership degrees $\mu_{p_1}(p_1)$ and $\mu_{p_2}(p_2)$ and the membership degrees $\mu_{p_{12}}(p_{12})$ of the convolutions p_{12}.

Given membership degrees $\mu_{p_{12}}(p_{12})$ of the convolutions p_{12}, we compute values of probability measure $P(A_{12})$ by using Definition 7.4.

For example, $P(A_{12})$ computed on the base of p_{12} considered above is as follows:

$$P(A_{12}) = b_{12} = 0.44$$

At the final stage, we construct B_{12}. For example, $\mu_{B_{12}}(0.44) = 0.8$.

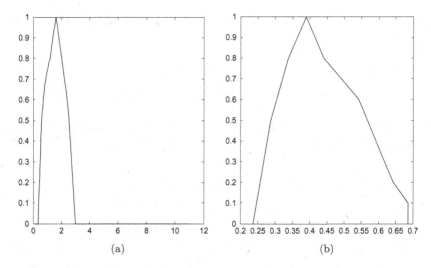

Fig. 7.3. The results of division of the discrete Z-numbers: (a) A_{12}, (b) B_{12}.

The constructed B_{12} is given below:

$$B_{12} = 0/0.24 + 0.5/0.29 + 0.8/0.34 + 1/0.38 + 0.8/0.44 + 0.7/0.49$$
$$+ 0.6/0.54 + 0.4/0.59 + 0.2/0.64$$
$$+ 0.1/0.69 + 0/0.68$$

The result $Z_{12} = (A_{12}, B_{12})$ of the standard division is obtained. A_{12}, B_{12} are shown in Fig. 7.3.

Chapter 8

Generalized Theory of Uncertainty

Uncertainty is an attribute of information. The path-breaking work of Shannon has led to a universal acceptance of the thesis that information is statistical in nature. Concomitantly, existing theories of uncertainty are based on probability theory. The generalized theory of uncertainty (GTU) departs from existing theories in essential ways [542].

First, the thesis that information is statistical in nature is replaced by a much more general thesis that information is a generalized constraint, with statistical uncertainty being a special, albeit important case. Equating information to a generalized constraint is the fundamental thesis of GTU.

Second, bivalence is abandoned throughout GTU, and the foundation of GTU is shifted from bivalent logic to fuzzy logic. As a consequence, in GTU everything is or is allowed to be a matter of degree or, equivalently, fuzzy. Concomitantly, all variables are, or are allowed to be granular, with a granule being a clump of values drawn together by a generalized constraint.

And third, one of the principal objectives of GTU is achievement of NL-capability, that is, the capability to operate on information described in natural language. NL-capability has high importance because much of human knowledge, including knowledge about probabilities, is described in natural language. NL-capability is the focus of attention in the present chapter. The centerpiece of GTU is the concept of a generalized constraint. The concept of a generalized constraint is motivated by the fact that most real-world constraints are elastic rather than rigid, and have a complex structure even when simple in appearance. The chapter concludes with examples of computation with uncertain information described in natural language.

213

8.1. Introduction

There is a deep-seated tradition in science of dealing with uncertainty whatever its form and nature-through the use of probability theory. Successes of this tradition are undeniable. But as we move further into the age of machine intelligence and automated decision-making, a basic limitation of probability theory becomes a serious problem. More specifically, in large measure, standard probability theory, call it PT, cannot deal with information described in natural language; that is, to put it simply, PT does not have NL-capability. Here are a few relatively simple examples:

Trip planning: I am planning to drive from Berkeley to Santa Barbara, with stopover for lunch in Monterey. Usually, it takes about two hours to get to Monterey. Usually, it takes about one hour to have lunch. It is likely that it will take about five hours to get from Monterey to Santa Barbara. At what time should I leave Berkeley to get to Santa Barbara, with high probability, before about 6 pm?

Balls-in-box: A box contains about 20 balls of various sizes. Most are large. What is the number of small balls? What is the probability that a ball drawn at random is neither small nor large?

Temperature: Usually, the temperature is not very low and not very high. What is the average temperature? *Tall Swedes*: Most Swedes are tall. How many are short? What is the average height of Swedes?

Flight delay: Usually, most United Airlines flights from San Francisco leave on time. What is the probability that my flight will be delayed?

Maximization: f is a function from reals to reals described as: If X is small then Y is small; if X is medium then Y is large; if X is large then Y is small. What is the maximum of f?

Expected value: X is a real-valued random variable. Usually, X is much larger than approximately a and much smaller than approximately b, where a and b are real numbers, with $a < b$. What is the expected value of X?

Vera's age: Vera has a son who is in mid-20s, and a daughter, who is in mid-30s. What is Vera's age? This example differs from other examples in that to answer the question what is needed is information drawn from world knowledge. More specifically: (a) child-bearing age ranges from about 16 to about 42; and (b) age of mother is the sum of the age of child and the age of mother when the child was born.

The generalized theory of uncertainty (GTU) differs from other theories in three important respects. First, the thesis that information is statistical in nature is replaced by a much more general thesis that information is a generalized constraint [528], with statistical uncertainty being a special, albeit important case. Equating information to a generalized constraint is the fundamental thesis of GTU. In symbolic form, the thesis may be expressed as

$$I(X) = GC(X)$$

where X is a variable taking values in U; $I(X)$ is information about X; and $GC(X)$ is a generalized constraint on X.

Second, bivalence is abandoned throughout GTU, and the foundation of GTU is shifted from bivalent logic to fuzzy logic [332, 513]. As a consequence, in GTU everything is or is allowed to be a matter of degree or, equivalently, fuzzy. Concomitantly, all variables are, or are allowed to be granular, with a granule being a clump of values defined by a generalized constraint [517, 518, 534, 536].

And third, one of the principal objectives of GTU is achievement of NL-capability. Why is NL-capability an important capability? Principally because much of human knowledge and real-world information is expressed in natural language. Basically, a natural language is a system for describing perceptions. Perceptions are intrinsically imprecise, reflecting the bounded ability of human sensory organs, and ultimately the brain, to resolve detail and store information. Imprecision of perception is passed on to natural languages. It is this imprecision that severely limits the ability of PT to deal with information described in natural language. NL-capability of GTU is the focus of attention in the present study.

A concomitant of GTU's NL-capability is its ability to deal with perception-based information (Fig. 8.1). Much of information about subjective probabilities is perception-based.

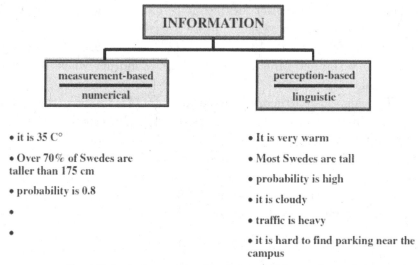

• measurement-based information may be viewed as a special case of perception-based information

• perception-based information is intrinsically imprecise

Fig. 8.1. Measurement-based versus perception-based information.

The centerpiece of GTU is the concept of a generalized constraint — a concept drawn from fuzzy logic. The principal distinguishing features of fuzzy logic are (a) graduation and (b) granulation. More specifically, in fuzzy logic everything is, or is allowed to be, graduated, that is, be a matter of degree or, more or less equivalently, fuzzy. Furthermore, in fuzzy logic all variables are allowed to be granulated, with a granule being a clump of values drawn together by indistinguishability, similarity, proximity or functionality (Fig. 8.2). Graduation and granulation underline the concept of a linguistic variable [511] — a concept which plays a key role in almost all applications of fuzzy logic [495].

More fundamentally, graduation and granulation have a position of centrality in human cognition. This is one of the basic reasons why fuzzy logic may be viewed in a model of human reasoning.

NL-Computation is the core of (precisiated natural language PNL) [539, 540]. Basically, PNL is a fuzzy-logic-based system for

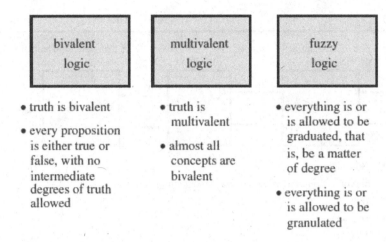

Fig. 8.2. Logical systems.

computation and deduction with information described in natural language. A forerunner of PNL is PRUF [527]. We begin with a brief exposition of the basics of NL-Computation in the context of GTU.

8.2. The Concept of NL-Computation

NL-Computation has a position of centrality in GTU. The basic structure of NL-Computation, viewed as the core of PNL, is shown in Fig. 8.3. The point of departure is a given proposition or, more generally, a system of propositions, p, which constitutes the initial information set described in a natural language (INL). In addition, what is given is a query, q, expressed in a natural language (QNL). The problem is to compute an answer to q given p, $\mathrm{ans}(q|p)$. In GTU, deduction of $\mathrm{ans}(q|p)$ involves these modules:

(a) precisiation module, P;
(b) protoform module, Pr; and
(c) computation/deduction module, C/D.

Informally, precisiation is an operation which precisiates its operand. The operand and the result of precisiation are referred to as precisiend and precisiand, respectively.

PRECISIATED NATURAL LANGUAGE (PNL)

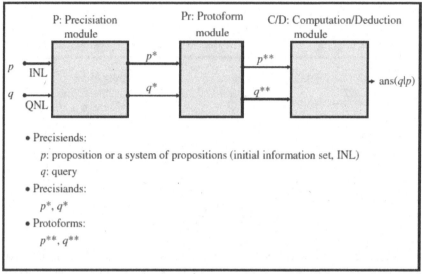

Fig. 8.3. NL-computation — basic structure (PNL).

The precisiation module operates on the initial information set, p, expressed as INL, and results in a precisiand, p^*. The protoform module serves as an interface between the precisiation module and the computation/deduction module. The input to Pr is a precisiand, p^*, and its output is a protoform of p^*, that is, its abstracted summary, p^{**}.

The computation/deduction module is basically a database (catalog) of deduction rules which are, for the most part, rules which govern generalized constraint propagation and counterpropagation. The principal deduction rule is the Extension Principle [501, 514]. The rules are protoformal, with each rule having a symbolic part and a computational part. Protoformal rules are grouped into modules, with each module comprising rules which are associated with a particular class of generalized constraints, e.g., possibilistic constraints, probabilistic constraints, veristic constraints, usuality constraints, etc. (Fig. 8.4).

The inputs to the C/D module are p^{**} and q^{**}. A module which plays an important role in C/D is the world knowledge module (WK).

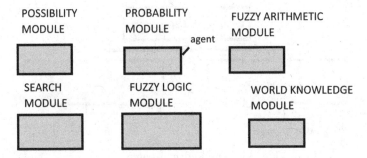

Fig. 8.4. Computational/deduction module.

World knowledge is the knowledge which humans acquire through experience, education and communication [539, 540]. Much of the information in WK is perception-based. Organization of knowledge in WK is a complex issue which is not addressed in the present chapter.

8.3. The Concept of Precisiation

The concept of precisiation has few precursors in the literature of logic, probability theory and philosophy of languages [90, 343]. The reason is that the conceptual structure of bivalent logic-on which the literature is based-is much too limited to allow a full development of the concept of precisiation. In GTU what is used for this purpose is the conceptual structure of fuzzy logic.

Precisiation and precision have many facets. More specifically, it is expedient to consider what may be labeled λ-precisiation, with λ being an indexical variable whose values identify various modalities of precisiation. In particular, it is important to differentiate between precision in value (v-precision) and precision in meaning (m-precision). For example, proposition $X = 5$ is v-precise and m-precise, but proposition $2 \leq X \leq 6$, is v-imprecise and m-precise. Similarly, proposition "X is a normally distributed random variable with mean 5 and variance 2," is v-imprecise and m-precise.

A further differentiation applies to m-precisiation. Thus, mh-precisiation is human-oriented meaning precisiation, while mm-precisiation is machine-oriented or, equivalently, mathematically

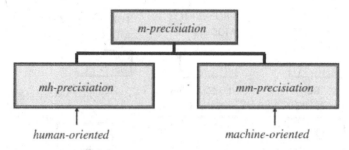

Fig. 8.5. *mh-* and *mm-*percisiation.

based meaning precisiation (Fig. 8.5). A dictionary definition may be viewed as a form of *mh*-precisiation, while a mathematical definition of a concept, e.g., stability, is *mm*-precisiation whose result is *mm*-precisiation of stability.

A more general illustration relates to representation of a function as a collection of fuzzy if-then rules — a mode of representation which is widely used in practical applications of fuzzy logic [133, 496]. More specifically, let f be a function from reals to reals which is represented as (Fig. 8.6).

$$f: \text{if } X \text{ is small then } Y \text{ is small,}$$
$$\text{if } X \text{ is medium than } Y \text{ is large,}$$
$$\text{if } X \text{ is large than } Y \text{ is small,}$$

where small, medium and large are labels of fuzzy sets. In this representation, the collection in question may be viewed as *mh*-precisiand of f. When the collection is interpreted as a fuzzy graph [512, 530] representation of f assumes the form.

$$f : \text{small} \times \text{small} + \text{medium} \times \text{large} + \text{large} \times \text{small}$$

which is a disjunction of Cartesian products of small, medium and large. This representation is *mm*-precisiand of f. In general, a precisiend has many precisiands. As an illustration consider the proposition "X is approximately a," or "X is *a" for short, where a is a real number. How can "X is *a" be precisiated? The simplest precisiand of "X is *a" is "$X = a$," (Fig. 8.7).

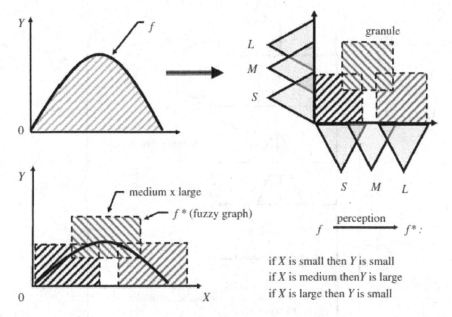

Fig. 8.6. Granular definition of a function.

This mode of precisiation is referred to as *s*-precisiation, with *s* standing for singular. This is a mode of precisiation which is widely used in science and especially in probability theory. In the latter case, most real-world probabilities are not known exactly but in practice are frequently computed with as if they are exact numbers. For example, if the probability of an event is stated to be 0.7, then it should be understood that 0.7 is actually *0.7, that is, approximately 0.7. The standard practice is to treat *0.7 as 0.7000..., that is, as an exact number.

Next in simplicity is representation of *a is an interval centering on *a*. This mode of precisiation is referred to as *cg*-precisiation, with *cg* standing for crisp-granular. Next is *fg*-precisiation of *a, with the precisiand being a fuzzy interval centering on *a*. Next is *p*-precisiation of *a, with the precisiand being a probability distribution centering on *a*, and so on.

An analogy is helpful in understanding the relationship between a precisiend and its precisiands. More specifically, a *mm*-precisiand,

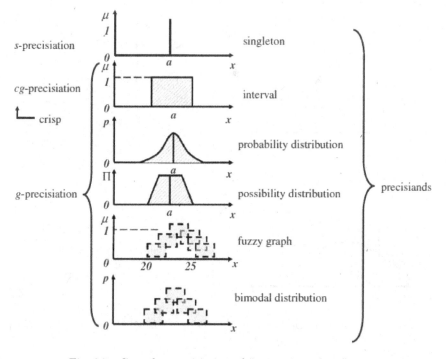

Fig. 8.7. Granular precisiation of "approximately a.", $* a$.

p^*, may be viewed as a model of precisiend, p, in the same sense as a differential equation may be viewed as a model of a physical system.

In the context of modeling, an important characteristic of a model is its "goodness of fit." In the context of NL-computation, an analogous concept is that of cointension. The concept is discussed in the following.

8.4. The Concept of Cointensive Precisiation

Precisiation is a prerequisite to computation with information described in natural language. To be useful, precisiation of a precisiend, p, should result in a precisiand, p^*, whose meaning, in some specified sense, should be close to that of p. Basically, cointension of p^* and p is the degree to which the meaning of p^* fits the meaning of p.

In dealing with meaning, it is necessary to differentiate between the intension or, equivalently, the intensional meaning, i-meaning of p and the extension, or equivalently, the extensional, e-meaning of p. The concepts of extension and intension are drawn from logic and, more particularly, from modal logic and possible world' semantics [63, 112, 259]. Basically, e-meaning is attribute-free and i-meaning is attribute-based. As a simple illustration, if A is a finite set in a universe of discourse, U, then the e-meaning of A, that is, its extension is the list of elements of A, $\{u_1, \ldots, u_n\}$, u_i being the name of ith element of A, with no attributes associated with u_i. Let $a(u_i)$ be an attribute-vector associated with each u_i. Then the intension of A is a recognition algorithm which, given $a(u_i)$, recognizes whether u_i is or is not an element of A. If A is a fuzzy set with membership function A then the e-meaning and i-meaning of A may be expressed compactly as

$$e\text{-meaning of } A : A = \{\mu_A(u_i)/u_i\}$$

where $\mu_A(u)/u$ means that $\mu_A(u)$ is the grade of membership of u_i in A; and

$$i\text{-meaning of } A : A = \{\mu_A(a(u_i))/u_i\}$$

with the understanding that in the i-meaning of A the membership function, A is defined on the attribute space. It should be noted that when A is defined through exemplification, it is said to be defined ostensively. Thus, o-meaning of A consists of exemplars of A. An ostensive definition may be viewed as a special case of extensional definition. A neural network may be viewed as a system which derives i-meaning from o-meaning.

Clearly, i-meaning is more informative than e-meaning. For this reason, cointension is defined in terms of intensions rather than extensions of precisiend and precisiand. Thus, meaning will be understood to be i-meaning, unless stated to the contrary. However, when the precisiend is a concept, which plays the role of definiendum and we know its extension but not its intension, cointension has to involve the extension of the definiendum (precisiend) and the intension of the definiens (precisiand).

As an illustration, let p be the concept of bear market. A dictionary definition of p — which may be viewed as a mh-precisiand of p — reads "A prolonged period in which investment prices fall, accompanied by widespread pessimism". A widely accepted quantitative definition of bear market is: We classify a bear market as a 30% decline after 50 days, or a 13 % decline after 145 days. This definition may be viewed as a mm-precisiand of bear market. Clearly, the quantitative definition, p^*, is not a good fit to the perception of the meaning of bear market which is the basis for the dictionary definition. In this sense, the quantitative definition of bear market is not cointensive.

Intensions are more informative than extensions in the sense that more can be inferred from propositions whose meaning is expressed intensionally rather than extensionally. The assertion will be precisiated at a later point. For the present, a simple example will suffice.

Consider the proposition p: Most Swedes are tall. Let U be a population of n Swedes, $U = (u_1, \ldots, u_n)$, $u_1 =$ name of ith Swede. A precisiand of p may be represented as Count(tall.Swedes) is most, where most is a fuzzy quantifier which is defined as a fuzzy subset of the unit interval [524, 525]. Let $\mu_{\text{tall}}(u_i)$, $i = 1, \ldots, n$ be the grade of membership of u_i in the fuzzy set of tall Swedes. Then the e-meaning of tall Swedes may be expressed in symbolic form as

$$\text{tall.Swedes} = \mu_{\text{tall}}(u_1)/u_1 + \cdots + \mu_{\text{tall}}(u_1)/u_n$$

Accordingly, the i-precisiand of p may be expressed as

$$\frac{1}{n}(\mu_{\text{tall}}(u_1) + \cdots + \mu_{\text{tall}}(u_n)) \text{is most}$$

Similarly, the i-precisiand of p may be represented as

$$\frac{1}{n}(\mu_{\text{tall}}(h_1) + \cdots + \mu_{\text{tall}}(h_n)) \text{is most}$$

where h_i is the height of u_i .

As will be seen later, given the e-precisiend of p we can compute the answer to the query: How many Swedes are not tall? The answer is 1-most (Fig. 8.8).

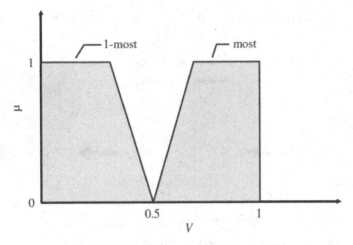

Fig. 8.8. "Most" and antonym of "most".

However, we cannot compute the answer to the query: How many Swedes are short? The same applies to the query: What is the average height of Swedes? As will be shown later, the answers to these queries can be computed given the i-precisiand of p.

The concept of cointensive precisiation has important implications for the way in which scientific concepts are defined. The standard practice is to define a concept within the conceptual structure of bivalent logic, leading to a bivalent definition under which the universe of discourse is partitioned into two classes: objects which fit the concept and those which do not, with no shades of gray allowed. Such definition is valid when the concept that is defined, the definiendum, is crisp, that is, bivalent. The problem is that in reality most scientific concepts are fuzzy, that is, are a matter of degree. Familiar examples are the concepts of causality, relevance, stability, independence and bear market. In general, when the definiendum (precisiend) is a fuzzy concept, the definiens (precisiand) is not cointensive, which is the case with the bivalent definition of bear market. More generally, bivalent definitions of fuzzy concepts are vulnerable to the Sorites (heap) paradox [395].

As an illustration, consider a bottle whose mouth is of diameter d, with a ball of diameter D placed on the bottle (Fig. 8.9).

- graduality of progression from stability to instability

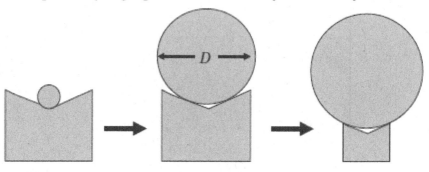

- Lyapounov's definition of stability leads to the counterintuitive conclusion that the system is stable no matter how large the ball is

- In reality, stability is a matter of degree

Fig. 8.9. Stability in a fuzzy concept.

When D is slightly larger than d, based on commonsense the system is stable. As D increases, the system becomes less and less stable. But Lyapounov's definition of stability leads to the conclusion that the system is stable for all values of D so long as D is greater than d. Clearly, this conclusion is counterintuitive. The problem is that under Lyapounov's bivalent definition of stability, a system is either stable or unstable, with no degrees of stability allowed.

What this example points to is the need for redefinition of many basic concepts in scientific theories. To achieve cointension, bivalence must be abandoned.

8.5. A Key Idea — The Meaning Postulate

In GTU, a proposition, p, is viewed as an answer to a question, q, of the form "What is the value of X?" Thus, p is a carrier of information about X. In this perspective, the meaning of p, $M(p)$, is the information which p carries about X. An important consequence of the fundamental thesis of GTU is what is referred to as the meaning postulate. In symbolic form, the postulate is expressed as $M(p) = GC(X(P))$, where $GC(X(P))$ is a generalized constraint on the variable which is constrained by p. In plain words, the meaning postulate assents that the meaning of a proposition may be represented as a generalized constraint. It is this postulate that makes the concept of a generalized constraint the centerpiece of GTU.

A point which should be noted is that the question to which p is an answer is not uniquely determined by p; hence, $X(p)$ is not uniquely defined by p. Generally, however, among the possible questions there is one which is most likely. For example, if p is "Monika is young," then the most likely question is "How old is Monika?" In this example, X is Age(Monika).

8.6.   The Concept of a Generalized Constraint

Constraints are ubiquitous. A typical constraint is an expression of the form $X \in C$, where X is the constrained variable and C is the set of values which X is allowed to take. A typical constraint is hard (inelastic) in the sense that if u is a value of X then u satisfies the constraint if and only if $u \in C$.

The problem with hard constraints is that most real-world constraints are not hard, meaning that most real-world constraints have some degree of elasticity. For example, the constraints "check-out time is 1 p.m.," and "speed limit is 100 km/hr," are, in reality, not hard. How can such constraints be defined? The concept of a generalized constraint is motivated by questions of this kind.

Real-world constraints may assume a variety of forms. They may be simple in appearance and yet have a complex structure. Reflecting this reality, a generalized constraint, $GC(X)$, is defined as an expression of the form

$$GC(X) : \text{isr } R$$

where X is the constrained variable; R is a constraining relation which, in general, is non-bivalent; and r is an indexing variable which identifies the modality of the constraint, that is, its semantics.

The constrained variable, X, may assume a variety of forms. In particular,

- X is an n-ary variable, $X = (X_1, \ldots, X_n)$,
- X is a proposition, e.g., X = Leslie is tall,
- X is a function,
- X is a function of another variable, $X = f(Y)$,
- X is conditioned on another variable, X/Y,
- X has a structure, e.g., X = Location(Residence(Carol)),
- X is a group variable. In this case, there is a group, $G[A]$ with each member of the group, $Name_i$, $i = 1, \ldots, n$, associated with an attribute-value, A_i. A_i may be vector valued. Symbolically,

$$G[A]: Name_1/A_1 + \cdots + Name_n/A_n$$

Basically, $G[A]$ is a relation.
- X is a generalized constraint, $X = Y$ isr R.

A generalized constraint is associated with a test-score function, $\text{ts}(u)$, [521, 522] which associates with each object, u, to which the constraint is applicable, the degree to which u satisfies the constraint. Usually, $\text{ts}(u)$ is a point in the unit interval. However, if necessary, the test-score may be a vector, an element of a semiring [382], an element of a lattice [181] or, more generally, an element of a partially ordered set, or a bimodal distribution — a constraint which will be described later. The test-score function defines the semantics of the constraint with which it is associated.

The constraining relation, R, is, or is allowed to be, non-bivalent (fuzzy). The principal modalities of generalized constraints are summarized in the following.

8.7.   Principal Modalities of Generalized Constraints

(a) *Possibilistic* (r = blank)

$$X \text{ is } R$$

with R playing the role of the possibility distribution of X. For example,

$$X \text{ is } [a, b]$$

means that $[a, b]$ is the set of possible values of X. Another example is

$$X \text{ is small}$$

In this case, the fuzzy set labeled small is the possibility distribution of X [130, 516]. If μ_{small} is the membership function of small, then the semantics of "X is small" is defined by

$$\text{Poss}\{X = u\} = \mu_{\text{small}}(u)$$

where u is a generic value of X.

(b) *Probabilistic* $(r = p)$

$$X \text{ isp } R$$

with R playing the role of the probability distribution of X. For example,

$$X \text{ isp } N(m, \sigma^2)$$

means that X is a normally distributed random variable with mean m and variance σ^2.

If X is a random variable which takes values in a finite set $\{u_1, \ldots, u_n\}$ with respective probabilities $p_1, \ldots, p_n$, then X may be expressed symbolically as

$$X \text{ isp } (p_1 \backslash u_1 + \cdots + p_n \backslash u_n)$$

with the semantics

$$\text{Prob}(X = u_i) = p_i, \quad i = 1, \ldots, n$$

What is important to note is that in GTU a probabilistic constraint is viewed as an instance of a generalized constraint.

When X is a generalized constraint, the expression

$$X \text{ is} p \ R$$

is interpreted as a probability qualification of X, with R being the probability of X, [518, 521, 522]. For example,

$$(X \text{ is small}) \text{ is} p \ likely$$

where small is a fuzzy subset of the real line, means that probability of the fuzzy event $\{X \text{ is small}\}$ is likely. More specifically, if X takes values in the interval $[a, b]$ and g is the probability density function of X, then the probability of the fuzzy even "X is small" may be expressed as [503]

$$\text{Prob}(X \text{ is small}) = \int_a^b \mu_{\text{small}}(u)g(u)du$$

Hence,

$$ts(g) = \mu_{\text{likely}} \left(\int_b^a g(u)\mu_{\text{small}}(u)du \right)$$

This expression for test-score function defines the semantics of probability qualification of a possibilistic constraint.

(c) *Veristic* $(r = v)$

$$X \text{ is} v \ R$$

where R plays the role of a verity (truth) distribution of X. In particular, if X takes values in a finite set $\{u_1, \ldots, u_n\}$ with respective verity (truth) values $t_1, \ldots, t_n$, then X may be expressed as

$$X \text{ is} v \ (t_1 \backslash u_1 + \cdots + t_n \backslash u_n)$$

meaning that $\text{Ver}(X = u_i) = t_i, i = 1, \ldots, n$.

For example, if Robert is half-German, quarter-French and quarter-Italian, then

$$\text{Ethnicity(Robert) is v } 0.5|\text{German} + 0.25| \text{ French} + 0.25|\text{Italian}.$$

when X is a generalized constraint, the expression

$$X \text{ isv } R$$

is interpreted as verity (truth) qualification of X. For example,

$$(X \text{ is small}) \text{ isv very true}$$

should be interpreted as "It is very true that X is small." The semantics of truth qualification is defined by [517]

$$\text{Ver}(X \text{ is } R) \rightarrow X \text{ is } \mu_R^{-1}(t)$$

where μ_R^{-1} is inverse of the membership function of R, and t is a fuzzy truth value which is a subset of $[0,1]$, Fig. 8.10.

There are two classes of fuzzy sets: (a) possibilistic, and (b) veristic. In the case of a possibilistic fuzzy set, the grade of membership is the degree of possibility. In the case of a veristic fuzzy set, the grade of membership is the degree of verity (truth). Unless stated to the contrary, a fuzzy set is assumed to be possibilistic.

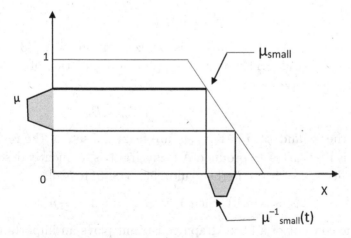

Fig. 8.10. Truth-qualification: $(X$ is small$)$ is t.

(d) *Usuality* $(r = u)$

$$X \text{ is}u \ R$$

The usuality constraint presupposes that X is a random variable, and that probability of the event $\{X \text{ is}u \ R\}$ is usually, where usually plays the role of a fuzzy probability which is a fuzzy number [236]. For example

$$X \text{ is}u \text{ small}$$

means that "usually X is small" or, equivalently,

$$\text{Prob}\{X \text{ is small}\} \text{ is usually}$$

In this expression, small may be interpreted as the usual value of X. The concept of a usual value has the potential of playing a significant role in decision analysis, since it is more informative than the concept of an expected value.

(e) *Random set* $(r = vs)$ In

$$X \text{ is}rs \ R$$

X is a fuzzy-set-valued random variable and R is a fuzzy random set.

(f) *Fuzzy graph*$(r = fq)$. In

$$X \text{ is}fg \ R$$

X is a function, f, and R is a fuzzy graph [512, 530] which constrains f (Fig. 8.11). A fuzzy graph is a disjunction of Cartesian granules expressed as

$$R = A_1 \times B_1 + \cdots + A_n \times B_n$$

where the A_i and B_i, $i = 1, \ldots, n$, are fuzzy subsets of the real line, and $\times$ is the Cartesian product. A fuzzy graph is frequently described as a collection of fuzzy if–then rules [53, 348, 511, 530].

$$R : \text{if } X \text{ is } A_i \text{ then } Y \text{ is } B_i, \quad i = 1, \ldots, n$$

The concept of a fuzzy-graph constraint plays an important role in applications of fuzzy logic [53, 124, 156, 224, 381, 495].

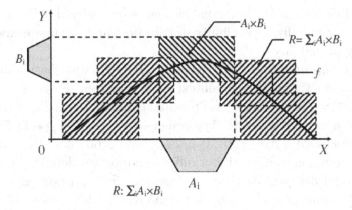

Fig. 8.11. Fuzzy graph.

8.8. The Concept of Bimodal Constraint/Distribution

In the bimodal constraint,

$$X \text{ is}bm \ R$$

R is a bimodal distribution of the form

$$R : \sum_i P_i \backslash A_i, i = 1, \ldots, n.$$

with the understanding that $\mathrm{Prob}(X \text{ is } A_i)$ is P_i [538]. That is, P_i is a granular value of $\mathrm{Prob}(X \text{ is } A_i)$, $i = 1, \ldots, n$.

To clarify the meaning of a bimodal distribution it is expedient to start with an example. I am considering buying Ford stock. I ask my stockbroker, "What is your perception of the near-term prospects for Ford stock?" He tells me, "A moderate decline is very likely; a steep decline is unlikely; and a moderate gain is not likely." My question is: What is the probability of a large gain?

Information provided by my stock broker may be represented as a collection of ordered pairs:

• Price: ((unlikely, steep decline), (very likely, moderate decline), (not likely, moderate gain)).

In this collection, the second element of an ordered pair is a fuzzy event or, generally, a possibility distribution, and the first element is a fuzzy probability.

The importance of the concept of a bimodal distribution derives from the fact that in the context of human-centric systems, most probability distributions are bimodal. Bimodal distributions can assume a variety of forms. The principal types are Type 1, Type 2 and Type 3 [517, 518, 521]. Types 1, 2 and 3 bimodal distributions have a common framework but differ in important detail (Fig. 8.12). A bimodal distribution may be viewed as an important generalization of standard probability distribution. For this reason, bimodal distributions of Types 1, 2, 3 are discussed in greater detail in the following.

- Type 1 (default): X is a random variable taking values in $U A_1, \ldots, A_n, A$, are events (fuzzy sets),

$$p_i = \text{Prob}(X \text{ is } A_i), \quad i = 1, \ldots, n$$

$$\sum_i p_i \text{ is unconstrained, } \text{Pi} = \text{granular value of } p_i$$

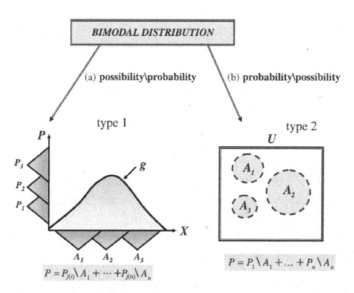

Fig. 8.12. Types 1 and Type bimodal distributions.

BD: bimodal distribution:

$$((P_1, A_1), \ldots, (P_n, A_n))$$

or, equivalently,

$$X \text{ is} bm \ (P_1 \backslash A_1 + \cdots + P_n \backslash A_n)$$

What is the granular probability, P, of A? In general, this probability is fuzzy-set-valued.

In basic bimodal distribution (BBD), X is a real-valued random variable, and X and P are granular (Fig. 8.13).

• Type 2 (fuzzy random set): X is a fuzzy-set-valued random variable with values

$$A_1, \ldots, A_n, A(\text{fuzzy sets})$$
$$p_i = \text{Prob}(X = A_i), \quad i = 1, \ldots, n$$

$$\text{Pi : granular value of } p_i$$

$$BD : X \text{ is} rs \ (P_1 \backslash A_1 + \cdots P_n \backslash A_n), \sum_i p_i = 1$$

What is the granular probability, P, of A? P is not definable. What are definable are (a) the expected value of the conditional possibility of A given BD, and (b) the expected value of the conditional necessity of A given BD.

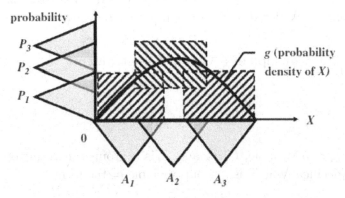

Fig. 8.13. Basic bimodal distribution.

- Type 3 (Dempster–Shafer) [121, 404, 409]: X is a random variable taking values $X_1, \ldots, X_n$ with probabilities $p_1, \ldots, p_n$. X_i is a random variable taking values in $A_i, i = 1, \ldots, n$. Probability distribution of X_i in $A_i, i = 1, \ldots, n$, is not specified,

$$X \text{ is} p \ (p_1 \backslash X_1 + \cdots + p_n \backslash X_n)$$

What is the probability, p, that X is in A? Because probability distributions of the X_i in the A_i are not specified, p is interval valued. What is important to note is that the concepts of upper and lower probabilities break down when the A_i are fuzzy sets [518].

In applying Dempster–Shafer theory, it is important to check on whether the data fit Type 3 model. In many cases, the correct model is Type 1 rather than Type 3.

The importance of bimodal distributions derives from the fact that in many realistic settings a bimodal distribution is the best approximation to our state of knowledge. An example is assessment of degree of relevance, since relevance is generally not well defined. If I am asked to assess the degree of relevance of a book on knowledge representation to summarization, my state of knowledge about the book may not be sufficient to justify an answer such as 0.7. A better approximation to my state of knowledge may be "likely to be high." Such an answer is an instance of a bimodal distribution.

What is the expected value of a bimodal distribution? This question is considered in the section on protoformal deduction rules.

8.9.   The Concept of a Group Constraint

In

$$X \text{ is} g \ R$$

X is a group variable, $G[A]$, and R is a group constraint on $G[A]$. More specifically, if X is a group variable of the form

$$G[A] : \text{Name}_1/A_i + \cdots + \text{Name}_n/A_n$$

or

$$G[A] : \sum_i \text{Name}_i / A_i, \text{ for short, } i = 1, \dots, n$$

then R is a constraint on the A_i, written in $G[A$ is $R]$. To illustrate, if we have a group of n Swedes, with Name$_i$ being the name of ith Swede, and A_i being the height of Name$_i$, then the proposition "most Swedes are tall," is a constraint on the A_i which may be expressed as [524, 539]

$$\frac{1}{n} \sum \text{Count (tall.Swedes) is most or, more explicitly,}$$

$$\frac{1}{n}\Big(\mu_{\text{tall}}(A_1) + \cdots + \mu_{\text{tall}}(A_n)\Big) \text{ is most}$$

where $A_i = \text{Height (Name}_i)$, $i = 1, \dots, n$, and most is a fuzzy quantifier which is interpreted as a fuzzy number [524, 525].

8.10. Primary Constraints, Composite Constraints and Standard Constraints

Among the principal generalized constraints there are three that play the role of primary generalized constraints. They are:

Possibilistic constraint: X is R,
Probabilistic constraint: X is$p$ R

and

Veristic constraint: X is$v$ R.

A special case of primary constraints is what may be called standard constraints: bivalent possibilistic, probabilistic and bivalent veristic. Standard constraints form the basis for the conceptual framework of bivalent logic and probability theory.

A generalized constraint is composite if it can be generated from other generalized constraints through conjunction, and/or projection and/or constraint propagation and/or qualification and/or possibly other operations. For example, a random-set constraint may be viewed as a conjunction of a probabilistic constraint and either a possibilistic or veristic constraint. The Dempster–Shafer theory of evidence is, in effect, a theory of possibilistic random-set constraints. The derivation graph of a composite constraint defines how it can be derived from primary constraints.

The three primary constraints — possibilistic, probabilistic and veristic — are closely related to a concept which has a position of centrality in human cognition — the concept of partiality. In the sense used here, partial means: a matter of degree or, more or less equivalently, fuzzy. In this sense, almost all human concepts are partial (fuzzy). Familiar examples of fuzzy concepts are: knowledge, understanding, friendship, love, beauty, intelligence, belief, causality, relevance, honesty, mountain and, most important, truth, likelihood and possibility. Is a specified concept, C, fuzzy? A simple test is: If C can be hedged, then it is fuzzy. For example, in the case of relevance, we can say: very relevant, quite relevant, slightly relevant, etc. Consequently, relevance is a fuzzy concept.

The three primary constraints may be likened to the three primary colors: red, blue and green. In terms of this analogy, existing theories of uncertainty may be viewed as theories of different mixtures of primary constraints. For example, the Dempster–Shafer theory of evidence is a theory of a mixture of probabilistic and possibilistic constraints. GTU embraces all possible mixtures. In this sense, the conceptual structure of GTU accommodates most, and perhaps all, of the existing theories of uncertainty.

8.11. The Generalized Constraint Language and Standard Constraint Language

A concept which has a position of centrality in GTU is that of generalized constraint language (GCL). Informally, GCL is the set of all generalized constraints together with the rules governing syntax, semantics and generation. Simple examples of elements of GCL are

$$(X \text{ is small}) \text{ is likely}$$
$$((X, Y) \text{ is } p\ A) \wedge (X \text{ is } B)$$
$$(X \text{ is } p\ A) \wedge ((X, Y) \text{ is } v\ B)$$
$$\text{Proj}_Y ((X \text{ is } A) \wedge (X, Y) \text{ is } p\ B)$$

where $\wedge$ is conjunction.

A very simple example of a semantic rule is:

$$(X \text{ is } A) \wedge (Y \text{ is } B)$$
$$\rightarrow \text{Poss}(X \text{ is } A) \wedge \text{Poss}(Y \text{ is } B) =_A (u) \wedge_B (v)$$

where u and v are generic values of X, Y; and A and B are the membership functions of A and B, respectively.

In principle, GCL is an infinite set. However, in most applications only a small subset of GCL is likely to be needed.

A key idea which underlies NL-Computation is embodied in the meaning postulate — a postulate which asserts that the meaning of a proposition, p, drawn from a natural language is representable as a generalized constraint. In the context of GCL, the meaning postulate asserts that p may be precisiated through translation into GCL. Transparency of translation may be enhanced through annotation. Simple example of annotation,

$$\text{Monika is young} \rightarrow X/\text{Age (Monika) is } R/\text{young}$$

In GTU, the set of all standard constraints together with the rules governing syntax, semantics and generation constitute the standard constraint language (SCL). SCL is a subset of GCL.

8.12. The Concept of Granular Value

The concept of a generalized constraint provides a basis for an important concept — the concept of a granular value. Let X be a variable taking values in a universe of discourse U, $U = \{u\}$. If a is an element of U, and it is known that the value of X is a, then a is referred to as a singular value of X. If there is some uncertainty about the value of X, the available information induces a restriction on the possible values of X which may be represented as a generalized constraint $GC(X)$, X isr R. Thus a generalized constraint defines a granule which is referred to as a granular value of X, $\text{Gr}(X)$ (Fig. 8.14). For example, if X is known to lie in the interval $[a, h]$, then $[a, h]$ is a granular value of X. Similarly, if X is$p$

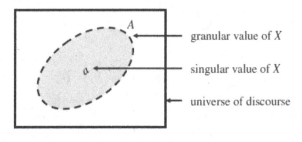

- singular: X is a $\longrightarrow$ singleton
- granular: X isr A $\longleftarrow$ granule
- a granule is defined by a generalized constraint

example:

    X: unemployment

    a: 7.3%

    A: high

Fig. 8.14. A granule defined as a generalized constraint.

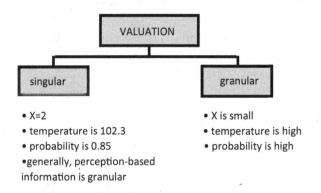

Fig. 8.15. Singular and granular values.

Nm^2, then Nm^2, is a granular value of X. What is important to note is that defining a granular value in terms of a generalized constraint makes a granular value mm-precise.

It is this characteristic of granular values that underlies the concept of a linguistic variable [514]. Symbolically, representing a granular value as a generalized constraint may be expressed as

$Gr(X) = GC(X)$. It should be noted that, in general, perception-based information is granular (Fig. 8.15).

The importance of the concept of a granular value derives from the fact that it plays a central role in computation with information described in natural language. More specifically, when a proposition expressed in a natural language is represented as a system of generalized constraints, it is, in effect, a system of granular values. Thus, computation with information described in natural language ultimately reduces to computation with granular values. Such computation is the province of Granular Computing [54, 264, 265, 291, 484, 517, 518, 534, 535].

8.13. The Concept of Protoform

The term "protoform" is an abbreviation of "prototypical form." Informally, a protoform, A, of an object, B, written as $A = PF(B)$, is an abstracted summary of B. Usually, B is a proposition, a system of propositions, question, command, scenario, decision problem, etc. More generally, B may be a relation, system, case, geometrical form or an object of arbitrary complexity. Usually, A is a symbolic expression, but, like B, it may be a complex object. The primary function of $PF(B)$ is to place in evidence the deep semantic structure of B (Fig. 8.16).

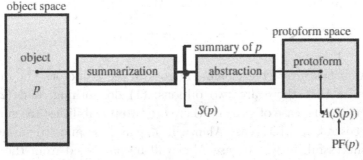

$S(p)$: summary of p
$PF(p)$: abstracted summary of p
    deep structure of p

Fig. 8.16. Definition of protoform of p.

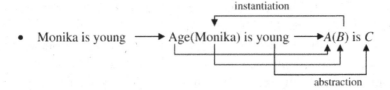

- Monika is young ——→ Age(Monika) is young ——→ A(B) is C

- Monika is much younger than Robert ——→
  Age(Monika), Age(Robert) is much.younger ——→ D(A(B), A(C)) is E
- What is Monika's age ——→ Age(Monika) is ?X ——→

  └ A(B) is ?X ┘

- Distance between New York and Boston is about 200 mi ——→ A(B, C) is R

- Usually Robert returns from work at about 6pm ——→

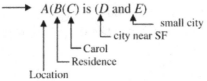

  Prob{A is B} is C
           └——— usually
        └— about 6 pm
     └ Time(Robert.returns.from.work)

- Carol lives in a small city near San Francisco ——→ Residence(Carol) is
  ((city.near.SF) and small.city))

  ——→ A(B(C) is (D and E)
              └——— small city
           └ city near SF
        └ Carol
        └ Residence
   Location

- Most Swedes are tall ——→ 1/n ΣCount(G[A is R]) is Q

Alan has severe back pain. He goes to see a doctor. The doctor tells him that there are two options: (1) do nothing; and (2) do surgery. In the case of surgery, there are two possibilities: (a) surgery is successful, in which case Alan will be pain free; and (b) surgery is not successful, in which case Alan will be paralyzed from the neck down. Question: Should Alan elect surgery?

I am planning to drive from Berkeley to Santa Barbara, with stopover for lunch in Monterey. Usually, it takes about two hours to get to Monterey. Usually, it takes about one hour to have lunch. It is likely that it will take about five hours to get from Monterey to Santa Barbara. At what time should I leave Berkeley to get to Santa Barbara, with high probability, before about 6 pm?

Abstraction has levels, just as summarization does, including no summarization and/or no abstraction. For this reason, an object may have a multiplicity of protoforms (Fig. 8.17). Conversely, many objects may have the same protoform. Such objects are said to be protoform-equivalent, or PF-equivalent, for short. For

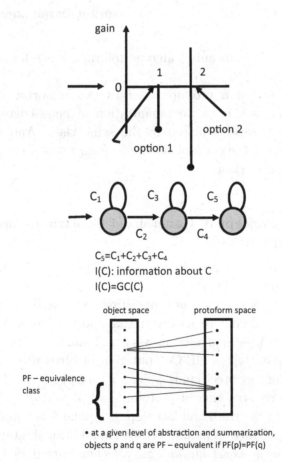

Fig. 8.17. Protoforms and PF-equivalence

example, p: Most Swedes are tall, and q: Few professors are rich, are PF-equivalent.

A protoform may be extensional (e-protoform) or intensional (i-protoform). For example,

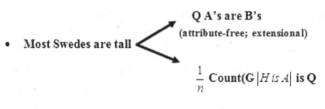

As in the case of meaning, an e-protoform is less informative than an i-protoform.

The concept of a protoform serves two important functions. First, it provides a basis for organization of knowledge, with PF-equivalent propositions placed in the same class. And second, in NL-Computation the concept of a protoform plays a pivotal role in computation/deduction.

8.14.   The Concept of Generalized-Constraint-Based Computation

In GTU, computation/deduction is treated as an instance of question-answering. With reference to Fig. 8.3, the point of departure is a proposition or a system of propositions, p, described in a natural language p is referred to as the initial information set, INL. The query, q, is likewise expressed in a natural language. As was stated earlier, the first step in NL-Computation involves precisiation of p and q, resulting in precisiands p^* and q^*, respectively. The second step involves construction of protoforms of p^* and q^*, p^{**} and q^{**}, respectively. In the third and last step, p^{**} and q^{**} are applied to the computation/deduction module, C/D. An additional internal source of information is world knowledge, wk. The output of C/D is an answer, ans$(q|p)$.

Examples

p: Monika is young p^*: Age(Monika) is young,
p^{**}: A(B) is C,
p: Most Swedes are tall $p*$: Count(tall.Swedes/Swedes) is most,
p^{**}: Count $(G[X$ is $A]/G[X])$ is Q.

The key idea in NL-Computation — the meaning postulate — plays a pivotal role in computation/deduction in GTU. More specifically, p^* may be viewed as a system of generalized constraints which induces a generalized constraint on ans$(q|p)$. In this sense, computation/deduction in GTU may be equated to generalized constraint propagation. More concretely, generalized constraint propagation is governed by what is referred to as the deduction principle. Informally, the basic idea behind this principle is the following.

Deduction principle

Assume that the answer to q can be completed if we know the values of variables $u_i, \ldots, u_n$. Thus,

$$ans(q \backslash p) = f(u_i, \ldots, u_n)$$

Generally, what we know are not the values of the u_i but a system of generalized constraints which represent the precisiand of p, p^*. Express the precisiand, p^*, as a generalized constraint on the u_i.

$$p^* : GC(u_i, \ldots, u_n)$$

At this point, what we have is $GC(u_i, \ldots, u_n)$ but what we need is the generalized constraint on $ans(q \backslash p)$, $ans(q \backslash p) = f(u_i, \ldots, u_n)$. To solve this basic problem — a problem which involves constraint propagation — what is needed is the extension principle of fuzzy logic [501, 514]. This principle will be discussed at a later point. At this juncture, a simple example will suffice. Assume that

$$p : \text{Most Swedes are tall}$$

and

$$q : \text{What is the average height of Swedes?}$$

Assume that we have a population of Swedes, $G = t(u_i, \ldots, u_n)$, with $h_i, i = 1, \ldots, n$, being the height of ith Swede. Precisiends of p and q may be expressed as

$$p^* : \frac{1}{n}(\mu_{\text{tall}}(h_1 t) + \cdots \mu_{\text{tall}}(h_n)) \text{ is most}$$

$$q^* : \text{ans}(q \backslash p) = \frac{1}{n}(h_1 + \cdots + h_n)$$

In this instance, what we are dealing with is propagation of the constraint on p^* to a constraint on $\text{ans}(q|p)$. Symbolically, the problem may be expressed as

$$\frac{\frac{1}{n}(\mu_{\text{tall}}(h_1) + \cdots + \mu_{\text{tall}}(h_n)) \text{is most}}{\frac{1}{n}(h_1 + \cdots + h_n)}$$

with the understanding that the premise and the consequent are fuzzy constraints. Let $\mu_{\text{ave}}(v)$ be the membership function of the average height. Application of this extension principle reduces computation of the membership function of $\text{ans}(q|p)$ to the solution of the variational problem

$$\mu_{\text{ave}}(v) = \sup_h \left(\mu_{\text{most}} \left(\frac{1}{n}(\mu_{\text{all}}(h_1) + \cdots + \mu_{\text{all}}(h_n)) \right) \right)$$

In this simple example, computation of the answer to query requires the use of just one rule of deduction — the extension principle. More generally, computation of the answer to a query involves application of a sequence of deduction rules drawn from the Computation/Deduction module. The Computation/Deduction module comprises a collection of agent-controlled modules and submodules, each of which contains protoformal deduction rules drawn from various fields and various modalities of generalized constraints. A protoformal deduction rule has a symbolic part, which is expressed in terms of protoforms; and a computational part which defines the computation that has to be carried out to arrive at a conclusion. The principal protoformal deduction rules are described in the following.

8.15. Protoformal Deduction Rules

There are many ways in which generalized constraints may be combined and propagated. The principal protoformal deduction rules are the following:

(a) *Conjunction (possibilistic)*

$$\frac{\begin{array}{l} \text{Symbolic} \\ X \text{ is } R \\ Y \text{ is } S \end{array}}{(X,Y) \text{ is } T} \qquad \begin{array}{l} \\ \text{Computational} \\ \\ T = R \times S \end{array}$$

where $\times$ is the Cartesian product.

(b) *Projection (possibilistic)*

$$\frac{\begin{array}{l} \text{Symbolic} \\ (X,Y) \text{ is } R \end{array}}{X \text{ is } S}, \quad \mu_S(u) = \mu_{\text{Proj}_X R(u)} = \max_v \mu_R(u,v)$$

where μ_R and μ_S are the membership functions of R and S, respectively.

(c) *Projection (probabilistic)*

$$\frac{\begin{array}{l} \text{Symbolic} \\ (X,Y) \text{ isp } R \end{array}}{X \text{ isp } S}, \quad p_S(u) = \int p_R(u,v)dv$$

where X and Y are real-valued random variables, and R and S are probability densities of (X,Y) and X, respectively.

(a) *Computational rule of inference* [501].

$$\frac{\begin{array}{l} \text{Symbolic} \\ X \text{ is } A \\ (X,Y) \text{ is } B \end{array}}{Y \text{ is } C} \quad \mu_C(v) = \max_u(\mu_A(u) \wedge \mu_B(u,v))$$

A, B and C are fuzzy sets with respective membership functions μ_A, μ_B, μ_C; $\wedge$ is min or t-norm (Fig. 8.18).

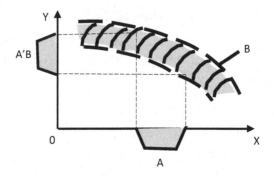

Fig. 8.18. Compositional rule of inference.

(b) *Intersection/product syllogism* [524, 525]

Symbolic	Computational
$Q_1 A$'s are B's	
$\dfrac{Q_2(A\&B)\text{'s are } C\text{'s}}{Q_3 A\text{' are } (B\&C)\text{'s}}$ $Q_3 = Q_1^* Q_2$	

Q_1 and Q_2 are fuzzy quantifiers; A, B, C are fuzzy sets; $*$ is product in fuzzy arithmetic [236].

(c) *Basic extension principle* [501]

$$\frac{X \text{ is } A}{g(x) \text{ is } B}$$

Symbolic   Computational

$$\mu_B(v) = \sup_u (\mu_A(u))$$

subject to

$$v = g(u)$$

g is a given function or functional; A and B are fuzzy sets (Fig. 8.19).

(d) *Extension principle* [514]

This is the principal deduction rule governing possibilistic constraint propagation (Fig. 8.20)

Symbolic Computational $\dfrac{f(X) \text{ is } A}{g(X) \text{ is } B} \mu_B(v) = \sup_u (\mu_B(f(u)))$

subject to $v = g(u)$

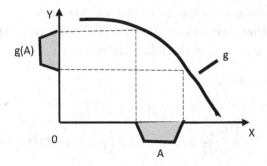

Fig. 8.19. Basic extension of principle.

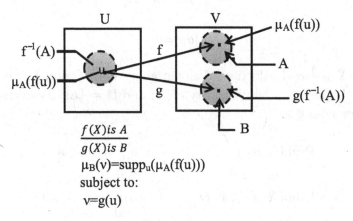

$$\frac{f(X) \text{ is } A}{g(X) \text{ is } B}$$

$\mu_B(v) = \text{supp}_u(\mu_A(f(u)))$
subject to:
$v = g(u)$

Fig. 8.20. Extension principle.

The extension principle is an instance of the generalized extension principle

$$Y = f(X)$$
$$Gr(Y) \text{ isr } Gr(X)$$

The generalized extension principle may be viewed as an answer to the following question: If f is a function from $U = \{X\}$ to $V = \{Y\}$ and I can compute the singular value of Y given a singular value of X, what is the granular value of Y given a granular value of X?

The extension principle is a primary deduction rule in the sense that many other deduction rules are derivable from the extension principle. An example is the following rule:

(e) *Probability rule*

Symbolic   Computational

$$\frac{\text{Prob}(X \text{ is } A)\text{is } B}{\text{Prob}(X \text{ is } C)\text{is } D} \qquad \mu_D(v) = \sup \left(\mu_B \left(\int_U \mu_A(u) r(u) du \right) \right)$$

subject to

$$v = \int_U \mu_C(u) r(u) du$$

$$\int_U r(u) du = 1$$

where X is a real-valued random variable; A, B, C and D are fuzzy sets: r is the probability density of X; and $U = \{u\}$. To derive this rule, we note that

$$\text{Prob}(X \text{ is } A) \text{ is } B \qquad \int_U r(u) \mu_A(u) du \text{ is } B$$

$$\text{Prob}(X \text{ is } C) \text{ is } D \qquad \int_U r(u) \mu_C(u) \, du \text{ is } D$$

which are generalized constraints of the form

$$f(r) \text{ is } B$$

$$g(r) \text{ is } D$$

Applying the extension principle to these expressions, we obtain the expression for D which appears in the basic probability rule.

(f) *Fuzzy-graph interpolation rule*

This rule is the most widely used rule in applications of fuzzy logic [513, 515]. We have a function, $Y = f(X)$, which is represented as a fuzzy graph (Fig. 8.21).

The question is: What is the value of Y when X is A? The A_i, B_i and A are fuzzy sets.

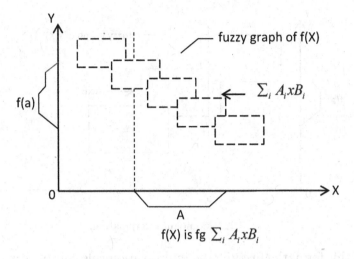

f(X) is fg $\sum_i A_i x B_i$

Fig. 8.21. Fuzzy-graph interpolation.

Symbolic part

$$X \text{ is } A$$
$$Y = f(X)$$
$$\frac{f(X) \text{ is } fg \ \sum_i A_i \times B_i}{Y \text{ is } C}$$

Computational part

$$C = \sum_i m_i \wedge B_i$$

where m_i is the degree to which A matches A_i

$$m_i = \sup_u (\mu_A(u) \wedge \mu_{A_i}(u)), \quad i = 1, \ldots, n$$

When A is a singleton, this rule reduces to

$$X = a$$
$$Y = f(X)$$
$$f(X) \text{ is } fg \ \sum_i A_i \times B_i, \quad i = 1, \ldots, n$$
$$Y = \sum_i \mu_{A_i}(a) \vee B$$

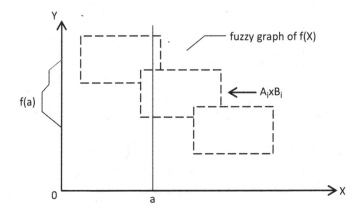

Fig. 8.22. Mamdani interpolation.

In this form, the fuzzy-graph interpolation rule coincides with the Mamdani rule — a rule which is widely used in control and related applications [288] (Fig. 8.22).

In addition to basic rules, the Computation/Deduction module contains a number of specialized modules and sub-modules. Of particular relevance to GTU are Probability module and Usuality submodule. A basic rule in Probability module is the bimodal distribution interpolation rule which is stated in the following.

(g) Bimodal distribution interpolation rule

With reference to Fig. 8.23, the symbolic and computational parts of this rule are:

$$\text{Symbolic} \quad \frac{\text{Prob}(X \text{ is } A_i) \text{ is } P_i}{\text{Prob}(X \text{ is } A) \text{ is } Q}, \quad i = 1, \dots, n$$

Computational

$$\mu_Q(v) = \sup_r \left(\mu_{P_1} \left(\int_U \mu_{A_1}(u) r(u) du \right) \right)$$

$$\wedge \cdots \wedge \mu_{P_n} \left(\int_U \mu_{A_n}(u) r(u) du \right)$$

$$\text{subject to } v = \int_U \mu_A(u) r(u) \int_U r(u) du = 1$$

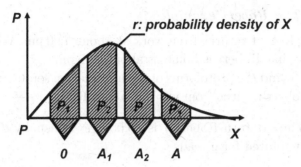

P_1 is P_1 granular value of p_i, i=1, ... N
(P_i, A_i) i=1...n are given
A is given
$(?P, A)$

Fig. 8.23. Interpolation of a bimodal distribution.

In this rule, X is a real-valued random variable; r is the probability density of X; and U is the domain of X.

What is the expected value, $E(X)$, of a bimodal distribution? The answer follows through application of the extension principle:

$$\mu_{E(X)}(v) = \sup_r \left(\mu_{P_1} \left(\int_U \mu_{A_1}(u) r(u) du \right) \right)$$

$$\wedge \cdots \wedge \mu_{P_n} \left(\int_U \mu_{A_n}(u) r(u) du \right)$$

subject to

$$v = \int_U u r(u) du$$

$$\int_U r(u) du = 1$$

$E(X)$ is a fuzzy subset of U.

8.16. Examples of Computation/Deduction

The following relatively simple examples are intended to illustrate application of deduction rules.

8.16.1.   *The Robert example*

p: Usually, Robert returns from work at about 6:00 pm. What is the probability that Robert is home at about 6:15 pm?

First, we find the protoforms of the information set and the query. Usually, Robert returns from work at about 6:00 pm $\longrightarrow$

$\longrightarrow$Prob(Time(Return(Robert)) is *6:00 pm) is usually B/usually, which in annotated form reads

Prob(X/Time(Return(Robert)) is A/*6:00 pm) is B/usually, where *a is an abbreviation of about a. Likewise, for the query, we have

$\longrightarrow$Prob(Time(Return(Robert)) is $\leq$ o*6:15 pm) is? D which in annotated form reads

$\longrightarrow$Prob(X/Time(Return(Robert)) is C/ $\leq$ o*6:15 pm) is D/usually,

where o is the operation of composition [12, 14, 348]. Searching the computation/deduction module, we find that the basic probability rule matches the protoforms of the data and the query

$$\frac{\text{Prob}(X \text{ is } A)\text{is } B}{\text{Prob}(X \text{ is } C)\text{is } D}$$

where

$$\mu_D(v) = \sup_r \left(\mu_B \left(\int_U \mu_A(u) r(u) du \right) \right)$$

subject to

$$v = \int_U \mu_C(u) r(u)$$

$$\int_U r(u) du = 1$$

and r is the probability density of X. Instantiating A, B, C and D, we obtain the answer to the query:

Probability that Robert is home at about 6:15 pm is D, where

$$\mu_D(v) = \sup_r \left(\mu_{\text{usually}} \left(\int_U \mu_{*6:00\,\text{pm}}(u)r(u)du \right) \right)$$

subject to

$$v = \int_U \mu_{\leq o*6:15\,\text{pm}}(u)r(u)du$$

and

$$\int_U r(u)du = 1$$

8.16.2.   *The tall Swedes problem*

We start with the information set

    p: Most Swedes are tall.

        Assume that the queries are:

    q_1: How many Swedes are not tall?

    q_2: How many are short?

    q_3: What is the average height of Swedes?

In our earlier discussion of this example, we found that p translates into a generalized constraint on the count density function, h. Thus,

$$p \longrightarrow \int_a^b h(u)\mu_{\text{all}}(u)du \text{ is most}$$

where a and b are the lower and upper bounds on the height of Swedes.

Precisiands of q_1, q_2 and q_3 may be expressed as

$$q_1 :\longrightarrow \int_a^b h(u)\mu_{\text{not.tall}}(u)du$$

$$q_2 :\longrightarrow \int_a^b h(u)\mu_{\text{short}}(u)du$$

$$q_3 :\longrightarrow \int_a^b uh(u)du$$

Considering q_1, we note that

$$\mu_{\text{not.tall}}(u) = 1 - \mu_{\text{tall}}(u)$$

Consequently,

$$q_1 :\longrightarrow 1 - \int_a^b h(u)\mu_{\text{tall}}(u)du$$

which may be rewritten as

$$\text{ans}(q_1) \longrightarrow 1\text{-most}$$

where 1-most plays the role of the antonym of most (Fig. 8.8).

Considering q_2, we have to compute

$$A : \int_a^b h(u)\mu_{\text{short}}(u)du$$

Given that $\int_a^b h(u)\mu_{\text{tall}}(u)du$, is most.

Applying the extension principle, we arrive at the desired answer to the query:

$$\mu_A(v) = \sup_h \left(\mu_{\text{most}} \left(\int_a^b h(u)\mu_{\text{tall}}(u)du \right) \right)$$

subject to

$$v = \int_a^b h(u)\mu_{\text{short}}(u)du$$

and

$$\int_a^b h(u)du = 1$$

Likewise, for q_3 we have as the answer

$$\mu_A(v) = \sup_h \left(\mu_{\text{most}} \left(\int_a^b h(u)\mu_{\text{tall}}(u)du \right) \right)$$

subject to

$$v = \int_a^b uh(u)du$$

and

$$\int_a^b h(u)du = 1$$

As an illustration of application of protoformal deduction to an instance of this example, consider

p: Most Swedes are tall
q: How many Swedes are short?

We start with the protoforms of p and q (see earlier example):

$$\text{Most Swedes are tall} \longrightarrow \frac{1}{n}\sum \text{Count}(G[A \text{ is } R])\text{is } Q$$

$$T \text{ Swedes are short} \longrightarrow \frac{1}{n}\sum \text{Count}(G[A \text{ is } S])\text{is } T$$

where

$$G[A] = \sum_i \text{Name}_i/A_i, i = 1,\ldots,n$$

An applicable deduction rule in symbolic form is

$$\frac{\frac{1}{n}\sum \text{Count}(G[A \text{ is } R])\text{is } Q}{\frac{1}{n}\sum \text{Count}(G[A \text{ is } S])\text{is } T}$$

The computational part of this rule is expressed as

$$\frac{\frac{1}{n}\sum_i \mu_R(A_i)\text{is } Q}{\frac{1}{n}\sum_i \mu_S(A_i)\text{is } T}$$

where

$$\mu_T(v) = \sup_{A_i,\ldots,A_n} \mu_Q\left(\sum_i \mu_R(A_i)\right)$$

subject to

$$v = \sum_i \mu_S(A_i)$$

What we see is that computation of the answer to the query, q, reduces to the solution of a variational problem, as it does in the earlier discussion of this example — a discussion in which protoformal deduction was not employed.

8.16.3. *Tall Swedes and tall Italians*

p: Most Swedes are much taller than most Italians

q: What is the difference in the average height of Swedes and the average height of Italians?

Step 1: Precisiation: translation of *p* into GCL

$$S = \{S_1, \ldots, S_n\} : \text{population of Swedes,}$$

$$I = \{I_1, \ldots, I_n\} : \text{population of Italians,}$$

$$g_i = \text{height of } S_i, \; g = (g_1, \ldots, g_m),$$

$$h_j = \text{height of } I_j, \; h = (h_1, \ldots, h_n),$$

$$\mu_{ij} = \mu_{\text{much.taller}}(g_i, h_j) = \text{degree to which } S_i$$
$$\text{is much taller than } I_j,$$

$$r_i = \tfrac{I}{n} \textstyle\sum_j \mu_{ij} = \text{Relative } \textstyle\sum \text{Count of Italians in relation}$$
$$\text{to whom } S_i \text{ is much taller,}$$

$$t_i = \mu_{\text{most}}(r_i) = \text{degree to which } S_i \text{ is much}$$
$$\text{taller than most Italians,}$$

$$v = \tfrac{1}{m} \textstyle\sum t_i = \text{Relative } \textstyle\sum \text{Count of Swedes who}$$
$$\text{are much taller than most Italians,}$$

$$ts(g, h) = \mu_{\text{most}}(v),$$

$$p \rightarrow \text{generalized constraint on } S \text{ and } I,$$

$$q : d = \tfrac{1}{m} \textstyle\sum_i g_i - \frac{1}{n} \textstyle\sum_j h_j.$$

Step 2: Deduction via extension principle

$$\mu_q(d) = \sup_{g,h} ts(g, h)$$

subject to

$$d = \frac{1}{m} \sum_i g_i - \frac{1}{n} \sum_j h_j$$

8.16.4. *Simplified trip planning*

Probably it will take about two hours to get from San Francisco to Monterey, and it will probably take about five hours to get from Monterey to Los Angeles. What is the probability of getting to Los

Angeles in less than about seven hours?

$$BD : (probably,^* \, 2) + (probably,^* \, 5)$$

$$\uparrow \qquad\qquad \uparrow$$

$$X \qquad\qquad Y$$

$$Z = X + Y$$

$$\uparrow \quad \uparrow \;\; \uparrow$$

$$w \quad\;\; u \;\;\; v \qquad\quad p_Z(w) = \int p_x(u) p_y(w - u)\, du$$

query: $\int p_Z(w)\mu_{\leq o^*7}(w)\, dw$ is? A

query relevant information: $\begin{cases} \pi_{pX} = \mu_{\text{probably}}\left(\int \mu_{*2}(u) p_X(u)\, du\right) \\ \pi_{pY} = \mu_{\text{probably}}\left(\int \mu_{*5}(u) p_Y(v)\, dv\right) \end{cases}$

$$\mu_A(t) = \sup_{p_X, p_Y} (\pi_X \wedge \pi_Y)$$

subject to

$$t = \int p_Z(w)\mu_{\leq o^*7}(w)\, dw$$

Part II

Applications and Advanced Topics of Fuzzy Logic

Chapter 9

Restriction-based Semantics

In restriction-based semantics, the meaning of propositions is defined as follows. It is needed to answer: what the restricted variable is; what restricting relation is; and how restricting relation restricts the restricted variable. In natural languages, restrictions are predominantly possibilistic. In this chapter, a comprehensive study of restriction-based semantics as a generalization of truth-conditional and possible-world semantics is given. Precisiation of propositions through the use of restriction-based semantics is discussed.

9.1. Precisiation of Meaning

Information is a restriction (constraints) on the values which a variable can take. Information is carried by propositions. For example, Vera is middle-aged. Carol lives in a small city near San Francisco. It is not very likely that Robert is rich. What is the information which is carried by p? To answer this question, it is necessary to understand the meaning of p. To compute with the information carried by p, it is necessary to precisiate the meaning of p. Precisiation of meaning of p = construction of a computational model of p.

Let's consider a simple example of problem-solving with information described in a natural language. Probably John is tall. What is the probability that John is short? Most Swedes are tall. What is the average height of Swedes? Usually Robert leaves office at about 5 pm. Usually it takes Robert about an hour to get home from work. At what time does Robert get home? Precisiation of meaning — a key to everyday reasoning and decision-making. The coming decade is likely to be a decade of automation of everyday reasoning and decision-making. In the world of automated reasoning and decision-making, computation with information described in a natural language is certain to play a prominent role. Precisiation of meaning is a prerequisite to computation with information described in a natural language. In turn, understanding of meaning is a prerequisite to precisiation of meaning.

Natural languages are intrinsically imprecise. Basically, a natural language is a system for describing perceptions. Perceptions are imprecise, reflecting the bounded ability of human sensory organs and ultimately the brain, to resolve detail and store information. Imprecision of perceptions is passed on to natural languages. There are many different forms of imprecision in natural languages. A principal source of imprecision is unsharpness of class boundaries.

Propositions:
Most Swedes are tall;
Icy roads are slippery;
Speed limit is 65 mph;
Check out time is 1 pm.

Commands:
Keep under refrigeration;
Handle with care.

We have to mention that unsharpness of class boundaries = fuzziness. Words and phrases are labels of classes with unsharp boundaries. Fuzziness of words is a concomitant of fuzziness of perceptions. Fuzziness of natural languages is rooted in unsharpness of class boundaries. Fuzzy set = precisiated (graduated) class with unsharp boundaries.

Graduation (precisiation) = association of a class which has unsharp boundaries with a scale of degrees — more concretely, with a membership function. Degrees are allowed to be fuzzy (fuzzy sets of type 2).

Humans have a remarkable capability to graduate perceptions without any measurements or any computations. More specifically, assume that I am given an object, a, and a class, A, and am asked to put a mark on a scale from 0 to 1 indicating my perception of the degree to which a fits A. Generally, I would have no difficulty in doing this.

If I am not sure what the degree is, and I am allowed to use a Z-mouse, I will put a fuzzy f-mark on the scale. A fuzzy f-mark reflects imprecision of my perception. In most cases, a crisp mark should be interpreted as the centroid of a fuzzy mark. For example, if I am asked to estimate the probability that Obama will be able to solve the financial crisis, and I put a crisp mark at 0.7, the crisp mark should be interpreted as the centroid of my fuzzy perception of the probability that Obama will be able to solve the financial crisis. What this points to is that more often than not fuzzy real-world probabilities are treated as if they were precise. Consider the following problem. What is the probability that Robert is home at 6:15 pm? Information set — information from which the answer is to be inferred (see Fig. 9.1).

p1: Usually Robert leaves office at about 5 pm.
p2: Usually it takes Robert about an hour to get home from work.

A Z-mouse serves primarily as a means of visual fuzzy data entry and retrieval. Computation of an answer to a question is carried out

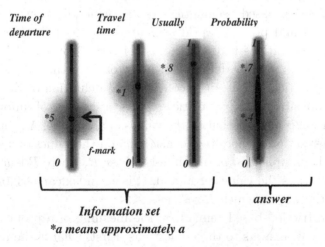

Fig. 9.1. Example of Z-mouse application.

through the use of the machinery of computing with words (CW or CWW). Precisiation of meaning is a prerequisite to computation with information described in natural language. Precisiation and computation employ the machinery of fuzzy logic.

Let's consider graduation of proposition. What is meant by graduation of propositions? If I were asked to graduate the proposition, p: Most Swedes are tall, what would I do? What is the connection between graduation of p and precisiation of p?

In general, a proposition, p, may be associated with a variety of attributes. A basic attribute is the truth-value of p, $t(p)$. In this perspective, graduation of p may be related to graduation of truth-value of p. As will be seen later, graduation of truth-value of p is a byproduct of precisiation of p.

The truth-value of p cannot be assessed in isolation. If I were asked what is the truth-value of p: Most Swedes are tall, I would have to know how most and tall are defined, and be given the distribution of heights of Swedes. Let us call the needed knowledge the information base, $\text{IB}(p)$.

The question is: How can the truth-value be computed given the information base, $\text{IB}(p)$? What is needed for this purpose is restriction-based semantics (RS). Restriction-based semantics is rooted in test-score semantics [521, 528].

Restriction-based semantics is a generalization of truth-conditional and possible-world semantics. In the following, precisiation of propositions through the use of restriction-based semantics is discussed in greater detail. The point of departure in restriction-based semantics, RS, is an unconventional definition of the concept of a proposition. A proposition, p, is a carrier of information. Information is a restriction on the values of a variable. A proposition, p, is a restriction (generalized constraint) on the values of a variable, X, which is implicit in p. In symbols, X isr R, where R is a relation which restricts the values of X and, r, is an indexical variable which defines the way in which R restricts X.

In restriction-based semantics, the meaning of a proposition, p, is defined by answers to three questions. First, what is the restricted variable, X? Second, what is the restricting relation, R? Third,

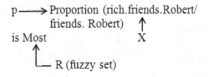

Fig. 9.2. Example of restrictions.

how does R restrict X? In natural languages, restrictions are predominantly possibilistic, expressed as X is R.

Example:

p: Most of Robert's friends are rich (Fig. 9.2).

9.1.1. *Canonical form of p: cf(p)*

When p is represented as a restriction, the expression X is$r$ R is referred to as the canonical form of p, $\mathrm{CF}(p)$. Thus, $\mathrm{CF}(p)$: X is$r$ R.

The concept of a canonical form of p has a position of centrality in precisiation of meaning of p. The canonical form of p may be interpreted as a generalized assignment statement.

In conclusion, the concept of a restriction is the centerpiece of restriction-based semantics. The importance of the concept of a restriction derives from the fact that it makes it possible to standardize precisiation of meaning by expressing a precisiated form of p as a restriction.

9.2. The Concept of Explanatory Database (ED)

In restriction-based semantics, the restricted variable, X, and the restricting relation, R, are described in a natural language. The concept of explanatory database, ED, serves to precisiate the meaning of X and R.

Generally, ED is represented as a collection of relations, with the names of relations drawn, but not exclusively, from the constituents of p [526].

For example, for the proposition, p: Most Swedes are tall, ED may be represented as

$$\text{ED} = \text{POPULATION.SWEDES[Name; Height]} + \text{TALL[Height; } \mu\text{]}$$
$$+ \text{MOST[Proportion;} \mu\text{]},$$

where $+$ plays the role of comma.

In relation to possible-world semantics, ED may be viewed as the description of a collection of possible-worlds, with the understanding that an instantiated ED is the description of a possible-world. More generally, an instantiated ED may be viewed as the description of a scenario. An instantiated ED may be viewed as a state of p, with ED playing the role of the state-space of p, SS(p). It is important to note that relations in ED are uninstantiated, that is, the values of database variables — entries in relations — are not specified. A database variable may be a scalar variable, and n-ary variable, a function or a relation. As an illustration, the database variables in p:

Most Swedes are tall, are μtall, μ most and $h1, \ldots, hn$, where hi is the height of Name $i, i = 1, \ldots, n$. Instantiated database variables constitute a state of p.

ED (state-space of p (SSp)) is shown in Fig. 9.3.

After X and R have been identified and the explanatory database, ED, has been constructed, X and R may be defined as functions of ED. As was noted earlier, definition of X and R may be viewed as precisiation of X and R. Precisiated X and R are denoted as X^* and R^*, respectively.

A canonical form, $\text{CF}^*(p)$, with precisiated values of X and R, X^* and R^*, will be referred to as a precisiated canonical form. In the following, construction of the precisiated canonical form of p is

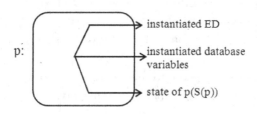

Fig. 9.3. State of p.

discussed in greater detail.

From p To $CF^*(p)$:

X^* is$r$ R^*

The concepts discussed so far provide a basis for a relatively straightforward procedure for constructing the precisiated canonical form of a given proposition, p. The precisiated canonical form may be viewed as a computational model of p. Effectively, the precisiated canonical form may be interpreted as a representation of precisiated meaning of p. A summary of the procedure for computing the precisiated canonical form of p is presented in the following.

Step 1. $\xrightarrow{\text{Clarification}}$

The first step is clarification, if needed, of the meaning of p. This step requires world knowledge.

Examples:

Overeating causes obesity $\xrightarrow{\text{Clarification}}$
Most of those who overeat are obese. Obesity is caused by overeating.
Clarification Most of those, who are obese, overeat.
Young men like young women.

$\xrightarrow{\text{Clarification Most young men like mostly young women}}$

Swedes are much taller than Italians $\xrightarrow{\text{Clarification}}$
Most Swedes are much taller than most Italians.

Step 2. Identification (explicitation) of X and R.

Identify the constrained variable, X, and the corresponding constraining relation, R.

Step 3. Construction of ED.

What information is needed — but not necessarily minimally — to precisiate (define) X and R? An answer to this question identifies the explanatory database, ED. Equivalently, ED may be viewed as an answer to the question: What information is needed — but not necessarily minimally — to compute the truth-value of p?

Step 4. Precisiation of X and R.

How can the information in ED be used to precisiate the values of X and R? This step leads to precisiated values of X and R, X^* and R^*, and thus results in the precisiated canonical form, $CF^*(p)$.

Precisiated X^* and R^* may be expressed as functions of ED and, more specifically, as functions of database variables, $v1, \ldots, vn$.

It is important to observe that in the case of possibilistic constraints, $CF^*(p)$ induces a possibilistic constraint on database variables, $v1, \ldots, vn$, in ED. This constraint may be interpreted as the possibility distribution of database variables in ED or, equivalently, as a possibility distribution on the state space, $SS(p)$, of p — a possibility distribution which is induced by p. The possibility distribution induced by p may be viewed as the intension of p.

Step 5. (Optional) Computation of truth-value of p. The truth-value of p depends on ED. The truth-value of p, $t(p, \text{ED})$, may be computed by assessing the degree to which the generalized constraint, X^* is$r$ R^*, is satisfied. It is important to observe that the possibility of an instantiated ED given p is equal to the truth-value of p given instantiated ED [521].

It is important to note that humans have no difficulty in learning how to use the procedure. The principal reason is: Humans have world knowledge. It is hard to build world knowledge into machines.

The generalized constraint on X^*, $GC(X^*)$, induces (converts into) a generalized constraint, $GC(V)$, on the database variables, $V = (v1, \ldots, vn)$ (Fig. 9.4). For possibilistic constraints, $GC(V)$ may be expressed as

$$f(V) \text{ is } A$$

where f is a function of database variables and A is a fuzzy relation (set) in the space of database variables.

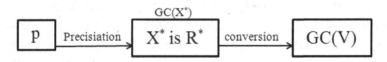

Fig. 9.4. Calculation of database variables.

Note. In the following example, $r =$ blank, that is, the generalized constraints are possibilistic.

1. p: Most Swedes are tall.

Step 1. Clarification. Clarification not needed.

Step 2. Identification (explicitation) of X and R.

X is identified as the proportion of tall Swedes among Swedes. Correspondingly, R is identified as Most.

Digression.

More specifically, if A and B are fuzzy sets in U, $U = \{u1, \ldots, un\}$, the $\sum$ Count (Cardinality) of A is defined as

$$\sum \text{Count}(A) = \sum_i \mu_A(u_i)$$

The relative $\sum$ Count of B in A is defined as

$$\sum \text{Count}(B/A) = \frac{\sum \text{Count}(A \cap B)}{\sum \text{Count}(A)} = \frac{\sum_i \mu_A(u_i) \wedge \mu_B(u_i))}{\sum_i \mu_A(u_i)}$$

where $\cap$ is intersection and $\wedge$ is min

In application to the example under consideration, assume that the height of ith Swede, Name i, is h_i and that the grade of membership of h_i in tall is $\mu_{\text{tall}}(h_i), i = 1, \ldots, n$. X may be expressed as

$$X = \frac{1}{n} \left(\sum_i \mu_{\text{tall}}(h_i) \right)$$

Step 3. Construction of ED.

The needed information is contained in the explanatory database, ED, where

ED = POPULATION.SWEDES[Name; Height] + TALL[Height;μ]

    + MOST[Proportion;μ]

Step 4. Precisiation of X and R.

In relation to ED, precisiated X and R may be expressed as

$$X^* = \frac{1}{n}\left(\sum_i \mu_{\text{tall}}(h_i)\right)$$

$$R^* = \text{MOST}[\text{Proportion};\mu]$$

The precisiated canonical form is expressed as

$$\text{CF}^*p = X^* \text{ is } R^*$$

where

$$X^* = \frac{1}{n}\left(\sum_i \mu_{\text{tall}}(h_i)\right)$$

$$R^* = \text{MOST}[\text{Proportion};\mu]$$

Step 5. The truth-value of p, $t(p, \text{ED})$, is the degree to which the constraint in step 4 is satisfied. More concretely,

$$t(p, ED) = \mu_{\text{most}}\left(\frac{1}{n}\sum_i \mu_{\text{tall}}(h_i)\right)$$

Note: The right-hand side of this equation may be viewed as a constraint on database variables $h_1, \ldots, h_n$, μ_{tall} and μ_{most}.

In conclusion, we have to mention that natural languages are pervasively imprecise, especially in the realm of meaning. The primary source of imprecision is the unsharpness of class boundaries. In this sense, words, phrases, propositions and commands in natural languages are preponderantly imprecise.

Precisiation of meaning is a prerequisite to achievement of higher levels of mechanization of natural language understanding. Precisiation of meaning plays a particularly important role in communication between humans and machines. Furthermore, precisiation of meaning is a prerequisite to problem-solving with information which is described in a natural language.

Despite its intrinsic importance, precisiation of meaning has drawn little, if any, attention within linguistics and computational linguistics. There is a reason. In large measure, theories of natural languages are based on bivalent logic.

A basic difference between a proposition drawn from a natural language and a proposition drawn from a mathematical language is that in the latter, the variables and the values assigned to them are explicit, whereas in the former the variables and the assigned values are implicit.

There is an additional difference. When p is drawn from a natural language, the assigned value is not sharply defined — typically it is fuzzy, as "most" is. When p is drawn from a mathematical language, the assigned value is sharply defined.

There is another important point. When p is drawn from a natural language, the value assigned to X is not really a value of X — it is a constraint (restriction) on the values which X is allowed to take. This suggests an unconventional definition of a proposition, p, drawn from a natural language. Specifically, a proposition is an implicit constraint on an implicit variable.

Constraints which we have in mind are not standard constraints — they are so-called generalized constraints.

Words and phrases in a natural language have elasticity. Another important point. What I have said so far explains why in the realm of natural languages most constraints are possibilistic. This is equivalent to saying, that in a natural language most words and phrases are labels of fuzzy sets.

Robert: Many thanks. You clarified what was not clear to me.

There is an analogy that may be of assistance. More specifically, the fuzzy set young may be represented as a chain linked to a spring, as shown in Fig. 9.5. The left end of the chain is fixed and the position of the right end of the spring represents the value of the variable Age (Robert).

The force that is applied to the right end of the spring is a measure of grade of membership. Initially, the length of the chain is 0, as is the length of the spring.

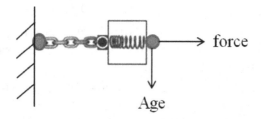

Fig. 9.5. Elasticity of meaning.

Elasticity of meaning is a basic characteristic of natural languages. Elasticity of meaning is a neglected issue in the literatures of linguistics, computational linguistics and philosophy of languages. There is a reason.

Traditional theories of natural language are based on bivalent logic. Bivalent logic, by itself or in combination with probability theory, is not the right tool for dealing with elasticity of meaning. What is needed for this purpose is fuzzy logic.

Unprecisiated (raw) propositions drawn from a natural language cannot be computed with. Precisiation is a prerequisite to computation. What is important to understand is that precisiation of meaning opens the door to computation with natural language.

Computation with natural language or, more or less equivalently, computing with words (CW or CWW), is largely unrelated to natural language processing.

More specifically, computation with natural language is focused on computation with information described in a natural language. Typically, what is involved is solution of a problem which is stated in a natural language. Let me go back to our example, p: Most Swedes are tall. Given this information, how can you compute the average height of Swedes?

A mathematician would say that the problem is ill-posed. It appears to be ill-posed for two reasons.

First, because the given information: Most Swedes are tall, is fuzzy, and second, because you assume that I am expecting you to come up with a crisp answer like "the average height of Swedes is 5' 10." Actually, what I expect is a fuzzy answer — it would be unreasonable to expect a crisp answer.

The problem becomes well-posed if p is precisiated. This is the essence of computing with words.

As we move further into the age of machine intelligence and automated reasoning, the complex of problems related to computation with information described in a natural language is certain to grow in visibility and importance.

Chapter 10

Granular Computing: Principles and Algorithms

Granular Computing is concerned with constructing and processing carried out at the level of information granules. Using information granules, we comprehend the world and interact with it, no matter which intelligent endeavor this may involve. The landscape of Granular Computing is immensely rich and involves set theory (interval mathematics), fuzzy sets, etc. in a highly synergetic environment. This chapter is a comprehensive study of this emerging paradigm and embraces its fundamentals, underlying methodological framework and a sound algorithmic environment.

10.1. Introduction

This study serves as a concise introduction to Granular Computing. Information granules and their computing form a cornerstone of this discipline. Our intent is to bring forward the concepts of information granules, discuss their formalizations and present pertinent algorithmic aspects. The concepts of information granules and information granularity offer a general perspective at information processing and entail far-reaching implications in numerous application areas. This is predominantly due to fact that information granules realize abstraction processes completed at various levels of hierarchy. This aspect is emphasized and exemplified through selected examples.

We focus on the fundamental constructs of Granular Computing [54, 55, 356], which are of importance when processing information granules and formulate some general ways in which the results are developed and interpreted. There are two main categories of algorithms studied here. The first one is concerned with a way of designing information granules. We introduce a principle of justifiable granularity along with its generalizations to deliver a way of forming information granules on a basis of available experimental evidence. It is emphasized how information granules are developed on a basis of some well-defined and intuitively supported objectives. It is also underlined a general way in which information granules of higher type arise. The second category of approaches, we show that information granularity can be regarded as a useful design asset augmenting the existing numeric constructs by forming so-called granular mappings considered and studied in system modeling and pattern recognition.

10.2.   Information Granularity: Selected Examples

Information granules are intuitively appealing constructs, which play a pivotal role in human cognitive and decision-making activities [54–57, 534, 536, 541]. We perceive complex phenomena by organizing existing knowledge along with available experimental evidence and structuring them in a form of some meaningful, semantically sound entities, which are central to all ensuing processes of describing the world, reasoning about the environment and support decision-making activities.

The term information granularity itself has emerged in different contexts and numerous areas of application. It carries various meanings. One can refer to Artificial Intelligence in which case information granularity is central to a way of problem solving through problem decomposition, where various subtasks could be formed and solved individually. Information granules and the area of intelligent computing revolving around them being termed Granular Computing are quite often presented with a direct association with the pioneering studies. He coined an informal yet highly descriptive and compelling concept of information granules. In a general way, by information granules one regards a collection of elements drawn together by their closeness (resemblance, proximity, functionality, etc.) articulated in terms of some useful spatial, temporal, or functional relationships. Subsequently, Granular Computing is about representing, constructing, processing, and communicating information granules.

It is again worth emphasizing that information granules permeate almost all human endeavors. No matter which problem is taken into consideration, we usually set it up in a certain conceptual framework composed of some generic and conceptually meaningful entities — information granules, which we regard to be of relevance to the problem formulation, further problem solving, and a way in which the findings are communicated to the community. Information granules realize a framework in which we formulate generic concepts by adopting a certain level of abstraction. Let us refer here to some areas, which offer compelling evidence as to the nature of underlying processing and interpretation in which information granules play a pivotal role.

10.2.1. *Image processing*

In spite of the continuous progress in the area, a human being assumes a dominant and very much uncontested position when it comes to understanding and interpreting images. Surely, we do not focus our attention on individual pixels and process them as such but group them together into a hierarchy of semantically meaningful constructs — familiar objects we deal with in everyday life. Such objects involve regions that consist of pixels or categories of pixels drawn together because of their proximity in the image, similar texture, color, etc. This remarkable and unchallenged ability of humans dwells on our effortless ability to construct information granules, manipulate them and arrive at sound conclusions.

10.2.2. *Processing and interpretation of time series*

From our perspective we can describe them in a semi-qualitative manner by pointing at specific regions of such signals. Medical specialists can effortlessly interpret various diagnostic signals including ECG or EEG recordings [351]. They distinguish some segments of such signals and interpret their combinations. In stock market, one analyzes numerous time series by looking at amplitudes, trends, and patterns. Experts can interpret temporal readings of sensors and assess a status of the monitored system. Again, in all these situations, the individual samples of the signals are not the focal point of the analysis, synthesis and the signal interpretation. We always granulate all phenomena (no matter if they are originally discrete or analog in their nature). When working with time series, information granulation occurs in time and in the feature space where the data are described.

10.2.3.   *Granulation of time*

Time is another important and omnipresent variable that is subjected to granulation. We use seconds, minutes, days, months, and years. Depending upon a specific problem we have in mind who the user is, the size of information granules (time intervals) could vary quite significantly. To the high-level management time intervals of quarters of year or a few years could be meaningful temporal information granules on basis of which one develops any predictive model. For those in charge of everyday operation of a dispatching center, minutes and hours could form a viable scale of time granulation. Long-term planning is very much different from day-to-day operation. For the designer of high-speed integrated circuits and digital systems, the temporal information granules concern nanoseconds, microseconds, and perhaps milliseconds. Granularity of information (in this case time) helps us focus on the most suitable level of detail.

10.2.4.   *Data summarization*

Information granules naturally emerge when dealing with data, including those coming in the form of data streams. The ultimate objective is to describe the underlying phenomenon in an easily understood way and at a certain level of abstraction. This requires that we use a vocabulary of commonly encountered terms (concepts) and discover relationships between them and possible linkages among the underlying concepts. Having a collection of detailed numeric weather data concerning temperature, humidity, wind speed, they are transformed into a linguistic description at the higher level of abstraction. It is noticeable that the notion of information granularity emerges with regard to several variables present in the data.

Information granules are examples of abstract entities which result as an abstraction process. As such they naturally give rise to hierarchical structures: the same problem or system can be perceived at different levels of specificity (detail) depending on the complexity of the problem, available computing resources, and particular needs to be addressed. A hierarchy of information granules is inherently visible in processing of information granules. The level of details (which is represented in terms of the size of information granules) becomes an essential facet facilitating a way a hierarchical processing of information with different levels of hierarchy indexed by the size of information granules.

Even such commonly encountered and simple examples presented above are convincing enough to lead us to ascertain that (a) information granules are the key components of knowledge representation and processing, (b) the level of granularity of information granules (their size, to be more descriptive) becomes crucial to the problem description and an overall strategy of problem solving, (c) hierarchy of information granules supports an important aspect of perception of phenomena and deliver a tangible way of dealing with complexity by focusing on the most essential facets of the problem, (d) there is no universal level of granularity of information; commonly the size of granules is problem-oriented and user dependent.

Human-centricity comes as an inherent feature of intelligent systems. It is anticipated that a two-way effective human–machine communication is imperative. Human perceive the world, reason, and communicate at some level of abstraction. Abstraction comes hand in hand with non-numeric constructs, which embrace collections of entities characterized by some notions of closeness, proximity, resemblance, or similarity. These collections are referred to as information granules. Processing of information granules is a fundamental way in which people process such entities. Granular Computing has emerged as a framework in which information granules are represented and manipulated by intelligent systems. The two-way communication of such intelligent systems with the users becomes substantially facilitated because of the usage of information granules.

By no means, the above quite descriptive definition of information granules is formal. It rather intends to emphasize the crux of the idea and link it to the human centricity and computing with perceptions rather than plain numbers.

What has been said so far touched upon a qualitative aspect of the problem. The visible challenge is to develop a computing framework within which all these representation and processing endeavors could be formally realized.

While the notions of information granularity and information granules themselves are convincing, they are not operational (algorithmically sound) until some formal models of information granules along with the related algorithmic framework have been introduced. In other words, to secure the algorithmic realization of Granular Computing, the *implicit* nature of information granules has to be translated into the constructs that are *explicit* in their nature, viz. described formally in which information granules can be efficiently computed with.

The common platform emerging within this context comes under the name of Granular Computing. In essence, it is an emerging paradigm of information processing. While we have already noticed a number of important conceptual and computational constructs built in the domain of system modeling, machine learning, image processing, pattern recognition, and data compression, in which various abstractions (and ensuing information granules) came into existence, Granular Computing becomes innovative and intellectually proactive endeavor that manifests in several fundamental ways:

- It identifies the essential commonalities between the surprisingly diversified problems and technologies used there, which could be cast into a unified framework known as a granular world. This is a fully operational processing entity that interacts with the external world (that could be another granular or numeric world) by collecting necessary granular information and returning the outcomes of the Granular Computing.
- With the emergence of the unified framework of granular processing, we get a better grasp as to the role of interaction between various formalisms and visualize a way in which they communicate.

- It brings together the existing plethora of formalisms of set theory (interval analysis) under the same banner by clearly visualizing that in spite of their visibly distinct underpinnings (and ensuing processing), they exhibit some fundamental commonalities. In this sense, Granular Computing establishes a stimulating environment of synergy between the individual approaches.
- By building upon the commonalities of the existing formal approaches, Granular Computing helps assemble heterogeneous and multifaceted models of processing of information granules by clearly recognizing the orthogonal nature of some of the existing and well established frameworks (say, probability theory coming with its probability density functions and fuzzy sets with their membership functions).
- Granular Computing fully acknowledges a notion of variable granularity, whose range could cover detailed numeric entities and very abstract and general information granules. It looks at the aspects of compatibility of such information granules and ensuing communication mechanisms of the granular worlds.
- Granular Computing gives rise to processing that is less time demanding than the one required when dealing with detailed numeric processing.
- Interestingly, the inception of information granules is highly motivated. We do not form information granules without reason. Information granules arise as an evident realization of the fundamental paradigm of abstraction.

On the one hand, Granular Computing as an emerging area brings a great deal of original, unique ideas. On the other, it dwells substantially on the existing well-established developments that have already happened in a number of individual areas. In a synergistic fashion, Granular Computing brings fundamental ideas of interval analysis, fuzzy sets and rough sets, facilitates building a unified view at them where, an overarching concept is the granularity of information itself. It helps identify main problems of processing and its key features, which are common to all the formalisms being considered.

Granular Computing forms a unified conceptual and computing platform. Yet, what is important, it directly benefits from the already existing and well-established concepts of information granules formed in the setting of set theory, fuzzy sets, rough sets and others. Reciprocally, the general investigations carried out under the rubric of Granular Computing offer some interesting and stimulating thoughts to be looked at within the realm of the specific formalism of sets, fuzzy sets, shadowed set or rough sets. There is a plethora of formal approaches towards characterization and processing information granules such as probabilistic sets [205], rough sets [344–346] and axiomatic set theory [279].

10.3. Formal Platforms of Information Granularity

There is a plethora of formal platforms in which information granules are conceptualized, defined and processed. In what follows, we highlight the main formalisms being used and provide their key characterization.

Sets (*intervals*) realize a concept of abstraction by introducing a notion of dichotomy. Dichotomy means that when describing real-world concepts, we admit that any individual element may belong to a given concept — information granule or has to be excluded from it. The notion of dichotomy is central to the two-valued logic where only two truth values (false-true) are considered. The discipline of interval analysis comes as one of the usage of sets composed of numbers [10, 316, 317]. Sets (intervals) are concisely characterized by a so-called characteristic functions taking on values in $\{0, 1\}$. Formally, a characteristic function describing a set A is defined as follows

$$A(x) = \begin{cases} 1 & \text{if } x \in A \\ 0 & \text{if } x \notin A \end{cases} \tag{10.1}$$

where $A(x)$ stands for a value of the characteristic function of set A at point x. With the emergence of digital technologies, interval mathematics has appeared as an important discipline encompassing a great deal of applications. The well-known set operations — union, intersection, and complement being the three fundamental constructs are expressed by means of the characteristic functions of the corresponding sets.

Fuzzy sets form an important and practically sound conceptual and algorithmic generalization of sets. By admitting partial membership of an element to a given information granule, we bring an important feature which makes the concept to be in rapport with reality. It helps working with the notions, where the principle of dichotomy is neither justified, nor advantageous. The description of fuzzy sets is realized in terms of membership functions taking on values in the unit interval. Formally, a fuzzy set A is described by a membership function mapping the elements of a universe X to the unit interval $[0, 1]$

$$A : X \rightarrow [0, 1] \tag{10.2}$$

The membership functions are therefore synonymous of fuzzy sets. Operations on fuzzy sets are realized in the same way as for sets. Given the fact that we are concerned with membership grades in $[0, 1]$ rather than 0s and 1s, there are a number of alternatives in the realization of fuzzy sets operators (logic *and or* operators, respectively). Those are implemented through so-called t-norms and t-conorms [242, 354].

Shadowed sets [347, 352] offer an interesting description of information granules by distinguishing among three categories of elements. Those are the elements, which (i) fully belong to the concept, (ii) are excluded from it (iii) their belongingness is completely *unknown*. Formally, these information granules are described as a mapping $X : X \rightarrow \{1, 0, [0, 1]\}$ where the elements with the membership quantified as the entire $[0, 1]$ interval are used to describe a shadow of the construct. Given the nature of the mapping here, shadowed sets can be sought as a granular description of fuzzy sets where the shadow is used to localize unknown membership values, which in fuzzy sets are distributed over the entire universe of discourse. Note that the shadow produces non-numeric descriptors of membership grades.

Probability-oriented information granules are expressed in the form of some probability density functions. They capture a collection of elements resulting from some experiment.

In virtue of the fundamental concept of probability, the granularity of information associates with a manifestation of occurrence of some elements. Probability function or probability density function are commonly encountered descriptors of experimental data. The abstraction offered by probabilities is apparent: instead of coping with huge masses of data, one produces their abstract manifestation in the form of a single or a few probability functions. Histograms are examples of probabilistic information granules arising as a concise characterization of one-dimensional data. They can be regarded as approximations of probability density functions.

Rough sets emphasize a roughness of description of a given concept X when being realized in terms of the indiscernibility relation provided in advance. The roughness of the description of X is manifested in terms of its lower and upper approximations using which a certain rough set is characterized.

Some other formal models of information granules involve axiomatic sets, soft sets, and intuitionistic sets (in which raised is a notion of membership and non-membership).

The choice of a certain formal setting of information granulation is mainly dictated by the formulation of the problem and the associated specifications coming with the problem. There is an interesting and a quite broad spectrum of views at information granules and their processing. The two extremes are quite visible here:

Symbolic perspective: A concept — information granule is viewed as a single symbol (entity). This view is very much present in the AI community, where computing revolves around symbolic processing. Symbols are subject to processing rules giving rise to results, which are again symbols coming from the same vocabulary one has started with.

Numeric perspective: Here, information granules are associated with a detailed numeric characterization. Fuzzy sets are profound examples with this regard. We start with numeric membership functions. All ensuing processing involves *numeric* membership grades so in essence it focuses on number crunching. The results are inherently numeric. The progress present here has resulted in a diversity of numeric constructs. Because of the commonly encountered numeric treatment of fuzzy sets, the same applies to logic operators (connectives) encountered in fuzzy sets.

There are a number of alternatives of describing information that are positioned in-between these two extremes or the descriptions could be made more in a multi-level fashion. For instance, one could have an information granule described by a fuzzy set whose membership grades are symbolic (ordered terms, say *small*, *medium*, *high*; all defined in the unit interval).

With regard to the formal settings of information granules as briefly highlighted above, it is instructive to mention that all of them offer some operational realization (in different ways, though) of implicit concepts by endowing them by a well-defined semantics. For instance, treated implicitly an information granule *small error* is regarded just as a symbol (and could be subject to symbolic processing as usually realized in Artificial Intelligence), however once explicitly articulated as an information granule, it comes associated with some semantics (becomes calibrated), thus coming with a sound operational description, say characteristic or membership function. In the formalism of fuzzy sets, the symbol *small* comes with the membership description, which could be further processed.

10.4. Characterization of Information Granules: Coverage and Specificity

The characterization of information granules is more challenging in comparison to a way in which a single numeric entity could be fully described. This is not surprising considering the abstract nature of the granule. In what follows, we introduce two measures that are of practical relevance and offer a useful insight into the nature and further usage of the granule in various constructs.

In a descriptive way, a level of abstraction captured by some information granules A is associated with the number of elements (data) embraced by the granule. For instance, these elements are the elements of the space or a collection of some experimental data. A certain measure of cardinality, which counts the number of elements involved in the information granule, forms a sound descriptor of information granularity. The higher the number of elements embraced by the information granule, the higher the abstraction of this granule and the lower its specificity becomes. Starting with a set theory formalism where A is a set, its cardinality is computed in the form of the following sum in the case of a finite universe of discourse $X = \{x_1, x_2, \ldots, x_n\}$:

$$\text{card}(A) = \sum_{i=1}^{n} A(x_i) \tag{10.3}$$

or an integral (when the universe is infinite and the integral of the membership function itself does exists)

$$\text{card}(A) = \int_x A(x)dx \tag{10.4}$$

where $A(x)$ is a formal description of the information granule (say, in the form of the characteristic function or membership function). For a fuzzy set, we count the number of its elements but one has to bear in mind that each element may belong with a certain degree of membership so the calculations carried out above involve the degrees of membership. In this case, one commonly refers to the cardinality as a δ — count of A. For rough sets, one can proceed in a similar manner as above by expressing the granularity of the lower and upper bounds of the rough set (roughness). In case of probabilistic information granules, one can consider its standard deviation as a sound descriptor of information granularity. The higher the coverage (cardinality), the higher the level of abstraction being associated with the information granule.

The specificity is about the level of detail being captured by the information granule. As the name stipulates, the specificity indicates how detailed information granule is. In other words, the specificity

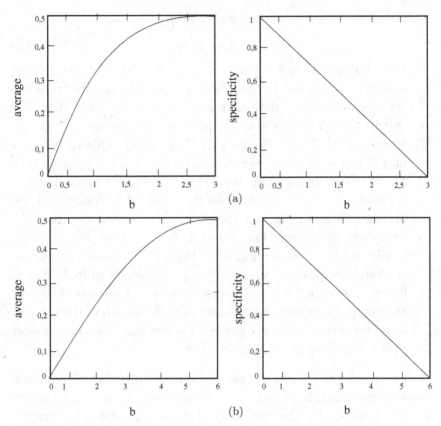

Fig. 10.1. Plots of coverage and specificity as a function of b: (a) $\sigma = 1.0$, (b) $\sigma = 1.0$.

can be determined by assessing the "size" of this fuzzy set. To explain the notion, we start with a case when information granule is an interval $[a, b]$, see Fig. 10.1(a). The specificity can be defined in the following way $1 - (b-a)/range$ where *range* is expressed as $y_{max} - y_{min}$ with y_{max} and y_{min} being the extreme values of assumed by the variable. This definition adheres to our perception of specificity: the broader the interval, the lower its specificity. In the boundary cases, when $a = b$, the specificity attains its maximal value equal to 1 whereas when the interval spreads across the entire space (range), the specificity value is zero. The above definition is a special case. In a general way, specificity is defined as a measure adhering to the conditions we have already outlined above:

$$sp : A \rightarrow [0, 1] \qquad (10.5)$$

(i) Boundary conditions $sp(\{x\}) = 1$, $sp(X) = 0$: A single-element information granule is the most specific. The specificity of the entire space is the minimal one (here we can request that it is equal to zero but this is not required in all situations).

(ii) Monotonicity if $A \subset B$ then $sp(A) \geq sp(B)$: This reflects our intuition that the more detailed information granule comes with the higher specificity. One has to note here that the requirement is general in the sense that the definition of inclusion and the details of computing the specificity are dependent upon the formalism of information granules. In the above example, we considered intervals, see Fig. 10.1. Here, the inclusion of intervals is straightforward; apparently $A = [a, b]$ is included in $B = [c, d]$ if the $a \geq c$ and $b \leq d$. The specificity defined above is just an example; any decreasing function of the length of the interval could serve as a viable alternative. For instance, one can consider $\exp(-|b - a|)$ as the specificity of A.

The technical details of specificity have to be redefined when considering some other formalisms of information granules. Consider a given fuzzy set B. The specificity of B can be defined by starting with the already formulated specificity of an interval. In virtue of the representation theorem stating that any fuzzy set can be described through a collection of it's α-cuts (which are intervals), we determine the specificity of the α-cut B_α.

$B_\alpha = \{y | B(y) \geq \alpha\}$ and then integrate the results over all values of the threshold α. Thus we have

$$sp(B) = \int_0^{\alpha_{max}} sp(B_\alpha) d\alpha = \int_0^{\alpha_{max}} \left(1 - \frac{h(\alpha)}{range}\right) d\alpha \qquad (10.6)$$

where $h(\alpha)$ stands for the length of the interval

$$h(\alpha) = |\max\{y | B^{-1}(y) = \alpha\} - \min\{y | B^{-1}(y) = \alpha\}| \qquad (10.7)$$

α_{max} is the maximal value of membership of B, $\alpha_{max} = hgt(B) = \sup_y B(y)$. For normal fuzzy set B, $\alpha_{max} = 1$. In other words, the specificity comes as an average of specificity values of the corresponding α-cuts. In practical situations, the integral standing in (10.6) is replaced by its discrete version involving summation carried out over some finite number of values of α.

To visualize the concepts of coverage and specificity as well as to emphasize the relationships between these two characteristics, we assume that the data are governed by the Gaussian probability density function $p(x)$ with a zero mean and some standard deviation. As the interval is symmetric, we are interested in determining an optimal value of its upper bound b. The coverage provided by the interval $[0, b]$ is expressed as the integral of the probability function

$$\text{cov}([0, b]) = \int_0^b p(x)dx \tag{10.8}$$

while the specificity (assuming that the $x_{\max}$ is set as 3) is defined in the following form

$$sp([0, b]) = 1 - \frac{b}{x_{\max}} \tag{10.9}$$

The plots of the coverage and the specificity measures being regarded as a function of b are shown in Fig. 10.1.

One can note that the coverage is a nonlinear and monotonically increasing function of b while the specificity (in the form specified above) is a linearly decreasing function of b. As becomes intuitively apparent, the increase in the coverage results in lower values of the specificity measure and vice versa. We will consider them as two essential criteria guiding the development of information granules.

10.5. The Design of Information Granules

Information granules are a manifestation of abstraction and as such have to reflect the existing real world and its phenomena. In what follows, we discuss two main approaches to the development of information granules.

First, the principle of justifiable granularity supports a construction of an information granule on a basis of some experimental evidence (typically those could be numeric experimental data) by striking a balance between the criterion of coverage and specificity.

Second, there is a plethora of clustering algorithms. Clustering can be sought as a synonym of information granulation when a large data set is represented (described) by a small of collection of clusters — information granules. Depending of the underlying formalism in which information granules are expressed, we encounter resulting clusters in the form of sets, fuzzy sets or rough sets. K-means is a representative example of clustering when clusters come in the form of sets.

Fuzzy C-means (FCM) is a representative of fuzzy clustering; the clusters come in the form of fuzzy sets whose membership functions are contained in a certain partition matrix. Clustering is a very well-established area with a lot of reference material easily found. In what follows, we focus on the principle of justifiable granularity while making some additional comments on linkages with clustering techniques.

10.5.1. *The principle of justifiable granularity*

The principle of justifiable granularity [356, 357, 359] delivers a comprehensive conceptual and algorithmic setting to develop information granules. The principle is general in the sense it shows a way of forming information granules without being restricted to certain formalism in which granules are formalized. Information granules are built by considering available experimental evidence.

Let us start with a simple scenario using which we illustrate the key components of this principle and deliver its underlying motivation. Consider a collection of one-dimensional numeric real-number data of interest (for which an information granule is to be formed) $X = \{x_1, x_2, \ldots, x_N\}$. Denote the largest and the smallest element in X by $x_{\min}$ and $x_{\max}$, respectively. On a basis of this experimental evidence X, we form an interval information granule A so that it satisfies the requirements of coverage and specificity. The first requirement implies that the information granule is justifiable, viz. it embraces (covers) as many elements of X as possible and can be sought as a sound representative. The quest for meeting the requirement of the well-defined semantics is quantified in terms of high specificity of A. In other words, for given $\boldsymbol{X}$, the interval A has to satisfy the requirement of high coverage and specificity; these two concepts have been already discussed in the previous chapter. In other words, the construction of $A = [a, b]$ leads to the optimization of its bounds a and b so that at the same time we maximize the coverage and specificity. It is known that these requirements are in conflict: the increase in the coverage values leads to lower values of specificity. To transform the two-objective optimization problem in a scalar version of the optimization, we consider the performance index built as a product of the coverage and specificity

$$V(a, b) = \text{cov}(A) * sp(A) \qquad (10.10)$$

and determine the solution $(a_{\text{opt}}, b_{\text{opt}})$ such that $V(a, b)$ becomes maximized.

The ensuing approach can be established as a two-phase algorithm. In phase one, we proceed with a formation of a numeric representative of $\boldsymbol{X}$ denoted by r, say a mean, median, or a modal value (denoted here by r) that can be regarded as a rough initial representative of $\boldsymbol{X}$. In the second phase, we separately determine the lower bound (a) and the upper bound (b) of the interval by maximizing the product of the coverage and specificity as specified by the optimization criterion. This simplifies the process of building the granule as we encounter two separate optimization tasks

$$\begin{aligned} a_{\text{opt}} &= \arg \text{Max}_a V(a), V(a) = \text{cov}([a, r]) * sp([a, r]) \\ b_{\text{opt}} &= \arg \text{Max}_a V(b), V(b) = \text{cov}([r, b]) * sp([r, b]) \end{aligned} \qquad (10.11)$$

We calculate $\text{cov}([r, b]) = \text{card}\{x_k | x_k \in [r, b]\}/N$. The specificity model has to be provided in advance. Its simplest version is expressed as $sp([r, b]) = 1 - |b - r|/(x_{\text{max}} - r)$ By sweeping through possible values of b positioned within the range $[r, x_{\text{max}}]$, we observe that the coverage is a stair-wise increasing function whereas the specificity decreases linearly, see Fig. 10.2. The maximum of the product can be easily determined.

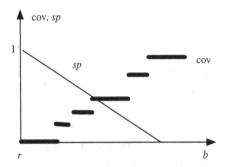

Fig. 10.2. Example plots of coverage and specificity (linear model) regarded as a function of b.

The determination of the optimal value of the lower bound of the interval a is completed in the same way as above. We determine the coverage by counting the data located to the left from the numeric representative r, namely $\text{cov}([a, r]) = \text{card}\{x_k | x_k \in [a, r]\}/N$ and compute the specificity as $sp([a, r]) = 1 - |a - r|/(r - x_{\min})$.

Some additional flexibility can be added to the optimized performance index by adjusting the impact of the specificity in the construction of the information granule. This is done by bringing a weight factor ξ as follows

$$V(a, b) = \text{cov}(A) * sp(A) \tag{10.12}$$

Note that the values of ξ lower than 1 discount the impact of specificity in the design of information granule; in the limit case this impact is eliminated when $\xi = 0$. The value of ξ set to 1 returns the original performance index whereas the values of ξ greater than 1 stress the importance of specificity by producing results that are more specific.

In case the data are governed by some given probability function $p(x)$, the coverage is computed as an integral $\text{cov}([r, b]) = \int_r^b p(x)dx$. The calculations of specificity are completed as before.

In case of n-dimensional multivariable data, $X = \{x_1, x_2, \ldots, x_n\}$, the principle is realized in a similar manner. For convenience, we assume that the data are normalized to $[0, 1]$ meaning that each coordinate of the normalized x_k assumes values positioned in $[0, 1]$. The numeric representative r is determined first and then the information granule is built around it. The coverage is expressed in the form of the following count

$$\text{cov}(A) = \text{card}\{x_k | \|x_k - r\|^2 \le n\rho^2\} \qquad (10.13)$$

Note that the geometry of the resulting information granule is implied by the form of the distance function $\|.\|$ used in (10.4). For the Euclidean distance, the granule is a circle. For the Tchebyshev one, we end up with hyper rectangular shapes. The specificity is expressed as $sp(A) = 1 - \rho$. For these two distance functions, the corresponding plots for a two-dimensional case are illustrated in Fig. 10.3.

So far we have presented the development of the principle of justifiable granularity when building an interval information granule.

When constructing an information granule in the form of a fuzzy set, the implementation of the principle has to be modified. Considering some predetermined form of the membership function, say a triangular one, the parameters of this fuzzy set (lower and upper bounds, a and b) are optimized. See Fig. 10.4.

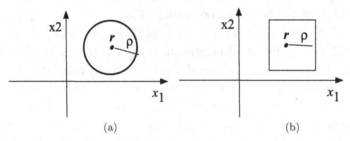

Fig. 10.3. Development of information granules in the two-dimensional case when using two distance functions: (a) Euclidean distance and (b) Tchebyshev distance.

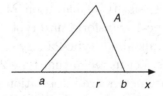

Fig. 10.4. Triangular membership function with adjustable (optimized) bounds a and b.

The coverage is replaced by a σ-count by summing up the membership grades of the data in A (in what follows we are concerned with the determination of the upper bound of the membership function, namely b)

$$\mathrm{cov}(A) = \sum_{k:x_k > r} A(x_k) \qquad (10.14)$$

The coverage computed to determine the lower bound (a) is expressed in the form

$$\mathrm{cov}(A) = \sum_{k:x_k < r} A(x_k) \qquad (10.15)$$

Several interesting and practically sound variants of the principle are also considered. Before moving to their discussion, we make a general observation. The principle supports an elevation of the type of information granules being constructed. This means that given a collection of experimental data in the form of information granules of type-n leads to an information granule of type $n + 1$. The raise in the type of information granule is a manifestation of the elevated abstraction of the resulting construct [356].

In particular, a collection of experimental data — numerical data viz. type-0 information granules lead to a single information granule of type-1, say an interval, fuzzy set or a probability function. When considering experimental evidence in the form of fuzzy sets or intervals (viz. type-1 information granules), the result becomes an information granule of type-2, say type-2 fuzzy set or an interval-valued interval. In essence, we end up with an information granule of elevated type in comparison to level of information granularity the available experimental evidence we have started with. This comes as a general regularity of elevation of type of information granularity data of type-1 transform into type-2, data of type-2 into type-3, etc. Hence we talk about type-2 fuzzy sets, granular intervals, imprecise probabilities. Let us recall that type-2 information granule is a granule whose parameters are information granules rather than numeric entities. Recall that type-2 fuzzy sets have membership functions whose membership grades are fuzzy sets defined in the

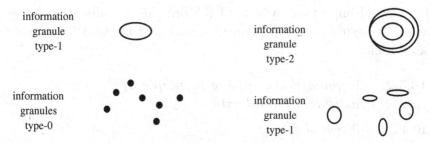

Fig. 10.5. Aggregation of experimental evidence through the principle of justifiable granularity: an elevation of type of information granularity.

unit interval or intervals contained in $[0, 1]$. Likewise imprecise probabilities come with probability values that are information granules. Figure 10.5 illustrates a hierarchy of information granules built successively by using the principle of justifiable granularity.

It is also worth noting that the principle of justifiable granularity applies to various formalisms of information granules and this makes this approach substantially general.

A brief note could be helpful on some linkages between the principle of justifiable granularity and clustering as there are some interesting linkages between them.

(i) The principle is concerned with a formation of a single information granule whereas in virtue of the underlying concept, clustering is about a formation of at least two clusters (information granules).

(ii) The principle of justifiable granularity can be used to augment the results of clustering. For instance in k-means as well as FCM, the algorithm returns a collection of prototypes which are numeric. One can enhance their representation capabilities by forming granular prototypes, which are built around the prototypes. In this sense, the principle of justifiable granularity enriches the results of clustering.

(iii) The principle of justifiable granularity could be initialized by the results of clustering in the sense the numeric prototype offers a starting point of the algorithm.

Several important variants of the principle are discussed below where its generic version becomes augmented by available domain knowledge.

10.5.2. *Augmentations of the principle of justifiable granularity*

10.5.2.1. *Weighted data*

The data can come in a weighted format meaning that each data point x_k is associated with a weight w_k assuming values in $[0, 1]$ and quantifying the relevance (importance) of the data. The higher the value of the weight w_k, the higher the importance of x_k becomes. Apparently, this situation generalized the previously discussed in which all w_k's can be treated as equal to 1. The computing the coverage is modified to accommodate the varying values of the weight. When forming an interval information granule, we consider the sum of the weights leading to the coverage expressed in the form (we are concerned with the optimization of the upper bound of the interval $[a, b]$)

$$\text{cov}([r, b]) = \sum_{k:x_k > r} w_k \qquad (10.16)$$

When building a fuzzy set, we additionally accommodate the values of the corresponding membership grades thus computing the coverage in the form (again the computations are concerned with the optimization of the upper bound of the support of A).

$$\text{cov}(A) = \sum_{k:x_k > r} \min(A(x_k), w_k) \qquad (10.17)$$

Note that the minimum operation leads to the conservative way of determining the contribution of x_k to the computing the coverage.

The definition of specificity and its computing is kept unchanged.

The approach presented here can be referred to filter-based (or context-based) principle of justifiable granularity. The weights associated with the data play a role of filter delivering some auxiliary information about the data for which an information granule is being constructed.

10.5.2.2. *Inhibitory data*

In a number of problems, especially in classification tasks, where we usually encounter data (patterns) belonging to several classes, an information granule is built for the data belonging to a given class. In terms of coverage, the objective is to embrace (cover) as much experimental evidence behind the given class, but at the same time an inclusion of data of inhibitory character (those coming from other classes) has to be penalized. This leads us to the modification of the coverage to accommodate the data of the inhibitory character. Consider the interval information granule and focus on the optimization of the upper bound. As usual, the numeric representative is determined by taking a weighted average of the excitatory data (r). Along with the excitatory data to be represented (x_k, w_k), the inhibitory data come in the form of the pairs (z_k, v_k). The weights w_k and v_k assume the values in the unit interval. The computing of the coverage has to take into consideration the discounting nature of the inhibitory data, namely

$$\text{cov}([r, b]) = \max \left(0, \sum_{k:x_k \geq r} w_k - \gamma \sum_{k:z_k \in [r,b]} v_k \right) \tag{10.18}$$

The alternative version of the coverage can be expressed as follows:

$$\text{cov}([r, b]) = \sum_{\substack{k:x_k \geq r \\ z_k \in [r,b]}} [\max(0, w_k - \gamma v_k)] \tag{10.19}$$

As seen above, the inhibitory data reduce to the reduction of the coverage; the non-negative parameter γ is used to control an impact coming from the inhibitory data. The specificity of the information granule is computed in the same way as done previously.

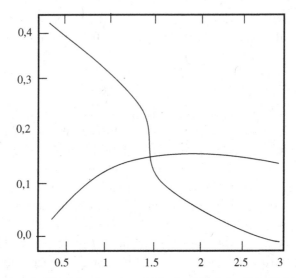

Fig. 10.6. Plots of pdfs of the data for which the principle of justifiable granularity is applied. Shown are also inhibitory data (governed by p_2).

We consider data governed by the normal probability function $N(0,1)$ $(p_1(x))$. The inhibitory data are also governed by the normal distribution $N(2,2)$ $(p_2(x))$. The plots of these pdfs are shown in Fig. 10.6. In virtue of the given pdfs, the coverage is easily computed as follows (here $\gamma = 1$), $\mathrm{cov} = \max(0, \int_0^b \rho_1(x)dx - \int_0^b \rho_2(x)dx$. We are interested in forming an optimal interval $[0,b]$ with the upper bound being optimized.

The optimal value of b is determined by maximizing the product of the above coverage and specificity (which in this case is taken as $1 - b/4$. $V = b_{\mathrm{opt}} = \arg\max_b V(b)$.

The plots of the maximized performance index V versus values of b are displayed in Fig. 10.7.

The maximum is clearly visible as it is achieved for $b = 1.05$. For comparison, when $\gamma = 0$ (so no inhibitory data are taken into consideration), the optimal value of b becomes higher and equal to 1.35 (which is not surprising as we are not penalizing by the inhibitory data). In this case, the corresponding plot of V is also shown in Fig. 10.7 (dotted curve).

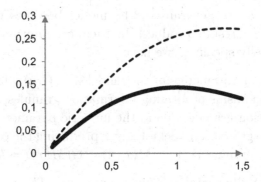

Fig. 10.7. Plots of V (b) for $\gamma = 1$ (solid line) and $\gamma = 0$ (dotted line).

10.6. Information Granularity as a Design Asset in System Modeling

The concept of the granular mapping (and model described by the mapping, in general) delivers a generalization of commonly encountered numeric mappings (models) no matter what their structure is [56, 283, 350]. In this sense, this conceptualization in the format of granular mappings offers an interesting and practically convincing direction. The constructs of this nature are valid for any formalism of information granules.

10.6.1. *Granular mappings*

A numeric mapping (model) M_0 constructed on a basis of a collection of training data $(\boldsymbol{x}_k, \text{target}_k)$, $\boldsymbol{x}_k \in R^n$ and target $t_k \in R$ and comes with a collection of its parameters a, where $a \in R^p$. In the buildup of the mapping, the values of the parameters are optimized yielding a vector a_{opt}. The estimation of the parameters is realized by minimizing a certain performance index Q (say, a sum of squared errors between target_k and $M_0(x_k)$), namely $a_{\text{opt}} = \arg \text{Min}_a Q(a)$. To compensate for inevitable errors of the model (as the values of the index Q are never equal identically to zero), we make the parameters of the model information granules, resulting in a vector of information granules $A = [A_1 A_2 \cdots A_p]$. These granules are built around original numeric values of a. In other words, we say that the model is embedded in the *granular* parameter space. The elements of the vector a are generalized, the model becomes granular and subsequently the results produced by them are information granules as well. Formally speaking, we have

- granulation of parameters of the model $A = G(a)$ where G stands for the mechanisms of forming information granules, viz. building an information granule around the numeric parameter,
- result of the granular model for any x producing the corresponding information granule Y, $Y = M(x, A) = G(M(x)) = M(x, G(a))$.

Figure 10.8 illustrates the underlying idea. The nonlinear mapping M endowed with some parameters approximates the data. We make the parameters of M in the form of intervals thus building the output of the mapping in the form of some interval. Note that the envelope of $y = M(x, a)$ denoted as Y (with the bounds y^- and y^+) covers most the data (leaving some out, which are of a clear outlier nature).

Information granulation is regarded as an essential design asset. By making the results of the model granular (and more abstract in this manner), we realize a better alignment of $G(M_0)$ with the data. Intuitively, we envision that the output of the granular model covers the corresponding target. Formally, let cov(target, Y) denote a certain coverage predicate (either being Boolean or multivalued) and quantifying an extent to which target is included (covered) in Y. The definition of coverage was introduced earlier in the study.

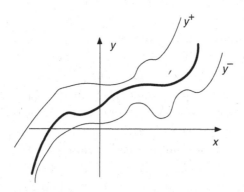

Fig. 10.8. Original numeric mapping along with the interval bounds.

The design asset is supplied in the form of a certain allowable level of information granularity ε which is a certain non-negative parameter being provided in advance. We allocate (distribute) the design asset by forming intervals around the parameters of the model. This is done in a way so that both the coverage measure and the specificity are maximized. The overall level of information granularity ε serves here as a constraint to be satisfied when allocating information granularity across the parameters of the model, namely $\sum_{i=1}^{p} \varepsilon_i = p\varepsilon$. The maximization of both the objectives is translated into the product of the coverage and specificity. In the sequel, the constraint-based optimization problem reads as follows:

$$V(\varepsilon_1, \varepsilon_2, \ldots, \varepsilon_n) = \left(\frac{1}{N} \sum_{k=1}^{N} \mathrm{cov}(\mathrm{target}_k, Y_k) \right) \left(\frac{1}{N} \sum_{k=1}^{N} sp(Y_k) \right)$$

$$\max_{\varepsilon_1, \varepsilon_2, \ldots, \varepsilon_n} V(\varepsilon_1, \varepsilon_2, \ldots, \varepsilon_n)$$

subject to

$$\sum_{i=1}^{p} \varepsilon_i = p\varepsilon \quad \text{and} \quad \varepsilon \geq 0 \tag{10.20}$$

The monotonicity property of the coverage measure is obvious: the higher the values of ε, the higher the resulting coverage and the lower the specificity of the result. As the two contributing criteria are evidently in conflict, one may anticipate that there is a sound compromise that might be established.

The numeric parameters of the mapping are elevated to their granular counterparts with intent of maximizing the performance index. Considering the ith parameter a_i, we form its interval-valued generalization built around its numeric value $[a_i^-, a_i^+]$. With the optimization, several protocols of allocation of information granularity are considered as follows:

Uniform allocation of information granularity

Here, we make a uniform allocation of information granularity across all parameters of the mapping. The interval information granule is expressed in the following form:

$$[\min(a_i(1 - \varepsilon/2), a_i(1 + \varepsilon/2)), \max(a_i(1 - \varepsilon/2), a_i(1 + \varepsilon/2))]$$
$$(10.21)$$

In case $a_i = 0$, the interval is built around zero as $[-\varepsilon/2, \varepsilon/2]$. Note that the balance of information granularity as expressed in (10.20) is obviously satisfied. There is no optimization here and this protocol can serve as a reference scenario that help quantify the performance when compared with realizing some mechanisms of allocation of information granularity.

Symmetric allocation of information granularity

Here, information granularity is allocated in the following form:

$$[\min(a_i(1 - \varepsilon_i), a_i(1 + \varepsilon_i)), \max(a_i(1 - \varepsilon_i), a_i(1 + \varepsilon_i))] \quad (10.22)$$

In this way an information granule is created symmetrically around a_i.

Asymmetric allocation of information granularity

In this scenario, we admit a formation of information granules in a more flexible manner as follows:

$$[\min(a_i(1 - \varepsilon_i^-), a_i(1 + \varepsilon_i^-)), \max(a_i(1 - \varepsilon_i^+), a_i(1 + \varepsilon_i^+))] \quad (10.23)$$

The number of parameters in this situation is larger than in the previous one as information granules are positioned asymmetrically. In this case we also require the satisfaction of the total balance of information granularity.

10.6.2.   *Granular aggregation: An enhancement of aggregation operations through allocation of information granularity*

In what follows, we look at a special case of the allocation of information granularity by looking at a concept of granular aggregation being a generalization of the well-known schemes of data (evidence) aggregation. The proposed approach works in the presence of a collection of the pairs of the data $(x(1), \text{target}(1))$, $(x(2),$

target(2)), ..., (x(N), target(N)) where $x(k)$ is an n-dimensional vector in the unit hypercube $[0, 1]^n$ and target(k) is in the $[0, 1]$ is regarded as an experimentally available result of aggregation of the components of $x(k)$. No matter what formal model of the aggregation of the elements of $x(k)$s is envisioned, it is very unlikely that the model returns the result that coincides with the value of the target(k). Denote the aggregation formula as Agg($w, x(k)$) where w is a weight vector of the aggregation operation. The values of w are not available and need to be optimized so that the aggregation mechanism returns the results as close as possible to the required target(k). For instance, an initial optimization schemes can optimize the vector of weights w so that the following distance becomes minimized $w_{opt} = \arg \min_w Q$.

$$Q = \sum_{k=1}^{N} (\text{target}(k) - \text{Agg}(w, x(k)))^2 \tag{10.24}$$

Evidently, it is unlikely to derive w such that Q attains the zero value. Nevertheless we can regard w_{opt} as an initial numeric estimate of the weight vector and further optimize it by making the weights granular (say interval-valued) by invoking the criterion guiding the optimal allocation of information granularity

In other words, w_{opt} is made granular leading to interval-valued W so that the product of the coverage and specificity attains the maximal value. The architecture of the overall system is illustrated in Fig. 10.9. The optimal allocation of information granularity is realized by following one of the protocols discussed above.

10.6.3. *Development of granular models of higher type*

In system modeling, granular models arise in a hierarchical way by raising a level of information granularity. The essence of the formation of such models can be concisely elaborated as follows; refer also to Fig. 10.10. The data available for the design of the model come as a collection of pairs (x_k, target_k), $k = 1, 2, \ldots, N$.

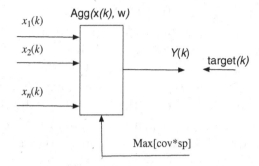

Fig. 10.9. Allocation of information granularity in aggregation problem.

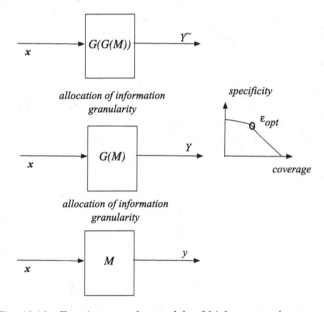

Fig. 10.10. Forming granular models of higher type: A concept.

An initial model M is numeric, viz. in terms of the terminology used here is a granular model of type-0. Through the process of an optimal allocation of information granularity, we form a granular model of type-1 by making the numeric parameters of the previous model granular. The level of information granularity used when forming the granular model $G(M)$ is selected on a basis of the coverage-specificity characteristics of the model. As shown in

Fig. 10.10, the optimal value of the level of information granularity is the one for which there is a substantial increase in the coverage value while still retaining the specificity value or eventually accepting its quite limited drop.

When assessing the performance of the granular model in terms of the coverage, one still may have a number of data that are not "covered" by the information granules of the type-1 model. More formally, the set of outlier O_1 comes in the form

$$O_1 = \{(x_k, \text{target}) | \text{target} x_k \notin GM(x_k)\} \qquad (10.25)$$

Those data can be regarded as type-1 granular outliers. To increase the coverage of the granular model, one elevates the level of type of information granules by making them type-2 information granules, which yields type-2 granular models denoted as $G(G(M))$.

For instance, when the parameters are intervals, type-2 information granules become granular intervals (viz. intervals whose bounds are information granules rather than single numeric values). In case of parameters in terms of fuzzy sets, the parameters are type-2 fuzzy sets. Again by invoking an optimal allocation of information granularity with the criterion of coverage determined for O_1, some outliers are covered by the results produced by $G(G(M))$. The remaining ones form O_2

$$O_2 = \{(x_k, \text{target}) \in O_1 | \text{target} x_k \notin G(G(M))(x_k)\} \qquad (10.26)$$

Those data can be thought as type-2 granular outliers.

10.7. Concluding Comments

In this study, we have focused on the conceptual and algorithmic developments of information granules. The principle of justifiable granularity delivers a general conceptual and algorithmic setting of building information granules. It is important to stress two key features that exhibit far-reaching implications. First, the principle motivates the construction of information granules on a basis of the essentials of these entities, namely experimental justification and semantic content. Second, it applies across various formalisms of information granules. The discussion presented here casts the commonly encountered fuzzy sets of type-2 (and interval-valued fuzzy sets, in particular) in an original setting in terms of their origin and the development by stressing their emergence in association with all practical situations where emerge various sources of data (knowledge) that require a certain type of aggregation.

The concepts of granular mappings are the cornerstone of granular calculations by expanding upon numerical mappings (being at the center of constructs of classifiers and predictors) and augmenting originally available numeric results. Again as in case of the principle of justifiable granularity, the quality of the information granules is evaluated and optimized *vis-à-vis* the coverage of the experimental data and their specificity.

Chapter 11

Complex Fuzzy Sets and Complex Fuzzy Logic. An Overview of Theory and Applications

Fuzzy logic, introduced by Zadeh along with his introduction of fuzzy sets, is a continuous multi-valued logic system. Hence, it is a generalization of the classical logic and the classical discrete multi-valued logic (e.g., Łukasiewicz' three/many-valued logic). Throughout the years Zadeh and other researches have introduced extensions to the theory of fuzzy setts and fuzzy logic. Notable extensions include linguistic variables, type-2 fuzzy sets, complex fuzzy numbers, and Z-numbers. Another important extension to the theory, namely the concepts of complex fuzzy logic and complex fuzzy sets, has been investigated by Kandel *et al.* This extension provides the basis for control and inference systems relating to complex phenomena that cannot be readily formalized via type-1 or type-2 fuzzy sets. Hence, in recent years, several researchers have used the new formalism, often in the context of hybrid neuro-fuzzy systems, to develop advanced complex fuzzy logic-based inference applications. In this chapter we reintroduce the concept of complex fuzzy sets and complex fuzzy logic and survey the current state of complex fuzzy logic, complex fuzzy sets theory, and related applications.

11.1. Introduction

The development of computers and the related attempt to automate human reasoning and inference have posed a challenge to researchers. Humans, and in many cases machines, are not always operating under strict and well-defined two-valued logic or discrete multi-valued logic. Their perception of sets and classes is not as crisp as implied by the traditional set and class theory. To capture this perception, L. A. Zadeh has introduced the theory of fuzzy sets and fuzzy logic [230, 252, 479, 501, 502, 514, 536]. The seminal paper [501], published by Zadeh in 1965, ignited tremendous interest among a large number of researchers. Following the introduction of the concepts of fuzzy logic and set theory, several researchers, [61, 432, 434], have established an axiomatic framework for these concepts.

The five decades that followed Zadeh's pioneering work have produced extensive research work and applications related to control theory [127, 266], artificial intelligence [117, 252, 273, 348], inference, and reasoning [195, 245]. In recent years, fuzzy logic has been applied in many areas, including fuzzy neural networks [281], neuro-fuzzy systems and other bio-inspired fuzzy systems [105], clustering [1, 209, 433], data mining [117, 211, 231], and software testing [6, 263]. In 1975 Zadeh introduced the concept of linguistic variable and the induced concept of type-2 (type-n) fuzzy sets [234, 366, 514]. Other notable extensions to the theory of fuzzy sets and fuzzy logic include complex fuzzy numbers [80], and Z-numbers [485].

Many natural phenomena are complex and cannot be modeled using one-dimensional classes and/or one-dimensional variables. For example, in pattern recognition, objects can be represented by a set of measurements and are regarded as vectors in a multi-dimensional space. Often, it is not practical to assume that this multi-dimensional information can be represented via a simple combination of variables and operators on one-dimensional clauses. Specifically, consider a set of values where each value is a member of a fuzzy set. This set, referred to as fuzzy set of type-2, cannot be compactly represented by basic operations on fuzzy sets of type-1 [234, 366, 514]. This type of sets however, can be represented via complex classes presented next.

Another important extension to the theory of fuzzy logic and fuzzy sets, namely complex fuzzy logic (CFL) and complex fuzzy sets (CFS), has been developed by Kandel and his coauthors [319, 368, 369, 434, 437]. Moses *et al.* introduced an aggregation of two fuzzy sets into one complex fuzzy set [368]. Next, Ramot *et al.* introduced the concept of a complex degree of membership represented in polar coordinates, where the amplitude is the degree of membership of an object in a CFS and the role of the phase is to add information which is generally related to spatial or temporal periodicity in the specific fuzzy set defined by the amplitude component. They used this formalism along with the theory of relations to establish the concept of CFL. Finally, Tamir *et al.* developed an axiomatically-based CFL system and used CFL to provide a new and general formalism of CFS. These formalisms significantly enhance the expressive power of type-1 and type-2 fuzzy sets [234, 366]. The successive definitions of the theory of CFL and CFS represent an evolution from a relatively naïve and restricted practice to a sound, well founded, practical, and axiomatically-based form. In recent years, several researchers have used the new formalism, often in the context of hybrid neuro-fuzzy systems to develop advanced complex fuzzy logic-based inference applications.

There is a substantial difference between the definitions of complex fuzzy numbers given by Buckley [80–84] and the concept of complex fuzzy sets or complex fuzzy logic. Buckley is concerned with generalizing the number theory while the CFL and CFS theories are concerned with the generalization of the fuzzy set theory and fuzzy logic [434, 435, 438]. Complex fuzzy numbers have been utilized in several numerical applications [285, 477, 556]. Yet, the concept of a complex fuzzy number is different from the concept of complex fuzzy sets or complex fuzzy classes. Recently, Zadeh introduced the concept of *Z-numbers*. A Z-number, $Z = (A, B)$, is an ordered pair of two fuzzy numbers. In this context A, provides a restriction on a real-valued variable X and B is a restriction on the degree of certainty that X is A [485]. Nevertheless, this concept is used to qualify the reliability of fuzzy quantities rather than to define complex fuzzy sets [434, 437].

The present chapter includes an introduction to the succession of definitions of CFL and CFS, concentrating on the axiomatic-based approach. In addition, the chapter includes a survey the current state of research into complex fuzzy logic, complex fuzzy set theory, and related applications.

11.2.   Complex Fuzzy Logic and Set Theory

The first formalization of complex fuzzy sets and complex fuzzy logic investigated by Kandel and his coauthors [319, 329] is a special case of the formalism presented by Tamir *et al.* [434]. Hence, in this section only two formalisms for complex fuzzy sets and complex fuzzy logic are considered: (1) the formal definitions provided by Ramot *et al.* [368], (2) the generalization of these concepts developed by Tamir *et al.* [434, 436–438].

11.2.1.   *Complex fuzzy sets* [368]

This section reviews the basic concepts and operations of complex fuzzy set as defined by Ramot *et al.* [126, 369]. According to Ramot *et al.* a complex fuzzy set S on a universe of discourse U is a set defined by a complex-valued grade of membership function $\mu_S(x)$ [368, 369]:

$$\mu_S(x) = r_S(x)e^{j\omega_S(x)} \tag{11.1}$$

where $j = \sqrt{-1}$. The function $\mu_S(x)$ maps U into the unit disc of the complex plane. This definition utilizes polar representation of complex numbers along with conventional fuzzy set definition; where $r_S(x)$, the amplitude part of the grade of member-ship, is a fuzzy function defined in the interval $[0, 1]$. On the other hand, $\omega_S(x)$ is a real-valued function standing for the phase part of the grade of membership.

In the definition provided by Ramot, the absolute value, or the amplitude part of the membership grade, behaves the same as in traditional fuzzy sets. Its value is mapped into the interval $[0, 1]$. On the other hand, the phase component of the expression is not a fuzzy function; it is a real-valued function that can get any real value. Furthermore, the grade of membership is not influenced by the phase. The phase role is to add information which is generally related to spatial or temporal periodicity in the specific fuzzy set defined by the amplitude component. For example, fuzzy information related to solar activity along with crisp information that relates to the date of measurement of the solar activity [368]. Another example where complex fuzzy set has an intuitive appeal comes from the stock market. Intuitively, the periodicity of the stock market along with fuzzy set-based estimate of the current values of stocks can be represented by a complex grade of membership such as the one proposed by Ramot. The amplitude conveys the information contained in a fuzzy set such as "strong stock" while the phase conveys a crisp information about the current phase in the presumed stock market cycle.

Following the basic definition of complex-valued grade of membership function Ramot *et al.* define the basic set operations such as complement, union, and intersection. Each of these operations is defined via a set of theorems [435].

11.2.2. *Complex fuzzy logic* [369]

There are several ways to define fuzzy logic, fuzzy inference, and fuzzy logic system (FLS). One of these ways is to use fuzzy set theory to define fuzzy relations, and then define logical operations, such as implication and negation, as well as inference rules, as special types of relations on fuzzy sets. Alternatively, fuzzy logic can be formalized as a direct generalization of classical logic. Under this "traditional" approach, notions that relate to the syntax and semantics of classical logic, such as propositions, interpretation, and inference are used to define fuzzy logic. Although the relations-based definition can be carefully formalized, it is generally less rigorous than the traditional approach.

Ramot *et al.* use the first approach [369]. They use the definition of complex fuzzy relations to define complex fuzzy logic via the definition of logical operations. Additionally, Ramot *et al.* restrict complex fuzzy logic to propositions of the form "X *is* A", where X is a variable that receives values x from a universal set U and A is a complex fuzzy set on U. They use this type of propositions to introduce implications of the form "*if* X *is* A *then* Y *is* B". Finally, they use modus ponens to produce a complex fuzzy inference system. Clearly their approach is limited due to two facts: (1) they rely on complex fuzzy sets and relations to define CFL and (2) their fuzzy inference system is limited to propositions on complex fuzzy sets.

These limitations are resolved via the axiomatically-based approach presented in Section 11.3.

11.3.   Generalized Complex Fuzzy Logic [434]

This section presents the generalized form of complex fuzzy logic investigated [434].

11.3.1.   *Propositional and first-order predicate complex fuzzy logic*

A complex fuzzy proposition P is a composition of two propositions each of which can accept a truth value in the interval [0,1]. In other words, the interpretation of a complex fuzzy proposition is a pair of truth values from the Cartesian interval $[0,1] \times [0,1]$. Alternatively, the interpretation can be formulated as a mapping to the unit circle. Formally a fuzzy interpretation of a complex fuzzy proposition P is an assignment of fuzzy truth value of the form $i(p_r) + j \cdot i(p_i)$, or of the form $i(r(p))e^{j\sigma i(\theta(p))}$, where σ is a scaling factor in the interval $(0, 2\pi]$, to P.

For example, consider a proposition of the form "$x \dots A \dots B \dots$," along with the definition of a linguistic variables and constants. Namely, a *linguistic variable* is a variable whose domain of values is comprised of formal or natural language words [514]. Generally, a linguistic variable is related to a fuzzy set such as {very young male, young male, old male, very old male} and can get any value from the set. A linguistic constant has a fixed and unmodified linguistic value, i.e., a single word or phrase from a formal or natural language.

Thus, in a proposition of the form "$x \dots A \dots B \dots$," where A and B are linguistic variables, $i(p_r)$ $(i(r(p)))$ can be assigned to the term A and $i(p_i)$ $(i(\theta(p)))$ can be assigned to term B.

Propositional CFL extends the definition of propositional fuzzy logic and first-order predicate CFL extends the notion of first-order predicate fuzzy logic. Nevertheless, since propositional CFL is a special case of first-order predicate CFL, we only present the formalism for first-order predicates CFL here.

Table 11.1. Basic LΠ∀ CFL connectives.

Operation	Interpretation
L-Implication	$i(P \longrightarrow_L Q) = \min(1, 1 - i(p_r) + i(q_r))$ $+ j \cdot \min(1, 1 - i(p_i) + i(q_i))$
Π-Implication	$i(P \longrightarrow_\Pi Q) = \min(1, i(p_r)/i(q_r)) + j \cdot \min(1, i(p_i)/i(q_i))$
Π-Conjunction	$i(P \otimes Q) = i(p_r) \cdot i(q_r)) + j \cdot (i(p_i) \cdot i(q_i))$

Table 11.2. Derived LΠ∀ CFL connectives.

Operation	Interpretation
L-Negation	$i('P) = 1 + j1 - i(P)$
Π-Delta	$\Delta(i(P)) = 1$ if $(i(P)) = 1 + j1$ else $\Delta(i(P)) = 0 + j0$
Equivalence	$i(P \longleftrightarrow Q) = i(P_r \longrightarrow_L Q_r) \otimes i(Q_r \longrightarrow_L P_r) + j \cdot i(P_i \longrightarrow_L Q_i)$ $\otimes i(Q_i \longrightarrow_L P_i)$
$P \ominus Q$	$i(P \ominus Q) = \max(0, i(p_r) - i(q_r)) + j \cdot \max(0, i(p_i) - i(q_i))$

Tables 11.1 and 11.2 present the basic and derived connectives of LΠ∀ CFL. In essence, the connectives are symmetric with respect to the real and imaginary parts of the predicates.

Following classical logic, LΠ∀ CFL extends, LΠ CFL. The primitives include constants, variables, arbitrary-arity functions and arbitrary-arity predicates. Formulae are constructed using the basic connectives defined in Table 11.1, derived connectives such as the connectives presented in Table 11.2, the truth constants, the quantifier ∀, and the identity sign =. The quantifier ∃ can be used to abbreviate formulae derived from the basic primitives and connectives. A fuzzy interpretation of a proposition $P(x_1, \ldots, x_n) = P_r(x_1, \ldots, x_n) + j \cdot P_i(x_1, \ldots, x_m)$ over a domain M is a mapping that assigns a fuzzy truth value to each $(n\text{-tuple}) \times (m\text{-tuple})$ of elements of M. As in the case of LΠ fuzzy logic, we closely follow the system used in Ref. [61].

The same axioms used for first-order predicate fuzzy logic are used for first-order predicate complex fuzzy logic; Modus ponens as well as product necessitation, and generalization are the rules of inference.

11.3.2.   *Complex fuzzy propositions and inference examples*

Consider the following propositions:

1. $P(x) \equiv$ "x is a destructive hurricane with high surge".
2. $Q(x) \equiv$ "x is a destructive hurricane with fast moving center".

Let A be the term "destructive hurricane." Let B be the term "high surge," and let C be the term "fast moving center." Hence, P is of the form: "x is a A with B" and Q is of the form "x is A with C." In this case, the terms "destructive hurricane," "high surge," and "fast moving center," are values assigned to the linguistic variables A, B, C. Furthermore, the term "destructive hurricane" can get fuzzy truth values (between 0 and 1) or fuzzy linguistic values such as: "catastriphic," "devastating," and "disastrous." Assume that the complex fuzzy interpretation (i.e., the degree of confidence or complex fuzzy truth value) of P is $pr + jpi$, while the complex fuzzy interpretation of Q is $qr + jqi$. Thus, the truth value of "x is a devastating hurricane" is pR, the truth value of "x is in a high surge" is pi, the truth value of "x is a catastriphic hurricane" is qr, and the truth value of "x is a fast moving center" is qi, Suppose that the term "moderate" stands for "non-destructive" which stands for "NOT destructive," the term "low" stands for "NOT high," and the term "slow" stands for "NOT fast." In this context, NOT is inter-pretend as the fuzzy negation operation. Note that this is not the only way to define these linguistic terms and it is used to exemplify the expressive power and the inference power of the logic. Then, the complex fuzzy interpretation of the noted composite propositions is:

(1) $f(0.'P) = (1 - p_r) + j(1 - p_I)$

That is, $'P$ denotes the proposition: "x is a moderate hurricane with a low surge." The confidence level in $'P$ is $(1-p_r)+j(1-p_i)$; where the fuzzy truth value of the term "x is a non-destructive hurricanes." is $(1 - p_r)$ and the fuzzy truth value of the term "low surge," is $(1 - p_i)$.

(2) $'P \longrightarrow 'Q = \min(1, q_r - p_r) + j \times \min(1, q_i - p_I)$

Thus, $('P \longrightarrow 'Q)$ denotes the proposition: If "x is a moderate hurricane with a low surge. THEN x is a moderate hurricane with low moving center." The truth values of individual terms, as well as the truth value of $'P \longrightarrow 'Q$ are calculated according to Table 11.1.

(3) $f(P \oplus 'Q) = \max(p_r, 1 - q_r) + j \times \max(p_i, 1 - q_i)$.

(4) That is, $f(P \oplus 'Q)$ denotes a proposition such as: "x is a destructive hurricane with high surge" OR. The truth values of individual terms, as well as the truth value of $P \oplus 'Q$ are calculated according to Table 11.1.

(5) $f('P \otimes Q) = \min(1 - p_r q_r) + j \times \min(1 - p_i, q_i)$.

That is, $('P \otimes Q)$ denotes the proposition "x is a moderate hurricane wit low surge" AND "x is a destructive hurricane with fast moving center."

The truth values of individual terms, as well as the truth value of $'P \otimes Q$ are calculated according to Table 11.1.

11.3.3. *Complex fuzzy inference example*

Assume that the degree of confidence in the proposition $R = 'P$ defined above is $r_r + jr_i$. Let $S = 'Q$ and assume that the degree of confidence in the fuzzy implication $T = R \longrightarrow S$ is $t_r + jt_i$. Then, using Modus ponens

$$R$$
$$\frac{R \longrightarrow S}{S}$$

one can infer S with a degree of confidence $\min(r_r, t_r) j \times \min(r_i, t_i)$. In other words if one is using:

"x is a non-destructive hurricane with a low surge"
IF "x is a non-destructive hurricane with a low surge" THEN
"x is non-destructive hurricane with slow moving center"
"x is non-destructive hurricane with slow moving center."

Hence, using Modus ponens one can infer:

"*x is moderate hurricane with slow moving center.*" with a degree of confidence of $\min(r_r, t_r) + j \times \min(r_i, t_i)$.

11.4.   Generalized Complex Fuzzy Class Theory [434]

The axiomatic fuzzy logic can serve as a basis for formal FCT. Similarly, axiomatic based complex fuzzy logic can serve as the basis for formal definition of complex fuzzy classes. In this section, we provide a formulation of complex fuzzy class theory (CFCT) that is based on the logic theory presented in Section 11.3.

The main components of FCT are:

(1) Variables:

    (a) Variables denoting objects (potentially complex objects).

    (b) Variables denoting crisp sets, i.e., a universe of discourse and its subsets.

    (c) Variables denoting complex fuzzy classes of order 1.

    (d) Variables denoting complex fuzzy classes of order n, that is, complex fuzzy classes of complex fuzzy classes of order $n-1$.

(2) The LΠ∀ CFL system along with its variables, connectives, predicates, and axioms as defined in Section 11.3.

(3) Additional predicates:

    (a) A binary predicate $\in (x, \Gamma)$ denoting membership of objects in complex fuzzy classes and/or in crisp sets.

(4) Additional axioms:

    (a) Instances of the comprehension schema (further explained below)

$$(\exists\Gamma)\Delta(\forall x)(x \in \Gamma \leftrightarrow P(x)) \qquad (11.2)$$

    where x is a complex fuzzy object, Γ is a complex fuzzy class, and $P()$ is a complex fuzzy predicate.

    (b) The axiom of extensionality

$$(\forall x)\Delta(x \in \Gamma \leftrightarrow x \in \Psi) \rightarrow \Gamma = \Psi \qquad (11.3)$$

where x is a complex fuzzy object, Γ is a complex fuzzy class, and $P()$ is a complex fuzzy predicate.

Note that a grade of membership is not a part of the above specified terms; yet it can be derived or defined using these terms.

The comprehension schema is used to "construct" classes. It has the basic form of: $(\forall x)(x \in \Gamma \leftrightarrow P(x))$. Intuitively, this schema refers to the class Γ of all the objects x that satisfy the predicate $P()$. Instances of this schema have the generic form: $(\exists \Gamma)(\forall x)(x \in \Gamma \leftrightarrow P(x))$. Associated with this schema are comprehension terms of the form: $\in \{x | P(x) \leftrightarrow P(y)\}$. The Δ operation introduced in Equation (11.3) is used to produce precise instances of the extensionality schema and ensure the conservatism of comprehension terms.

Fixing a standard model over the CFCT enables the definition of commonly used terms, set operations, and definitions, as well as proving CFCT theorems. Some of these elements are listed here:

(1) The complex characteristic function $\chi_{x \in \Gamma} \equiv \chi_\Gamma$ and the grade of membership function $\mu_{x \in \Gamma} \equiv \mu_\Gamma$.

(2) Complex class constants, α-cuts, iterated complements, and primitive binary operations, such as union, intersection, etc. These operations are constructed using the schema $O_P(\Gamma) \equiv \{x | P(x \in \Gamma)\}$. Table 11.3 lists some of these elements.

(3) Uniform and supreme relations defined in Ref. [61] enable the definition of fuzzy class relations such as inclusion.

(4) Theorems, primitive fuzzy class operations, and fuzzy class relations [61].

Table 11.3.   Derived primitive class operations.

Term	Symbol	P	Comments
Empty complex class	Θ	0	
Universal complex class	Φ	1	
Strict complement	$\backslash \Gamma$	$\sim$	$\sim$ stands for Gödel (G) negation
Complex class intersection	$\cap$	$\oplus$	$\oplus$ stands for a G, Ł, or Π conjunction t-norm
Complex class union	$\cup$	$\vee$	$\vee$ stands for a G, Ł, or Π disjunction

Following the axiomatically-based definition of grade of membership, can formulate a basis for the definition of "membership grade based" complement, union, and intersection.

11.4.1. *Complex fuzzy classes and connectives examples*

In order to provide a concrete example, we define the following complex fuzzy classes using the comprehension schema. Let the universe of discourse be the set of all the stocks that were available for trading on the opening of the New York stock exchange (NYSE) market on January 5, 2015 along with a set of attributes related to historical price performance of each of these stocks.

Consider the following complex propositions:

$P(x) = $ "x is a volatile stock in a strong portfolio".
$Q(x) = $ "x is a stock in a decline trend in a strong portfolio".

Then, the proposition: $(\exists \Gamma)\Delta(\forall x)(x \in \Gamma \leftrightarrow (P(x) \otimes Q(x)))$ where x is any member of the universe of discourse, defines a complex fuzzy class Γ that can be "described" as the class of "volatile stocks in a decline trend in strong portfolios." On the other hand, the proposition $(\exists \Gamma)\Delta(\forall x)(x \in \Gamma \leftrightarrow ('P(x) \vee Q(x)))$ where x is any member of the universe of discourse, defines a complex fuzzy class Γ that can be "described" as the class of "non-volatile stocks in a decline trend in strong portfolios".

11.5. Pure Complex Fuzzy Classes

Often it is useful to define complex fuzzy sets via membership functions rather than through axioms. To this end, Tamir *et al.* have introduced the concept of pure complex fuzzy sets [435]. This concept is reviewed in this section.

The Cartesian representation of the pure complex grade of membership is given in the following way:

$$\mu(V, x) = \mu_r(V) + j\mu_i(z) \tag{11.4}$$

where $\mu_r(V)$ and $\mu_i(z)$, the real and imaginary components of the pure complex fuzzy grade of membership, are real value fuzzy grades of membership. That is, $\mu_r(V)$ and $\mu_i(z)$ can get any value in the interval $[0, 1]$. The polar representation of the pure complex grade of membership is given by:

$$\mu(V, x) = r(V)e^{j\sigma\phi(z)} \tag{11.5}$$

where $r(V)$ and $\phi(z)$, the amplitude and phase components of the pure complex fuzzy grade of membership, are real value fuzzy grades of membership. That is, they can get any value in the interval $[0, 1]$. The scaling factor σ is in the interval $(0, 2\pi]$. It is used to control the behavior of the phase within the unit circle according to the specific application. Typical values of σ are $\{1, \frac{\pi}{2}\pi, 2\pi\}$.

The main difference between pure complex fuzzy grades of membership and the complex fuzzy grade of membership proposed by Ramot *et al.* [368, 369] is that both components of the membership grade are fuzzy functions that convey information about a fuzzy set.

11.6. Recent Developments in the Theory and Applications of CFL and CFS

In this section, we review recent literature on complex fuzzy logic and complex fuzzy sets. First we review papers that enhance the theoretical basis of CFL/CFS. Next, we outline some of the recent reports on CFL/CFS related applications.

11.6.1. *Advances in the theoretical foundations of CFL/CFS*

Yager *et al.* have presented the idea of Pythagorean membership grades and the related idea of Pythagorean fuzzy subsets [486]. They have focused on the negation operation and its relationship to the Pythagorean Theorem. Additionally, they examined the basic set operations for the case of Pythagorean fuzzy subsets. Yager *et al.* further note that the idea of Pythagorean membership grades can provide an interesting semantics for complex number-valued membership grades used in complex fuzzy sets.

Greenfield *et al.* [185] have compared and contrasted the FCS formalism proposed by Ramot *et ul.* [368] as well as the "innovation of pure complex fuzzy sets, proposed by Tamir *et al.* [435]" with type-2 fuzzy sets [234, 366]. They have concentrated on the rationales, applications, definitions, and structures of these constructs. In addition, they have compared pure complex fuzzy sets with type-2 fuzzy sets in relation to inference operations. They have concluded that complex fuzzy sets and type-2 fuzzy sets differ in their roles and applications. They have identified similarities between pure complex fuzzy sets and type-2 fuzzy sets; but concluded that type-2 fuzzy sets were isomorphic to pure complex fuzzy sets.

Apolloni *et al.* propose to define and manage a complex fuzzy set by computing its membership function using a few variables quantized into a few elementary granules and elementary functions connecting the variables [37].

Guosheng *et al.* have introduced three complex fuzzy reasoning schemes: Principal Axis, Phase Parameters, and Concurrence Reasoning Scheme [193]. They have demonstrated that a variety of conjunction operators and implication operators can be selected to compose the corresponding instances of complex reasoning schemes.

Guangquan *et al.* have investigated various operation properties of complex fuzzy relations [186]. They have defined a distance measure for evaluating the differences between the grades as well as the phases of two complex fuzzy relations. Furthermore, they have used the distance measure to define δ-equalities of complex fuzzy relations. Finally, they have examined fuzzy inference in the framework of δ-equalities of complex fuzzy relations.

Tamir *et al.* have proposed a complex fuzzy logic (CFL) system that is based on the extended post multi-valued logic system (EPS) of order $p > 2$, and have demonstrated its utility for reasoning with fuzzy facts and rules. The advantage of this formalism is that it is discrete. Hence, it better fits real time applications, digital signal processing, and embedded systems that use integer processing units.

11.6.2. *Applications of CFL/CFS*

A group of researchers working along with Dick have developed the concept of adaptive neuro fuzzy complex inference system (ANCFIS) and explored related applications by integrating complex fuzzy logic into adaptive neuro fuzzy inference system (ANFIS) = [101].

Man *et al.* have extended the concept of ANFIS and introduced ACNFIS [290]. They have applied ANCFIS in time series forecasting. They compared ACNFIS to three commonly cited time series datasets and demonstrated that ACNFIS was able to accurately model relatively periodic data.

An extension of this work, including synthetic time series and several real-world forecasting problems, is presented by Zhifei *et al.* [557]. They have found that ANCFIS performs well on these problems and is also very parsimonious. Their work demonstrates the utility of complex fuzzy logic on real-world problems.

Aghakhani *et al.* have developed an online learning algorithm for ACNFIS and applied it to time series prediction [7]. Their experimental results show that the online technique is comparable to existing results, although slightly inferior to the off-line ANCFIS results.

Yazdanbaksh *et al.* applied ANCFIS to the problem of short-term forecasts of Photovoltaic power generation [493]. They compared ANFIS and radial basis function networks against ANCFIS. Their experimental results have demonstrated that the ANCFIS-based approach was more accurate in predicting power output on a simulated solar cell. Additionally, in a recent paper Yazdanbaksh *et al.* presented a recommended approach to determining input windows that balances the accuracy and computation time [494].

Another group that is active in exploring CFL/CFS applications is led by Li [273, 275]. Li *et al.* have proposed a novel complex neuro-fuzzy autoregressive integrated moving average (ARIMA) computing approach and applied it to the problem of time-series forecasting [274]. They have found that their new formalism, referred to as CNFS-ARIMA, has excellent nonlinear mapping capability for time-series forecasting.

Additionally, Li *et al.* have presented a neuro-fuzzy approach using complex fuzzy sets (CNFS) for the problem of knowledge discovery [272]. They have devised a hybrid learning algorithm to evolve the CNFS for modeling accuracy, combining artificial bee colony algorithm and recursive least squares estimator method. They have tested the CNFS-based approach in knowledge discovery through experimentation, and concluded that the proposed approach outperforms comparable approaches.

Another application of CNFS presented by Li *et al.* is adaptive image noise canceling [271]. Two cases of image restoration have been used to test the proposed approach and have shown a good restoration quality. Additionally, Li *et al.* have presented a hybrid learning method that enables efficient and quick CNFS convergence procedure and applied the hybrid learning-based CNFS to the problem of function approximation [271, 273]. They have concluded that the CNFS shows much better performance than its traditional neuro-fuzzy counterpart and other compared approaches.

Ma *et al.* applied complex fuzzy sets to the problem of multiple periodic factor prediction (MPFP) [285]. They have developed a product-sum aggregation operator (PSAO), which is a set of complex fuzzy sets. PSAO has been used to integrate information with uncertainty and periodicity. Next, they have developed a PSAO-based prediction (PSAOP) method to generate solutions for MPFP problems. The experimental results indicate that the proposed PSAOP method effectively handles the uncertainty and periodicity in the information of multiple periodic factors simultaneously and can generate accurate predictions for MPFP problems.

Tamir *et al.* have considered numerous applications of CFL [231, 436–440]. They have introduced several soft computing based methods and tools for disaster mitigation [231] and epidemic crises prediction [439]. Additionally, they have demonstrated the potential use of complex fuzzy graphs as well as incremental fuzzy clustering in the context of complex and high order fuzzy logic systems. Additionally, they have developed an axiomatic based framework for discrete complex fuzzy logic and set theory [436].

In Ref. [440], Tamir *et al.* have presented a complex fuzzy logic based inference system used to account for the intricate relations between software engineering constraints such as quality, software features, and development effort. The new model concentrates on the requirements specifications part of the software engineering process.

Moreover, the new model significantly improves the expressive power and inference capability of the soft computing component in a soft computing-based quantitative software engineering paradigm.

11.7. Conclusion

We have reviewed the theoretical basis of complex fuzzy logic and complex fuzzy sets and the current state of related applications. We have surveyed the research related to the underlying theory as well as recent applications of the theory in complex fuzzy-based algorithms and complex fuzzy inference systems.

The concepts of complex fuzzy logic and complex fuzzy sets have undergone an evolutionary process since they were first introduced [319]. The initial definitions were practical but somewhat naïve and limited [126, 329, 368, 369]. The introduction of axiomatically-based approach [434, 437, 438] has enabled extending the concepts, maintaining practicality, and providing a solid foundation for further theoretical development. Several applications of the new theories have emerged; based on recent reports this area of applications is gaining momentum.

Chapter 12

Introduction to Fuzzy Logic Control

Recently, fuzzy control systems have been widely used for automatic control of complex processes. This type of control systems, being a qualitatively new class of control systems, proved to be very effective in control of complex nonlinear uncertain dynamic objects for which the classical deterministic and stochastic controllers are unable to operate. Fuzzy controller is a knowledge-based controller in which fuzzy logic is used to represent knowledge and logical inference.

In this chapter, comprehensive outline of the fuzzy control systems is described. Their advantages and disadvantages, and comparison with classical control systems are provided.

12.1. Introduction

Fuzzy set theory has been used successfully in virtually all the technical fields, including control, modeling, image/signal processing and expert systems. The most successful and active field, however, is fuzzy control.

The first fuzzy control (i.e., fuzzy logic control) applications were introduced in the mid-70s with the work of Prof. E. H. Mamdani and his associates at the University of London in United Kingdom in 1974 [287]. The concept and theoretical foundation of fuzzy control and systems, however, had been developed first a few years earlier (e.g., [508, 510, 511]) by Professor L.A. Zadeh, who demonstrated that a family of logical rules with fuzzy predicates could result in a control algorithm that had a performance comparable to the conventional industrial controllers.

327

The idea of linguistic control algorithms was a brilliant generalization of the human experience to use linguistic rules with vague predicates in order to formulate control actions. The formalization of this concept by fuzzy set theory brought it to the field of control by using the apparatus of approximate reasoning.

The main paradigm of fuzzy control is that the control algorithm is a knowledge-based algorithm, described by the methods of fuzzy logic. The fuzzy logic control system is essentially an expert knowledge-based system that contains the control algorithm in a simple rule-base. The knowledge encoded in the rule-base is derived from human experience and intuition and from theoretical and practical understanding of the dynamics of the controlled object. The machinery of approximate reasoning converts the knowledge embedded in the rule-base into a crisp (non-fuzzy) control algorithm.

Most of the early fuzzy control applications followed Mamdani's approach — these were rule-based controllers with fuzzy predicates and reasoning mechanism [288, 480, 498], implementing nonlinear PI, PD or PID-like control strategies. The focus was on solving specific control problems, e.g., climate control (Matsushita), subway control (Hitachi), dishwasher and locomotive wheel slip control (General Electric), control of prepaint anticorrosion process (Ford Motor Company), vehicle transmissions (Honda, General Motors, & Nissan), etc. [76, 239, 405, 406, 423]. Utilizing some of the main advantages of fuzzy control — implementation of intuitive control strategies based on human experience, no requirements for an explicit plant model, and rapid prototyping of the control algorithm — these applications gained quick success.

Today, the synergy among fuzzy control, neural networks, evolutionary computing, machine learning, probabilistic/possibilistic reasoning, bio-inspired computational intelligence methodologies, and other soft-computing theory establishes the foundations of a broader control area — intelligent control. Fuzzy control methods are also widely used as a tool in conjunction with the conventional control, diagnosis, pattern recognition, signal processing, knowledge-based algorithms and systems where they are introduced within the framework of heuristic strategies at a higher control level (supervisory control, formalization of heuristic task and goals) or/and synergistically with control algorithms that require subjective information, which can be difficult to formalize within the framework of conventional controllers [76].

In this chapter, we will first introduce the configuration and operation of typical fuzzy controllers, both single-input single-output (SISO) and multiple-input single-output (MISO) types. We will then unveil that fuzzy controllers are actually conventional nonlinear controllers with peculiar but advantageous structural changes with input state. Based on this insightful view, we will point out what the advantages and disadvantages of fuzzy control are and when they should and should not be utilized in practice. Finally, we discuss various analytical issues in fuzzy control.

12.2. The Mamdani Fuzzy Controller

Figure 12.1 depicts the structure of a fuzzy control system, which comprises typical SISO Mamdani fuzzy controller and a system (plant) under control. The plant may be linear or nonlinear and its model may or may not be mathematically known. Virtually, all the real-world fuzzy controllers use digital computers for implementation. Hence, fuzzy controllers are discrete-time controllers. For practical purpose, there is no point to consider fuzzy controllers as continuous-time controllers and we certainly will not do so in this chapter.

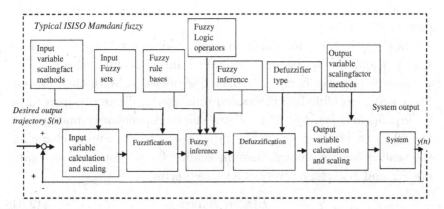

Fig. 12.1. Structure of typical SISO Mamdani fuzzy control systems.

The major components of the typical fuzzy controller are defined by the theory of approximate reasoning and follow the calculus of fuzzy systems. Consequently, the structure of the controller is modular and comprises the main fuzzy system operations and components — fuzzification module, fuzzy rule-base, fuzzy inference mechanism, and defuzzification module.

12.2.1.   *Fuzzification module*

In Fig. 12.1, the system output is designated by $y(n)$, where n is a positive integer. The sampling time is nT, where T is the sampling period. However, as a notational convention, we will use n, instead of nT, to represent the sampling time.

The desired system output trajectory is denoted $S(n)$, which can be either constant or time-varying. At time n, $y(n)$ and $S(n)$ are used to compute input variables of the fuzzy controller. In many cases, error and change of error (we call it rate for convenience) of $y(n)$ are used as input variables. The reason for two input variables only is that the number of fuzzy rules needed increases dramatically with the increase of the number of input variables (we will explain this in detail later). The input variables then are

$$e(n) = S(n) - y(n) \qquad (12.1)$$

$$r(n) = e(n) - e(n-1) = y(n-1) - y(n) \qquad (12.2)$$

Both $e(n)$ and $r(n)$ have their ranges, and we assume them to be $[a_1, b_1]$ and $[a_2, b_2]$, respectively, which are their respective universes of discourse.

Scaling factors are used to scale the input variables before fuzzification. These factors are called input scaling factors. The purpose is to make fuzzy controller design easier. With them, input fuzzy sets are defined on the scaled universes of discourse, instead of on $[a_1, b_1]$ and $[a_2, b_2]$. This allows one to conveniently manipulate the effective fuzzification of the input variables by simply changing the scaling factors' values. Assume scaling factors for error and rate are K_e and K_r, respectively. The scaled error is

$$E(n) = K_e e(n) \qquad (12.3)$$

and the scaled rate is

$$R(n) = K_r r(n) \tag{12.4}$$

Without loss of generality, $E(n)$ and $R(n)$ are assumed to be defined on $[A_1, B_1]$ and $[A_2, B_2]$, respectively.

The scaled variables are then fuzzified by partitioning into input fuzzy sets. Input fuzzy sets are fuzzy sets that are defined on $[A_1, B_1]$ and $[A_2, B_2]$. Two arrays of fuzzy sets are needed: one for $E(n)$ and the other for $R(n)$. Figure 12.2 shows four input fuzzy sets for $E(n)$, hypothetically used by the fuzzy controller. The membership functions are purposely selected as a mixture of three different types, namely, triangular, trapezoidal and bell-shaped. The use of "Positive" and "Negative" in the linguistic names is necessary because $e(n)$ and $r(n)$ can be positive and negative.

Suppose that $K_e = 2$ and at time $n = n^*$, $e(n^*) = 1.2$. Then, $E(n^*) = 2.4$. The fuzzification results, shown in Fig. 12.2, are membership value 0.2 for fuzzy set "Positive Small" and 0.6 for "Positive Large". The membership values for "Negative Small" and "Negative Large" are 0.

Fuzzification can be formulated mathematically. For mathematical convenience, the linguistic naming system should be replaced by a numerical index system. For instance, one may use A_i, $i = -2$,

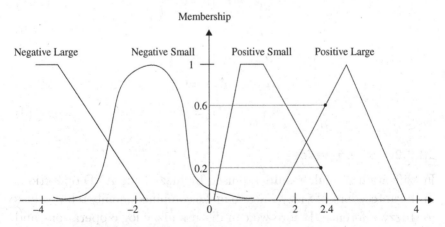

Fig. 12.2. Demonstration of how fuzzification of input variables works.

$-1, 1, 2$, to represent the four fuzzy sets for $E(n)$. Thus, $\{A_{-2}, A_{-1}, A_1, A_2\}$ symbolizes $\{$"Negative Large", "Negative Small", "Positive Small", "Positive Large"$\}$. Such an indexing system is essential as it makes the mathematical analysis of fuzzy control possible. Now, the example fuzzification of $e(n^*) = 1.2$ can be described as

$$\mu_{A_2}(e(n^*)) = 0.6 \tag{12.5}$$

$$\mu_{A_1}(e(n^*)) = 0.2 \tag{12.6}$$

$$\mu_{A_{-1}}(e(n^*)) = 0 \tag{12.7}$$

$$\mu_{A_{-2}}(e(n^*)) = 0 \tag{12.8}$$

Now, let us look at the fuzzification of $R(n)$. The fuzzy controller supposedly uses fuzzy sets $\{B_{-2}, B_{-1}, B_0, B_1, B_2\}$ for $R(n)$, which symbolize $\{$"Negative Large," "Negative Small", "Approximately Zero", "Positive Small", "Positive Large"$\}$. The specific definitions of these fuzzy sets are not given, as they are unimportant for the point we are going to make. Assume that $R(n^*) = 3.5$ is computed from $r(n^*) = 7$ and $K_r = 0.5$ and the fuzzification results are (see Fig. 12.4 for the graphical definitions of B_{-1} and B_0)

$$\mu_{B_2}(r(n^*)) = 0 \tag{12.9}$$

$$\mu_{B_1}(r(n^*)) = 0 \tag{12.10}$$

$$\mu_{B_0}(r(n^*)) = 0.3 \tag{12.11}$$

$$\mu_{B_{-1}}(r(n^*)) = 0.5 \tag{12.12}$$

$$\mu_{B_{-2}}(r(n^*)) = 0 \tag{12.13}$$

12.2.2. *Fuzzy rules*

Fuzzification module results are used by fuzzy logic AND operations in the antecedent of fuzzy rules to make combined membership values for fuzzy inference. Before we can discuss fuzzy logic operations and fuzzy inference in the next section, we first need to study fuzzy rules.

An example of a fuzzy rule is

IF $E(n)$ is Positive Large AND $R(n)$ is Negative Small

THEN $u(n)$ (or $\Delta u(n)$) is Positive Medium   (12.14)

where "Positive Large" and "Negative Small" are input fuzzy sets and "Positive Medium" is an output fuzzy set. The output variable can either be fuzzy controller output, $u(n)$, or increment of controller output, $\Delta u(n)$. In essence, rule (12.4) states that if system output is significantly smaller, then the desired system output and system output is decreasing slowly, the controller output should be positive medium (or increment of controller output should be moderate if $\Delta u(n)$ is used in the rule consequent instead).

We will use $u(n)$ and $\Delta u(n)$ to represent, respectively, output and incremental output of a fuzzy controller. The scaled versions are denoted as $U(n)$ and $\Delta U(n)$, respectively (see below).

The quantity, linguistic names, symbolic names and membership functions of output fuzzy sets are all design parameters determined by the controller developer. Linguistic names are similar to those of input fuzzy sets; they can be symbolized as well in similar fashion. In theory, output fuzzy sets can be any shapes. Nevertheless, numerous successful applications of fuzzy control have led to the extensive use of singleton fuzzy sets. Figure 12.3 shows five example singleton output fuzzy sets. Using singleton fuzzy sets is by no means

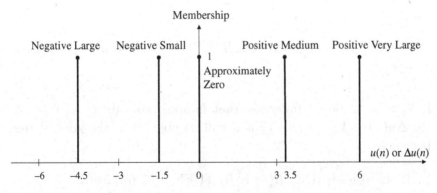

Fig. 12.3. Example membership functions of singleton output fuzzy sets.

restrictive, both mathematically and functionally. We will discuss mostly the fuzzy controllers using singleton output fuzzy sets due to their enormous popularity and practicality.

The number of output fuzzy sets relates to the number of input fuzzy sets. If there are N_1 and N_2 distinct input fuzzy sets for $E(n)$ and $R(n)$, respectively, then there are $N_1 \times N_2$ different combinations of the input fuzzy sets. Thus, $N_1 \times N_2$ different fuzzy rules are needed. Subsequently, up to $N_1 \times N_2$ different output fuzzy sets may be required. But, the actual amount in practice is usually markedly less than this maximum. Fuzzy rules are often so designed that some of them use the same output fuzzy sets, reducing significantly the number of different output fuzzy sets needed. The number of output fuzzy sets ranges somewhere between three and seven; a larger quantity is usually unnecessary.

A modest amount of fuzzy rules usually suffices for a typical fuzzy controller. The exact quantity is determined by the number of input fuzzy sets. A $N_1 \times N_2$ two-dimensional table is often used to conveniently represent $N_1 \times N_2$ rules, but this table scheme is not applicable when more than two input variables are involved. Given a particular application, fuzzy rules may be designed by the controller developer and/or by the expert operating the system. Rule design is an empirical process partially depending on trial and error effort. There does not exist a set of fuzzy rules universally applicable to any systems with guaranteed superior control performance.

Using the numerical indexing system, a general fuzzy rule is expressed as

$$\text{IF } E(n) \text{ is } A_i \text{ AND } R(n) \text{ is } B_j \text{ THEN } u(n) \text{ (or } \Delta u(n)) \quad (12.15)$$
$$\text{is } V_k$$

If V_k is a singleton fuzzy set that is non-zero only at $u(n) = V_k$ (or $\Delta u(n) = V_k$), where V_k is a real number, then the general rule becomes

$$\text{IF } E(n) \text{ is } A_i \text{ AND } R(n) \text{ is } B_j \text{ THEN } u(n) \text{ (or } \Delta u(n)) \text{ is } V_k$$
$$(12.16)$$

For any fuzzy rule, output fuzzy set is always related to input fuzzy sets in a certain way because the rule represents the knowledge or experience of the human being. For instance, in rule (12.14), output fuzzy set "Positive Medium" is linked to input fuzzy sets "Positive Large" for $E(n)$ and "Negative Small" for $R(n)$. More generally, in rule (12.16), V_k depends on A_i and B_j; this dependence can be represented by relating indexes of A_i and B_j to V_k as follows (the same can be said to rule (12.15), but we will not go into detail as it does not use singleton output fuzzy set):

$$\text{IF} \quad E(n) \text{ is } A_i \text{ AND } R(n) \text{ is } B_j \text{ THEN} u(n) \text{ (or } \Delta u(n)) \text{ is} \tag{12.17}$$
$$V_{f(i,j)}$$

where $k = f(i,j)$. $f()$ can be any function of i and j as long as its value is an integer at every combination of i and j because the index for V_k must be integer. Without loss of generality, we introduce another function $h(i,j)$ and let

$$h(i,j) = V_{f(i,j)} = V_k \tag{12.18}$$

Obviously, $h()$ can be any function and its value at i and j does not have to be integer. Now, fuzzy rule (12.17) can be expressed as

$$\text{IF } E(n) \text{ is } A_i \text{ AND } R(n) \text{ is } B_j \text{ THEN } u(n)(\text{or } \Delta u(n)) \text{ is } h(i,j)$$

At any sampling time, usually only a handful number of fuzzy rules are activated. A fuzzy rule is activated if, after fuzzification, the membership values of the input fuzzy sets for $E(n)$ and $R(n)$ are both non-zero for the rule. An activated rule contributes its share in the calculation of new controller output. If, on the other hand, either of the membership values is zero, the rule will not be activated and subsequently will make no contribution. This principle of determining rule activation applies to all the fuzzy rules.

Continue our concrete demonstration. For the fuzzification results in the last section, among the total 20 fuzzy rules (i.e., $N_1 = 4$

and $N_2 = 5$), only the following four will be activated at time n^*:

$$\text{IF } E(n) \text{ is } A_1 \text{ AND } R(n) \text{ is } B_{-1}$$
$$\text{THEN } u(n) \text{ (or } \Delta u(n)) \text{ is } h(1, -1) \tag{12.19}$$

$$\text{IF } E(n) \text{ is } A_1 \text{ AND } R(n) \text{ is } B_0$$
$$\text{THEN } u(n) \text{ (or } \Delta u(n)) \text{ is } h(1, 0) \tag{12.20}$$

$$\text{IF } E(n) \text{ is } A_2 \text{ AND } R(n) \text{ is } B_{-1}$$
$$\text{THEN } u(n) \text{ (or } \Delta u(n)) \text{ is } h(2, -1) \tag{12.21}$$

$$\text{IF } E(n) \text{ is } A_2 \text{ AND } R(n) \text{ is } B_0$$
$$\text{THEN } u(n) \text{ (or } \Delta u(n)) \text{ is } h(2, 0) \tag{12.22}$$

Due to the fuzzification, at time n^*, the membership values for "$E(n)$ is A_1", "$E(n)$ is A_2", "$R(n)$ is B_{-1}" and "$R(n)$ is B_0" are 0.2, 0.6, 0.5 and 0.3, respectively (see (12.5)–(12.13)). These membership values now need to be combined by fuzzy logic AND operations.

In fuzzy control, the most widely used AND operators are Zadeh AND operator and product AND operator. Use of other types is rare. For any specific fuzzy controller, it is customary to employ only one type of AND operator for all the fuzzy rules. The reason is perhaps to keep fuzzy rules and hence controllers simple. Theoretically, a mixture of different fuzzy AND operators may be used in different fuzzy rules and/or in a fuzzy rule if three or more input variables are involved.

12.2.3. *Fuzzy inference mechanism and defuzzification*

The fuzzy inference mechanism applies the methods of fuzzy reasoning to evaluate the rules. First, the membership values produced by the Fuzzification Module are aggregated by fuzzy logic AND operation in the rule antecedent producing the degree of firing the rule. Second, the fuzzy inference (Fig. 12.1) relates the degree of firing to the rule consequent and aggregates the rules. Third, the defuzzification operator transforms the fuzzy output generated by the rule-base into a deterministic value.

Following are the degrees of firing for the four fuzzy rules (12.19)–(12.22) using Zadeh fuzzy logic AND:

$$\mu_{Z1} = \min(\mu_{A_1}(e(n^*)), \mu_{B_{-1}}(r(n^*))) = \min(0.2, 0.5)$$

$$= 0.2 \text{ for } h(1, -1)$$

$$\mu_{Z2} = \min(\mu_{A_1}(e(n^*)), \mu_{B_0}(r(n^*))) = \min(0.2, 0.3) = 0.2 \text{ for } h(1, 0)$$

$$\mu_{Z3} = \min(\mu_{A_2}(e(n^*)), \mu_{B_{-1}}(r(n^*))) = \min(0.6, 0.5)$$

$$= 0.5 \text{ for } h(2, -1)$$

$$\mu_{Z4} = \min(\mu_{A_2}(e(n^*)), \mu_{B_0}(r(n^*))) = \min(0.6, 0.3) = 0.3 \text{ for } h(2, 0)$$

and product fuzzy logic AND operator, respectively:

$$\mu_{P1} = \mu_{A_1}(e(n^*)) \times \mu_{B_{-1}}(r(n^*)) = 0.2 \times 0.5 = 0.1 \text{ for } h(1, -1)$$

$$\mu_{P2} = \mu_{A_1}(e(n^*)) \times \mu_{B_0}(r(n^*)) = 0.2 \times 0.3 = 0.06 \text{ for } h(1, 0)$$

$$\mu_{P3} = \mu_{A_2}(e(n^*)) \times \mu_{B_{-1}}(r(n^*)) = 0.6 \times 0.5 = 0.3 \text{ for } h(2, -1)$$

$$\mu_{P4} = \mu_{A_2}(e(n*)) \times \mu_{B_0}(r(n^*)) = 0.6 \times 0.3 = 0.18 \text{ for } h(2, 0)$$

The degree of firing characterizes the compatibility of the numerical input $(e(n^*), r(n^*))$ to the fuzzy sets of the rule antecedent.

Due to space constraint, we will not discuss the variety of methods of fuzzy inference, rule aggregation, and defuzzification. We should only mention that for the special case of singleton consequents, most of these methods collapse into a defuzzified output that is defined by the weighted average of output fuzzy set weighted by the normalized degrees of firing the rules.

The following example shows the calculation of defuzzified controller output $U(n^*)$, assuming $h(1, -1) = 10$, $h(1, 0) = h(2, -1) = 5$, $h(2, 0) = 8$, $K_u = 1$ and $K_{\Delta u} = 1$.

$$U(n^*)$$

$$= K_u \frac{\mu_{Z1} \cdot h(1, -1) + \mu_{Z2} \cdot h(1, 0) + \mu_{Z3} \cdot h(2, -1) + \mu_{Z4} \cdot h(2, 0)}{\mu_{Z1} + \mu_{Z2} + \mu_{Z3} + \mu_{Z4}}$$

$$= 6.583$$

$U(n^*)$ is the new output of the fuzzy controller at time n^*. It is applied to the system to achieve control.

If the defuzzification result is $\Delta U(n^*)$ instead of $U(n^*)$, the new fuzzy controller output should be

$$U(n^*) = U(n^* - 1) + \Delta U(n^*)$$

where $U(n^* - 1)$ is fuzzy controller output at time $n^* - 1$.

The fuzzification, fuzzy inference and defuzzification operations repeat in every sampling period. That is, we have shown, with a step-by-step example, how a typical fuzzy controller works. Figure 12.4 provides a graphical description of these steps for the above example where Zadeh fuzzy logic AND and OR operators are used.

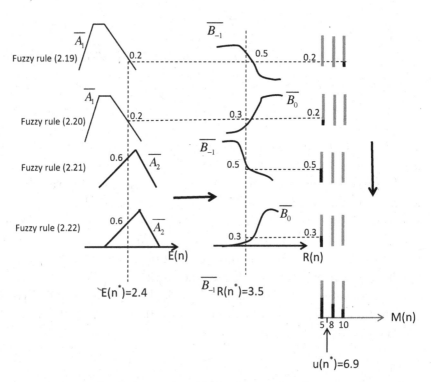

Fig. 12.4. A graphical description of the fuzzy controller example to show concretely how fuzzification, fuzzy inference, and defuzzification operations work.

Thus far, we have described each and every step of how a fuzzy controller computes new output from the input variables. These steps constitute merely a procedure and are numerical only. In comparison with conventional controllers, what is needed is the explicit structure of the fuzzy controller behind this procedure that relates input variables to output variables. As is, this fuzzy controller is a black-box and analytically unknown. It produces an output signal after an input signal is fed.

12.3.   Design of Fuzzy Controllers

12.3.1.   *Selection of membership functions*

First, input fuzzy sets must cover entire scaled universes of discourse so that any value of input variables will produce at least one non-zero membership value. The number of input fuzzy sets, their linguistic names and shapes are design parameters determined by the fuzzy controller developer. The basis for the developer's decision includes the characteristics of the system to be controlled, control operator's knowledge and experience on the system, the developer's experience with fuzzy control as well as personal preference. At present, proper determination of the design parameters is, to a great extent, more an art than science. No mathematically rigorous formulas or procedures exist to accomplish the design of input fuzzy sets. What do exist in the literature are rules of the thumb and empirical knowledge accumulated through many years of practice and studies.

Usually, 2–13 fuzzy sets are used for each input variable and a larger number is uncommon. Different numbers of fuzzy sets may be used for different input variables. The shape of fuzzy sets may be different for the same input variable or different input variables. Each input fuzzy set is assigned a linguistic name, preferably unique. The common names include "Negative Large," "Negative Medium," "Negative Small," "Approximately Zero," "Positive Small," "Positive Medium" and "Positive Large." They are often abbreviated as NL, NM, NS, AZ, PS, PM and PL. Of course, one may employ any other linguistic names that he/she prefers. Different naming will not affect fuzzification result as long as the membership functions remain unchanged.

The most widely used types of input fuzzy sets are triangular, trapezoidal, Gaussian and bell-shaped. Regardless of the shape, input fuzzy sets are usually required to be so positioned that (1) any two adjacent membership functions overlap once, and (2) at any sampling time, two non-zero membership values are yielded by the fuzzification of each input variable. The rationale behind the requirements is to limit the number of fuzzy rules executed at any time to an adequate level.

These two requirements are unachievable, however, for Gaussian input fuzzy sets as Gaussian function has two infinitely long "tails". This type of fuzzy sets is used in the literature largely because the function and its derivatives are smooth and continuous, making the mathematical analysis more tractable and simpler, as compared to the other three types of membership functions.

12.3.2. *Rule-base*

The concept of a rule-base is crucial for fuzzy controller design [157]. It is also one reason for criticism toward fuzzy control because, in general, there are no systematic tools for forming the rule-base of the fuzzy controller. We shall outline two notable methods. The first is based on intuitive knowledge and experience — the fuzzy controller is designed as a simple expert system. Different sources of knowledge, resulting in the formulation of alternative rule-bases, can be considered. One reasonable source is the knowledge, based on the experience of an operator, controlling a given process. This allows the introduction of "rule of thumb" experience in the control strategy. Most fuzzy controllers combine an approach based on the operator's experience with a good understanding of systems and control theory. Almost all fuzzy controllers developed in the 1970s and 1980s were of this type. The satisfactory results, obtained with the industrial applications of fuzzy control [406, 423], confirm this direction in the construction of fuzzy controllers.

The second and more formal approach to the construction of the rule-base of the fuzzy controller is based on the use of meta-rules. For example, the following meta-rules capture the common-sense control strategy [157]:

MR1: *If the error e(n) and its change r(n) are zero, then maintain present control setting.*

MR2: *If the error e(n) is tending to zero at a satisfactory rate r(n), then maintain present control setting.*

MR3: *If the error e(n) is not self-correcting, then control action Δu(n) is not zero and depends on the sign and magnitude of e(n) and r(n).*

The rule-base in Table 12.1 is derived from the meta-rules and represents a control strategy that can be applied to a wide class of objects (e.g., steam engine, heat exchanger, temperature contour of a bioreactor, and room temperature) whose dynamics is approximated by a first-order system with a dead time T_d and time constant T:

$$S(s) = \frac{e^{-T_d s}}{1 + T s}$$

Table 12.1. Example of a rule-base derived from the meta-rules [157].

Meta-rules representing the control strategy for plants that can be approximated by a first-order system with a dead time
1   If the error $e(n)$ is positive AND the change of the error $r(n)$ is approximately zero THEN the change of the control $\Delta u(n)$ is positive.
2   If the error $e(n)$ is negative AND the change of the error $r(n)$ is approximately zero THEN the change of the control $\Delta u(n)$ is negative.
3   If the error $e(n)$ is approximately zero AND the change of the error $r(n)$ is approximately zero THEN the change of the control $\Delta u(n)$ is approximately zero.
4   If the error $e(k)$ is approximately zero AND the change of the error $r(n)$ is positive THEN the change of the control $\Delta u(n)$ is positive.
5   If the error $e(n)$ is approximately zero AND the change of the error $r(n)$ is negative THEN the change of the control $\Delta u(n)$ is negative.

12.3.3.   *Implementation*

For finite universes of the input and output, which is always the case for real-world applications, the mapping can be approximated by a look-up-table (LUT). For a predefined rule-base and membership functions, the LUT can be calculated in advance as part of the fuzzy controller design process. The output of the fuzzy controller can be inferred from the LUT by interpolation. This simple LUT eliminates the tedious calculations of the degrees of firing — an operation that might require significant computational resource and time.

12.4.   Multiple-Output, Single-Input (MISO) Mamdani Fuzzy Controllers

We now generalize the above SISO fuzzy controller to typical MISO fuzzy controllers whose structure is shown in Fig. 12.5. Structurewise, it is the same as the SISO fuzzy controller (Fig. 12.1) except that more input variables are involved.

Assume there are M input variables, $x_i(n)$, which represent different physical variables and their derivatives (e.g., temperature, pressure, speed, velocity and acceleration). Every variable is scaled by a scaling factor, and the result is denoted as $X_i(n)$. Suppose that P_i input fuzzy sets are used to fuzzify $X_i(n)$. The total number of fuzzy rules is

$$\Omega = \prod_{i=1}^{M} P_i \qquad (12.23)$$

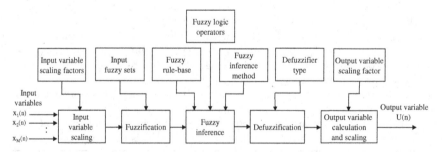

Fig. 12.5.   Structure of typical MISO fuzzy controllers.

The number of fuzzy rules grows very quickly with the increase of the number of input variables. It can be quite large even for a relatively small amount of input variables and input fuzzy sets. For example, if $M = 4$ and $P_i = 3$, $\Omega = 256$.

Represent input fuzzy set for $X_i(n)$ in the jth fuzzy rule by $A_{I_{i,j}}$, where $I_{i,j}$ is an integer index whose range is determined by the number of fuzzy sets for $X_i(n)$. The jth rule is like:

$$\text{IF } X_1(n) \text{ is } A_{I_{1,j}} \text{ AND } \cdots\cdots \text{ AND } X_M(n) \text{ is } A_{I_{M,j}} \quad (12.24)$$

$$\text{THEN } u(n) \text{ (or } \Delta u(n)) \text{ is } h(I_{1,j},\ldots,I_{M,j})$$

where $h(I_{1,j},\ldots,I_{M,j})$ represents a singleton output fuzzy set that is non-zero only at $u(n) = h(I_{1,j},\ldots,I_{M,j})$ or at $\Delta u(n) = h(I_{1,j}, \ldots,I_{M,j})$.

Suppose that after fuzzification, fuzzy logic AND operations, and fuzzy inference using any one of the fuzzy inference methods in [156], the combined membership value from antecedent of the jth rule is $\mu_j(x, A)$, where x is a vector containing all the M input variables and A is a vector involving all the input fuzzy sets. We use $\mu_j(x, A)$ to signify the fact that the combined membership value is the function of all the input variables and input fuzzy sets. Then, after defuzzification by using the generalized defuzzifier [155], output of the fuzzy controllers at time n is

$$U(n) \text{ (or } \Delta U(n)) = K_u \frac{\sum_{j=1}^{\Omega} \mu_j^{\alpha}(x, A) \cdot h(I_{1,j},\ldots,I_{M,j})}{\sum_{j=1}^{\Omega} \mu_j^{\alpha}(x, A)} \quad (12.25)$$

Although the summation is from 1 to Ω, only a small number of $\mu_j(x, A)$ is actually non-zero at any sampling time. K_u should be replaced by $K_{\Delta u}$ if the left-hand side of the equation is $\Delta U(n)$.

If fuzzy logic OR operations are used to combine memberships for the same output fuzzy sets in all the fuzzy rules, the result is $\varpi(n)$ membership values, denoted as $\hat{\mu}_j(x, A)$, for $\varpi(n)$ distinctive singleton output fuzzy sets, $h(\hat{I}_{1,j},\ldots,\hat{I}_{M,j})$. Here, $\hat{I}_{i,j}$ is a new index, $j = 1,\ldots,\varpi(n)$ and $\varpi(n) \leq \Omega$. We use notation $\varpi(n)$ to signalize that the number of distinctive output fuzzy sets may be different at different times. The defuzzifier output is

$$U(n) \text{ (or } \Delta U(n)) = K_u \frac{\sum_{j=1}^{\varpi(n)} \hat{\mu}_j^\alpha(x, A) \cdot h(\hat{I}_{1,j}, \dots, \hat{I}_{M,j})}{\sum_{j=1}^{\varpi(n)} \hat{\mu}_j^\alpha(x, A)} \quad (12.26)$$

12.5. Takagi–Sugeno (TS) Fuzzy Controllers

The structure of typical SISO TS fuzzy controllers is depicted in Fig. 12.6.

It is similar to, but not the same as, the structure of the typical SISO Mamdani fuzzy controllers, as shown in Fig. 12.1. There exist four differences between the Mamdani and TS structures. First, TS fuzzy controllers do not use scaling factors for input and output variables. The scaling is implicitly achieved by the TS rule structure: each input variable is multiplied by a coefficient in the consequent of every fuzzy rule. The coefficient is not specifically used for scaling, but part of its effect can be imaged as scaling. The second difference is that TS fuzzy controllers use (linear) functions of input variables as rule consequent whereas Mamdani fuzzy controllers use fuzzy sets. Third, TS fuzzy controllers do not need to use fuzzy logic OR operators in fuzzy rules, because there are no identical rule consequent. Finally, TS fuzzy controllers have only one fuzzy inference method to use. In comparison, many choices exist for Mamdani fuzzy controllers.

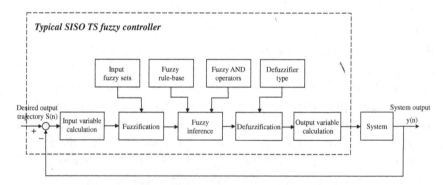

Fig. 12.6. Structure of typical SISO TS fuzzy control systems.

The structure of MISO TS fuzzy controllers is almost the same as that of the SISO ones, with the major difference being more input variables. We now introduce their operation, which contains SISO ones as a special case. The operation is the repeated cycle of the same three steps executed by Mamdani fuzzy controllers: fuzzification, fuzzy inference and defuzzification.

TS fuzzy controllers use the same fuzzification as Mamdani ones do. Assume that TS fuzzy controllers use Ω fuzzy rules with linear consequent (Ω is defined above), the jth rule is like

$$\text{IF } x_1(n) \text{ is } A_{I_{1,j}} \text{ AND } \cdots\cdots \text{ AND } x_M(n) \text{ is } A_{I_{M,j}} \quad (12.27)$$

$$\text{THEN } U(n) \text{ (or } \Delta U(n)) = a_j + a_{1j}x_1(n) + \cdots + a_{Mj}x_M(n)$$

where a_{ij} are constant parameters. TS fuzzy controllers combine the membership values in the antecedent in the same way as the Mamdani fuzzy controllers do and use the same common fuzzy logic AND operators. However, TS fuzzy controllers do not use fuzzy logic OR operation to combine membership values from different rules, as there are not identical rule consequents to begin with.

Suppose that after fuzzification and fuzzy logic AND operation, the combined membership for the consequent of the jth rule is $\mu_j(x, A)$. TS fuzzy controllers simply use the product of $\mu_j(x, A)$ and the linear function in the rule consequent as fuzzy inference result for the jth rule. After defuzzification by, say, the generalized defuzzifier, output of the TS fuzzy controllers is

$$U(n)(\text{or } \Delta U(n))$$

$$= \frac{\sum_{j=1}^{\Omega} \mu_j^{\alpha}(x, A)(a_j + a_{1j}x_1(n) + \cdots + a_{Mj}x_M(n))}{\sum_{j=1}^{\Omega} \mu_j^{\alpha}(x, A)}$$

$$= \frac{\sum_{j=1}^{\Omega} \mu_j^{\alpha}(x, A)\left(a_j + \sum_{i=1}^{M} a_{ij}x_i(n)\right)}{\sum_{j=1}^{\Omega} \mu_j^{\alpha}(x, A)} \quad (12.28)$$

Again, at any specific sampling time, many rules are not activated due to zero membership values of input fuzzy sets after fuzzification.

What rules are executed depends on the values of input variables as well as the definitions of input fuzzy sets.

TS fuzzy rule (12.27) reduces to Mamdani fuzzy rule (12.24), if (1) $a_{ij} = 0$ for all i and j, and (2) $a_{0j} = h(I_{1,j}, \ldots, I_{M,j})$ for all j, where $h(I_{1,j}, \ldots, I_{M,j})$ represents singleton fuzzy sets. That is to say that a Mamdani fuzzy rule with singleton output fuzzy set is a special type of TS rules.

12.6. Fuzzy Control Versus Conventional Control

To the seemingly simple question "what is fuzzy control," people with different technical backgrounds have offered different answers. Computer AI scientists often think that fuzzy control methodology can emulate human knowledge and experience because fuzzy sets, fuzzy logic and fuzzy rules capture and represent the essence of human expertise. Control engineers see fuzzy control as a form of "intelligent" control and hence consider it to be superior to conventional control in certain aspects. Practitioners in industry view fuzzy control as a powerful and cost-effective means to solve complicated real-world control problems in a rather effective fashion.

Our answer is from the viewpoint of conventional control technology, and reveals the nature of fuzzy control in relation to conventional control. According to the mathematical representations of the Mamdani fuzzy controllers in (12.25) and the TS fuzzy controllers in (12.28), it should be clear that fuzzy control does nothing but generate nonlinear mapping from input variables to output variables. Simply put, fuzzy control is nonlinear control; a fuzzy controller is a nonlinear controller.

Moreover, fuzzy control is nonlinear variable structure control. Take the SISO Mamdani fuzzy controller described above as an example. In fuzzification, which input fuzzy sets will yield non-zero membership values depends on the values of $e(n)$ and $r(n)$, which in turn decide which fuzzy rules will be activated in fuzzy inference. This is to say that which input and output fuzzy sets will be used in defuzzification vary as the values of $e(n)$ and $r(n)$ change from one sampling time to another. These time-dependent changes of the controller structure make the fuzzy controllers nonlinear variable structure controllers. By the same token, MISO TS fuzzy controllers described in (12.28) are also nonlinear variable structure controllers.

12.6.1. *Advantages of fuzzy control*

The biggest advantage of fuzzy control is that it provides an effective and efficient methodology to develop nonlinear controllers in practice without using highly advanced mathematics. Making a fuzzy controller requires describing human control knowledge/experience linguistically and captures them in the form of fuzzy sets, fuzzy logic operation and fuzzy rules. Fuzzy control can be used to emulate human expert knowledge and experience, and is ideal for solving problems where imprecision and vagueness are present and verbal description is necessary. Unlike the traditional mathematical model-based controller design methodology, explicit system model is not needed by fuzzy control. Rather, system model is implicitly built into fuzzy rules, fuzzy logic operation and fuzzy sets in a vague manner. Fuzzy rules relate input fuzzy sets describing state variables of the system, e.g., $e(n)$ and $r(n)$, to fuzzy controller output. In this sense, fuzzy control combines the system modeling task and the system control task into one task. By avoiding a separate modeling task, which can be much more challenging than the control task in many nonlinear situations, control problems can usually be solved more efficiently and effectively. Countless applications of fuzzy control around the world have proved this point.

Conventional nonlinear control is powerful if the nonlinear system model is mathematically available. It is well known, though, that accurately establishing a nonlinear system model is generally difficult because correct identification of nonlinear system structure is not easy, which significantly limits the application scope of nonlinear control.

Fuzzy control has also created a paradigm for developing nonlinear and multiple-input multiple-output (MIMO) controllers without using complicated and sophisticated linear/nonlinear control theory and mathematics. This is in sharp contrast to conventional control technology, especially the nonlinear one. By manipulating various components of a fuzzy controller, such as the scaling factors, fuzzy sets and fuzzy rules, coupled with computer simulation and trial-and-error effort, it is often possible for a non-control professional to build a rather well-performing fuzzy controller. This advantage makes fuzzy control practical and powerful in solving real-world problems and it explains why fuzzy control has especially been popular in the industry.

A number of excellent fuzzy system development software packages, including MATLAB Fuzzy Logic Toolbox^{TM}, are in the market to facilitate the development tasks.

12.6.2.   *Disadvantages of fuzzy control*

From a conventional control standpoint, the advantages of fuzzy control come with a price, at least at this stage of the technology. After all, nothing is perfect and everything has two faces.

First of all, fuzzy controllers have often been used as black-box controllers. In many applications, fuzzy control users were satisfied once trial-and-error effort produced satisfactory control performance. Rigorous or analytical investigation was often not pursued or simply ignored. As stated earlier, fuzzy control is nonlinear variable structure control. As such, deriving their analytical structures (see (12.25) and (12.28)) should be the first step for analytical study. Yet, even this step is very difficult and many times impossible. Indeed, for many fuzzy controllers, especially those involving complicated fuzzy sets, numerous fuzzy rules and multiple input variables, the task can be extremely hard. Without accurate mathematical structure of a fuzzy controller, precise analysis and design of a fuzzy control system in the spirit of conventional control is technically difficult, if not impossible. This is true even when the system model is mathematically available.

None of the existing fuzzy system development software packages can help in this regard either, as they share a common flaw — no analytical capabilities. They are unable to derive the analytical structure of a fuzzy controller, let alone mathematically design a system and determine its stability or any other system properties.

Second, a fuzzy controller usually has (far) more design parameters than a comparable conventional controller. To make matters worse, learning how to construct a good fuzzy controller is, to a large extent, more an art than science.

Subsequently, fuzzy control design may require more tuning and trial-and-error effort. Compared to the industrially dominant PID control that has only three design parameters, the number of design parameters for a fuzzy controller can become overwhelmingly large. They range from the number and shape of input and output fuzzy sets, scaling factors, fuzzy AND and OR operators to fuzzy rules to defuzzifier. Worse yet, there do not exist clear relationships between these parameters and controller's performance.

At present, developers must partially rely on the empirical rules of thumb and *ad hoc* procedures in the literature to make successful fuzzy control applications. Although there exist a great deal of such knowledge, it is not sufficient, especially for fuzzy control novices. Fuzzy controllers are nonlinear controllers. As such, the generality of the knowledge is rather limited.

Any design and/or tuning procedure can hardly be generalized to cover a broad range of fuzzy control problems. As a result, trial-and-error effort and extensive computer simulation are often necessary. Neither stability nor performance of the fuzzy control system under development can rigorously be guaranteed. This empirical approach, while effective for some applications, is impractical and unsafe for applications in some fields, such as aerospace, nuclear engineering and, particularly, biomedicine.

These two drawbacks of fuzzy control are inherent. They are quite serious, especially in comparison with conventional control technology. Nevertheless, they are moderate and reasonable tradeoffs to pay for the biggest advantage of fuzzy control — capable of control without system mathematical model.

Furthermore, these two major problems are at least partially solvable and have been resolved to a certain degree. We will show the resolutions in the next chapter.

12.7.   Applicability of Fuzzy Control

There exist literally a countless number of different types of systems in practice. Hence, as with any control technology, it is essential that the applicability of fuzzy control be well defined, which apparently relates to the strengths and limitations of fuzzy control examined in the last section. Fuzzy control is likely most desirable if (1) mathematical model of the system to be controlled is unavailable, but the system is known to be significantly nonlinear, time-varying or with time-delay, and/or (2) PID control cannot generate satisfactory system performance.

Given the strengths of fuzzy control, the first criterion is natural and logical. We need to stress the second criterion: It is practically important to know whether PID control can solve the control problem of interest before fuzzy control is attempted. PID controllers have been used to control about 90% industrial processes worldwide. PID control techniques are well developed and numerous control system design and gain tuning methods have been developed. When the system to be controlled is linear and its mathematical model is available, design and implementation of linear PID control is effective and efficient. Note that using PID control does not necessarily require system model. In the absence of the system model, one can still achieve satisfactory PID control performance in practice by manually tuning, in a trial-and-error fashion, the proportional-gain, integral-gain and derivative-gain. This is true if the system is linear or somewhat nonlinear. Better yet, there exist many different types of PID controllers. The most commonly used one is the linear PID controller but often nonlinear ones, such as the anti-windup PID controller, are also employed. Properly adding nonlinearity to linear PID control can lead to desirable nonlinear control effect. Time has already proved that PID control, though simple, is effective and can produce satisfactory results quickly for the majority of control problems, especially those in process control. This is the case even when the system of interest is nonlinear, time-varying or associated with time-delay, as long as they are not too severe. Moreover, PID control is still an area of active research at present. Many theoretical and empirical results in the literatures have dealt with various aspects of PID control systems, including system analysis and design.

Fuzzy control should be used if at least one of the two criteria holds. This is the case even if control expert knowledge and experience are unavailable. Practically speaking, it is possible for one to achieve satisfactory fuzzy control of nonlinear systems through extensive computer simulation and trial-and-error effort without expert knowledge. Utilizing available expert knowledge/experience can reduce development cost and time, particularly when the system is rather complex. But this is not a prerequisite for using fuzzy control.

Even when the system of interest is nonlinear, time-varying or associated with time-delay and its model is explicitly given, it is often still advantageous to apply fuzzy control provided that designing an adequate nonlinear controller is difficult. Unlike linear control theory, there does not exist general nonlinear control and system theory universally applicable to any nonlinear, time-varying or time-delay systems. When the nonlinear system of interest is complicated, or a MIMO one, classical control may be ineffective or even unusable. Furthermore, many of the existing nonlinear control techniques require highly sophisticated control and mathematics background, such as differential geometry. They are inaccessible to many of the engineers in the field.

Fuzzy control should not be employed if the system to be controlled is linear, regardless of the availability of its explicit model. For linear systems, there is no advantage to use fuzzy control. PID control and various other types of linear controllers can effectively solve the control problem with significantly less effort, time and cost. Likewise, fuzzy control should be avoided if the system of interest is nonlinear, time-varying or associated with time-delay, but PID control can yield satisfactory control result.

In summary, PID control should be tried first whenever possible. Fuzzy control becomes a choice only after PID control fails or PID control is not applicable in the first place.

Chapter 13

Fuzzy Decision-Making

The existing decision models have been successfully applied to solving many decision problems in management, business, economics, and other fields, but nowadays arises a need to develop more realistic decision models. The main drawback of the existing utility theories starting from von Neumann–Moregnstern expected utility to the advanced non-expected models is that they are designed for laboratory examples with simple, well-defined gambles which do not adequately enough reflect real decision situations. In real-life decision-making problems preferences are vague and decision-relevant information is imperfect as described in natural language (NL). Vagueness of preferences and imperfect decision-relevant information require using suitable utility model which would be fundamentally different to the existing precise utility models. Precise utility models cannot reflect vagueness of preferences, vagueness of objective conditions and outcomes, imprecise beliefs, etc. The time has come for a new generation of decision theories. In this study, we propose a decision theory, which is capable to deal with vague preferences and imperfect information. The theory discussed here is based on a fuzzy-valued non-expected utility model representing linguistic preference relations and imprecise beliefs.

13.1. Introduction

Decision-making theory is a holy grail of numerous studies in management science, economics and other areas. It comprises a broad diversity of approaches to modeling behavior of a decision-maker (DM) realized under various information frameworks. In essence, the solution to the decision-making problem is defined by a preferences framework and a type of decision-relevant information. In its turn preference and decision-relevant information frameworks are closely related. One of the approaches to formally describe preferences on the base of decision-relevant information is the use of a utility function. Utility function is a quantitative representation of preferences of a DM and any scientifically grounded utility model comes with the underlying preference assumptions.

The existing utility models are developed within the three main directions of decision-making theory: decision-making under ignorance, decision-making under risk and decision-making under ambiguity.

Decision-making under ignorance [169, 207] is characterized by an absence of any information about probabilities of events. Unfortunately, this is an ideal view on decision-relevant information, because in real-life a DM almost always has some limited information about probabilities. The decision-making methods developed for situations of ignorance include Laplace insufficient reason criterion, Savage minimax regret criterion, Hurwitz criterion, Wald maximin solution rule, etc. Maximin solution rule models extreme pessimism in decision-making, whereas its generalization, Hurwitz criterion uses linear combination of pessimistic and optimistic solutions.

In decision-making under risk [98, 365, 398, 447, 448, 454] it is supposed that precise objective or subjective probabilities of states of nature and precise outcomes are available. Subjective probabilities [398] are used when objective probabilities are unknown. The main methods of decision-making under risk are von Neumann and Morgenstern expected utility (EU) [454], subjective expected utility (SEU) [398] and Kahneman and Tversky Prospect theory (OPT) [153, 447]. As it was shown by many experiments, the use of precise objective or subjective probabilities appeared non-realistic [31, 89, 140, 177]. On the other hand, even if objective probabilities were known, beliefs of a DM do not coincide with them but are affected by some kind of distortion — they are transformed into so-called decision weights [153, 325, 447].

A large number of studies is devoted to decision-making under ambiguity [58, 89, 100, 138, 145, 147, 159, 170–172, 177, 192, 212,

233]. Ambiguity is commonly referred to as uncertainty with respect to probabilities — the cases when probabilities are not known or are supposed to vary within some range. The terms "uncertainty" and "ambiguity" are not always clearly distinguished and defined but, in general, are related to non-probabilistic uncertainty. In turn, decision-making under uncertainty often is considered as an extreme non-probabilistic case — when no information on probabilities is available. From the other side, this case is also termed as decision-making under complete ignorance. At the same time, sometimes, this is considered as ambiguity represented by simultaneous consideration of all the probability distributions. The studies on decision-making under ambiguity are conducted in two directions — a development of models based on multiple probability distributions, called multiple priors models [175, 178], and a formation of approaches based on non-additive measures [457–459, 465]. Mainly, these models consider so-called ambiguity aversion as a property of human behavior to generally prefer outcomes related to non-ambiguous events to those related to ambiguous ones.

The well-known approach developed for multiple priors is maximin EU (MMEU) and its development [89, 92, 100, 144–147, 168, 170–172, 176, 243, 365]. In this criterion, an alternative is evaluated by minimal or maximal EU with respect to all possible probability distributions. In Ref. [172], they suggest to use convex combination of minimal and maximal expected utilities.

In general, multiple priors are much more adequate but still a poor formulation of probability-relevant information available for a DM–in real-world problems, a DM usually has some information that allows determining which priors are more and which are less relevant. For addressing this issue, models with second-order probabilities were suggested [58, 102, 244, 407]. In Ref. [244], they suggest so-called "smooth ambiguity" model which generalizes the existing MMEU models. In this model, a subjective probability measure reflects DM's belief on whether a considered subset of multiple priors contains a "true" prior. The use of these models is a step toward forming a more adequate information structure. However, a construction of a second-order probability distribution over first-order probabilities become doubtful as the latter cannot be known precisely [89]. Second-order precise probability model is a non-realistic description of human beliefs characterized by imprecision and associated with some psychological aspects that need to be considered as well. The other disadvantage of the belief representation suggested in Ref. [244] is that the problem of investigation of consistency of subjective probability-relevant information is not discussed — consistent multiple priors are supposed to be given in advance. However, a verification of consistency of beliefs becomes a very important problem. An extensive investigation of this issue is covered in Ref. [457].

The alternative approach to model imperfect information about probabilities is the use of imprecise probabilities, cf. [44, 139, 166, 191, 220, 221, 280, 349, 450, 451, 457]. Some intuitively acceptable and useful interpretations of imprecise probabilities are interval probabilities [139, 191], fuzzy (linguistic) probabilities [154, 482], to name a few viable alternatives. The first fundamental study in this framework was the Walley's theory of imprecise probabilities [457]. The key concept of the theory is the lower prevision, which can be used to model evaluations like lower and upper probabilities, belief functions, additive probability measures, etc. and does not impose any assumptions on the type of probability distributions. However, this theory often requires solving very complicated optimization problems.

In Ref. [191], they suggest an approach for decisions based on interval probabilities where the latter are obtained on the base of pairwise comparison of likelihood of events.

The important class of approaches to problems when a DM is uncertain about probabilities deals with imprecise hierarchical models [115, 154, 183, 322, 452, 553]. In these models, imprecise probabilities of states of nature are assigned at the first (lower) level. The second level is used to represent imprecise probability describing a DM's or experts' confidence about imprecise probability being assigned at the first level. However, most of the works devoted to hierarchical models deals with a large number of optimization problems.

One of the main models in this realm of application of non-additive measures (fuzzy measures) is Choquet expected utility (CEU) based on the Choquet integral [104]. As mentioned in Ref. [483], fuzzy measure is a unified description of various types of characterizations of uncertainty such as randomness, lack of specificity, and imprecision [72, 122, 123, 219, 430, 456].

CEU is a one of the most successful utility models, it is used as a criterion of decision-making under ambiguity and decision-making under risk.

Concerning real-world information about probabilities, Savage wrote [398]: ... *there seem to be some probability relations about which we feel relatively 'sure' as compared with others.... The notion of 'sure' and 'unsure' introduced here is vague, and my complaint is precisely that neither the theory of personal probability as it is developed in this book, nor any other device known to me renders the notion less vague.* In our opinion, the issue is that real relevant information perceived by DMs involves possibilistic uncertainty. Fuzzy probabilities [86, 115, 143, 256, 354, 360, 431, 482] are tools for addressing this issue to a significant extent.

Fuzzy probabilities are successful interpretation for linguistic estimates of probabilities such as "this is likely", "probability is low", etc. [514, 538].

In comparison to multiple priors consideration, for majority of cases, a DM has some additional linguistic information coming from his experience or even naturally present which reflects unequal levels of belief or possibility for different probability distributions. This means, that it is more adequate to consider sets of probability distributions as fuzzy sets which allow for taking into account various degrees of belief or possibility for different probability distributions. This involves second-order uncertainty, namely, probability-possibility modeling of information.

Different types of decision-relevant information require an application of different theories for solving a decision-making problem. In order to view the situations of decision-relevant information that one can be faced with and the utility models that can be applied, let us look at Table 13.1.

Table 13.1. Classification of decision-relevant information.

Outcomes	Utilities	Probabilities			
		Precise	Complete ignorance	Ambiguous	Imperfect
Complete					
Precise	Precise	Situation 1	Situation 2	Situation 3	Situation 4
	Fuzzy	Situation 5	Situation 6	Situation 7	Situation 8
Ignorance	Precise	Situation 9	Situation 10	Situation 11	Situation 12
	Fuzzy	Situation 13	Situation 14	Situation 15	Situation 16
Ambiguous	Precise	Situation 17	Situation 18	Situation 19	Situation 20
	Fuzzy	Situation 21	Situation 22	Situation 23	Situation 24
Imperfect	Precise	Situation 25	Situation 26	Situation 27	Situation 28
	Fuzzy	Situation 29	Situation 30	Situation 31	Situation 32

In Table 13.1, we identify three important coordinates (dimensions) essential to our investigations. The first one concerns information available for probabilities, the second captures information about outcomes, while the third looks at the nature of utilities and their description. The first two dimensions include precise information (risk), ignorance (absence of information), ambiguous information, and imperfect information. Two main types of utilities are considered, namely precise and fuzzy. Decision-relevant information setups are represented at the crossing of these coordinates; those are cells containing Situations from 1 to 32. They capture combinations of various types of probabilities, outcomes, and utilities. The most developed scenarios are those positioned in entries numbered from 1 to 4 (precise utility models). A limited attention has paid to situations 5–8 with fuzzy utilities, which are considered in Refs. [32, 77, 174, 293]. For the situations 9–12 with complete ignorance with respect to outcomes and with precise utilities a few works related to interactive obtaining of information were suggested. For situations 13–16, in our opinion, no works were suggested. Few studies are devoted to the situations with ambiguous outcomes (situations 17–20) [206, 210, 212] and precise utilities and no works to ambiguous outcomes with fuzzy utilities are available (situations 21–24). For situations 25–32 a very few studies were reported including the existing fuzzy utility models [32, 77, 174, 293]. In this study, we consider the case with imperfect probabilities, imperfect outcomes, and fuzzy utilities (situation 32) for which all other situations excluding those with complete ignorance (as there is no information) are subsumed by it. Unfortunately, for this situation no adequate utility model has been established so far.

Fuzzy logic [17, 18, 449, 531, 534] has emerged as a tool to handle vague estimates. There is a significant number of studies devoted to fuzzy and linguistic preference relations (FPR and LPR, for short) [167, 336–338]. They are motivated by the fact that vagueness is more adequately articulated in terms of fuzzy concepts. As a result, fuzzy degree-based preference axiomatization arises as a more adequate representation as it is closer to the essentials of human thinking [360, 532]. In view of this, LPR form a natural generalization of classical preference relations to underline the human-like utility model.

Along the direction of imperfect information and vague preference-based models, a series of works was devoted to the fuzzy utility models and decisions under fuzzy uncertainty [11, 32, 73, 77, 116, 174, 188, 192, 293]. In Ref. [77], they presented axioms for LPR in terms of linguistic probability distributions over fuzzy outcomes and defined fuzzy expected utility on this basis. But, unfortunately, an existence of a fuzzy utility function has not been proved. Reference [73] is an extensive work devoted to the representation of FPR. In this paper, an existence of a utility function representing a fuzzy pre-order is proved. However, in this work a utility function itself is considered as a non-fuzzy real-valued function. In Ref. [293], it is formulated conditions for existence and continuity of a numerical and fuzzy-valued expected utility under some standard conditions of a FPR (viz. reflexivity, transitivity, continuity, etc.). The author proves theorems on existence of a fuzzy expected utility for the cases of probabilistic and possibilistic information on states of nature. The possibilistic case, as it is correctly identified by the author, appears to be more adequate to deal with real-world problems. However, in this model, probabilities and outcomes are considered as numerical entities. This notably limits the use of the suggested model for real-life decision problems where almost all the information is described in NL. A new approach for decision-making under possibilistic information on states of nature when probabilistic information is absent is considered in Ref. [192]. In Ref. [174], they suggest representation of a fuzzy preference relation by fuzzy number-valued EU on the basis of fuzzy random variables. However, an existence of a fuzzy utility function has not been shown. In Ref. [32], they consider a fuzzy utility as a fuzzy-valued Choquet integral with a real-valued fuzzy measure obtained based on a set of possible probability distributions and with a fuzzy integrand. Unfortunately, the existence of the suggested fuzzy utility is not proved.

The existing decision theories yield good results, but nowadays there is a need in generation of more realistic theories. The problem is that the existing theories are good for laboratory examples with simple, well-defined gambles. The existing approaches to model impreciseness of beliefs are based on non-realistic and complicated techniques which are far from adequate modeling vagueness of perceptions. At the same time, the use of Savage's formulation of states of nature as "a space of mutually exclusive and exhaustive states" is inadequate to real decision problems, when DM often cannot exhaustively determine all possible objective conditions and cannot precisely differentiate between them. From the other side, in the existing theories they use numerical description of outcomes as results of actions under various events. However, a DM almost always cannot precisely determine future outcomes and have to use imprecise quantities like *high profit*, *medium cost* etc.

Despite that development of preference frameworks has passed a long way the modern preferences frameworks lack an important feature of human-like preferences: human-like preferences are vague [360] and are described in NL. Humans compare alternatives using linguistic techniques like "much better", "much worse", "a little better", "almost equivalent", etc. [532]. Such vague estimates cannot be handled and described in terms of classical logic.

In real-life decision problems, the relevant information on states of nature, probabilities, outcomes and utilities is imperfect as perception-based and described in NL [16, 20, 21, 24, 28, 29]. As Prof. Zadeh states, imperfect information is information which in one or more regards is imprecise, uncertain, incomplete, unreliable, vague or partially true [545]. Moreover, real-life problems are characterized by a second-order uncertainty, or uncertainty^2, for short. The cases of uncertainty^2 are fuzzy probabilities, second-order probabilities, type-2 fuzzy sets, etc. [542].

In this chapter, we construct fundamentals of the theory of decision-making with imperfect information for solving problems when all the relevant in formation is NL-described. The suggested theory utilizes fuzzy logic and fuzzy mathematics [59, 318] and is capable of dealing with the second-order uncertainty represented by fuzzy probabilities. The theory is based on the representation theorems on a fuzzy number-valued utility represented as a fuzzy-valued Choquet integral with a fuzzy integrand and a fuzzy-valued fuzzy measure for the framework of linguistic preferences, fuzzy states of nature, fuzzy probabilities, and fuzzy outcomes.

As opposed to the existing approaches with imprecise beliefs like multiple priors models (e.g., MMEU), second-order precise and imprecise beliefs models (smooth ambiguity and hierarchical models), models with non-additive beliefs (e.g., CEU, Prospect theory), etc. the suggested theory uses fuzzy probabilities and fuzzy-valued fuzzy measures [22, 189, 190, 256, 322, 555] which are closer to DMs' beliefs described in NL. In the suggested theory, in contrast to the existing theories, a state of nature is considered as a fuzzy set taking into account that in real problems not only beliefs but also underlying events are often described in NL. This helps to model vagueness and proximity of real-objective conditions. For evaluation of outcomes, in the developed theory we use fuzzy numbers as more reliable for NL-based descriptions than numerical values used in the existing decision models like MMEU, CEU etc, especially when one deals with non-monetary outcomes like health, time, reputation, quality, etc. [415].

In the suggested theory, we use linguistic preference relation which, as opposed to classical logic-based preference relations used the existing theories, are able to adequately describe human preferences under imperfect information described in NL. Fuzzy-valued utility function used in the suggested theory, as opposed to its numerical counterpart used in the famous theories like MMEU, CEU, prospect theory, etc. is a natural interpretation quantifying vague preferences and imprecise beliefs.

13.2. Definitions

Let E^n [125, 258] be a space of all fuzzy subsets of R^n. These subsets satisfy the conditions of normality, convexity, and are upper semicontinuous with compact support. It is obvious that E^1 is the set of fuzzy numbers defined over R. Then let us denote by $E^1_{[0,1]}$ the corresponding space of fuzzy numbers defined over the unit interval $[0,1]$.

Definition 13.1 (Fuzzy Hausdorff distance [19, 23]). Let $V, W \in E^n$. The fuzzy Hausdorff distance d_{fH} between V and W is defined as

$$d_{fH}(V,W) = \bigcup_{r \in [0,1]} r \left[d_H(V^1, W^1), \sup_{r \leq \bar{r} \leq 1} d_H(V^{\bar{r}}, W^{\bar{r}}) \right]$$

where d_H is the Hausdorff distance *[125, 258]* and V^1, W^1 denote the cores of fuzzy sets V, W respectively.

Example 13.1. Let V and W be triangular fuzzy sets $V = (2, 3, 4)$ and $W = (6, 8, 12)$. Then the fuzzy Hausdorff distance d_{fH} between V and W is defined as a triangular fuzzy set $d_{fH}(V,W) = (5, 5, 8)$.

Definition 13.1 is a generalization of Definition 2.6 given by Zhang G-Q in Ref. [555].

Let Ω be a non-empty set and $F(\Omega) = \{V | \mu_{\tilde{V}} : \Omega \to [0,1]\}$ be the class of all fuzzy subsets of Ω.

Definition 13.2 (Hukuhara difference [125, 258]). Let $X, Y \in E^n$. If there exists $Z \in E^n$ such that $X = Y + Z$, then Z is called a Hukuhara difference of X and Y is denoted as $X -_h Y$.

Note that with the standard fuzzy difference for Z produced of X and Y, $X \neq Y + Z$. We use Hukuhara difference when we need $X = Y + Z$.

Example 13.2. Let X and Y be triangular fuzzy sets $X = (3, 7, 11)$ and $Y = (1, 2, 3)$. Then Hukuhara difference of X and Y is $X -_h Y = (3, 7, 11) -_h (1, 2, 3) = (3 - 1, 7 - 2, 11 - 3) = (2, 5, 8)$.

Indeed, $Y + (X -_h Y) = (1, 2, 3) + (2, 5, 8) = (3, 7, 11) = X$.

Definition 13.3 ([555, 558]). A subclass F of $F(\Omega)$ is called a fuzzy σ-algebra if it has the following properties:

(1) $\emptyset, \Omega \in F$
(2) if $V \in F$, then $V^c \in F$
(3) if $\{V_n\} \subset F$, then $\bigcup_{n=1}^{\infty} V_n \in F$

Definition 13.4 ([555]). Let A be a fuzzy number. For every positive real number M, there exists a $r_0 \in (0, 1]$ such that $M < A_2^{r_0}$ or $A_1^{r_0} < -M$. Then A is called fuzzy infinity, denoted by ∞.

Definition 13.5 ([555]). For $A, B \in E^1$, we say that $A \leq B$, if for every $r \in (0, 1]$,
$A_1^r \leq B_1^r$ and $A_2^r \leq B_2^r$.
We consider that $A < B$, if $A \leq B$, and there exists an $r_0 \in (0, 1]$ such that
$A_1^{r_0} < B_1^{r_0}$, or $A_2^{r_0} < B_2^{r_0}$.
We consider that $A = B$ if $A \leq B$, and $B \leq A$
Denote $E_+^1 = \{A \in E | A \geq 0\}$.

Definition 13.6 ([555]). A fuzzy number-valued fuzzy measure ((z) fuzzy measure) on F is a fuzzy number-valued fuzzy set function $\eta : F \to E_+^1$ with the properties:

(1) $\eta(\emptyset) = 0$;
(2) if $V \subset W$ then $\eta(V) \leq \eta(W)$;
(3) if $V_1 \subset V_2 \subset \cdots V_n \subset \cdots \in F$, then $\eta(\bigcup_{n=1}^{\infty} V_n) = \lim_{n \to \infty} \eta(V_n)$;
(4) if $V_1 \supset V_2 \supset \cdots V_n \in F$, and there exists n_0 such that $\eta(V_{n_0}) \neq \infty$, then $\eta(\bigcap_{n=1}^{\infty} V_n) = \lim_{n \to \infty} \eta(V_n)$.

Here limits are taken in terms of the d_{fH} distance.

Example 13.3. Let $\Omega = [0, 1]$. Consider values of a fuzzy number-valued fuzzy measure η for some fuzzy subsets $s_i \subset \Omega, i = \overline{1, 3}$ and their unions. Let $s_i, i = \overline{1, 3}$ be triangular fuzzy sets $s_1 = (0, 0; 0.5)$, $s_2 = (0; 0.5; 1)$, $s_3 = (0.5; 1; 1)$. Then the corresponding values of the

Table 13.2. The values of the fuzzy number-valued fuzzy measure η.

$B \subset S$	s_1	s_2	s_3	$s_1 \cup s_2$	$s_1 \cup s_3$	$s_2 \cup s_3$
$\eta_{Pl}(B)$	(0.3,0.4,0.4)	(0,0.1,0.1)	(0.3,0.5,0.5)	(0.3,0.5,0.5)	(0.6,0.9,0.9)	(0.3,0.6,0.6)

fuzzy number-valued fuzzy measure η can be as the triangular fuzzy numbers given in Table 13.2.

$(\Omega, \mathbf{F}(\Omega))$ is called a fuzzy measurable space and $(\Omega, \mathbf{F}(\Omega), \eta)$ is called a (z) fuzzy measure space.

Definition 13.7 ([555]). Let $(\Omega, \mathbf{F}(\Omega), \eta)$ be a (z) fuzzy measure space. A mapping $f : \Omega \to (-\infty, +\infty)$ is called a fuzzy measurable function if $\chi_{F_\beta} \in \mathbf{F}(\Omega)$, where $F_\beta = \{\omega \in \Omega | f(\omega) \geq \beta\}$ and

$$\chi_{F_\beta}(\omega) = \begin{cases} 1 & \text{iff } \omega \in F_\beta \\ 0 & \text{iff } \omega \notin F_\beta \end{cases}$$

with $\beta \in (-\infty, +\infty)$. Let $\mathbb{N}_R$ be the set of all closed intervals of the real line.

Definition 13.8 ([489]). $\bar{f} : \Omega \to \mathbb{N}_R$ is fuzzy measurable if both $f_1(\omega)$, the left end point of interval $\bar{f}(\omega)$, and $f_2(\omega)$, the right end point of interval $\bar{f}(\omega)$, are fuzzy measurable functions of ω.

Definition 13.9 ([489]). Let $\bar{f} : \Omega \to \mathbb{N}_R$ be a fuzzy measurable interval-valued function on Ω and η be a fuzzy number-valued fuzzy measure on $\mathbf{F}$. The Choquet integral of $\bar{f}$ with respect to η is defined by: $\int \bar{f} d\eta = \{\int f d\eta | f(\omega) \in \bar{f}(\omega) \forall \omega \in \Omega, f : \Omega \to \mathbb{R} \text{ is fuzzy measurable}\}$.

Definition 13.10 ([489]). A fuzzy-valued function $f : \Omega \to E^1$ is fuzzy measurable if its r-cut $\bar{f}^r(\omega) = \{y | \mu_{\bar{f}(\omega)}(y) \geq r\}$ is a fuzzy measurable set function for every $r \in (0, 1]$, where $\mu_{f(\omega)}$ is the membership function of the value of f at ω.

Definition 13.11 ([489]). Let $f : \Omega \to E^1$ be a fuzzy measurable fuzzy-valued function on Ω and η be a fuzzy-number-valued fuzzy measure on F. The Choquet integral of f with respect to η is defined by

$$\int_\Omega f d\eta = \cup_{r \in [0,1]} r \int_\Omega \bar{f}^r d\eta$$

Definition 13.12 ([77]). The set of linguistic probabilities $P^l = \{P_1, \ldots, P_i, \ldots, P_n\}$ and corresponding values $\{X_1, \ldots, X_i, \ldots, X_n\}$ of a random variable X are called a distribution of linguistic probabilities of this random variable.

Definition 13.13 (Fuzzy set-valued random variable [77]). Let a discrete variable X takes a value from the set $\{X_1, \ldots, X_n\}$ of possible linguistic values, each of which is a fuzzy variable $\langle x_i, U_x, X_i \rangle$ described by a fuzzy set $X_i = \int_{U_x} \mu_{x_i(x)}/x$. Let the probability that X take a linguistic value X_i to be characterized by a linguistic probability $P_i \in P^l$, $P^l = \{P|P \in E^1_{[0,1]}\}$. The variable X is then called a fuzzy set-valued random variable.

Definition 13.14 (Linguistic lottery [77]). Linguistic lottery is a fuzzy set-valued random variable with known linguistic probability distribution. Linguistic lottery is represented by a vector

$$L = (P_1, X_1; \ldots; P_i, X_i; \ldots; P_n, X_n)$$

Example 13.4. Let us have the linguistic lottery $L = (P_1, X_1; P_2, X_2; P_3, X_3)$, where P_i and X_i are described by triangular and trapezoidal fuzzy numbers defined over [0,1]: $X_1 = (0.1, 0.3, 0.5)$ ("small"), $X_2 = (0.3, 0.5, 0.7)$ ("medium"), $X_3 = (0.5, 0.7, 0.9)$ ("large"), $P_1 = (0.5, 0.7, 0.9)$("high"), $P_2 = (0.0, 0.2, 0.4)$("low"), $P_3 = (0.0, 0.0, 0.1, 0.4)$ ("very low"). Then the considered linguistic lottery is $L = ((0.5, 0.7, 0.9), (0.1, 0.3, 0.5); (0.0, 0.2, 0.4), (0.3, 0.5, 0.7) (0.0, 0.0, 0.1, 0.4), (0.5, 0.7, 0.9))$.

13.3. Decision Model

In our study, we generalize the axiomatizations of decision-making problem used by Anscombe and Aumann [36] and Schmeidler [402, 403], which are constructed for perfect information framework. For real-world problems, probabilities, outcomes and utilities are not exactly known and are described in natural language. Taking into account that such problems are essentially characterized by imperfect information relevant to decision-making, our generalization involves the following aspects: (1) Spaces of fuzzy sets [125, 258] instead of a classical framework are used for modeling states of nature and outcomes. (2) Fuzzy probabilities are considered instead of numerical probability distributions. (3) Linguistic preference relation (LPR) [77, 532] is used instead of binary logic-based preference relations. (4) Fuzzy number-valued utility functions [23, 125, 258] are used instead of real-valued utility functions. (5) Fuzzy number-valued fuzzy measure [555] is used instead of a real-valued non-additive probability.

These aspects form fundamentally a new statement of the problem — the problem of decision-making with imperfect information. This problem is characterized by second-order uncertainty, namely by fuzzy probabilities. In this framework, we prove representation theorems for a fuzzy-valued utility function. Fuzzy-valued utility function will be described as a fuzzy-valued Choquet integral [28, 489] with fuzzy number-valued integrand and fuzzy number-valued fuzzy measure. Fuzzy number-valued integrand will be used to model imprecise linguistic utility evaluations. It is contemplated that fuzzy number-valued fuzzy measure that can be generated by fuzzy probabilities will better reflect the features of impreciseness and non-additivity related to human behavior. The fuzzy utility model we consider here is a generalization of Schmeidler's CEU and is more suitable for human evaluations and vision of decision problem and related information.

Let $S = \{S_1, \ldots, S_n\} \subset E^n$ be a set of fuzzy states of the nature, $X = \{X_1, \ldots, X_n\} \subset E^n$ be a set of fuzzy outcomes, Y be a set of *distributions of linguistic probabilities* over X, i.e., Y is a set of *fuzzy number-valued functions* [59, 125, 258]: $Y = \{y | y : X \rightarrow E^1_{[0,1]}\}$. For notational simplicity we identify X with the subset $\{y \in Y | y(X) = 1$ for some $X \in X\}$ of Y. Denote by F_S a σ-algebra of subsets of S. Denote by A_0 the set of all F_S-measurable [318, 489] fuzzy finite-valued step functions [460] from S to Y and denote by A_c the constant fuzzy functions in A_0. We call a function $f : S \rightarrow Y$ a fuzzy finite-valued step function if there is a finite partition of S to $H_i \subset S, i = 1, 2, \ldots, n, H_j \cap H_k = \emptyset$, for $j \neq k$, such that $f(S) = y_i$ for all $S \in H_i$. In this case $g : S \rightarrow Y$ is called a constant fuzzy function if for some $g(S) = y$ for all $S \in S$, $y \in Y$. Thus the constant fuzzy function is a special case of a fuzzy finite-valued step function.

Let A be a convex subset [323] of Y^S which includes A_c. Y can be considered as a subset of some linear space, and Y^S can then be considered as a subspace of the linear space of all fuzzy functions from S to the first linear space. Let us now define convex combinations in Y pointwise [323]: for y and z in Y, and $\lambda \in (0, 1)$, $\lambda y + (1 - \lambda)z = r$, where $r(X) = \lambda y(X) + (1 - \lambda)z(X)$, $y(X), z(X) \in E^1_{[0,1]}$. The latter expression is defined based in the Zadeh's extension principle. Let $\mu_{r(X)}, \mu_{y(X)}, \mu_{z(X)} : [0, 1] \rightarrow [0, 1]$ denote the membership functions of fuzzy numbers $r(X), y(X), z(X)$, respectively. Then for $\mu_{r(X)} : [0, 1] \rightarrow [0, 1]$ we have:

$$\mu_{r(X)}(r(X)) = \sup_{\substack{r(X) = \lambda y(X) + (1 - \lambda)z()X \\ y(X) + z(X) \leq 1}} \min (\mu_{y(X)}, (y(X)), \mu_{z(X)}, (z(X))),$$

where $r(X), y(X), z(X) \in [0, 1]$

Convex combinations in A are also defined pointwise, i.e., for f and g in A $\lambda f + (1 - \lambda)g = h$, where $\lambda f(S) + (1 - \lambda)g(S) = h(S)$ on S.

To model LPR, let's introduce a linguistic variable "degree of preference" with term-set $T = (T_1, \ldots, T_n)$. Terms can be labeled, for example, as "equivalence", "little preference", "high preference", and can each be described by a fuzzy number defined over some scale, for example, $[0,1]$. The fact that preference of f against g is described by some $t_i \in T$ is expressed as fT_ig. We denote LPR as $\succsim_l$ and below we sometimes, for simplicity, write $f \succsim^i_l g$ or $f \succ^i_l g$ instead of fT_ig.

368	*Fuzzy Logic Theory and Applications*

Definition 13.15. Two acts f and g in Y^S are said to be co-monotonic if there are no S_i and S_j in S, $f(S_i) \succ_l f(S_j)$ and $g(S_j) \succ_l g(S_i)$ hold.

Two real-valued functions a and b are co-monotonic iff $(a(S_i) - a(S_j))(b(S_i) - b(S_j)) \geq 0$ for all S_i and S_j in S.

For a fuzzy number-valued function $a : S \to E^1$ denote by a^r, $r \in (0,1]$ its r-cut and note that $a^r = [a_1^r, a_2^r]$, where $a_1^r, a_2^r : \mathsf{S} \to \mathsf{R}$.

Two fuzzy functions $a, b : \mathsf{S} \to E^1$ are said to be co-monotonic iff the real-valued functions $a_1^r, b_1^r : \mathsf{S} \to \mathsf{R}$, $a_2^r, b_2^r : \mathsf{S} \to \mathsf{R}$, $r \in (0,1]$ are co-monotonic.

A constant act $f = y^\mathsf{S}$ for some y in Y, and any act g are co-monotonic. An act f whose statewise lotteries $\{f(S)\}$ are mutually indifferent, i.e., $f(S) \sim_l y$ for all S in S, and any act g are co-monotonic.

In the suggested framework, we extend a classical neo-Bayesian nomenclature as follows: elements of X are fuzzy outcomes; elements of Y are linguistic lotteries; elements of A are fuzzy acts; elements of S are fuzzy states of nature; and elements of $\tilde{\mathsf{F}}_\mathsf{S}$ are fuzzy events.

It is common knowledge that under degrees of uncertainty humans evaluate alternatives or choices linguistically using certain evaluation techniques such as "much worse", "a little better", "much better", "almost equivalent", etc. In contrast to the classical preference relation, imposed on choices made by humans, LPR consistently expresses "degree of preference" allowing the analysis of preferences under uncertainty.

Below we give a series of axioms of the LPR $\succsim_l$ over A [28].

(i) Weak-order:

(a) Completeness of LPR. Any two alternatives are comparable with respect to LPR: for all f and g in A: $f \succsim_l g$ or $g \succsim_l f$. This means that for all f and g there exists such $T_i \in T$ that $f \succsim_l^i g$ or $g \succsim_l^i f$.

(b) Transitivity. For all f, g and h in A: If $f \succsim_l g$ and $g \succsim_l h$ then $f \succsim_l h$. This means that if there exist such

$T_i \in$ T and $T_j \in$ T that $f \succsim_l^i g$ and $g \succsim_l^j h$, then there exists such $T_k \in$ T that $f \succsim_l^k h$. Transitivity of LPR is defined on the base of the extension principle and fuzzy preference relation [532]. This axiom states that any two alternatives are comparable and assumes one of the fundamental properties of preferences (transitivity) for the case of fuzzy information.

(ii) **Co-monotonic Independence:** For all pairwise co-monotonic acts f, g and h in A if $f \succsim_l g$, then $\alpha f + (1-\alpha)h \succsim_l \alpha g + (1-\alpha)h$ for all $\alpha \in (0, 1)$. This means that if there exist such $T_i \in$ T that $f \succsim_l^i g$ then there exists such $T_k \in$ T that $\alpha f + (1 - \alpha)h \succsim_l^k \alpha g + (1 - \alpha)h$, with f, g and h pairwise co-monotonic. The axiom extends the independency property for co-monotonic actions as opposed to independence axiom for the case of fuzzy information.

(iii) **Continuity:** For all f, g and h in A: if $f \succ_l g$ and $g \succ_l h$ then there are α and β in $(0, 1)$ such that $\alpha f + (1 - \alpha)h \succ_l g \succ_l \beta f + (1 - \beta)h$. This means that if there exist such $T_i \in$ T and $T_j \in$ T that $f \succsim_l^i g$ and $g \succsim_l^j h$ then there exist such $T_k \in$ T and $T_m \in$ T that define preference of $\alpha f + (1 - \alpha)h \succsim_l^k g \succsim_l^m \beta g + (1 - \beta)h$. The axiom is an extension of classical continuity axiom for the case of fuzzy information.

(iv) **Monotonicity:** For all f and g in A: If $f(S) \succsim_l g(S)$ on S then $f \succsim_l g$.

This means that if for any $S \in$ S there exists such $T \in$ T that $f(S) \succsim_l g(S)$, then there exists $T_i \in$ T such that $f \succsim_l^i g$. The axiom is an extension of the classical monotonicity axiom for the case of fuzzy information.

(v) **Nondegeneracy:** Not for all $f, g \in$ A, $f \succsim_l g$.

LPR $\succsim_l$ on A induces LPR denoted also by $\succsim_l$ on Y: $y \succsim_l z$ iff $y^S \succsim_l z^S$, where y^S and z^S denotes the constant functions y and z on S.

The presented axioms are formulated to reflect human preferences under a mixture of fuzzy and probabilistic information.

Such formulation requires the use of a fuzzy-valued utility function. Formally, it is required to use a fuzzy-valued utility function U such that

$$\forall f, g \in \mathsf{A}, f \succsim_l g \Leftrightarrow U(f) \geq U(g)$$

The problem of decision-making with imperfect information consists in determination of an optimal $f^* \in \mathsf{A}$, that is, $f^* \in \mathsf{A}$ for which $U(f^*) = \max_{f \in A} U(f)$.

Fuzzy utility function U we adopt will be described as a fuzzy number-valued Choquet integral with respect to a fuzzy number-valued fuzzy measure. In its turn fuzzy number-valued fuzzy measure can be obtained from NL-described knowledge about probability distribution over S. NL-described knowledge about probability distribution over S is expressed as $P^l = P_1/S_1 + P_2/S_2 + P_3/S_3 = $ small/small + high/medium + small/large, with the understanding that a term such as high/medium means that the probability, that $S_2 \in \mathsf{S}$ is medium, is high. So, P^l is a linguistic (fuzzy) probability distribution.

In the discussions above, we have mentioned the necessity of the use of a fuzzy utility function as a suitable quantifying representation of vague preferences. Below we present a definition of a fuzzy number-valued utility function representing LPR (i)–(v) over an arbitrary set Z of alternatives.

Definition 13.16 ([16, 28]). Fuzzy number-valued function $U(\cdot) :$ $\mathsf{Z} \to \mathsf{E}^1$ is a utility function if it represents linguistic preferences $\succsim_l$ such that for any pair of alternatives $Z_1, Z_2 \in \mathsf{Z}$, $Z_1 \succsim_l^i Z_2$ holds if and only if $U(Z_1) \geq U(Z_2)$, where T_i is determined on the base of $d_{fH}(U(Z_1), U(Z_2))$.

Here we consider a set Z of alternatives as if they are a set A of actions $f : \mathsf{S} \to \mathsf{Y}$.

Below we present representation theorems showing the existence of a fuzzy number-valued Choquet-integral-based fuzzy utility function [16, 28] that represents LPR defined over the set A of alternatives under conditions of linguistic probability distribution P^l over a set S.

Theorem 13.1. *Assume that LPR $\succsim_l$ on* $\mathbf{A} = \mathbf{A}_0$ *satisfies* (i) *weak order,* (ii) *continuity,* (iii) *co-monotonic independence,* (iv) *monotonicity, and* (v) *nondegeneracy. Then there exists a unique fuzzy number-valued fuzzy measure η on F_S and an affine fuzzy number-valued function u on* $\mathbf{Y}$ *such that for all f and g in* $\mathbf{A}$:

$$f \succsim_l g \quad \text{iff} \quad \int_S u(f(S))d\eta \geq \int_S u(g(S))d\eta$$

where u is unique up to positive linear transformations.

Theorem 13.2. *For a nonconstant affine fuzzy number-valued function u on* $\mathbf{Y}$ *and a fuzzy number-valued fuzzy measure η on* F_S *a fuzzy number-valued Choquet integral induces such LPR on* $\mathbf{A}$ *that satisfies conditions* (i)−(v). *Additionally, u is unique up to positive linear transformations.*

The direct theorem (Theorem 13.1) provides conditions for existence of the suggested fuzzy utility function representing LPR defined over a set of fuzzy actions under conditions of fuzzy probabilities. LPR formulated by using a series of axioms reflects the essence of human-like preferences under conditions of imperfect information. The converse theorem (Theorem 13.2) provides conditions under which a fuzzy utility function described as a fuzzy number-valued Choquet integral with a fuzzy number-valued integrand and a fuzzy number-valued fuzzy measure induces the formulated LPR.

The proofs of Theorems 13.1 and 13.2 are given in the appendix.

In brief, a value of fuzzy utility function U for action f is determined as a fuzzy number-valued Choquet integral [16, 22, 26, 28]:

$$U(f) = \int_S u(f(S))d\eta_{\tilde{P}^l}$$

$$= \sum_{i=1}^n \left(u(f(S_{(i)})) -_h u(f(S_{(i+1)})) \right) \cdot \eta_{\tilde{P}^l}(H_{(i)}) \quad (13.1)$$

Here, $\eta_{P^l}()$ is a fuzzy number-valued fuzzy measure obtained from linguistic probability distribution over S[22, 26, 28] and $u(f(S))$ is a fuzzy number-valued utility function used to describe NL-based evaluations of utilities, (i) means that utilities are ranked such that $u(f(S_{(1)})) \geq \cdots \geq u(f(S_{(n)}))$, $H_{(i)} = \{S_{(1)}, \ldots, S_{(i)}\}$, $u(f_j$ $(S_{(n+1)})) = 0$, and for each (i) there exists $u(f(S_{(i)})) -_h u(f(S_{(i+1)}))$. Multiplication $\cdot$ is realized in the sense of the Zadeh's extension principle. An optimal $f^* \in A$, that is $f^* \in A$ for which $U(f^*) = \max_{f \in A} \{\int_S u(f(S)) d\eta_{Pl}\}$, can be determined by using a suitable fuzzy ranking method.

The crucial problem in the determination of an overall fuzzy utility of an alternative is a construction of a fuzzy number-valued fuzzy measure η_{Pl}. We will consider η_{Pl} as a fuzzy number-valued lower probability constructed from linguistic probability distribution P^l. Linguistic probability distribution $\tilde{P}^l$ implies that a state $S_i \in S$ is assigned a linguistic probability P_i that can be described by a fuzzy number defined over [0,1]. However, fuzzy probabilities P_i cannot initially be assigned for all $S_i \in S$ [534]. Initial data are represented by fuzzy probabilities for $n - 1$ fuzzy states of nature whereas for one of the given fuzzy states the probability is unknown. Subsequently, it becomes necessary to determine unknown fuzzy probability $P(s_j) = P_j$ [531]. In the framework of Computing with Words [18, 304, 536, 537], the problem of obtaining the unknown fuzzy probability for state s_j given fuzzy probabilities of all other states is a problem of propagation of generalized constraints [531, 542, 544]. Formally this problem is formulated as [77, 542]

Given

$$P(S_i) = P_i; S_i \in E^n, P_i \in E^1_{[0,1]}, \quad i = \{1, \ldots, j-1, j+1, \ldots, n\} \, (13.2)$$

find unknown

$$P(S_j) = P_j, P_j \in E^1_{[0,1]} \tag{13.3}$$

It reduces to a variational problem of constructing the membership function $\mu_{P_j}(\cdot)$ of an unknown fuzzy probability P_j:

$$\mu_{P_j}(p_j) = \sup_\rho \min_{i=\{1,\ldots,j-1,j+1,\ldots,n\}} \left(\mu_{P_i} \left(\int_S \mu_{S_i}(s)\rho(s)ds \right) \right) \tag{13.4}$$

subject to

$$\int_S \mu_{s_j}(s)\rho(s)ds = p_j, \quad \int_S \rho(s)ds = 1 \qquad (13.5)$$

Here, $\mu_{S_j}(s)$ is the membership function of a fuzzy state S_j.

When P_j has been determined, linguistic probability distribution P^l for all states S_i is determined:.

$$P^l = P_1/S_1 + P_2/S_2 + \cdots + P_n/S_n$$

If we have linguistic probability distribution over fuzzy values of some fuzzy set-valued random variable s, the important problem that arises is the verification of its consistency, completeness, and redundancy [11, 77]. Given consistent, complete and not redundant linguistic probability distribution P^l we can obtain from it a fuzzy set P^ρ of possible probability distributions $\rho(s)$. We can construct a fuzzy measure from P^ρ as its lower probability function (lower prevision) [328] by taking into account a degree of correspondence of $\rho(s)$ to P^l. Lower prevision is a unifying measure as opposed to the other existing additive and non-additive measures [458, 459]. We denote the fuzzy-number-valued fuzzy measure by η_{P^l} [16, 22, 28, 29, 555] because it is derived from the given linguistic probability distribution P^l. A degree of membership of an arbitrary probability distribution $\rho(s)$ to P (a degree of correspondence of $\rho(s)$ to P^l) can be obtained by the formula

$$\pi_P(\rho(s)) = \min_{i=\overline{1,n}}(\pi_{P_i}(p_i))$$

where $p_i = \int_S \rho(s)\mu_{S_i}(s)ds$ is numeric probability of fuzzy state S_i defined by $\rho(s)$. Furthermore $\pi_{P_i}(p_i) = \mu_{P_i}\left(\int_S \rho(s)\mu_{S_i}(s)ds\right)$ is the membership degree of p_i to P_i.

To derive a fuzzy-number-valued fuzzy measure η_{P^l} we use the following formulas [28]:

$$\eta_{P^l}(\mathrm{H}) = \bigcup_{r\in(0,1]} r\left[\eta_{P_1^{lr}}(\mathrm{H}), \eta_{P_2^{lr}}(\mathrm{H})\right] \qquad (13.6)$$

where

$$\eta_{Pl_1^r}(\mathrm{H}) = \inf\left\{ \int_S \rho(s)\mu_\mathrm{H}(s)ds \,\middle|\, \rho(s) \in P^{\rho^r} \right\},$$

$$\eta_{Pl_2^r}(\mathrm{H}) = \inf\left\{ \int_S \rho(s)\mu_\mathrm{H}(s)ds \,\middle|\, \rho(s) \in \mathrm{core}(P^\rho) \right\} \qquad (13.7)$$

$$P^{\rho^r} = \left\{ \rho(s) \,\middle|\, \min_{i=\overline{1,n}}(\pi_{P_i}(p_i)) \geq r \right\}, \quad \mathrm{core}(P^\rho) = P^{\rho^{r=1}}, \quad \mathrm{H} \subset S$$

The support of η_{Pl} is defined as supp $\eta_{Pl} = cl\left(\bigcup_{r\in(0,1]} \eta_{Pl}^r\right)$.

For special case, when states of nature are just some elements, fuzzy number-valued fuzzy measure η_{Pl} is defined as

$$\eta_{Pl}(\mathrm{H}) = \bigcup_{r\in(0,1]} r\left[\eta_{Pl_1^r}(\mathrm{H}), \eta_{Pl_2^r}(\mathrm{H})\right], \quad \mathrm{H} \subset S = \{S_1, \ldots, S_n\}$$

where

$$\eta_{Pl}^r(\mathrm{H}) = \inf\left\{ \sum_{s_i\in\mathrm{H}} p(s_i) \,\middle|\, (p(s_1), \ldots, p(s_n)) \in P^{\rho^r} \right\}$$

$$P^{\rho^r} = \left\{ (p(s_1), \ldots, p(s_n)) \in P_1^r \times \cdots \times P_n^r \,\middle|\, \sum_{i=1}^n p(s_i) = 1 \right\}$$

here $P_1^r, \ldots, P_n^r$ are r-cuts of fuzzy probabilities $P_1, \ldots, P_n$ respectively, $p(s_1), \ldots, p(s_n)$ are basic probabilities for $P_1, \ldots, P_n$ respectively, $\times$ denotes the Cartesian product.

13.4. Examples

13.4.1. *Zadeh's two boxes problem*

Assume that we have two open boxes, A and B, each containing 20 black and white balls. A ball is picked at random. If I pick a white ball from A, I win $a1$ dollars; if I pick a black ball, I lose $a2$ dollars. Similarly, if I pick a white ball from B, I win $b1$ dollars; and if I pick a black ball, I lose $b2$ dollars. I am shown the boxes for a few seconds, not enough to count the balls. I form a perception of the number of white and black balls in each box. At the same time, assume that

I do not know the exact amounts of dollars I can gain or lose — $a1$, $a2$, $b1$, $b2$ — but only perception-based approximate values for them are provided in form of linguistic imprecise evaluations.

Given perception-based information on probabilities, gains and losses, which box should I choose?

Solution. Let us denote boxes as A and B colors of balls as w (white) and b (black), respectively.

The set of possible events will be represented as $\{Aw, Bw, Ab, Bb\}$, where Aw means "a white ball picked from box A", Bb means "a black ball picked from box B". Then the set of the states of nature is: $S = \{S_1, S_2, S_3, S_4\}$, where $S_1 = (Aw, Bw)$, $S_2 = (Aw, Bb)$, $S_3 = (Ab, Bw)$, $S_4 = (Ab, Bb)$.

Denote probabilities of the events as $P(Aw)$, $P(Bw)$, $P(Ab)$, $P(Bb)$. Then the probabilities of the states are defined as

$$P_1 = P(Aw, Bw) = P(Aw)P(Bw)$$

$$P_2 = P(Aw, Bb) = P(Aw)P(Bb)$$

$$P_3 = P(Ab, Bw) = P(Ab)P(Bw)$$

$$P_4 = P(Ab, Bb) = P(Ab)P(Bb)$$

Denote the outcomes of the events as $X(Aw)$, $X(Bw)$, $X(Ab)$, $X(Bb)$, where $X(Aw)$ denotes the outcome faced when a white ball picked from box, etc.

The alternatives are: f_1 (means choosing box A), f_2 (means choosing box B).

As alternatives map states to outcomes, we write

$$f_1(S_1) = X(Aw)$$

$$f_1(S_2) = X(Aw)$$

$$f_1(S_3) = X(Ab)$$

$$f_1(S_4) = X(Ab)$$

$$f_2(S_1) = X(Bw)$$

$$f_2(S_2) = X(Bb)$$

$$f_2(S_3) = X(Bw)$$
$$f_2(S_4) = X(Bb)$$

Assume that imperfect decision-relevant information is treated by using fuzzy outcomes and fuzzy probabilities given in form of the following triangular and trapezoidal fuzzy numbers, respectively:

$$X(Aw) = \$(15, 20, 25), X(Ab) = \$(-10, -5, 0)$$
$$X(Bw) = \$(80, 100, 120), X(Bb) = \$(-25, -20, -15)$$
$$P(Aw) = (0.25, 0.35, 0.5, 0.6), \quad P(Bw) = (0.1, 0.2, 0.25, 0.35)$$

Then the unknown probabilities are

$$P(Ab) = (0.4, 0.5, 0.65, 0.75), \quad P(Bb) = (0.65, 0.75, 0.8, 0.9)$$

The probabilities of the states of nature are computed as follows:

$$P(Aw, Bw) = (0.25, 0.35, 0.5, 0.6) \cdot (0.1, 0.2, 0.25, 0.35)$$
$$= (0.025, 0.35, 0.5, 0.6)$$
$$P(Aw, Bb) = (0.25, 0.35, 0.5, 0.6) \cdot (0.65, 0.75, 0.8, 0.9)$$
$$= (0.1625, 0.2625, 0.4, 0.54)$$
$$P(Ab, Bw) = (0.4, 0.5, 0.65, 0.75) \cdot (0.1, 0.2, 0.25, 0.35)$$
$$= (0.04, 0.1, 0.1625, 0.2625)$$
$$P(Ab, Bb) = (0.4, 0.5, 0.65, 0.75) \cdot (0.65, 0.75, 0.8, 0.9)$$
$$= (0.26, 0.375, 0.52, 0.675)$$

An overall utility for an alternative $f_j, j = 1, 2$ will be determined as a fuzzy-valued Choquet integral [16, 28]:

$$\begin{aligned}
U(f_j) &= (u(f_j(S_{(1)})) -_h u(f_j(S_{(2)})))\eta_{\tilde{P}^l}(\{S_{(1)}\}) \\
&+ (u(f_j(S_{(2)})) -_h u(f_j(S_{(3)})))\eta_{\tilde{P}^l}(\{S_{(1)}, S_{(2)}\}) \\
&+ (u(f_j(S_{(3)})) -_h u(f_j(S_{(4)})))\eta_{\tilde{P}^l}(\{S_{(1)}, S_{(2)}, S_{(3)}\}) \\
&+ (u(f_j(s_{(4)})))\eta_{\tilde{P}^l}(\{S_{(1)}, S_{(2)}, S_{(3)}, S_{(4)}\})
\end{aligned}$$

Here (i) means that the states are ordered such that: $u(f_j(S_{(1)})) \geq u(f_j(S_{(2)})) \geq u(f_j(S_{(3)})) \geq u(f_j(S_{(4)}))$, and $u(f_j(S_{(i)}))$ denotes utility of an outcome we face taking action f_j at a state $S_{(i)}$, where $\eta_{Pl}(\cdot)$ is a fuzzy number-valued fuzzy measure. For simplicity, we define $u(f_j(S_i))$ to be numerically equal to the corresponding outcomes $f_j(S_i)$. The ordered fuzzy utilities $u(f_j(S_{(i)}))$ will be:

$$u(f_1(S_{(1)})) = u(f_1(S_1)) = (15, 20, 25)$$
$$u(f_1(S_{(2)})) = u(f_1(S_2)) = (15, 20, 25)$$
$$u(f_1(S_{(3)})) = u(f_1(S_3)) = (-10, -5, 0)$$
$$u(f_1(S_{(4)})) = u(f_1(S_4)) = (-10, -5, 0)$$

$$u(f_2(S_{(1)})) = u(f_2(S_1)) = (80, 100, 120)$$
$$u(f_2(S_{(2)})) = u(f_2(S_3)) = (80, 100, 120)$$
$$u(f_2(S_{(3)})) = u(f_2(S_2)) = (-25, -20, -15)$$
$$u(f_2(S_{(4)})) = u(f_1(S_4)) = (-25, -20, -15)$$

Then the overall utilities of the alternatives are determined as follows:

$$U(f_1) = (25, 25, 25)\eta_{\tilde{P}l}\left(\{S_1, S_2\}\right) + (-10, -5, 0)$$
$$U(f_2) = (105, 120, 135)\eta_{\tilde{P}l}\left(\{S_1, S_3\}\right) + (-25, -20, -15)$$

The r-cuts of $\eta_{Pl}\left(\{S_1, S_2\}\right), \eta_{Pl}\left(\{S_1, S_3\}\right)$ are found as numerical solutions to problem (13.6) and (13.7):

$$\eta_{Pl}^r(\{S_1, S_2\})$$
$$= \inf \left\{ p(S_1) + p(S_2) \,\middle|\, \begin{array}{l} (p(S_1), p(S_2), p(S_3)) \in \\ P_1^r \times P_2^r \times P_3^r, p(S_1) + p(S_2) + p(S_3) = 1 \end{array} \right\}$$

$$\eta_{Pl}^r(\{S_1, S_3\})$$
$$= \inf \left\{ p(S_1) + p(S_3) \,\middle|\, \begin{array}{l} (p(S_1), p(S_2), p(S_3)) \in \\ P_1^r \times P_2^r \times P_3^r, p(S_1) + p(S_2) + p(S_3) = 1 \end{array} \right\}$$

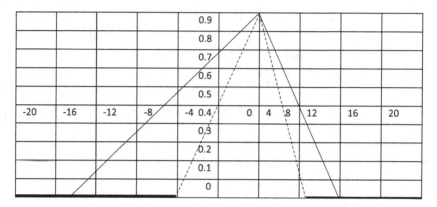

Fig. 13.1. Computed fuzzy overall utilities $U(f_1)$ (dashed), $U(f_2)$(solid).

The values of $\eta_{Pl}(\{S_1, S_2\}), \eta_{Pl}(\{S_1, S_3\})$ we found are triangular fuzzy numbers $\eta_{Pl}(\{S_1, S_2\}) = (0.25, 0.35, 0.35)$, $\eta_{Pl}(\{S_1, S_3\}) = (0.1, 0.2, 0.2)$.

Now we can compute fuzzy overall utilities $U(f_1), U(f_2)$. The computed $U(f_1), U(f_2)$ approximated by triangular fuzzy numbers are shown in Fig. 13.1.

Applying Jaccard comparison method we find that

$$U(f_1) \geq U(f_2) \text{ with degree } 0.83$$

$$U(f_2) \geq U(f_1) \text{ with degree } 0.59$$

We determine the linguistic degree of the preference as it is shown in Fig. 13.2. According to Fig. 13.2, f_1 (choosing box A) has medium preference over f_2 (choosing box B).

The decision-relevant information we considered in this problem is characterized by imperfect (fuzzy) probabilities, imperfect (fuzzy) outcomes and fuzzy utilities. Such type of decision-relevant information is presented in Cell 32 of Table 13.1. We have also solved the Zadeh's problem for special cases when only probabilities or outcomes are imprecise. Below we shortly present the results:

(1) The case of imprecise probabilities described as fuzzy numbers $P(Aw) = T(0.25, 0.35, 0.5, 0.6)$, $P(Bw) = T(0.1, 0.2, 0.25, 0.35)$ and exactly known outcomes $a1 = \$20$, $a2 = -\$5$, $b1 = \$100$, $b2 = -\$20$. This is the situation presented in Cell 4 in Table 13.1

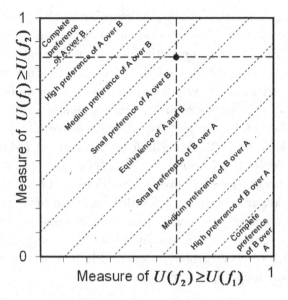

Fig. 13.2. Linguistic preferences.

(see Introduction) — information on probabilities is imperfect and information on outcomes and utilities is precise (as we determine utilities to be numerically equal to outcomes). In this case, the suggested fuzzy utility model degenerates to a fuzzy-valued utility described as Choquet integral with *numeric* integrand and *fuzzy number-valued* fuzzy measure. The obtained fuzzy overall utilities for this case are $U(f_1) = (1.25, 3.75, 3.75)$ and $U(f_2) = (-8, 4, 4)$. According to the Jaccard index, $U(f_1) \geq U(f_2)$ with degree 0.708 and $U(f_2) \geq U(f_1)$ with degree 0.266, which implies the medium preference of f_1 over f_2. In this case we have more strong preference of f_1 over f_2 than that obtained for the case of fuzzy probabilities and fuzzy outcomes (small preference of f_1 over f_2). The reason for this is that in the present case information is more precise (outcomes are exactly known) and also ambiguity aversion resulted from fuzzy probabilities is more clearly observed (whereas in the previous case it is weaken behind impreciseness of outcomes).

(2) The case of imprecise outcomes described as fuzzy numbers $a1 = \$(15, 20, 25)$, $a2 = \$(-10, -5, 0)$, $b1 = \$(80, 100, 120)$, $b2 = \$(-25, -20, -15)$ and precise probabilities $P(Aw) = 0.4$,

$P(Bw) = 0.2$. This is the situation presented in Cell 29 in Table 13.1 (see Introduction) — information on probabilities is precise and information on outcomes and utilities is imperfect (as we determine utilities to be numerically equal to outcomes). In this case the suggested fuzzy utility model degenerates to a fuzzy-valued expected utility with fuzzy number-valued integrand and crisp probability measure. The obtained fuzzy overall utilities are $U(f_1) = (0, 5, 10)$ and $U(f_2) = (-4, 4, 12)$. According to the Jaccard index, $U(f_1) \geq U(f_2)$ with degree 0.915 and $U(f_2) \geq U(f_1)$ with degree 0.651, which implies low preference of f_1 over f_2. So, despite that in this case the situation is less uncertain than for the case with fuzzy probabilities and fuzzy outcomes, we have in essence the same preference of f_1 over f_2. The reason for this is that for this case ambiguity aversion is absent (due to exact probabilities) and impreciseness of outcomes does not allow for a higher preference.

13.4.2. *Investment problem*

An economic agent considers the following alternatives to make a decision for short-term investment of up to 1 year: common bonds, stocks of enterprise, fixed-term deposit. Suppose that the agent evaluates each alternative under the following states of economy that may take place during a year: strong growth, moderate growth, stable economy, recession. Having examined the relationships between the yields on the alternative investments and the states of economy on the base of the past experience, the economic agent notes the following trends:

The first action will yield high income if there is strong growth in economy, medium income — if there is moderate growth in economy, less than medium income under stable economy and small income if recession occurs

The second action will yield very high income if there is strong growth in economy, medium income if there is moderate growth in economy, small income under stable economy and a notable loss if recession occurs.

The third action will yield approximately the same medium income in all the considered states of economy.

It is also supposed that strong growth will take place with a medium probability, moderate growth will take place with a less than medium probability, stable economy — with a small probability and recession — with a very small probability.

What option to choose?

Let's denote the three possible actions (alternatives) as f_1 (common bonds), f_2 (stocks of enterprise), f_3 (fixed-term deposit). Let's denote the fuzzy states of nature (the economy) as follows: S_1 ("strong growth"), S_2 ("moderate growth"), S_3 ("stable"), S_4 ("recession"). The fuzzy states of nature are shown in Fig. 13.3.

Let the fuzzy probabilities of the above fuzzy states be denoted as: P_1 ("medium"), P_2 ("less than medium"), P_3 ("small"), P_4 ("very small" — unknown membership function). So, it is needed to compute unknown fuzzy probability P_4. The membership function of P_4 will be obtained as the numerical solution of the problems (13.4)–(13.5) as follows:

$$\mu_{P_4}(p_4) = \max_\rho \min\left(\mu_{P_1}\left(\sum_{k=1}^{K} \mu_{s_1}(\sigma_k)\rho(\sigma_k)\Delta_k \right) \right.$$

$$\left. \mu_{P_2}\left(\sum_{k=1}^{K} \mu_{s_2}(\sigma_k)\rho(\sigma_k)\Delta_k \right), \ \mu_{P_3}\left(\sum_{k=1}^{K} \mu_{s_3}(\sigma_k)\rho(\sigma_k)\Delta_k \right) \right)$$

subject to

$$\sum_{k=1}^{K} \mu_{s_4}(\sigma_k)\rho(\sigma_k)\Delta_k = p_4$$

$$\sum_{k=1}^{K} \rho(\sigma_k)\Delta_k = 1, \quad \Delta_k = \sigma_{k+1} - \sigma_k, \quad k = 1, \ldots, K-1$$

The fuzzy probabilities P_1 ("medium"), P_2 ("less than medium"), P_3 ("small"), P_4 ("very small" — computed) are shown in Fig. 13.4.

The linguistic evaluations of the outcomes X_{ji} obtained by taking action f_j at a state S_i are shown in Table 13.3.

The membership functions of X_{ji} on the scale $[-2, 15]$ are given in Fig. 13.5.

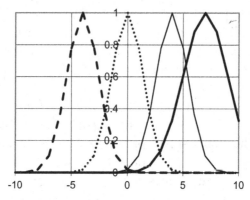

Fig. 13.3. Fuzzy states of economy: S_1 (thick line), S_2 (thin line), S_3 (dotted line), S_4 (dashed line).

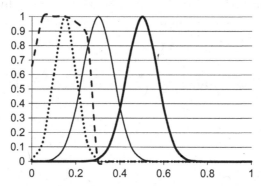

Fig. 13.4. Fuzzy probabilities $\tilde{P}_1$ (thick line), $\tilde{P}_2$ (thin line), $\tilde{P}_3$ (dotted), $\tilde{P}_4$ (dashed).

Table 13.3. Fuzzy values of the outcomes.

	(S_1)	(S_2)	(S_3)	(S_4)
Alternative 1 (f_1)	X_{11} = high income	X_{12} = medium income	X_{13} = less than medium income	X_{14} = small income
Alternative 2 (f_2)	X_{21} = very high income	X_{22} = medium income	X_{23} = small income	X_{24} = notable loss
Alternative 3 (f_3)	X_{31} = medium income	X_{32} = medium income	X_{33} = medium income	X_{34} = medium income

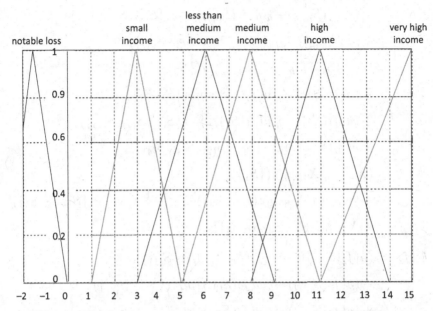

Fig. 13.5. Scaled fuzzy outcomes X_{ji} (from left to right): notable loss (X_{24}), small income (X_{14}, X_{23}), less than medium income(X_{13}), medium income (X_{12}, X_{22}, X_{31}, X_{32}, X_{33}, X_{34}), high income (X_{11}), very high income (X_{21}).

Overall fuzzy utilities for the actions f_1, f_2, f_3 are computed as follows:

$$U(f_j) = \sum_{i=1}^{3} \left(u(f_j(S_{(i)})) -_h u(f_j(S_{(i+1)}))\right) \cdot \eta_{P^l}(H_{(i)})$$

where (i) means that utilities are ranked such that $u(f_j(S_{(1)})) \geq \cdots \geq u(f_j(S_{(n)}))$, $\eta_{P^l}()$ is a fuzzy number-valued measure, $H_{(i)} = \{S_{(1)}, \dots, S_{(i)}\}$, $u(f_j(S_{(4)})) = 0$.

For simplicity, we consider utilities $u(f_j(S_i))$ to be numerically equal to the corresponding fuzzy outcomes $u(f_j(S_i)) = X_{ji}$ Then according to the suggested method, the overall utilities for the actions f_1, f_2, f_3 would be:

$$U(f_1) = (u(f_1(S_{(1)})) -_h u(f_1(S_{(2)})))\eta_{P^l}(\{S_{(1)}\})$$
$$+ (u(f_1(S_{(2)})) -_h u(f_1(S_{(3)})))\eta_{P^l}(\{S_{(1)}, S_{(2)}\})$$

$$+ (u(f_1(S_{(3)})) -_h u(f_1(S_{(4)})))\eta_{Pl}(\{S_{(1)}, S_{(2)}, s_{(3)}\})$$

$$+ u(f_1(S_{(4)})))\eta_{Pl}(\{S_{(1)}, S_{(2)}, S_{(3)}, S_{(4)}\})$$

$$= (u(f_1(S_1)) -_h u(f_1(S_2)))\eta_{Pl}(\{S_1\})$$

$$+ (u(f_1(S_2)) -_h u(f_1(S_3)))\eta_{Pl}(\{S_1, S_2\})$$

$$+ (u(f_1(S_3)) -_h u(f_1(S_4)))\eta_{Pl}(\{S_{(1)}, S_{(2)}, S_{(3)}\})$$

$$+ u(f_1(S_{(4)})))\eta_{Pl}(\{S_{(1)}, S_{(2)}, S_{(3)}, S_{(4)}\})$$

$$= (X_{11} -_h X_{12})\eta_{Pl}(\{S_1\})$$

$$+ (X_{12} -_h X_{13})\eta_{Pl}(\{S_1, S_2\})(X_{13} -_h X_{14})\eta_{Pl}(\{S_1, S_2, S_3\})$$

$$+ X_{14}\eta_{Pl}(\{S_1, S_2, S_3, S_4\})$$

$$U(f_2) = (u(f_2(S_{(1)})) -_h u(f_2(S_{(2)})))\eta_{Pl}(\{S_{(1)}\})$$

$$+ (u(f_2(S_{(2)})) -_h u(f_2(S_{(3)})))\eta_{Pl}(\{S_{(1)}, S_{(2)}\})$$

$$+ (u(f_2(S_{(3)})) -_h u(f_2(S_{(4)})))\eta_{Pl}(\{S_{(1)}, S_{(2)}, S_{(3)}\})$$

$$+ u(f_2(S_{(4)})))\eta_{Pl}(\{S_{(1)}, S_{(2)}, S_{(3)}, S_{(4)}\})$$

$$= (u(f_2(S_1)) -_h u(f_2(S_2)))\eta_{Pl}(\{S_1\})$$

$$+ (u(f_2(S_2)) -_h u(f_2(S_3)))\eta_{Pl}(\{S_1, S_2\})$$

$$+ (u(f_2(S_3)) -_h u(f_2(S_4)))\eta_{Pl}(\{S_{(1)}, S_{(2)}, S_{(3)}\})$$

$$+ u(f_2(S_{(4)})))\eta_{Pl}(\{S_{(1)}, S_{(2)}, S_{(3)}, S_{(4)}\})$$

$$= (X_{21} -_h X_{22})\eta_{Pl}(\{S_1\})$$

$$+ (X_{22} -_h X_{23})\eta_{Pl}(\{S_1, S_2\})(X_{23} -_h X_{24})\eta_{Pl}(\{S_1, S_2, S_3\})$$

$$+ X_{24}\eta_{Pl}(\{S_1, S_2, S_3, S_4\})$$

$$U(f_3) = (u(f_3(S_{(1)})) -_h u(f_3(S_{(2)})))\eta_{Pl}(\{S_{(1)}\})$$

$$+ (u(f_3(\tilde{S}_{(2)})) -_h u(f_3(S_{(3)})))\eta_{Pl}(\{S_{(1)}, S_{(2)}\})$$

$$+ (u(f_3(S_{(3)})) -_h u(f_3(S_{(4)})))\eta_{Pl}(\{S_{(1)}, S_{(2)}, S_{(3)}\})$$

$$+ u(f_3(S_{(4)})))\eta_{Pl}(\{S_{(1)}, S_{(2)}, S_{(3)}, S_{(4)}\})$$

$$= (u(f_3(S_1)) -_h u(f_3(S_2)))\eta_{Pl}(\{S_1\})$$

$$+ (u(f_3(S_2)) -_h u(f_3(S_3)))\eta_{Pl}(\{S_1, S_2\})$$

$$+ (u(f_3(S_3)) -_h u(f_3(S_4)))\eta_{\tilde{P}l}(\{S_{(1)}, S_{(2)}, S_{(3)}\})$$

$$+ u(f_3(S_{(4)})))\eta_{Pl}(\{S_{(1)}, S_{(2)}, S_{(3)}, S_{(4)}\})$$

$$-= (X_{31} -_h X_{32})\eta_{Pl}(\{S_1\}) + (X_{32} -_h X_{33})\eta_{Pl}(\{S_1, S_2\})$$

$$+ (X_{33} -_h X_{34})\eta_{Pl}(\{S_1, S_2, S_3\}) + X_{34}\eta_{Pl}(\{S_1, S_2, S_3, S_4\})$$

$$= X_{34}\eta_{Pl}(\{S_1, S_2, S_3, S_4\})$$

Here η_{Pl} is the fuzzy probability-based fuzzy number-valued fuzzy measure obtained as lower prevision. We need to compute $\eta_{Pl}(H)$ for $H = \{S_1\}$, $H = \{S_1, S_2\}$ and $H = \{S_1, S_2, S_3\}$, that is for $H = \{S_1, \ldots, S_l\}$, $l = 1, \ldots, 3$. When $H = \{S_1, S_2, S_3, S_4\} = S$ then $\eta_{Pl}(H) = 1$. r-cuts of $\eta_{Pl}(H)$ will be computed as numerical solutions to problem (13.7) as follows (by taking into account that $\mu_H(s) = \max(\mu_{S_1}(s), \ldots, \mu_{S_l}(s))$):

$$\eta_{P_1^l}{}^r(\{S_1, \ldots, S_l\}) = \min_{(p(\sigma_1), \ldots, p(\sigma_K)) \in P^{\rho^r}}$$

$$\times \sum_{k=1}^{K} p(\sigma_k) \max(\mu_{S_1}(\sigma_k), \ldots, \mu_{S_l}(\sigma_k)) \Delta_k$$

$$\eta_{P_2^l}{}^r(\{S_1, \ldots, S_l\}) = \min_{(p(\sigma_1), \ldots, p(\sigma_K)) \in core(P^\rho)}$$

$$\times \sum_{k=1}^{K} p(\sigma_k) \max(\mu_{S_1}(\sigma_k), \ldots, \mu_{S_l}(\sigma_k)) \Delta_k$$

$$l = 1, \ldots, 3$$

$$P^{\rho^r} = \left\{ (p(\sigma_1), \ldots, p(\sigma_K)) \left| \sum_{k=1}^{K} p(\sigma_k)\Delta_k = 1, \min_{i=\overline{1,4}}(\pi_{P_i}(p_i)) \geq r \right. \right\}$$

subject to

$$\pi_{P_i}(p_i) = \mu_{\tilde{P}_i}\left(\sum_{k=1}^{K} p(\sigma_k)\mu_{s_i}(\sigma_k)\Delta_k \right), \quad i = \overline{1,4}$$

The computed membership functions for values of $\eta_{Pl}(B)$ for states S_1 ("strong growth"), S_2 ("moderate growth"), S_3 ("stable"), S_4 ("recession") (corresponds to the unknown probability Γ_4) are as given in Fig. 13.6.

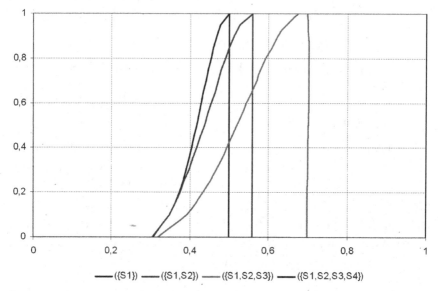

——({S1}) ——({S1,S2}) ——({S1,S2,S3}) ——({S1,S2,S3,S4})

Fig. 13.6. Values of $\eta_{Pl}()$ for states of economy S_1 ("strong growth"), $\{S_1, S_2\}$ ("strong growth", moderate growth"), $\{S_1, S_2, S_3\}$ ("strong growth", "moderate growth", "stable"), $\{S_1, S_2, S_3, S_4\}$ ("strong growth", "moderate growth", "stable", "recession").

Finally, we calculate fuzzy overall utilities $U(f_1)$, $U(f_2)$, and $U(f_3)$. The membership functions for $U(f_1)$, $U(f_2)$, and $U(f_3)$ are shown in Fig. 13.7.

We use here the Jaccard compatibility-based rating [408] to compare fuzzy numbers $U(f_1), U(f_2), U(f_3)$. By realizing a pairwise comparison, we arrive at the following results:

$$U(f_1) \geq U(f_2) \text{ with degree } 0.99$$
$$U(f_2) \geq U(f_1) \text{ with degree } 0.78$$
$$U(f_1) \geq U(f_3) \text{ with degree } 0.89$$
$$U(f_3) \geq U(f_1) \text{ with degree } 0.95$$
$$U(f_2) \geq U(f_3) \text{ with degree } 0.71$$
$$U(f_3) \geq U(f_2) \text{ with degree } 0.99$$

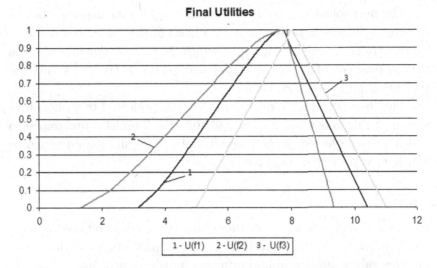

Fig. 13.7. Computed final fuzzy utilities $U(f_1), U(f_2), U(f_3)$.

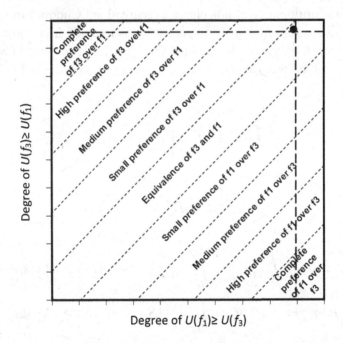

Fig. 13.8. Linguistic preference.

The best solution is to choose the action f_3 (time deposit). Let us determine linguistic preferences on a basis of the calculated degrees. To determine linguistic degree to which f_3 is preferred to f_1 on the base of degrees of $U(f_3) \geq U(f_1)$ and $U(f_1) \geq U(f_3)$ we use the scheme displayed in Fig. 13.8.

The linguistic preference to which f_3 is preferred to f_1 is equivalence. Analogously, we have found that the linguistic preference to which f_1 is preferred to f_2 is small and the linguistic preference to which f_3 is preferred to f_2 is also small.

Appendix

Here, we provide the proofs of the representation theorems on a fuzzy utility function expressed in the form of Choquet integral with a fuzzy number-valued integrand and a fuzzy number-valued fuzzy measure.

Auxiliary results. In the presented work, we extend the results in [402]. Our approach extends classical real-valued Choquet integral of a real-valued function with respect to a real-valued non-additive set function to a fuzzy number-valued Choquet integral [489] of a fuzzy number-valued function with respect to a fuzzy number-valued fuzzy measure η:

$$I(a) = \int_S a d\eta = \int_0^\infty \eta(\{S \in S | a(S) \geq \alpha\}) d\alpha \qquad (\text{A.1})$$

where $a : S \to E^1$. In r-cuts we will have

$$[I(a)]^r = [I_1^r(a_1^r), I_2^r(a_2^r)]$$

where

$$I_1^r(a_1^r) = \int_S a_1^r d\eta_1^r = \int_0^\infty \eta_1^r(\{S \in \text{Sn} | a_1^r(S) \geq \alpha_1^r\}) d\alpha_1^r$$

$$I_2^r(a_2^r) = \int_S a_2^r d\eta_2^r = \int_0^\infty \eta_2^r(\{S \in \text{Sn} | a_2^r(S) \geq \alpha_2^r\}) d\alpha_2^r$$

Here, $I_1^r, I_2^r : \mathcal{C} \to \mathcal{R}$ are monotonic and homogenous functions, where $\mathcal{C}$ is the space of bounded, F_S-measurable, and real-valued functions on $\mathcal{S}$. $[\tilde{I}(a)]^r = [I_1^r(a_1^r), I_2^r(a_2^r)]$ is an r-cut of a fuzzy number because $I_1^r(a_1^r) \leq I_1^{\bar{r}}(a_1^{\bar{r}})$, $I_2^r(a_2^r) \geq I_2^{\bar{r}}(a_2^{\bar{r}})$ for $r \leq \bar{r}$ and $I_1^r(a_1^r) \leq I_2^r(a_2^r)$ due to monotonicity property of $I_1^r, I_2^r : \mathcal{C} \to \mathcal{R}$ and the fact that $\eta_1^r(a_1^r) \leq \eta_2^r(a_2^r)$.

Denote $\mathcal{S}^*$ the indicator function of $\mathcal{S}$.

Theorem 13.3. *Let $I : \mathrm{B} \to \mathrm{E}^1$, where $\mathcal{B}$ is the space of bounded, $\mathrm{F_S}$-measurable, fuzzy number-valued functions on $\mathcal{S}$, satisfying $I(\mathrm{S}^*) = 1$, be given. Assume also that the functional I satisfies:*

(i) *Co-monotonic additivity: for co-monotonic $a, b \in \mathrm{B}$, $I(a + b) = I(a) + I(b)$ holds.*

(ii) *Monotonicity: if $a(S) \geq b(S)$ for all $S \in \mathrm{S}$ then $I(a) \geq I(b)$.*

Under these conditions, defining $\eta(\mathrm{H}) = I(\mathrm{H}^*)$ for all $\mathrm{H} \in \mathrm{F_S}$, where $\mathcal{H}^*$ denotes the indicator function of $\mathcal{H}$, we have

$$I(a) = \int_0^\infty \eta(a \geq \alpha)d\alpha + \int_{-\infty}^0 (\eta(a \geq \alpha) - 1)d\alpha, \quad \forall a \in \mathrm{B} \quad (\mathrm{A.2})$$

such that

$$I_1^r(a_1^r) = \int_0^\infty \eta_1^r(a_1^r \geq \alpha_1^r)d\alpha_1^r + \int_{-\infty}^0 (\eta_1^r(a_1^r \geq \alpha_1^r) - 1)d\alpha_1^r$$

$$I_2^r(a_2^r) = \int_0^\infty \eta_2^r(a_2^r \geq \alpha_2^r)d\alpha_2^r + \int_{-\infty}^0 (\eta_2^r(a_2^r \geq \alpha_2^r) - 1)d\alpha_2^r$$

Note that co-monotonically additive and monotonic I on $\mathcal{B}$ satisfies $I(\lambda a) = \lambda I(a)$ for $\lambda > 0$. Indeed, r-cut of $I(\lambda a)$ is defined as $[I(\lambda a)]^r = [I_1^r([\lambda a]_1^r), I_2^r([\lambda a]_2^r)]$, where $[\lambda a]_1^r = \lambda a_1^r$, $[\lambda a]_2^r = \lambda a_2^r$ because $\lambda > 0$. So, $I_1^r(\lambda a_1^r) = \lambda I_1^r(a_1^r)$, $I_2^r(\lambda a_2^r) = \lambda I_2^r(a_2^r)$.

Thus, we will have:

$$[I(\lambda a)]^r = [I_1^r(\lambda a_1^r), I_2^r(\lambda a_2^r)] = [\lambda I_1^r(a_1^r), \lambda I_2^r(a_2^r)]$$

$$= \lambda [I_1^r(a_1^r), I_2^r(a_2^r)] = \lambda [I(a)]^r$$

So, $I(\lambda a) = \lambda I(a)$, $\lambda > 0$.

Remark 13.1. The integrand in (A.1) can be compactly expressed as follows:

$$a^*(\alpha) = \begin{cases} \eta(a \geq \alpha), & \alpha \geq 0 \\ \eta(a \geq \alpha) - \eta(S), & \alpha < 0 \end{cases}$$

in sense that

$$a_1^{*r}(\alpha) = a_1^{*r}(\alpha_1^r) = \begin{cases} \eta_1^r(a_1^r \geq \alpha_1^r), & \alpha_1^r \geq 0 \\ \eta_1^r(a_1^r \geq \alpha_1^r) - \eta_1^r(S), & \alpha_1^r < 0 \end{cases}$$

$$a_2^{*r}(\alpha) = a_2^{*r}(\alpha_2^r) = \begin{cases} \eta_2^r(a_2^r \geq \alpha_2^r), & \alpha_2^r \geq 0 \\ \eta_2^r(a_2^r \geq \alpha_2^r) - \eta_2^r(S), & \alpha_2^r < 0 \end{cases}$$

If a_1^r, a_2^r are non-negative, then $a_1^{*r}, a_2^{*r} = 0$ for $\alpha_1^r, \alpha_2^r < 0$. If θ_1^r, θ_2^r are negative lower bounds of a_1^r, a_2^r, respectively then $a_1^{*r}(\alpha_1^r) = 0$ and $a_2^{*r}(\alpha_2^r) = 0$ for $\alpha_1^r \leq \theta_1^r$ and $\alpha_2^r \leq \theta_2^r$, respectively. If $\vartheta_1^r, \vartheta_2^r$ are upper bound of a_1^r, a_2^r, respectively, then r-cuts of (A.2) are equivalent to

$$I_1^r(a_1^r) = \int_{\theta_1^r}^{\vartheta_1^r} a_1^{*r}(\alpha_1^r) d\alpha_1^r$$

$$I_2^r(a_2^r) = \int_{\theta_2^r}^{\vartheta_2^r} a_2^{*r}(\alpha_2^r) d\alpha_2^r$$

So, (13.3) is equivalent to $I(a) = \int_\theta^\vartheta a^*(\alpha) d\alpha$ (the fact that $\vartheta_1^r, \vartheta_2^r$ and θ_1^r, θ_2^r can be considered as endpoints of r-cut of a fuzzy number is obvious). As $I_1^r, I_2^r : \mathcal{C} \to \mathcal{R}$ are co-monotonically additive and monotonic, then, based on the results for such functionals obtained [402], we can claim that r-cuts of (13.2) are implied by r-cuts of (A.1), and hence, ((A.2) is implied by (A.1)).

Proof of Theorem 13.3. Remark 13.1 allows proof of (A.1) for non-negative fuzzy number-valued functions only. Assuming that (A.1) holds for any fuzzy finite step function, we will prove it for an arbitrary non-negative F_S-measurable fuzzy number-valued function

[489] a bounded by some $\lambda \in E^1$ (that is, $0 \le a(S) \le \lambda$, hold for all $S \in S$). For $n = 1, 2, \ldots$ and $1 \le k \le 2^n$ we define:

$$H_n^{k,1,r} = \{S \in S | \lambda_1^r (k-1)/2^n < [a(S)]_1^r \le \lambda_1^r k/2^n\} \quad \text{and}$$

$$\mathcal{H}_n^{k,2,r} = \{\tilde{S} \in \mathcal{S} | \lambda_2^r (k-1)/2^n < [\tilde{a}(\tilde{S})]_2^r \le \lambda_2^r k/2^n\}$$

Define also

$$[a_n(S)_1^r = \lambda_1^r (k-1)/2^n, \quad [a_n(S)]_2^r = \lambda_2^r (k-1)/2^n$$

$$[b_n(S)]_1^r = \lambda_1^r k/2^n, \quad [b_n(S)]_2^r = \lambda_2^r k/2^n$$

Thus, for all S and n

$$[a_n(S)]_1^r \le [a_{n+1}(S)]_1^r \le [a(S)]_1^r \le [b_{n+1}(S)]_1^r \le [b_n(S)]_1^r \quad \text{and}$$

$$[a_n(S)]_2^r \le [a_{n+1}(S)]_2^r \le [a(S)]_2^r \le [b_{n+1}(S)]_2^r \le [b_{n(S)}]_2^r$$

hold. So, for all S and n $a_n(S) \le a_{n+1}(S) \le a(S) \le b_{n+1}(S) \le b_n(S)$ hold. Monotonicity of $I_1^r, I_2^r : \mathcal{C} \to \mathcal{R}$ implies $I_1^r(a_{n1}^r) \le I_1^r(a_1^r) \le I_1^r(b_{n1}^r)$, $I_2^r(a_{n2}^r) \le I_2^r(a_2^r) \le I_2^r(b_{n2}^r)$, in turn co-monotonic additivity of $I_1^r, I_2^r : \mathcal{C} \to \mathcal{R}$ implies $0 \le I_1^r(b_{n1}^r) - I_1^r(a_{n1}^r) = \lambda_1^r/2^n \to 0$ and $= \lambda_2^r/2^n \to 0$, $n \to \infty$.

Based on the assumption about fuzzy finite step functions, it follows that

$$I_1^r(a_{n1}^r) = \int_0^{\lambda_1^r} \eta_1^r(a_{n1}^r \ge \alpha_1^r) d\alpha_1^r, \quad I_2^r(a_{n2}^r) = \int_0^{\lambda_2^r} \eta_2^r(a_{n2}^r \ge \alpha_2^r) d\alpha_2^r$$

and

$$I_1^r(b_{n1}^r) = \int_0^{\lambda_1^r} \eta_1^r(b_{n1}^r \ge \alpha_1^r) d\alpha_1^r, \quad I_2^r(b_{n2}^r) = \int_0^{\lambda_2^r} \eta_2^r(b_{n2}^r \ge \alpha_2^r) d\alpha_2^r$$

The monotonicity of η_1^r, η_2^r and the definitions of $a_{n1}^r, b_{n1}^r, a_{n2}^r, b_{n2}^r$, $n = 1, 2, \ldots$, imply $\eta_1^r(a_{n1}^r \ge \alpha_1^r) \le \eta_1^r(a_1^r \ge \alpha_1^r) \le \eta_1^r(b_{n1}^r \ge \alpha_1^r)$,

$\eta_2^r(a_{n2}^r \geq \alpha_2^r) \leq \eta_2^r(a_2^r \geq \alpha_2^r) \leq \; \leq \eta_2^r(b_{n2}^r \geq \alpha_2^r)$ From these inequalities it follows that:

$$\int_0^{\lambda_1^r} \eta_1^r(a_{n1}^r \geq \alpha_1^r)d\alpha_1^r$$

$$\leq \int_0^{\lambda_1^r} \eta_1^r(a_1^r \geq \alpha_1^r)d\alpha_1^r \leq \int_0^{\lambda_1^r} \eta_1^r(b_{n1}^r \geq \alpha_1^r)d\alpha_1^r$$

and

$$\int_0^{\lambda_2^r} \eta_2^r(a_{n2}^r \geq \alpha_2^r)d\alpha_2^r \leq \int_0^{\lambda_2^r} \eta_2^r(a_2^r \geq \alpha_2^r)d\alpha_2^r$$

$$\leq \int_0^{\lambda_2^r} \eta_2^r(b_{n2}^r \geq \alpha_2^r)d\alpha_2^r$$

hold.

So,

$$I_1^r(a_1^r) = \int_0^{\lambda_1^r} \eta_1^r(a_1^r \geq \alpha_1^r)d\alpha_1^r \qquad ,$$

$$I_2^r(a_2^r) = \int_0^{\lambda_2^r} \eta_2^r(a_2^r \geq \alpha_2^r)d\alpha_2^r$$

that is,

$$I(a) = \int_0^{\lambda} \eta(a \geq \alpha)d\alpha$$

Let us now prove that (A.1) holds for fuzzy finite step functions. Any non-negative fuzzy step function $a \in B$ has a unique r-cut representation

$$a_1^r = \sum_{i=1}^k \alpha_{i1}^r \mathcal{H}_i^*, \quad a_2^r = \sum_{i=1}^k \alpha_{i2}^r \mathcal{H}_i^*$$

for some k, where $\alpha_{11}^r > \alpha_{21}^r > \cdots > \alpha_{k1}^r$, $\alpha_{12}^r > \alpha_{22}^r > \cdots > \alpha_{k2}^r$ and the sets $\mathcal{H}_i$, $i = 1, \ldots, k$ are pairwise disjoint. Defining $\alpha_{k+11}^r = 0$,

$\alpha_{k+12}^r = 0$ we have:

$$\int_0^{\alpha_{11}^r} \eta_1^r(a_1^r \ge \alpha_1^r)d\alpha_1^r = \sum_{i=1}^{k}(\alpha_{i1}^r - \alpha_{i+11}^r)\eta_1^r\left(\bigcup_{j=1}^{i}\mathcal{H}_j\right)$$

$$\int_0^{\alpha_{12}^r} \eta_2^r(a_2^r \ge \alpha_2^r)d\alpha_2^r = \sum_{i=1}^{k}(\alpha_{i2}^r - \alpha_{i+12}^r)\eta_2^r\left(\bigcup_{j=1}^{i}\mathcal{H}_j\right)$$

So,

$$\int_0^{\alpha_1} \eta(a \ge \alpha)d\alpha = \sum_{i=1}^{k}(\alpha_i -_h \alpha_{i+1})\eta\left(\bigcup_{j=1}^{i}H_j\right) \qquad \text{(A.3)}$$

Note that throughout the paper we use the Hukuhara difference. The induction hypothesis implies that for $k < n$

$$I(a) = \sum_{i=1}^{k}(\alpha_i -_h \alpha_{i+1})\eta\left(\bigcup_{j=1}^{i}H_j\right) \qquad \text{(A.4)}$$

We need to prove it for $k = n$. Note that for $k = 1$ $I_1^r(\alpha_1^r\mathcal{H}^*) = \alpha_1^r\eta_1^r(\mathcal{H}^*)$, and $I_2^r(\alpha_2^r\mathcal{H}^*) = \alpha_2^r\eta_2^r(\mathcal{H}^*)$ hold, i.e., $I(\alpha\mathcal{H}^*) = \alpha\eta(H^*)$ holds.

Given endpoints of r-cut of a as

$$a_1^r = \sum_{i=1}^{k}\alpha_{i1}^r\mathcal{H}_i^*, \quad a_2^r = \sum_{i=1}^{k}\alpha_{i2}^r\mathcal{H}_i^*, \quad a = b + c$$

where

$$b_1^r = \sum_{i=1}^{k-1}(\alpha_{i1}^r - \alpha_{i+11}^r)\mathcal{H}_i^*, \quad b_2^r = \sum_{i=1}^{k-1}(\alpha_{i2}^r - \alpha_{i+12}^r)\mathcal{H}_i^*$$

$$c_1^r = \alpha_{k1}^r\left(\sum_{i=1}^{k}\mathcal{H}_j^*\right), \quad c_2^r = \alpha_{k2}^r\left(\sum_{i=1}^{k}\mathcal{H}_j^*\right)$$

From the induction hypothesis $(k - 1 < n)$,

$$I(b) = \sum_{i=1}^{k-1} ((\alpha_i -_h \alpha_k) -_h (\alpha_{i+1} -_h \alpha_k)) \eta \left(\bigcup_{j=1}^{i} H_j \right)$$

$$= \sum_{i=1}^{k-1} (\alpha_i -_h \alpha_{i+1}) \eta \left(\bigcup_{j=1}^{i} H_j \right)$$

and

$$I(c) = \alpha_k \eta \left(\bigcup_{j=1}^{i} H_j \right)$$

Thus,

$$I(b) + I(c) = \sum_{i=1}^{k} (\alpha_i -_h \alpha_{i+1}) \eta \left(\bigcup_{j=1}^{i} H_j \right)$$

From the other side, as b and c are co-monotonic, $I(a) = I(b) + I(c)$ and (A.4) for $k = n$ has been proved. The proof is completed. □

Remark 13.2. From the opposite direction of Theorem 13.3 it follows that if a fuzzy functional I is defined by (A.2) with respect to some fuzzy number-valued fuzzy measure, then it satisfies co-monotonic additivity and monotonicity. One can easily obtain the proof by reversing the proof of Theorem 13.3 as follows. For a functional I defined by (A.2) with respect to some fuzzy number-valued fuzzy measure η, it is needed to prove that it is co-monotonically additive and monotonic. Monotonicity of I follows from the fact that $a \geq b$ on $\mathcal{S}$ implies $a^* \geq b^*$ on $\mathcal{E}^1$.

So, at first it is needed to show co-monotonic additivity for fuzzy finite step functions in $\mathcal{B}$. To this end the following two claims are given.

Claim 13.1. *Two fuzzy finite step functions $b, c \in$ B are co-monotonic if there exists an integer k, a partition of $\mathcal{S}$ into k pairwise disjoint elements $(\mathcal{H}_i)_{i=1}^{k}$ of $F_\mathcal{S}$, and two k-lists of fuzzy numbers*

$\beta_1 \geq \beta_2 \geq \cdots \geq \beta_k$ and $\gamma_1 \geq \gamma_2 \geq \cdots \geq \gamma_k$ such that $b = \sum_{i=1}^{k} \beta_i H_i^*$ and $c = \sum_{i=1}^{k} \gamma_i H_i^*$. The proof is obvious.

Claim 13.2. *Let* $(\mathcal{H}_i)_{i=1}^{k}$ *be* F_S-*measurable finite partition of* S *(if* $i \neq j$, *then* $\mathcal{H}_i \cap \mathcal{H}_j = \emptyset$) *and let* $a = \sum_{i=1}^{k} \alpha_i H_i^*$ *with* $\alpha_1 \geq \alpha_2 \geq \cdots \geq \alpha_k$. *Then for any fuzzy number-valued fuzzy measure* $\eta : F_S \to E^1$ *we have:*

$$\int_{-\infty}^{\infty} a^*(\alpha) d\alpha = \sum_{i=1}^{k} (\alpha_i -_h \alpha_{i+1}) \eta \left(\bigcup_{j=1}^{i} H_j \right) \qquad (A.5)$$

with $\alpha_{k=1} = 0$.

For $I(a)$ defined by the left side of (A.5) for fuzzy finite step functions, formula (A.5) and Claim 13.1 imply additivity for co-monotonic fuzzy finite step functions. Extension of this result to any co-monotonic functions in $\mathcal{B}$ is obtained by computing appropriate limits in metrics d_{fH}.

It can be easily shown that Theorem 13.3 and its converse hold if $\mathcal{B}$ is substituted by $\mathcal{B}_0$, the set of all fuzzy finite step functions in $\mathcal{B}$. Also, for co-monotonically additive and monotonic $I : B_0 \to E^1$ there exists a unique extension to all of $\mathcal{B}$, which satisfies co-monotonic additivity and monotonicity. To prove this it is needed to pass to r-cuts of I and then easily apply the facts that $\mathcal{B}$ is the (sup) norm closure of $\mathcal{B}_0$ in $(\mathcal{E}^1)^S$ in metrics d_{fH} and that monotonicity implies norm continuity.

Now let $\mathcal{B}(\mathcal{K})$ denote the set of functions in $\mathcal{B}$ with values in $\mathcal{K}$, and suppose that $K \supset \{v \in E^1 | -\gamma \leq v \leq \gamma\}$, where $\gamma \geq 0$, $-\gamma = -1\gamma$.

Corollary 13.1. *Let* $I : B(K) \to E^1$ *be given such that*

(1) *for all* $\lambda \in K$ $I(\lambda S^*) = \lambda$,
(2) *if* a, b *and* c *are pairwise co-monotonic, and* $I(a) > I(b)$, *then* $I(\alpha a + (1 - \alpha)c) > I(\alpha b + (1 - \alpha)c)$, $\alpha \in (0, 1)$,
(3) *if* $a \geq b$ *on* S, *then* $I(a) > I(b)$.

Then, defining $\eta(H) = I(H^*)$ on F_S we will have for all $a \in B(K)$:

$$I(a) = \int_0^\infty \eta(a \geq \alpha)d\alpha + \int_{-\infty}^0 (\eta(a \geq \alpha) - 1)d\alpha$$

The proof consists in extending I on $\mathcal{B}(\mathcal{K})$ to I on $\mathcal{B}$ and showing that conditions of Theorem 13.3. are satisfied. As I is homogeneous on $\mathcal{B}(\mathcal{K})$ it can be uniquely extended to a homogeneous function on $\mathcal{B}$. Next, by homogeneity, the extended functional I satisfies monotonicity on $\mathcal{B}$. Co-monotonic additivity of I on $\mathcal{B}$ follows from the following Lemma and homogeneity property.

Lemma 13.1. *Given the conditions of the corollary, let a and b in $\mathcal{B}(\mathcal{K})$ be co-monotonic such that $d_{fH}(a(S), 0) \geq -1 + \varepsilon$, $d_{fH}(b(S), 0) \leq 1 - \varepsilon$ for some $\varepsilon > 0$ and let $0 < \lambda < 1$. Then $I(\lambda a + (1 - \lambda)b) = \lambda I(a) + (1 - \lambda)I(b)$.*

Proof. Denote $I(a) = \alpha$ and $I(b) = \beta$. By a condition of the Lemma, and by (i) and (iii) of the Corollary it is true that $\alpha S^*, \beta S^* \in B(K)$, $I(\alpha S^*) = \alpha$ and $I(\beta S^*) = \beta$.

We need to prove that $I(\lambda a + (1 - \lambda)b) = \lambda I(a) + (1 - \lambda)I(b)$. Suppose that $I(\lambda a + (1 - \lambda)b) > \lambda I(a) + (1 - \lambda)I(b)$ (the case of the other inequality is treated in a similar manner).

Let $0 < \delta < \varepsilon$. Then by (i) $I(a) < I((\alpha + \delta)S^*)$, $I(b) < I((\beta + \delta)S^*)$. Now

$$\lambda\alpha + (1 - \lambda)\beta + \delta = I(\lambda(\alpha + \delta)S^* + (1 - \lambda)(\beta + \delta)S^*)$$
$$> I(\lambda a + (1 - \lambda)(\beta + \delta)S^*)$$
$$\gg I(\lambda a + (1 - \lambda)b)$$

The equality follows from (i) and each of the two inequalities follows from (ii). The inequality above holds for any δ $(0 < \delta < \varepsilon)$, so we get the required contradiction. The proof is completed. □

Remark 13.3. The corollary holds if $\mathcal{B}(\mathcal{K})$ is replaced by $\mathcal{B}_0(\mathcal{K})$ the set of bounded, F_S-measurable, fuzzy finite step functions on S with values in $\mathcal{K}$. The same is true for the Lemma.

Proof of Theorem 13.1

Step 1. At this step we show the existence of an affine fuzzy number-valued function defined over $\mathcal{Y}$.

Affinity of u implies $u(y) = \sum_{X \in X} y(X) u(X)$ defined as follows:

$$\mu_{u(y)}(u(y)) = \sup_{\substack{u(y) = \sum_{X \in X} y(X) u(X) \\ \sum_{X \in X} y(X) = 1}} \min$$

$$\times \left(\mu_{u(X)}(u(X)), \mu_{y(X)}(y(X)) \right)$$

Positive linear transformation u' of u implies $u' = au(y) + b, a \in E_+^1, b \in E^1$, where addition and multiplication is defined on the base of Zadeh's extension principle.

Using the implications from von Neumann–Morgenstern theorem, we suppose that there exists a fuzzy number-valued function u representing LPR $\succsim_l$ induced on $\mathcal{Y}$. Now, from nondegeneracy axiom it follows that there exist such f^* and f_* in $\mathcal{A}_0$ that $f^* \succ_l f_*$. From monotonicity axiom it follows existence of a state S in $\mathcal{S}$ such that $f^*(S) \equiv y^* \succ_l f_*(S) \equiv y_*$. Since u is given up to a positive linear transformation, suppose that $u(y_*) = -v$ and $u(y^*) = v, v \in E_+^1$. We denote $K = u(Y)$ which is a convex subset [323] of $\mathcal{E}^1$ with $-v, v \in K$.

Step 2. At this step we show the existence of an affine fuzzy number-valued function defined over A_0.

Denote by $M_f = \{\alpha f + (1 - \alpha) y^S | y \in Y \text{ and } \alpha \in [0, 1]\}$ for an arbitrary $f \in A_0$. It is clear that M_f is convex and any two acts in M_f are co-monotonic. So we can claim that there exists an affine fuzzy number-valued function over M_f representing the corresponding LPR $\succsim_l$. By using positive linear transformation we can define for this function denoted J_f: $J_f(y_*^S) = -v$ and $J_f(y^{*S}) = v$. For any $h \in M_f \cap M_g$, $J_f(h) = J_g(h)$ hold. This allows to define fuzzy number-valued function $J(f) = J_f(f)$ on A_0, which represents the LPR $\succsim_l$ on A_0 and satisfies for all y in $\mathcal{Y}$: $J(y^S) = u(y)$.

Step 3. At this step we show the existence of a fuzzy number-valued functional [460] defined on the base of u and J_f.

Denote by $\mathcal{B}_0(\mathcal{K})$ the F_S-measurable, $\mathcal{K}$-valued fuzzy finite step functions on $\mathcal{S}$. By means of u let us define onto function

$\Phi : A_0 \to B_0(K)$ as $\Phi(f)(S) = u(f(S))$, $S \in S, f \in A_0$. If $\Phi(f) = \Phi(g)$ then $f \sim_l g$ (it follows from monotonicity). So, $\Phi(f) = \Phi(g)$ implies $J(f) = J(g)$.

Define a fuzzy number-valued function I on $B_0(\mathcal{K})$ as follows: $I(a) = J(f)$ for $a \in B_0(K)$, where $f \in A_0$ is such that $\Phi(f) = a$. I is well defined as J is constant fuzzy number-valued function (that is, $\exists v \in E^1, J(f) = v, \forall f \in A$) on $\Phi^{-1}(a)$.

Fuzzy number-valued function I satisfies the following conditions:

(i) for all α in $\mathcal{K}$:$I(\alpha S^*) = \alpha$. Indeed, let $y \in Y$ be such that $u(y) = \alpha$, hence $J(y^S) = \alpha$ and $\Phi(y^S) = \alpha S^*$ implying $I(\alpha S^*) = \alpha$,

(ii) for all pairwise co-monotonic functions a, b and c in $B_0(\mathcal{K})$ and $\alpha \in [0, 1]$: if $I(a) > I(b)$, then $I(\alpha a + (1-\alpha)c) > I(\alpha b + (1-\alpha)c)$. This is true because Φ preserves co-monotonicity,

(iii) if $a(s) \geq b(s)$ on S for a and b in $B_0(\mathcal{K})$ then $I(a) \geq I(b)$. This is true because Φ preserves monotonicity.

Step 4. This step completes the proof of Theorem 13.1.

From the Corollary and Remark 13.3 for a fuzzy number-valued function on $B_0(\mathcal{K})$, which satisfies conditions (i), (ii), and (iii) above, it follows that the fuzzy number-valued fuzzy measure η on F_S defined by $\eta(H) = I(H^*)$ satisfies

$$I(a) \geq I(b) \quad \text{iff} \quad \int_S a d\eta \geq \int_S b d\eta, \quad \forall a, b \in B_0(K) \qquad \text{(A.6)}$$

Hence, for all f and g in $\mathcal{A}_0$:

$$f_l \succsim g \quad \text{iff} \quad \int_S \Phi(f) d\eta \geq \int_S \Phi(g) d\eta$$

The proof is completed.

Proof of Theorem 13.2

Step 1. At this step we show that LPR, which is induced by u and η on $\mathcal{A}_0$, satisfies axioms (i)–(v).

To prove this theorem we use Remarks 13.1–13.3, Theorem 13.3 and other results given above, which show that I on $B_0(\mathcal{K})$ defined by (A.6) satisfies conditions (i)–(iii). Secondly, we can see that J is defined as a combination of Φ and I. Thus, the LPR on $\mathcal{A}_0$ induced by J satisfies all the required conditions because Φ preserves monotonicity and co-monotonicity and $\int_S a d\eta$ is a (sup) norm continuous function on a in metrics d_{fH} (this is based on the analogous property of endpoints of r-cuts of $\int_S a d\eta$ that are classical functionals of the type considered by Schmeidler [402]).

Step 2. At this step we show the uniqueness of the fuzzy utility representation.

In order to prove the uniqueness property of the utility representation suppose that there exists an affine fuzzy number-valued function u' on $\mathcal{Y}$ and a fuzzy number-valued fuzzy measure η' on F_S such that for all f and g in $\mathcal{A}_0$:

$$f_1 \succsim g \quad \text{iff} \quad \int_S u'(f(S))d\eta' \geq \int_S u'(g(S))d\eta' \qquad (A.7)$$

Monotonicity of η' can be derived. Considering (A.7) for all $f, g \in A_c$ we obtain, based on implications of von Neumann and Morgenstern theorem and Zadeh's extension principle, that u' is a positive linear transformation of u. But (A.7) is preserved for positive linear transformation of a fuzzy utility. Hence, to prove that $\eta' = \eta$ we may assume w.l.o.g. that $u' = u$. For an arbitrary $\mathcal{H}$ in F_S let f in $\mathcal{A}_0$ be such that $\Phi(f) = \lambda H^*, \lambda \in E^1$. Then $\int_S \Phi(f)d\eta = v\eta(H)$ and $\int_S \Phi(f)d\eta' = v\eta'(H)$. Let y in $\mathcal{Y}$ be such that $u(y) = v\eta(H)$. Then $f \sim_l y^S$, which implies $u(y) = u'(y) = \int_S u'(y)d\eta' = v\eta'(H)$. So, $v\eta(H) = v\eta'(H)$, and therefore, $\eta(H) = \eta'(H)$. The proof is completed. $\qquad\qquad\square$

Note that for a special case the suggested decision making model and utility representation reduce to the one suggested by Schmeidler in Ref. [403].

If S is a finite set $S = \{S_1, \ldots, S_n\}$, $U(f)$ is determined as follows:

$$U(f) = \sum_{i=1}^{n}(u(f(S_{(i)})) -_h u(f(S_{(i+1)})))\eta(H_{(i)}) \qquad (A.8)$$

Subscript $(\cdot)$ shows that the indices are permuted in order to have $u(f(S_{(1)})) \geq \cdots \geq u(f(S_{(n)}))$, using some fuzzy ranking method,

$u(f(S_{(n+1)})) = 0$, and $\mathrm{H}_{(i)} = \{S_{(1)}, \ldots, S_{(i)}\}$. Here, η is a fuzzy-number-valued fuzzy measure that can be obtained from linguistic probability distribution P^l on the base of the methodology presented in Ref. [16]. For this case we denote a fuzzynumber-valued fuzzy measure η_{P^l}. The optimal action f^* is found as an action with a fuzzy utility value $U(f^*) = \max_{f \in A}\{\int_S u(f(S))d\eta_{P^l}\}$. If $\mathcal{A}$ is a finite set $\mathrm{A} = \{f_1, \ldots, f_m\}$, then after determining fuzzy utility values for all alternatives, the best alternative can be found using some fuzzy ranking method.

Chapter 14

Selected Interpretability Aspects of Fuzzy Systems for Classification

Two conflicting goals are often involved in the design of fuzzy rule-based systems: accuracy maximization and interpretability maximization. A number of approaches have been proposed for finding a fuzzy rule-based system with a good accuracy–interpretability tradeoff. Formulation of the accuracy maximization is usually straightforward in each application area of fuzzy rule-based systems such as classification, regression and forecasting. Formulation of the interpretability maximization, however, is not so easy. This is because various aspects of fuzzy rule-based systems are related to their interpretability. In this chapter, we activate discussions on how to measure the interpretability of fuzzy rule-based systems which are used for classification purposes.

14.1. Introduction

Systems using the fuzzy set theory [501] are excellent for advanced research and engineering applications in the field of classification, nonlinear modeling, identification, control, prediction, medical diagnostics, industrial diagnostics, economics, biometrics, image processing, etc. Such systems have several important advantages that distinguish them from other alternative solutions. Their advantages can be summarized as follows:

- Fuzzy systems allow us to describe phenomena and concepts that are ambiguous and imprecise.
- Fuzzy systems use a very intuitive rule notation in the form of if... then..., which consists of antecedents and consequences of

401

the rules, and input and output linguistic variables among others. Particularly important are linguistic systems [287, 288, 385, 389, 529], in which the values of linguistic variables are represented by fuzzy sets. Knowledge accumulated in these systems provides very good opportunities for its interpretation.

- Fuzzy systems significantly support nonlinear modeling. In particular, they allow us to extract readable knowledge (in the form of fuzzy rules) from phenomena and objects for which a model is still not known or it is a so-called black box [222, 426].

- Fuzzy systems can be combined with other approaches, thus creating various kinds of hierarchical systems or systems encoding fuzzy rules in the form of tree structures [401]. Such systems are one of the basic tools for data mining.

- Fuzzy systems provide a good framework for creating a variety of extensions which, for example, enable processing of imprecise information (uncertainty). Such extensions are used in systems based on the terms of a so-called rough-fuzzy set, fuzzy-rough set, interval-valued fuzzy set, fuzzy-valued fuzzy set, etc. [298, 333, 334, 421, 551]. They usually add extensive information on reliability of a generated response to the system output, which makes it harder to take care of readability of the knowledge stored in them.

- Fuzzy systems may (but do not have to) use knowledge and skills of so-called experts and they are able to extract knowledge from numeric data.

- Fuzzy systems can be implemented in hardware. Support in this area could include the use of chips field programmable gate array (FPGA). Since the first hardware solutions supporting fuzzy systems were introduced [487], other technologies have also been used in this field, e.g., complementary metal-oxide semiconductor (CMOS), very large scale integration (VLSI), etc. [552].

- Fuzzy systems can be easily adapted to create an online fuzzy rules base. It is particularly important in the case of issues of nonlinear modeling performed in cooperation with non-invasive online identification (for the object).

- Fuzzy systems support operation and analysis of Internet social networks. Such networks have recently gained in importance and have become an indispensable form of communication. Prediction of missing connections, activity analysis and modeling aspects are only some of the examples of application areas in which fuzzy systems are an important tool [173, 371]).

In this chapter, we consider practical aspects of designing fuzzy systems aimed at broadly defined interpretability. The purpose of this chapter is to show that the term interpretability goes far beyond the concept of readability of a fuzzy set and fuzzy rules (most often discussed in the literature).

In the literature a number of papers on the subject of interpretability of fuzzy systems can be found. Their authors have proposed among the others:

- Solutions aimed at reducing the number of fuzzy rules [9, 35, 164, 184, 218, 278, 292], reducing the number of fuzzy sets [187] and aimed at reducing the number of system inputs [35, 108, 442, 453]. Limitations were also related to the number of antecedences in fuzzy rules. The optimal number was most often set to Miller number, which equals 7 ± 2 [33, 35, 218, 363]. Miller number was designated in 1956 by George Miller and it represents the maximum pieces of information that can be directly distinguished by a human [309]. The use of restrictions in a system structure was often associated with a reduction of redundant elements and merging of similar ones [108, 187, 215, 237, 372, 412].

- Solutions related to correct notation of fuzzy rules [35, 278], correct activation of fuzzy rules [33, 148, 292], distinguishability and interdependence of fuzzy sets (e.g., their overlapping) [296, 297, 363] as well as solutions on issues such as: complementarity, fitting in with data, etc. [79, 152, 164].

- Solutions related to fuzzy systems construction aimed at interpretability. In Refs. [107, 108, 110, 134, 373, 384, 386, 387, 391–393, 414, 417], the use of additional weights of importance of the rules, antecedences, consequences and system inputs was proposed. In Refs. [400], a dynamic· structure of connections between fuzzy sets and rules was considered. It aimed at, among others, reducing system complexity and simplifying the rule-based notation. In Refs. [108, 151], parameterized triangular norms were used (as precise aggregation operators) in order to increase accuracy, and in Ref. [151], the authors reviewed parameterized triangular norms in terms of their suitability for the construction of fuzzy systems. In Ref. [108], the authors used an extended (precise) defuzzification mechanism in which the number of discretization points does not have to be equal to the number of rules. This was suggested, among others, in order to increase accuracy of the system with a fixed number of rules and to provide opportunities to reduce the complexity of rules.

14.1.1. *Attempts at systematizing solutions for interpretability of fuzzy systems*

- The literature abounds in numerous attempts to systematize solutions for interpretability [165, 411, 413]. The systematics presented in Ref. [165] deserves a special attention. Its authors have proposed division of solutions for interpretability into four groups of quadrants: (a) quadrant concerning solutions aimed at reducing complexity at fuzzy rules level (it takes into account, among others, the number of fuzzy rules, the number of antecedences in each rule and using Miller number), (b) quadrant concerning solutions aimed at reducing the complexity at the fuzzy partitioning level (it takes into account, among others, the number of fuzzy sets associated with various inputs and outputs and the number of inputs), (c) quadrant concerning solutions aimed at increasing semantic readability at the fuzzy rules' level (it takes into account, among others, the consistency of the rules, activation level of rules and readability of rule-based notation), and (d) quadrant concerning solutions aimed at increasing semantic readability at the fuzzy partitioning level (it takes into account, among others, a coverage degree of the input data by fuzzy sets, normalization of fuzzy sets, distinctness of fuzzy sets and fuzzy sets complementarity).
- An interesting semantics has also been described in Ref. [34], which can complement the semantics proposed in Ref. [165]. In this semantic interpretability criteria were divided in terms of their readability of the knowledge accumulated in the system and

a different importance was symbolically assigned to the criteria. There are: (a) very important criteria (for the complexity of fuzzy rules and notation readability), (b) important criteria (for the semantics of rules and fuzzy sets, including the criteria for ordering fuzzy sets, semantic phrases used; sharing of fuzzy sets by a number of rules, etc.), and (c) the least important criteria (for the normalization of fuzzy sets, their complementarity, coverage of input data area, etc.).

14.1.2. *Solutions proposed in this chapter*

- The solutions proposed in this chapter can be summarized as follows: (a) In this chapter, the issue of interpretability has been treated comprehensively in terms of semantics considered in Section 14.4. Moreover, the developed interpretability criteria apply to all aspects of fuzzy system designing. In particular, they include, among others, interpretability of fuzzy sets and rules, parameterized triangular norms, weights of importance and discretization points. This approach gives a broader look at the issue of interpretability. (b) In this chapter, a hybrid algorithm for selection of the structure and parameters of a fuzzy system, constructed on the basis of the genetic [141, 160, 488, 497] and the imperialist [43] algorithms is introduced. The vast majority of algorithms presented in the literature can select system parameters only when its structure has been indicated by the designer (selected earlier by trial and error).

- It can be noted that the solutions presented in this chapter relate to interpretability directly and indirectly. The direct approach formulates appropriate criteria (Section 1.4) and uses them in the automatic process of fuzzy system selection. The indirect approach uses precise aggregation and inference operators in system design. They were proposed in our previous works [108, 109, 388, 390] and called flexible. Their use allows for achieving good accuracy with a simpler system structure. Therefore, it makes a good starting point for direct impact on interpretability of a fuzzy system. The use of the learning algorithm also affects the indirect impact on interpretability. It creates a good opportunity to nd an appropriate trade-off between interpretability and accuracy.

14.2. Description of a Fuzzy System for Classification

Further on in this paper a multi-input, multi-output logical-type flexible fuzzy system will be considered [108, 109, 389, 391]. This system performs mapping $X \to Y$, where $X \subset R^n$ and $Y \subset R^m$.

14.2.1. *Rule base*

The rule base of the considered system consists of a collection of N fuzzy rules R^k, $k = 1, \ldots, N$. Each rule R^k takes the following form:

$$
R^k : \left[\left(\begin{array}{c} \text{IF } (\bar{x} \text{ is } A_1^k | w_{k,1}^A \text{ AND} \cdots \text{AND}(\bar{x}_n \text{ is } A_n^k) | w_{k,n}^A) \\ \text{THEN } (y_1 \text{ is } B_1^k) | w_{1,k}^B, \ldots, (y_m \text{ is } B_m^k) | w_{m,k}^B \end{array} \right) | w_k^{rule} \right]
$$

$$(14.1)$$

where n is the number of inputs, m is the number of outputs, $\bar{x} = [\bar{x}_1, \ldots, \bar{x}_n] \in X$ is a vector of input signals (input linguistic variables for the singleton type fuzzification used [389], $y = [y_1, \ldots, y_m] \in Y$ is a vector of output linguistic variables, $A_1^k, \ldots, A_n^k$ are input fuzzy sets characterized by membership functions $\mu_{A_i^k}(x_i)$ ($i = 1, \ldots, n$), $B_1^k, \ldots, B_m^k$ are output fuzzy sets characterized by membership functions $\mu_{B_j^k}(y_j)$ ($j = 1, \ldots, m$), $w_{k,i}^A \in [0, 1]$ are weights of input fuzzy sets, $w_{j,k}^B \in [0, 1]$ are weights of output fuzzy sets, and $w_k^{rule} \in [0, 1]$ are weights of rules.

Fuzzy sets A_i^k and B_j^k are fuzzy values of linguistic variables representing values such as "very low", "low", "medium low", "medium", "medium high", "high", "very high", "near [value]", etc. [501]. Later in this chapter, we consider the system, in which membership functions $\mu_{A_i^k}(x_i)$ and $\mu_{B_j^k}(y_j)$ of fuzzy sets A_i^k and B_j^k are Gaussian functions, represented as follows:

$$
\mu(x) = \exp\left(-\left(\frac{x - \bar{x}}{\sigma} \right)^2 \right)
$$

$$(14.2)$$

Selection of a membership function allowed us to give more detailed information in Sections 14.3.1 and 14.4.2. The Gaussian function reflects well the industrial, natural, medical and social processes; however, our solutions may be related to any other membership function.

The flexibility of system (14.3) is a result of using: (a) weights in the rule base, (b) precise aggregation operators of antecedences and rules (Section 14.2.3), (c) precise inference operators (Section 14.2.3), and (d) a precise defuzzification process (Section 14.2.2).

14.2.2. *Defuzzification process*

Defuzzification is used to determine output signals of fuzzy system $\bar{y}_j$ for given input signals. This is carried out as follows:

$$
\bar{y}_j = \frac{\displaystyle\sum_{r=1}^{R_j} \bar{y}_{j,r}^{def} \cdot \overset{N}{\underset{k=1}{\overset{\leftrightarrow *}{T}}} \left\{ \overset{*}{S} \left\{ \begin{array}{c} 1 - \tau_k(\bar{x}), \mu_{B_j^k}(\bar{y}_{j,r}^{def}); \\ 1, w_{j,k}^B, p^{imp} \\ w_k^{rule}, p^{agr} \end{array} \right\}; \right\}}{\displaystyle\sum_{r=1}^{R_j} \overset{N}{\underset{k=1}{\overset{\leftrightarrow *}{T}}} \left\{ \overset{*}{S} \left\{ \begin{array}{c} 1 - \tau_k(\bar{x}), \mu_{B_j^k}(\bar{y}_{j,r}^{def}); \\ 1, w_{j,k}^B, p^{imp} \\ w_k^{rule}, p^{agr} \end{array} \right\}; \right\}}
\tag{14.3}
$$

where $\tau_k(\bar{x})$ is the activation level of the rule k. It is determined for the input signals vector $\bar{x}$ and defined as follows:

$$
\tau_k(\bar{x}) = \overset{n}{\underset{i=1}{\overset{\leftrightarrow *}{T}}} \left\{ \mu_{A_i^k}(\bar{x}_i); w_{k,i}^A, p^\tau \right\}
\tag{14.4}
$$

and $\overset{\leftrightarrow *}{T}\{.\}$ and $\overset{\leftrightarrow *}{S}\{.\}$ are Dombi parameterized triangular norms with weights of arguments (Section 14.2.3), p^τ is a shape parameter of t-norm used for aggregation of antecedences, p^{imp} is a shape parameter of t-conorm used for inference, p^{agr} is a shape parameter of t-norm used for aggregation of inferences from rules, and $\bar{y}_{j,r}^{def}$ $(r = 1, \ldots, R_j)$ are discretization points.

Discretization points are points in space Y, which are related to the defuzzification and they are independent of the rule base (14.1). In these points discretization of output fuzzy sets and fuzzy sets obtained in response to the input signals of system $\bar{x}$ is performed. The most frequently used defuzzification methods (Center of area, Center of gravity, Fuzzy mean, Weighted fuzzy mean, Quality method, etc., [270, 391] associate the number of discretization points with the number of output fuzzy sets (rules). In the system considered in this paper, the number of discretization points R_j for any output j does not have to equal the number of rules N. This creates good opportunities for increasing the interpretability and accuracy of the fuzzy system. This issue was discussed in detail in our previous papers [108, 109, 111]. In these papers, detailed information on derivation of the formula (14.3) and linking it with the rule base of the form (14.1) can also be found.

14.2.3. *Aggregation and inference operators*

In this section parameterized Dombi-type triangular norms with weights of arguments, used in Eqs. (14.3) and (14.4), are considered. Their use contributes indirectly to an increase of the interpretability of system (14.3).

This is due to high working precision of these operators, which allows for achieving the expected accuracy of system (14.3) with a smaller number of rules N.

Parameterized Dombi-type triangular norms with weights of arguments have the following form:

$$\begin{cases} \overset{\leftrightarrow^*}{T}\{a;w,p\} = \overset{\leftrightarrow^{*n}}{\underset{i=1}{T}}\left\{\begin{matrix} a_i; \\ w_i, p \end{matrix}\right\} = \left(1 + \left(\sum_{i=1}^{n}\left(\frac{w_i \cdot (1 - a_i)}{1 - w_i \cdot (1 - a_i)}\right)^p\right)^{\frac{1}{p}}\right)^{-1} \\[4ex] \overset{\leftrightarrow^*}{S}\{a;w,p\} = \overset{\leftrightarrow^{*n}}{\underset{i=1}{S}}\left\{\begin{matrix} a_i; \\ w_i, p \end{matrix}\right\} = 1 - \left(1 + \left(\sum_{i=1}^{n}\left(\frac{w_i \cdot a_i}{1 - w_i \cdot a_i}\right)^p\right)^{\frac{1}{p}}\right)^{-1} \end{cases}$$

$$(14.5)$$

where $p > 0$ and parameters $w_1, \ldots, w_n \in [0,1]$ are weights of arguments $a_1, \ldots, a_n \in [0,1]$. Operators of the form (14.5) were formed from the combination of two types of triangular norms. The first type comprises parameterized Dombi-type triangular norms (marked with the symbol $\div$). Their way of working depends on the value of the parameter p. By changing value of the parameter p it is possible to achieve similar behavior to typical non-parametric norms, such as min/max norms, Hamacher norms, Lukasiewicz norms, algebraic norms, etc. Apart from the Dombi-type norms, in the literature many other types of parameterized triangular norms (e.g., Frank, Dubois and Prade, Schweizer and Skalar, Weber, Yager, Yu, etc.) can be found. The second type of triangular norms used in the construction of operators of the form (14.5) are standard triangular norms with weights of arguments (marked with the symbol $*$) [108, 109, 388]. They can be described as follows:

$$
\begin{cases}
T^*\{a; w\} = \underset{i=1}{\overset{n}{T^*}}\{a_i; w_i\} = \underset{i=1}{\overset{n}{T}}\{1 - w_i \cdot (1 - a_i)\} \\[2mm]
S^*\{a; w\} = \underset{i=1}{\overset{n}{S^*}}\{a_i; w_i\} = \underset{i=1}{\overset{n}{S}}\{a_i \cdot w_i\}
\end{cases}
\tag{14.6}
$$

Examples of triangular norms with weights of arguments are standard algebraic norms:

$$
\begin{cases}
T^*\{a; w\} = \prod_{i=1}^{n} (1 + (a_i - 1) \cdot w_i) \\[2mm]
S^*\{a; w\} = 1 - \prod_{i=1}^{n} (1 - a_i \cdot w_i)
\end{cases}
\tag{14.7}
$$

The idea of operation of triangular norms with weights of arguments (especially the idea of reducing arguments with weights equal to 0) can be summarized as follows: $T^*\{a_1, a_2, w_1, 0\} = a_1$, $T\{a_1, a_2\} = T^*\{a_1, a_2, 1, 1\}$, $S^*\{a_1, a_2, w_1, 0\} = a_1$ $S^*\{a_1, a_2, 1, 1\} == S\{a_1, a_2\}$. More detailed information on the operators of the forms (14.5)–(14.7) can be found in our previous papers [108, 109, 388].

14.3. A Hybrid Genetic-Imperialist Algorithm for Automatic Selection of Structure and Parameters of a Fuzzy System

In this section, we focus on a hybrid multi-population algorithm, which was created by combining the genetic algorithm [208] and the imperialist algorithm [43]. It will be denoted as the GIA. The proposed algorithm aims at selection of the structure and parameters of the fuzzy system (14.3). The genetic algorithm is meant to select a fuzzy system structure while the applied imperialist algorithm is meant to select fuzzy system parameters.

The idea of the imperialist algorithm is inspired by the social evolution whereas the idea of the genetic algorithm is inspired by the biological evolution of species. Each individual of a population in the terminology of the imperialist algorithm is a country. Imperialists are selected from these countries. They are countries with the best value of the evaluation function (i.e., the lowest possible value in the case of the considered problem of minimizing an evaluation function).

Imperialists create empires, for which other countries are colonies. Colonies are subject of evolutionary operations referring to the social evolution. These operations are assimilation and revolution. In addition, a binary mutation of the colony is performed (part encoding structure). It is derived from the genetic algorithm. Evolutionary operations change the balance of power of given empires. After this change, a decision is made whether the process of the social evolution should continue, or whether the solution (a fuzzy system encoded in an individual of a population) meeting the stopping criterion of the algorithm has been obtained.

The proposed algorithm belongs to so-called population-based algorithms. They provide a method for solving optimization problems. They can be defined as search procedures based on the mechanisms of natural selection and inheritance and they use the evolutionary principle of survival of the fittest individuals. What differs population algorithms from traditional optimization methods, among others, is that they: (a) do not process task parameters directly, but their encoded form, (b) do not conduct a search starting from a single point, but from a population of points, (c) use only the objective function and not its derivatives, and (d) use probabilistic, not deterministic selection rules. Owing it to the above mentioned features, population algorithms have the advantage over other optimization techniques such as analytical, inspection, random methods, etc. [4, 5, 9, 38, 47, 48, 52, 97, 103, 106, 109, 110, 114, 118, 137, 142, 163, 182, 200, 208, 215, 254, 255, 260, 261, 308, 310, 339, 410, 416, 490].

14.3.1. *Encoding of potential solutions*

Encoding of population of potential solutions used in the algorithm refers to the Pittsburgh approach [216]. A single individual of the population (X_{ch}) is therefore an object that encodes the complete structure of the fuzzy system (14.3) (X_{ch}^{str}) and its parameters (X_{ch}^{par}):

$$X_{ch} = \{X_{ch}^{str}, X_{ch}^{par}\} \qquad (14.8)$$

Part X_{ch}^{str} of the individual X_{ch}^{str} encodes the whole structure of the fuzzy system (14.3) in a binary form, which has the following form:

$$X_{ch}^{str} = \left\{ \begin{array}{c} x_1, \ldots, x_n \\ A_1^1, \ldots, A_n^1, \ldots, A_1^{N\,max}, \ldots, A_n^{N\,max} \\ B_1^1, \ldots, B_m^1, \ldots, B_1^{N\,max}, \ldots, B_m^{N\,max} \\ \text{rule}_1, \ldots, \text{rule}_{N\,max} \\ \bar{y}_{1,1}^{def}, \ldots, \bar{y}_{1,R\,max}^{def}, \ldots, \bar{y}_{m,1}^{def}, \ldots, \bar{y}_{m,R\,max}^{def} \end{array} \right\}$$

$$= \{X_{ch,1}^{str}, \ldots, X_{ch,L^{str}}^{str}\} \qquad (14.9)$$

where ch = 1; ::::; Npop is the index of an individual in a population, Npop is the number of individuals in a population, Nmax is the maximum (allowed) number of rules in system (14.3) (selected individually for the considered problem), Rmax is the maximum (allowed) number of discretization points in system (14.3) (also selected individually for the considered problem) and L^{str} is the number of the individual components X_{ch}^{str} (referred to as genes from now on), which is determined as follows:

$$L^{str} = N\max \cdot (n + m + 1) + n + R\max \cdot m \qquad (14.10)$$

In the encoding procedure of X_{ch}^{str} it is assumed that each individual of the population encodes the maximum number of rules Nmax and discretization points Rmax. The algorithm searches the real number of system (14.3) rules in the range $N \in [1, N\max]$ and the real number of discretization points in the range $R_j \in [1, R\max]$ $(j = 1, \ldots m)$. Therefore, it is a different approach than in the conventional methods of learning, in which the user (mostly using the trial-and-error method) had to clearly indicate N and R_j.

The principle adopted in the encoding procedure X_{ch}^{str} is such that the gene with value 0 of the individual X_{ch}^{str} excludes the associated element from the target system structure (14.3) and vice versa. This element can be: a rule (rule$_k$, $k = 1; : : : ; N$max), an input fuzzy set (A_i^k, $i = 1; \ldots; n, k = 1; \ldots; N$max), an output fuzzy set (B_j^k; $j = 1; \ldots; m; k = 1; \ldots; N$max), an input ($x_i$, $i = 1; \ldots; n$) and a discretization point ($\bar{y}^r, r = 1; \ldots; R$max).

Part X_{ch}^{par} of the individual X_{ch} encodes the real parameters of the fuzzy system and it has the following form: $\bar{x}_{1,1}^A, \sigma_{1,1}^A \ldots, \bar{x}_{n,1}^A, \sigma_{n,1}^A, .$

$$X_{ch}^{par} = \left\{ \begin{array}{c} \bar{x}_{1,1}^A, \sigma_{1,1}^A, \ldots, \bar{x}_{n,1}^A, \sigma_{n,1}^A, \ldots \\ \bar{x}_{N\max}^A, \sigma_{1,N\max}^A, \ldots, \bar{x}_{n,N\max}^A, \sigma_{n,N\max}^A, \\ \bar{y}_{1,1}^B, \sigma_{1,1}^B, \ldots, \bar{y}_{m,1}^B, \sigma_{m,1}^B, \ldots \\ \bar{y}_{1,N\max}^B, \sigma_{1,N\max}^B, \ldots, \bar{y}_{m,N\max}^B, \sigma_{m,N\max}^B, \\ w_{1,1}^A, \ldots, w_{1,n}^A, \ldots, w_{N\max,1}^A, \ldots, w_{N\max,n}^A, \\ w_{1,1}^B, \ldots, w_{m,1}^B, \ldots, w_{1,N\max}^B, \ldots, w_{m,N\max}^B, \\ w_1^{rule}, \ldots, w_{N\max}^{rule}, \\ p^r, p^{imp}, p^{agr}, \\ \bar{y}_{1,1}^{def}, \bar{y}_{1,R\max}^{def}, \ldots, \bar{y}_{m,1}^{def}, \bar{y}_{m,R\max}^{def}, \end{array} \right\}$$

$$= \{ X_{ch,1}^{par}, \ldots, X_{ch,L^{par}}^{par} \} \qquad (14.11)$$

where $\{\bar{x}^A_{i,k}, \bar{\sigma}^A_{i,k}\}$ are membership function parameters (14.2) of input fuzzy sets $A^k_1, \ldots, A^k_n$, $\{\bar{y}^B_{i,k}, \bar{\sigma}^B_{i,k}\}$ membership function parameters (14.2) of output fuzzy sets $B^k_1, \ldots, B^k_m$ and L^{par} is the number of components of individual $X^{\mathrm{par}}_{\mathrm{ch}}$, determined as follows:

$$L^{\mathrm{par}} = N \max \cdot (3 \cdot n + 3 \cdot m + 1) + R \max \cdot m + 3 \qquad (14.12)$$

In the encoding procedure of $X^{\mathrm{par}}_{\mathrm{ch}}$ it is assumed that only genes $X^{\mathrm{par}}_{\mathrm{ch}}$, whose counterparts in $X^{\mathrm{str}}_{\mathrm{ch}}$ are equal to 1, are considered in the construction of system (14.3). Moreover, analyzing $X^{\mathrm{str}}_{\mathrm{ch}}$ of the form (14.9) the actual number of inputs encoded in the individual X_{ch} can be easily indicated;

$$\mathrm{noi}(\mathrm{ch}) = \sum_{i=1}^{n} X^{\mathrm{str}}_{\mathrm{ch}}\{x_i\} \qquad (14.13)$$

where $X^{\mathrm{str}}_{\mathrm{ch}}\{x_i\}$ is the parameter of the individual $X^{\mathrm{str}}_{\mathrm{ch}}$ associated with the input x_i. The adoption of this notation greatly facilitated, among others, notation of interpretability criteria considered in Section 14.4. Similarly to noi (ch), the actual number of rules nor (ch), the actual number of discretization points nodfo (ch; j) for the input j, the number of input fuzzy sets noifs (ch), the number of output fuzzy sets noofs (ch), and the number of output fuzzy sets noofsfo (ch; j) for the output j can be determined. These functions are used in Section 14.4.

14.3.2. *Evaluation of potential solutions*

As already mentioned, each individual in the population (X_{ch}) encodes parameters $X^{\mathrm{par}}_{\mathrm{ch}}$ (formula (14.11)) and structure $X^{\mathrm{str}}_{\mathrm{ch}}$ (formula (14.9)) of a single system (14.3). The purpose of the algorithm is to minimize the value of the evaluation function specified for the individual X_{ch} in the following way:

$$ff(X_{\mathrm{ch}}) = T^* \left\{ \begin{matrix} ff\,\mathrm{acc}(X_{\mathrm{ch}}), ff\,\mathrm{int}(X_{\mathrm{ch}}) \\ w_{ff\mathrm{acc}}, w_{ff\,\mathrm{int}} \end{matrix} \right\} \qquad (14.14)$$

where component ffacc (X_{ch}) specifies the percentage accuracy of system (14.3), component ffint (X_{ch}) specifies interpretability of system (14.3) according to the adopted interpretability criteria, T f g is a weighted algebraic triangular norm of the form (14.7), $w_{ff\text{acc}}$ $[0;1]$ represents weight of the component ffacc (X_{ch}) and $w_{ff\text{ int}}$ $[0;1]$ represents weight of the component ffint (X_{ch}). Values of weights $w_{ff\text{acc}}$ and $w_{ff\text{ int}}$ result from expectations of the user regarding the ratio between the accuracy of system (14.3) and its interpretability. Component ffint (X_{ch}) takes into account interpretability criteria proposed in Section 14.4. Their aggregation is realized as follows:

$$ff \ \text{int}(X_{\text{ch}}) = T^* \left\{ \begin{matrix} ff\,\text{acc}_A(X_{\text{ch}}), ff \ \text{int}_B(X_{\text{ch}}), \ldots; \\ w_{ff \ \text{int } A}, w_{ff \ \text{int}|B}, \cdots \end{matrix} \right\} \qquad (14.15)$$

where $ff \ \text{int}_A(\cdot)$ $ff \ \text{int}_B(\cdot), \ldots$ are functions representing considered interpretability criteria defined in Section 14.4, $w_{ff \ \text{int } A} \in [0,1]$, $w_{ff \ \text{int } B} \in [0,1], \ldots$ are weights of importance of function $ff \ \text{int}_A(\cdot) ff \ \text{int}_B(\cdot), \ldots$ and $T^*\{\cdot\}$ is weighted algebraic triangular norm of the form (14.7). The values of weights in Eq. (14.15) can be selected on the basis of suggestions given in the paper [34], which was done in our simulations.

In most applications, the objective adopted in the design phase is to obtain a single fuzzy system. It is expected that the system will be characterized by good accuracy and interpretability. But if it was necessary to obtain a set of solutions with different proportions of accuracy-interpretability (in terms of Eq. (14.14)), then possibilities offered by the methods based on Pareto fronts [119] could be used instead of criteria aggregation.

14.3.3. *Processing of potential solutions*

The hybrid genetic-imperialist algorithm works as shown in the block diagram presented in Fig. 14.1. The purpose of the algorithm is a systematic improvement of solutions in the sense of the adopted evaluation function (e.g., function in the form (14.14)). The considered

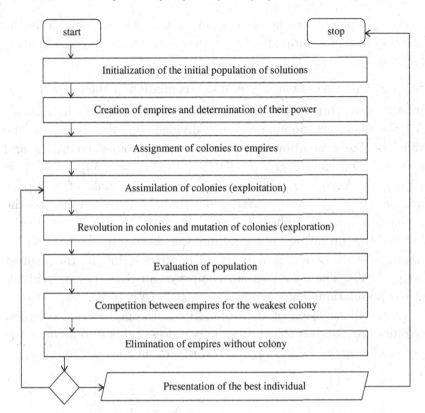

Fig. 14.1. Block scheme of the hybrid genetic-imperialist algorithm for automatic selection of structure and parameters of a fuzzy system.

algorithm uses encoding presented in Section 14.3.1 and the way of evaluating of individuals presented in Section 14.3.2.

Step 1. Initialization of the algorithm.

Initialization of a population is performed before the start of the algorithm. In the basic initialization procedure of the population the genes of all individuals (countries) X_{ch}, $ch = 1; ::::; N_{pop}$ can be initialized randomly. Thus, binary values of the genes of the part X_{ch}^{str} encoding fuzzy system structure can be drawn from the set $X_{ch}^{str} \in \{0; 1\}$, where the gene index $g = 1; : : : ; L^{str}$. Value 1 of the gene means that the connection associated with this gene occurs in the fuzzy system structure. Real values of genes of the part $X_{\text{ch}}^{\text{par}}$ encoding fuzzy system parameters can be drawn from the range determined individually for the problem under consideration ($X_{\text{ch}.g}^{\text{par}} \in [\underline{X}_g^{\text{par}}, \bar{X}_g^{\text{par}}]$).

Step 2. Creation of empires and determination of their power.

In the procedure used for creation of empires all individuals X_{ch} of a given population are divided on the basis of the value of the evaluation function into two groups: countries and empires. The empire group (denoted as $Xi_k = \{Xi_k^{\text{str}}, Xi_k^{\text{par}}\} = \{Xi_{k,1}, \ldots, Xi_{k,L^{\text{str}}+L^{\text{par}}}\}$) contains those individuals of the population ($k = 1; : : : ; Ni$) which have the best value of the evaluation function. The number of empires Ni can be set freely, but in the literature a suggestion has been found that $Ni = \text{round}(\frac{N\text{pop}}{10})$ (round($\cdot$) is a function approximating to the nearest integer) [43]. The colony group comprises all the other individuals of the population. Their number is equal to $N\text{pop }Ni$.

After the division of the population into empires and colonies, colonies are assigned to empires. This process takes into account the power of empires P_k ($k = 1; \ldots; Ni$) determined as follows:

$$Pi_k = \left| \frac{ff(Xi_k) - \max\limits_{s=1,\ldots,Ni}\{ff(Xi_s)\}}{\sum\limits_{q=1}^{N_i}(ff(Xi_q) - \max\limits_{s=1,\ldots,Ni}\{ff(Xi_s)\}} \right| \tag{14.16}$$

where the numerator and the denominator take into account the normalized value of the evaluation function for the problem of minimizing the value of the evaluation function. $Nic_k = \text{int}(Ni \cdot Pi_k)$ colonies are randomly assigned to each empire. Colonies assigned to the empire k will be denoted as:

$$Xic_{k,r} = \{Xic_{k,r}^{\text{str}}, Xic_{k,r}^{\text{par}}\} = \{Xic_{k,r,1}, \ldots, Xic_{k,r,L^{\text{str}}+L^{\text{par}}}\} \tag{14.17}$$

where $k = 1; : : : ; Ni$ and $r = 1; : : : ; Nic_k$. The system of empires and their colonies created in this step is subject to changes described in the subsequent steps.

Step 3. Changes in colonies.

The purpose of making changes in colonies is exploitation and exploration of the search space of considerations. Exploitation is meant to make colonies similar to empires (as individuals with the best values of the evaluation function) for which they have been assigned. This is realized using an assimilation operator typical of the imperialist algorithm. On the other hand, exploration is meant to introduce random changes in the population allowing for finding unknown good solutions. This is implemented using a revolution operator typical of the imperialist algorithm, and a mutation operator typical of the genetic algorithm.

The assimilation operator processes the part Xc_r^{par} of individual Xc_r, which encode fuzzy system parameters. It allows colonies to move toward empires, but at the same time it introduces a small o set by a randomly selected angle. Its operation can be defined as follows:

$$Xic_{k,r,g}^{par} := \{Xi_{k,g}^{par}, Xic_{k,r,g}^{par}\} \cdot U_r(0,2) \cdot U_g(-\gamma, \gamma) \qquad (14.18)$$

where U_r (0; 2) is a random number from the range (0; 2) generated for the purposes of assimilation of the colony r, $U_g(-\gamma, \gamma)$ is a random number from the range (;) generated individually for each gene g of the colony r, > 0 is a parameter of the algorithm determining intensity of the random 0 set. The assimilation operator allows empires to keep their strong position as good solutions in the sense of the evaluation function value. It also prevents the algorithm from making those changes in individuals of the population which would make it impossible to find the optimal solution in terms of the adopted criteria.

After the assimilation process, revolution and mutation of the colonies are performed in the population. In contrast to the assimilation, revolution and mutation only affect a subset of the genes of the colony. It is implemented in such way that for each gene of each colony a real number from the range [0; 1] is drawn. If the number value is lower than so-called revolution and mutation probability $p_{rm} \in [0.1]$ (being parameter of the algorithm and working in a similar way to the probability of mutation in genetic algorithms), then this gene is subject to evolution or mutation. Revolution mainly refers to the genes encoding fuzzy system parameters (Xc_r^{par}) while mutation, on the other hand, refers to the genes encoding the fuzzy system structure (Xc_r^{str}). The operation of the revolution operator can be expressed as follows:

$$Xic_{k,r,g}^{\text{par}} := \{\underline{X}_g^{\text{par}} + (\bar{X}_g^{\text{par}} - \underline{X}_g^{\text{par}}) \cdot U_g(0,1) \tag{14.19}$$

where $\underline{X}_g^{\text{par}}$ is the minimum allowed value of the gene g $\bar{X}_g^{\text{par}}$ is the maximum allowed value of the gene g.

On the other hand, operation of the mutation operator consists in changing the value of the binary gene encoding the information on using (or blocking) of the associated component of a fuzzy system to the opposite information (i.e., from 1 to 0 or vice versa). Since the revolution and mutation affect colonies significantly, the value of parameter p_{rm} cannot be too large so as not to cause degeneration of the population.

Step 4. Changes in empires.

Changes in empires are implemented in two stages. The first one involves competition of each empire Xi_k with its best colony $(Xic_{k,r})$. The base of this competition is the value of the evaluation function. The second stage involves moving the weakest colony of the weakest empire to another empire. The process of determining of the weakest empire takes into account the total power of empires and the probability of the weakest colony acquisition, which is determined on the basis of that power. The total power of empires is determined as follows:

$$C_k = f\!f(Xi_k + \zeta \cdot \frac{\sum\limits_{r=1}^{Nci_k} f\!f(Xic_{k,r})}{Nci_k} \tag{14.20}$$

is $\zeta \in [0,1]$ is a coefficient of colony importance (algorithm parameter). With the total power of empires having been computed, the probability of acquiring of the weakest colony is determined for each empire (similar as in formula (14.16)):

$$Pic_k = \left| \frac{C_k - \max\limits_{s=1,\ldots,Ni} C_s}{\sum\limits_{q=1}^{N_i} C_q - \max\limits_{s=1,\ldots,Ni} C_s} \right| \qquad (14.21)$$

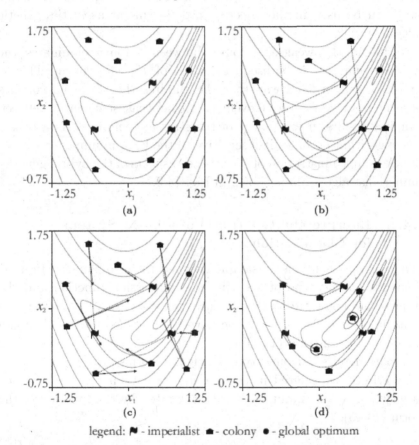

legend: ⚑ - imperialist ⬟ - colony ● - global optimum

Fig. 14.2. Illustration of the selected aspects of the operation of the hybrid genetic-imperialist algorithm in a two-dimensional space shown for the Rosenbrock function (determined by the formula $f(x) = (1x_1)^2 + 10x_2x_1^{2\,2}$, with the minimum in point $x_1 = 1$; $x_2 = 1$): (a) division of the population into imperialists and colonies, (b) creation of empires, (c) assimilation and revolution, (d) acquisition of empires by colonies with a better value of the evaluation function (denoted in circles).

The sum of probabilities of the weakest colony acquisition for all empires is equal to 1. For the most powerful empire this probability is the highest and for the weakest one it equals 0. To indicate the empire which will acquire the weakest colony, we can use the roulette wheel method. Then, each empire has to be associated with a segment of the wheel, whose size is proportional to the probability of acquiring the worst colony Pic_k. The virtual roulette wheel prepared in this way can be used in the selection process similar as in the genetic algorithm [392].

Moving the weakest colonies between empires eliminates the weakest empires in subsequent steps of the algorithm. This is implemented in such way that the empires that have no colonies are removed. Moreover, movement of the weakest colonies between empires results in weakening of the strongest empires. As a result, the algorithm becomes less sensitive to the local minima.

A sample illustration of the selected aspects of the hybrid genetic-imperialist algorithm is shown in Fig. 14.2.

14.4.   Interpretability Criteria of a Fuzzy System for Classification

This section contains a sample way of their implementation. It depends on the type of the applied membership function and the type of the aggregation and inference operators used. Due to this, the criteria described in this section have been defined for the Gaussian membership function (14.2) and the operators built on the basis of the parameterized Dombi-type triangular norms of the form (14.5). The criteria considered in this section have been designed in such a way so as to be minimized and aggregated by the function of the form (14.15).

14.4.1.   *Complexity evaluation criterion*

This criterion allows us to evaluate complexity of the fuzzy system (14.3). It bases on the genes analysis of the individual X_{ch}^{str} encoding the structure of the form (14.9). It takes into account the number of fuzzy rules of the form (14.1), input fuzzy sets, output fuzzy sets, inputs and discretization points. The method of operation of

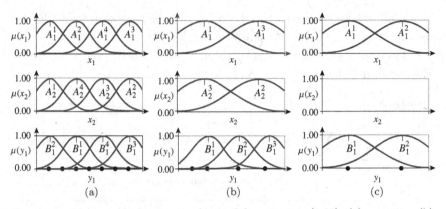

Fig. 14.3. Three exemplary cases obtained for criterion (1.22): (a) negative, (b) intermediate, (c) preferred (low complexity of system (1.3), low criterion value). Discretization points are denoted as black circles.

the considered criterion is shown in Fig. 14.3 and it is expressed as follows:

$$ff \, \mathrm{int}_A(X_{\mathrm{ch}}) = \frac{noifs(\mathrm{ch}) + noofs(\mathrm{ch}) + nod(\mathrm{ch})}{N\mathrm{max} \cdot (n + m) + R\mathrm{max} \cdot m} \tag{14.22}$$

where the functions *fnoifs* ( ) ; *noofs* ( ) ; *nod* ( )*g* have been considered.

14.4.2. *Fuzzy sets readability evaluation criterion*

In this section, two criteria related to readability of fuzzy sets are proposed. The first one concerns the position of fuzzy sets while the other refers to the consistency of their shape. The criteria have been adapted to the membership function (14.2) considered in this chapter, but they can be easily adapted to some other membership functions.

Fuzzy sets position evaluation criterion.

The criterion under consideration makes it possible to evaluate the correctness of the input and output fuzzy sets' distribution. Incorrect distribution of fuzzy sets results from their overlapping and their remoteness. The distribution of fuzzy sets can be evaluated, among others, by analyzing the intersections of adjacent fuzzy sets. The considered criterion takes into account two points of intersection for each pair of adjacent fuzzy sets. The use of the first intersection point allows us to assess the distance between fuzzy sets while the use of the other allows us to assess overlapping.

The method of operation of the considered criterion is shown in Fig. 14.5 and it is expressed as follows:

$f \, \mathrm{int}_B(X_{\mathrm{ch}})$

$$= \frac{\frac{1}{2} \cdot \displaystyle\sum_{i=1}^{noi(\mathrm{ch})} \sum_{k=1}^{noifsfi(\mathrm{ch},i)-1} \left(|c_{\mathrm{int}B} - \mathrm{interMax}(A_i^k, A_i^{k+1})| + \mathrm{interMin}(A_i^k, A_i^{k+1}) \right)}{\dfrac{\displaystyle\sum_{i=1}^{noi(\mathrm{ch})} \left(noisfi(\mathrm{ch},i) - 1 \right)}{2}}$$

$$+ \frac{\frac{1}{2} \cdot \displaystyle\sum_{j=1}^{m} \sum_{k=1}^{noofsfo(\mathrm{ch},j)-1} \left(|c_{\mathrm{int}B} - \mathrm{interMax}(B_j^k, B_j^{k+1})| + \mathrm{interMin}(B_j^k, B_j^{k+1}) \right)}{\dfrac{\displaystyle\sum_{j=1}^{m} \left(noofsfo(\mathrm{ch},j) - 1 \right)}{2}}$$

$$(14.23)$$

where $c_{\mathrm{int}\,B} \in (0,1)$ determines the desired value of the membership function at the intersection point between two adjacent fuzzy sets (in the simulations we assumed the value 0.5), the functions $\{noi(\cdot), noifsfi(\cdot)\, mnoofsfo(\cdot)\}$ are considered in Section 14.3.1, the functions $\{\mathrm{interMax}(\cdot), \mathrm{interMin}(\cdot)\}$ determine the values of two intersection points of the fuzzy sets (Fig. 14.4). For the fuzzy sets expressed by the Gaussian function of the form (14.2) they take the following form:

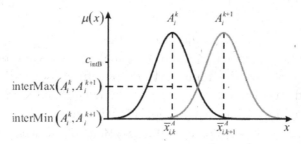

Fig. 14.4. Graphical interpretation of the intersection points of fuzzy sets and the desired intersection points of fuzzy sets.

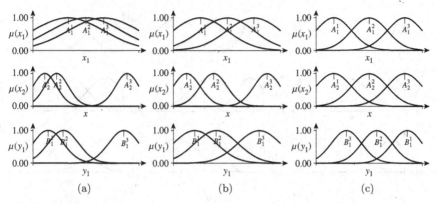

Fig. 14.5. Three exemplary cases obtained for criterion (14.23): (a) negative, (b) intermediate, (c) preferred (correct distribution of fuzzy sets, low criterion value).

$$\begin{cases} \mathrm{interMin}(A_i^k, A_i^{k+1}) = \exp\left(-\dfrac{(X_{\mathrm{ch}}^{\mathrm{sup}\,p}\{\bar{x}_{i,k}^A\} - X_{\mathrm{ch}}^{\mathrm{sup}\,p}\{\bar{x}_{i,k+1}^A\})^2}{(X_{\mathrm{ch}}^{\mathrm{sup}\,p}\{\sigma_{i,k}^A\} - X_{\mathrm{ch}}^{\mathrm{sup}\,p}\{\sigma_{i,k+1}^A\})^2}\right), \\[2mm] \mathrm{interMax}(A_i^k, A_i^{k+1}) = \exp\left(-\dfrac{(X_{\mathrm{ch}}^{\mathrm{sup}\,p}\{\bar{x}_{i,k}^A\} - X_{\mathrm{ch}}^{\mathrm{sup}\,p}\{\bar{x}_{i,k+1}^A\})^2}{(X_{\mathrm{ch}}^{\mathrm{sup}\,p}\{\sigma_{i,k}^A\} - X_{\mathrm{ch}}^{\mathrm{sup}\,p}\{\sigma_{i,k+1}^A\})^2}\right) \end{cases}$$

$$(14.24)$$

where $X_{\mathrm{ch}}^{\mathrm{sup}\,p}$ is a temporary set of the fuzzy system parameters containing the parameters of the input and output fuzzy sets sorted ascending in relation to the centers of these sets:

$$X_{\mathrm{ch}}^{\mathrm{supp}}$$

$$= \begin{cases} \bar{x}_{1,1}^A, \sigma_{1,1}^A, \ldots, \bar{x}_{1,noifsfi(\mathrm{ch},1)}^A, \sigma_{1,noifsfi(\mathrm{ch},1)}^A, \ldots, \\ \bar{x}_{noi(\mathrm{ch}),1}^A, \sigma_{noi(\mathrm{ch}),1}^A, \ldots, \bar{x}_{noi(\mathrm{ch}),noifsfi(\mathrm{ch},noi(\mathrm{ch}))}^A, \\ \sigma_{noi(\mathrm{ch}),noifsfi(\mathrm{ch},noi(\mathrm{ch}))}^A, \\ \bar{y}_{1,1}^B, \sigma_{1,1}^B, \ldots, \bar{y}_{1,noofsfo(\mathrm{ch},1)}^B, \sigma_{1,noofsfo(\mathrm{ch},1)}^B, \ldots, \\ \bar{y}_{m,1}^B, \sigma_{m,1}^B, \ldots, \bar{y}_{m,noofsfo(\mathrm{ch},m)}^B, \sigma_{m,noofsfo(\mathrm{ch},m)}^B \end{cases}$$

$$(14.25)$$

The criterion (14.23) takes values close to 0 when values of the function $\mathrm{interMax}(\cdot) \approx c_{\mathrm{int}\,B}$ and values of the function $\mathrm{interMax}(\cdot) \approx 0$ (Fig. 14.4). In this case, the position of fuzzy sets can be considered as readable.

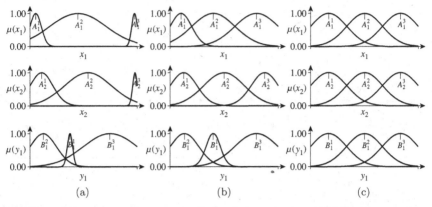

Fig. 14.6. Three exemplary cases obtained for criterion (14.26): (a) negative, (b) intermediate, (c) preferred (minor differences between the widths of fuzzy sets, low criterion value).

14.4.2.1. *Criterion for assessing similarity of fuzzy sets width*

The considered criterion is a cohesion measure of the widths of input and output fuzzy sets. It is of a great importance for semantic readability of the fuzzy system (14.3) rule base, because it facilitates the understanding of the rule-based notation (14.1).

The method of operation of this criterion is shown in Fig. 14.6 and it is expressed as follows:

$$ffint_C(X_{ch})$$

$$= \frac{1}{2} \cdot \left(\frac{\displaystyle\sum_{i=1}^{noi(ch)} \sum_{k1=1}^{noifsfi(ch,i)-1} \sum_{k2=k1+1}^{noifsfi(ch,i)} \text{sim}_{\text{width}}(A_i^{k1}, A_i^{k2})}{\displaystyle\sum_{i=1}^{noi(ch)} \binom{noifsfi(ch,i)}{2}} \right.$$

$$\left. + \frac{\displaystyle\sum_{j=1}^{noi(ch)} \sum_{k1=1}^{noofsfi(ch,j)-1} \sum_{k2=k1+1}^{noofsfi(ch,j)} \text{sim}_{\text{width}}(B_j^{k1}, B_j^{k2})}{\displaystyle\sum_{j=1}^{m} \binom{noofsfi(ch,j)}{2}} \right)$$

$$(14.26)$$

where $\binom{n}{k}$ is the Newton's binomial, the function $\mathrm{sim_{width}}(\cdot)$ is used to determine similarity of width of the membership function of fuzzy sets. For the sets expressed by the Gaussian function (14.2) it may take the following form:

$$\mathrm{sim_{width}}(A_i^{k1}, A_i^{k2}) = \frac{|X_{\mathrm{ch}}^{\mathrm{supp}}\{\sigma_{i,k1}^A\} - X_{\mathrm{ch}}^{\mathrm{supp}}\{\sigma_{i,k2}^A\}|}{\max\{X_{\mathrm{ch}}^{\mathrm{supp}}\{\sigma_{i,k1}^A\}, X_{\mathrm{ch}}^{\mathrm{supp}}\{\sigma_{i,k2}^A\}\}} \quad (14.27)$$

where $X_{\mathrm{ch}}^{\mathrm{supp}}$ is a temporary set of the system parameters of the form (14.25).

14.4.3. *Fuzzy rules readability evaluation criteria*

In this section, two criteria related to the readability of fuzzy rules are presented: the criterion considering uniformity of covering data points with input fuzzy sets and the criterion limiting the number of simultaneously activated fuzzy rules.

Criterion for assessing coverage of the data space by input fuzzy sets.

The considered criterion allows one to evaluate matching of input fuzzy sets to the input data. For properly positioned input fuzzy sets associated with the input i, the sum of memberships determined for the signal given on the input i is equal to 1. This assumption is valid for all system inputs (14.3) and it is evaluated in the context of the whole learning sequence $\{\bar{x}_z, d_z\}$ $(z = 1, \ldots, Z)$.

The method of operation of the considered criterion is shown in Fig. 14.7 and it is expressed as follows:

$$f\!f\mathrm{int}_D(X_{\mathrm{ch}})$$

$$= \frac{\displaystyle\sum_{z=1}^{Z}\sum_{i=1}^{n}\left(X_{\mathrm{ch}}^{\mathrm{str}}\{x_i\} \cdot \max\left\{0, \mathrm{neg}_Z\left(\sum_{k=1}^{N\,\max}\left(\frac{X_{\mathrm{ch}}^{\mathrm{str}}\{\mathrm{rule}_k\}\cdot}{\mu_{A_i^k}(\bar{x}_{z,i}^L)}\right)\right)\right\}\right)}{Z \cdot noi(\mathrm{ch})}$$

$$(14.28)$$

where $\mathrm{neg}_Z(\cdot)$ is Zadeh's negation ($\mathrm{neg}_Z(a) = 1 - a$), $\bar{x}_{z,i}^L$ is the value of input signal i from the set z of learning sequence.

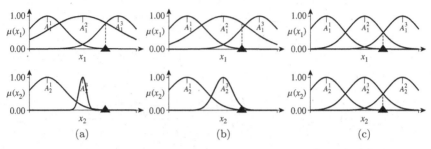

Fig. 14.7. Three exemplary cases obtained for criterion (14.28): (a) negative, (b) intermediate, (c) preferred (good matching of fuzzy sets to the data, low criterion value). Location of the signals coming from the learning sequence sample is denoted as a triangle.

Criterion (14.28) takes values close to 0 when for each set from the learning sequence the sum of its membership in input fuzzy sets is equal to 1 or more. In this case uniformity of coverage of the data space by input fuzzy sets can be regarded as satisfactory. The criterion of the form (14.28) is complementary to the criterion of the form (14.26) related to similarity of fuzzy sets width and the criterion (14.23) related to the readability of fuzzy sets position.

14.4.3.1. *Criterion for assessing fuzzy rules activity*

The considered criterion makes it possible to evaluate activation level of the rules (14.1) in system (14.3). The proper rule activation level is achieved when for each set from the learning sequence activation of a single rule from the rule base occurs and activation of the other rules is minimal. Activation level of the rule k of system (14.3) is expressed using Eq. (14.4).

The method of operation of the considered criterion is shown in Fig. 14.8 and it is expressed as follows:

$$ff\mathrm{int}_E(X_{\mathrm{ch}}) = \mathrm{neg}_Z\left(\frac{1}{Z}\cdot\sum_{z=1}^{Z}\frac{\max\limits_{k=1,\ldots,N_{\max}}\{X_{\mathrm{ch}}^{\mathrm{str}}\{\mathrm{rule}_k\}\cdot\tau_k(\bar{x}_z)\}}{\sum\limits_{k=1}^{N\max}X_{\mathrm{ch}}^{\mathrm{str}}\{\mathrm{rule}_k\}\cdot\tau_k(\bar{x}_z)}\right)$$

$$(14.29)$$

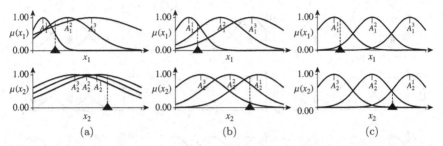

Fig. 14.8. Three exemplary cases obtained for criterion (14.29): (a) negative, (b) intermediate, (c) preferred (a small number of fuzzy rules activated at the same time, low criterion value). Location of signals coming from the learning sequence sample is denoted as a triangle.

where $\tau_k(\cdot)$ is the activity level of the rule k for the set from the learning sequence z (e.g., expressed by the formula (14.4) for system of the form (14.3)).

14.4.4. *Criterion for assessing the readability of weights values in the fuzzy rule base*

The use of weights in the rules base of the fuzzy system has many advantages: (a) it increases the flexibility of the problem description, (b) it allows for the introduction of a hierarchy of importance in the rules base, and (c) it increases the accuracy of the system [108, 217, 388, 414]. However, weights in the rule base may sometimes affect readability of fuzzy systems [374]. In system of the form (14.3), weights have specified interpretation in the context of rules of the form (14.1) and dedicated aggregation operators of the forms (14.5) and (14.6), used for their processing. Therefore, it seems that this usage of weights positively affects the readability of system (14.3).

The considered criterion allows us to evaluate readability of weights values from the rule base of the form (14.1) of system (14.3). Preferred values of weights are those which are close to the values of the set $f0:0;\ 0:5;\ 1:0g$. Then, they can be easily labeled as: not important, important, and very important.

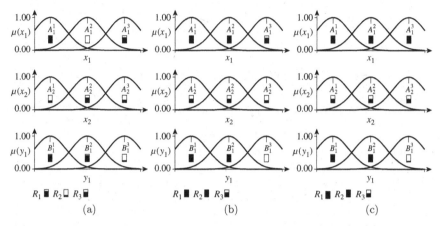

Fig. 14.9. Three exemplary cases obtained for criterion (14.30): (a) negative, (b) intermediate, (c) preferred (good readability of weights, low criterion value). Weights' values are denoted as rectangles. Black rectangles indicate value of weight equal to 1.0 and white ones indicate value of weight equal to 0.0.

The method of operation of the considered criterion is shown in Fig. 14.9 and it is expressed as follows:

$$
\begin{aligned}
&f\!f\mathrm{int}_F(X_{\mathrm{ch}}) \\
&= \mathrm{neg}_Z \left(\frac{1}{noifs(\mathrm{ch}) + noofs(\mathrm{ch}) + nor(\mathrm{ch})} \right. \\
&\qquad \cdot \sum_{k=1}^{N\,\max} X_{\mathrm{ch}}^{\mathrm{str}}\{\mathrm{rule}_k\} \\
&\qquad\quad \left(\sum_{i=1}^{n} X_{\mathrm{ch}}^{\mathrm{str}}\{x_i\} \cdot X_{\mathrm{ch}}^{\mathrm{str}}\{A_i^k\} \cdot \mu_w(w_{i,k}^A) \right. \\
&\qquad\quad \left. + \sum_{j=1}^{m} X_{\mathrm{ch}}^{\mathrm{str}}\{B_j^k\} \cdot \mu_w(w_{i,k}^B) \right. \\
&\qquad\quad \left.\left. + \sum_{k=1}^{N\,\max} \mu_w(w_k^{rule}) \right)\right)
\end{aligned}
$$

$$(14.30)$$

where $\mu_w(\cdot)$ is a function promoting obtaining the values of 0.0, 0.5 and 1.0 expressed by the formula:

$$
\mu_w(x) = \begin{cases}
\dfrac{a - x}{a} & \text{for } x \in [0, a] \\[2mm]
\dfrac{x - a}{b - a} & \text{for } x \in (a, b] \\[2mm]
\dfrac{c - x}{c - b} & \text{for } x \in (b, c] \\[2mm]
\dfrac{x - c}{1 - c} & \text{for } x \in (c, 1]
\end{cases}
\tag{14.31}
$$

where $a = 0.25$, $b = 0.50$, and $c = 0.75$.

The criterion (14.30) takes values close to 0 when all weights take the values close to the values from the set $\{0.0, 0.5, 1.0\}$.

14.4.5. *Criterion for assessing the readability of aggregation and inference operators*

The considered criterion allows one to evaluate readability of the shape parameter of parametrized triangular norms with weights of arguments of the form (14.5) described in Section 14.2.3. In system (14.3) these norms are used for aggregation of antecedences (they have a parameter p), generation of inferences from the rules (they have a parameter p^{imp}) and aggregation of inferences from the rules (they have a parameter p^{agr}). The precision of their operation can usually achieve a better accuracy of the system [108, 151, 391]. This allows for a better use of abilities of the rule base (14.1) without substantially increasing the number of rules. Moreover, application of the norms of the form (14.5) facilitates the selection of aggregation operators for system (14.3), which takes place automatically by changing the shape parameter and not by the trial-and-error method.

The readable parameter of the norms (14.5) is the one for which norms (14.5) approximate the shape of the typical, nonparametric

Table 14.1. A set of values of the parameter of Dombi-type parametrized triangular norms of the form (1.5), for which their shape approximates the shape of typical and non-para-metric triangular norms.

Parameter value	Non-parametrized norm	Similarity
$p = 0.00$	Drastic	Full
$p = 0.43$	Algebraic	High
$p = 0.71$	Lukasiewicz	High
$p = 1.00$	Hamacher	Full
$p \to \infty$	Min/max	Full

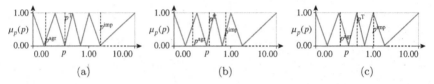

(a)   (b)   (c)

Fig. 14.10. Three exemplary cases obtained for criterion (14.32): (a) negative, (b) intermediate, (c) preferred (good readability of parameters of Dombi-type norm, low criterion value).

triangular norms. This is because it is assumed that operation of nonparametric norms (e.g., minimum/maximum operator) is more intuitive. Table 14.1 contains a set of selected values of the parameter of Dombi-type parametrized triangular norms of the form (14.5), for which their shape approximates the shape of typical and non-parametric triangular norms [242]. The data presented in the table were generated for the two-argument norms with an accuracy of 0.01.

The method of operation of the considered criterion is shown in Fig. 14.10 and it is expressed as follows:

$$ff\ \mathrm{int}_G(X_{\mathrm{ch}}) = \mathrm{neg}_z \left(\frac{1}{3} \cdot \left(\begin{array}{l} \mu_p(X_{\mathrm{ch}}^{\mathrm{par}}\{p^\tau\}) \\ + \mu_p(X_{\mathrm{ch}}^{\mathrm{par}}\{p^{\mathrm{imp}}\}) \\ + \mu_p(X_{\mathrm{ch}}^{\mathrm{par}}\{p^{\mathrm{agr}}\}) \end{array} \right) \right) \qquad (14.32)$$

where $\mu_p(\cdot)$ is a function promoting obtaining the expected values, adapted to the type of the triangular norms applied. Sample values for the Dombi-type triangular norms are presented in Table 14.1, and the function $\mu_p(\cdot)$ dedicated to them is described by the formula:

$$\mu_p(x) = \begin{cases} \dfrac{a-x}{a} & \text{for } x \in [0, a] \\[2mm] \dfrac{x-a}{b-a} & \text{for } x \in (a, b] \\[2mm] \dfrac{c-x}{c-b} & \text{for } x \in (b, c] \\[2mm] \dfrac{x-c}{d-c} & \text{for } x \in (c, d] \\[2mm] \dfrac{e-x}{e-d} & \text{for } x \in (d, e] \\[2mm] \dfrac{x-e}{f-e} & \text{for } x \in (e, f] \end{cases} \tag{14.33}$$

where $a = 0.21$, $b = 0.43$, $c = 0.57$, $d = 0.71$, $e = 0.85$, and $f = 10.00$.

14.4.6.   *Criterion for assessing the defuzzification mechanism*

Defuzzification mechanism does not have a direct impact on interpretability of a fuzzy system. However, this criterion can be used to evaluate useful-ness of discretization points of a given defuzzification procedure. Then, the evaluation criterion of the defuzzification mechanism of a fuzzy system encoded in the individual of the population X_{ch} of the form (14.8) can be defined as follows:

$$\mathit{ff} \; \text{int}_H(X_{\text{ch}})$$

$$= \text{neg}_Z \left(\frac{\displaystyle\sum_{j=1}^{m} \sum_{r=1}^{R\max} \left(X_{\text{ch}}^{\text{str}}\{\bar{y}_{j,r}^{\text{def}}\} \cdot \max_{k=1,\dots,N_{\max}} \left\{ \begin{matrix} X_{\text{ch}}^{\text{str}}\{B_j^k\} \cdot \\ \cdot \mu_y(\mu_{B_j^k}(\bar{y}_{j,r}^{\text{def}})) \end{matrix} \right\} \right)}{\displaystyle\sum_{j=1}^{m} \sum_{r=1}^{R\max} X_{\text{ch}}^{\text{str}}\{\bar{y}_{j,r}^{\text{def}}\}} \right)$$

$$\tag{14.34}$$

where μ_y is the function used to control discretization points activity. It can have the following form:

$$\mu_y(x) = \begin{cases} 1 & \text{for } x \geq c_{\text{int}H} \\ 0 & \text{for } x < c_{\text{int}H} \end{cases} \tag{14.35}$$

where $c_{\text{int}H} \in [0,1]$ is the minimum expected value of the membership function for discretization points (the parameter used for evaluation of discretization points activity).

The criterion (14.34) determines the number of active discretization points in relation to the total number of discretization points. It takes values equal to 0 when all discretization points are active.

An active discretization point is the one for which the membership function of any output fuzzy set is greater than or equal to the constant $c_{\text{int}H}$.

In practice different criteria relating to defuzzification mechanism can be defined. They can verify not only inclusion of the output data in the subdomain, but also similarity to the characteristic points of this subdomain. Such points can be centers of gravity of output fuzzy sets, points of their intersection, fuzzy sets characteristic points B'_j, etc.

14.5. Simulations

The issues examined in the simulations is shown in Table 14.2. The purpose of the simulations was to obtain systems of the forms (14.3) characterized by the lowest value of the fitness function (14.14).

Table 14.2. The issues examined in the simulation.

Item no.	Problem name	No. of input attr.	No. of output attr.	No. of sets	Problem label
1.	Banknote authentication [Lohweg *et al.* (2013)]	4	2	1372	BAU
2.	Diabetic retinopathy [Antal and Hajdu(2014)]	19	2	1151	DRD
3.	Fertility [Gil *et al.* (2012)]	9	2	100	FER
4.	Wilt [Johnson *et al.* (2013)]	5	2	4489	WIL

The method of conducting simulations and interpreting the results can be summarized as follows:

- We used the flexible fuzzy system of the form (14.3). It was further referred as S2. Moreover, a non-flexible fuzzy system of the form (14.3), with static weights values set to 1, triangular Dombi norms replaced with algebraic norms and static discretization points set as centers of output fuzzy sets, was tested. It was further referred as S1.
- We used the hybrid genetic-imperialist algorithm to select a structure and parameters of the flexible and non-flexible fuzzy system. In this process the interpretability criteria were taken into account.
- The simulations were performed for seven different variants of weights of the evaluation function (14.14): from the one focused on accuracy (W1) to the one focused on interpretability (W7) (see Table 14.3).
- The simulations were performed taking into account all the criteria described in Section 14.4. The function of the form (14.15) was used for aggregation of these criteria. They have the following weights values:

$$w_{ff\text{int A}} = 0.5, w_{ff\text{int B}} = 1.0, w_{ff\text{int C}} = 0.5,$$

$$w_{ff\text{int D}} = 0.5, w_{ff\text{int E}} = 0.2, w_{ff\text{int F}} = 0.2,$$

$$w_{ff\text{int G}} = 0.2, w_{ff\text{int H}} = 0.2$$

These values refer to the semantics presented in Ref. [33].

Table 14.3. A set of variants of the weights of the evaluation function (14.14).

Variant	$w_{ff\text{acc}}$	$w_{ff\text{int}}$	Description
1	1.00	0.10	focused on high accuracy
W2	0.85	0.25	focused on accuracy
W3	0.70	0.40	intermediate between W2 and W4 taking into account the compromise
W4	0.55	0.55	between interpretability and accuracy
W5	0.40	0.70	intermediate between W4 and W6
W6	0.25	0.85	focused on interpretability
W7	0.10	1.00	focused on good interpretability

- Each simulation (for each variant) was repeated 100 times, each time drawing a population of individuals of the form (14.8). The obtained results were averaged and are presented in Table 14.4 and Fig. 14.16. Due to the varying complexity of the considered simulation problems, Fig. 14.16 is indicative.

A set of parameters of the hybrid genetic-imperialist algorithm is given in Table 14.4 and a set of parameters of the fuzzy system of the form (14.3) is presented in Table 14.5.

The remarks on the way of interpretation of fuzzy rules of the form (14.1) obtained in simulations can be summarized as follows:

- Weights symbols in notation of rules of the form (14.1) were replaced by linguistic labels (Table 14.6). They are: v when weight value is greater than 0.75 (very important), i when weight value is in the range [0.25, 0.75] (important), n when weight value is less than 0.25 (not important).

Table 14.4. A set of parameters of the hybrid genetic-imperialist algorithm.

	Item no. parameter	Notation	Value
1.	Number of iterations	$Niter$	1000
2.	Number of countries	$Npop$	100
3.	Number of empires	Ni	10
4.	Random o set angle of colony	γ	0.15
5.	Probability of revolution and mutation	prm	0.15
6.	Colony importance coefficient	ζ	0.20

Table 14.5. A set of parameters of the fuzzy system (14.3) described in Section 14.2.

Description	Notation	Value
Maximum number of rules	Nmax	7
Maximum number of discretization points	Rmax	21
Minimum value of Dombi-norm parameters	$\underline{p}$	0.00
Maximum value of Dombi-norm parameters	$\overline{p}$	10.00
Expected intersection point of fuzzy sets	$c_{\text{int } B}$	0.50
Parameter of distribution of discretization points	$c_{\text{int} H}$	0.10

Table 14.6. A set of sample rules of the form (14.1) of the fuzzy system S2 described by the formula (14.3) for variant W6.

BAU:

$R^1 : IF$ $\begin{pmatrix} Variance\ is\ low|i\ AND \\ Skewness\ is\ low|i \end{pmatrix}$ $THEN$ $\begin{pmatrix} True\ is\ low|i\ AND \\ False\ is\ high|i \end{pmatrix}$ $|v$

$R^2 : IF$ $\begin{pmatrix} Variance\ is\ medium|v\ AND \\ Skewness\ is\ high|i\ AND \\ Kurtosis\ is\ high|i \end{pmatrix}$ $THEN$ $\begin{pmatrix} True\ is\ medium|i\ AND \\ False\ is\ medium|i \end{pmatrix}$ $|i$

$R^3 : IF$ $\begin{pmatrix} Variance\ is\ high|i\ AND \\ Kurtosis\ is\ low|i\ AND \\ Entropy\ is\ near-2.73|i \end{pmatrix}$ $THEN$ $\begin{pmatrix} True\ is\ high|i\ AND \\ False\ is\ low|i \end{pmatrix}$ $|i$

DRD:

$R^1 : IF$ $\begin{pmatrix} Prescreening\ is\ near\ 0.56|i\ AND \\ MA_{0.5}\ is\ high|i\ AND \\ EX_1\ is\ near\ 240.15|i\ AND \\ EX_3\ is\ low|i\ AND \\ EX_5\ is\ near\ 28.10|i\ AND \\ EX_8\ is\ near\ 1.56|i\ AND \\ Distance\ is\ high|i \end{pmatrix}$ $THEN(NoSigns\ is\ near\ 0.82|v)|i$

$R^2 : IF$ $(MA_{0.7}\ is\ high|i)$ $THEN(DRSigns\ is\ low|i)|i$

$R^3 : IF$ $\begin{pmatrix} MA_{0.5}\ is\ low\ |i\ AND \\ MA_{0.7}\ is\ low\ |i\ AND \\ MA_{0.8}\ is\ near\ 65.18|i\ AND \\ MA_{0.9}\ is\ near\ 80.55|i\ AND \\ MA_{1.0}\ is\ near\ 68.93|i\ AND \\ EX_3\ is\ high|i\ AND \\ EX_6\ is\ near\ 13.02|i\ AND \\ Distance\ is\ low|i\ AND \\ Diameter\ is\ near\ 0.12|v\ AND \\ Binres\ is\ near\ 0.46|i \end{pmatrix}$ $THEN(DRSigns\ is\ high|i)|i$

(Continued)

Table 14.6. (*Continued*)

FER:

$$
\begin{cases}
R^1 : IF \begin{pmatrix} Age \ is \ near \ 0.77|i \ AND \\ Disease \ is \ near \ 0.67|i \ AND \\ Trauma \ is \ high|i \ AND \\ Alcohol \ is \ high \ |i \ AND \\ Sitting \ is \ near \ 0.66|i \end{pmatrix} THEN \begin{pmatrix} Altered \ is \ near \ 0.63|i \ AND \\ Normal \ is \ low \ |i \end{pmatrix} |i \\[4mm]
R^2 : IF \quad (Surgical \ is \ low|i) \qquad THEN(Normal \ is \ medium|i)|i \\[4mm]
R^3 : IF \begin{pmatrix} Trauma \ is \ low \ |n \ AND \\ Surgical \ is \ high \ |v AND \\ Fevers \ is \ near \ -0.18|n \ AND \\ Alcohol \ is \ low \ |i \ AND \\ Smoking \ is \ near \ -0.54|i \end{pmatrix} THEN(Normal \ is \ high|i)|i
\end{cases}
$$

WIL:

$$
\begin{cases}
R^1 : IF \begin{pmatrix} GLCM_{Pan} \ is \ near \ 126.69|i \ AND \\ Mean_G \ is \ high|i \end{pmatrix} THEN(Diseased \ is \ near \ 0.85|v)|i \\[4mm]
R^2 : IF \begin{pmatrix} Mean_G \ is \ low \ |i \ AND \\ Mean_{NIR} \ is \ near \ 731.30|v AND \\ SD_{Pan} \ is \ high|i \end{pmatrix} THEN(Normal \ is \ high|i)|i \\[4mm]
R^3 : IF \begin{pmatrix} Mean_R \ is \ near \ 139.70|v AND \\ SD_{Pan} \ is \ low|v \end{pmatrix} THEN(Normal \ is \ low|v)|i
\end{cases}
$$

- Names of input fuzzy sets A_i^k and output fuzzy sets B_j^k in notation of rules of the form (14.1) were replaced by the following linguistic labels: "very low", "low", "medium", "high", "very high" (Table 14.6). Fuzzy sets, which were reduced in the system, were not included in the notation of rules (14.1). Sometimes in the literature these sets are described as "don't care" sets [391]. If the fuzzy system has only one fuzzy set assigned to a specific input or output, its label is set to "near [value]".
- Names of inputs and outputs in notation of the rules of the form (14.1) were replaced by linguistic labels taken from the description of the described simulation problems (Table 14.6).

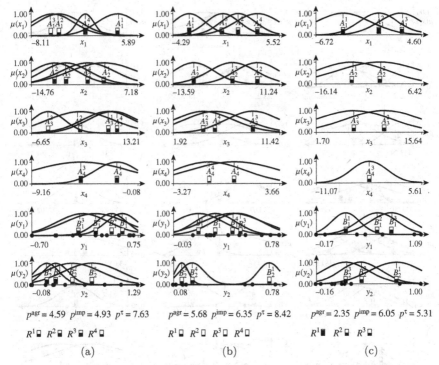

Fig. 14.11. Exemplary representation of the fuzzy system S2 rules (14.3) for the BAU problem and variants: (a) W2, (b) W4, (c) W6.

The conclusions from the simulations can be summarized as follows:

- The fuzzy sets for variants W1 and W2 (column a in Figs. 14.11 and 14.12) are characterized by low readability. However, the systems related to these sets work with high accuracy (Table 14.7).
- The fuzzy sets for variant W4 (column b in Figs. 14.11 and 14.12) have good interpretability. Number of rules for this variant is in the range from 3 to 4 with a good accuracy of the system (Table 14.7). This is a good basis for interpretation of these rules.
- The fuzzy sets for variant W6 (column c in Figs. 14.11 and 14.12), have very good interpretability. In these cases reduction of system outputs often occurs, and the number of rules is usually equal to 3. Moreover, the system accuracy is acceptable (Table 14.7).

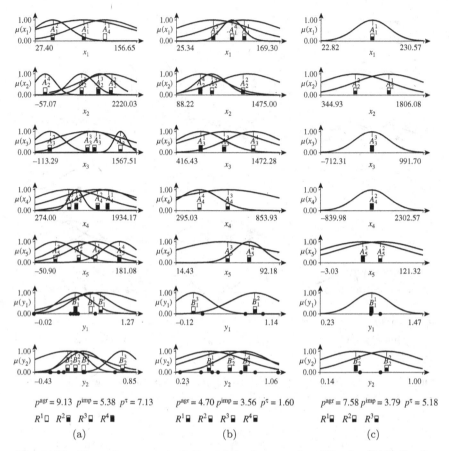

Fig. 14.12. Exemplary representation of the fuzzy system S2 rules (14.3) for the WIL problem and variants: (a) W2, (b) W4, (c) W6.

- The results for intermediate variants W3 and W5 and extreme variants W1 and W7 are shown in Table 14.7 and in Fig. 14.16. They show dependence between the system accuracy (14.3) and its interpretability. The results are (as expected) differential. This is also reflected in Figs. 14.11 and 14.12.
- The average number of rules, input fuzzy sets, output fuzzy sets, inputs and discretization points was different for different simulation variants (Fig. 14.16).

Values of these components decrease for cases characterized by greater interpretability.

Table 14.7. A summary of the mean values of the components used to evaluate system (14.3): percentage accuracy for the test set (test.acc.), percentage accuracy for the learning set (learn.acc.), no. of rules, value of the component expressed by (14.15) $\overline{ff}$int.

System	Problem	Criterion	W_1	W_2	W_3	W_4	W_5	W_6	W_7
S1	BAU	test.acc.	98.928	98.967	98.528	98.420	98.296	98.290	98.285
		learn.acc.	97.927	97.864	97.702	97.369	97.683	96.661	96.645
		no. of rules	3.220	3.140	3.100	3.020	3.020	3.020	3.040
		$\overline{ff}$int	0.399	0.388	0.342	0.335	0.323	0.313	0.308
	DRD	test.acc.	69.710	69.251	69.193	67.837	66.580	65.614	63.014
		learn.acc	65.957	65.391	65.957	64.209	63.783	62.522	60.957
		no. of rules	3.550	3.650	3.200	3.000	3.000	3.000	3.000
		$\overline{ff}$int	0.469	0.462	0.428	0.384	0.333	0.330	0.284
	FER	test.acc.	93.593	93.963	92.667	91.380	89.000	88.100	88.167
		learn.acc	86.667	86.333	86.000	85.667	85.333	85.000	84.500
		no. of rules	3.333	3.400	3.233	3.267	3.067	3.033	3.000
		$\overline{ff}$int	0.418	0.439	0.400	0.405	0.300	0.231	0.183
	WIL	test.acc.	94.912	95.089	94.821	94.754	94.754	94.754	94.753
		learn.acc	94.754	94.814	94.754	94.754	94.754	94.754	94.754
		no. of rules	3.033	3.067	3.000	3.000	3.000	3.000	3.000
		$\overline{ff}$int	0.150	0.163	0.138	0.101	0.103	0.104	0.088
S2	BAU	test.acc.	99.846	99.830	99.781	99.711	99.800	99.657	99.565
		learn.acc	99.662	99.562	99.570	99.243	98.978	98.832	99.002
		no. of rules	3.600	3.900	3.700	3.600	3.433	3.500	3.400
		$\overline{ff}$int	0.566	0.560	0.580	0.548	0.533	0.517	0.539

(*Continued*)

Table 14.7. (*Continued*)

System	Problem	Criterion	W_1	W_2	W_3	W_4	W_5	W_6	W_7
	DRD	test.acc.	70.000	69.797	68.319	66.541	63.894	62.039	60.406
		learn.acc	66.996	66.826	65.913	63.913	61.043	59.217	58.348
		no. of rules	4.600	4.250	3.700	3.000	3.000	3.000	3.000
		$\overline{ff}$int	0.590	0.584	0.475	0.434	0.395	0.387	0.373
	FER	test.acc.	94.407	94.370	93.444	92.778	89.444	88.167	88.556
		learn.acc	88.667	88.667	88.333	87.500	86.333	86.250	84.500
		no. of rules	3.633	3.733	3.467	3.200	3.000	3.000	3.000
		$\overline{ff}$int	0.517	0.518	0.498	0.463	0.330	0.281	0.279
	WIL	test.acc.	95.663	95.456	95.169	95.072	94.754	94.754	94.754
		learn.acc	95.513	95.513	95.134	95.134	94.754	94.754	94.754
		no. of rules	3.000	3.100	3.000	3.100	3.000	3.000	3.000
		$\overline{ff}$int	0.328	0.312	0.301	0.265	0.220	0.217	0.220

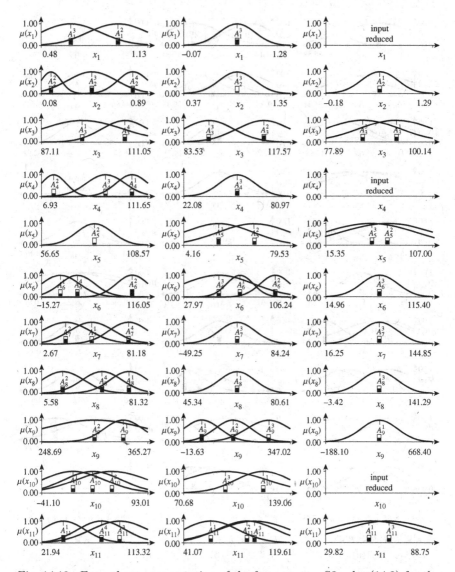

Fig. 14.13. Exemplary representation of the fuzzy system S2 rules (14.3) for the DRD problem and variants: (a) W2, (b) W4, (c) W6.

- Readability of non-flexible system S1 is slightly better than readability of flexible system S2 which stems from the fact that it does

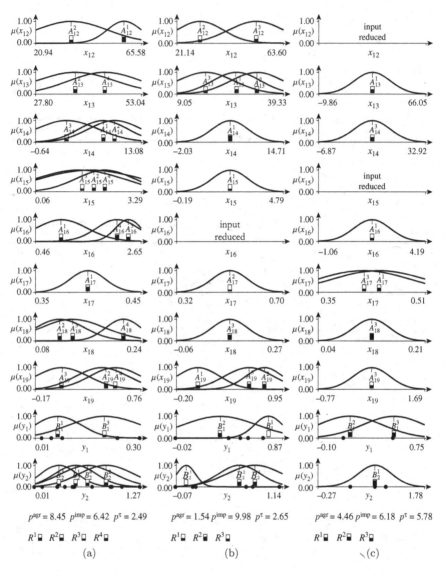

Fig. 14.13. (*Continued*)

not include weights, triangular norms and discretization points criteria.

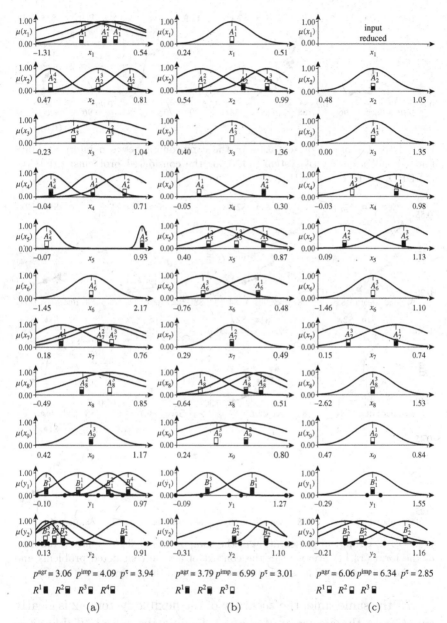

Fig. 14.14. Exemplary representation of the fuzzy system S2 rules (14.3) for the FER problem and variants: (a) W2, (b) W4, (c) W6.

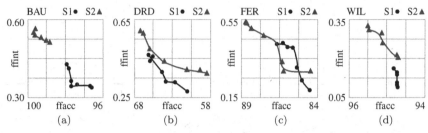

Fig. 14.15. Graphical presentation of the compromise between interpretability ffint (·) and accuracy of system (14.3) for the considered problems: (a) BAU, (b) DRD, (c) FER, (d) WIL.

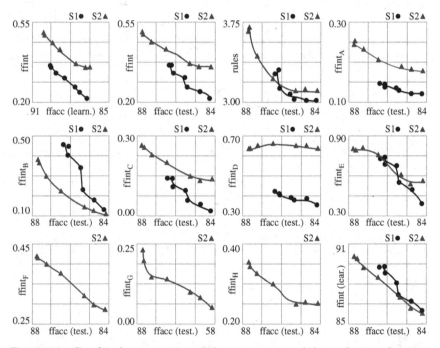

Fig. 14.16. Graphical presentation of the components of the evaluation function of the form (14.14) averaged in the context of all the considered problems and performed 100 times. These values were referred to the component $ff\mathrm{acc}$ (·).

At the same time, the accuracy of the flexible system S2 is clearly superior to the accuracy of the non-flexible system S1 (Table 14.7, Fig. 14.15).

Chapter 15

Fuzzy Reinforcement Learning

In this chapter, we discuss fuzzy reinforcement learning (FRL). The field of reinforcement learning (RL) can be classified into two generations RL1 and RL2 based on the invention of Q-Learning by Watkins [466]. RL1 was suffering from a major short coming that here was no analytical proof of convergence for RL. Using Q-Learning, this problem was solved when Tsitsiklis and Konda [250] analytically proved convergence of RL. We describe FRL1 which was the first generation of fuzzy RL. The most significant result of FRL1 was the generalized approximate-reasoning-based intelligent control (GARIC) [65] architecture. GARIC combined the state of the art in reinforcement learning with fuzzy logic. We then discuss how GARIC can be used for performance evaluation [68]. FRL1 was followed by FRL2. The most significant development of FRL2 was the invention of the actor-critic-based fuzzy reinforcement learning algorithm (ACFRL) [70]. The ACFRL algorithm has been followed by fuzzy Q-learning to solve fuzzy dynamic programming (FDP).

15.1. The GARIC Architecture

Berenji and Khedkar were the first to combine Fuzzy Logic and Reinforcement Learning [65]. Berenji shows a demonstration of GARIC on Cart-Pole balancing. Figure 15.1 shows the architecture of GARIC. It includes three learning units. The first unit is the action selection network (ASN). The second unit is the action evaluation network (AEN). The third unit is the stochastic action modification

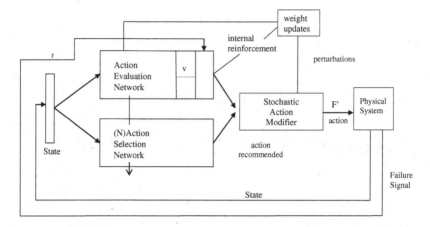

Fig. 15.1. GARIC architecture.

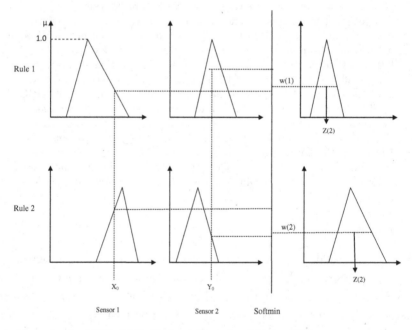

Fig. 15.2. Refine of membership function.

(SAM) unit. GARIC used triangular membership functions. It was shown in Ref. [65] how one can further refine the membership functions as shown in Fig. 15.2. We can assist the AEN by providing fuzzy rules as shown in Fig. 15.3.

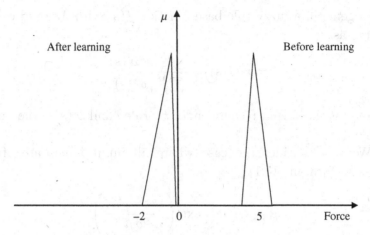

Fig. 15.3. Fuzzy rules.

15.2.   The ACFRL Algorithm

The main structure in the ACFRL algorithm is a fuzzy rule base actor, which decides on the action that should be taken in each state of the environment.

A fuzzy rule base is a function f that maps an input vector s in R^K into an output vector a in R^m.

In this chapter, we consider only multiple-input-single-output (MISO) fuzzy systems $f : R^K \rightarrow R$.

A fuzzy rule base consists of a collection of fuzzy rules. A fuzzy rule i is a function f_i that maps an input vector s in R^K into a scalar a in R. We will consider fuzzy rules of the Takagi–Sugeno–Kang (TSK) form [64, 69].

Rule i; IF s_1 is S_1^i and s_2 is S_2^i and

$$s_K \text{ is } S_K^i \text{ THEN a is } \bar{a}^i = a_0^i + \sum_{j=1}^{K} a_j^i s_j$$

where S_j^i are the input labels in rule i and a_j^i are tunable coefficients. Each label is a membership function $\mu : R \rightarrow R$ that maps its input into a degree to which this input belongs to the fuzzy category (linguistic term) described by this label.

In general, a fuzzy rule base function $f(s)$ with M rules can be written as

$$a = f(s) = \frac{\sum_{i=1}^{M} \bar{a}^i \omega^i(s)}{\sum_{j=1}^{M} \omega^i(s)} \tag{15.1}$$

where π^i is the output recommended by rule i and $\omega^i(s)$ is the weight of rule i.

We will consider the case where all input labels are of the Gaussian form in (15.1)

$$\mu_{S_j^i}(s_j) = b_j^i \exp\left(\frac{(s_j - \bar{s}_j^i)^2}{2\sigma_j{i}^2}\right) \tag{15.2}$$

The product inference is used for computing the weight of each rule: $\omega^i(s) = \prod_{j=1}^{K} \mu_{S_j^i}(s_j)$.

Wang [423] proved that a fuzzy rule base with the above specifications can approximate any continuous function on a compact input set arbitrarily well if the following parameters are allowed to vary: $\bar{s}_j^i, \sigma_j^i, b_j^i$, and $\bar{a}^i$.

His result obviously applies when $\bar{a}^i = a_0^i + \sum_{j=1}^{\pi} a_j^i s_j$, as in TSK rules, in which case a_j^i become the variable parameters. Making these substitutions into (15.1), we get

$$a = f(s) = \frac{\displaystyle\sum_{i=1}^{M} \bar{a}^i \left(\prod_{j=1}^{K} b_j^i\right) \exp\left(-\sum_{j=1}^{K} \frac{\left(s_j - \bar{s}_j^i\right)^2}{2(\sigma_j^i)^2}\right)}{\displaystyle\sum_{i=1}^{M} \left(\prod_{j=1}^{K} b_j^i\right) \exp\left(-\sum_{j=1}^{K} \frac{\left(s_j - \bar{s}_j^i\right)^2}{2(\sigma_j^i)^2}\right)} \tag{15.3}$$

Recently, Konda and Tsitsiklis [66, 250] presented a simulation-based AC algorithm and proved convergence of actor's parameters to a local optimum for actors that satisfy certain assumptions. The ACFRL algorithm was developed by instantiating their algorithm with a fuzzy rulebase actor and proving that such an actor satisfies assumptions necessary for convergence.

ACFRL algorithm requires the actors to specify a probability distribution over the action space instead of a single action.

Therefore, we have modified the traditional fuzzy actor structure in (15.3) by using a Gaussian probability distribution with a mean $\bar{a}^i$ and a variance σ^i instead of $\bar{a}^i$. That is, the probability of taking action a when the state s is encountered is given by

$$\pi_\theta(s,a) = \frac{\sum_{i=1}^{M} \exp\left(-\frac{(\bar{a}^i - a)^2}{a(\sigma^i)^2}\right) \left(\prod_{j=1}^{K} b_j^i\right) \exp\left(-\sum_{j=1}^{K} \frac{(s_j - \bar{s}_j^i)^2}{2(\sigma_j^i)^2}\right)}{\sum_{i=1}^{M} \left(\prod_{j=1}^{K} b_j^i\right) \exp\left(-\sum_{j=1}^{K} \frac{(s_j - \bar{s}_j^i)^2}{2(\sigma_j^i)^2}\right)}$$

(15.4)

where θ is the vector of all tunable parameters in the fuzzy rulebase actor.

Equations (15.1) and (15.4) show that the fuzzy rulebase actor used in the ACFRL algorithm is just a weighted combination of radial basis functions of input variables, a commonly used model in statistical regression. Therefore, it can be interpreted as a particular implementation of a randomized stationary policy, which is the view we will take in the next section when proving its convergence.

The ACFRL critic is completely determined by the actor's structure and does not need to be chosen independently. The critic approximates the Q-values of state-action pairs using a linear combination of partial derivatives with respect to actor's parameters

$$Q_p^\theta(s,a) = \sum_{i=1}^{p} p^i \frac{\partial}{\partial \theta_i} \ln \pi_\theta(s,a)$$

(15.5)

where $p = (p^1, \ldots, p^n)$ denotes the parameter vector of the critic.

In problems where no well-defined episodes exist, the critic also stores p, the estimate of the average reward under the current policy, which is updated according to

$$p_{t+1} = p_t + \alpha_t(r_t - p_t)$$

(15.6)

The critic's parameter vector p is updated as follows:

$$p_{t+1} = p_t + \alpha_t(r_t - p_t + Q_{p_t}^{\theta_t}(s_{t+1}, a_{t+1}) - Q_{p_t}^{\theta_t}(s_t, a_t))z_t \qquad (15.7)$$

where a_t is the critic's learning rate at time t and z_t is an n-vector representing the eligibility trace. In problems with well-defined episodes, the average cost term p is not necessary and can be removed from the above equations. The vector z_t is updated as follows:

$$z_{t+1} = \lambda z_t + \nabla \ln \pi_{\theta_t}(s_{t+1}, a_{t+1}) \qquad (15.8)$$

For the purposes of the current paper, we have simplified the update equation for actor's parameters presented by Konda and Tsitsiklis [66] by restricting θ to be bounded. In practice, this does not reduce the power of the algorithm since the optimal parameter values are finite in well-designed actors. The resulting update equation is

$$\theta_{t+1} = \Gamma(\theta_t - \beta_t Q_{p_t}^{\theta_t}(s_{t+1}, a_{t+1})\nabla \ln \pi_{\theta_t}(s_{t+1}, a_{t+1})) \qquad (15.9)$$

where β_t is the actor's learning rate at time t and Γ is a truncation operator to keep the parameters within a bounded region. We further require that π^i and $\bar{s}_j^i$ stay different for all rules i, so as to avoid redundancy among the rules.

Q-Learning

Q-Leaning finds an optimal action-selection policy for any Markov decision process. It learns an action-value function. A policy is a rule that an agent follows in selecting actions given the state it is in. The invention of *Q*-Learning was very important in RL. It advanced RL11 to RL2. Similarly the progress of FRL1 to FRL2 is due to *Q*-Learning. *Q*-Learning is able to compare the expected utility of the available actions. It is proven that for any finite MDP, *Q*-Learning can find an optimal policy.

Assuming there are S states and A actions per state. The learning rate is $\gamma(0 \leq \gamma \leq 1)$. The *Q*-Learning learns Q. It learns a function that calculate the quantity of a state-action combination. The core of the algorithm is a simple value iteration update. The Q gets updated as

$$Q(s_t, a_t) \leftarrow \underbrace{Q(s_t, a_t)}_{\text{old value}} + \underbrace{\alpha_t}_{\text{learning rate}}$$

$$\cdot \left(\underbrace{r_{t+1}}_{\text{reward}} + \underbrace{\gamma}_{\text{discount rate}} \cdot \overbrace{\underbrace{\max_a Q(s_{t+1,a})}_{\text{estimate of optimal future value}}}^{\text{learned value}} - \underbrace{Q(s_t, a_t)}_{\text{old value}} \right)$$

15.3. Fuzzy Q-Learning to Solve Fuzzy Dynamic Programming

Bellman and Zadeh [62] introduced fuzzy dynamic programming (FDP). They invented a sophisticated functional equations approach and applied it to a typical robot navigation problems. However, Berenji [67] showed that using a fuzzy Q-Learning approach solves the problem and produces the same result as Bellman and Zadeh [62].

Initialize FQ values

Until FQ values converge or max. # of trials do {

1. $x \leftarrow$ current state.
2. Select the action with the highest FQ. If multiple exist, select randomly among them.
3. Apply action, observe the new state (y) and reward (r).
4. Update $FQ(x, a) \leftarrow FQ(x, a) + \beta[(r + \gamma V(y) \wedge C(x, a) - FQ(x, a)]$ where $\wedge$ represents a conjunction or an "and" operator (e.g., the "minimum")}.

Chapter 16

Adaptive Neuro-Fuzzy Inference Systems (ANFISs)

System modeling based on conventional mathematical tools (e.g., differential equations) is not well suited for dealing with ill-defined and uncertain systems. By contrast, a fuzzy inference system employing fuzzy if-then rules can model the qualitative aspects of human knowledge and reasoning processes without employing precise quantitative analyses. In this chapter, we consider a novel architecture called the Adaptive Network-based Fuzzy Inference System, or simply ANFIS, which can serve as a basis for constructing a set of fuzzy if-then rules with appropriate membership functions to generate the stipulated input–output pairs. Modeling of nonlinear functions and prediction of chaotic time series are considered.

16.1. Introduction

In this chapter, we propose a class of adaptive networks that are functionally equivalent to fuzzy inference systems. The proposed architecture is referred to as adaptive neuro-fuzzy inference system (ANFIS), which stands for adaptive network-based fuzzy inference system or semantically equivalently, ANFIS. We describe how to decompose the parameter set to facilitate the hybrid learning rule for ANFIS architectures representing both the Sugeno and Tsukamoto fuzzy models. We also demonstrate that under certain minor constraints, the radial basis function network (RBFN) is functionally equivalent to the ANFIS architecture for the Sugeno fuzzy model. The effectiveness of ANFIS with the hybrid learning rule is tested through four simulation examples: Example 1 models a two-dimensional sinc function; Example 2 models a three-input nonlinear function that was used as a benchmark problem for other fuzzy modeling approaches; Example 3 explains how to identify nonlinear components in an online control system; and Example 4 predicts the Mackey–Glass chaotic time series. The results from ANFIS are compared extensively with connectionist approaches and conventional statistical methods.

Note that similar network structures were also proposed independently by Lin and Lee [277] and Wang and Mendel [463].

16.2.   ANFIS Architecture

For simplicity, we assume that the fuzzy inference system under consideration has two inputs x and y and one output z. For a first-order Sugeno fuzzy model [424, 427, 428], a common rule set with two fuzzy if-then rules is the following:

Rule 1: If x is A_1 and y is B_1, then $f_1 = p_1x + q_1y + r_1$;
Rule 2: If x is A_2 and y is B_2, then $f_2 = p_2x + q_2y + r_2$.

Figure 16.1(a) illustrates the reasoning mechanism for this Sugeno model; the corresponding equivalent ANFIS architecture is as shown in Fig. 16.1(b), where nodes of the same layer have similar functions, as described next. (Here, we denote the output of the ith node in layer 1 as $O_{l,i}$.)

Layer 1. Every node i in this layer is an adaptive node with a node function

$$O_{1,i} = \mu_{A_i}(x) \qquad \text{for } i = 1, 2 \quad \text{or}$$

$$O_{1,i} = \mu_{B_{i-2}}(y) \quad \text{for } i = 3, 4 \qquad (16.1)$$

where x (or y) is the input to node i and A_i (or B_{i-2}) is a linguistic label (such as "small" or "large") associated with this node. In other words, $O_{1,i}$ is the membership grade of a fuzzy set $A(= A_1, A_2, B_1,$ or $B_2)$ and it species the degree to which the given input x (or y) satisfies the quantifier A. Here, the membership function for A can be any appropriate parameterized membership function, such as the

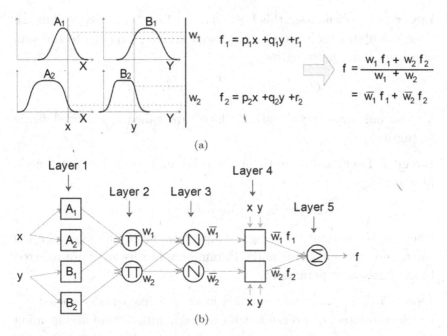

(a)

(b)

Fig. 16.1. (a) A two-input first-order Sugeno fuzzy model with two rules; (b) equivalent ANFIS architecture.

generalized bell function:

$$\mu_A(x) = \frac{1}{1 + \left|\frac{x - c_i}{a_i}\right|^{2b}}$$ (16.2)

where $\{a_i, b_i, c_i\}$ is the parameter set. As the values of these parameters change, the bell-shaped function varies accordingly, thus exhibiting various forms of membership functions for fuzzy set A. Parameters in this layer are referred to as premise parameters.

Layer 2. Every node in this layer is a fixed node labeled, whose output is the product of all the incoming signals:

$$O_{2,i} = w_i = \mu_{A_i}(x)\mu_{B_i}(y), \quad i = 1, 2$$ (16.3)

each node output represents the ring strength of a rule. In general, any other t-norm operators that perform fuzzy AND can be used as the node function in this layer.

Layer 3. Every node in this layer is a fixed node labeled N. The ith node calculates the ratio of the ith rule's firing strength to the sum of all rules' firing strengths:

$$O_{3,i} = \bar{w}_i = \frac{w_i}{w_1 + w_2}, \quad i = 1, 2 \tag{16.4}$$

for convenience, outputs of this layer are called normalized firing strengths.

Layer 4. Every node i in this layer is an adaptive node with a node function

$$O_{4,i} = \bar{w}_i f_i = \bar{w}_i (p_i x + q_i y + r_i) \tag{16.5}$$

where $\bar{w}_i$ is a normalized firing strength from layer 3 and $\{p_i, q_i, r_i\}$ is the parameter set of this node. Parameters in this layer are referred to as consequent parameters.

Layer 5. The single node in this layer is a fixed node labeled $\sum$, which computes the overall output as the summation of all incoming signals:

$$\text{over all output} = O_{5,1} = \sum_i \bar{w}_i f_i = \frac{\sum_i w_i f_i}{\sum_i w_i} \tag{16.6}$$

Thus, we have constructed an adaptive network that is functionally equivalent to a Sugeno fuzzy model. Note that the structure of this adaptive network is not unique; we can combine layers 3 and 4 to obtain an equivalent network with only four layers. By the same token, we can perform the weight normalization at the last layer; Fig. 16.2 illustrates an ANFIS of this type. In the extreme case, we can even shrink the whole network into a single adaptive node with the same parameter set. Obviously, the assignment of node functions and the network configuration are arbitrary, as long as each node and each layer perform meaningful and modular functionalities.

The extension from Sugeno ANFIS to Tsukamoto ANFIS is straightforward, as shown in Fig. 16.3, where the output of each rule (f_i, $i = 1, 2$) is induced jointly by a consequent membership function and a ring strength. For the Mamdani fuzzy inference system with max–min composition, a corresponding ANFIS can be constructed

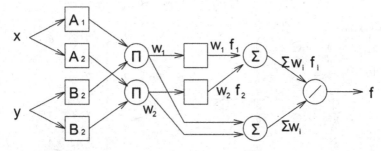

Fig. 16.2. ANFIS architecture for the Sugeno fuzzy model, where weight normalization is performed at the very last layer.

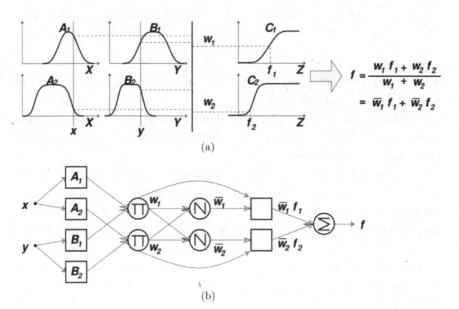

Fig. 16.3. (a) A two-input two-rule Tsukamoto fuzzy model; (b) equivalent ANFIS architecture.

if discrete approximations are used to replace the integrals in the centroid defuzzification scheme. However, the resulting ANFIS is much more complicated than either Sugeno ANFIS or Tsukamoto ANFIS. The extra complexity in structure and computation of Mamdani ANFIS with max–min composition does not necessarily imply better learning capability or approximation power. If we

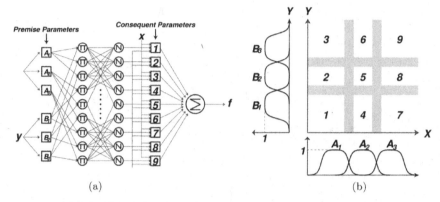

Fig. 16.4. (a) ANFIS architecture for a two-input Sugeno fuzzy model with nine rules; (b) the input space that are partitioned into nine fuzzy regions.

adopt sum–product composition and centroid defuzzification for a Mamdani fuzzy model.

Throughout this chapter, we shall concentrate on the ANFIS architectures for the first-order Sugeno fuzzy model because of its transparency and efficiency.

Figure 16.4(a) is an ANFIS architecture that is equivalent to a two-input first-order Sugeno fuzzy model with nine rules, where each input is assumed to have three associated MFs. Figure 16.4(b) illustrates how the two-dimensional input space is partitioned into nine overlapping fuzzy regions, each of which is governed by a fuzzy if-then rule. In other words, the premise part of a rule defines a fuzzy region, while the consequent part specifies the output within the region.

Next we shall demonstrate how to apply the hybrid learning algorithms developed to identify ANFIS parameters.

16.3. Hybrid Learning Algorithm

From the ANFIS architecture shown in Fig. 16.1(b), we observe that when the values of the premise parameters are fixed, the overall output can be expressed as a linear combination of the consequent parameters. In symbols, the output f in Fig. 16.1(b) can be rewritten as

$$f = \frac{w_1}{w_1 + w_2} f_1 + \frac{w_2}{w_1 + w_2} f_2$$
$$= \bar{w}_1(p_1 x + q_1 y + r_1) + \bar{w}_1(p_2 x + q_2 y + r_2)$$
$$= (\bar{w}_1 x)p_1 + (\bar{w}_1 y)q_1 + (\bar{w}_1)r_1 + (\bar{w}_2 x)p_2 + (\bar{w}_2 y)q_2 + (\bar{w}_2)r_2$$

$$(16.7)$$

which is linear in the consequent parameters p_1, q_1, r_1, p_2, q_2, and r_2. From this observation, we have

$$S = \text{set of total parameters,}$$
$$S_1 = \text{set of premise (nonlinear) parameters,}$$
$$S_2 = \text{set of consequent (linear) parameters}$$

$H(\cdot)$ and $F(\cdot, \cdot)$ are the identity function and the function of the fuzzy inference system, respectively. Therefore, the hybrid learning algorithm can be applied directly. More specifically, in the forward pass of the hybrid learning algorithm, node outputs go forward until layer 4 and the consequent parameters are identified by the least-squares method. In the backward pass, the error signals propagate backward and the premise parameters are updated by gradient descent. Table 16.1 summarizes the activities in each pass.

The consequent parameters thus identified are optimal under the condition that the premise parameters are fixed. Accordingly, the hybrid approach converges much faster since it reduces the search space dimensions of the original pure backpropagation method. Thus, we should always look for the possibility of decomposing the parameter set in the first place. For Tsukamoto ANFIS, this can be achieved if the membership function on the consequent part of each rule is replaced by a piecewise linear approximation with two

Table 16.1. Two passes in the hybrid learning procedure for ANFIS.

	Forward pass	Backward pass
Premise parameters	Fixed	Gradient descent
Consequent parameters	Least-squares estimator	Fixed
Signals	Node outputs	Error signals

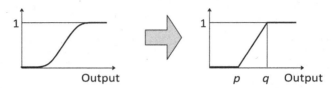

Fig. 16.5. Piecewise linear approximation of consequent MFs in Tsukamoto ANFIS.

consequent parameters, as shown in Fig. 16.5. In this case, again, the consequent parameters constitute the linear parameter set S_2 and the hybrid learning rule can be employed as before.

There are several ways of combining gradient descent and the least-squares method. We can choose one of these methods according to the available computing resources and required performance level.

As pointed out by a reviewer of the original ANFIS paper [377], the learning mechanisms should not be applied to determine membership functions in Sugeno ANFIS, since they convey a linguistic and subjective descriptions of possibly ill-defined concepts. We think this is a case-by-case situation and the decision should be left to the user. In principle, if the size of the available input–output dataset is large, then ne-tuning of the membership functions is recommended (or even necessary), since human-determined membership functions are seldom optimal in terms of reproducing desired outputs. However, if the dataset is too small, then it probably does not contain enough information about the target system. In this situation, the human-determined membership functions represent important information that might not be reflected in the dataset; therefore, the membership functions should be kept fixed throughout the learning process.

If the membership functions are fixed and only the consequent part is adjusted, Sugeno ANFIS can be viewed as a functional-link network [240, 340], where the "enhanced representations" of the input variables are obtained via the membership functions. These enhanced representations determined by human experts apparently provide more insight into the target system than the functional expansion or the tensor (outer product) models [340]. By updating the membership functions, we are actually tuning this enhanced representation for better performance.

Because the update formulas for the premise and consequent parameters are decoupled in the hybrid learning rule (see Table 16.1), further speedup of learning is possible by using variants of the gradient method or other optimization techniques on the premise parameters, such as conjugate gradient descent, second-order back-propagation [342], quick propagation [149], and many others.

16.4. Learning Methods That Cross-Fertilize ANFIS and RBFN

Under certain minor conditions, an RBFN is functionally equivalent to a FIS, and thus adaptive FIS, including ANFIS and CANFIS. This functional equivalence provides a shortcut for better understanding both ANFIS/CANFIS and RBFNs in the sense that developments in either literature cross-fertilize the other. In this section, we briefly describe a variety of adaptive learning mechanisms that can be used for both adaptive FIS and RBFN.

An adaptive FIS usually consists of two distinct modifiable parts: the antecedent part and the consequent part. These two parts can be adapted by different optimization methods, one of which is the hybrid learning procedure combining (steepest descent SD) and (least-squares estimator LSE). Possible combinations of SD and LSE are also discussed in the same section. These learning schemes are equally applicable to RBFNs.

Conversely, the analysis and learning algorithms for RBFNs are also applicable to adaptive FIS (ANFIS/CANFIS). The RBFN approximation capability may be further improved with supervised adjustments of the center and shape of receptive field functions [268, 471]. Besides using a supervised learning scheme alone to update all modifiable parameters, a variety of two-phase training algorithms for RBFNs have been reported. A typical scheme is to x the receptive field (radial basis) functions first and then adjust the weights of the output layer. There are several schemes proposed to determine the center positions (u_i) of the receptive field functions.

Lowe discussed selection of fixed centers based on standard deviations of training data [282]. Moody and Darken discussed unsupervised or self-organized selection of centers u_i by means of vector quantization or clustering techniques [313, 315]. Then the width parameters σ_i are determined by taking the average distance to the first several nearest neighbors of u_i's. Nowlan [335] employed the so-called soft competition among Gaussian hidden units to locate the centers. (This soft-competitive method is based on the maximum likelihood estimator, in contrast to the so-called hard competition such as the k-means winner-take-all algorithm.) Once these nonlinear parameters are fixed and the receptive fields are frozen, the linear parameters (i.e., the weights of the output layer) can be updated by either the least-squares method or the gradient method.

Chen *et al.* [99] used an alternative method that employs the orthogonal least-squares algorithm to determine the u_i's and C_i's while keeping the σ_i's at a pre-determined constant. Other RBFN analyses, such as generalization properties [78] and sequential adaptation [229], among others [227, 321], are all applicable to adaptive FIS (ANFIS/CANFIS).

16.5.   ANFIS as a Universal Approximator

This section explains an interesting property that when the number of rules is not restricted, a zero-order Sugeno model has unlimited approximation power for matching any nonlinear function arbitrarily well on a compact set. This fact is intuitively reasonable. However, to give a mathematical proof, we need to apply the Stone–Weierstrass theorem [232, 383].

16.5.1.   *Stone–Weierstrass theorem*

Let domain D be a compact space of N dimensions, and let $\mathcal{F}$ be a set of continuous real-valued functions on D satisfying the following criteria:

1. Identity function: The constant $f(x) = 1$ is in $\mathcal{F}$.
2. Separability: For any two points $x_1 \neq x_2$ in D, there is an $\mathcal{F}$ in $\mathcal{F}$ such that $f(x_1) \neq f(x_2)$.

3. Algebraic closure: If f and g are any two functions in $\mathcal{F}$, then fg and $af + bg$ are in F for any two real numbers a and b.

Then $\mathcal{F}$ is dense in $C(D)$, the set of continuous real-valued functions on D. In other words, for any $\varepsilon > 0$ and any function g in C(D), there is a function f in $\mathcal{F}$ such that $|g(x) - f(x)| < \varepsilon$ for all $x \in D$.

In applications of fuzzy inference systems, the domain in which we operate is almost always compact. It is a standard result in real analysis that every closed and bounded set in R^N is compact. In what follows, we shall describe how to apply the Stone–Weierstrass theorem to show the universal approximation power of the zero-order Sugeno model.

Identity Function: The first hypothesis of the Stone–Weierstrass theorem requires that our fuzzy inference system be able to compute the identity function $f(x) = 1$. An obvious way to compute this function is to set the consequence part of each rule equal to 1. A fuzzy inference system with only one rule suffices to satisfy this requirement.

Separability: The second hypothesis of the Stone–Weierstrass theorem requires that our fuzzy inference system be able to compute functions that have different values for different points. [Without this requirement, the trivial set of functions $f:f(x) = c, \; c \in R$ would satisfy the Stone–Weierstrass theorem.] Again, this is obviously achievable by any fuzzy inference system with appropriate parameters.

Algebraic Closure|Additive: The third hypothesis of the Stone–Weierstrass theorem requires that our fuzzy inference systems be invariant under addition and multiplication. Suppose that we have two fuzzy inference systems S and $\hat{S}$; each of them has two rules, and the final output of each system is specified as

$$S : z = \frac{w_1 f_1 + w_2 f_2}{w_1 + w_2} \qquad (16.8)$$

and

$$\hat{S} : \hat{z} = \frac{\hat{w}_1 \hat{f}_1 + \hat{w}_2 \hat{f}_2}{\hat{w}_1 + \hat{w}_2} \qquad (16.9)$$

Then the sum of z and $\hat{z}$ is equal to

$$az + b\hat{z}$$

$$= a \frac{w_1 f_1 + w_2 f_2}{w_1 + w_2} + b \frac{\hat{w}_1 \hat{f}_1 + \hat{w}_2 \hat{f}_2}{\hat{w}_1 + \hat{w}_2}$$

$$= \frac{w_1 \hat{w}_1 (af_1 + b\hat{f}_1) + w_1 \hat{w}_2 (af_1 + b\hat{f}_2) + w_2 \hat{w}_1 (af_2 + b\hat{f}_1) + w_2 \hat{w}_2 (af_2 + b\hat{f}_2)}{w_1 \hat{w}_1 + w_1 \hat{w}_2 + w_2 \hat{w}_1 + w_2 \hat{w}_2}$$

Thus, we can construct a four-rule fuzzy inference system that computes $az + b\hat{z}$, where the firing strength and the output of each rule are defined by $w_i \hat{w}_j$ and $af_i + b\hat{f}_i$, $(i, j = 1$ or $2)$, respectively.

16.5.2. *Algebraic closure — Multiplicative*

Invariantness under multiplication is the final feature we must demonstrate before we can conclude that the Stone–Weierstrass theorem can be applied to the zero-order Sugeno fuzzy model. The product of the outputs of two fuzzy inference systems z and $\hat{z}$ can be expressed as

$$z\hat{z} = \frac{w_1 \hat{w}_1 f_1 \hat{f}_1 + w_1 \hat{w}_2 f_1 \hat{f}_2 + w_2 \hat{w}_1 f_2 \hat{f}_1 + w_2 \hat{w}_2 f_2 \hat{f}_2}{w_1 \hat{w}_1 + w_1 \hat{w}_2 + w_2 \hat{w}_1 + w_2 \hat{w}_2} \qquad (16.10)$$

Thus, we can construct a four-rule fuzzy inference system that computes $z\hat{z}$, where the firing strength and the output of each rule are defined by $w_i \hat{w}_j$ and $f_i \hat{f}_j$ $(i; j = 1$ or $2)$, respectively.

From the preceding description, we conclude that the ANFIS architectures that compute $az + b\hat{z}$ and $z\hat{z}$ are of the same class as those of S and $\hat{S}$ if and only if the membership functions used are invariant under multiplication. One class of MFs that satisfy this property is the scaled Gaussian membership function [462, 464]:

$$\mu_{A_i}(x) = k_i \exp \left[- \left(\frac{x - c_i}{a_i} \right)^2 \right]. \qquad (16.11)$$

Another class of MFs that are invariant under the product operator is MFs for crisp sets, which assume values of either 0 or 1. MFs of this kind can be viewed as a special case of either the generalized bell MF with parameter b approaching ∞, or as the trapezoidal MF with $a = b$ and $c = d$.

Therefore, with an appropriate class of membership functions, a zero-order Sugeno model can satisfy the four criteria of the Stone–Weierstrass theorem. That is, for any given $\varepsilon > 0$ and any real-valued function g, there is a zero-order Sugeno model S such that $|g(\vec{x}) - S(\vec{x})| < \varepsilon$ for all $\vec{x}$ in the underlying compact set. The preceding argument of universal approximation power applies to other types of fuzzy models as well, since the zero-order Sugeno model is a special case of the Mamdani fuzzy model, the Tsukamoto fuzzy model, and other higher-order Sugeno models.

However, caution should be taken in accepting this claim, since there has been no mention of how to construct the Sugeno model according to a given training dataset; the Stone–Weierstrass theorem yields only an existence theorem, but not a constructive method.

16.6. Simulation Examples

This section presents simulation results of the ANFIS architecture for the Sugeno fuzzy model. In the first two examples, ANFIS is used to model two nonlinear functions; the results are compared with those achieved by backpropagation MLP approaches and other earlier work on fuzzy modeling. In the third example, we use ANFIS for online identification of a nonlinear component in a discrete control system. In the last example, we predict a chaotic time series using ANFIS and demonstrate its superiority to several standard statistical and neural network approaches. The purpose of these examples is to give a detailed description of how to use ANFIS and how it performs.

16.6.1. *Practical considerations*

In a conventional fuzzy inference system, the number of rules is determined by an expert who is familiar with the target system to be modeled. In our simulation, however, no expert is available and the number of MFs assigned to each input variable is chosen empirically — that is, by plotting the datasets and examining them visually, or simply by trial and error. For datasets with more than three inputs, visualization techniques are not very effective and most of the time we have to rely on trial and error. This situation is similar to that of neural networks; there is just no simple way to determine in advance the minimal number of hidden units needed to achieve a desired performance level. (There are several other techniques for determining the numbers of MFs and rules, such as CART and clustering methods. But here we shall not use them since the purpose of this section is to demonstrate the learning capability of ANFIS.)

If we choose the grid partition, the number of MFs on each input variable uniquely determines the number of rules. The initial values of premise parameters are set in such a way that the centers of the MFs are equally spaced along the range of each input variable. Moreover, these MFs satisfy the condition of ϵ-completeness [266] with $\epsilon = 0.5$, which means that given a value x of one of the inputs in the operating range, we can always find a linguistic label A such that $\mu_A(x) \geq \epsilon$. In this manner, the fuzzy inference system can provide smooth transition and sufficient overlap from one linguistic label to another. Although we did not attempt to maintain the ϵ-completeness during the training process, it can be easily achieved by using a constrained gradient method [476]. Figure 16.6 shows a typical initial MF setting when the number of MFs is four and the input range is [0; 12].

Throughout the simulation examples presented in this section, all the membership functions used are the generalized bell function

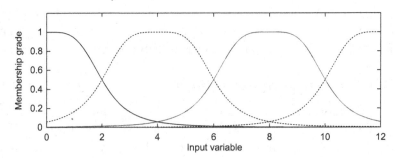

Fig. 16.6. A typical initial MF setting, where input range is assumed to be [0; 12] (MATLAB file: init_ mf.m).

defined in Eq. (16.2):

$$\mu_{A_i}(x) = \text{gbell}(x; a, b, c) = \frac{1}{1 + \left|\frac{x-c}{a}\right|^{2b}} \tag{16.12}$$

which contains three fitting parameters, a, b, and c. Each of these parameters has a physical meaning: c determines the center of the MF; a is half the width of the MF; and b (together with a) controls the slopes at the crossover points (where the MF value is 0.5).

We mentioned that the step size may κ influence the speed of convergence. In the simulation reported next, we use two heuristic guidelines to update the step size adaptively.

16.6.2. *Example 1: Modeling a two-input sinc function*

In this example, we use ANFIS to model a two-dimensional since equation defined by

$$z = \sin c(x, y) = \frac{\sin(x)\sin(y)}{xy} \tag{16.13}$$

From the evenly distributed grid points of the input range $[-10, 10] \times [-10, 10]$ of the preceding equation, 121 training data pairs were obtained. The ANFIS used here contains 16 rules, with four membership functions assigned to each input variable. The total number of fitting parameters is 72, including 24 premise (nonlinear) parameters and 48 consequent (linear) parameters. (We also tried ANFIS models with four rules and nine rules, but these models are too simple to describe the highly nonlinear sinc function.)

Figure 16.7 shows the RMSE curves for both a 2-18-1 backpropagation MLP and the ANFIS architecture used here. Each curve is the result of averaging 10 error curves from 10 runs. For the MLP, these 10 runs were started from different sets of initial random weights. For ANFIS, these 10 runs correspond to 10κ values ranging from 0.01 to 0.10.

The backpropagation MLP, which contained 73 fitting parameters (connection weights and thresholds), was trained with quick propagation [149], which is considered one of the best learning

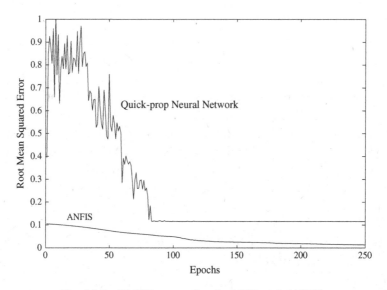

Fig. 16.7. RMSE curves for the MLP and ANFIS.

algorithms for backpropagation MLPs. Figure 16.7 shows how ANFIS approximates a highly nonlinear surface more effectively than an MLP. It should be emphasized that for the same number of epochs (250 in Fig. 16.7), the ANFIS model did take longer since the hybrid learning rule involves more computation. However, even we increased the training epochs for the MLP, its performance stayed the same since its error curve levels off after 100 epochs, as shown in Fig. 16.7.

The poor performance of MLPs seems due to their structure: The learning processes could become trapped in local minima because of the randomly initialized weights, or some neurons could be pushed into saturation during the training. Either of these two situations can significantly decrease the approximation power of MLPs.

The training data and reconstructed surfaces at different epochs during training are depicted in Fig. 16.8.

Since the error measure is always computed after a forward pass (that is, the first half of a whole epoch) is completed, the epoch numbers shown in the caption of Fig. 16.8 always end with 0.5. Note that the reconstructed surface after 0.5 epochs is the result after identifying consequent parameters using LSE for the first time; yet it already looks similar to the training data surface.

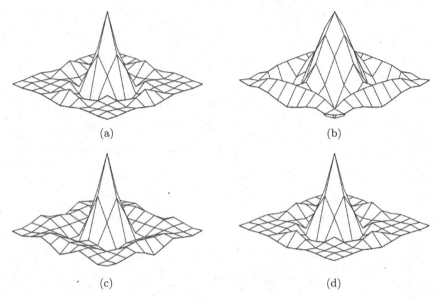

(a)

(b)

(c)

(d)

Fig. 16.8. Training data (a) and reconstructed surfaces at 0.5 (b), 99.5 (c), and 249.5 (d) epochs in Example 1 (MATLAB file: trn_2in.m).

Figure 16.9 lists the initial and final membership functions. It is interesting to observe that the sharp changes in the training data surface around the origin are accounted for by the membership functions moving toward the origin. Theoretically, the final MFs on both x and y should be symmetric with respect to the origin. However, they are not symmetric, due to computer truncation errors and the approximated initial conditions used for bootstrapping the recursive least-squares estimator.

16.6.3. *Example 2: Modeling a three-input nonlinear function*

The training data in this example were obtained from a three-input nonlinear equation defined by

$$\text{output} = (1 + x^{0.5} + y^{-1} + z^{-1.5})^2 \qquad (16.14)$$

This equation was also used by Takagi and Hayashi [429], Sugeno and Kang [424], and Kondo [249] to test their modeling approaches.

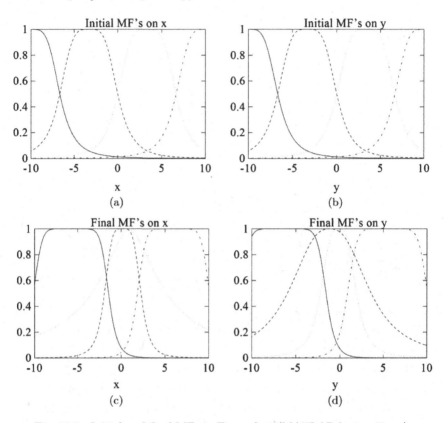

Fig. 16.9.   Initial and final MFs in Example 1 (MATLAB le: trn 2in.m).

Here, the ANFIS architecture (see Fig. 16.10) contains eight rules, with two membership functions assigned to each input variable.

A total of 216 training data and 125 checking data were sampled uniformly from the input ranges $[1; 6] \times [1; 6] \times [1; 6]$ and $[1.5; 5.5] \times [1.5; 5.5] \times [1.5; 5.5]$, respectively. The training data were used for training ANFIS, while the checking data were used for verifying the identified ANFIS only. To allow comparison, we use the same performance index adopted in Refs. [249, 424]:

$$\text{APE} = \text{average percentage error} = \frac{1}{P} \sum_{i=1}^{P} \frac{|T(i) - O(i)|}{|T(i)|} \cdot 100\%$$

$$(16.15)$$

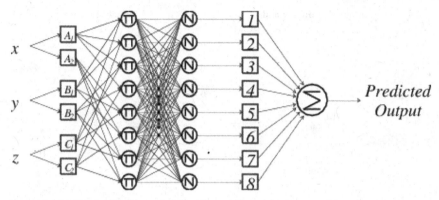

Fig. 16.10. The ANFIS model for Example 2 (the connections from inputs to layer 4 are not shown).

where P is the number of data pairs, and $T(i)$ and $O(i)$ are the ith desired output and predicted output, respectively.

Figure 16.11 illustrates the membership functions before and after training. The training error curves with different initial step sizes ($\kappa = 0.01$ to 0.09) are shown in Fig. 16.12(a), which indicates that the initial value of does not have a critical influence on the final performance as long as is not too large. Figure 16.12(b) shows the training and checking error curves with initial step size equal to 0.1. After 199.5 epochs, the final results were $APE_{trn} = 0 : 043\%$ and $APE_{chk} = 1 : 066\%$, which are listed in Table 16.2 along with the results of other earlier work [249, 424]. Here, ANFIS achieves the best performance at the cost of requiring more training data.

16.6.4. *Example 3: Online identification in control systems*

Here we repeat a simulation example from Ref. [324], where a 1-20-10-1 backpropagation MLP is employed to identify a nonlinear component in a control system, except that here we use ANFIS instead to show its superiority. The plant under consideration is governed by the following difference equation:

$$y(k + 1) = 0.3y(k) + 0.6y(k - 1) + f(u(k)) \qquad (16.16)$$

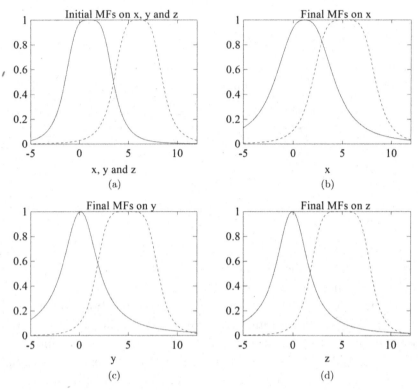

Fig. 16.11. Example 2: (a) MFs before learning; (b), (c), (d) MFs after learning (MATLAB file: trn_3in.m).

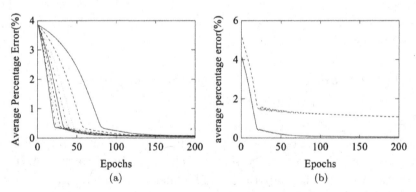

Fig. 16.12. Error curves of Example 2: (a) nine training error curves for nine initial step sizes from 0.01 (rightmost) to 0.09 (leftmost); (b) training (solid line) and checking (dashed line) error curves with initial step size equal to 0.1 (MATLAB file:trn_3in.m).

Table 16.2. Example 2: Comparisons with earlier work.

Model	Training error	Checking error	Parameters number	Training data size	Checking data size
ANFIS	0.043%	1.066%	50	216	125
GMDH model [249]	4.7%	5.7%	—	20	20
Fuzzy model 1 [424]	1.5%	2.1%	22	20	20
Fuzzy model 2 [424]	0.59%	3.4%	32	20	20

where $y(k)$ and $u(k)$ are the output and input, respectively, at time step k. The unknown function $f(\cdot)$ has the form

$$f(u) = 0.6\sin(\pi u) + 0.3\sin(3\pi u) + 0.1\sin(5\pi u) \qquad (16.17)$$

In order to identify the plant, a series-parallel model governed by the difference equation was used, where $F(\cdot)$ is the function implemented by ANFIS and its parameters are updated at each time step.

$$\hat{y}(k+1) = 0.3\hat{y}(k) + 0.6\hat{y}(k-1) + F(u(k)) \qquad (16.18)$$

Here, the ANFIS architecture has seven MFs on its input (thus seven rules with 35 fitting parameters) and the online learning paradigm adopted has a learning rate $\eta = 0.1$ and a forgetting factor $= 0 : 99$. The input to the plant and the model was a sinusoid $u(k) = \sin(2\pi k/250)$; the adaptation started at $k = 1$ and stopped at $k = 250$. As shown in Fig. 16.13, the output of the model follows the output of the plant almost immediately.

Comparisons with existing works are given in Table 16.2: Example 2: comparisons with earlier work. The last three rows are from Ref. [424]. even after the adaptation was stopped at $k = 250$ and the u(k) was changed to $0.5\sin(2\pi k/250) + 0.5\sin(2\pi k/25)$. In comparison, the MLP in Ref. [324] failed to follow the plant when the adaptation was stopped at $k = 500$, and the identification

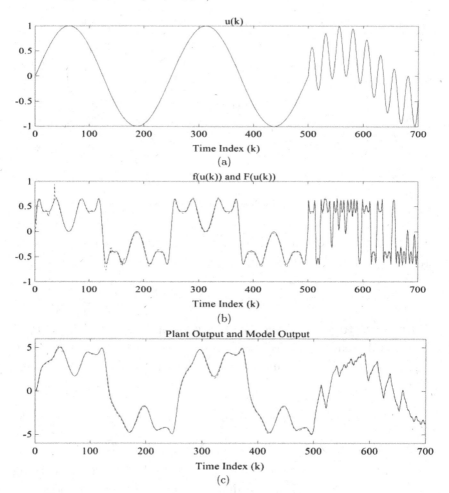

Fig. 16.13. Example 3: (a) $u(k)$; (b) $f(u(k))$ and $F(u(k))$; (c) plant and model outputs.

procedure had to continue for 50,000 time steps using a random input. Table 16.3 summarizes the comparison.

In the preceding simulation, the number of rules is determined by trial and error. If the number of MFs is below seven, then the model output will not follow the plant output satisfactorily after 250 adaptations. By using the more effective online learning, we can decrease the number of rules.

Table 16.3. Example 3: Comparison with MLP identifier [324].

Method	Parameter number	Time steps of adaptation
MLP	261	50000
ANFIS	35	250

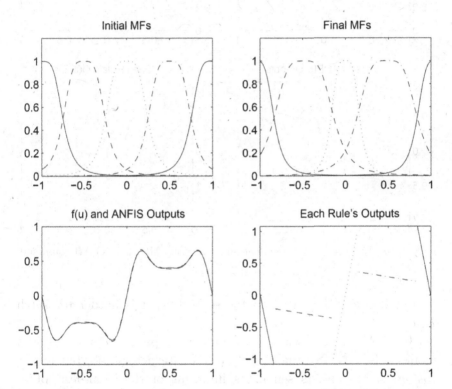

Fig. 16.14. Example 3: Offline learning with five MFs (MATLAB command: trn_1in(5)).

Figures 16.14–16.16 show the results after 49.5 epochs of offline learning when the number of MFs is 5, 4, and 3, respectively. From these figures, it is obvious that ANFIS is a good model even when as few as three MFs are used. However, as the number of rules becomes smaller, the relationship between $F(u)$ and each rule's

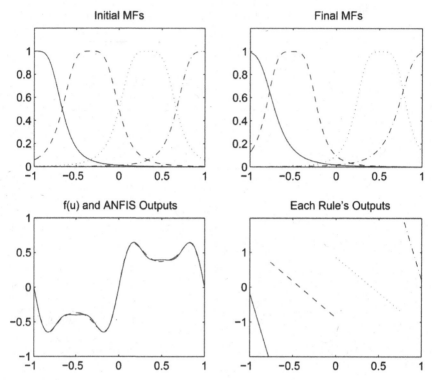

Fig. 16.15. Example 3: On line learning with four MFs (MATLAB command: trn_1in(4)).

output becomes less clear, in the sense that it is harder to sketch $F(u)$ from each rule's output.

In other words, when the number of parameters is reduced moderately, ANFIS usually still does a satisfactory job, but at the cost of sacrificing its semantics in terms of the local-description nature of fuzzy if-then rules. In this case, ANFIS is less of a structured knowledge representation and more like a black-box model, such as a backpropagation MLP.

16.6.5.   *Example 4: Predicting chaotic time series*

Examples 1–3 demonstrate the capability of ANFIS for modeling nonlinear functions. In this example, we demonstrate how ANFIS can be employed to predict future values of a chaotic time series.

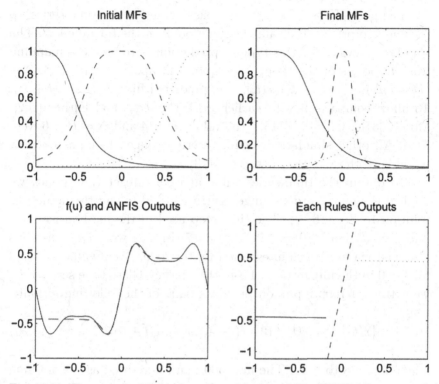

Fig. 16.16. Example 3: Off-line learning with three MFs (MATLAB command: trn_lin(3)).

The performance obtained in this example is compared with the results of a cascade-correlation neural network approach [113] and the conventional autoregressive (AR) model.

The time series used in our simulation is generated by the chaotic Mackey–Glass differential delay equation [286] defined as

$$\dot{x}(t) = \frac{0.2x(t - \tau)}{1 + x^{10}(t - \tau)} - 0.1x(t) . \tag{16.19}$$

The prediction of future values of this time series is a benchmark problem that has been used and reported by a number of connectionist researchers, such as Lapedes and Farber [262], Moody [315], Jones *et al.* [227], Crowder [113], and Sanger [396].

The goal of the task is to use past values of the time series up to time t to predict the value at some point in the future $t + P$. The standard method for this type of prediction is to create a mapping from D points of the time series spaced Δ apart — that is, $[x(t - (D - 1)\Delta), \ldots, x(t - \Delta), x(t)]$, to a predicted future value $x(t + P)$. To allow comparison with earlier work (Lapedes and Farber [262], Moody [315], Crowder [113]), the values $D = 4$ and $\Delta = P = 6$ were used. All other simulation settings were arranged to be as close as possible to those reported in Ref. [113].

To obtain the time series value at each integer time point, we applied the fourth-order Runge–Kutta method to end the numerical solution to Eq. (16.19). The time step used in the method was 0.1, initial condition $x(0) = 1.2$, and $= 17$. In this way, $x(t)$ was thus obtained via numerical integration for 0 t 2000. [We assume $x(t) = 0$ for $t < 0$ in the integration.] From the Mackey-Glass time series $x(t)$, we extracted 1000 input–output data pairs of the following format:

$$[x(t - 18), x(t - 12), x(t - 6), x(t); x(t + 6)], \qquad (16.20)$$

where $t = 118$ to 1117. The first 500 pairs were used as the training dataset for ANFIS, while the remaining 500 pairs were the checking dataset for validating the identified ANFIS. The number of MFs assigned to each input of the ANFIS was set to two, so the number of rules is 16.

Figure 16.17(a) depicts the initial membership functions for each input variable. The ANFIS used here contains a total of 104 fitting parameters, of which 24 are premise (nonlinear) parameters and 80 are consequent (linear) parameters. After 499.5 epochs, we had $\text{RMSE}_{\text{trn}} = 0 : 0016$ and $\text{RMSE}_{\text{chk}} = 0 : 0015$, which are much better than the results of the other approaches, as will be explained later.

The desired and predicted values for both training data and checking data are essentially the same in Fig. 16.18(a); the differences between them can only be seen on a much finer scale, as shown in Fig. 16.18(b). Figure 16.17(b) is the final membership functions; Fig. 16.19 shows the RMSE curves, which indicate that most of the learning was done in the first 100 epochs.

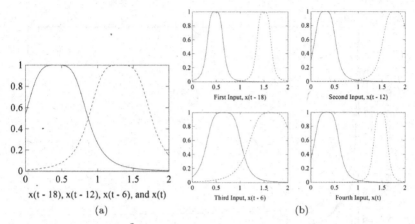

Fig. 16.17. Membership functions in chaotic time series prediction: (a) initial MFs for all four inputs; (b) MFs after learning (MATLAB file: trn_4in.m).

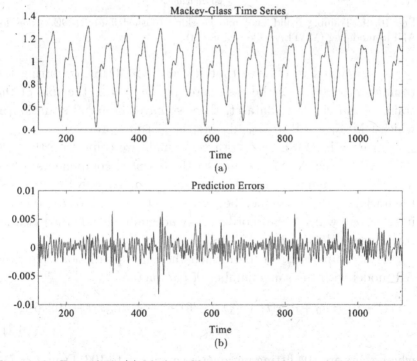

Fig. 16.18. Example 3, (a) Mackey–Glass time series from $t = 124$ to 1123 and six-step-ahead prediction (which is indistinguishable from the time series here); (b) prediction error (MATLAB file: trn_4in.m).

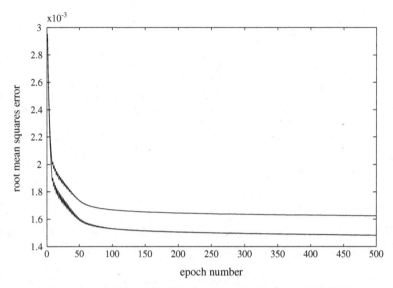

Fig. 16.19. Training (solid line) and checking (dashed line) RMSE curves for ANFIS modeling (MATLAB file: trn_4in.m).

It is unusual to observe that $\text{RMSE}_\text{trn} > \text{RMSE}_\text{chk}$ during the training process, as is the case here. (If we change the role of the training and checking dataset, then we have the usual situation in which $\text{RMSE}_\text{trn} < \text{RMSE}_\text{chk}$ during the learning process.)

Since both RMSEs are both very small, we conjecture that (1) the ANFIS used here has captured the essential components of the underlying dynamics; and (2) the training data contain the effects of the initial conditions [remember that we set $x(t) = 0$ for $t \leq 0$ in the integration], which might not be easily accounted for by the essential components identified by ANFIS.

As a comparison, we performed the same prediction using the AR model with the same number of parameters:

$$x(t + 6) = a_0 + a_1 x(t) + a_2 x(t - 6) + \cdots + a_{103} x(t - 102^*6),$$

$$(16.21)$$

where there are 104 fitting parameters a_k, $k = 0$ to 103. From $t = 712$ to 1711, we extracted 1000 data pairs, of which the first 500 were

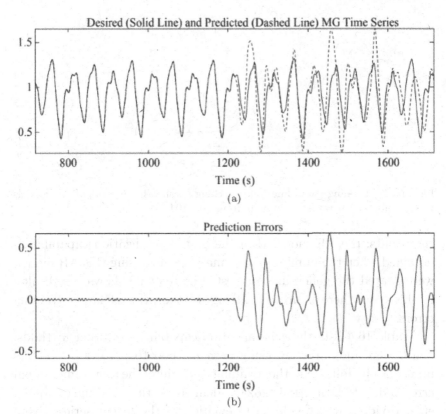

Fig. 16.20. (a) Mackey–Glass time series (solid line) from $t = 718$ to 1717 and six-step-ahead prediction (dashed line) by AR model with parameter $= 104$; (b) prediction errors (the first 500 data points are training data, while the remaining are for validation).

used to identify a_k and the remainder were used for checking. The results obtained through the standard least-squares method were $\mathrm{RMSE_{trn}} = 0 : 005$ and $\mathrm{RMSE_{chk}} = 0 : 078$, which are much worse. Figure 16.20 shows the predicted values and the prediction errors. Obviously, the over-parameterization of the AR model causes over-fitting in the training data, which produces large errors in the checking data. To search for an appropriate AR model in terms of the best generalization capability, we tried different AR models with the number of parameters varying from 2 to 104. Figure 16.21 displays

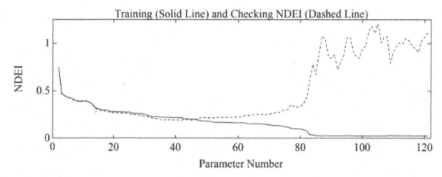

Fig. 16.21. Training (solid line) and checking (dashed line) errors of AR models with numbers of parameters varying from 2 to 104.

the results; the AR model with the best generalization capability is obtained when the number of parameters is 45. Using this AR model, we repeated the generalization test. Figure 16.22 shows the results; in this case, there is no over-fitting, at the price of larger training errors.

Table 16.4 lists the generalization capabilities of other methods, which were measured by using each method to predict 500 points immediately following the training set. Here the non-dimensional error index (NDEI) [113, 262] is defined as the root mean square error divided by the standard deviation of the target series. (Note that the average relative variance used in Refs. [468, 469] is equal to the square of NDEI.) The remarkable generalization capability of ANFIS, we believe, is derived from the following facts:

- ANFIS can achieve a highly nonlinear mapping, as shown in Examples 1–3. Therefore, it is superior to common linear methods in reproducing nonlinear time series.
- The ANFIS used here has 104 adjustable parameters, far fewer than those used in the cascade-correlation NN (693, the median) and backpropagation MLP (about 540) listed in Table 16.4.
- Although not based on *a priori* knowledge, the initial parameters of ANFIS are intuitively reasonable and all the input space is covered properly; this results in fast convergence to good parameter values that captures the underlying dynamics.

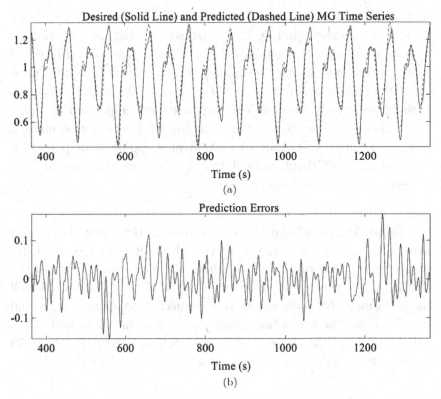

Fig. 16.22. Example 3, (a) Mackey–Glass time series (solid line) from $t = 364$ to 1363, and six-step-ahead prediction (dashed line) by the best AR model with 45 parameters; (b) prediction errors.

Table 16.4. Results of the tests.

Method	Training cases	Non-dimensional error index
ANFIS	500	0.036
AR model	500	0.39
Cascaded-correlation NN	500	0.32
Backpropagation MLP	500	0.05
6th-order polynomial	500	0.85
Linear predictive method	2000	0.60
LRF	500	0.10–0.25
LRF	10000	0.025–0.05
MRH	500	0.05
MRH	10000	0.02

- ANFIS consists of fuzzy rules which are local mappings (which are called local experts in Ref. [228]) instead of global ones. These local mappings facilitate the minimal disturbance principle [474], which states that the adaptation should not only reduce the output error for the current training pattern but also minimize disturbance to response already learned. This is particularly important in online learning. We also found that the use of least-squares method to determine the output of each local mapping is of particular importance. Without using LSE, the learning time would have been 5 to 10 times longer.

Tables 16.5 and 16.6 list the results of the more challenging generalization test, in which P is 84 and 85 for rows 1–6 and 7–10, respectively. The results of the first six rows were obtained by iterating the prediction of $P = 6$ until $P = 84$. ANFIS still outperformed these statistical and connectionist approaches in all cases except where a substantially larger amount of training data were used (e.g., the last row of Tables 16.5 and 16.6). Figure 16.23 depicts the generalization test results for ANFIS when $P = 84$.

Table 16.5. FULLY TEST FOR LAD-class AND LDA-distance.

	LDA-class with 2 classes # of transformed inputs			LDA-class with 3 classes # of transformed inputs		
DataSet	2	3	4	2	3	4
PHB	4.903	5.003	5.147	4.784	4.993	5.177
ABALONE	2.290	2.153	2.148	2.364	2.345	2.339
Auto-MPG	9.347	10.282	104.569	19.233	204.777	237.690
Stock	10.151	10.760	11.117	9.616	12.397	45.452
AirFoil	65.985	26.736	25.955	11.638	42.615	27.601
Weather Ankara	13.845	6.173	10.611	9.547	8.874	8.811
Wizmir	13.495	14.846	24.435	11.515	14.863	13.146
Yacht	15.739	19.124	22.122	74.046	90.713	26.072
Concrete	16.312	16.027	15.528	16.264	15.885	15.521
Friedman	3.704	3.392	3.079	4.123	3.823	2.271

Table 16.6. FULLY TEST FOR LAD-class AND LDA-distance.

DataSet	LDA-class with 4 classes # of transformed inputs			LDA-distance # of transformed inputs		
	2	3	4	2	3	4
PHB	4.445	4.729	6.028	5.522	7.326	13.764
ABALONE	2.367	2.305	2.301	2.342	2.296	2.263
Auto-MPG	127.485	299.177	1184.210	40.753	54.901	400.700
Stock	6.332	11.160	14.340	12.928	11.582	32.227
AirFoil	10.629	64.972	22.892	10.216	8.887	6.716
Weather Ankara	11.683	11.749	11.755	14.417	14.122	14.540
Wizmir	9.731	8.705	8.761	12.936	12.464	12.710
Yacht	25.041	170.312	62.313	16.255	31.794	26.430
Concrete	16.102	15.696	15.168	15.668	14.800	13.544
Friedman	4.929	4.076	3.836	4.504	4.136	1.847

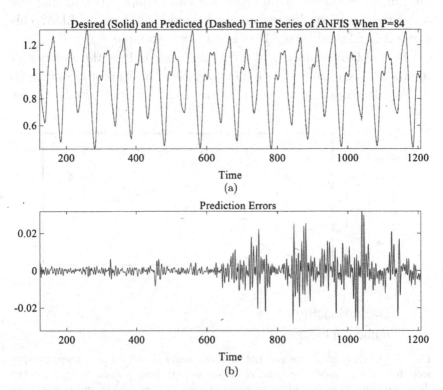

Fig. 16.23. Generalization test of ANFIS for $P = 84$.

16.6.6.   *Example 5: Dimensionality reduction for ANFIS*

In this example, we use ANFIS to model a two-dimensional sinc equation defined by in this example, we propose another way of using LDA for regression. That is, we can simply transform a regression task into a classification one by partitioning the output variable into several intervals and assign data points with target values in an interval to a class. That is, the number of intervals is equal to the number of classes. Usually we want to make the class sizes as evenly as possible.

Thus, the separating point for 2 interval (thus 2-class task) is the median of the target output, and the separating points for 3 intervals (thus 3-class task) are the 33% and 67% percentile points, and so on. Once the classes are defined, we can employ LDA to find the linear transform for dimensionality reduction as the usual LDA. This method is referred to as LDA-class in this example.

Both LDA-distance and LDA-class can reduce the number of inputs for regression. We shall employ them as a preprocessing step for ANFIS modeling, as shown in Fig. 16.24. In other words, we use

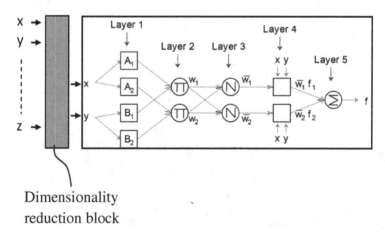

Dimensionality
reduction block

Fig. 16.24. Example 5, we put the dimensionality reduction as a preprocessing step for ANFIS modeling (one direction of our future work is to view the dimensionality reduction block as an additional layer of ANFIS and training the integrated system as a whole for better performance).

LDA-distance or LDA-class to reduce the input dimension first, and then use the transformed inputs for the common ANFIS training. The typical number of inputs is usually 2, 3, or 4, which can greatly speed up ANFIS training and hopefully prevent overfitting due to the use of much less parameters.

To compare the performance between LDA-distance and LDA-class for dimensionality reduction of ANFIS, here we use 10 datasets to evaluate the performance. All the experiments were conducted in MATLAB R2016a, with a platform of Microsoft 64-bits Win 7 OS, Intel Core(TM) i7-2670QM Processor @2.20GHz, 32GB RAM. The regression datasets used in our experiments include 4 (BHP, Auto-MPG, AirFoil, Yacht) from UCI Machine Learning Repository [39] and 6 (ABALONE, Stock, Weather Ankara, Wizmir, Concrete, Friedman) from KEEL [248]. In order to achieve a better estimate of the modeling performance of ANFIS, we use 3-fold cross validation for each dataset. For LDA-distance, the weight function used here is $f(x) = \sqrt{|\|x\| - \tau|}$, where the threshold τ can be represented as a multiple of the standard deviation p_y of the target variable y such that $\tau = \alpha p_y$. Typical range for is 0.1 to 1.0 ($\alpha \in [0.1 1.0]$), and here we set equal to 0.3 in our implementation. For LDA-class, we varied the number of classes in our experiments to see its effect on the final performance of ANFIS modeling. For ANFIS architecture, we adopted grid partitioning and used 2 MFs for each (transformed) input, so the number of rules is equal to 2 to the number of inputs. For training, we adopted the default options shown next:

- Number of training epoch is 100.
- Initial step size is 0.01.
- Step size decreasing rate is 0.5.
- Step size increasing rate is 1.5.

Table 16.7 summarizes the overall results of our experiments over 10 datasets for regression, where the best performance in the same category (or with the same number of transformed inputs) is marked in bold font. It can be observed that the proposed LDA-class with 2 classes can achieve the most bold-font figures among all. However,

Table 16.7. The value of RMSE for LDA-class with 2 classes and LDA-distance.

DataSet	LDA-class with 2 classes # of transformed inputs			LDA-distance # of transformed inputs		
	2	3	4	2	3	4
PHB	**4.903**	**5.003**	**5.147**	5.522	7.326	13.764
ABALONE	**2.290**	**2.153**	**2.148**	2.342	2.296	2.263
Auto-MPG	**9.347**	**10.282**	**104.569**	40.753	54.901	400.700
Stock	**10.151**	**10.760**	**11.117**	12.928	11.582	32.227
AirFoil	65.985	26.736	25.955	**10.216**	**8.887**	**6.716**
Weather Ankara	**13.845**	**6.173**	**10.611**	14.417	14.122	14.540
Wizmir	13.495	14.846	24.435	**12.936**	**12.464**	**12.710**
Yacht	**15.739**	**19.124**	**22.122**	16.255	31.794	26.430
Concrete	16.312	16.027	15.528	**15.668**	**14.800**	**13.544**
Friedman	**3.704**	**3.392**	**3.079**	4.504	4.136	**1.847**

Table 16.8. Comparison of generalization capability for $P = 6$ (the last four rows are from Ref. [113]).

Method	Training cases	Non-dimensional error index
ANFIS	500	
AR model	500	0.007
Cascaded-correlation NN	500	0.19
Backpropagation MLP	500	0.06
6th-order polynomial	500	0.02
Linear predictive method	2000	0.55

LDA-distance has an overwhelming winning over the datasets of AirFoil and Concrete. The underlying reason for this is yet to be investigated. (AirFoil is NASAs dataset obtained from a series of aerodynamic and acoustic tests of two and three-dimensional airfoil blade sections conducted in an anechoic wind tunnel. Concrete is a dataset used to predict the strength of concrete compressive.) Table 16.8 compares LDA-class (with 2 classes) with LDA-distance directly. The winning rate of LDA-class is about 67%.

We have arbitrarily selected the first three datasets (BHP, ABALONE, Audo-MPG) to plot their performance of different methods with respect to the number of transformed inputs, as shown

BHP

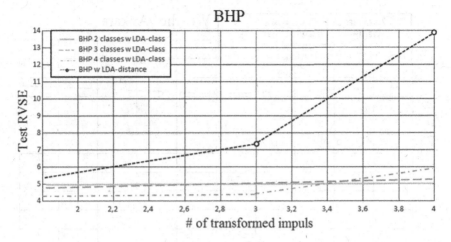

Fig. 16.25. BPH dataset.

ABALONE

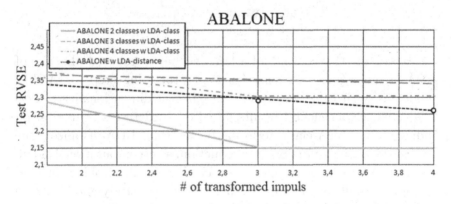

Fig. 16.26. ABALONE dataset.

in Figs. 16.25–16.27, respectively. As we increase the number of transformed inputs, the test RMSE does not go up rapidly, indicating that the problem of over fitting is not likely to happen due to the limited number of transformed inputs. In other words, the proposed dimensionality reduction method can provide a sufficient yet parsimonious model that is just the right size for the give dataset for regression.

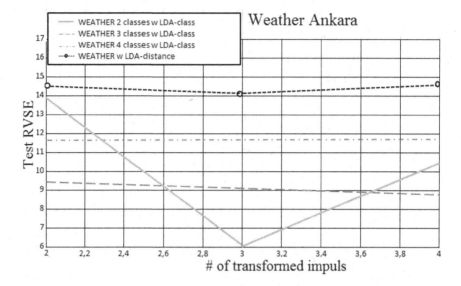

Fig. 16.27.   Weather Ankara dataset.

Based on the concept of LDA, we have proposed the use of LDA-distance and LDA-class as a preprocessing step for ANFIS modeling, such that the problem of curse of dimensionality can be alleviated. Experimental results based on 10 datasets for regression indicate that LDA-class performs better than LDA-distance. Due to the effective dimensionality reduction, the computation load in training ANFIS is significantly lessened, and the problem of over fitting is less likely to happen. This is an initial study and there are several future directions to extend this work, including:

- Regard the input transform as an extra layer of ANFIS and invoke the hybrid learning algorithm to update all the parameters (input transform plus the original ANFIS) as a whole to have a tightly coupled system with better performance.
- Explore the use of fuzzy LDA [214] as a preprocessing step for dimensionality reduction of ANFIS.
- Try out other schemes of input partitioning, including tree partitioning and scatter partitioning [378].

16.7. Extensions and Advanced Topics

Because of the extreme flexibility of adaptive networks, ANFIS can be generalized in a number of different ways. For instance, the membership functions can be changed to any of the parameterized MFs. Furthermore, we can replace the nodes in layer 2 with the parameterized t-norm and let the learning rule decide the best t-norm operator for a specific application. Moreover, the realization of rules with OR'ed antecedents, linguistic hedges, and multiple outputs can be put into ANFIS accordingly.

Another important issue in the training of ANFIS is how to preserve some intuitive features that make the resulting fuzzy rules easy to interpret. These features include ϵ-completeness [266], moderate fuzziness, and reasonably shaped membership functions. Although we did not pursue these directions in our discussion, most of these features can be preserved by maintaining certain constraints or by modifying the error measure, as explained next.

- The requirement of ϵ-completeness ensures that for any given value of an input variable, there is at least an MF with grade greater than or equal to ϵ. This guarantees that the whole input space is covered properly if ϵ is greater than zero. The ϵ-completeness can be maintained by the constrained gradient descent [476]. For instance, suppose that $\epsilon = 0.5$ and the adjacent membership functions are of the generalized bell MF in Eq. (16.2) with parameter sets $\{a_i, b_i, c_i\}$ and $\{a_{i+1}, b_{i+1}, c_{i+1}\}$. Then ϵ-completeness is satisfied if $c_i + a_i \geq c_{i+1} - a_{i+1}$, and the satisfaction of this constraint is guaranteed throughout the training if the constrained gradient descent is employed.

- Moderate fuzziness refers to the requirement that within most regions of the input space, there should be a dominant fuzzy if-then rule with a ring strength close to unity that accounts for the final output, instead of multiple rules with similar ring strengths. This prevents neighboring MFs from having too much overlap and makes the rule set more informative. In particular, this eliminates one of the most unpleasant situations that an MF goes under the other one. An simple way to keep moderate fuzziness is to use a modified error measure

$$E' = E + \beta \sum_{i=1}^{P} [-\bar{w}_i \ln(\bar{w}_i)] \qquad (16.22)$$

where E is the original squared error; β is a weighting constant; P is the size of the training dataset; and $\bar{w}_i$ is the normalized firing strength of the ith rule. The second term $\sum_{i=1}^{P} [-\bar{w}_i \ln(\bar{w}_i)]$ in the preceding equation is Shannon's information entropy [375], and its value is minimized whenever there is a $\bar{w}_i$ equal to one. Since this modified error measure is not based on data fitting alone, the ANFIS thus trained also has a potentially better generalization capability. The improvement of generalization by using an error measure based on both data fitting and weight elimination has been reported in the neural network literature [468, 469].

- The easiest way to maintain reasonably shape for each MF is to parameterize the MF correctly to reflect adequate constrains. For one thing, we want all the MFs to remain bell-shaped regardless of their parameter values. This is not true for the generalized bell MF in Eq. (16.2) if $b_i < 0$; a quick fix is to replace b_i with $b_i^2 + k$, where k is a positive fixed constant.

Throughout this chapter, we have assumed that the structure of ANFIS is fixed and that the parameter identification is solved through the hybrid learning rule. However, to make the whole approach more complete, the structure identification [424, 425] (which is concerned with the selection of an appropriate input-space partition style, the number of membership functions on each input, and so on) is equally important to the successful application of ANFIS, especially for modeling problems with a large of inputs. Effective partitioning of the input space can decrease the number of rules and thus increase the speed in both the learning and application phases. Advances in neural network structure identification [150, 269] may shed some light on this.

Fuzzy control is by far the most successful application of fuzzy set theory and fuzzy inference systems. The adaptive capability of ANFIS makes it almost directly applicable to adaptive control and learning control. In fact, ANFIS can replace almost any neural network in a control system and perform the same function.

The active role of neural networks in signal processing [251, 473] also suggests similar applications for ANFIS. The nonlinearity and structured knowledge representation of ANFIS are its primary advantages over classical linear approaches in adaptive filtering [201] and adaptive signal processing [472], such as identification, inverse modeling, predictive coding, adaptive channel equalization, adaptive interference (noise or echo) canceling, and so on.

By employing the adaptive network as a common framework, we can construct other adaptive fuzzy models that are tailored for applications such as data classification and feature extraction.

Chapter 17

Fuzzy Expert Systems

Expert system (ES) is a computer-based intelligent system that emulates
the mental abilities of a human expert. It performs in all respects like
a human expert. Usually, human experts' belief and knowledge are
imprecise and uncertain, and described by fuzzy concepts. Widespread
interest in fuzzy ESs can be attributed to these systems' ability to aid
various institutions in solving important practical, real-world problems.
In this chapter, we discuss different types of ESs, emphasizing on the
fuzzy ES ESPLAN created by the author.

17.1. Introduction

ES was introduced by the "father of expert system" Edwars Feigen-
baum, with the "DENDRAL" and "MYSIN" system.

There are many different types of expert systems.

Diagnosis types of ES are used to recommend remedies to illnesses,
mechanical problems etc.

Repair ES can define repair strategies and suggest a plan for the
repair of the item. This type ES is used in the automotive repair
field and similar areas.

Instructional ES is used for individualized training or instruction in
a diverse field. The system presents material in an order determined

by its evaluation of the user's ability and current knowledge and monitors the progress of the student, altering the sequence depending on this progress.

Interpretive ES have the ability to analyze data to define its usefulness. These are used in mineral, gas and oil deposits exploration, image analysis and speech understanding.

Predictive ES are intended to "guess" at the possible outcomes of observed situations.

Planning ES act as a tool by performing tasks such as costing, material ordering, production scheduling, etc.

Monitoring and control ES monitor operations and control certain functions. They are often used for decision making in the nuclear energy industry, air traffic control, etc.

Classification ES is intended to classify the goals on base of various features. One of the most important application of fuzzy logic is Fuzzy ES, that use fuzzy data and rules for decision making ability of a human expert.

In Ref. [499], authors described the immune ES that protects the human body using fuzzy cognitive map (FCM). ES for medical diagnosis and health management is described in Ref. [197]. Fuzzy ES to detect the heart disease is given in Ref. [397]. Intelligent ES for hardware fault detection for computer system is investigated in Ref. [419].

Application of fuzzy ES in teacher's performance evaluation is considered in Ref. [238].

17.2.   Fuzzy Expert Systems Using Bayes-Shortliffe Approach

17.2.1.   *Structure of the system*

In this section, some aspects of the shell of expert systems planning (ESPLAN) [17, 18], are considered. Namely, here the problems will be discussed connected with fuzzy knowledge representation in knowledge base of this system and the inference organization.

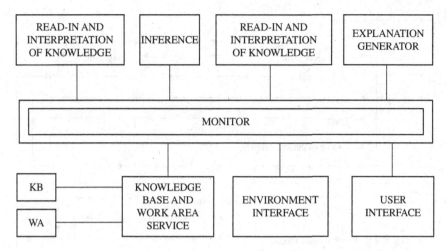

Fig. 17.1. Structure of the expert system.

The mathematical description of knowledge in the shell of expert systems ESPLAN is based on fuzzy interpretation of antecedents and consequents in production rules. The common structure of developed expert systems is shown in Fig. 17.1.

17.2.2. *Knowledge representation*

For the knowledge representation in the ESPLAN shell the antecedent of each rule contains a conjunction of logical connectives like (Fig. 17.2): <name of object> $\left\{ \begin{matrix} = \\ \neq \end{matrix} \right\}$ <linguistic value> named elementary antecedent (for instance, "IF quantity of petroleum = great AND demanded output of residual oil $\neq$ little AND ...").

The consequent of the rule is a list of imperatives, among which may be some operator-functions (i.e., input and output of objects' values, operations with segments of a knowledge base, etc). Each rule may be complemented with a confidence degree cf $\in [0, 100]$ and with the author's comments on the rule. For example, let us take a rule from the knowledge base (Fig. 17.2):

IF the remainder of local petroleum = great
THEN the load of 17th unit = great
CONFIDENCE 90

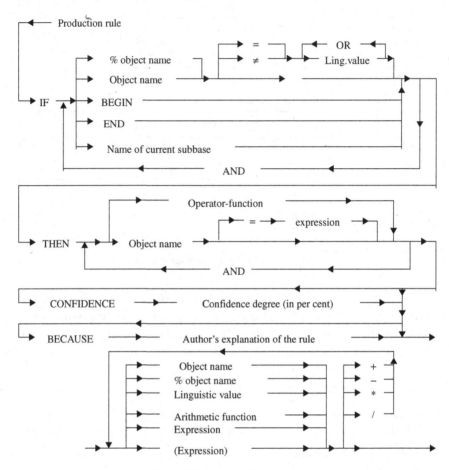

Fig. 17.2. Production rules.

BECAUSE "if there is great remainder, then the 17th unit may be completely loaded"

For appropriate interpretation of linguistic values in ESPLAN the fuzzy sets theory is used. Each linguistic value has a corresponding membership function which is built using parametric LR-representation (Fig. 17.3).

So, each membership function is defined by four parameters: α_l — left deviation, a_1 — left peak, a_2 — right peak, α_r — right deviation, i.e., $\mu_a(x) = (\alpha_l, a_1, a_2, \alpha_r)$.

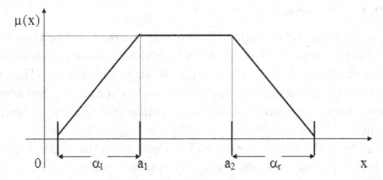

Fig. 17.3. Membership function.

So we have an analytic form of membership function [17, 18]:

$$\mu_a(x) = \begin{cases} 1 - \dfrac{a_1 - x}{\alpha_l} & \text{if } a_1 - \alpha_l \leq x \leq a_1 \\[2mm] 1 & \text{if } a_1 \leq x \leq a_2 \\[2mm] 1 - \dfrac{x - a_2}{\alpha_r} & \text{if } a_2 \leq x \leq a_2 + \alpha_r \\[2mm] 0 & \text{in other cases} \end{cases}$$

The graphical representation of membership function is a trapezoid with the tops a_l and a_r and plumb deviations α_l and α_r, respectively. Such representation allows the definition of unimodal membership functions, but knowledge representation language of ESPLAN also allows definition of polimodal membership functions using construction "OR". For instance, "low OR near 50". The result of interpretation is a disjunction (max) of membership functions of composite elements.

The subsystem of fuzzy arithmetic and linguistic values processing (see Fig. 17.1) provides automatic interpretation of linguistic values like "high", "low", "OK", "near...", "from ... to ..." and so on; i.e., for each linguistic value this subsystem automatically computes α_l, a_1, a_2 and α_r using universes of corresponding variable. The user of the system may define new linguistic values, modify built-in ones and explicitly prescribe a membership function in any place where linguistic values are useful.

17.2.3. *Inference*

Efficiency of inference engine considerably depends on the knowledge base internal organization. That is why ESPLAN realizes paradigm of "network of production rules" similar to semantic network. Here the nodes are rules and vertexes are objects. Inference mechanism acts as follows. First, some objects take some values (initial data). Then, all production rules, containing each of these objects in antecedent, are chosen from the knowledge base. For these rules the truth degree is computed (in other words, the system estimates the truth degree of the fact that current values of objects correspond to values fixed in antecedents). If the truth degree exceeds some threshold then imperatives from consequent are executed. At that time the same objects as well as a new one take new values and the process continues till work area contains "active" objects ("active" object means untested one).

The assigned value of the object is also complemented by a number, named confidence degree, which is equal to the truth degree of the rule.

A truth degree of a rule's antecedent is calculated according to the following algorithm [17].

Let us consider an antecedent of a rule in the form:

$$\text{IF ... AND } w_i \begin{Bmatrix} = \\ \neq \end{Bmatrix} a_{ji} \text{ AND ... AND } w_k \begin{Bmatrix} = \\ \neq \end{Bmatrix} a_{jk} \text{ AND ...}$$

Confidence degree of the rule $CF \in {]}0,100]$.

Objects w_i, w_k etc. have current values of the form (v, cf) in the work area (here v is linguistic value with its membership function, $cf \in {]}0,100]$ is confidence degree of the value v). Truth value of kth elementary antecedent is:

$r_k = \text{Poss}(v_k|a_{jk})^*cf_k$, if the sign is "="
and $r_k = (1 - \text{Poss}(v_k|a_k))^*cf_k$, if the sign is "$\neq$"
$\text{Poss}(v|a) = \max\limits_{u} \min(\mu_v(u), \mu_a(u)) \in [0, 1]$.

For the LR-representation of membership function.

$$\text{Poss}(v|a) = \begin{cases} 1 - \dfrac{v_1 - a_2}{\gamma_l + \alpha_r} & \text{if } 0 < v_1 - a_2 < \gamma_l + \alpha_r \\ 1 & \text{if } \max(a_1, v_1) \le \min(a_2, v_2) \\ 1 - \dfrac{a_1 - v_2}{\alpha_l + \gamma_r} & \text{if } 0 < a_1 - v_2 < \alpha_l + \gamma_r \\ 0 & \text{otherwise} \end{cases}$$

The truth degree of the rule:

$$R_j = (\min_k r_k) * \frac{CF_j}{100}$$

After the inference is over, the user may obtain for each object the list of its values with confidence degree which are accumulated in the work area. The desirable value of the object may be obtained using one of the developed algorithms:

$$w_i : (v_i^n, cf_i^n), n = \overline{1, S},$$

S is total number of values.

Calculation of resulting value:

I. Last $- v_i^s$

II. The value with maximum confidence degree $- v_i^m / cf_i^m = \max_n cf_i^n$

III. The value $\underline{v}_i = \Lambda_n (v_i^n * cf_i^n)$, or $\bar{v}_i = V_n (v_i^n * cf_i^n)$

IV. The average value $\bar{v}_i = \dfrac{\sum_n v_i^n * cf_i^n}{\sum_n cf_i^n}$

IF $x_1 = a_1^j$ AND $x_2 = a_2^j$ AND ... THEN $y_1 = b_1^j$ AND $y_2 = b_2^j$ AND ...

IF ... THEN $Y_1 = \text{AVRG } (y_1)$ AND $Y_2 = \text{AVRG } (y_2)$ AND ...

ESPLAN has a built-in function AVRG which calculates the average value. This function simplifies the organization of compositional inference with possibility measures. As a possibility measure here a confidence degree is used. So, the compositional relation is given as a set of production rules like:

IF $x_1 = a_1^j$ AND $x_2 = a_2^j$ AND ... THEN $y_1 = b_1^j$ AND $y_2 = b_2^j$ AND ...,

where j is a number of a rule (similar to the row of the compositional relation matrix). After all these rules have been executed (with different truth degrees) the next rule (rules) ought to be executed:

IF ... THEN $Y_1 =$ AVRG (y_1) AND $Y_2 =$ AVRG (y_2) AND ...

The approach based on construction of compositional relations is often used for synthesis of control systems for technological processes. Particularly, it was used for the construction of a knowledge base for the control of initial oil-refinery unit.

17.3.   Examples

17.3.1.   *The expert system for scheduling of oil-refinery production*

Here we consider some aspects of system's application for solving the tasks of scheduling oil-refinery production. The process was partitioned into four main subprocesses — initial oil-refinery, catalytic cracking, catalytic reforming, and petrol compounding.

{Distribution of petroleum among units 15, 16, 17}

. . . .

{Description of objects: shortname, fullname, minimal
value, maximal value, unit of measurement}
OB(S_100, "Plan on local petroleum", 10,30, "thous.tons");
OB(P_106, "Plan on output of residual oil",1,3,"thous.tons");
OB(R_106, "Real output of residual oil",1,3,"thous.tons");
OB(IN_42_106,"Input of residual oil at the unit 42",0.5,1.5, "thous.tons");
OB(E_17_106, "Yield efficiency for residual oil at the unit 17");

. . . .

IF . . .
THEN . . .
AND P3=(P_106+IN_42_106)/E_17_106
AND P31=TP_17-P3
BECAUSE "Computing necessary load of 17-th unit to provide the plan with respect to the residual oil and the load unit 42";
IF P31=Less 0
THEN IN_17_100=TP_17 AND OUT_17_106=IN_17_100*E_17_106
AND R_106=OUT_17_106-IN_42_106
AND DISPLAY("Power of 17-th unit is insufficient for the load")
AND DISPLAY("of the unit 42 and demanded plan on residual oil")
BECAUSE "Necessary load of 17th unit is greater than the top capacity of the unit"

17.3.2. *Fuzzy hypotheses generating and accounting systems*

Using ESPLAN one may construct hypotheses generating and accounting systems. Such system contains the rules:

IF <condition$_j$> THEN $X = A_j$ CONFIDENCE CF$_j$

Here, "$X = A_j$" is a hypothesis that the object X takes the value A_j. Using some preliminary information, this system generates elements $X = (A_j, R_j)$, where R_j is a truth degree of jth rule. In order to account the hypothesis (i.e., to estimate the truth degree that X takes the value A_0) the recurrent Bayes–Shortliffe formula (see Chapter 6), generalized for the case of fuzzy hypotheses, is used [419]:

$$P_0 = 0$$

$$P_j = P_{j-1} + cf_j * \text{Poss}(A_0/A) * \left(1 - \frac{P_{j-1}}{100}\right)$$

This formula is realized as a built-in function BS:

IF END THEN P = BS(X, A_0);

These systems were implemented in two problem domains: medical diagnostics and forecasting of social conflicts.

In a case of medical diagnostics the structure of knowledge has the form:

IF ... AND symptom $_k$ $\left\{\begin{matrix}=\\\neq\end{matrix}\right\}$ value $_{jk}$ AND ... .

THEN diagnosis $_1$ = $\left\{\begin{matrix}\text{yes}\\\text{no}\end{matrix}\right\}$ CONFIDENCE CF$_j$;

. . . .

IF END THEN Probability_of_diagnosis$_1$ = BS(diagnosis$_1$, yes)-BS(diagnosis$_1$,no).

There was developed the system for the diagnosis of approximately 40 venous and arterial diseases, concerning its stages. The distinctive feature of the system is the capability of describing symptoms using fuzzy values.

17.3.3.   *Forecasting of conflicts*

There were also developed models that forecast conflicts and produce current advices. For this purpose approximately 70 factors had been chosen, some of them described current situation, others had an influence on the current situation. Having based on these factors, approximately 1500 causal relations were obtained like

IF illegal activities in region1 = positive
AND punishment for these activities = negative
THEN illegal activities in region2 = increase
CONFIDENCE 60.

Here "positive" and "negative" are linguistic values with membership functions, defined at the range $[0, 100]$, with peaks in points 100 and 0, respectively. Other linguistic values like "little", "big", etc. are also used in these models. The exploitation of the system demonstrated its sufficiently high adequacy to real processes. Moreover, one of the most important products of the system is availability of full explanation (i.e., motivation) of the forecasts. This explanation allows conducting a profound analysis of social processes.

In case of forecasting of social conflicts the structure of the knowledge base has the form:

IF ... AND factor $_k$ $\left\{ \begin{array}{c} = \\ \neq \end{array} \right\}$ value $_{jk}$ AND ...

THEN hypothesis_factor $_1$ $= \left\{ \begin{array}{c} \text{increase} \\ \text{decrease} \end{array} \right\}$ CONFIDENCE CF$_j$;

. . . .

IF END THEN forecast_factor$_1$ = BS(hypothesis_factor$_1$,increase)-

BS(hypothesis_factor$_1$,decrease).

Chapter 18

Application of Logistic Regression Analysis to Fuzzy Cognitive Maps

In this chapter, we will consider the model construction of complex systems with fuzzy cognitive maps, which provide us with a quite simple method for simulating the diversified phenomena of the real world. Since several mathematical methods for examining these maps are available already, we will in turn focus on the statistical aspects and in particular on the logistic regression models.

18.1. Introduction

Fuzzy systems have proven to be powerful tools in model construction because they enable us to design these models quite effortlessly and in a human-like manner [534]. Typical application areas are control, decision making and robotics. Fuzzy systems also apply well when we examine the complex phenomena in the real world.

Our models may yield both unique and general probability estimations of the magnitude of the output values according to their input values. Hence, unlike in many prevailing studies, which only seem to provide more or less unique outcomes, our models may also provide us with important additional information concerning their general mathematical properties.

This chapter is dedicated to my friend, great mentor and source of inspiration, Professor Lotfi Zadeh.

18.2. Fuzzy Cognitive Maps

The fuzzy cognitive maps (FCM) stem from the ideas of Robert Axelrod and Bart Kosko [45, 253], and they are used for simulating and forecasting such phenomena of the real world which consist of numerous variables and their interrelationships. They may also include feedback operations, and hence in these systems everything may depend upon everything else. We usually apply these maps to such simulations in which we aim to forecast the complex phenomena on the time axis [88, 91, 179, 199, 330, 420, 422]. In statistics the structural equation models are used for this purpose (e.g., Mplus^{TM}, LISREL^{TM}, AMOS^{TM}) as well as time series analysis, but the fuzzy cognitive maps are usually simpler and more robust in model construction.

The traditional Axelrod's cognitive maps base on classical bivalent or trivalent logic and mathematics and hence they can only model more or less coarsely the relationships [45]. Kosko enhanced these maps by applying the Hebbian neural networks and using the numeric variable values which usually range from 0 to 1, and these values denote the degrees of activation of the variables or concepts. The degrees of relationship between the variables, in turn, may range from -1 to 1 in which case the benchmarks -1, 1 and 0 denote full negative effect, full positive effect and no effect, respectively [253].

Due to the mathematical properties of the numeric cognitive maps, in iterations on the time axis the values of its variables may oscillate (limit cycles), are chaotic or finally become stable (fixed-point attractors). For example, in control applications our goal is usually to achieve certain fixed points.

If (empiric) data, history data, in a given period of time is unavailable, we only operate with a priori maps, and thus we apply human intuition or expertise in our constructions, otherwise we can also construct a posteriori maps and then we apply such methods as statistics (e.g., regression and path analysis), neural networks or evolutionary computing. Hence, appropriate data as well as such reasoning as abduction or induction can yield usable FCMs in an automatic manner.

However, the numeric FCMs can only establish monotonic causal interrelationships between the variables, whereas fuzzy linguistic cognitive maps enable us to avoid this problem [91]. The latter approach is also more user-friendly due to its linguistic nature. Below we only focus on the numeric FCMs because they are closely related to logistic regression modeling.

If the standard methods are used in FCM simulations, the concept (node) values range from zero to unity and the weights or intensities of the interrelationships in the connection matrices belong to the closed intervals from -1 to 1 [179, 253]. Hence, in the basic FCM computer simulations we may apply the matrix product, $*$,

$$V_{t+1} = f(V_t^* M) \qquad (18.1)$$

in which the state vector, V_t, contains m concept values at time t, M is an $m \times m$ connection matrix, f is the transformation function and vector V_{t+1} contains the new concept values at time $t+1$ [253]. The function f is usually the logistic or sigmoid function,

$$f(x) = 1/(1 + \exp(-\lambda x)) \qquad (18.2)$$

in which exp is the exponential function and parameter lambda λ, is positive value [179, 358, 420] (Fig. 18.1). This function transforms the preliminary output values into the closed interval from 0 to 1. Quite often lambda has the values of 1 or 5, and we will use the former value below because then the outputs have larger dispersions [199].

In the real-world FCM applications on the time axis the preceding values of concepts are usually relevant in the succeeding iteration. Thus, in our computations the diagonals of our connection matrices may also contain non-zero values, and then values of 1 are often used. Examples are provided in Section 18.4.

The FCMs seem to have certain mathematical analogy with logistic regression analysis, and thus we consider next this subject matter.

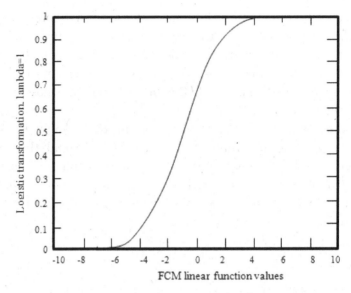

Fig. 18.1. Transformation function (18.2) when $\lambda = 1$.

18.3. Logistic and Multinomial Logistic Regression Analysis

We consider first a logistic regression model in which case we have a dichotomous dependent, or response variable, Y, which usually has values 0 or 1, and thus it refers to two groups of observations [161]. Then, we may establish that in the former group (values of 0) certain phenomenon or characteristic will not occur, whereas in the latter group it will occur. For example, in the Medical case-control research the cases (values of 1) and controls (reference set, values of 0) are usually the persons having or not having a certain disease, respectively, and we would like to predict the probability of having this disease.

If we now, for the sake of simplicity, only compare the probabilities of having the disease between two gender groups of persons, males and females, we should first calculate the odds to the disease in these groups,

- Odds1 = Probability of females having the disease/Probability of females not having the disease

- Odds2 = Probability of males having the disease/Probability of males not having the disease

If within this predictor, the females denote the reference group, the odds ratio (OR) is Odds2/Odds1, and this statistic plays an essential role in logistic regression analysis. If OR > 1, males have higher risks of having the disease, whereas OR < 1 denotes lower risk. This reasoning is applied to the dichotomous predictors when we estimate person's probability of having the disease.

More generally, the stochastic response variable, Y, then provides us with the probabilities of persons having the disease according to the logistic function

$$Y = 1/(1 + \exp(-Z)) \qquad (18.3)$$

in which $Z = \sum_i w_i X_i + C$, C is the constant and exp is the exponential function, i.e., Z is a linear regression function of its predictors, X_i, and their coefficients, w_i, $i = 1, 2, \ldots, m$. In fact, $\exp(w_i) = OR_i$ We notice that (18.3) is identical to the transformation function (18.2) when lambda $= 1$.

With the continuous predictors, if $w_i > 0$, then the higher values of X_i, the higher the risk of having the disease, whereas $w_i < 0$ denotes lower risk. Hence, with continuous predictors we examine the coefficients w_i, which are the logarithmic values of their odds, whereas with the discrete variables we focus on the corresponding OR values as above (non-dichotomous discrete variables should first be transformed into dichotomous dummy variables).

The iterative maximum likelihood method is applied to finding the appropriate statistical regression model in (18.3). In practice, the zero-model with only containing the constant C is constructed first, and then its goodness-of-fit value, $-2 \cdot \log$Likelihood value, is compared to the corresponding tentative values of model (18.3) when the coefficients w_i and C are used as the optimization parameters. The best final model has the lowest goodness-of-fit value compared to the zero-model [161].

Table 18.1 presents a simple statistical example with SPSS^{TM}, in which case we aim to predict the risk of having certain disease

Table 18.1. Logistic regression statistics for predicting disease.

	w	S.E.	Wald	df	Sig.	OR	95% C.I. for OR	
							Lower	Upper
Age	0.027	0.009	9.608	1	0.002	1.027	1.010	1.045
Sector (1)	1.182	0.337	12.298	1	0.000	3.260	1.684	6.310
Constant	−2.160	0.344	39.436	1	0.000	0.115		

according to person's age and his/her residential area (sectors 1 and 2) in a given data set. Wald's tests indicate that both of these variables are relevant in this model because we notice them to be significant. We notice first that the older the person, the higher the risk (odds) of having the disease because the corresponding regression coefficient value, w, is positive (0.027). Since here the residential area number 1 was the reference set, we also notice that in the area number 2 it is higher risk of having the disease because the OR value > 1, in fact, in the area 2 the odds is 3.260 times higher than in area 1. The 95 % confidence limits are quite narrow, and thus the OR values are quite reliable.

Hence, logistic regression analysis enables us to perform risk analysis, and below we apply it to the FCM models when we estimate the possible new values of a given concept, i.e., these concept values will be our response variables and the preceding concept values are our predictors. We also notice that both FCM and this analysis apply similar logistic functions even though they have distinct interpretations. Since logistic regression analysis presupposes dichotomous response variables, we will also apply multinomial logistic regression models below in which case multi-valued discrete response variables are also possible, but otherwise analogous outcomes are obtained.

18.4.   Application Examples

We will consider two well-known examples below, the city-health and process control of liquid tank models [267, 341, 420]. Since the prevailing FCM methods have already been applied to their simulations quite much [179], we focus on their statistical aspects, in particular our regression models. In this manner, we may provide additional information to these model simulations.

18.4.1. *The city-health model*

The city-health model contains seven concepts as follows:

1. Number of people in the city
2. Migration into city
3. Modernization
4. Amount of garbage
5. Sanitation facilities
6. Number of diseases
7. Bacteria per area

and their FCM interrelationships, the connection matrix, are presented in Table 18.2 [267]. For example, the concept Nr_people is only directly affected by Migration with weight 0.5 and Nr_diseases with weight −0.3.

If we apply this table to our FCM iterations with $\lambda = 1$ by using (18.1) and (18.2), we will achieve the fixed-point attractors quite rapidly as is shown in Table 18.3 and Fig. 18.2. In the real-world FCM applications the preceding values of concepts are usually relevant in the succeeding iteration, and thus in computations the

Table 18.2. City-health connection matrix.

	Nr_ people	Migra- tion	Moderni- zation	Garbage	Sani- tation	Nr_ diseases	Bacteria
Nr_people	0	0	0.6	0.9	0	0	0
Migration	0.5	0	0	0	0	0	0
Modernization	0	0.6	0	0	0.8	0	0
Garbage	0	0	0	0	0	0	0.9
Sanitation	0	0	0	0	0	−0.8	−0.9
Nr_diseases	−0.3	0	0	0	0	0	0
Bacteria	0	0	0	0	0	0.8	0

Table 18.3. Descriptive statistics of possible concept values in city-health model prior to logistic transformation.

	N	Range	Minimum	Maximum	Mean	Std. deviation
Nr_people	1000	0.55	0.49	1.05	0.8005	0.10357
Migration	1000	0.53	0.8	1.33	1.1008	0.09994
Modernization	1000	0.51	0.8	1.31	1.0701	0.10222
Garbage	1000	0.61	0.95	1.56	1.2916	0.12389
Sanitation	1000	0.62	0.9	1.52	1.2555	0.11739
Nr_diseases	1000	1.09	−0.01	1.08	0.546	0.20023
Bacteria	1000	1.01	0.1	1.11	0.6278	0.17801

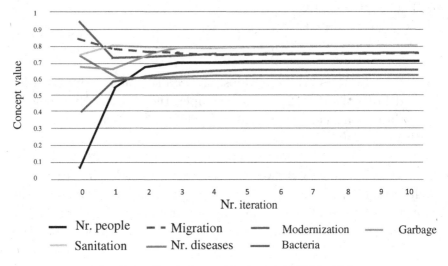

Fig. 18.2. Simulation results based on Table 18.4.

diagonals of our connection matrices also should contain non-zero values. However, in our first example we are not applying this idea but we rather follow the original modeling with zero diagonal.

Table 18.3 presents approximately the possible values of each concept prior to the logistic transformation when 1000 random initial concept vectors are used because we are unable to use all initial vector combinations due to computational explosion. Mainly non-negative values are obtained. After the logistic transformation, the most concept values will thus be greater than 0.5. These outcomes thus indicate that mainly high concept values are obtained in iterations. The values prior to the logistic transformation are relevant to our examinations below because then we are independent of the various versions of the logistic functions.

Table 18.3 and Fig. 18.2 present a simulation example with transformed values in a given period of time (iterations) when iteration 0 denotes the random initial input vector. In our city-health model any initial vector values will lead to similar fixed-point attractors. Table 18.4 also provides an example on a history data set of the FCM.

Our aim is to examine how the concept values can be predicted according to the other concepts. This type of FCM studies has been performed already by applying graph and path analysis [179], but we use statistical methods instead.

First, we apply decision analysis for having the overall vision on the interrelationships between the concepts. Second, we apply logistic regression models for our predictions.

As a concrete example, we only focus here on the concept Number of diseases which will be our dependent variable. The SPSS^{TM} decision tree tool with exhaustive CHAID method provides a roadmap for selecting the relevant predictors (Fig. 18.3), and

Table 18.4. Iteration example with city-health model.

Iterations	Nr_ people	Migration	Moderni- zation	Garbage	Sani- tation	Nr_ diseases	Bacteria
0	0.036	0.849	0.934	0.679	0.758	0.743	0.392
1	0.559	0.804	0.722	0.671	0.818	0.611	0.580
2	0.685	0.775	0.742	0.764	0.802	0.603	0.610
3	0.709	0.772	0.760	0.799	0.801	0.611	0.640
4	0.713	0.774	0.766	0.808	0.804	0.618	0.654
5	0.714	0.774	0.767	0.810	0.805	0.622	0.659
6	0.714	0.775	0.768	0.810	0.805	0.624	0.660
7	0.714	0.775	0.768	0.810	0.805	0.624	0.660
8	0.714	0.775	0.768	0.810	0.805	0.624	0.660
9	0.714	0.775	0.768	0.810	0.805	0.624	0.660
10	0.714	0.775	0.768	0.810	0.805	0.624	0.660

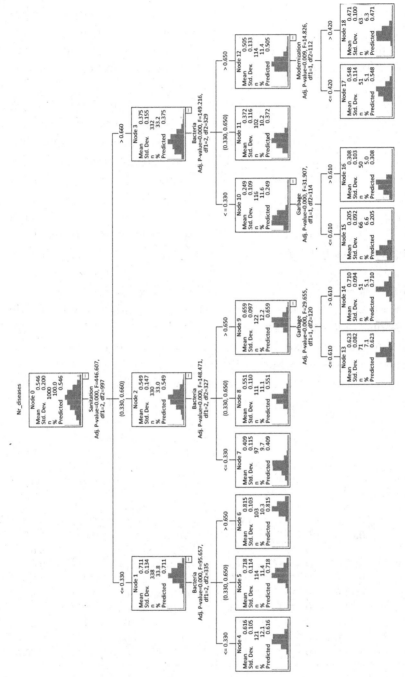

Fig. 18.3. Decision tree of the relevant predictors to Nr_diseases.

the concepts Sanitation, Bacteria, Garbage and Modernization seem essential in this sense. Hence, the essential indirect effects on the dependent concept are also taken into consideration.

For example, by following its paths, this decision tree indicates that if Sanitation > 0.66 and Bacteria < 0.33 and Garbage > 0.61, then the average value of Nr_diseases is 0.31.

Figure 18.4 depicts the distribution of the possible values of Nr_diseases prior to the logistic transformation. Hence, its mean, 0.55, was applied when the corresponding dichotomous concept, Nr_diseases_binned, was created for the logistic regression analysis,

- Nr_diseases_binned = 0, when Nr_diseases $\leq$ 0.55,
- Nr_diseases_binned = 1, when Nr_diseases > 0.55.

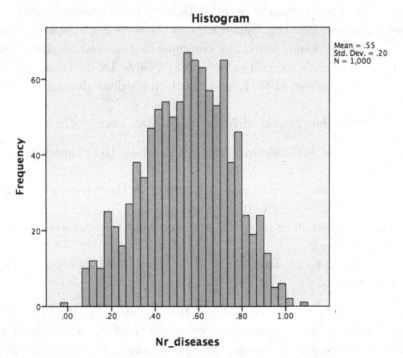

Fig. 18.4. Distribution of the possible values of Nr_diseases prior to their transformations.

Table 18.5. Logistic regression statistics for predicting high values of Nr_diseases.

| | w | S.E. | Wald | df | Sig. | OR | 95% C.I. for OR | |
							Lower	Upper
Moderni-zation	−2.748	0.448	37.619	1	0.000	0.064	0.027	0.154
Garbage	4.802	0.527	83.163	1	0.000	121.808	43.393	341.930
Sanitation	−13.551	0.965	197.181	1	0.000	0.000	0.000	0.000
Bacteria	9.735	0.776	157.454	1	0.000	16894.641	3693.085	77287.394
Constant	0.886	0.405	4.789	1	0.029	2.424		

We will refer to these values as low and high number of diseases, respectively.

We may now construct such logistic regression model which can yield the probabilities of obtaining high concept values to the dependent concept. When various stepwise regression methods were applied, their outcomes corresponded to our decision tree with Nagelkerke's rsquare value of 0.81 (Table 18.5). These rsquare values ranges from 0 to 1, and the latter values denote the best fitting.

We may thus reason with the weights, w, among others,

- the increase in Modernization will decrease the chances to high Nr_diseases.
- The increase in Garbage will increase the chances to high Nr_diseases.
- The increase in Sanitation will decrease the chances to high Nr_diseases.
- The increase in Bacteria will increase the chances to high Nr_diseases.

These results also correspond to our intuition and the FCM relationships. In fact, we may even reason that, for example, if we increase one unit in Garbage, the odds for obtaining high number of diseases is OR = 121.808 times higher, and according to its confidence interval, CI, at least 43.393 times higher.

If we now formulate the linear function according to the coefficients w in Table 18.5,

$$\text{Nr\_diseases} = -2.748 \cdot \text{Modernization } 4.802 \cdot \text{Garbage}$$
$$- 13.551 \cdot \text{Sanitation } 9.735 \cdot \text{Bacteria} + 0.886$$

$$(18.5)$$

we may calculate the individual predicted probabilities of obtaining the high number of diseases with (18.3) (Fig. 18.5),

$$\text{Prob}(\text{Nr\_diseases}_{high}) = 1/(1 + \exp(-\text{Nr\_diseases})) \qquad (18.6)$$

For example, if Modernization = 0.44, Garbage = 0.27, Sanitation = 0.10 and Bacteria = 0.35, the probability of high number of diseases = 0.95.

If the discrete dependent concept has more than two values, we may apply multinomial logistic regression models instead. Consider now, for example, the binned concept, Nr_diseases_binned, with three values,

- Nr_diseases_binned = 1, when Nr_diseases ≤ 0.46,
- Nr_diseases_binned = 2, when $0.47 \leq$ Nr_diseases ≤ 0.64,
- Nr_diseases_binned = 3, when Nr_diseases ≥ 0.65,

in which case each class contains approximately one third of the observations, and we may refer to these classes as low, average and high number of diseases, respectively. We used the lowest group as our reference set.

Our model with the similar predictors as above yielded Nagelkerke's rsquare value of 0.85 and the regression coefficients in Table 18.6.

In this context we actually obtain two binary logistic models and the comparisons are drawn between low and average as well as between low and high values of Nr_diseases. In both cases we may reason with the values of w,

- the increase in Modernization will decrease the chances to average or high Nr_diseases.

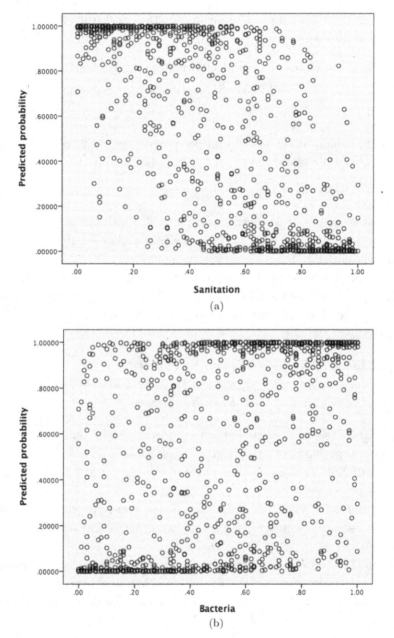

Fig. 18.5. The probabilities of high values for Nr_disease according to sanitation (a) and bacteria (b).

Table 18.6. Multinomial logistic regression statistics for predicting average and high values of Nr_diseases.

Nr_diseases_binned	w	Std. error	Wald	df	Sig.	OR
Average						
Intercept	3.983	0.547	52.936	1	0.000	
Modernization	−3.215	0.514	39.185	1	0.000	0.040
Garbage	4.462	0.578	59.519	1	0.000	86.7
Sanitation	−14.203	1.140	155.079	1	0.000	6.790E-7
Bacteria	9.809	0.862	129.572	1	0.000	18190.8
High						
Intercept	3.780	0.682	30.715	1	0.000	
Modernization	−6.974	0.713	95.634	1	0.000	0.001
Garbage	8.709	0.786	122.858	1	0.000	6056.5
Sanitation	−28.106	1.604	307.173	1	0.000	6.221E-13
Bacteria	18.762	1.177	254.125	1	0.000	140651867.8

- The increase in Garbage will increase the chances to average or high Nr_diseases.
- The increase in Sanitation will decrease the chances to average or high Nr_diseases.
- The increase in Bacteria will increase the chances to average or high Nr_diseases.

For example, if one unit increase in Garbage, the OR values indicate that the odds for average and high number of diseases are 86.663 and 6056.483 times higher, respectively. The linear functions are formulated as above, and the unique probabilities by applying then the logistic function,

$$\text{Nr\_diseases}_{\text{average}} = -3.215 \cdot \text{Modernization} + 4.462 \cdot \text{Garbage}$$
$$- 14.203 \cdot \text{Sanitation} + 9.809 \cdot \text{Bacteria} + 3.983$$
$$(18.7)$$

$$\text{Nr\_diseases}_{\text{high}} = -6.974 \cdot \text{Modernization} + 8.709 \cdot \text{Garbage}$$
$$- 28.106 \cdot \text{Sanitation} + 18.762 \cdot \text{Bacteria} + 3.780$$
$$(18.8)$$

Here again, our conclusions correspond our intuition and the FCM relationships.

If we applied ordinary linear regression analysis instead, we might obtain too coarse models because, in principle, the FCMs will yield nonlinear models. Fuzzy models, on the other hand, would be useful to nonlinear modeling, but this subject matter is precluded in this context because it has already been studied elsewhere, for example in Refs. [91, 330].

18.4.2. *The liquid tank model*

Our second example considers the control problem presented in Refs. [341, 420]. In this model two valves, valve1 and valve2, supply different liquids into the tank. These liquids are mixed for a certain chemical reaction, and our goal is to maintain the desired liquid level (amount of liquid) and specific liquid gravity in the tank. The third valve, valve3, is used to drain liquid from the tank.

Our FCM model applies the connection matrix presented in Table 18.7, and now the preceding values of the dependent concepts are also used in simulations (diagonal values are 1). We also use the transformed concept values with $\lambda = 1$ in this context because then our results correspond better to the original problem-setting.

Tables 18.8 and 18.9 present the possible concept values prior to and after our transformation when 1000 random initial concept values were used. Table 18.10 and Fig. 18.6 provide examples on our simulations when iteration 0 denotes random initial vector, and the fixed-point attractors are achieved already after a few iterations.

We will first focus on predicting the liquid levels in the tank. Hence, Liquid_level_binned is our dependent concept in our

Table 18.7. Connection matrix of the liquid tank model.

	Liquid level	Valve1	Valve2	Valve3	Gravity
Liquid level	1	−0.207	−0.112	0.064	0.264
Valve1	0.298	1	0.061	0.069	0.067
Valve2	0.356	0.062	1	0.063	0.061
Valve3	−0.516	0.07	0.063	1	0.068
Gauge	0.064	0.468	0.06	0.268	1

Table 18.8. Descriptive statistics of possible concept values prior to transformation.

	N	Range	Minimum	Maximum	Mean	Std. deviation
Liquid level	1000	1.77	−0.22	1.55	0.5830	0.34792
Valve1	1000	1.56	−0.08	1.47	0.6760	0.33109
Valve2	1000	1.14	−0.03	1.11	0.5419	0.29284
Valve3	1000	1.30	0.08	1.38	0.7404	0.30320
Gravity	1000	1.33	0.08	1.41	0.7150	0.29568

Table 18.9. Descriptive statistics of possible concept values after transformation.

	N	Range	Minimum	Maximum	Mean	Std. deviation
Liquid level	1000	0.38	0.45	0.83	0.6379	0.07886
Valve1_new	1000	0.33	0.48	0.81	0.6589	0.07305
Valve2_new	1000	0.26	0.49	0.75	0.6297	0.06763
Valve3_new	1000	0.28	0.52	0.80	0.6736	0.06573
Gravity	1000	0.28	0.52	0.80	0.6683	0.06460

Table 18.10. Iteration example with liquid tank model.

Iteration nr.	Liquid level	Valve1	Valve2	Valve3	Gravity
0	0.1	0.45	0.37	0.04	0.01
1	0.586	0.613	0.596	0.526	0.523
2	0.678	0.692	0.653	0.686	0.688
3	0.691	0.724	0.669	0.732	0.731
4	0.693	0.734	0.674	0.743	0.741
5	0.693	0.737	0.675	0.746	0.744
6	0.693	0.738	0.676	0.747	0.744
7	0.693	0.738	0.676	0.747	0.744
8	0.693	0.738	0.676	0.747	0.744

multinomial logistic regression model. We created three groups for our dependent concept by applying the class limits in Refs. [341, 420],

- if Liquid_level < 0.68, the level is low,
- If $0.68 \leq$ Liquid_level ≤ 0.70, the level is appropriate (the given goal level),
- If Liquid level > 0.70, the level is high.

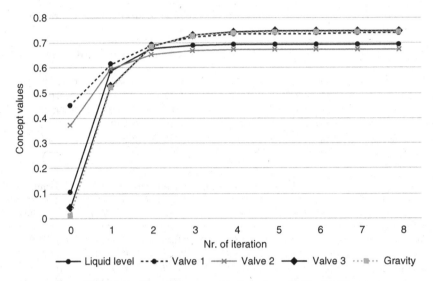

Fig. 18.6. Simulation results based on Table 18.10.

The goal level will be our reference set. By applying stepwise multinomial logistic regression when the possible predictors are the preceding liquid level and the other concepts, yielded the final model with Nagelkerke's rsquare of 0.979, and these results are in Table 18.11. Wald's tests indicate that our predictors seem the only relevant concepts to this model.

If we examine the regression coefficients in this Table from the standpoint of the goal values of the liquid level, we may reason, among others,

- the increased flows in valve1 and valve2 will cause lower risk to achieve low liquid level from the goal level,
- the increased flow in valve3 will cause higher risk to achieve low liquid level from the goal level,
- the increased flows in valve1 and valve2 will cause higher risk to achieve high liquid level from the goal level,
- the increased flow in valve3 will cause lower risk to achieve high liquid level from the goal level.

Table 18.11. Multinomial logistic regression statistics for predicting low and high levels of Nr_diseases.

Liquid_level_binned		w	Std. error	Wald	df	Sig.
Low	Intercept	79.136	14.739	28.827	1	0.000
	Liquid_level	−109.707	20.377	28.985	1	0.000
	Valve1	−33.785	6.341	28.392	1	0.000
	Valve2	−40.126	7.551	28.238	1	0.000
	Valve3	54.930	10.236	28.797	1	0.000
High	Intercept	−126.517	30.898	16.766	1	0.000
	Liquid_level	151.329	37.194	16.554	1	0.000
	Valve1	45.568	11.036	17.049	1	0.000
	Valve2	52.309	12.773	16.772	1	0.000
	Valve3	−79.126	19.380	16.670	1	0.000

Hence, these examples correspond well to the basic principles for controlling this system with the FCM.

The specific probabilities of low and high levels may be calculated the with the linear regression equations, and then with the logistic function as above,

$$\text{Liquid\_level}_{\text{low}} = -109.707 \cdot \text{Liquid\_level} - 33.785 \cdot \text{valve1}$$
$$- 40.126 \cdot \text{valve2} + 54.930 \cdot \text{valve3} + 79.136$$
$$(18.9)$$

$$\text{Liquid\_level}_{\text{high}} = 151.329 \cdot \text{Liquid\_level} + 45.568 \cdot \text{valve1}$$
$$+ 52.309 \cdot \text{valve2} - 79.126 \cdot \text{valve3} - 126.517$$
$$(18.10)$$

This system also aims to keep the gravity between the values 0.74 and 0.80 [341, 420]. As Table 18.9 and Fig. 18.7 indicate, its possible values are actually either below or within these limits. Hence, we may apply binary logistic regression analysis here and the concept values below the goal interval constitute our reference set.

In our regression model with the valve1 and valve2 and the preceding gravity as the predictors and the new gravity as the dependent

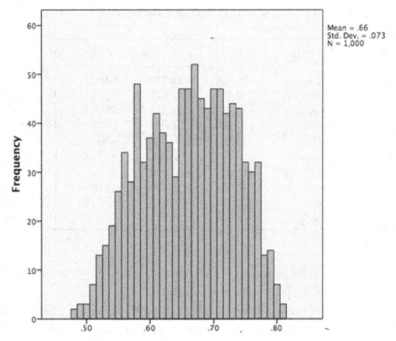

Fig. 18.7. Distribution of the possible values of gravity after their transformations.

Table 18.12. Logistic regression statistics for predicting appropriate gravity.

	w	S.E.	Wald	df	Sig.	OR
Valve1	29.775	3.301	81.378	1	0.000	8531E+12
Valve2	3.819	0.795	23.082	1	0.000	45.551
Gravity	13.439	1.571	73.197	1	0.000	686354.793
Constant	−33.075	3.623	83.359	1	0.000	0.000

concept, we obtained Nagelkerke's rsquare of 0.87 according to the stepwise regression methods. The coefficients in Table 18.12 indicate that the increases in the predictor concepts will increase the chances to achieve the goal values for the gravity with respect to its low values.

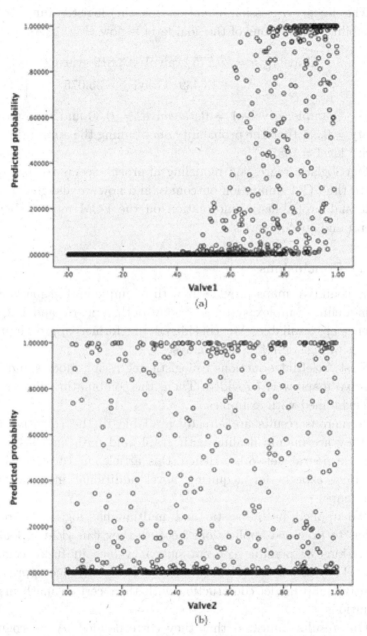

Fig. 18.8. The probabilities of goal values for Nr_disease according to valve1 (a) and valve2 (b).

The linear regression equation for the logistic function and probability calculations of the goal level is now (Fig. 18.8),

$$\text{Gravity}_{\text{goal}} = 29.775 \cdot \text{valve1} + 3.819 \cdot \text{valve2}$$
$$+ 13.439 \cdot \text{Gravity} - 33.075 \quad (18.11)$$

For example, if valve1 = 0.97, valve2 = 0.30 and the preceding gravity = 0.38, then the probability of obtaining the appropriate new gravity level = 0.87.

Our logistic regression modeling approach seems to correspond well to the FCM simulation outcomes, and now we also may acquire additional probabilistic information on the FCM models, both at general and specific levels.

18.5. Conclusions

Fuzzy cognitive maps provide us with a simple and usable method for modeling complex systems. Today both numeric and linguistic systems are available. We considered the former approach in the context of logistic regression analyses.

First, brief introductions to logistic regression models and fuzzy cognitive maps were provided. Then, the combination of these two were examined with examples.

Numerous results are already available to the cognitive maps but they are mainly dealing with graph and path analysis as well with the neural networks. Hence, this article, in turn, considered statistical aspects for acquiring novel additional information on these maps.

We applied both logistic and multinomial logistic regression models to practical applications because they can yield probability estimations of possible concept output values in fuzzy cognitive maps. They also seem to adopt more or less analogous approach to cognitive map model construction with their certain mathematical resolutions.

Our results indicated that they corresponded to the cognitive map simulations and with our approach we may also acquire both general and unique predictions on the possible values of the concepts when their initial values are given. This information, in turn, is important when we study the general features of the complex systems.

Our results above only provide certain general guidelines to this problem area and thus further studies are expected in the future.

Acknowledgments

I express my thanks to Prof. Rafik Aliev for having this opportunity to contribute to this book and also honor Lotfi Zadeh's memory.

Chapter 19

Fuzzy Logic in Medicine

The characteristics of the human body are quite different from person to person. This fact makes it difficult to examine, diagnose, care and cure humans. The complexity of their clinical practice and health care should be manipulated by a dynamic and human-centered theory in computers. The most appropriate one is fuzzy logic. Fuzzy logic would play a primary role in future medical and health care systems. We consider applications of fuzzy logic to process the signal of brain imaging and evaluate medical checkup data.

19.1. Introduction

Fuzzy logic has been employed in medical and health care studies. For example, 5,369 papers were found by searching by "Fuzzy" and "Medical" in IEEE Xplore database. Fuzzy logic has the following abilities:

(1) Fuzzy membership function has high ability to represent and manipulate bio-signals of human body.
(2) Fuzzy inference has high adaptability to various human body characteristics.
(3) Fuzzy logic provides a way to represent and manipulate imprecise and uncompleted information of human body.
(4) Fuzzy logic demonstrates knowledge of physician in a transparent style.

Thus, fuzzy logic provides a promising framework to develop medical and human health care systems. A fusion between fuzzy logic and pattern recognition led many successful tasks [71, 75, 198].

This chapter mainly introduces a results of fuzzy signal processing and a health checkup data analysis method on fuzzy interval [0, 1].

19.2. Fuzzy Signal Processing-Trans-Skull Brain Imaging

A conventional ultrasonography system can non-invasively provide human tissue and blood flow velocity information with real-time processing. In general, since the human skull prevents the disclosure of brain anatomy, we usually placed the sensor at the anterior and superior attachment site of the upper ear (the posterior temporal window) in adults. Due to this limitation, the conventional system cannot obtain transcranial information from arbitrary places in the skull. This section describes a transcranial sonography system [196] that can visualize the shape of the skull and brain surface from any point to examine skull fracture and brain disease such as cerebral atrophy, and epidural or subdural hematoma. In this system, we develop anatomical knowledge of the human head, and we employ the following fuzzy inference to determine the skull and brain surface.

Figure 19.1 shows an overview of our experimental system using models and human head. The model is placed into a water bath,

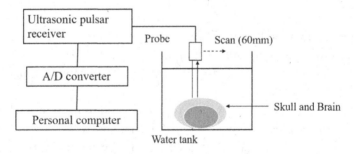

Fig. 19.1. Overview of the experimental system.

and ultrasound data are acquired from the model. When using a human head, a water bath is placed at the front of the head, and intracranial brain tissue data are collected. The ultrasonic pulsar receiver transmits and receives ultrasonic waves via the probe. A personal computer records the ultrasonic waveform data through an A/D converter. The sampling interval is 10 ns. The data obtained using this system include reflected echoes from the acrylic (or skull) surface, bottom, and intracranial soft tissue. We use an ultrasonic focus probe whose center frequency is 1 MHz, selected for its skull penetration in our past works. The model is scanned at intervals of 1.0 mm. In this method, first, the three starting boundary positions, A1, A2 and B in 1st waveform data are manually determined by considering layer head structure of skull, CSF and brain surface from human forehead, where first x denotes A1, second one does A2, and third one is B as shown in Fig. 19.2. and extract the one-wavelength echoes in the 1st data set. Second, by applying the information of each echo to the neighboring data set (2nd data), we calculate a fuzzy degree, which shows the possibility of a position at a point along the boundary. The position with the highest fuzzy degree is accepted as the echo position in the 2nd data set. Thus, the three boundary positions (A1, A2 and B) are determined from the 2nd data set. This process is repeated for all 61 ultrasound waveform data.

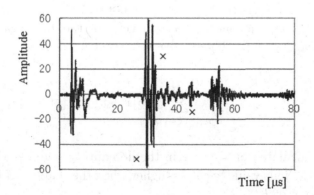

Fig. 19.2. Ultrasonic waveform.

We consider the changes in characteristic values, knowledge of shape, amplitude, and location, from 1st data to 2nd data, to determine the echo positions.

- *Knowledge of shape*: The changes to the *shape* are small.
- *Knowledge of amplitude*: The changes in the *amplitude* are small.
- *Knowledge of location*: The changes in *location* are small.

To convert these knowledge characteristics to fuzzy if-then rules and calculate the fuzzy degrees, three characteristic values, λ_f, λ_a and λ_{th} are introduced.

The notation $F[ti]$ $(ti = 0, 1, 2, \ldots)$ denotes the signal of the 1st data and $S[tj]$ $(tj = 0, 1, 2, \ldots)$ denotes the signal of the 2nd data. For each of A1, A2 and B, we manually extract one-wavelength echo in the 1st data at time ti. The notation $F[n]$ denotes the amplitude of this echo $(n = -(k-1)/2, -(k-1)/2 + 1, \ldots, (k-1)/2, t_a = 0)$, where odd number k denotes the sample number of $F[n]$. The echo position we determine in the 2nd data is denoted by time x: $x \in tj$. In the following calculations, we move the one wavelength $F[n]$ from $t_a - m(k-1)/2$ to $t_a + m(k-1)/2$ in the domain $[t_a - m(k-1)/2, t_a + m(k-1)/2]$ at the tj in 2nd data, where coefficient $m = 3$ is experimentally determined.

19.2.1.   *Characteristics with respect to echo shape, λ_f*

The first characteristic value, λ_f, denotes a criterion fitting the shapes between the one-wavelength echo of the 1st data and the wave of the 2nd data. The degree $\lambda_f(x)$ is defined by,

$$\lambda_f(x) = \sum_{n=-(k-1)/2}^{(k-1)/2} S[x+n] \times F[n] \tag{19.1}$$

$\lambda_f(x)$ is calculated on every x in the domain $[t_a - m(k-1)/2, t_a + m(k-1)/2]$. This value becomes higher when the shape of S is similar to the shape of F.

19.2.2. *Characteristics with respect to magnitude of echo amplitude,* λ_α

The second characteristic value, λ_α, denotes the criterion of closeness between the magnitude of peak to the amplitude peak of the one-wavelength echo of 1st data and the wave of 2nd data. The degree $\lambda_\alpha(x)$ is defined by

$$\lambda_\alpha(x) = |\alpha_x - \alpha_{ta}| \tag{19.2}$$

where the notation α_x denotes the maximal magnitude of $S[x]$ for $[x - (k-1)/2,\ x + (k-1)/2]$, and the notation α_{ta} denotes the maximal magnitude of $F[n]$. $\lambda_\alpha(x)$ is calculated for every x. $\lambda_\alpha(x)$ becomes lower when the amplitude magnitude of S becomes more similar to that of $F[n]$.

19.2.3. *Characteristic value with respect to location,* λ_{th}

The third characteristic value, λ_{th}, denotes the criterion of closeness between the location of the 1st data echo and the 2nd data wave. $\lambda_{th}(x)$ is defined by

$$\lambda_{th}(x) = x - t_a \tag{19.3}$$

$\lambda_{th}(x)$ is calculated for every x. λ_{th} becomes lower when the location of S is closer to the location of F. Using these three characteristic values, the following fuzzy if-then rule is defined to select a suitable next position for each of A1, A2 and B:

IF $\quad$ $\lambda_f(x)$ is high, $\quad$ [Knowledge 1]

AND $\quad$ $\lambda_\alpha(x)$ is low, $\quad$ [Knowledge 2]

AND $\quad$ $\lambda_{th}(x)$ is low, $\quad$ [Knowledge 3]

THEN $\quad$ the fuzzy degree $\mu_{\text{total}}(x)$ for position is *high*.

Figures 19.3(a)–19.3(c) show the defined fuzzy membership functions, SHAPE, MAGNITUDE and LOCATION for λ_f, λ_α and λ_{th}, respectively. After we calculate every $\lambda(x)$ on the domain $[t_a - m(k-1)/2,\ t_a + m(k-1)/2]$, the maximum values, shown

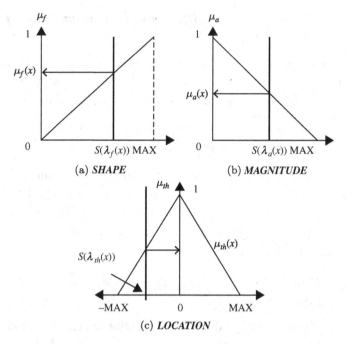

Fig. 19.3. Fuzzy membership functions.

by MAX in Fig. 19.3, are calculated. Then, the fuzzy membership functions are formed. The fuzzy degrees $\mu_f(x), \mu_a(x)$ and $\mu_{th}(x)$ are calculated by

$$\mu_f(x) = \min(\text{SHAPE}, s(\lambda_f(x))$$
$$\mu_a(x) = \min(\text{MAGNITUDE}, s(\lambda_a(x)) \qquad (19.4)$$
$$\mu_{th}(x) = \min(\text{LOCATION}, s(\lambda_{th}(x))$$

where a singleton function $s(\lambda_\beta(x) : \beta = f, a, th)$ is defined as $s(\lambda_\beta(x)) = 1$ if $x = \lambda_b$; otherwise on domain λ_β.

The fuzzy degrees $\mu_f(x)$, $\mu_a(x)$ and $\mu_{th}(x)$ represent the possibility that position x is the target echo position with respect to the shape, magnitude and location, respectively.

The fuzzy if-then rule can be combined with the following arithmetic product to calculate the total degree:

$$\mu_{\text{total}}(x) = \mu_f(x) \times \mu_a(x) \times \mu_{th}(x) \qquad (19.5)$$

After we calculate every $\mu_{\text{total}}(x)$ on the domain $[t_a - m(k-1)/2, t_a + m(k-1)/2]$, we determine position x of $S[tj]$ as the target echo by finding the x with the highest fuzzy degree $\mu_{\text{total}}(x)$. This process is applied to the determination of position of $A1$, and $A2$ and B, for 2nd data. In the same way, the process is repeated for all 61 data. We applied this method to determine the boundaries of the three positions in all data. We calculate the distances from the time-amplitude plane. First, we measured the thickness of skull x_i and distance between bottom and brain surface y_i. Suffix i denotes number of scan data. The thickness x_i' and distance y_i' between skull bottom and brain surface from the determined positions are calculated. Notation x_i' denotes the skull thickness. We calculate time difference t_{1i}' between skull surface and skull bottom, and then calculate the thickness x_i' by

$$x_i' = \frac{1}{2}t_{1i}' \times v_i' \qquad (19.6)$$

where v_i' is the velocity. On the other hand, time difference of y_i' is t_{2i}' between skull bottom and brain surface. We calculate the distance y_i' by

$$y_i' = \frac{1}{2}t_{2i}' \times v_i' \qquad (19.7)$$

The ultrasound velocity in water is 1480 m/s. We visualize an image on distances by these distances x_i' and y_i'. First, the animal model with brain tissue is tested. The width of the cattle brain is 55 mm. We acquired data for three lines. Sixty-one data were acquired for each line, and formed an image. Experimental results are shown in Fig. 19.4(a). Lines A1 and A2 represent skull surface and skull bottom, respectively. Line B represents the brain tissue surface on the domain of 60 mm.

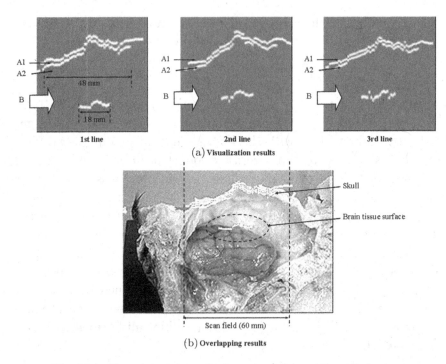

Fig. 19.4. Experimental results for animal data with cattle brain.

Figure 19.4(b) visualizes an overlapped image. The extracted lines (A1, A2 and B) exactly matched the skull boundaries and brain tissue surface. Next, we applied the proposed method to two human subjects. Two healthy male volunteers (ages 23 and 24 years old) were employed for the present study. A water bath was placed on the frontal portion of the head, and we acquired data of two lines in each subject.

In the human experiment, we determine four lines A0 (skin surface), A1 (Skull head), A2 (skull bottom) and B (Brain surface). We can easily extend our method for determining A1, A2 and B into the method for determining A0, A1, A2 and B. The extended method is applied to the subjects. The experimental results are shown in Figs. 19.5 and 19.6.

Figure 19.5(a) shows the visualization results for the four lines of the 1st subject. Figure 19.6(a) shows the visualization results for

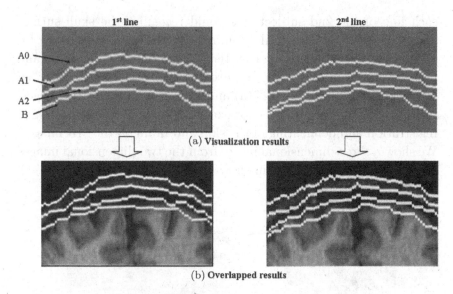

(a) **Visualization results**

(b) **Overlapped results**

Fig. 19.5. Experimental results of 1st subject.

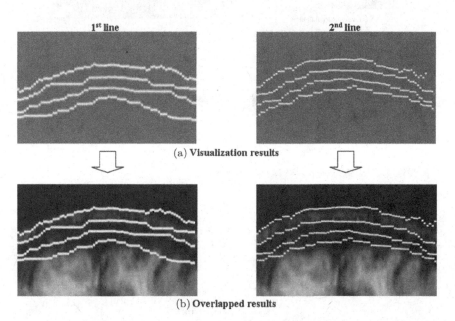

(a) **Visualization results**

(b) **Overlapped results**

Fig. 19.6. Experimental results of 2nd subject.

each line of the 2nd subject. We could recognize the skull surface
and skull bottom, and could confirm the brain tissue surface for
all images. Consequently, our system can visualize skull shape and
brain tissue from every line. Figures 19.5(b) and 19.6(b) show an
overlapped image of Figs. 19.5(a) and 19.6(a) with their MR images,
respectively. This accuracy is not exact but includes the errors of the
registration and delineating of the skin and brain on the MR images.
We show a three-dimensional image from the two-dimensional images
of Fig. 19.7(b) on the domain shown in Fig. 19.7(a).

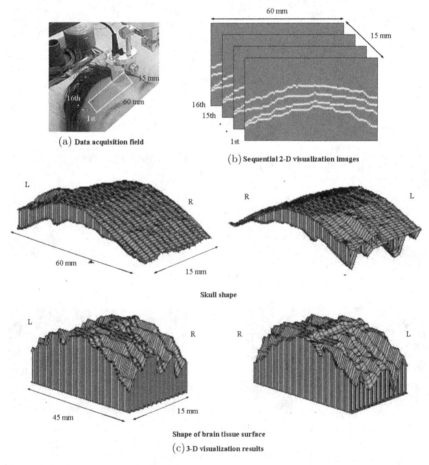

(a) Data acquisition field

(b) Sequential 2-D visualization images

Skull shape

Shape of brain tissue surface

(c) 3-D visualization results

Fig. 19.7. Three-dimensional experimental results.

The three-dimensional resultant images for collecting two-dimensional visualization images are shown in Fig. 19.7(c). In this, the upper figure shows the skull shape and lower figure shows the brain tissue surface. We can see that this fuzzy system could roughly provide the three-dimensional shape of the skull and the shape of the brain tissue surface.

Thus, fuzzy membership functions plays a primary role in this signal processing. It is proved that fuzzy membership function has high ability to represent and manipulate bio-signal from human body.

19.3. Health Checkup Data Analysis

This section describes a fuzzy logic approach for evaluating medical checkup data [202, 203]. Fuzzy degree for medical checkup data represents a normality of health condition. We call this fuzzy normal degree. The higher degree demonstrates normal conditions and lower degree does abnormal ones. Japanese Society of Human Dry Duck has reported about these reference intervals in April 2014 [203]. They studied to make the reference intervals for medical checkup data in all medical examination institutes for 1.5 million subjects, and they made reference intervals based on a standard of the Clinical Laboratory Standard Institute (CLSI). The intervals show Table 19.1.

We define fuzzy membership functions from this table. The fuzzy degree is obtained from each inspection item. We define fuzzy membership functions from Table 19.1, and we show an analysis method based on fuzzy logic. Fuzzy normal degree is considered as an attribute value in closed interval [0, 1]. To convert health data, state of health is defined that absolutely healthy is 1.0, and unhealthy is 0.0. We treat the fuzzy degree as a unified evaluation index for every item. We employ twelve medical checkup data: body mass index (BMI), systolic blood pressure (SBP), diastolic blood pressure (DBP), triglyceride (TG), high-density lipoprotein cholesterol (HDL), low-density lipoprotein cholesterol (LDL), serum glutamic-oxaloacetic transaminase (GOT), serum glutamate pyruvate transaminase (GPT), gamma-glutamyl trans peptidase (GTP),

Table 19.1. A reference interval.

Inspection item	Gender (M/F)	Division and range of value				Function pattern
		A	B	C	D	
BMI (kg/m²)	M	18.5–27.7		–18.4, 27.8–		2
	F	16.8–26.1		–16.7, 26.2–		2
SBP (mmHg)	M/F	88–147		147–159	160–	3
DBP (mmHg)	M/F	51–94		95–99	100–	3
TG (mg/dL)	M	39–198		199–399	–38, 400–	6
	F	32–134	135–199	200–399	–31, 400–	5
HDL (mg/dL)	M	40–92		30–39, 93–119	–29, 120–	4
	F	49–106		30–48, 106–119	–29, 120–	4
LDL (mg/dL)	M	72–178		60–71, 178–179	–59, 180–	4
	F	73–183		–72, 184–		2
GOT (U/L)	M	13–29	30–35	36–50	51–	1
	F	13–28	29–35	36–50	51–	1
GPT (U/L)	M	10–37	38–40	41–50	51–	1
	F	8–25	26–40	41–50	51–	1
GTP (IU/L)	M	12–84		85–100	101–	3
	F	8–25	26–80	81–100	101–	1
HbA1c (%)	M	4.63–5.67		5.68–6.12	6.12–	3
	F	4.62–5.67		5.68–6.12	6.12–	3
CRE (mg/dL)	M	0.66–1.08	1.08–1.09	1.10–1.29	1.30–	1
	F	0.47–0.82		0.83–0.99	1.00–	3
UA (mg/dL)	M	3.6–7.9		–3.5, 7.9–8.9	9.0–	3
	F	2.6–5.9	6.0–7.5	–2.5, 7.5–8.9	9.0–	1

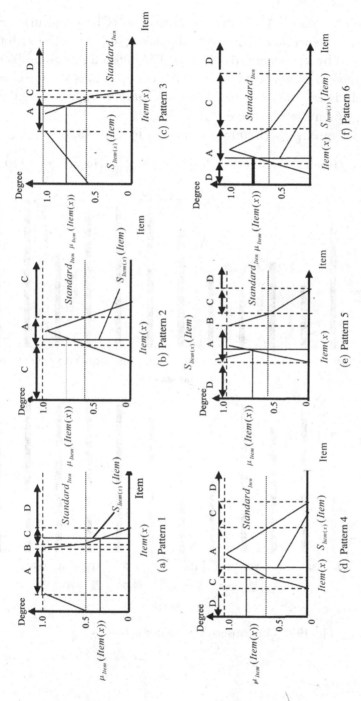

Fig. 19.8. Fuzzy membership functions used in health checkup data analysis.

glycated hemoglobin A1c (HbA1c), creatinine (CRE) and uric acid (UA). Each inspection item meets diagnostic criteria. The criteria were formed by four standard divisions. The division A is no problem. The division B is abnormality a little. The divisions C and D are abnormal. Fuzzy membership functions $Standard_{Item}$ are defined each inspection item in Table 19.1 by Fig. 19.8.

Fuzzy degree $\mu_{Item}(Item(x))$ is defined by Eq. (19.8).

$$\mu_{Item}(Item(x)) = \min(Standard_{Item}, S_{Item(x)}(Item)) \qquad (19.8)$$

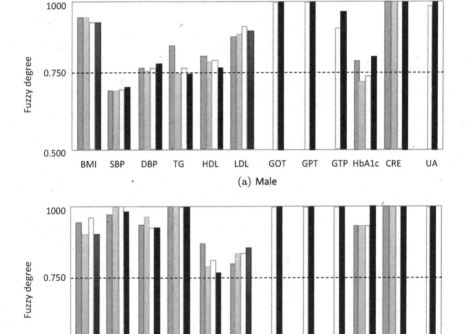

Fig. 19.9. Comparison every health indices by year.

Here, the notation Item denotes an index of inspection item. The notation Item(x) denotes a raw value of the Item, and the notation x does an examinee of the health check. The notation $S_{\text{Item}(x)}$(Item) is a fuzzy singleton function defined as $S_{\text{Items}(x)}$(Item) $= 1$ if Item $=$ Item(x); $=0$, otherwise. As the input data, we employed National Health and Nutrition Survey which MHLW reported from 2008 through 2011. Results of the survey publish as frequency distribution data on the website of MHLW. These data consist of results of separating by gender and age class, and include the mean and standard deviation. The composition of the number of people was different. These data excluded persons who are taking medicine and injecting to reduce inspection value. We converted mean of Japanese health data into fuzzy normal degrees in this method. Figure 19.9 shows these fuzzy degrees of each year. By converting the raw values of items into the fuzzy normal degree, it is easy for us to understand which items is becoming worse and which item should be improved.

For example, this figure suggested that males were worse at SBP; LDL of females was worse; tendency to improve year by year. Figure 19.10 shows fuzzy normal degrees of BMI and HbA1c for

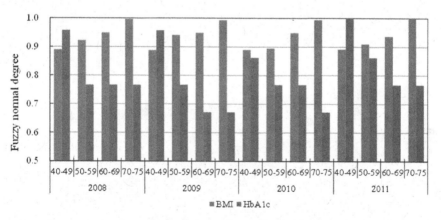

Fig. 19.10. Comparison of fuzzy normal degrees of BMI and HbA1c (male).

male. This figure shows BMI was improved but HbA1c was worsened according to getting older for every year. Thus, fuzzy logic can represent the criteria of medical checkup in a unified form, and provides a framework to treat every items by the fuzzy normal degree. In addition, Refs. [203, 226] demonstrate the disease index for several diseases and a degree of total health condition etc. This scheme would also be applied personal health care by designing fuzzy membership functions of Fig. 19.8 to adapt the characteristics of a user. Thus, fuzzy logic has high ability to manipulate our dynamic daily health data being different from person to person.

Bibliography

1. Aaron, B., Tamir, D. E., Rishe, N. D., and Kandel, A. (2014) Dynamic incremental fuzzy C-means clustering, in *Proc. 6th Int. Conf. Pervasive Patterns and Applications*, Venice, Italy, pp. 28–37.
2. Abu Aarqob, O. A., Shawagfeh, N. T., and AbuGhneim, O. A. (2008) Functions defined on fuzzy real numbers according to Zadeh's extension, *Int. Math. Forum* 3(16), 763–776.
3. Adamo, J. M. (1980) Fuzzy decision trees, *Fuzzy Sets Syst.* 4, 207–219.
4. Adeli, H. and Hung, S. L. (1994) *Machine Learning: Neural Networks, Genetic Algorithms, and Fuzzy Systems*, Wiley, New York, USA.
5. Affenzeller, M., Winkler, S., Wagner, S., and Beham, A. (2009) *Genetic Algorithms and Genetic Programming: Modern Concepts and Practical Applications*, Chapman and Hall/CRC, New York, USA.
6. Agarwal, D., Tamir, D. E., Last, M., and Kandel, A. (2012) A comparative study of software testing using artificial neural networks and info-fuzzy networks, *IEEE Trans. Syst., Man, Cyb.* 42(5), 1183–1193.
7. Aghakhani, S. and Dick, S. (2010) An on-line learning algorithm for complex fuzzy logic, in *Proc. IEEE Int. Conf. Fuzzy Systems*, pp. 1–7.
8. Aho, A. V. and Ullman, J. D. (1973) *The Theory of Parsing, Translation and Compiling*, Prentice-Hall, Englewood Cliffs, N.J., p. 1.
9. Alcal, R., Ducange, P., Herrera, F., Lazzerini, B., and Marcelloni, F. (2009) A multi-objective evolutionary approach to concurrently learn rule and data base soft linguistic fuzzy rule-based systems, *IEEE Trans. Fuzzy Syst.* 17, 1106–1122.
10. Alefeld, J. and Herzberger, G. (1983) *Introduction to Interval Computations*, Academic Press, New York.
11. Alexeyev, A. V., Borisov, A. N., Glushkov, V. I., Krumberg, O. A., Merkuryeva, G. V., Popov, V. A., and Slyadz, N. N. (1987) A Linguistic approach to decision-making problems, *Fuzzy Sets Syst.* 22, 25–41.

12. Aliev, R. A., Aliev, F. T., and Babaev, M. D. (1991) *Fuzzy Process Control and Knowledge Engineering*, Verlag TUV Rheinland, Klon.
13. Aliev, R. A., Mamedova, G. A., and Tserkovny, A. E. (1991) *Fuzzy Control Systems*, Energoatomizdat, Moscow (in Russian).
14. Aliev, R. A., Bonfig, K. W., and Aliev, F. T. (1993) *Messen, Steuern und Regeln mit Fuzzy-Logik*, Franzis-Verlag, München (in German).
15. Aliev, R. A. (1995) *Fuzzy Knowledge Based Intelligent Robots*, Radop o Svyaz, Moscow (in Russian).
16. Aliev, R. A. and Huseynov, O. H. (2014) *Decision Theory with Imperfect Information*, World Scientific, New Jersey, London, Singapore, 444 p.
17. Aliev, R. A. and Aliev, R. R. (2001) *Soft Computing and its Applications*, World Scientific, Singapore.
18. Aliev, R. A., Fazlollahi, B., and Aliev, R. R. (2004) *Soft Computing and its Applications in Business and Economics*, Springer-Verlag, Berlin, Heidelberg.
19. Aliev, R. A. (2013) *Fundamentals of the Fuzzy Logic-Based Generalized Theory of Decisions*, Springer, New York, Berlin.
20. Aliev, R. A. and Tserkovny, A. E. (2011) Systemic approach to fuzzy logic formalization for approximate reasoning, *Inform. Sci.* 181, 1045–1059.
21. Aliev, R. A. (2009) Decision and stability analysis in fuzzy economics, in *Annual Meeting NAFIPS*, USA, pp. 1–2.
22. Aliev, R. A., Huseynov, O. H., and Aliev, R. R. (2009) Decision making with imprecise probabilities and its application, in *Proc. ICSCCW*, pp. 1–5.
23. Aliev, R. A. and Pedrycz, W. (2009) Fundamentals of a fuzzy-logic-based generalized theory of stability, *IEEE T. Syst., Man, Cyb., Part B: Cyb.* 39(4), 971–988.
24. Aliev, R. A., Pedrycz, W., and Huseynov, O. H. (2013) Behavioral decision making with combined states under imperfect information, *Int. J. Inf. Tech. Decis.* 12(3), 619–645.
25. Aliev, R. A., Huseynov, O. H., Aliyev, R. R., and Alizadeh, A. V. (2015) *The Arithmetic of Z-Numbers. Theory and Applications*, World Scientific, Singapore.
26. Aliev R. A., Aliyev, B. F., Gardashova, L. A., and Huseynov, O. H. (2010) Selection of an optimal treatment method for acute periodontitis disease, *J. Med. Syst.* 36(2), 639–646.
27. Aliev, R. A. and Huseynov, O. H. (2014) Fuzzy geometry-based decision making with unprecisiated visual information, *Int. J. Inf. Tech. Decis.* 13(05), 1051–1073.
28. Aliev, R. A., Pedrycz, W., Fazlollahi, B., Huseynov, O. H., Alizadeh, A. V., and Guirimov, B. G. (2012) Fuzzy logic-based generalized decision theory with imperfect information, *Inform. Sci.* 189, 18–42.
29. Aliev, R. A., Pedrycz, W., Kreinovich, V., and Huseynov, O. H. (2016) The general theory of decisions, *Inform. Sci.* 327(10), 125–148.
30. Aliev, R. A., Alizadeh. A. V., and Huseynov, O. H. (2015) The arithmetic of discrete Z-numbers, *Inform. Sci.* 290, 134–155.

31. Allais, M. and Hagen, O. (1979) *Expected Utility Hypotheses and the Allais Paradox: Contemporary Discussions of the Decisions Under Uncertainty with Allais' Rejoinder*, D. Reidel Publishing Co., Dordrecht.

32. Alo, R., De Korvin, A., and Modave, F. (2002) Using fuzzy functions to select an optimal action in decision theory, in *Proc. NAFIPS*, pp. 348–353.

33. Alonso, J. M. (2010) Modeling highly interpretable fuzzy systems, *Eur. Centre Soft Comput.* http://dottorato.di.uniba.it/previous/seminari/hilk-bari-june-2010-print[1].pdf.

34. Alonso, J. M., Magdalena, L., and Cordon, O. (2010) Embedding HILK in a three-objective evolutionary algorithm with the aim of modeling highly interpretable fuzzy rule-based classifiers, in *4th Int. Workshop on Genetic and Evolving Fuzzy Systems* (GEFS2010), pp. 15–20.

35. Alonso, J. M. and Magdalena, L. (2011) HILK++: An interpretability-guided fuzzy modeling methodology for learning readable and comprehensible fuzzy rule-based classifiers, *Soft Comput.* 15(10), 1959–1980.

36. Anscombe, F. J. and Aumann, R. J. (1963) A definition of subjective probability, *Ann. Math. Stat.* 34, 199–205.

37. Apolloni, B., Pedrycz, W., Bassis, S., and Malchiodi, D. (2008) Granular constructs, *The Puzzle of Granular Computation*, Springer, Berlin, Heidelberg, pp. 343–384.

38. Arora, R. K. (2015) *Optimization: Algorithms and Applications*, Chapman and Hall/CRC. New York, USA.

39. Asuncion, A. and Newman, D. J. (2007) Uci machine learning repository, http://mlearn.ics.uci.edu/MLRepository.html.

40. Atanassov, K. (1999) *Intuitionistic Fuzzy Sets*, Springer Physica-Verlag, Berlin.

41. Atanasov, K. and Ban, A. (2000) On an operator over intuitionistic fuzzy sets, *Comptes Rendus de I'Academic bulgare des Sciences, Tome* 53(5), 39–42.

42. Atanasov, K. (2006) On the implications and negations over intuitionistic fuzzy sets, in *Proc. Free University of Burgas Conf.*

43. Atashpaz-Gargari, E. and Lucas, C. (2007) Imperialist competitive algorithm: An algorithm for optimization inspired by imperialistic competition, *IEEE C. Evol. Comput.* 7, 4661–4666.

44. Augustin, T., Miranda, E., and Vejnarova, J. (2009) Imprecise probability models and their applications, *Int. J. Approx. Reason.* 50(4), 581–582.

45. Axelrod, R. (1976) *Structure of Decision, the Cognitive Maps of Political Elites*, Princeton, University Press, Princeton.

46. Baas, S. J. and Kwakernaak, H. (1977) Rating and ranking of multi-aspect alternatives using fuzzy sets, *Automatica* 13, 47–58.

47. Back, T. (1996) *Evolutionary Algorithms in Theory and Practice: Evolution Strategies, Evolutionary Programming, Genetic Algorithms*, Oxford University Press, Oxford.

48. Back, T., Fogel, D. B., and Michalewicz, Z. (2000) *Evolutionary Computation 1: Basic Algorithms and Operators*, CRC Press, New York, USA.

49. Baldwin, J. F. and Pilsworth, B. W. (1979) A model of fuzzy reasoning through multivalued logic and set theory, *Int. J. Man-Machines Studies* 11, 351–380.
50. Ban, A. I. and Gal, S. G. (2002) *Defects of Properties in Mathematics Quantitative Characterizations*, Series on Concrete and Applicable Mathematics, vol 5, World Scientific, Singapore.
51. Bandler, W. and Kohout, L. (1980) Fuzzy power sets and fuzzy implications operators, *Fuzzy Sets Syst.* 4(1), 13–30.
52. Banzhaf, W., Nordin, P., Keller, R. E., and Francone, F. D. (1997) *Genetic Programming: An Introduction*, Morgan Kaufmann, San Francisco, CA, USA.
53. Bardossy, A. and Duckstein, L. (1995) *Fuzzy Rule-Based Modelling with Application to Geophysical Biological and Engineering Syst.* CRC Press, Boca Raton, FL.
54. Bargiela, A. and Pedrycz, W. (2002) *Granular Computing*, Kluwer Academic Publisher, Dordrecht.
55. Bargiela, A. and Pedrycz, W. (2003) *Granular Computing: An Introduction*, Kluwer Academic Publisher, Dordrecht.
56. Bargiela, A. and Pedrycz, W. (2005) Granular mappings, *IEEE T. Syst., Man, Cyb.s-Part A* 35(2), 292–297.
57. Bargiela, A. and Pedrycz, W. (2008) Toward a theory of granular computing for human-centered information processing, *IEEE T.Fuzzy Syst.* 16(2), 320–330.
58. Becker, J. and Sarin, R. (1990) Economics of ambiguity in probability, Working paper, UCLA Graduate School of Management.
59. Bede, B. and Gal, S. G. (2005) Generalizations of the differentiability of fuzzy-number-valued functions with applications to fuzzy differential equations, *Fuzzy. Set. Syst.* 151, 581–599.
60. Bede, B. and Stefanini, L. (2013) Generalized differentiability of fuzzy-valued functions, *Fuzzy Set. Syst.* 230, 119–141.
61. Běhounek, L. and Cintula. P. (2005) Fuzzy class theory, *Fuzzy Sets and Syst.* 154(1), 34–55.
62. Bellman, R. E. and Zadeh, L. A. (1970) Decision making in a fuzzy environment, *Man. Sci.* 17(4).
63. Belohlavek, R. and Vychodil, V. (2006) *Attribute Implications in a Fuzzy Setting*, ICFCA Lect. Notes Art. Intel., 3874. Springer, Heidelberg, pp. 45–60.
64. Berenji, H. R. (1991) Refinement of approximate reasoning-based controllers by reinforcement learning, in *Proc. 8th Int. Workshop on Mach. Learning*, Morgan Kaufmann, San Mateo, CA, pp. 475–479.
65. Berenji, H. R. and Khedkar, P. (1992) Learning and tuning fuzzy logic controllers through reinforcements, *IEEE Trans. Neur. Net.* 3(5), 724–740.
66. Berenji, H. R. (1993) Fuzzy reinforcement learning and dynamic programming, in *Int. Conf. Art. Intel, Workshop on Fuzzy Logic Control*, Chambery, France.

67. Berenji, H. R. (1996) Fuzzy Q-Learning for generalization of reinforcement learning, in *5th IEEE Int. Conf. Fuzzy Systems,* New Orleans, Louisiana, pp. 2208–2214.

68. Berenji, H. R. and Khedkar, P. (1998) Using fuzzy logic for performance evaluation in reinforcement learning, *Int. J. Approx. Reason.* 18(1–2), 131–144.

69. Berenji, H. R. and Vengerov, D. (2001) Convergent actor critic-based fuzzy reinforcement learning apparatus and method, US patent 6,917,925 B2, Filed.

70. Berenji, H. R. and Vengerov, D. (2003) A convergent actor-critic based FRL algorithm with application to power management of wireless transmitters, *IEEE T. Fuzzy Syst.* 11(4), 478–485.

71. Bezdek, J. C., Keller, J., Krisnapuram, R., and Pal, N. (1999) *Fuzzy Models and Algorithms for Pattern Recognition and Image Processing,* Springer.

72. Billot, A. (1992) From fuzzy set theory to non-additive probabilities: How have economists reacted? *Fuzzy Sets Syst.* 49, 75–90.

73. Billot, A. (1995) An existence theorem for fuzzy utility functions: A new elementary proof, *Fuzzy Sets Syst.* 74, 271–276.

74. Birkhoff, G. (1948) *Lattice Theory,* Am. Math. Soc. Colloq. Publication, New York.

75. Bloch, I. (2015) *Handbook of Biomedical Imaging "Fuzzy Methods in Medical Imaging,"* Springer, US, pp. 25–44.

76. Bonissone, P. (1994) *Fuzzy Logic Controllers: An Industrial Reality,* IEEE Press, New York, pp. 316–327.

77. Borisov, A. N., Alekseyev, A. V. Merkuryeva, G. V., Slyadz, N. N., and Gluschkov, V. I. (1989) *Fuzzy Information Processing in Decision Making Systems,* Radio i Svyaz, Moscow (in Russian).

78. Botros, S. M. and Atkeson, C. G. (1991) Generalization properties of radial basis functions, *Adv. Neur. Inf. Proc. Syst. III,* Morgan Kaufmann, San Mateo, CA, pp. 707–713.

79. Botta, A., Lazzerini, B., Marcelloni, F., and Stefanescu, D. C. (2009) Context adaptation of fuzzy systems through a multi-objective evolutionary approach based on a novel interpretability index, *Soft Comput.* 13, 437–449.

80. Buckley, J. J. (1989) Fuzzy complex numbers, *Fuzzy Sets Syst.* 33(1), 333–345.

81. Buckley, J. J. and Qu, Y. (1990) Solving linear and quadratic fuzzy equations, *Fuzzy Sets Syst.* 38(1), 43–59.

82. Buckley, J. J. and Qu, Y. (1991) Fuzzy complex analysis I: Differentiation, *Fuzzy Sets Syst.* 41(1), 269–284.

83. Buckley, J. J. and Qu, Y. (1991) Solving fuzzy equations: A new solution concept, *Fuzzy Sets Syst.* 41(1), 291–301.

84. Buckley, J. J. (1992) Fuzzy complex analysis II: Integration, *Fuzzy Sets Syst.* 49(1), 171–179.

85. Buckley, J. and Eslami, E. (1997) Fuzzy plane geometry I: Points and lines, *Fuzzy Sets Syst.* 86, 179–187.

86. Buckley, J. J. (2003) Fuzzy probability and statistics, *Stud. Fuz. Soft Comput.*, Springer, p. 196.

87. Buckley, J. J. and Leonard, J. J. (2008) Monte Carlo methods in fuzzy optimization, C-4, *Stud. Fuz. Soft Comput.*, Springer-Verlag, Heidelberg, Germany.

88. Buruzs, M., Hatwágner, M., and Kóczy, L. T. (2015) Expert-based method of integrated waste management systems for developing fuzzy cognitive map, *Stud. Fuz. Soft Comput.* 319, 111–137.

89. Camerer, C. and Weber M. (1992) Recent developments in modeling preferences, *J Risk Uncertainty* 5, 325–370.

90. Carnap, R. (1950) *The Logical Foundations of Probability*, University of Chicago Press, Chicago, *J. Symbolic Logic* 16(3), 205–207.

91. Carvalho, J. P. and Tome, J. (2009) Rule based fuzzy cognitive maps in socio-economic systems, in *Proc. IFSA Cong.*, Lisbon, pp. 1821–1826.

92. Casadesus-Masanell, R., Klibanoff, P. and Ozdenoren, E. (2000) Maxmin expected utility through statewise combinations, *Econ. Lett.* 66, 49–54.

93. Casasnovas, J. and Riera, J. V. (2006) On the addition of discrete fuzzy numbers, *Wseas Trans. Math.* 5(5), 549–554.

94. Casasnovas, J. and Riera, J. V. (2012) Weighted means of subjective evaluations, in R. Seizing, V. Sanz (eds.), *Soft Comput. Hum. Soc. Sci.*, Springer, Berlin, Heidelberg, pp. 323–345.

95. Castillo, O. and Melin, P. (2008) *Type-2 Fuzzy Logic: Theory and Applications*, Springer, Berlin.

96. Castillo, O. and Melin, P. (2012) A review on the design and optimization of interval type-2 fuzzy controllers, *Appl. Soft Comput.* 12(4), 1267–1278.

97. Chambers, L. D. (2000) *The Practical Handbook of Genetic Algorithms: Applications*, Chapman and Hall/CRC, New York, USA.

98. Chateauneuf, A. and Wakker, P. (1999) An axiomatization of cumulative prospect theory for decision under risk, *J Risk Uncertainty* 18(2), 137–145.

99. Chen, S. C., Cowan, F. N., and Grant, P. M. (1991) Orthogonal least squares learning algorithm for radial basis function networks, 2(2), 302–309.

100. Chen, Z. and Epstein, L. G. (2002) Ambiguity, risk, and asset returns in continuous time, *Econometrica* 70, 1403–1443.

101. Chen, Z., Aghakhani, S., Man, J., and Dick, S. (2009) ANCFIS: A neuro-fuzzy architecture employing complex fuzzy sets, *IEEE T. Fuzzy Syst.* 19(2), 305–322.

102. Chew, S. H., Karni, E., and Safra, Z. (1987) Risk aversion in the theory of expected utility with rank-dependent probabilities, *J. Econ. Theory* 42, 370–381.

103. Chiong, R. (2010) *Nature-Inspired Algorithms for Optimisation*, Springer, New York ,USA.

104. Choquet, G. (1953) Theory of capacities, *Annales de 'Institut Fourier* 5, 131–295.

105. Constantin, V. (1995) *Fuzzy Logic and Neuro Fuzzy Applications Explained*, Prentice Hall.

106. Cox, E. (2005) *Fuzzy Modeling and Genetic Algorithms for Data Mining and Exploration*, Morgan Kaufmann, USA.

107. Cpałka, K. and Rutkowski, L. (2005) Flexible takagi-sugeno fuzzy systems, Neural Networks, in *Proc. IEEE IJCNN*, 3, 1764–1769.

108. Cpałka, K. (2009) A new method for design and reduction of neuro-fuzzy classification systems, *IEEE Trans. Neur. Net.* 20, 701–714.

109. Cpałka, K. (2009) On evolutionary designing and learning of flexible neuro-fuzzy structures for nonlinear classification, *Nonlinear Anal. Series A: Theory, Meth. Appl.*, 71, 1659–1672.

110. Cpałka, K., Rebrova, O., Nowicki, R., and Rutkowski, L. (2013) On design of flexible neuro-fuzzy systems for nonlinear modelling, *Int. J. General Syst.* 42(6), 706–720.

111. Cpałka, K. (2017) *Design of Interpretable Fuzzy Systems*, Springer, Switzerland.

112. Cresswell, M. J. (1973) *Logic and Languages*, Methuen, London, UK.

113. Crowder, R. S. (1990) III. Predicting the Mackey-Glass timeseries with cascade-correlation learning, in *Proc. 1990 Connect. Models Summer School*, D. Touretzky, G. Hinton, and T. Sejnowski (eds.), Carnegic Mellon University, pp. 117–123.

114. Dasgupta, D. and Michalewicz, Z. (2001) *Evolutionary Algorithms in Engineering Applications*, Springer, New York, USA.

115. De Cooman, G. (2005) A behavioral model for vague probability assessments, *Fuzzy Sets Syst.* 154, 305–308.

116. De Wilde, P. (2004) Fuzzy utility and equilibria, *IEEE T. Syst., Man, Cyb., Part B: Cyb.* 34(4) 1774–1785.

117. De, S. P. and Krishna, P. R. (2004) A new approach to mining fuzzy databases using nearest neighbor classification by exploiting attribute hierarchies, *Int. J. Intel. Syst.* 19(12), 1277–1290.

118. Deb, K. and Kalyanmoy, D. (2001) *Multi-Objective Optimization Using Evolutionary Algorithms*, Wiley, England.

119. Deb, K., Pratap, A., Agarwal, S., and Meyarivan, T. (2002) A fast and elitist multi-objective genetic algorithm: NSGA-II, *IEEE T. Evol. Comput.* 6, 182–197.

120. Deluca, A. and Termini, S. (1978) A definition of non-probabilistic entropy in the setting of fuzzy sets theory, *Inform. Control*, 9, 613–626.

121. Dempster, A. P. (1967) Upper and lower probabilities induced by a multivalued mapping. *Ann. Math. Statist.* 38, 325–329.

122. Denneberg, D. (1994) *Non-Additive Measure and Integral*, Kluwer Academic Publisher, Boston, p. 196.

123. Denneberg, D. (2000) Non-additive measure and integral, basic concepts and their role for applications, *Fuzzy Measures and Integrals: Theory Applications*, Physica-Verlag, pp. 42–69.

124. Di Nola, A., Sessa, S., Pedrycz, W., and Sanchez, E. (1989) *Fuzzy Relation Equations and Their Applications to Knowledge Engineering*, Kluwer, Dordrecht.

125. Diamond, P. and Kloeden, P. (1994) *Metric Spaces of Fuzzy Sets, Theory and Applications*, World Scientific, Singapore.

126. Dick, S. (2005) Towards complex fuzzy logic, *IEEE Trans. Fuzzy Syst.* 13(1), 405–414.

127. Drianko, D., Hellendorf, H., and Reinfrank, M. (1993) *An Introduction to Fuzzy Control*, Springer-Verlag, Berlin, Heidelberg, Germany.

128. Dubois, D. and Prade, H. (1978) Operations on fuzzy numbers, *Int. J. Syst. Sci.* 9, 613–626.

129. Dubois, D. and Prade, H. (1982) Towards fuzzy differential calculus, *Fuzzy Sets Syst.* 1–17.

130. Dubois, D. and Prade, H. (1988) Representation and combination of uncertainty with belief functions and possibility measures, *Comput. Intell.* 4, 244–264.

131. Dubois, D. and Prade, H. (1990) Rough fuzzy sets and fuzzy rough sets, *Int. J. General Syst.* 17(2–3), 191–209.

132. Dubois, D. and Prade, H. (1992) Putting rough sets and fuzzy sets together, *Intel. Decision Support*, Kluwer Academic Publisher, Dordreccht, pp. 203–232.

133. Dubois, D. and Parde, H. (1996) *Fuzzy Information Engineering: A Guided Tour of Applications*, Wiley, New York.

134. Duch, W., Korbicz, J., Rutkowski, L. and Tadeusiewicz, R. (2013) Biocybernetics and biomedical engineering, *EXIT* (Warszawa).

135. Efstathiou, J. and Rajkovic. V. (1979) Multiattribute decision-making using a fuzzy heuristic approach, *IEEE Trans. Syst. Man, Cybern. SMC-9*, 326–333.

136. Efstathiou, J. and Tong, R. M. (1980) Ranking fuzzy sets using linguistic preference relations, in *Proc. 10th Int. Symp. Multiple-Valued Logic*, Northwestern University, Evanston, IL.

137. Eiben, A. E. and Smith, J. E. (2015) *Introduction to Evolutionary Computing*, Springer, Berlin, Heidelberg, Germany.

138. Einhorn, H. and Hogarth, R. (1985) Ambiguity and uncertainty in probabilistic inference, *Psychol. Rev.* 92, 433–461.

139. Ekenberg, L. and Thorbiornson, J. (2001) Second–order decision analysis, *Int. J. Uncertainty, Fuzz. Knowl. Based Syst.* 9(1), 13–37.

140. Ellsberg, D. (1961) Risk, ambiguity and the savage axioms, *Quarterly J. Econ.* 75, 643–669.

141. El-Samak, A. F. and Ashour, W. (2015) Optimization of traveling salesman problem using affinity propagation clustering and genetic algorithm, *J. Art. Intel. Soft Comput. Res.* 5, 239–246.

142. Engelbrecht, A. P. (2006) *Fundamentals of Computational Swarm Intelligence*, John Wiley & Sons, NJ, USA.

143. En-lin, L. and You-ming, Z. (2003) Random variable with fuzzy probability, *Appl. Math. Mech.* 24(4), 491–498.

144. Epstein, L. G. and Wanf, T. (1994) Intertemporal asset pricing under knightian uncertainty, *Econometrica* 62, 283–322.

145. Epstein, L. G. (1999) A definition of uncertainty aversion, *Rev. Econ. Stud.* 66, 579–608.

146. Epstein, L. G. and Zhang, J. (2001) Subjective probabilities on subjectively unambiguous events, *Econometrica* 69, 265–306.

147. Epstein, L. G. and Schneider, M. (2008) Ambiguity, information quality and asset pricing, *J. Fin.* 63(1), 197–228.

148. Espinosa, J. and Vandewalle, J. (2000) Constructing fuzzy models with linguistic integrity from numerical data-AFRELI algorithm, *IEEE Trans. Fuzzy Syst.* 8, 591–600.

149. Fahlman, S. E. (1988) Faster-learning variations on back-propagation: An empirical study, in D. Touretzky, G. Hinton, T. Sejnowski (eds.), in *Proc. 1988 Connect. Models Summer School*, Carnegic Mellon University, pp. 38–51.

150. Fahlman, S. E. and Lebiere, C. (1990) The cascade-correlation learning architecture, in D. S. Touretzky, G. Hinton, and T. Sejnowski (eds.), *Adv. Neur. Inf. Proc. Syst. II*, Morgan Kaufmann, San Mateo, CA.

151. Farahbod, F. Eftekhari, M. (2012) Comparison of different T-norm operators in classification problems, *Int. J. Fuzzy Logic Syst.* 2(3), 33–41.

152. Fazendeiro, P., de, Oliveira. and Pedrycz, W. (2007) A multiobjective design of a patient and anaesthetist-friendly neuromuscular blockade controller, *IEEE T. Biomed. Eng.* 54, 1667–1678.

153. Fenema, H. and Wakker, P. (1997) Original and cumulative prospect theory: A discussion of empirical differences, *J. Behav. Decis. Making* 10, 53–64.

154. Ferson, S., Ginsburg, L., and Kreinovich, V. (2002) Uncertainty in risk analysis: Towards a general second-order approach combining interval, probabilistic, and fuzzy techniques, in *Proc. FUZZ-IEEE*, pp. 1342–1347.

155. Filev, D. P. and Yager, R. R. (1991) A generalized defuzzification method via BAD distributions, *Int. J. Intel. Syst.* 6, 687–697.

156. Filev, D. and Yager, R. R. (1994) *Essentials of Fuzzy Modeling and Control*, Wiley-Interscience, New York.

157. Filev, D. and Syed, F. (2010) Applied control systems: Blending fuzzy logic with conventional control systems, *Int. J. General Syst.* 39, 395–414.

158. Flores, R., Barros, L., and Bassanezi, R. (2001) A note on Zadeh's extensions, *Fuzzy sets syst.* 117, 327–331.

159. Franke, G. (1978) Expected utility with ambiguous probabilities and irrational parameters, *Theory Deci.* 9, 267–283.

160. Fraser, A. and Burnell, D. (1970) *Computer Models in Genetics*, New York.

161. Freedman, D. (2005) *Statistical Models: Theory and Practice*, Cambridge University Press.

162. Fukami, S., Mizumoto, M., and Tanaka, K. (1980) Some consideration of fuzzy conditional inference, *Fuzzy Sets Syst.* 4, 243–273.

163. Gabryel, M., Cpalka, K., and Rutkowski, L. (2005) Evolutionary strategies for learning of neuro-fuzzy systems, in *Proc. I Workshop on Genetic Fuzzy Systems*, Granada, pp. 119–123.

164. Gacto, M. J., Alcal, R., and Herrera, F. (2010) Integration of an index to preserve the semantic interpretability in the multi-objective evolutionary rule selection and tuning of linguistic fuzzy systems, *IEEE Trans. Fuzzy Syst.* 18(3), 515–531.

165. Gacto, M. J., Alcal, R., and Herrera, F. (2011) Interpretability of linguistic fuzzy rule-based systems: An overview of interpretability measures, *Inf. Sci.* 181(20), 4340–4360.

166. Gajdosa, T., Hayashib, T., Tallona, J.-M., and Vergnauda, J.-C. (2008) Attitude toward imprecise information, *J. Econ. Theory* 140(1), 27–65.

167. Genç, S., Emre Boran, F., Akay, D., and Xu, Z. (2010) Interval multiplicative transitivity for consistency, missing values and priority weights of interval fuzzy preference relations, *Inform. Sci.* 180(24), 4877–4891.

168. Ghirardato, P., Klibanoff, P., and Marinacci, M. (1998) Additivity with multiple priors, *J. Math. Econ.* 30, 405–420.

169. Ghirardato, P. (2001) Coping with ignorance: Unforeseen contingencies and non-additive uncertainty, *Econ. Theor.* 17, 247–276.

170. Ghirardato, P. and Marinacci, M. (2001) Range convexity and ambiguity averse preferences, *Econ. Theor.* 17, 599–617.

171. Ghirardato, P. and Marinacci, M. (2002) Ambiguity made precise: A comparative foundation, *J. Econ. Theor.* 102, 251–289.

172. Ghirardato, P., Maccheroni, F., and Marinacci, M. (2004) Differentiating ambiguity and ambiguity attitude, *J. Econ. Theor.* 118, 133–173.

173. Gibilisco, M. B., Gowen, A. M., Albert, K. E., Mordeson, J. N., Wierman, M. J., and Clark, T. D. (2014) *Fuzzy Social Choice Theory*, Springer.

174. Gil, M. A. and Jain, P. (1992) Comparison of experiments in statistical decision problems with fuzzy utilities, *IEEE Trans. Systems, Man, Cyb.* 22(4), 662–670.

175. Gilboa, I. and Schmeidler, D. (1989) Maximin expected utility with a non-unique prior, *J. Math. Eco.* 18, 141–153.

176. Gilboa, I., Andrew, W. P., and Schmeidler, D. (2008) Probability and uncertainty in economic modeling, *J. Econ. Pers.* 22(3), 173–188.

177. Gilboa, I. (2009) *Theory of Decision Under Uncertainty*, Cambridge University Press, Wiley.

178. Gilboa, I., Maccheroni, F., Marinacci, M., and Schmeidler, D. (2010) Objective and subjective rationality in a multiple prior model, *Econometrica* 78(2), 755–770.

179. Glykas, M. (2010) *Fuzzy Cognitive Maps*, Springer, Berlin, Germany.

180. Goetschel, R. and Voxman, W. (1986) Elementary fuzzy calculus, *Fuzzy Sets Syst.* 18, 31–43.

181. Goguen, J. A. (1969) The logic of inexact concepts, *Synthese* 19, 325–373.

182. Goldberg, D. E. (1989) *Genetic Algorithms in Search, Optimization, and Machine Learning*, Addison-Wesley Professional, USA.

183. Good. I. J. (1962) Subjective probability as the measure of a non-measurable set, *Logic, Methodology and Philosophy of Science*, Stanford University Press, California, pp. 319–329.

184. Gorzalczany, M. B. and Rudzinski, F. (2012) Accuracy vs interpretability of fuzzy rule-based classifiers: An evolutionary approach, in *Proc. 2012 Int. Conf. Swarm Evolutionary Computation*, pp. 222–230.

185. Greenfield, S. and Chiclana, F. (2013) Fuzzy in 3-D: Contrasting complex fuzzy sets with type-2 fuzzy sets, in *Proc. Joint Ann. Meeting IFSA World Cong. and NAFIPS*, pp. 1237–1242.

186. Guangquan, Z., Dillon, T. S., Kai-Yuan, C., Jun, M., and Jie, L. (2010) Delta-equalities of complex fuzzy relations, in *Proc. IEEE Int. 24th Conf. Adv. Inf. Net. Appl.*, pp. 1218–1224.

187. Guillaume, S. and Charnomordic, B. (2004) Generating an interpretable family of fuzzy partitions from data, *IEEE Trans. Fuzzy Syst.* 12(3), 324–335.

188. Guo, P. and Tanaka, H. (2003) Decision analysis based on fused double exponential possibility distributions, *Eur. J. Oper. Res.* 148, 467–479.

189. Guo, C. and Zhang, D. (2004) On set-valued fuzzy measures, *Inf. Sci.* 160(1–4), 13–25.

190. Guo, C. and Zhang, D. (2007) On choquet integrals of fuzzy-valued functions with respect to fuzzy-valued fuzzy measures, *Int. Conf. Mach. Learning Cyb.* vol. 7, pp. 3653–3656.

191. Guo, P. and Tanaka, H. (2010) Decision making with interval probabilities, *Eur. J. Oper. Res.* 203, 444–454.

192. Guo, P. (2011) One-shot decision theory, *IEEE Tran. Syst. Man Cyb. Part A* 41(5), 917–926.

193. Guosheng, C. and Jianwei, Y. (2010) Complex fuzzy reasoning schemes, in *Proc. 3rd Int. Conf. Information Computation*, pp. 29–32.

194. Halmos, P. R. (1960) *Naive Set Theory*, Van Nostrand, New York.

195. Halpern, J. Y. (2003) *Reasoning about Uncertainty*, MIT Press, USA.

196. Hata, Y., Kobashi, S., Kondo, K., Kitamura, Y. T., and Yanagida, T. (2005) Transcranial ultrasonography system for visualizing skull and brain surface aided by fuzzy expert system, *IEEE Trans. Syst. Man Cyb.* 35(6), 1360–1373.

197. Hata, Y., Syoji, K., and Hiroshi, N. (2009) Human health care system of systems, *IEEE Syst. J.* 3(2), 231–238.

198. Hata, Y. (2015) Computational intelligence and medical applications, *Encycl. Life Support Syst. (UNESCO EOLSS)* 172–201.

199. Hatwagner, M. F., Niskanen, V. A. and Koczy, L. T. (2017) Behavioral analysis of fuzzy cognitive map models by simulation, in *Proc. IFSA '17 Congress*.

200. Haupt, R. L. and Haupt, S. E. (1998) *Practical Genetic Algorithms*, 2nd edn., Wiley, USA.

201. Haykin, S. S. (1991) *Adaptive Filter Theory*, 2nd edn., Prentice Hall, Upper Saddle River, NJ.

202. Higuchi, S. and Hata, Y. (2014) Fuzzy dependency analysis for medical checkup reference, in *Proc. 2014 IEEE Int. Conf. Systems, Man and Cybernetics*, SMC, pp. 4010–4015.

203. Higuchi, S. and Hata, Y. (2014) Fuzzy logic approach to health checkup data analysis, in *Proc. 2014 World Automation Congress*, WAC.

204. Hintikka, J. and Suppes, P. (1966) *Aspects of Inductive Logic*, North-Holland Publishing Co., Amsterdam, p. 1.

205. Hirota, K. (1981) Concepts of probabilistic sets, *Fuzzy Sets Syst.* 5(1), 31–46.

206. Ho Joanna, L. Y., Keller, L. R., and Keltyka, P. (2002) Effects of outcome and probabilistic ambiguity on managerial choices, *J Risk Uncertainty* 24(1), 47–74.

207. Hogarth, R. M. and Kunreuther, H. (1995) Decision making under ignorance: Arguing with yourself, *J. Risk Uncertainty* 10(1) 15–36.

208. Holland, J. H. (1992) *Adaptation in Natural and Artificial Systems: An Introductory Analysis with Applications to Biology, Control, and Artificial Intelligence*, A Bradford Book, USA.

209. Höppner, F., Klawonn, F., Kruse, R., and Runkler, K. (1999) *Fuzzy Cluster Analysis: Methods for Classification, Data Analysis and Image Recognition*, Wiley, New York, USA.

210. Hsu, M., Bhatt, M., Adolphs, R. *et al.*, (2005) Neural systems responding to degrees of uncertainty in human decision-making, *Science* 310(5754), 1680–1683.

211. Hu, D., Li, H., and Yu, X. (2009) The information content of fuzzy relations and fuzzy rules, *Comp. & Math. Appl.* 57(2), 202–216.

212. Huettel, S. A., Stowe, C. J., Gordon, E. M. *et al.*, (2006) Neural signatures of economic preferences for risk and ambiguity, *Neuron* 49, 765–775.

213. Humberto, B., Francisco, H., and Javier M. (2008) Fuzzy sets and their extensions: Representation, aggregation and models.

214. Hyoun-Joo Go, Keun-Chang Kwak, Mann-Jun Kwon, and Myung-Geun Chun. (2005) Iris pattern recognition using fuzzy lda method, in *Int. Conf. Knowl.-Based Intelligence Information Engineering System*, Springer, pp. 364–370.

215. Icke, I. and Rosenberg, A. (2011) Multi-objective genetic programming for visual analytics, in S. Silva *et al.* (eds.), *EuroGP 2011*, LNCS, 6621, pp. 322–334.

216. Ishibuchi, H., Nakashima, T., and Murata, T. (1997) Comparison of the Michigan and Pittsburgh approaches to the design of fuzzy classification systems, *Elect. Commun. Japan Part 3*, 80(12), 379–387.

217. Ishibuchi, H. (2005) Rule weight specification in fuzzy rule-based classification systems, *IEEE Trans. Fuzzy Syst.* 13(4), 428–436.

218. Ishibuchi, H. and Nojima, Y. (2007) Analysis of interpretability-accuracy tradeoff fuzzy systems by multiobjective fuzzy genetics-based machine learning, *Int. J. Approx.Reason.* 44, 4–31.

219. Jaffray, J.-Y. (1991) Belief functions, convex capacities, and decision making, *Math. Psychology: Current Developments*, Springer, New York, pp. 127–134.

220. Jaffray, J.-Y. and Philippe, F. (1997) On the existence of subjective upper and lower probabilities, *Math. Oper. Res.* 22, 165–185.

221. Jaffray, J.-Y. (1999) Rational decision making with imprecise probabilities, in *Proc. 1st Int. Symposium on Imprecise Prob. Their Applications*, Belgium, Imprecise Probability Project, pp. 324–332.

222. Jager, T. (2012) *Black-Box Models of Computation in Cryptology*, Vieweg+Teubner Verlag, Heidelberg, Germany.

223. Jain, R. (1976) Decision-making in the presence of fuzzy variables, *IEEE Trans Syst. Man Cyb. SMC-6*, pp. 698–703.

224. Jamshidi, M., Titli, A., Zadeh, L. A., and Boverie, S. (1997) Applications of fuzzy logic—towards high machine intelligence quotient systems. *Environment Intelligence Manufacturing System*, Prentice-Hall, Upper Saddle River, NJ.

225. Janis, V. (1998) Fuzzy mappings and fuzzy methods for crisp mappings, *Math* 6, 31–47.

226. Japanese Society of Human Dry Dock, http://www.ningen-dock.jp/html.

227. Jones, R. D., Lee, Y. C., Barnes, C. W., Flake, G. W., Lee, K., and Lewis, P. S. (1990) Function approximation and time series prediction with neural networks, in *Proc. IEEE Int. Joint Conf. Neural Network*, pp. 649–665.

228. Jordan, M. I. and Jacobs, R. A. (1993) Hierarchical mixtures of experts and the EM algorithm, Technical report, M.I.T.

229. Kadirkamanathan, V., Niranjan, M., and Fallside, F. (1991) Sequential adaptation of radial basis function neural networks, *Advances in Neural Information Processing Systems III*, Morgan Kaufmann, San Mateo, CA, pp. 721–727.

230. Kandel, A. (1987) *Fuzzy Mathematical Techniques with Applications*, Addison Wesley.

231. Kandel, A., Tamir, D. E., and Rishe, N. D. (2014) Fuzzy logic and data mining in disaster mitigation, *Impr. Disaster Resilience Mit. – IT Means Tools*, Springer Netherlands, pp. 167–186.

232. Kantorovich, L. V. and Akilov, G. P. (1982) *Functional Analysis*, 2nd edn. Pergamon, Oxford.

233. Karni, E. (1985) *Decision Making under Uncertainty: The Case of State Dependent Preferences*, Harvard University Press, Cambridge.

234. Karnik, N. N., Mendel, J. M., and Liang, Q. (1999) Type-2 fuzzy logic systems. *IEEE Trans. Fuzzy Syst.* 7(6), 643–658.

235. Karnik, N. N. and Mendel, J. M. (2001) Operations on type-2 fuzzy sets, *Fuzzy Set. Syst.* 122, 327–348.

236. Kaufman, A. and Gupta, M. M. (1985) *Introduction to Fuzzy Arithmetic: Theory and Applications*, Van Nostrand Reinhold Company, New York.

237. Kenesei, T. and Abonyi, J. (2007) Interpretable support vector machines in regression and classification-application in process engineering, *Hung. J. Industr. Chem.* 35, 101–108.

238. Khan, A. R., Amin, H. U., and Rehman, Z. U. (2011) *Application of Expert System with Fuzzy Logic in Teachers Performance Evaluation*, Institute of Computing & Information Technology (ICIT), Gomal University, Pakistan.

239. Kickert, W. and Mamdani, E. (1978) Analysis of a fuzzy logic controller, *Fuzzy Sets Syst.* 12, 29–44.

240. Klassen, M. S. and Pao, Y.-H. (1988) Characteristics of the functional-link net: A higher order delta rule net, *IEEE Proc. Int. Conf. Neural Network*, San Diego.

241. Kleene, S. C. (1952) *Introduction to Metamathematics*, Van Nostrand, New York, p. 334.

242. Klement, P., Mesiar, R., and Pap, E. (2000) *Triangular Norms*, Kluwer Academic Publishers, Dordrecht.

243. Klibanoff, P. (2001) Characterizing uncertainty aversion through preference for mixtures, *Social Choice Welfare* 18, 289–301.

244. Klibanoff, P., Marinacci, M., and Mukerji, S. (2005) A smooth model of decision making under ambiguity, *Econometrica* 73(6), 1849–1892.

245. Klir, G. J. and Tina, A. (1988) *Fuzzy Sets, Uncertainty, and Information.* Prentice Hall, USA.

246. Klir, G. and Yuan, B. (1995) *Fuzzy Sets and Fuzzy Logic: Theory and Applications*, Prentice Hall, New Jersey.

247. Klir, G. J. (2004) Generalized information theory: Aims, results, and open problems, *Reliab. Eng. Syst. Saf.* 85(1–3), 21–38.

248. Knowledge extraction based on evolutionary learning. http://sci2s.ugr.es/keel/datasets.php.

249. Kondo, T. (1986) Revised GMDH algorithm estimating degree of the complete polynomial, *T. Soc. Instr. Control Eng.* 22(9), 928–934 (Japanese).

250. Konda, V. R. and Tsitsiklis, J. N. (2002) Actor-critic algorithms, *Adv. Neur. Inf.* 12, 143–147.

251. Kosko, B. (1991) *Neural Networks for Signal Processing*, Prentice Hall, Upper Saddle River, NJ.

252. Kosko, B. (1993) Fuzzy logic, *Sci. Am.* 269(1).

253. Kosko, B. (1997) *Fuzzy Engineering*, Prentice Hall, Upper Saddle River, New Jersey,

254. Koza, J. R. (1992) *Genetic Programming: On the Programming of Computers by Means of Natural Selection*, Bradford Book, USA.

255. Krasnogor, N., Melin-Batista, B., Moreno-Prez, J. A., Moreno-Vega, J. M., and Pelta, D. A. (2009) *Nature Inspired Cooperative Strategies for Optimization (NICSO 2008)*, Springer, Heidelberg, Germany.

256. Krzysztof, P. (1986) On the Bayes formula for fuzzy probability measures, *Fuzzy Sets Syst.* 18(2), 183–185.

257. Lakoff, G. (1972) Hedges: A study in meaning criteria and the logic of fuzzy concepts, in *Papers from 8th Reg. Meet. Chicago Linguistic Society*, pp. 183–228.

258. Lakshmikantham, V. and Mohapatra, R. (2003) *Theory of Fuzzy Differential Equations and Inclusions*, Taylor & Francis, London, New York.

259. Lambert, K. and Van Fraassen, B. C. (1970) Meaning relations, possible objects and possible worlds, *Philos. Probl. Logic* 29, 1–19.

260. Lapa, K. and Cpałka, K. (2016) Nonlinear pattern classification using fuzzy system and hybrid genetic-imperialist algorithm, *Adv. Intel. Syst. Comput.* 432, 159–171.

261. Lapa, K. and Cpałka, K. (2016) On the application of a hybrid genetic-firework algorithm for controllers structure and parameters selection, *Adv. Intel. Syst. Comput.* 429, 111–123.

262. Lapedes, A. S. and Farber, R. (1987) Nonlinear signal processing using neural networks: Prediction and system modeling, Technical Report LA-UR-87-2662, Los Alamos Nat. Lab., New Mexico 87545.

263. Last, M., Friedman, M., and Kandel, A. (2003) The data mining approach to automated software testing, in *Proc. 9th ACM Int. Conf. Knowl. Disc. Data Mining*, pp. 388–396.

264. Lawry, J. (2001) A methodology for computing with words, *Int. J. Approx. Reason* 28, 51–89.

265. Lawry, J., Shanahan, J. G., and Ralescu, A. L. (2003) *Modelling with Words — Learning, Fusion, and Reasoning within a Formal Linguistic Representation Framework*, Springer, Berlin.

266. Lee, C.-C. (1990) Fuzzy logic in control systems, *Fuzzy Logic Controller — Part 1.* 20(2), 404–418.

267. Lee, K. C., Lee, W. J., Kwon, O. B., Han, J. H., and Yu, P. I. (1998) Strategic planning simulation based on fuzzy cognitive map knowledge and differential game, *Simulation* 71(5), 316–327.

268. Lee, S. and Kil, R. M. (1991) A Gaussian potential function network with hierarchically self-organizing learning. *J. Neural Networ.* 4(2), 207–224.

269. Lee, T.-C. (1991) *Structure Level Adaptation for Artificial Neural Networks*, Kluwer Academic, Boston.

270. Leekwijck, W. V. and Kerre, E. E. (1999) Defuzzification: Criteria and classification, *Fuzzy Sets Syst.* 108(2), 159–178.

271. Li, C. and Chan, F. (2011) Complex-fuzzy adaptive image restoration an artificial-bee-colony-based learning approach, *Intelligence Informatics Database Systems*, Springer, Berlin Heidelberg, pp. 90–99.

272. Li, C. and Chiang, T. (2011) Function approximation with complex neuro-fuzzy system using complex fuzzy sets A new approach, *New Gen. Comput.* 29(3), 261–276.

273. Li, C. and Chan, F. (2012) Knowledge discovery by an intelligent approach using complex fuzzy sets, *Intelligence Informatics Database System*, Springer, Berlin Heidelberg, pp. 320–329.

274. Li, C. and Chiang, T. -. (2013) Complex neurofuzzy ARIMA Forecasting — A new approach using complex fuzzy sets, *IEEE Trans. Fuzzy Syst.* 21(3), 567–584.

275. Li, Y. and Jang, T. Y. (1996) Complex adaptive fuzzy inference systems, in *Proc. Asian Conf. Soft Comp. Intel. Syst. Inf. Proc.* pp. 551–556.

276. Lifschitz V. (1990) *Formalizing Common Sense*, Ablex Publishing Corp., NJ.

277. Lin, C.-T. and Lee, C. S. G. (1991) Neural-network-based fuzzy logic control and decision system, *IEEE T Comput.* 40(12), 1320–1336.

278. Liu, F., Quek, C., and Ng, G. S. (2007) A novel generic hebbian ordering-based fuzzy rule base reduction approach to Mamdani neuro-fuzzy system, *Neur. Comput.* 19, 1656–1680.

279. Liu, X. and Pedrycz, W. (2009) *Axiomatic Fuzzy Set Theory and Its Applications*, Springer-Verlag, Berlin.

280. Lossin, S.-H. (2005) Decision making with imprecise and fuzzy probabilities — A Comparison, in *Proc. 4th Int. Symp. Imprecise Prob. Their Appl.*, pp. 222–229.

281. Lou, X., Hou, W., Li, Y., and Wang, Z. (2007) A fuzzy neural network model for predicting clothing thermal comfort, *Comput. Math. Appl.* 53(12), 1840–1846.

282. Lowe, D. (1989) Adaptive radial basis function nonlinearities, and the problem of generalization, in *Proc. 1st IEEE Int. Conf. Art. Neur. Net*, London, UK, pp. 171–175.

283. Lu, W., Pedrycz, W., Liu, X., Yang, J., and Li, P. (2014) The modeling of time series based on fuzzy information granules, *Expert Syst. Appl.* 41, (8–15), 3799–3808.

284. Lukasiewicz, J. (1951) *Aristotle's Syllogistic*, Clarendon Press, Oxford.

285. Ma, S., Peng, D., and Li, D. (2009) Fuzzy complex value measure and fuzzy complex value measurable function, *Fuzzy Inf. Eng.* 54, 187–192.

286. Mackey, M. C. and Glass, L. (1977) Oscillation and chaos in physiological control systems, *Science* 197, 287–289.

287. Mamdani, E. H. (1974) Application of fuzzy algorithms for simple dynamic plant, *Proc. IEEE* 121, 1585–1588.

288. Mamdani, E. and Assilian, S. (1975) An experiment in linguistic synthesis with a fuzzy logic controller, *Int. J. Man Mac. Stud.* 7(1) 1–13.

289. Mamdani, E. H. (1977) Applications of fuzzy logic to approximate reasoning using linguistic systems, *IEEE Trans. Comput.* C-26, 1182–1191.

290. Man, J. Y., Chen, Z., and Dick, S. (2007) Towards inductive learning of complex fuzzy inference systems, *PAM NAFIPS*, pp. 415–420.

291. Mares, M. (1994) *Computation Over Fuzzy Quantities*, CRC, Boca Raton, FL.

292. Marquez, A. A., Marquez, F. A., and Peregrin, A. (2010) A multi-objective evolutionary algorithm with an interpretability improvement mechanism for linguistic fuzzy systems with adaptive defuzzification, in *IEEE Int. Conf. Fuzzy*, pp. 1–7.

293. Mathieu-Nicot, B. (1986) Fuzzy expected utility, *Fuzzy Sets Syst.* 20(2) 163–173.

294. Mayburov, S. (2008) Fuzzy geometry of phase space and quantization of massive fields, *J Phys A: Math Theor.* 41, 1–10.

295. Melin, P. (2012) *Modular Neural Networks and Type-2 Fuzzy Systems for Pattern Recognition*, Springer, Berlin.

296. Mencar, C., Castellano, G., and Fanelli, A. M. (2007) On the role of interpretability in fuzzy data mining, *J Uncertainty Fuzz. Knowl. Based Syst.* 521–537.

297. Mencar, C., Castiello, C., Cannone, R., and Fanelli, A. M. (2011) Interpretability assessment of fuzzy knowledge bases: A cointension based approach, *Int. J. Approx Reason.* 52(4), 501–518.

298. Mendel, J. M. (2001) *Uncertain Rule-Based Fuzzy Logic Systems: Introduction and New Directions*, Prentice Hall, USA.

299. Mendel, J. M. (2002) An architecture for making judgments using computing with words, *Int. J. Appl. Math. Comput. Sci.* 12(3), 325–335.

300. Mendel, J. M. and John, R. I. (2002) Type–2 fuzzy sets made simple, *IEEE T. Fuzzy Syst.* 2(10), 117–127.

301. Mendel, J. M. (2003) Fuzzy Sets for Words: A New Beginning, in *Proc. 12th IEEE Int. Conf. Fuzzy Systems, FUZZ*, pp. 37–42.

302. Mendel, J. M., Jhon, R. I., and Liu, F. (2006) Interval type-2 fuzzy logic systems made simple, *IEEE T. Fuzzy Syst.* 6(14), 808–821.

303. Mendel, J. M. (2007) Advances in type-2 fuzzy set syst, *Inf. Sci.*, 177, 84–110.

304. Mendel, J. M. (2007) Computing with words and its relationships with fuzzistics, *Inf. Sci.* 179(8), 988–1006.

305. Mendel, J. M. (2007) Type-2 Fuzzy Set System: An overview, *IEEE Comput Intell M.*, 2, 20–29.

306. Mendel, J. M. and Wu, D. (2010) *Perceptual Computing: Aiding People in Making Subjective Judgments*, IEEE Press and Wiley, New York.

307. Mendel, J. (2014) *Type-2 Fuzzy Logic Control: Introduction to Theory and Application*, Wiley-IEEE Press, New-Jersey.

308. Michalewicz, Z. (1996) *Genetic Algorithms+Data Structures=Evolution Programs*, Springer, Germany.

309. Miller, G. A. (1956) The magical number seven, plus or minus two: Some limits on our capacity for processing information, *The Psychol. Rev.* 63, 81–97.

310. Mitchell, M. (1996) *An Introduction to Genetic Algorithms*, The MIT Press.

311. Mizumoto, M. and Tanaka, K. (1979) Some properties of fuzzy number, *Advances in Fuzzy Set Theory and Applications*, North-Holland, Amsterdam, pp. 153–164.

312. Mizumoto, M. (1982) Fuzzy conditional inference under max-composition, *Inform. Sci.* 27, 183–209.

313. Moody, J. and Darken, C. (1988) Learning with localized receptive fields, in *Proc. 1988 Con. Models Summer School*, Carnegie Mellon University, Morgan Kaufmann, San Mateo, CA.

314. Moody, J. (1989) Fast learning in multi-resolution hierarchies, in D. S. Touretzky (ed.), *Advances in Neural Information I*, Morgan Kaufmann, San Mateo, CA, pp. 29–39.

315. Moody, J. and Darken, C. (1989) Fast learning in networks of locally-tuned processing units, *Neur. Comput.* 1, 281–294.

316. Moore, R. (1996) *Interval Analysis*, Prentice Hall, Englewood Cliffs.
317. Moore, R., Kearfott, R. B., and Cloud, M. J. (2009) *Intro. Interval Anal.*, SIAM, Philadelphia.
318. Mordeson, J. N. and Nair, P. S. (2001) *Fuzzy Mathematics: An Introduction for Engineers and Scientists*, Springer, Heidelberg, Germany.
319. Moses, D., Degani, O., Teodorescu, H., Friedman, M., and Kandel, A. (1999) Linguistic coordinate transformations for complex fuzzy sets, in *IEEE Int. Conf. Fuzzy Systems*, pp. 1340–1345.
320. Mueller, E. (2006) *Commonsense Reasoning*, Morgan Kaufmann, San Francisco, CA.
321. Musavi, M. T., Ahmed, W., Chan, K. H., Faris, K. B., and Hummels, D. M. (1992) On the training of radial basis function classifiers, *J. Neural Networ.* 5(4), 595–603.
322. Musayev, A. F., Alizadeh, A. V., Guirimov, B. G., and Huseynov, O. H. (2009) Computational framework for the method of decision making with imprecise probabilities, in *Fifth* ICSCCW, Famagusta, North Cyprus, pp. 287–290.
323. Nanda, S. (1991) Fuzzy linear spaces over valued fields, *Fuzzy Set Syst.* 42(3), 351–354.
324. Narendra, K. S. and Parthsarathy, K. (1990) Identification and control of dynamical systems using neural networks. *IEEE T Neural Networ.* 1(1), 4–27.
325. Narukawa, Y. and Murofushi, T. (2004) Decision modeling using the choquet integral, *Lect. Notes Comput. Sci.* 3131, 183–193.
326. Negoita, C. V. and Ralescu, D. A. (1975) *Applications of Fuzzy Sets to Systems Analysis*, Wiley John Wiley & Sons, New York.
327. Nguyen, H. (1978) A not on the extension principle for Fuzzy sets, *J. Math. Anal. Appl.* 64, 369–380.
328. Nguyen, H. T. and Walker, E. A. (2000) *A First Course in Fuzzy Logic*, CRC Press, Boca Raton.
329. Nguyen, H. T., Kandel, A., and Kreinovich, V. (2000) Complex fuzzy sets: Towards new foundations, in *IEEE Int. Conf. Fuzzy*, pp. 1045–1048.
330. Niskanen, V. A. (2016) Concept map approach to approximate reasoning with fuzzy extended logic, Fuzzy technology: Present applications and future technology. *Stud. Fuzz. Soft Comput.* 335, 47–70.
331. Nodyen, H. T. (1977) On fuzziness and linguistic probabilities, *J. Math. Anal. Appl.* 61, 658–671.
332. Novak, V., Perfilieva, I., and Mockor, J. (1999) *Mathematical Principles of Fuzzy Logic*, Kluwer, Boston/Dordrecht.
333. Nowicki, R. (2008) On combining neuro-fuzzy architectures with the rough set theory to solve classification problems with incomplete data, *IEEE T. Knowl. Data Eng.* 39, 1239–1253.
334. Nowicki, R. (2009) Rough neuro-fuzzy structures for classification with missing data, *IEEE T. Syst. Man Cyb., Part B* 39, 1334–1347.

335. Nowlan, S. J. (1989) Maximum likelihood competitive learning, in D. J. Touretzky (ed.), *Advances Neural Information 2*, San Mateo, CA, Morgan Kaufmann, pp. 574–582.

336. Orlovsky, S. A. (1978) Decision-making with a fuzzy preference relation, *Fuzzy Set Syst.* 1, 155–167.

337. Ovchinnikov, S. (1991) On fuzzy preference relations, *Int. J. Intel. Syst.* 6, 225–234.

338. Ovchinnikov, S. (1991) On modeling fuzzy preference relations, *Lect. Notes Comput. Sci.* 521, 154–164.

339. Pal, S. K. and Wang, P. P. (1996) *Genetic Algorithms for Pattern Recognition*, CRC Press, Florida, USA.

340. Pao, Y.-H. (1989) *Adaptive Pattern Recognition and Neural Networks*, Addison-Wesley, Reading, MA, pp. 197–222.

341. Papageorgiou, E., Stylios, E., and Groumpos, P. (2003) *Fuzzy Cognitive Map Learning Based on Nonlinear Hebbian Rule*, 2903, Springer, pp. 256–268.

342. Parker, D. B. (1987) Optimal algorithms for adaptive networks: 2nd order back propagation, 2nd order direct propagation and 2nd order Hebbian learning, in *Proc. IEEE Int. Conf. Neural Network*, pp. 593–600.

343. Partee, B. (1976) *Montague Grammar*, Academic, New York.

344. Pawlak, Z. (1982) Rough sets, *Int. J. Inform. Comp. Sci.* 11(15), pp. 341–356.

345. Pawlak, Z. and Skowron, A. (2007) Rough sets and Boolean reasoning, *Inform. Sci.* 177(1), 41–73.

346. Pawlak, Z. and Skowron, A. (2007) Rudiments of rough sets, *Inform. Sci.* 177(1), 3–27.

347. Pedrycz, W. (1998) Shadowed sets: Representing and processing fuzzy sets, *IEEE T. Syst. Man Cyb., Part B* 28, 103–109.

348. Pedrycz, W. and Gomide, F. (1998) *An Introduction to Fuzzy Sets*, MIT Press, Cambridge, MA.

349. Pedrycz, W. and Peters, J. F. (1998) Computational intelligence in software engineering, *Adv. Fuzzy Syst. Appl. Theor.* 16, 485, Singapore.

350. Pedrycz, W. and Bargiela, A. (2002) Granular clustering: A granular signature of data, *IEEE Trans. Syst., Man Cyb.* 32, 212–224.

351. Pedrycz, W. and Gacek, A. (2002) Temporal granulation and its application to signal analysis, *Inform. Sci.* 143(1–4), 47–71.

352. Pedrycz, W. (2005) Interpretation of clusters in the framework of shadowed sets, *Pattern Recogn. Lett.* 26, 15, 2439–2449.

353. Pedrycz, W. and Gomide F. (2007) *Rule-Based System/Model (FRBS). Fuzzy Systems Engineering, Toward Human-Centric Comput.*, NJ.

354. Pedrycz, W. and Gomide, F. (2007) *Fuzzy Systems Engineering: Toward Human-Centric Comput.*, John Wiley, Hoboken, NJ.

355. Pedrycz, W., Skowron, A., and Kreinovich, V. (2008) *Handbook of Granular Computing, C-25 On Type-2 Fuzzy Sets as Granular 'Models for Words*, Wiley, England, pp. 553–574.

356. Pedrycz, W. (2013) *Granular Computing*, CRC Press, Boca Raton, FL.
357. Pedrycz, W. and Homenda, W. (2013) Building the fundamentals of granular computing: A principle of justifiable granularity, *Appl. Soft Comput.* 13, 4209–4218.
358. Pedrycz, W., Jastrzebska, A., and Homenda, W. (2016) Design of fuzzy cognitive maps for modeling time series, *IEEE T. Fuzzy Syst.* 24(1), 120–130.
359. Pedrycz, W. and Wang, X. (2016) Designing fuzzy sets with the use of the parametric principle of justifiable granularity, *IEEE T. Fuzzy Syst.* 24(2), 489–496.
360. Pena, J.P-P. and Piggins, A. (2007) Strategy-proof fuzzy aggregation rules, *J. Math. Econ.* 43, 564–580.
361. Perfilieva, I. (2007) Fuzzy transforms: A challenge to conventional transforms, *Adv. Imag. Elect. Phys.* 147, 137–196.
362. Poston, T. (1971) Fuzzy geometry, Ph.D. Thesis, University of Warwick.
363. Pulkkinen, P. and Koivisto, H. (2010) A dynamically constrained multi-objective genetic fuzzy system for regression problems, *IEEE Trans. Fuzzy Syst.* 18(1), 161–177.
364. Puri, M. and Ralescu, D. (1983) Differential of fuzzy function, *J. Math. Anal. Appl.* 91, 552–558.
365. Quiggin, J. (1982) A theory of anticipated utility, *J. Econ. Behav. Organ.* 3(4), 323–343.
366. Qilian, L. and Mendel, J. M. (2000) Interval type-2 fuzzy logic systems, in *Proc. Ninth IEEE Int. Conf. Fuzzy Syst.* 8(5), 328–333.
367. Radzikowska, M. and Kerre, E. E. (2002) A comparative study of fuzzy rough sets, *Fuzzy Set Syst.* 126, 137–155.
368. Ramot, D., Milo, R., Friedman, M., and Kandel, A. (2002) Complex fuzzy sets. *IEEE T. Fuzzy Syst.* 10(2), 171–186.
369. Ramot, D., Friedman, M., Langhoz, G., and Kandel, A. (2003) Complex fuzzy logic, *IEEE T. Fuzzy Syst.* 11(4), 450–464.
370. Rescher, N. (1969) *Many-Valued Logic*, McGraw-Hill, New York, pp. 54–125.
371. Reznik, L. and Dimitrov, V. (2013) *Fuzzy Systems Design: Social and Engineering Applications*, Physica. The Netherlands.
372. Riid, A. and Rustern, E. (2010) Interpretability improvement of fuzzy systems: Reducing the number of unique singletons in zeroth order Takagi-Sugeno systems, *IEEE Int. Conf. Fuzzy System*, pp. 1–6.
373. Riid, A. and Rustern, E. (2011) *Interpretability, Interpolation and Rule Weights in Linguistic Fuzzy Modeling*, pp. 91–98.
374. Riid, A. and Rustern, E. (2014) Adaptability, interpretability and rule weights in fuzzy rule-based systems, *Inf. Sc.* 257(1), 301–312.
375. Robert G. Gallager. *Information Theory and Reliable Communication*, John Wiley & Sons.
376. Roe, J. (1996) Index theory, coarse geometry, and topology of manifolds, in *Reg. Conf. Ser. Math.*, Island.

377. Roger Jang, J.-S. (1993) ANFIS: Adaptive-Network-based Fuzzy Inference Systems, *IEEE T Syst Mn Cyb.* 23(3), 665–685.

378. Roger Jang, J.-S., Chuen-Tsai Sun, and Eiji Mizutani (1997) *Neuro-Fuzzy and Soft Computing: A Computational Approach to Learning and Machine Intelligence*, MATLAB Curriculum Series, Prentice Hall, Upper Saddle River, NJ.

379. Rosenfeld, A. (1990) Fuzzy rectangles, *Pattern Recogn. Lett.* 11, 677–679.

380. Rosenfeld, A. (1998) Fuzzy geometry: An updated overview, *Inf. Sc.* 110(3–4), 127–133.

381. Ross, T. J. (2004) *Fuzzy Logic with Engineering Applications*, 2nd edn., Wiley, New York.

382. Rossi, F. and Codognet, P. (2003) *Soft Constraints, Special Issue on Constraints*, Vol. 8, issue 1, Kluwer, Dordrecht.

383. Royden, H. L. (1968) *Real Analysis*. 2nd edn., Macmillan, New York.

384. Rutkowski, L. and Cpałka, K. (2001) A general approach to neuro-fuzzy systems, Fuzzy Systems, in *10th IEEE Int. Conf. Melbourne*, pp. 1428–1431.

385. Rutkowska, D. (2002) *Neuro-Fuzzy Architectures and Hybrid Learning*, Springer, Germany.

386. Rutkowski, L. and Cpałka, K. (2002) Compromise approach to neuro-fuzzy systems, in *2nd Euro-Int. Sym. Comput. Intel. Loc.*, pp. 85–90.

387. Rutkowski, L. and Cpałka, K. (2002) A neuro-fuzzy controller with a compromise fuzzy reasoning, *Control Cybernet.* 31(2), 297–308.

388. Rutkowski, L. and Cpałka, K. (2003) Flexible neuro-fuzzy systems, *IEEE Trans, Neur. Net.* 14, 554–574.

389. Rutkowski, L. (2004) *Flexible Neuro-Fuzzy Systems: Structures, Learning and Performance Evaluation*, Springer.

390. Rutkowski, L. and Cpałka, K. (2005) Designing and learning of adjustable Quasi-triangular norms with applications to Neuro-fuzzy systems, *IEEE Trans. Fuzzy Systs* 13, 140–151.

391. Rutkowski, L. (2008) *Computational Intelligence*, Springer, Germany.

392. Rutkowski, L. Przybyl, A., Cpałka, K., and Er, M. J. (2010) Online speed pro le generation for industrial machine tool based on neuro-fuzzy approach, *Lect. Notes Artif. Intel.* 114, 645–650.

393. Rutkowski, L. Przyby l, A., and Cpałka, K. (2012) Novel online speed pro le generation for industrial machine tool based on flexible Neuro-fuzzy approximation, *IEEE Trans. Industr. Elect.* 59(2), 1238–1247.

394. Sadeghian, A., Mendel, J. M., and Tahayori, H. (2013) *Advances in Type-2 Fuzzy Set Systems. Theory and Applications*, Springer, New York.

395. Sainsbury, R. M. (1995) *Paradoxes*, Cambridge University Press, Cambridge.

396. Sanger, T. D. (1991) A tree-structured adaptive network for function approximate in high-dimensional spaces, *IEEE T Neural Networ.* 2(2), 285–293.

397. Sanjeev, K. and Gursimranjeet, K. (2013) Detection of heart diseases using fuzzy logic, Department of EC, Punjab Technical University AICT, Amritsar, Punjab, India.

398. Savage, L. J. (1954) *The Foundations of Statistics*, Wiley, New York.
399. Savage, R. I. (1968) *Statistic Uncertainity and Behavior*, Houghton-Mifflin, Boston.
400. Scherer, R. (2010) Neuro-fuzzy systems with relation matrix, *Art. Intel. Soft Comput.* 6113, 210–215.
401. Scherer, R. (2012) *Multiple Fuzzy Classification Systems*, Springer, Germany.
402. Schmeidler, D. (1986) Integral representation without additivity, *Proc. Am. Math. Soc.* 97(2), 255–261.
403. Schmeidler, D. (1989) Subjective probability and expected utility without additivity, *Econometrica* 57(3), 571–587.
404. Schum, D. (1994) *Evidential Foundations of Probabilistic Reasoning*, Wiley, New York.
405. Schwartz, D. G. and Klir, G. J. (1991) Fuzzy logic flowers in Japan, *IEEE Spectrum* 29, 32–35.
406. Schwartz, D. G., Klir, G. J., Lewis, H. W., and Ezawa, Y. (1994) Applications of fuzzy sets and approximate reasoning, *Proc. IEEE* 82, 482–498.
407. Segal, U. (1987) The Ellsberg paradox and risk aversion: An anticipated utility approach, *Int. Econ. Rev.* 28, 175–202.
408. Setnes, M. (1997) Compatibility-based ranking of fuzzy numbers, in *Annual Meeting of the NAFIPS*, pp. 305–310.
409. Shafer, G. (1976) *A Mathematical Theory of Evidence*, Princeton University Press, Princeton, NJ.
410. Sher, G. I. (2013) *Handbook of Neuroevolution Through Erlang*, Springer, Germany.
411. Shukla, P. K. and Tripathi, S. P. (2012) A review on the interpretability-accuracy trade-off in EMOFS, 3, pp. 256–277.
412. Shukla, P. K. and Tripathi, S. P. (2014) Handling high dimensionality and interpretability-accuracy Trade-off issues in evolutionary multiobjective fuzzy classifiers, *Int. J. Sci. & Eng. Res.* 5(6), 665–671.
413. Shukla, P. K. and Tripathi, S. P. (2014) A new approach for tuning interval type-2 fuzzy knowledge bases using genetic algorithms, *J. Uncertainty Anal. Appl.* 2(4), 1–15.
414. Siminski, K. (2010) Rule weights in a Neuro-fuzzy system with a hierarchical domain partition, *Int. J. Appl. Math. Comput. Sci.* 20(2), 337–347.
415. Simon, H. (1997) *Models of Bounded Rationality: Empirically Grounded Economic Reason, 3*, MIT Press, Cambridge, MA.
416. Simon, D. (2013) *Evolutionary Optimization Algorithms*, Wiley, USA.
417. Singh, L., Kumar, S., and Paul, S. (2008) Automatic simultaneous architecture and parameter search in fuzzy neural network learning using novel variable length crossover differential evolution, in *IEEE Int. Conf. Fuzzy Systems*, pp. 1795–1802.
418. Smith, V. (1969) Measuring nonmonetary utilities in uncertain choices: The Ellsberg Urn, *Quart. J. Econ.* 83, 324–329.

419. Sourav, M., Sumanta, C., and Biswarup, N. (2013) Diagnosis and troubleshooting of computer foults based on expert system and artificial intelligence, *Int. J. Pure Appl. Math.* 83(5), 717–729.

420. Stach, W., Kurgan, L. and Pedrycz, W. (2010) Expert-based and computational methods for developing fuzzy Cognitive Maps, *Fuzzy Cognitive Maps*, pp. 24–41, Springer, Germany.

421. Starczewski, J. (2013) *Advanced Concepts in Fuzzy Logic and Systems with Membership Uncertainty*, Springer, Germany.

422. Stylios, C. and Groumpos, P. (2004) Modeling complex systems using fuzzy cognitive maps, *IEEE Trans. Syst., Man Cyb. A* 34(1), 155–162.

423. Sugeno, M. (1985) *Industrial Applications of Fuzzy Control*, Elsevier Science Pub. Co., Japan.

424. Sugeno, M. and Kang, G. T. (1988) *Structure Identification of Fuzzy Model*, 28, pp. 15–33,

425. Sun, C.-T.(1994) Rulebase structure identification in an adaptive network based fuzzy inference system, *IEEE Fuzzy Syst.* 2(1), 64–73.

426. Suykens, J. A. K. and Vandewalle, J. P. L. (1998) *Nonlinear Modeling: Adv.Black-Box Techniques*, Springer, Germany.

427. Takagi, T. and Sugeno, M. (1983) Derivation of fuzzy control rules from human operator's control actions, in *Proc. IFAC Sym. Fuzzy Inf., Knowledge Representation and Decision Analysis*, pp. 55–60.

428. Takagi, T. and Sugeno, M. (1985) Fuzzy identification of systems and its applications to modeling and control, *IEEE T Syst Man Cyb.* 15, 116–132.

429. Takagi, H. and Hayashi, I. (1991) NN-driven fuzzy reasoning, *Int. J. Approx. Reason.* 5(3), 191–212.

430. Takahagi, E. (2008) A fuzzy measure identification method by diamond pairwise comparisons and φ_s transformation, *J. Fuzz Optim. Decision Mak.* 7(3), 219–232.

431. Talasova, J. and Pavlacka, O. (2006) Fuzzy probability spaces and their applications in decision making, *Austrian J. Statis.* 35, 347–356.

432. Tamir, D. E. and Kandel, A. (1990) An axiomatic approach to fuzzy set theory, *Inform. Sci.* 52(1), pp. 75–83.

433. Tamir, D. E. and Kandel, A. (2010) The pyramid fuzzy C-means algorithm, *Int. J. Comput. Intel. Control* 2(2), 65–77.

434. Tamir, D. E. and Kandel, A. (2011) Axiomatic theory of complex fuzzy logic and complex fuzzy classes, *Int. J. Comp., Commun. Control* 6(3), 508–522.

435. Tamir, D. E. and Kandel, A. (2011) A new interpretation of complex membership grade, *Int. J. Intel. Syst.* 26(4), 285–312.

436. Tamir, D. E., Last, M., Teodorescu, N. H., and Kandel, A. (2012) Discrete complex fuzzy logic, in *Proc. NAFIPSC*, USA, pp. 1–6.

437. Tamir, D. E., Last, M., and Kandel, A. (2013) *Complex Fuzzy Logic, On Fuzziness*, Springer-Verlag, pp. 665–672.

438. Tamir, D. E., Last, M., and Kandel, A. (2013) The theory and applications of generalized complex fuzzy propositional logic, *Soft Computing: State of the Art Theory and Novel Applications*, Springer Series on Studies in Fuzziness and Soft Computing, Springer-Verlag, pp. 177–192.

439. Tamir, D. E., Rishe, N. D., Last, M., and Kandel, A. (2014) Soft computing based epidemical crisis prediction, *Intelligent Methods for Cyberwarfare*, Springer-Verlag, pp. 43–76.

440. Tamir, D. E., Mueller, C. J., and Kandel, A. (2015) Complex fuzzy logic reasoning based methodologies for quantitative software engineering, *Computational Intelligence and Quantitative Software Engineering*, Springer-Verlag.

441. Tanaka, J., Okuda, T., and Asai, K. (1979) Fuzzy information and decision in statistical model, *Advances in Fuzzy Set Theory Applications*, North-Holland, Amsterdam, pp. 300–320.

442. Tikk, D., Gedeon, T., and Wong, K. (2003) A feature ranking algorithm for fuzzy modeling problems, *Interpretability Issues in Fuzzy Modeling*, Springer-Verlag, pp. 176–192.

443. Tong, R. M. and Bonissone, P. P. (1980) A linguistic approach to decision-making with fuzzy sets, *IEEE Trans. Syst., Man. Cyb.*, SMC-10, 716–723.

444. Toulmin, S. (2003) *The Uses of Argument*, Cambridge University Press, UK.

445. Trillas, E., Moraga, C., Guadarrama, S., Cubillo, S. and Castieira, E. (2007) Computing with antonyms, *Studies in Fuzzy Computation*, Springer-Verlag, Berlin Heidelberg, pp. 133–153.

446. Tsang, E. C. C., Chen, Q., Zhao, S., Yeung, D. S., and Wang, X. (2008) Hybridization of fuzzy and rough Sets: Present and future, pp. 45–62.

447. Tversky, A. and Kahneman, D. (1979) Prospect theory: An analysis of decision under uncertainty, *Econometrica* 47, 263–291.

448. Tversky, A. and Kahneman, D. (1992) Advances in prospect theory: Cumulative representation of uncertainty, *J. Risk Uncertainty* 5(4), 297–323.

449. Tzafestas, S. G., Chen, C. S., Fokuda, T., Harashima, F., Schmidt, G., Sinha, N. K., Tabak, D., and Valavanis K. (2006) Fuzzy logic applications in engineering science, *Microprocessor-based and Intelligence in System Engineering*, Springer, Netherlands, Vol. 29, pp. 11–30.

450. Utkin, L. V. and Augustin, T. (2003) Decision making with imprecise second-order probabilities, in *Proc. 3rd Int. Symp. Imprecises Prob. Applications*, Lugano, Switzerland, pp. 545–559.

451. Utkin, L. V. (2005) Imprecise second-order hierarchical uncertainty model, *Int. J. Uncertainty, Fuz. Knowl. Based Syst.* 13(2), 177–193.

452. Utkin, L. V. (2007) *Analysis of Risk and Decision Making Under Incomplete Information*, SPb, Nauka, Russian.

453. Vanhoucke, V. and Silipo, R. (2003) *Interpretability in Multidimensional Classification, Interpretability Issues in Fuzzy Modeling*, Springer-Verlag, pp. 193–217.

454. Von Neumann, J. and Morgenstern, O. (1944) *Theory of Games and Economic Behaviour*, Princeton University Press.

455. Voxman, W. (2001) Canonical representations of discrete fuzzy numbers, *Fuzzy Set Syst.* 54, 457–466.
456. Wakker, P. (1989) Continuous subjective expected utility with non-additive probabilities, *J. Math. Econ.* 18, 1–27.
457. Walley, P. (1991) *Statistical Reasoning with Imprecise Probabilities. Monographs on Statistics and Applied Probability*, Chapman and Hall, London, New York.
458. Walley, P. (1996) Measures of uncertainty in expert systems, *Art. Intel.* 83(1), 1–58.
459. Walley, P. and De Cooman, G. A. (2001) Behavioral model for linguistic uncertainty, *Inform. Sci.* 134(1–4), 1–37.
460. Wang, G. and Li, X. (1999) On the convergence of the fuzzy valued functional defined by μ-integrable fuzzy valued functions, *Fuzzy Set Syst.* 107(2), 219–226.
461. Wang, G., Wu, C., and Zhao, C. (2005) Representation and operations of discrete fuzzy numbers, *Southeast Asian Bulletin Math.* 28, 1003–1010.
462. Wang, L.-X. (1992) Fuzzy systems are universal approximators, in *IEEE Int. Conf. Fuzzy Systems*, San Diego.
463. Wang, L.-X. and Mendel, J. M. (1992) Back-propagation fuzzy systems as nonlinear dynamic system identifiers, in *IEEE Int. Conf. Fuzzy Systems*, San Diego.
464. Wang, L.-X. and Mendel, J. M. (1992) Fuzzy basis function, universal approximation, and orthogonal least squares learning. *IEEE T Neural Networ.* 3(5), 807–814.
465. Wang, Z. and Wang, W. (1995) Extension of lower probabilities and coherence of belief measures, in *Lect. Notes Comput. Sci.* 945, 62–69.
466. Watkins, C. (1989) Learning from delayed rewards, Ph.D dissertation. Cambridge University, Cambridge, U.K.
467. Watson, S. R., Wfiss, J. J., and Donell, M. L. (1979) Fuzzy decision analysis, *IEEE Trans Syst. Man. Cybern*, SMC-9, 1–9.
468. Weigend, A. A., Rumelhart, D. E., and Huberman, B. A. (1990) Back-propagation, weight-elimination and time series prediction, in *Proc. 1990 Connect. Models Summer School*, Carnegic Mellon University, pp. 105–116.
469. Weigend, A. S., Rumelhart, D. E., and Huberman, B. A. (1991) Generalization by weight-elimination with application to forecasting, *Advances in Neural Informatics Processing System III, pages* Morgan Kaufmann, San Mateo, CA, pp. 875–882.
470. Werthner, H. (1994) *Qualitative Reasoning: Modeling and the Generation of Behavior*, Springer, Wien, Germany.
471. Wettschereck, D. and Dietterich, T. (1992) Improving the performance of radial basis function networks by learning center locations, *Advances in Neural Informatics Processing System* 4, San Mateo, CA, Morgan Kaufmann, pp. 1133–1140.
472. Widrow B. and Stearns, D. (1985) *Adaptive Signal Processing*, Prentice Hall, Upper Saddle River, NJ.

473. Widrow B. and Winter R. (1988) Neural nets for adaptive ltering and adaptive pattern recognition, *IEEE Comp.*, pp. 25–39.
474. Widrow, B. and Lehr, M. A. (1990) 30 years of adaptive neural networks: Perceptron, madline, and backpropagation, *Proc. IEEE* 78(9), 1415–1442.
475. Williamson, R. C. (1989) Probabilistic arithmetic, Ph.D. dissertation, University of Queensland, Australia, http://theorem.anu.edu.au/ ∼williams/papers/thesis 300.
476. Wismer, D. A. and Chattergy, R. (1978) *Introduction to Nonlinear Optimization: A Problem Solving Approach*, North-Holland, Amsterdam, vol. 6, pp. 139–162.
477. Wu, C. and Qiu, J. (1999) Some remarks for fuzzy complex analysis, *Fuzzy Set Syst.* 106(1), 231–238.
478. Yager, R. R. (1980) Fuzzy sets. probabilities and decision, *J. Cyb.* 10, 1–18.
479. Yager, R. R. (1987) *Fuzzy Sets and Applications*, Selected Papers by L.A. Zadeh. Wiley.
480. Yager, R. R. and Filev, D. (1994) *Essentials of Fuzzy Modeling and Control*, John Wiley & Sons, New York.
481. Yager, R. R. (1998) On measures of specificity, *Comput. Intel. Soft Comput. Fuzzy-Neuro Integ. Appl.*, Springer-Verlag, Berlin, pp. 94–113.
482. Yager, R. R. (1999) Decision making with fuzzy probability assessments, *IEEE T. Fuzzy Syst.* 7(4), 462–467.
483. Yager, R. R. (2001) A general approach to uncertainty representation using fuzzy measures, in *Proc. 4th Int FLAIRS*, pp. 619–623.
484. Yager, R. R. (2006) Perception based granular probabilities in risk modeling and decision making, *IEEE Trans. Fuzzy Syst.* 14, 129–139.
485. Yager, R. R. (2012) On a view of zadeh Z-numbers. *Adv. Comp. Intelligence*, 299, pp. 90–101.
486. Yager, R. R. and Abbasov, A. M. (2013) Pythagorean membership grades, complex numbers, and decision making, *Int. J. Intel. Syst.* 28(5), 436–452.
487. Yamakawa, T. and Miki, T. (1986) The current mode fuzzy logic integrated circuits fabricated by the standard CMOS process, *IEEE Trans. Comput.* C-35, 161–167.
488. Yang, C. H., Moi, S. H., Lin, Y. D., and Chuang, L. Y. (2016) Genetic algorithm combined with a local search method for identifying susceptibility genes, *J. Art. Intell. Soft Comput.* 6, 203–212.
489. Yang, R., Wang, Z., Heng, P.-A., and Leung, K.-S. (2005) Fuzzy numbers and fuzzification of the Choquet integral, *Fuzzy Set Syst.* 153(1), 95–113.
490. Yang, X. S. (2014) *Nature-Inspired Optimization Algorithms*, Elsevier, England.
491. Yavuz, E., Çoşkun, H., and Talo, Ö. (2016) Cesàro summability of integrals of fuzzy-number-valued functions, *A1 Math. Stat.* 67, 38–49.
492. Yavuz, E. and Çoşkun, H. (2017) On the limits of logarithmic summable fuzzy-number-valued functions at infinity, *J. Math. Anal.* 8, 116–124.

493. Yazdanbaksh, O., Krahn, A. and Dick, S. (2013) Predicting solar power output using complex fuzzy logic, in *Proc. Joint IFSA World Cong. and NAFIPS Annual Meeting*, pp. 1243–1248.

494. Yazdanbakhsh, O. and Dick, S. (2015) Time-series forecasting via complex fuzzy logic, pp. 147–165.

495. Yen, J., Langari, R., and Zadeh, L. A. (1995) *Industrial Applications of Fuzzy Logic and Intelligent Systems*, IEEE, New York.

496. Yen, J. and Langari, R. (1998) *Fuzzy Logic: Intelligence, Control and Information*, 1st edn., Prentice-Hall, Englewood Cliffs, NJ.

497. Yin, Z., O'Sullivan, C., and Brabazon, A. (2016) An analysis of the performance of genetic programming for realised volatility forecast, *J. Art. Intel. Soft Comput. Res.* 6, 155–172.

498. Ying, H. (2000) *Fuzzy Control and Modelling: Analytical Foundations and Applications*, IEEE Press.

499. Yue, H., Yue, G. and Yi, G. (2007) Application study in decision support with fuzzy cognitive map. *Int. J. Comput.* 1(3), 324–331.

500. Zadeh, L. A. and Desoer, C. A. (1963) *Linear System Theory — The State Space Approach*, McGraw-HillBook Co., New York.

501. Zadeh, L. A. (1965) Fuzzy sets, *Inf. Control* 8(1), 338–353.

502. Zadeh, L. A. (1968) Fuzzy algorithms, *Inf. Control* 12(2), 94–102.

503. Zadeh, L. A. (1968) Probability measures of fuzzy events, *J. Math. Anal. Appl.* 23, 421–427.

504. Zadeh, L. A. (1968) The concept of state in system theory, *Network and Switching Theory*, Academic Press, New York.

505. Zadeh, L. A. (1969) The concepts of system, aggregate and state in system theory, *Syst. Theory*, Academic Press, New York.

506. Zadeh, L. A. (1971) Fuzzy orderings, *Inform. Sci.* 3, 117–200.

507. Zadeh, L. A. (1971) Similarity relations and fuzzy orderings, *Inform. Sci.* 3, 177–200.

508. Zadeh, L. A. (1971) Toward a theory of fuzzy systems, *Aspects of Network and System Theory*, Rineheart and Winston, pp. 469–490.

509. Zadeh, L. A. (1972) A fuzzy-set-theoretic interpretation of linguistic hedges, *J. Cyb.* 2(3), 4–34.

510. Zadeh, L. A. (1972) A rationale for fuzzy control, *J. Dyn. Syst., Measurement, and Control* 3, 123–126.

511. Zadeh, L. A. (1973) Outline of a new approach to the analysis of complex systems and decision processes, *IEEE T. Syst., Man Cyb.* 3, 28–44.

512. Zadeh, L. A. (1974) On the analysis of large scale systems, *Syst Appr. Envir. Prob.* Vandenhoeck and Ruprecht, Gottingen, pp. 23–37.

513. Zadeh, L. A. (1975) Fuzzy logic and approximate reasoning, *Synthese* 30, 407–428.

514. Zadeh, L. A. (1975) The concept of a linguistic variable and its application to approximate reasoning, P I-III, *Inform. Sci.* I(8), 199–249; II(8), 301–357; III(9), 43–80.

515. Zadeh, L. A. (1976) A fuzzy-algorithmic approach to the definition of complex or imprecise concepts, memorandum No. ERL-M474, *Electron. Res. Lab.* 8(3), 249–291.

516. Zadeh, L. A. (1978) Fuzzy sets as a basis for a theory of possibility, *Fuzzy Set Syst.* 1, 3–28.

517. Zadeh, L. A. (1979) A theory of approximate reasoning, in Hayes J., Michie D., Mikulich, L.I. (eds.), *Machine Intelligence*, vol. 9, Halstead Press, New York, pp. 149–194.

518. Zadeh, L. A. (1979) Fuzzy sets and information granularity, in Gupta, M., Ragade, R., Yager, R. (eds.), *Advances in Fuzzy Set Theory and Applications*, Amsterdam, pp. 3–18.

519. Zadeh, L. A. (1979) *Possibility Theory and Soft Data Analysis*, Electronics Research Laboratory Memorandum M 79/58, 69-120, Boulder, Westview Press.

520. Zadeh, L. A. (1979) Liar's paradox and truth-qualification principle, ERL Memorandum M79/34, University of California, Berkeley.

521. Zadeh, L. A. (1981) Possibility theory, soft data analysis, *Math. Frontiers of the Society and Policy Science*, Westview Press, Boulder, CO, pp. 69–129.

522. Zadeh, L. A. (1981) Test-score semantics for natural languages and meaning representation via PRUF, *Empir. Semantics*, Brockmeyer, Bochum, W. Germany, pp. 281–349.

523. Zadeh, L. A. (1982) Test-score semantics and meaning representation via PRUF. *Empir. Semantics*, Bochum, Brockmeyer, pp. 281–349.

524. Zadeh, L. A. (1983) A computational approach to fuzzy quantifiers in natural languages, *Comput. Math. App.* 9, 149–184.

525. Zadeh, L. A. (1983) A fuzzy-set-theoretic approach to the compositionality of meaning: Propositions, dispositions and canonical forms, *J. Semantics* 3, 253–272.

526. Zadeh, L. A. (1984) *Fuzzy Sets and Commonsense Reasoning*, Institute of Cognitive Studies report 21, Berkeley.

527. Zadeh, L. A. (1984) Precisiation of meaning via translation into PRUF, *Cognitive Constraints on Communication*, Reidel, Dordrecht, pp. 373–402.

528. Zadeh, L. A. (1986) Outline of a computational approach to meaning and knowledge representation based on the concept of a generalized assignment statement, in *Proc. Int. Seminar on Art. Intel. Man–Mac. Systems*, Springer, Heidelberg, pp. 198–211.

529. Zadeh, L. A. and Kacprzyk, J. (1992) *Fuzzy Logic for the Management of Uncertainty*, John Wiley & Sons, Inc.

530. Zadeh, L. A. (1996) Fuzzy logic and the calculi of fuzzy rules and fuzzy graphs, *Multiple-Valued Logic* 1, 1–38.

531. Zadeh, L. A. (1996) Fuzzy logic = computing with words, *IEEE T. Fuzzy Syst.* 4(2), 103–111.

532. Zadeh, L. A. (1996) Linguistic characterization of preference relations as a basis for choice in social systems, *Fuzzy Sets, Fuzzy Logic, Fuzzy System*, World Scientific Publishing Co.

533. Zadeh, L. A. (1996) Quantitative fuzzy semantics, *Fuzzy Sets, Fuzzy Logic, and Fuzzy Systems*, 105–122.

534. Zadeh, L. A. (1997) Toward a theory of fuzzy information granulation and its centrality in human reasoning and fuzzy logic, *Fuzzy Set. Syst.* 90(2), 111–127.

535. Zadeh, L. A. (1998) Some reflections on soft computing granular computing and their roles in the conception, design and utilization of information/intelligent systems, *Soft Comput.* 2, 23–25.

536. Zadeh, L. A. (1999) From computing with numbers to computing with words — from manipulation of measurements to manipulation of perceptions. *IEEE T Circuits Syst.* 45(1), 105–119.

537. Zadeh, L. A. (2001) A new direction in AI — toward a computational theory of perceptions, *AI Mag.* 22(1), 73–84.

538. Zadeh, L. A. (2002) Toward a perception-based theory of probabilistic reasoning with imprecise probabilities, *J. Statist. Plann. Inference* 105, 233–264.

539. Zadeh, L. A. (2004) A note on web intelligence, world knowledge and fuzzy logic, *Data Knowl. Eng.* 50, 291–304.

540. Zadeh, L. A. (2004) Precisiated natural language (PNL), *AI Mag.* 25(3), 74–91.

541. Zadeh L. A. (2005) Toward a generalized theory of uncertainty (GTU) — An outline, *Inform. Sci.* 172, 1–40.

542. Zadeh, L. A. (2006) Generalized theory of uncertainty (GTU) — principal concepts and ideas, *Comput. Stat. Data An.* 51, 15–46.

543. Zadeh, L. A. (2008) Computation with imprecise probabilities, in *Proc. 8th Int. Conf. Application of Fuzzy System and Soft Comp. ICAFS*, pp. 1–3.

544. Zadeh, L. A. (2008) Is there a need for fuzzy logic? *Inform. Sci.* 178(13), 2751–2779.

545. Zadeh, L. A. (2009) Computing with words and perceptions — A paradigm shift, in *Proc. IEEE Int. Conf. Inform. Reuse and Integ.*

546. Zadeh, L. A. (2009) Fuzzy logic, *Encyclopedia of Computational and System Science*, Springer, Berlin.

547. Zadeh, L. A., Aliev, R. A., Fazlollahi, B., Alizadeh, A. V., Guirimov, B. G., and Huseynov, O. H. (2009) Decision theory with imprecise probabilities, *Appl. Fuzzy Logic Soft Comput. Comm., Plan. Manag. Uncertainty*.

548. Zadeh, L. A. (2010) A note on Z-numbers, *Inform. Sci.* 181, 2923–2932.

549. Zadeh, L. A. (2012) Computing with words — principal concepts and ideas, in *Studies in Fuzziness and Soft Computing*, vol. 277, Springer, Berlin Heidelberg.

550. Zadeh, L. A. (2013) A restriction-centered theory of reasoning and computation, in *Int. Conf. Soft Computing and Software Eng.* (PowerPoint presentation).

551. Zadeh, L. A. (2016) A very simple formula for aggregation and multicriteria optimization, *Int. J. Uncertainty, Fuzz. Know. Based Syst.* 24(6), 961–962.

552. Zavala, A. H. and Nieto, O. C. (2012) Fuzzy hardware: A retrospective and analysis, *IEEE Trans. Fuzzy Syst.* 20, 623–635.

553. Zeinalova, L. M. (2010) Decision making under the second-order imprecise probability, in *Proc. 8th ICAFS*, pp. 108–122.
554. Zhai, D. and Mendel, J. (2011) Uncertainty measures for general type-2 fuzzy sets, *Inform. Sci.* 181(3), 503–518.
555. Zhang, G-Q. (1992) Fuzzy number-valued fuzzy measure and fuzzy number-valued fuzzy integral on the fuzzy set, *Fuzzy Set. Syst.* 49, 357–376.
556. Zhang, G., Dillon, T. S., Cai, K., Ma, J., and Lu, J. (2009) Operation properties and delta equalities of complex fuzzy sets, *Int. J. Approx. Reason.* 50(8), 1227–1249.
557. Zhifei, C., Aghakhani, S., Man, J., and Dick, S. (2011) ANCFIS: A neurofuzzy architecture employing complex fuzzy sets, *IEEE Int. Conf. Fuzzy Syst.* 19(2), 305–322.
558. Zhong, Q. (1990) On fuzzy measure and fuzzy integral on fuzzy set, *Fuzzy Set. Syst.* 37(1), 77–92.

Index

A

A fuzzy-number-valued function, 164

Absolute value of fuzzy number, 55

Adaptive neuro-fuzzy inference systems, 453

Addition of continuous Z-numbers, 197

Addition of discrete fuzzy numbers, 202

Addition of the discrete Z-numbers, 210

Aggregation, 408

Aggregation operation, 40

Algebraic product, 34

Algebraic sum, 37

ALI1-logic, 86

ALI2-logic, 86

ALI3-logic, 86

ANFIS, 453

ANFIS architecture, 454

Approximate reasoning, 66–67, 80

Arithmetic operations on fuzzy numbers, 45

Automated reasoning, 264

B

Bell-shaped membership functions, 25

Bimodal constraint, 233

Bimodal distribution, 235

Bimodal distribution interpolation rule, 252

Bounded difference, 35

Bounded sum, 38

Boundedness, 13

Brain imaging, 532

C

Cardinality, 271

Cardinality of a fuzzy set, 22

Cartesian product of fuzzy sets, 41

Chaotic time series, 476

Characterization of information granules, 287

Choquet expected utility, 357

Classification ES, 496

Cointensive precisiation, 222

Co-monotonic independence, 369

Compatibility conditions, 195

Complex fuzzy logic, 309–310, 312

Complex fuzzy propositions, 316

Complex fuzzy sets, 309, 312

Complexity evaluation criterion, 420

Complement of a fuzzy set, 5

Completeness of rules, 187

Composite constraints, 237

Composition of two fuzzy relations, 10

Computation with natural language, 274

Computation with restrictions, 129

Computational rule of inference, 247

Concentration and dilation of fuzzy sets, 41

Concept of a generalized constraint, 227

Concept of precisiation, 219

Concept of protoform, 241

Concepts of coverage, 291

Conditional logical inference rule, 101

Consistency of rules, 187

Containment, 5

Context-free grammar, 71

Continuity, 369

Continuous Z-numbers, 193

Convex fuzzy set, 14

Convexity, 12

D

Data summarization, 280

Decision making under ambiguity, 354

Decision making under ignorance, 354

Decision making under risk, 354

Decision model, 366

Defuzzification, 336

Defuzzification process, 407

Derivative of a fuzzy graph, 124

Derivatives of fuzzy functions, 166

Diagnosis, 495

Difference of fuzzy sets, 43

Discrete Z-numbers, 202, 205

Division of discrete Z-numbers, 211

Division of two fuzzy numbers, 52

Drastic intersection, 36

Drastic union, 39

E

Expert system for scheduling, 502

Explanatory database, 267

Extended fuzzy logic, 113

Extension principle, 45

Extensions of fuzzy sets, 56

Equality of fuzzy sets, 19

Elasticity of meaning, 274

Embedded fuzzy sets, 58

Encoding of population, 411

ESPLAN, 496

f-concurrent, 121

f-geometry and f-transformation, 118

f-triangle, 121

F

Fitness function, 432

Flexibility of system, 407

f-mark, 265

Function, 4

Functional fuzzy rule base, 185

Fuzzification module, 330

Fuzzy arithmetic, 44

Fuzzy clusters, 187

Fuzzy cognitive map, 496, 507–508

Fuzzy conditional inference rule, 102

Fuzzy control, 327

Fuzzy controllers, 339

Fuzzy decision making, 353

Fuzzy dynamic programming, 451

Fuzzy expert systems, 495

Fuzzy functions, 163

Fuzzy granule, 192

Fuzzy graph 185, 232

Fuzzy Hausdorff distance, 362

Fuzzy hypotheses generating and accounting systems, 503

Fuzzy implication, 185

Fuzzy implication rule base, 185

Fuzzy inference mechanism, 336

Fuzzy logic, 65, 68

Fuzzy logic control, 327

Fuzzy logic in medicine, 531

Fuzzy minimum and maximum of fuzzy numbers, 52
Fuzzy n-cube representation, 24
Fuzzy number, 44
Fuzzy number-valued fuzzy measure, 364
Fuzzy probabilities, 147, 357
Fuzzy random number, 192
Fuzzy random variable, 192
Fuzzy reinforcement learning, 445
Fuzzy relation, 184
Fuzzy rulebase function, 448
Fuzzy rule-based system, 183
Fuzzy rules, 332
Fuzzy rules activity, 426
Fuzzy set inclusion, 22
Fuzzy sets, 3
Fuzzy sets readability evaluation criterion, 421
Fuzzy set-valued random variable, 365
Fuzzy signal processing, 532
Fuzzy standard intersection and union, 30
Fuzzy state, 179
Fuzzy system for classification, 406, 420
Fuzzy systems, 169, 402
Fuzzy truth-values 65
Fuzzy-graph constraint, 232
Fuzzy-graph interpolation rule, 250
Fuzzy-set-valued random variable, 192, 235
Fuzzy-valued non-expected utility, 353

G

G-logic, 86
G43-logic, 86
Generalized constraint language, 238
Generalized differentiability concepts, 166
Generalized means, 40
Generalized theory of uncertainty, 215

Genetic-imperialist algorithm, 410
Goal programming, 195
Graduation, 216, 264
Graduation of propositions, 266
Granular aggregation, 304
Granular Computing, 277, 283
Granular definition of a function, 221
Granular mappings, 278, 301
Granular models, 305
Granular value, 239
Granularity of information, 281
Granulation, 186, 216
Granulation of time, 280
Group constraint, 236

H

Height of a fuzzy set, 20
Hukuhara difference, 362
Hukuhara difference of discrete fuzzy numbers, 203
Human-centricity, 281
Hybrid learning algorithm, 458

I

Identification in control systems, 471
Imperfect information, 353
Imprecise beliefs, 353
Imprecise hierarchical models, 356
Imprecise probability, 356
Imprecise truth tables, 66
Imprecision of my perception, 265
Inference operators, 408
Information granularity, 277–278
Informativeness, 192
Inhibitory data, 299
Instructional ES, 495
Integrable, 165
Interpretability criteria, 420
Interpretability of fuzzy systems, 404
Interpretive ES, 495
Intersection of two fuzzy sets, 6
Intuitionistic fuzzy sets, 60
Investment problem, 380

J

Justifiable granularity, 291

K

KD-logic, 86

L

α-level fuzzy sets 19
L-logic, 86
Largest fuzzy set, 6
Level of granularity, 281
Linguistic approximation, 78
Linguistic lottery, 365
Linguistic preference relations, 353
Linguistic probabilities, 366
Linguistic terms, 206
Linguistic truth-values, 70
Linguistic variables, 184
Logistic regression analysis, 509

M

Mamdani fuzzy controller, 329
Meaning of a proposition, 267
Measurable function, 165
Measure, 289
Measure of reliability, 189
Membership, 4
Membership function, 173
Memoryless fuzzy system, 182
Min-logic, 85
Monitoring and control ES, 496
Monotonicity, 369
Multiple priors, 355
Multiplication of continuous
    Z-numbers, 201
Multiplication of discrete fuzzy
    numbers, 204

N

Natural language, 189
Neutrosophic set, 63
NL-computation, 217
Nondegeneracy, 369

Non-memoryless fuzzy systems,
    176
Normal and subnormal sets, 20

O

Operations on linguistic truth-values,
    75
Ordered weighted averaging
    operations, 40

P

Parameterized triangular norms, 407
Pittsburgh approach, 411
Planning ES, 496
Possibilistic constraints, 228
Possibilistic restriction, 126, 194
Power of fuzzy sets, 41
Precisiation of meaning, 272
Predictive ES, 496
Probabilistic constraints, 229
Probabilistic restriction, 127
Probability measure of a discrete
    fuzzy number, 202
Probability rule, 250
Probability-oriented information
    granules, 286
Probability measure, 193
Prospect theory, 362
Protoformal deduction rules, 247

Q

Q-Learning, 450

R

Random set, 232
Reasoning with Z-information, 189
Repair ES, 495
Restriction concept, 125
Restriction-based semantics, 267
Revolution and mutation of the
    colonies, 417
Revolution operator, 417
Riemann integrable, 164
Rough sets, 62, 286
Rule base, 185, 406

S

S-logic, 85
$S^\#$-logic, 85
Semantic rule, 70
Separation of convex fuzzy sets, 16
Shadow of a fuzzy set, 15
Shadowed sets, 285
Sigma-count, 149
Similarity of fuzzy sets, 424
Soft constraint, 194
Specificity 192, 288–289
Specificity of the information granule, 299
Stability in a fuzzy concept, 226
Standard constraint language, 238
Standard constraints, 237
Standard division of discrete fuzzy numbers, 204
Standard fuzzy complement, 32
Standard intersection, 34
Standard subtraction of discrete fuzzy numbers, 203
Standard union, 37
State at time, 177
State equations, 178
State equations for fuzzy systems, 172
Strict and strong convexity, 14
Strongly generalized Hukuhara differentiable, 166
Subtraction of fuzzy numbers, 50
Sugeno fuzzy model, 453
Syntactic rule, 70

T

Takagi–Sugeno (TS) fuzzy controllers, 344
T-conorms, 36
T-norms, 33
Trapezoidal membership functions, 26
Triangular membership functions, 25
Truth qualification, 140
Truth value, 269
Type-2 fuzzy number, 59
Type-2 fuzzy set, 56
Type-2 fuzzy sets and numbers, 56

U

Union of two fuzzy sets, 5
Universal approximator, 462
Usuality constraints, 232

V

Vague preference-based models, 359
Vagueness of preferences, 353
Veristic constraints, 218

W

Weak-order, 368

Z

Z-information, 189
Z-number, 189
Z-restriction, 127
Z-valuation, 190
Z-mouse, 265

Printed in the United States
By Bookmasters